SP
STA

GUI

# CHAMPIONS LEAGUE03-04



ABSOLUTE
PUBLISHING LTD

# Angus Loughran's
## GUIDE TO THE
# CHAMPIONS LEAGUE 03-04

First published in Great Britain in 2003 by Absolute Publishing Ltd


**ABSOLUTE PUBLISHING LTD**
**197-199 CITY ROAD, LONDON EC1V 1JN, UK**

Printed and bound by Cox and Wyman, Reading, Berkshire
ISBN: 0 9542304 42



**AUTHOR** ANGUS LOUGHRAN
**PUBLISHER** PETER LEVINGER
**STATISTICS** CHRIS RHYS, MARYAN MAHIEU
**ADDITIONAL STATISTICS** ROB BATEMAN - OPTA
**ADDITIONAL REPORTING** REUTERS
**SERIES EDITORS** GLYN WILMSHURST, ANDY TONGUE, MATTHEW WEINER
**ART EDITOR** JOHN PAUL YETTON
**DESIGNER** DAMON COGMAN
**COVER PHOTOGRAPHY** GETTY IMAGES

# CONTENTS


FOREWORD BY ANGUS LOUGHRAN **6**

CHAMPIONS LEAGUE DRAW **7**

BETTING ANALYSIS **12**

QUALIFYING ROUNDS **16**

RECORDS AND STATISTICS **22**

GROUP A **40**

GROUP B **62**

GROUP C **85**

GROUP D **104**

GROUP E **126**

GROUP F **151**

GROUP G **171**

GROUP H **194**

COMPETITION HISTORY **215**

# FOREWORD

## BY ANGUS LOUGHRAN

As we begin another exciting season of Champions League football, the key difference from last year is the abolition of the second group stage in favour of a knockout last 16. The move should benefit the competition, as knockout football offers fantastic excitement, yet it remains important for the commercial side of Champions League that each club is guaranteed a certain number of matches as a reward for making it into Europe's elite competition.

As usual, six matches are guaranteed in the first group stage and the team that finishes third in each section will enter the UEFA Cup in the New Year. This means that as long as a club avoids last place in the group, they will play a minimum of eight games in European competition this season. The last 16 will see the eight group winners meet the eight group runners-up. No teams from the same country can meet at this stage, and clubs cannot be drawn against the team they played in the group phase. For example, if Ajax and Milan both qualify from Group H, they cannot meet in the last 16. Likewise Chelsea and Manchester United cannot be paired together in the second round even if one was a group winner and one was a runner-up. Once we reach the quarter-finals there is a free draw and any two clubs can meet for a second time or play teams of the same nationality.

Real Madrid are the obvious favourites for the title with Manchester United most bookmakers' choice as second favourites. Bayern Munich, who had disappointing campaign last year, are highly fancied this time round along with defending champions Milan and last year's runners-up Juventus. London clubs Chelsea and Arsenal are certain to make impact, with Claudio Ranieri's side handed an excellent draw giving them a real opportunity to progress. There are always surprises with Galatasaray looking under-rated by the bookies at 100-1. Overall, I would expect the majority of the fancied teams to make it through the first stage, ensuring a wonderful last 16 with big names in Europe battling it out for one of the most prestigious prizes in sport, a victory in the Champions League final.

In Britain, television viewers are in for a treat. Under the new TV deal, ITV, who have provided Champions League coverage from the start, are showing two live games every Tuesday during the group stage. Their first choice will be on ITV1 with a second game covered live by ITV2. There is also a highlights package later in the evening. On Wednesdays, Sky will show all eight matches live via their traditional sports channels and their digital interactive service. Never before have armchair fans had it so good and, for those prepared to pay the premium, the choice of live action on Wednesdays will now be completely in their hands. This is of course a major bonus for punters who will now be able to watch whichever game most directly affects their bet.

When contemplating Champions League wagers, it is certainly worth shopping round for speciality markets, as well as the usual outright group and match betting. Firms like the Tote and Fred Done offer a fantastic range of bets and plenty of opportunities for the betting public to add to their enjoyment of this festival of football.

# CHAMPIONS LEAGUE GROUPS

## GROUP A

**FC BAYERN MUNICH**
(Germany)
**OLYMPIQUE LYONNAIS**
(France)
**CELTIC FC**
(Scotland)
**RSC ANDERLECHT**
(Belgium)

## GROUP B

**ARSENAL FC**
(England)
**INTERNAZIONALE MILAN**
(Italy)
**FC DYNAMO KYIV**
(Ukraine)
**FC LOKOMOTIV MOSCOW**
(Russia)

## GROUP C

**RC DEPORTIVO CORUNA**
(Spain)
**PSV EINDHOVEN**
(Netherlands)
**AS MONACO**
(France)
**AEK ATHENS**
(Greece)

## GROUP D

**JUVENTUS FC**
(Italy)
**GALATASARAY SK**
(Turkey)
**REAL SOCIEDAD**
(Spain)
**FC OLYMPIAKOS PIRAEUS**
(Greece)

## GROUP E

**MANCHESTER UNITED**
(England)
**PANATHAIKOS**
(Greece)
**GLASGOW RANGERS FC**
(Scotland)
**VFB STUTTGART**
(Germany)

## GROUP F

**REAL MADRID CF**
(Spain)
**FC PORTO**
(Portugal)
**OLYMPIQUE DE MARSEILLE**
(France)
**PARTIZAN BELGRADE**
(Yugoslavia)

## GROUP G

**CHELSEA FC**
(England)
**SS LAZIO**
(Italy)
**AC SPARTA PRAGUE**
(Czechoslovakia)
**BESIKTAS JK**
(Turkey)

## GROUP H

**AC MILAN**
(Italy)
**CELTA VIGO**
(Spain)
**AFC AJAX**
(Netherlands)
**FC BRUGES**
(Belgium)

# CHAMPIONS LEAGUE FIXTURES

## TUESDAY, OCTOBER 16

### GROUP E
Manchester United v Panathinaikos
Rangers v Stuttgart

### GROUP F
Partizan Belgrade v Porto
Real Madrid v Marseille

### GROUP G
Besiktas v Lazio
Sparta Prague v Chelsea

### GROUP H
Club Brugge v Celta
AC Milan v Ajax Amsterdam

## WEDNESDAY, OCTOBER 17

### GROUP A
Bayern Munchen v Celtic
Olympique Lyon v Anderlecht

### GROUP B
Arsenal v Internazionale
Dynamo Kyiv v Lokomotiv Moscow

### GROUP C
AEK Athens v Deportivo La Coruna
PSV Eindhoven v Monaco

### GROUP D
Juventus v Galatasaray
Real Sociedad v Olympiakos

## TUESDAY, OCTOBER 30

### GROUP A
Anderlecht v Bayern Munchen
Celtic v Lyon

### GROUP B
Internazionale v Dynamo Kyiv
Lokomotiv Moscow v Arsenal

### GROUP C
Deportivo La Coruna v PSV
Monaco v AEK

### GROUP D
Galatasaray v Real Sociedad
Olympiakos v Juventus

## WEDNESDAY, SEPTEMBER 1

### GROUP E
Panathinaikos v Rangers
Stuttgart v Manchester United

### GROUP F
Marseille v Partizan
Porto v Real Madrid

### GROUP G
Chelsea v Besiktas
Lazio v Sparta Prague

### GROUP H
Ajax v Club Brugge
Celta v AC Milan

# CHAMPIONS LEAGUE FIXTURES

## TUESDAY, OCTOBER 21

### GROUP A
Anderlecht v Celtic
Lyon v Bayern Munchen

### GROUP B
Dynamo Kyiv v Arsenal
Lokomotiv Moscow v Internazionale

### GROUP C
AEK Athens v PSV
Deportivo La Coruna v Monaco

### GROUP D
Galatasaray v Olympiakos
Juventus v Real Sociedad

## WEDNESDAY, OCTOBER 22

### GROUP E
Rangers v Manchester United
Stuttgart v Panathinaikos

### GROUP F
Marseille v Porto
Real Madrid v Partizan Belgrade

### GROUP G
Chelsea v Lazio
Sparta Prague v Besiktas

### GROUP H
Ajax v Celta Vigo
AC Milan v Club Brugge

## TUESDAY, NOVEMBER 4

### GROUP E
Manchester United v Rangers
Panathinaikos v Stuttgart

### GROUP F
Partizan Belgrade v Real Madrid
Porto v Marseille

### GROUP G
Besiktas v Sparta Prague
Lazio v Chelsea

### GROUP H
Celta Vigo v Ajax
Club Brugge v Milan

## WEDNESDAY, NOVEMBER 5

### GROUP A
Bayern Munchen v Lyon
Celtic v Anderlecht

### GROUP B
Arsenal v Dynamo Kyiv
Internazionale v Lokomotiv Moscow

### GROUP C
Monaco v Deportivo
PSV v AEK

### GROUP D
Olympiakos v Galatasaray
Real Sociedad v Juventus

# CHAMPIONS LEAGUE FIXTURES

## TUESDAY, NOVEMBER 25

### GROUP A
Anderlecht v Lyon
Celtic v Bayern Munchen

### GROUP B
Internazionale v Arsenal
Lokomotiv Moscow v Dynamo Kyiv

### GROUP C
Deportivo v AEK
Monaco v PSV

### GROUP D
Galatasaray v Juventus
Olympiakos v Real Sociedad

## WEDNESDAY, NOVEMBER 26

### GROUP E
Panathinaikos v Man. United
Stuttgart v Rangers

### GROUP F
Marseille v Real Madrid
Porto v Partizan

### GROUP G
Chelsea v Sparta
Lazio v Besiktas

### GROUP H
Ajax v AC Milan
Celta v Club Brugge

## TUESDAY, DECEMBER 9

### GROUP E
Man. United v Stuttgart
Rangers v Panathinaikos

### GROUP F
Partizan v Marseille
Real Madrid v Porto

### GROUP G
Besiktas v Chelsea
Sparta v Lazio

### GROUP H
Club Brugge v Ajax
AC Milan v Celta

## WEDNESDAY, DECEMBER 9

### GROUP A
Bayern v Anderlecht
Lyon v Celtic

### GROUP B
Arsenal v Lokomotiv Moscow
Dynamo Kyiv v Internazionale

### GROUP C
AEK v Monaco
PSV v Deportivo

### GROUP D
Juventus v Olympiakos
Real Sociedad v Galatasaray

## SECOND GROUP STAGE

First knock-out round 1st leg - 24 & 25 February 2004
First knock-out round 2nd leg - 09 & 10 March 2004

## QUARTER FINALS

1st leg - 23 & 24 March 2004
2nd leg - 06 & 07 April 2004

## SEMI FINALS

1st leg - 20 & 21 April 2004
2nd leg - 04 & 05 May 2004

## CHAMPIONS LEAGUE CUP FINAL

Wednesday 26 May, 2004

**Arena AufSchalke, Germany**

# BETTING ANALYSIS

BY ANGUS LOUGHRAN

## GROUP A

Bayern Munich are the obvious favourites to top the group although, after last year's disappointment when they were eliminated in the first stage, nothing should be taken for granted. The German side will have an added incentive this year as the Champions League final is being held in their country. Lyon could be the dark horses of the group even though French sides have a disappointing record in this competition. Scottish teams have no great Champions League pedigree either but Celtic, who had such a marvellous run to reach last year's UEFA Cup final, will be particularly hard to beat, especially at Celtic Park where no one will relish facing them in front of their fanatical fans. Anderlecht are in the Champions League for the fifth time and have only once been past the first group stage. On that occasion, in 2000, they qualified despite losing 5-1 at Old Trafford to Manchester United and 4-0 to Dynamo Kiev. A strong performance in their last three matches booked a place in the second phase. Nevertheless, I expect Bayern Munich and Celtic to make it through Group A.

**TO QUALIFY: BAYERN MUNICH AND CELTIC**

## GROUP B

It would be a major surprise if it were not Arsenal and Inter who qualify from Group B. The key date is November 25 when the teams meet in the San Siro. European experience in is vital although Arsenal have been disappointing in the Champions League (particularly at home) in recent seasons with their best effort reaching the quarter finals in 2001 when they lost to Valencia. Inter suffered a strange season last year losing to city rivals AC Milan on away goals in the Champions League semi-final, even though the 'away' goals came on their own pitch! Dynamo Kiev and Lokomotiv Moscow will both provide stiff opposition at home and it is these matches which will effectively decide the group. If either of these Eastern European sides can win all their home games it could allow them to slip through the back door.

**TO QUALIFY: INTER MILAN AND ARSENAL**

## GROUP C

A very tough group with Deportivo La Coruna the clear favourites and each of the other three teams holding strong claims to qualify. AEK Athens are the outsiders but they performed with great credit in their group last year and gave Real Madrid plenty to think about in their two matches. They could easily qualify as the second-placed team. PSV Eindhoven and Monaco performed well in their domestic leagues last season and will both fancy their chances of reaching last 16. Deportivo have played with a high level of consistency in this competition over the last few seasons but have been found wanting when the action gets serious and, although I see them winning this group, they are a frustrating side to follow.

**TO QUALIFY: DEPORTIVO LA CORUNA AND AEK ATHENS**

## GROUP D

On paper, Juventus should have few problems in this fascinating section which is sure to have a political dimension. Galatasaray and Olympiakos are paired together offering a rare European clash between Turkey and Greece, which is sure to have a massive off-the-field impact in both countries. Expect hostile atmospheres at both venues. I feel sorry for Real Sociedad who crept into the last Spanish Champions League place only to be drawn into this tricky group. Galatasaray can edge them out for second place behind Juventus who, as last year's beaten finalists, will be desperate to go one better this time round.

**TO QUALIFY: JUVENTUS AND GALATASARAY**

## GROUP E

There is plenty of British interest in Group E as one would expect with Manchester United and Rangers being drawn together. The bookies are offer 33-1 on Rangers doing the double over the English side with 7-4 on the reverse results in United's favour. Even though both matches will be huge spectacles, United must have been delighted with the draw. I expect them to top the group. However, who will finish second will is another matter with Rangers having as good a chance as Stuttgart – beaten by Celtic in the UEFA Cup last season - and Panathinaikos, who will cause for problems everyone at home. This group looks sure to go down to the wire with Rangers versus Panathinaikos on December 9 likely to be the crucial match.

**TO QUALIFY: MANCHESTER UNITED AND GLASGOW RANGERS**

# CHAMPIONS LEAGUE BETTING

## GROUP F

Real Madrid start as hot favourites to win and the summer signing of David Beckham has been well-received by their fans. Porto are regular opponents in this competition having lost twice to Real in the first group stage in 1997. The Portuguese side did manage a home victory in 1999, but lost 3-1 in the Bernabeu and found Madrid too good on both occasions in 2002 when they were paired together in the second group stage. There was certainly a feeling of deja vu at the draw. The conquerors of Newcastle, Partizan Belgrade, were the shock qualifiers and have been dismissed as 250-1 outsiders for the title and 40 -1 for the group. This is an insult to a club who performed with great credit when beating Sir Bobby Robson side over two legs. They will be aiming for second place but a more realistic goal is finishing third and qualifying for the latter stages of the UEFA Cup. Marseilles are typically French. One is always unsure which Marseilles will turn up. On their day they could trouble anyone including Madrid but they can also be a very frustrating side to watch.

**TO QUALIFY: REAL MADRID AND PORTO**

## GROUP G

Chelsea and Lazio met in a pre-season friendly and there are plenty of links between the two clubs. I expect both to qualify with the key clash coming in Rome on Tuesday, November 4 which will probably decide who wins the group. Roman Abramovich has ploughed millions into the club who have a real sporting of rewarding his investment with a decent run in the Champions League. Although Besiktas in Istanbul and Sparta Prague are both difficult places to go, both Chelsea and Lazio could not have wished for a better draw. It would be a shock if either were eliminated in the first phase.

**TO QUALIFY: CHELSEA AND LAZIO**

## GROUP H

Milan are hot favourites to win the group with regular Champions League rivals Ajax, who they beat in the quarter-finals last year with the final kick of match, the main dangers. Both sides will expect to qualify with Celta Vigo, who will be strong at home, heading for the UEFA Cup spot. Bruges' chance is not an obvious one but any side that can successfully come through a two-legged qualifier against Borussia Dortmund should not be underestimated. Nevertheless, Ajax should get better of Bruges in two potentially exciting contests, given great rivalry between Holland and Belgium. I expect the Dutch side to qualify with Milan.

**TO QUALIFY: AC MILAN AND AJAX**

# Betting conclusion...

Juventus are my tip to win this season's Champions League. Marcello Lippi has kept together the same group of players who were so unfortunate not to triumph in last year's final when they suffered penalty heartache at the hands of AC Milan. They will be desperate to go one better this time around and Lippi is likely to make the Champions League his team's number one priority. Their semi-final second-leg victory over Real Madrid was in my view the most impressive performance of last season by any European team.

With Juventus leading the charge, the Italian challenge looks particularly strong, but it would be wrong to write off the English teams. Chelsea look the best value and could certainly give each-way backers a run for their money. Romanian striker Adrian Mutu is set to become one of the stars of the season given the quality of service he can expect from Chelsea's new-look midfield.

Of the big outsiders, Monaco with Didier Deschamps at the helm, look a sporting bet. The Frenchman has a wealth of Champions League experience and his team could surprise a few people.

The usual suspects - Raul, Ronaldo and Ruud Van Nistelrooy - head the market for top goal scorer in the Champions League but punters could be rewarded by taking a chance with Bayern Munich's Roy Makaay. His team have plenty to prove following last year's disappointment when they finished bottom of their group and Makaay, who joined from Deportivo La Coruna in the summer, is a forward of genuine quality.

# CHAMPIONS LEAGUE QUALIFYING ROUNDS

*Note: Country of competing club named at entry to competition*

## 1st QUALIFYING ROUND

**FC PYUNIK EREVEAN** (Armenia) **1** — **KR REJKAVIK** (Iceland) **0**
*(Pacajian 61)*
**KR REJKAVIK 1** — **FC PYUNIK 1**
*(B Gunnlaugsson 82pen)* — *(Mkrtichian 72)*
**FC PYUNIK WON 2-1 ON AGGREGATE**

---

**FC SHERIFF** (Moldova) **1** — **FC FLORA TALLINN** (Estonia) **0**
*(Tudor 88)*
**FC FLORA TIRASPOL 1** — **FC SHERIFF TIRASPOL 1**
*(Viikmae 88)* — *(Nesteruc 81)*
**FC SHERIFF WON 2-1 ON AGGREGATE**

---

**HB TORSHAVN** (Faroes) **0** — **FBK KAUNAS** (Lithuania) **1**
*(Opic 75)*
**FBK KAUNAS 4** — **HB TORSHAVN 1**
*(Beniusis 5,77, Kancelskis 37, Opic 41)* — *(R Jakobsen 9)*
**FBK KAUNAS WON 5-1 ON AGGREGATE**

---

**FC BATE BORISOV** (Belarus) **1** — **BOHEMIAN FC** (Ireland) **0**
*(Lashankov 25)*
**BOHEMIAN FC 3** — **FC BATE 0**
*(Caffrey 36, Ryan 45, Crowe 58)*
**BOHEMIAN FC WON 3-1 ON AGGREGATE**

---

**CS GREVENMACHER** (Luxembourg) **0** — **FK LEOTAR TREBINJE** (Bos-Herz) **0**
**FK LEOTAR TREBINJE 2** — **CS GREVENMACHER 0**
*(Kerkez 24, 85)*
**FK LEOTAR TREBINJE WON 2-0 ON AGGREGATE**

---

# CHAMPIONS LEAGUE QUALIFYING

**FK VARDAR SKOPJE** (Macedonia) **3 BARRY TOWN AFC** (Wales) **0**
*(Dos Santos 38, 70,Ristovski 49)*

| | |
|---|---|
| **BARRY TOWN AFC 2** | **FK VARDAR 1** |
| *(Jarman 1, Moralee 63)* | *(Dos Santos 61)* |

**FK VARDAR WON 4-2 ON AGGREGATE**

---

| | |
|---|---|
| **GLENTORAN FC** (N Ireland) **0** | **HJK HELSINKI** (Finland) **0** |
| **HJK HELSINKI 1** | **GLENTORAN FC 0** |
| *(Makela 75)* | |

**HJK HELSINKI WON 1-0 ON AGGREGATE**

---

| | |
|---|---|
| **SLIEMA WANDERERS FC** (Malta) **2** | **SKONTO FC RIGA** (Latvia) **0** |
| *(Bogdanovic 62, Doncic 65pen)* | |
| **SKONTO FC 3** | **SLIEMA WANDERERS 1** |
| *(Buitkaus 15, Verpakovskis 64, Dedura 75)* | *(Brincat 90)* |

**SLIEMA WANDERERS WON ON AWAY GOAL AFTER 3-3 DRAW**

---

| | |
|---|---|
| **OMONIA AC NICOSIA** (Cyprus) **0** | **FC IRTYSH PAVOLDAR** (Kazakhstan) **0** |
| **FC IRTYSH 1** | **OMONIA AC NICOSIA 2** |
| *(Agejev 21)* | *(Rauffmann 61, Georgiu 90)* |

**OMONIA AC NICOSIA WON 2-1 ON AGGREGATE**

---

| | |
|---|---|
| **FC DINAMO TBLISI** (Georgia) **3** | **KF TIRANA** (Albania) **0** |
| *(Melkadze 6, Anchabadze 45, Daraselia 50pen)* | |
| **KF TIRANA 3** | **FC DINAMO TBLISI 0** |
| *(Lici 13, Fortuzi 63, Halili 80)* | |

**KF TIRANA WON 4-2 ON PENALTIES AFTER 3-3 DRAW**

---

## 2nd QUALIFYING ROUND

| | |
|---|---|
| **BOHEMIAN FC 0** | **ROSENBORG BK** (Norway) **1** |
| | *(Karadas 35)* |
| **ROSENBORG BK 4** | **BOHEMIAN FC 0** |
| *(Karadas 43, Brattbakk 51, Strand 68, F Johnsen 76)* | |

**ROSENBORG BK WON 5-0 ON AGGREGATE**

---

| | |
|---|---|
| **MSK ZILINA** (Slovakia) **1** | **MACCABI TEL AVIV** (Israel) **0** |
| *(Bazik 86)* | |
| **MACCABI TEL AVIV FC 1** | **MSK ZILINA 1** |
| *(Penstil 25)* | *(Sninsky 16)* |

**MSK ZILINA WON 2-1 ON AGGREGATE**

**FC KOBENHAVN** (Denmark) **4** **SLIEMA WANDERERS FC 1**

| | |
|---|---|
| *(Zuma 24, Roell Larsen 28pen,70, Jonsson 45)* | *(Doncic 50)* |
| **SLIEMA WANDERERS FC 0** | **FC KOBEMHAVN 6** |
| | *(Jonsson 17, 43, Norregaard 39, Chetcuti 46og, Zuma 49, Roell Larsen 65)* |

**FC KOBENHAVN WON 10-1 ON AGGREGATE**

---

| | |
|---|---|
| **PARTIZAN BELGRADE** (Serbia & Mont) **1** | **DJURGARDENS IF** (Sweden) **1** |
| *(Ilic 59)* | *(Mekondele 72)* |
| **DJURDGARDENS IF 2** | **FK PARTIZAN 2** |
| *(Johansson 10, Wowoah 77)* | *(Ilic 62, Malbasa 67)* |

**FK PARTIZAN WON ON AWAY GOALS AFTER 3-3 DRAW**

---

| | |
|---|---|
| **NK MARIBOR** (Slovenia) **1** | **NK DINAMO ZAGREB** (Croatia) **1** |
| *(Pekic 37)* | *(Kranjcar 33)* |
| **NK DINAMO 2** | **NK MARIBOR 1** |
| *(Mijatovic 60, Drpic 63)* | *(Balajic 11)* |

**NK DINAMO WON 3-2 ON AGGREGATE**

---

| | |
|---|---|
| **MTK HUNGARIA FC** (Hungary) **3** | **HJK HELSINKI 1** |
| *(Welton 38, 43, Rednic 90)* | *(Kottila 54)* |
| **HJK HELSINKI 1** | **MTK HUNGARIA FC 0** |
| *(Maekelae 64)* | |

**MTK HUNGARIA FC WON 3-2 ON AGGREGATE**

---

| | |
|---|---|
| **AFC RAPID BUCURESTI** (Romania) **0** | **RSC ANDERLECHT** (Belgium) **0** |
| **RSC ANDERLECHT 3** | **AFC RAPID BUCURESTI 2** |
| *(Jestrovic 51, Zetterberg 52, Seol 74)* | *(Ilyes 42, Bratu 43)* |

**RSC ANDERLECHT WON 3-2 ON AGGREGATE**

---

| | |
|---|---|
| **FBK KAUNAS 0** | **CELTIC FC** (Scotland) **4** |
| | *(Larsson 12, Sutton 28, Maloney 54, Miller 87)* |
| **CELTIC FC 1** | **FBK KAUNAS 0** |
| *(Gvildys 21og)* | |

**CELTIC FC WON 5-0 ON AGGREGATE**

---

| | |
|---|---|
| **WISLA KRAKOW** (Poland) **5** | **OMONIA AC 2** |
| *(Zurawski 11, 49, Frankowski 19, Baszczynski 45, Dubicki 70)* | *(Rauffmann 74pen, 85pen)* |
| **OMONIA AC 2** | **WISLA KRAKOW 2** |
| *(Rauffmann 16, Charlambous 51)* | *(Zurawski 5, 72)* |

**WISLA KRAKOW WON 7-4 ON AGGREGATE**

---

| | |
|---|---|
| **FK LEOTAR TREBINJE 1** | **SK SLAVIA PRAHA** (Czech Republic) **2** |

| | |
|---|---|
| *(Delibasic 44pen)* | *(Da Silva 16, Dostalek 49pen)* |
| **SK SLAVIA PRAGUE 2** | **FK LEOTAR 0** |
| *(Kuka 43, Skaacel 74)* | |

**SK SLAVIA PRAGUE WON 3-1 ON AGGREGATE**

| | |
|---|---|
| **PFC CSKA MOSKVA** (Russia) **1** | **FK VARDAR SKOPJE 2** |
| *(Kirichenko 90)* | *(Grozdanovski 54, Dos Santos 64)* |
| **FK VARDAR SKOPJE 1** | **PFC CSKA MOSCOW 1** |
| *(Dos Santos 65)* | *(Gogniyev 21)* |

**FK VARDAR SKOPJE WON 3-2 ON AGGREGATE**

| | |
|---|---|
| **KF TIRANA 1** | **GRAZER AK** (Austria) **5** |
| *(Xhafa 5)* | *(Bazina 14, Aufhauser 33, Naumoski 41, 82, Standfest 55)* |
| **GRAZER AK 2** | **KF TIRANA 1** |
| *(Sick 14, Kollmann 86)* | *(Agolli 90)* |

**GRAZER AK WON 7-3 ON AGGREGATE**

| | |
|---|---|
| **FC PYUNIK 0** | **PFC CSKA SOFIA** (Bulgaria) **2** |
| *(Yanchev 19, Mugasi 46)* | |
| **PFC CSKA SOFIA 1** | **FC PYUNIK 0** |
| *(Lima 90)* | |

**PFC CSKA SOFIA WON 3-0 ON AGGREGATE**

| | |
|---|---|
| **FC SHERIFF 0** | **FC SHAKHTAR DONETSK** (Ukraine) **0** |
| **FC SHAKHTAR 2** | **FC SHERIFF 0** |
| *(Vukic 60, Brandao 88)* | |

**FC SHAKHTAR WON 2-0 ON AGGREGATE**

| | |
|---|---|
| **FK AUSTRIA WIEN** (Austria) **0** | **OLYMPIQUE DE MARSEILLE** (France) **1** |
| | *(Sytchev 4)* |
| **OLYMPIQUE DE MARSEILLE 0** | **FK AUSTRIA WIEN 0** |

**OLYMPIQUE DE MARSEILLE WON 1-0 ON AGGREGATE**

## 3rd QUALIFYING ROUND

| | |
|---|---|
| **ROSENBORG BK 0** | **RC DEPORTIVO LA CORUNA** (Spain) **0** |
| **RC DEPORTIVO LA CORUNA 1** | **ROSNBORG BK 0** |
| *(Luque 16)* | |

**RC DEPORTIVO WON 1-0 ON AGGREGATE**

| | |
|---|---|
| **FK VARDAR SKOPJE 2** | **AC SPARTA PRAHA** (Czech Rep) **3** |

| | |
|---|---|
| *(Oliveira 60, Georgievski 75)* | *(Poborsky 36, 89, Gluscevic 40)* |
| **AC SPARTA PRAHA 2** | **FK VARDAR SKOPJE 2** |
| *(Poborsky 34, Sionko 82)* | *(Georgievski 30, Chinedu 67)* |

**AC SPARTA WON 5-4 ON AGGREGATE**

---

| | |
|---|---|
| **MTK HUNGARIA FC 0** | **CELTIC FC 4** |
| | *(Larsson 17, Agathe 36, Petrov 70, Sutton 90)* |
| **CELTIC FC 1** | **MTK HUNGARIA 0** |
| *(Sutton 13)* | |

**CELTIC FC WON 5-0 ON AGGREGATE**

---

| | |
|---|---|
| **RANGERS FC** (Scotland) **1** | **FC KOBENHAVN 1** |
| *(Lovenkrands 7)* | *(Jonsson 51)* |
| **FC KOBENHAVN 1** | **RANGERS FC 2** |
| *(Alvaro Santos 83)* | *(Arteta 58pen, Arveladze 86)* |

**RANGERS FC WON 3-2 ON AGGREGATE**

---

| | |
|---|---|
| **CLUB BRUGGE KV** (Belgium) **2** | **BV BORUSSIA DORTMUND** (Germany) **1** |
| *(Ceh 32, Verheyen 44)* | *(Amoroso 52)* |
| **BV BORUSSIA DORTMUND 2** | **CLUB BRUGGE KV 1** |
| *(Amoroso 3, Ewerthon 86)* | *(Mendoza 27)* |

**CLUB BRUGGE KV WON 4-2 ON PENALIES AFTER 2-2 DRAW**

---

| | |
|---|---|
| **FC SHAKHTAR DONETSK 1** | **FC LOKOMOTIV MOSKVA** (Russia) **0** |
| *(Vukic 58pen)* | |
| **FC LOKOMOTIV MOSKVA 3** | **FC SHAKHTAR 1** |
| *(Ashvetia 20, 45, Ignashevich 86pen)* | *(Lewandowski 71* |

**FC LOKOMOTIV WON 3-2 ON AGGREGATE**

---

| | |
|---|---|
| **S.S.LAZIO** (Italy) **3** | **SL BENFICA** (Portugal) **1** |
| *(Corradi 16, Fiore 52, Mihajlovic 80)* | *(Simao 64)* |
| **SL BENFICA 0** | **S.S.LAZIO 1** |
| | *(Cesar 28)* |

**S.S.LAZIO WON 4-1 ON AGGREGATE**

---

| | |
|---|---|
| **FC DYNAMO KYIV** (Ukraine) **3** | **NK DINAMO ZAGREB 1** |
| *(Fyodorov 33, Leko 39, Gusev 82)* | *(Kranjcar 41)* |
| **NK DINAMO ZAGREB 0** | **FC DYNAMO KYIV 2** |
| | *(Shatskikh 46, Rincon 70)* |

**FC DYNAMO KYIV WON 5-1 ON AGGREGATE**

---

| | |
|---|---|
| **GRASSHOPPER-CLUB** (Switzerland) **1** | **AEK ATHENS FC** (Greece) **0** |

# CHAMPIONS LEAGUE QUALIFYING

| | |
|---|---|
| *(Nunez 83)* | |
| **AEK ATHENS 3** | **GRASSHOPPER-CLUB 1** |
| *(Katsouranis 21, Liberopoulos 25, Castillo 39og)* | *(Nunez 68)* |

**AEK ATHENS WON 3-2 ON AGGREGATE**

---

| | |
|---|---|
| **MSK ZILINA** (Slovakia) **0** | **CHELSEA FC** (England) **2** |
| | *(Gudjohnsen 42, Drahno 76og)* |
| **CHELSEA FC 3** | **MSK ZILNA 0** |
| *(Johnson 32, Huth 67, Hasselbaink 78)* | |

**CHELSEA FC WON 5-0 ON AGGREGATE**

---

| | |
|---|---|
| **RC CELTA DE VIGO** (Spain) **3** | **SK SLAVIA PRAHA** (Czech Rep) **0** |
| *(Mostovoi 18, Jesuli 49, Edu 55)* | |
| **SK SLAVIA PRAHA 2** | **RC CELTA DE VIGO 0** |
| *(R Dostalek 18, Hrdlicka 30)* | |

**RC CELTA WON 3-2 ON AGGREGATE**

---

| | |
|---|---|
| **FK PARTIZAN BELGRADE 0** | **NEWCASTLE UNITED FC** (England) **1** |
| | *(Solano 38)* |
| **NEWCASTLE UNITED FC 0** | **FK PARTIZAN BELGRADE 1** |
| | *(Iliev 50)* |

**FK PARTIZAN WON 4-3 ON PENALTIES AFTER 1-1 DRAW**

---

| | |
|---|---|
| **GALATASARAY SK** (Turkey) **3** | **PFC CSKA SOFIA 0** |
| *(Hasan Sas 3, Hakan Sukur 6, Arif 37)* | |
| **PFC CSKA SOFIA 0** | **GALATASARAY SK 3** |
| | *(Cesar Prates 28, Sabri 53, Arif 86)* |

**GALATASARAY SK WON 6-0 ON AGGREGATE**

---

| | |
|---|---|
| **RSC ANDERLECHT 3** | **WISLA KRAKOW 1** |
| *(Jestrovic 11, Lovre 36, Dindane 59)* | *(Zurawski 77pen)* |
| **WISLA KRAKOW 0** | **RSC ANDERLECHT 1** |
| | *(Dindane 84)* |

**RSC ANDERLECHT WON 4-1 ON AGGREGATE**

---

| | |
|---|---|
| **GRAZER AK 1** | **AFC AJAX** (Holland) **1** |
| *(Pogatetz 56)* | *(Sneijder 79)* |
| **AFC AJAX 2** | **GRAZER AK 1** |
| *(Ibrahimovic 15, Galasek 104pen)* | *(Kollmann 40)* |

**AFC AJAX WON 2-1 ON AGGREGATE**

(AFTER EXTRA TIME SILVER GOAL)

---

# CHAMPIONS LEAGUE RECORDS 1992-2003

## MOST SUCCESSIVE WINS
9 Barcelona (9/02 to 02/03)
8 Borussia Dortmund (12/96 to 10/97)
5 Man Utd (11/02 to 02/03)

## MOST SUCCESSIVE DEFEATS
7 Spartak Moscow (1/01 to 11/02) – ongoing
Fenerbahce (12/96 to 10/01) – ongoing

## LONGEST UNBEATEN RUNS
19 Ajax (9/94 to 3/96), Bayern Munich (3/01 to 4/02)
16 Manchester Utd (3/98 to 9/99 and 10/01 to 10/02)
14 Barcelona (5/02 to 4/03)

## LONGEST RUNS WITHOUT A WIN
17 Spartak Moscow (12/00 to 11/02) – ongoing
12 AEK Athens (9/94 to 11/02) – ongoing, Rangers (4/93 to 10/96)

## MOST SUCCESSIVE HOME WINS
10 Juventus (3/96 to 12/97)
9 Real Madrid (3/96 to 12/98)
8 Bayern Munich (11/99 to 10/00), Real Madrid (5/00 to 4/01)
7 Ajax (12/94 to 3/96), Arsenal (3/01 to 2/02), Barcelona (10/99 to 9/00)

## MOST SUCCESSIVE HOME DEFEATS
4 PSV Eindhoven (12/92 to 9/97), Sturm Graz (9/98 to 9/99)
3 Bayer Leverkusen (11/02 to 3/03) - ongoing, Deportivo La Coruna (3/02 to 9/02), Fenerbahce (9/01 to 10/01) – ongoing, Kosice (9/97 to 12/97) – ongoing, Lokomotiv Moscow (11/02 to 3/03) - ongoing, Maribor (9/99 to 10/99) – ongoing, Sparta Prague (10/01 to 2/02), Spartak Moscow (9/02 to 11/02) – ongoing

## MOST SUCCESSIVE AWAY WINS

**7** Ajax (11/95 to 3/97)
**4** Barcelona (9/02 to 11/02)

## MOST SUCCESSIVE AWAY DEFEATS

**11** Rosenborg (11/99 to 9/02)
**10** Spartak Moscow (10/00 to 11/02) – ongoing
**8** Galatasaray (3/94 to 11/97)
**7** Dynamo Kiev (9/00 to 9/02), Olympiakos (3/99 to 11/00), Porto (3/97 to 11/98)
**6** Arsenal (3/01 to 11/01), Besiktas (9/97 to 11/00) – ongoing
**5** Marseille (9/99 to 3/00) – ongoing, Olympiakos (9/01 to 10/02) – ongoing, Sporting Lisbon (11/97 to 10/00) – ongoing

## LONGEST UNBEATEN HOME RUNS

**29** Bayern Munich (3/98 to 4/02)
**20** Valencia (9/99 to 11/02)
**16** Juventus (3/96 to 3/99)
**15** Manchester Utd (10/97 to 3/00)
**14** Real Madrid (3/96 to 12/99)
**13** Galatasaray (11/99 to 2/02), Olympiakos (9/97 to 10/00), Manchester Utd (10/01 to 04/03) - ongoing
**12** Arsenal (9/00 to 2/02), Rosenborg (11/96 to 11/99)
**11** AC Milan (9/99 to 10/02)
**10** Barcelona (11/98 to 9/00), Real Madrid (3/00 to 4/01), Real Madrid (9/01 to 10/02), Spartak Moscow (10/94 to 9/99), Juventus (9/01 to 12/02)
**9** Ajax (9/94 to 3/96), Barcelona (12/93 to 10/97), Borussia Dortmund (12/96 to 9/99), AC Milan (11/92 to 11/94), Porto (11/97 to 12/99)

## LONGEST UNBEATEN AWAY RUNS

**14** Ajax (9/94 to 3/97)
**9** Manchester Utd (10/01 to 10/02)
**8** Bayern Munich (4/01 to 3/02)

## MOST SUCCESSIVE GAMES SCORING

**22** Bayern Munich (9/98 to 3/00)
**20** Barcelona (11/98 to 9/00)
**19** Juventus (3/96 to 11/97)
**15** Feyenoord (9/97 to 2/00), Real Madrid (11/01 to 10/02)

## MOST SUCCESSIVE GAMES WITHOUT SCORING

**5** Bordeaux (10/99 to 3/00), Galatasaray (12/93 to 3/94), Legia Warsaw (11/95 to 3/96) – ongoing, Porto (3/97 to 10/97), Sturm Graz (11/98 to 9/99)

## MOST SUCCESSIVE CLEAN SHEETS

6 Ajax (10/95 to 3/96), Panathinaikos (11/95 to 4/96)
5 Ajax (11/94 to 4/95), AC Milan (12/94 to 4/95), Real Madrid (3/98 to 9/98)

## MOST SUCCESSIVE GAMES WITHOUT KEEPING A CLEAN SHEET

18 PSV Eindhoven (11/97 to 10/00), Spartak Moscow (11/00 to 11/02) – ongoing
17 Rosenborg (11/99 to 10/01)
15 Arsenal (3/01 to 3/02)
14 Rangers (9/95 to 9/99)
13 Bayern Munich (11/99 to 9/00), Dynamo Kiev (4/99 to 3/00), Olympiakos (11/00 to 11/02) – ongoing
12 IFK Gothenburg (3/95 to 11/97)
12 Deportivo (03/02 to 02/03)

## MOST APPEARANCES

| | | |
|---|---|---|
| **GARY NEVILLE** | Manchester United FC | **78** |
| **RAUL GONZALEZ** | Real Madrid CF | **78** |
| **DAVID BECKHAM** | Manchester United FC | **77** |
| **ROBERTO CARLOS** | Real Madrid CF | **76** |
| **FRANK DE BOER** | AFC Ajax, FC Barcelona | **75** |
| **RYAN GIGGS** | Manchester United FC | **70** |
| **OLIVER KAHN** | FC Bayern Munchen | **69** |
| **OLE GUNNAR SOLSKJAER** | Manchester United FC | **69** |
| **PAUL SCHOLES** | Manchester United FC | **68** |
| **PATRICK KLUIVERT** | AFC Ajax, FC Barcelona | **68** |
| **FERNANDO HIERRO** | Real Madrid CF | **68** |
| **PAOLO MALDINI** | Milan AC | **65** |
| **MICHAEL REIZIGER** | AFC Ajax, Milan AC, FC Barcelona | **64** |
| **EDGAR DAVIDS** | AFC Ajax, Milan AC, Juventus FC | **64** |
| **LUIS FIGO** | FC Barcelona, Real Madrid CF | **64** |
| **ROY KEANE** | Manchester United FC | **62** |
| **NICKY BUTT** | Manchester United FC | **62** |
| **DIDIER DESCHAMPS** | Marseille, Juventus FC, Chelsea FC, Valencia CF | **61** |
| **SAMMY KUFFOUR** | FC Bayern Munchen | **61** |
| **GIOVANE ELBER** | FC Bayern Munchen | **60** |
| **ALESSANDRO DEL PIERO** | Juventus FC | **60** |
| **DENIS IRWIN** | Manchester United FC | **59** |
| **ALESSIO TACCHINARDI** | Juventus FC | **59** |
| **ZINEDINE ZIDANE** | Juventus FC, Real Madrid CF | **58** |

# CHAMPIONS LEAGUE RECORDS

## TOP GOAL SCORERS

| | | |
|---|---|---|
| **RAUL GONZALEZ** | Real Madrid FC | **43** |
| **RUUD VAN NISTELROOY** | Manchester United FC | **30** |
| **PATRICK KLUIVERT** | AFC Ajax 9, FC Barcelona 15 | **29** |
| **ALESSANDRO DEL PIERO** | Juventus FC | **29** |
| **FILIPPO INZAGHI** | Juventus FC 17, Milan AC 10 | **27** |
| **THIERRY HENRY** | AS Monaco 7, Arsenal FC 19 | **26** |
| **MARIO JARDEL** | FC Porto 19, SK Galatasaray 6 | **25** |
| **RIVALDO** | FC Barcelona 22, Milan AC 22 | **24** |
| **ANDREI SHEVCHENKO** | FC Dynamo Kyiv 14, Milan AC 10 | **24** |
| **JARI LITMANEN** | AFC Ajax 20, FC Barcelona , Liverpool 3, | **23** |
| **GIOVANE ELBER** | FC Bayern Munchen | **21** |
| **MARCO SIMONE** | Milan AC 11, PSG 3, AS Monaco 6 | **20** |
| **SERHII REBROV** | FC Dynamo Kyiv | **19** |
| **LUIS ENRIQUE** | FC Barcelona | **19** |
| **ANDY COLE** | Manchester United FC | **18** |
| **RYAN GIGGS** | Manchester United FC | **18** |
| **FERNANDO MORIENTES** | Real Madrid FC | **17** |
| **PAUL SCHOLES** | Manchester United FC | **17** |
| **OLE GUNNAR SOLSKJAER** | Manchester United FC | **17** |
| **LUIS FIGO** | FC Barcelona 7, Real Madrid FC 10 | **17** |
| **DAVID TREZEGUET** | AS Monaco 4, Juventus FC 13 | **17** |
| **DAVID BECKHAM** | Manchester United FC | **14** |
| **JOHN CAREW** | Rosenborg 5, Valencia CF 8 | **13** |
| **HERNAN CRESPO** | AC Parma 2, SS Lazio 2, Inter Milan 9 | **13** |
| **GUTI** | Real Madrid FC | **13** |
| **CARSTEN JANCKER** | FC Bayern Munchen | **13** |
| **JAN KOLLER** | Anderlecht FC 3, BV Borussia Dortmund 10 | **13** |
| **ROBERTO CARLOS** | Real Madrid FC | **13** |
| **SONNY ANDERSON** | FC Barcelona 3, Olympique Lyon 10 | **13** |
| **SIMONE INZAGHI** | SS Lazio | **12** |
| **ROY KEANE** | Manchester United FC | **12** |
| **ROY MAKAAY** | RC Deportivo Coruna | **12** |
| **PAULO SERGIO** | FC Bayern Munchen | **12** |
| **DIEGO TRISTAN** | RC Deportivo Coruna | **12** |
| **IVAN HELGUERA** | Real Madrid FC | **11** |
| **CLAUDIO LOPEZ** | Valencia CF 5, SS Lazio 6 | **11** |
| **JAVEIR SAVIOLA** | FC Barcelona | **11** |

## CLUBS WHO HAVE PLAYED IN THE FINALS

**4** Milan AC (1993, 1994, 1995, 2003), Juventus FC (1996, 1997, 1998, 2003)
**3** Real Madrid CF (1998, 2000, 2002)
**2** AFC Ajax (1995, 1996), FC Bayern Munchen (1999, 2001), Valencia (2000, 2001)
**1** Olympique de Marseille (1993), FC Barcelona (1994), Borussia Dortmund (1997), Manchester United FC (1999), Bayer 04 Leverkusen(2002)

## WINNERS OF THE CHAMPIONS LEAGUE FINAL

**3** Real Madrid CF (1998, 2000, 2002)
**2** Milan AC (1994, 2003)
**1** Olympique de Marseille (1993), AFC Ajax (1995), Juventus FC (1996), Borussia Dortmund (1997), Manchester United FC (1999), FC Bayern Munchen (2001)

## RUNNERS-UP IN THE CHAMPIONS LEAGUE

**3** Juventus FC (1997, 1998, 2003)
**2** Milan AC (1993, 1995), Valencia (2000, 2001)
**1** FC Barcelona (1994), AFC Ajax (1996), FC Bayern Munchen (1999), Bayer 04 Leverkusen(2002)

## BIGGEST WINS IN THE FINAL

Milan AC 4 v FC Barcelona 0 (1994)
Real Madrid CF 3 v Valencia CF 0 (2000)
Borussia Dortmund 3 v Juventus FC 1 (1997)

## BIGGEST WINS

| | |
|---|---|
| Paris Saint-Germain FC 7 v Rosenborg BK 2 | 24.10.00 |
| Olympique de Marseille 6 v CSKA Moscow 0 | 17.03.93 |
| Leeds United AFC 6 v Besiktas JK 0 | 26.09.00 |
| Real Madrid CF 6 v Ferencvarosi TC 1 | 18.10.95 |
| Real Madrid CF 6 v SK Sturm Graz 1 | 21.10.98 |
| Rosenborg BK 6 v Helsingborgs IF 1 | 26.09.00 |
| Brondby IF 2 v Manchester United FC 6 | 21.10.98 |

## FEWEST WINS

CSKA Moscow (1992/93)
AEK Athens (1994/95)
SK Rapid Wien (1996/97)
FS Kosice (1997/98)
K.Lierse SK (1997/98)
AIK Solna (1999/00)
Willem II (1999/00)
**They all failed to record a single victory in their only appearance in the group stage.*

## MOST GOALS IN A SEASON

| | | |
|---|---|---|
| 12 | RUUD VAN NISTELROOY (Manchester United FC) | 2002/2003 |
| 10 | RUUD VAN NISTELROOY (Manchester United FC) | 2001/2002 |
| 10 | JARDEL (FC Porto) | 1999/00 |
| 10 | RIVALDO (FC Barcelona) | 1999/00 |
| 10 | RAUL (Real Madrid CF) | 1999/00 |
| 9 | JARI LITMANEN (AFC Ajax) | 1995/96 |
| 9 | SIMONE INZAGHI (S.S.Lazio) | 1999/00 |
| 8 | ANDRII SHEVCHENKO (FC Dynamo Kyiv) | 1998/99 |
| 8 | DWIGHT YORKE (Manchester United FC) | 1998/99 |
| 8 | TORE ANDRE FLO (Chelsea FC) | 1999/00 |
| 8 | SERHII REBROV (FC Dynamo Kyiv) | 1999/00 |
| 8 | DAVID TREZEGUET (Juventus FC) | 2001/02 |

## TOP GOALSCORER IN A SEASON

| | | |
|---|---|---|
| 5 | FRANCK SAUZEE (Olympique de Marseille) | 1992/93 |
| 5 | HRISTO STOITCHKOV (FC Barcelona) | 1993/94 |
| 7 | GEORGE WEAH (Paris Saint-Germain FC) | 1994/95 |
| 9 | JARI LITMANEN (AFC Ajax) | 1995/96 |
| 5 | MILINKO PANTIC (Club Atletico de Madrid) | 1996/97 |
| 10 | ALESSANDRO DEL PIERO (Juventus FC) | 1997/98 |
| 8 | ANDRII SHEVCHENKO (FC Dynamo Kyiv) | 1998/99 |
| | DWIGHT YORKE (Manchester United FC) | |
| 10 | JARDEL (FC Porto) | 1999/00 |
| | RIVALDO (FC Barcelona) | |
| | RAUL (Real Madrid CF) | |
| 7 | RAUL (Real Madrid CF) | 2000/01 |
| 10 | RUUD VAN NISTELROOY (Manchester United FC) | 2001/02 |
| 12 | RUUD VAN NISTELROOY (Manchester United FC) | 2002/03 |

# CHAMPIONS LEAGUE 2002-2003 STATISTICS

**PROVIDED BY OPTA**

## PLAYER CROSSES

| PLAYER | TEAM NAME | CROSSES | CROSSING ACCURACY |
|---|---|---|---|
| FIGO | REAL MADRID | 186 | 22% |
| NEDVED | JUVENTUS | 116 | 28% |
| CAFU | ROMA | 114 | 28% |
| ROBERT | NEWCASTLE UNITED | 97 | 26% |
| VICENTE | VALENCIA | 95 | 28% |
| VAN DER MEYDE | AJAX | 88 | 26% |
| RUI COSTA | MILAN | 76 | 18% |
| HENRY | ARSENAL | 74 | 22% |
| BECKHAM | MANCHESTER UNITED | 73 | 29% |
| HAKAN YAKIN | BASEL | 71 | 34% |
| RECOBA | INTERNAZIONALE | 63 | 27% |
| ROBERTO CARLOS | REAL MADRID | 63 | 11% |
| BABIC | BAYER LEVERKUSEN | 61 | 20% |
| CONCEICAO | INTERNAZIONALE | 59 | 27% |
| DEL PIERO | JUVENTUS | 59 | 24% |
| MENDIETA | BARCELONA | 58 | 14% |
| SOLANO | NEWCASTLE UNITED | 57 | 33% |
| GIGGS | MANCHESTER UNITED | 54 | 33% |
| FRAN | DEPORTIVO DE LA CORUÑA | 54 | 22% |
| VÍCTOR | DEPORTIVO DE LA CORUÑA | 54 | 15% |

# CHAMPIONS LEAGUE 02-03 STATISTICS

## PLAYER ASSISTS

| PLAYER | TEAM NAME | ASSISTS |
|---|---|---|
| RAÚL | REAL MADRID | 6 |
| RUI COSTA | MILAN | 6 |
| AIMAR | VALENCIA | 5 |
| CAREW | VALENCIA | 5 |
| CARRIÈRE | LYON | 5 |
| SOLSKJAER | MANCHESTER UNITED | 5 |
| VERON | MANCHESTER UNITED | 5 |
| CAMORANESI | JUVENTUS | 4 |
| DAVIDS | JUVENTUS | 4 |
| HAKAN YAKIN | BASEL | 4 |
| RIQUELME | BARCELONA | 4 |
| ROSICKY | BORUSSIA DORTMUND | 4 |
| SEEDORF | MILAN | 4 |
| ZIDANE | REAL MADRID | 4 |

## PLAYER OFF-SIDES

| PLAYER | TEAM NAME | OFFSIDES |
|---|---|---|
| INZAGHI | MILAN | 32 |
| VIERI | INTERNAZIONALE | 27 |
| GIMENEZ | BASEL | 22 |
| IBRAHIMOVIC | AJAX | 21 |
| ROSSI | BASEL | 20 |
| MAKAAY | DEPORTIVO DE LA CORUÑA | 19 |
| KLUIVERT | BARCELONA | 18 |
| CAFU | ROMA | 17 |
| SAVIOLA | BARCELONA | 17 |
| KEZMAN | PSV EINDHOVEN | 17 |
| NIKOLAIDIS | AEK ATHENS | 17 |
| TREZEGUET | JUVENTUS | 17 |
| TOTTI | ROMA | 16 |
| HENRY | ARSENAL | 15 |
| VAN NISTELROOY | MANCHESTER UNITED | 15 |
| DI VAIO | JUVENTUS | 15 |
| RONALDO | REAL MADRID | 14 |

# CHAMPIONS LEAGUE 02-03 STATISTICS

## PLAYER PASSES

| PLAYER | TEAM NAME | PASSES | PASSING ACCURACY |
|---|---|---|---|
| ROBERTO CARLOS | REAL MADRID | 930 | 85% |
| ZIDANE | REAL MADRID | 910 | 88% |
| XAVI | BARCELONA | 897 | 90% |
| ZIDANE | REAL MADRID | 820 | 83% |
| TACCHINARDI | JUVENTUS | 756 | 84% |
| MÍCHEL SALGADO | REAL MADRID | 728 | 90% |
| THURAM | JUVENTUS | 719 | 82% |
| ZANETTI | INTERNAZIONALE | 717 | 88% |
| DE BOER | BARCELONA | 708 | 89% |
| VIEIRA | ARSENAL | 707 | 82% |
| MAKELELE | REAL MADRID | 705 | 86% |
| RUI COSTA | MILAN | 692 | 81% |
| MALDINI | MILAN | 690 | 80% |
| BARAJA | VALENCIA | 687 | 80% |
| SEEDORF | MILAN | 675 | 80% |
| PIRLO | MILAN | 662 | 81% |
| GATTUSO | MILAN | 659 | 83% |
| GUTI | REAL MADRID | 618 | 88% |
| LOSKOV | LOKOMOTIV MOSCOW | 616 | 75% |
| MOTTA | BARCELONA | 613 | 89% |

## GOALKEEPERS

| PLAYER | TEAM NAME | SAVES | SAVES-TO-SHOTS RATIO |
|---|---|---|---|
| TOLDO | INTERNAZIONALE | 81 | 81% |
| BUFFON | JUVENTUS | 68 | 81% |
| ZUBERBUHLER | BASEL | 51 | 70% |
| CASILLAS | REAL MADRID | 50 | 70% |
| LEHMANN | BORUSSIA DORTMUND | 47 | 80% |
| OVCHINNIKOV | LOKOMOTIV MOSCOW | 43 | 72% |
| DIDA | MILAN | 36 | 88% |
| AWAT | MACCABI HAIFA | 36 | 75% |
| BUTT | BAYER LEVERKUSEN | 36 | 67% |

| | | | |
|---|---|---|---|
| **CAÑIZARES** | VALENCIA | 34 | **74%** |
| **JUANMI** | DEPORTIVO DE LA CORUÑA | 32 | **63%** |
| **GIVEN** | NEWCASTLE UNITED | 32 | **62%** |
| **ANTONIOLI** | ROMA | 30 | **77%** |
| **CHIOTIS** | AEK ATHENS | 29 | **81%** |
| **LOBONT** | AJAX | 25 | **81%** |
| **BONANO** | BARCELONA | 24 | **83%** |
| **VERLINDEN** | CLUB BRUGGE | 22 | **76%** |
| **BARTHEZ** | MANCHESTER UNITED | 22 | **65%** |
| **ZOETEBIER** | FEYENOORD | 21 | **84%** |
| **MONDRAGON** | GALATASARAY | 21 | **68%** |

## PLAYER SCORING

| PLAYER | TEAM NAME | GOALS | CHANCE CONVERSION |
|---|---|---|---|
| **VAN NISTELROOY** | MANCHESTER UNITED | 12 | **34%** |
| **INZAGHI** | MILAN | 10 | **34%** |
| **CRESPO** | INTERNAZIONALE | 9 | **31%** |
| **MAKAAY** | DEPORTIVO DE LA CORUÑA | 9 | **23%** |
| **RAÚL** | REAL MADRID | 9 | **22%** |
| **KOLLER** | BORUSSIA DORTMUND | 8 | **32%** |
| **SAVIOLA** | BARCELONA | 7 | **29%** |
| **HENRY** | ARSENAL | 7 | **16%** |
| **SHEARER** | NEWCASTLE UNITED | 6 | **23%** |
| **RONALDO** | REAL MADRID | 6 | **21%** |
| **AIYEGBENI** | MACCABI HAIFA | 5 | **42%** |
| **GUTI** | REAL MADRID | 5 | **31%** |
| **GIGGS** | MANCHESTER UNITED | 5 | **29%** |
| **ANDERSON** | LYON | 5 | **23%** |
| **GIMENEZ** | BASEL | 5 | **23%** |
| **ROSSI** | BASEL | 5 | **22%** |
| **KLUIVERT** | BARCELONA | 5 | **16%** |
| **IBRAHIMOVIC** | AJAX | 5 | **15%** |
| **NEDVED** | JUVENTUS | 5 | **14%** |
| **DEL PIERO** | JUVENTUS | 5 | **12%** |
| **CAREW** | VALENCIA | 5 | **12%** |

# CHAMPIONS LEAGUE 02-03 STATISTICS

## PLAYER SHOOTING

| PLAYER | TEAM NAME | SHOTS ATTEMPTED | SHOOTING ACCURACY |
|---|---|---|---|
| HENRY | ARSENAL | 43 | 49% |
| CAREW | VALENCIA | 42 | 45% |
| RAÚL | REAL MADRID | 41 | 59% |
| DEL PIERO | JUVENTUS | 41 | 49% |
| MAKAAY | DEPORTIVO DE LA CORUÑA | 39 | 62% |
| ROBERTO CARLOS | REAL MADRID | 39 | 36% |
| NEDVED | JUVENTUS | 37 | 46% |
| VAN NISTELROOY | MANCHESTER UNITED | 35 | 74% |
| HAKAN YAKIN | BASEL | 35 | 43% |
| BARAJA | VALENCIA | 34 | 44% |
| IBRAHIMOVIC | AJAX | 33 | 58% |
| KLUIVERT | BARCELONA | 31 | 55% |
| RONALDO | REAL MADRID | 29 | 69% |
| INZAGHI | MILAN | 29 | 66% |
| CRESPO | INTERNAZIONALE | 29 | 59% |
| ROBERT | NEWCASTLE UNITED | 28 | 36% |
| VIERI | INTERNAZIONALE | 27 | 48% |
| SHEARER | NEWCASTLE UNITED | 26 | 54% |
| BELLAMY | NEWCASTLE UNITED | 26 | 46% |
| ZIDANE | REAL MADRID | 25 | 60% |

## PLAYER TACKLES

| PLAYER | TEAM NAME | TACKLES | SUCCESS |
|---|---|---|---|
| GATTUSO | MILAN | 103 | 77% |
| GALÁSEK | AJAX | 77 | 66% |
| DAVIDS | JUVENTUS | 71 | 80% |
| ZANETTI | INTERNAZIONALE | 70 | 86% |
| TACCHINARDI | JUVENTUS | 65 | 78% |
| ALBELDA | VALENCIA | 65 | 71% |
| MALDINI | MILAN | 64 | 78% |
| NESTA | MILAN | 63 | 79% |
| PUYOL | BARCELONA | 63 | 78% |
| VIEIRA | ARSENAL | 58 | 74% |

| | | | |
|---|---|---|---|
| MONTERO | JUVENTUS | 56 | 70% |
| HAAS | BASEL | 54 | 80% |
| MÍCHEL SALGADO | REAL MADRID | 54 | 72% |
| SCALONI | DEPORTIVO DE LA CORUÑA | 53 | 74% |
| CHIVU | AJAX | 53 | 66% |
| KALADZE | MILAN | 52 | 75% |
| I. HELGUERA | REAL MADRID | 52 | 63% |
| SPEED | NEWCASTLE UNITED | 52 | 63% |
| BARAJA | VALENCIA | 50 | 76% |
| FRINGS | BORUSSIA DORTMUND | 49 | 73% |

## PLAYER FOULS

| PLAYER | TEAM NAME | FOULS | YELLOW CARDS | RED CARDS | DISC POINTS |
|---|---|---|---|---|---|
| TACCHINARDI | JUVENTUS | 36 | 9 | 0 | 63 |
| GATTUSO | MILAN | 39 | 5 | 0 | 54 |
| DAVIDS | JUVENTUS | 34 | 3 | 1 | 49 |
| EMERSON | ROMA | 39 | 3 | 0 | 48 |
| IBRAHIMOVIC | AJAX | 42 | 2 | 0 | 48 |
| CANNAVARO | INTERNAZIONALE | 26 | 4 | 1 | 44 |
| VIEIRA | ARSENAL | 33 | 3 | 0 | 42 |
| ALBELDA | VALENCIA | 28 | 2 | 1 | 40 |
| SAMUEL | ROMA | 25 | 5 | 0 | 40 |
| MONTERO | JUVENTUS | 27 | 4 | 0 | 39 |
| I. HELGUERA | REAL MADRID | 30 | 3 | 0 | 39 |
| EVSEEV | LOKOMOTIV MOSCOW | 26 | 4 | 0 | 38 |
| CHIVU | AJAX | 17 | 4 | 1 | 35 |
| LOSKOV | LOKOMOTIV MOSCOW | 20 | 3 | 1 | 35 |
| GABRI | BARCELONA | 20 | 5 | 0 | 35 |
| GALÁSEK | AJAX | 26 | 3 | 0 | 35 |
| FRINGS | BORUSSIA DORTMUND | 29 | 2 | 0 | 35 |
| SALGADO | REAL MADRID | 29 | 2 | 0 | 35 |
| TOMMASI | ROMA | 29 | 2 | 0 | 35 |
| SHEARER | NEWCASTLE UNITED | 32 | 1 | 0 | 35 |

**FOUL = 1PT, YELLOW = 3PTS, RED = 6PTS**

# CHAMPIONS LEAGUE 02-03 STATISTICS

## TEAM TACKLING

| TEAM NAME | TACKLES ATTEMPTED | TACKLE SUCCESS RATE |
|---|---|---|
| FC DINAMO KIEV | 267 | 82.4% |
| BAYER 04 LEVERKUSEN | 272 | 79.8% |
| FC BAYERN MUNCHEN | 161 | 79.5% |
| KRC GENK | 180 | 79.4% |
| INTERNAZIONALE FC | 452 | 78.3% |
| OLYMPIAKOS PIRAEUS FC | 161 | 78.3% |
| RC LENS | 183 | 78.1% |
| AJ AUXERRE | 191 | 78.0% |
| MACCABI HAIFA | 149 | 77.9% |
| FEYENOORD | 174 | 77.6% |
| AC MILAN | 629 | 76.3% |
| ROSENBORG BK | 124 | 75.0% |
| JUVENTUS FC | 572 | 74.8% |
| ARSENAL FC | 377 | 74.8% |
| VALENCIA | 435 | 74.7% |
| AS ROMA | 388 | 74.0% |
| BASEL | 388 | 73.7% |
| AEK ATHENS | 176 | 72.7% |
| NEWCASTLE UNITED FC | 362 | 71.5% |
| BV BORUSSIA DORTMUND | 390 | 71.3% |
| LIVERPOOL FC | 205 | 71.2% |
| RC DEPORTIVO DE LA CORUÑA | 380 | 70.5% |
| GALATASARAY SK | 183 | 70.5% |
| MANCHESTER UNITED FC | 498 | 70.3% |
| REAL MADRID CF | 457 | 70.0% |
| LYON | 137 | 69.3% |
| AFC AJAX | 472 | 69.3% |
| PSV EINDHOVEN | 175 | 69.1% |
| FC BARCELONA | 407 | 68.6% |
| CLUB BRUGGE KV | 202 | 68.3% |
| SPARTAK MOSCOW | 197 | 66.0% |
| FC LOKOMOTIV MOSCOW | 363 | 65.6% |

## CHAMPIONS LEAGUE 02-03 STATISTICS

### TEAM SHOOTING

| TEAM NAME | TOTAL SHOTS ATTEMPTED | SHOOTING ACCURACY |
|---|---|---|
| LIVERPOOL FC | 82 | 61.0% |
| MANCHESTER UNITED FC | 175 | 53.7% |
| LYON | 86 | 53.5% |
| MACCABI HAIFA | 63 | 52.4% |
| INTERNAZIONALE FC | 147 | 49.7% |
| REAL MADRID CF | 239 | 49.0% |
| FC BARCELONA | 163 | 48.5% |
| ARSENAL FC | 136 | 47.1% |
| AEK ATHENS | 51 | 47.1% |
| VALENCIA CF | 203 | 46.8% |
| FEYENOORD | 64 | 45.3% |
| NEWCASTLE UNITED FC | 152 | 44.1% |
| OLYMPIAKOS PIRAEUS FC | 66 | 43.9% |
| RC DEPORTIVO DE LA CORUÑA | 139 | 43.9% |
| AC MILAN | 171 | 43.9% |
| CLUB BRUGGE KV | 70 | 42.9% |
| RC LENS | 57 | 42.1% |
| BASEL | 141 | 40.4% |
| FC LOKOMOTIV MOSCOW | 120 | 40.0% |
| JUVENTUS FC | 207 | 39.1% |
| AFC AJAX | 151 | 39.1% |
| PSV EINDHOVEN | 75 | 38.7% |
| FC DINAMO KIEV | 73 | 38.4% |
| KRC GENK | 69 | 37.7% |
| FC BAYERN MUNCHEN | 88 | 37.5% |
| SPARTAK MOSCOW | 48 | 37.5% |
| ROSENBORG BK | 63 | 36.5% |
| BV BORUSSIA DORTMUND | 121 | 34.7% |
| BAYER 04 LEVERKUSEN | 139 | 33.8% |
| AS ROMA | 130 | 30.8% |
| AJ AUXERRE | 46 | 30.4% |
| GALATASARAY SK | 63 | 30.2% |

# CHAMPIONS LEAGUE 02-03 STATISTICS

## TEAM PASSING

| TEAM NAME | TOTAL PASSES | PASSING ACCURACY |
|---|---|---|
| REAL MADRID CF | 8541 | 85.4% |
| FC BARCELONA | 7359 | 85.0% |
| PSV EINDHOVEN | 3315 | 84.3% |
| OLYMPIAKOS PIRAEUS FC | 2697 | 82.4% |
| MANCHESTER UNITED FC | 6475 | 80.9% |
| LYON | 2784 | 80.7% |
| FC BAYERN MUNCHEN | 2610 | 80.3% |
| AFC AJAX | 5656 | 80.3% |
| AC MILAN | 7600 | 80.2% |
| BAYER 04 LEVERKUSEN | 5275 | 79.8% |
| ARSENAL FC | 5598 | 79.8% |
| JUVENTUS FC | 7194 | 79.6% |
| FEYENOORD | 2635 | 78.9% |
| LIVERPOOL | 2482 | 78.8% |
| RC DEPORTIVO DE LA CORUÑA | 5293 | 78.7% |
| VALENCIA CF | 5935 | 78.4% |
| AS ROMA | 5063 | 78.3% |
| BV BORUSSIA DORTMUND | 5136 | 77.9% |
| GALATASARAY SK | 2534 | 77.9% |
| KRC GENK | 2185 | 76.7% |
| MACCABI HAIFA | 2177 | 76.6% |
| INTERNAZIONALE FC | 5893 | 76.5% |
| NEWCASTLE UNITED FC | 4677 | 76.1% |
| ROSENBORG BK | 2382 | 75.7% |
| AEK ATHENS | 2205 | 75.7% |
| RC LENS | 2152 | 75.3% |
| CLUB BRUGGE KV | 2204 | 75.0% |
| FC LOKOMOTIV MOSCOW | 4790 | 74.8% |
| BASEL | 4157 | 74.7% |
| SPARTAK MOSCOW | 2454 | 74.6% |
| AJ AUXERRE | 2349 | 74.4% |
| FC DINAMO KIEV | 2098 | 73.5% |

# CHAMPIONS LEAGUE 02-03 STATISTICS

## TEAM GOALS

| TEAM NAME | GOALS | CHANCE CONVERSION |
|---|---|---|
| MACCABI HAIFA | 12 | 19% |
| MANCHESTER UNITED FC | 32 | 18% |
| RC LENS | 11 | 18% |
| FC BARCELONA | 27 | 16% |
| INTERNAZIONALE FC | 26 | 16% |
| OLYMPIAKOS PIRAEUS FC | 11 | 15% |
| LIVERPOOL FC | 12 | 15% |
| JUVENTUS FC | 30 | 14% |
| LYON | 12 | 14% |
| AEK ATHENS | 7 | 14% |
| REAL MADRID CF | 33 | 13% |
| BV BORUSSIA DORTMUND | 16 | 12% |
| AC MILAN | 21 | 12% |
| RC DEPORTIVO DE LA CORUÑA | 18 | 12% |
| BASEL | 17 | 12% |
| VALENCIA CF | 24 | 12% |
| ARSENAL FC | 15 | 11% |
| NEWCASTLE UNITED | 16 | 11% |
| FC BAYERN MUNCHEN | 9 | 10% |
| BAYER 04 LEVERKUSEN | 14 | 10% |
| AFC AJAX | 14 | 9% |
| AJ AUXERRE | 4 | 9% |
| FC DINAMO KIEV | 6 | 8% |
| GALATASARAY SK | 5 | 8% |
| AS ROMA | 10 | 8% |
| CLUB BRUGGE KV | 5 | 7% |
| FC LOKOMOTIV MOSCOW | 8 | 7% |
| PSV EINDHOVEN | 5 | 7% |
| ROSENBORG BK | 4 | 6% |
| FEYENOORD | 4 | 6% |
| KRC GENK | 2 | 3% |
| SPARTAK MOSCOW | 1 | 2% |

## TEAM CROSSING

| TEAM NAME | CROSSES ATTEMPTED | CROSSING ACCURACY |
|---|---|---|
| LIVERPOOL FC | 138 | 37.0% |
| CLUB BRUGGE KV | 149 | 32.9% |
| VALENCIA CF | 375 | 31.7% |
| MACCABI HAIFA | 57 | 31.6% |
| BASEL | 219 | 30.1% |
| LENS | 119 | 28.6% |
| ROSENBORG BK | 176 | 28.4% |
| PSV EINDHOVEN | 140 | 27.9% |
| KRC GENK | 148 | 27.7% |
| OLYMPIAKOS PIRAEUS FC | 117 | 27.4% |
| LYON | 127 | 26.8% |
| FC BAYERN MUNCHEN | 176 | 26.1% |
| GALATASARAY SK | 142 | 26.1% |
| NEWCASTLE UNITED FC | 275 | 25.8% |
| AS ROMA | 305 | 25.6% |
| JUVENTUS FC | 413 | 24.9% |
| MANCHESTER UNITED FC | 323 | 24.8% |
| AFC AJAX | 292 | 24.7% |
| FEYENOORD | 130 | 24.6% |
| BARCELONA | 298 | 24.5% |
| ARSENAL FC | 223 | 24.2% |
| RC DEPORTIVO DE LA CORUÑA | 318 | 24.2% |
| INTERNAZIONALE FC | 325 | 24.0% |
| FC DINAMO KIEV | 109 | 22.9% |
| SPARTAK MOSCOW | 98 | 21.4% |
| BV BORUSSIA DORTMUND | 262 | 21.0% |
| BAYER 04 LEVERKUSEN | 282 | 20.9% |
| AC MILAN | 384 | 20.8% |
| AEK ATHENS | 123 | 20.3% |
| AJ AUXERRE | 115 | 20.0% |
| FC LOKOMOTIV MOSCOW | 157 | 19.1% |
| REAL MADRID CF | 388 | 19.1% |

## TEAM OF THE SEASON

**FRANCESCO TOLDO**
INTER MILAN
1,395

**JAVIER ZANETTI**
INTER MILAN
1,106

**ALESSANDRO NESTA**
AC MILAN
1,136

**CRISTIAN CHIVU**
AFC AJAX
1,293

**ROBERTO CARLOS**
REAL MADRID CF
1,313

**ZINEDINE ZIDANE**
REAL MADRID CF
1,516

**RUBEN BARAJA**
VALENCIA CF
1,537

**JUAN SEBASTION VERON**
MANCHESTER UNITED
1,514

**PAVEL NEDVED**
JUVENTUS FC
1,120

**RUUD VAN NISTELROOY**
MANCHESTER UNITED
1,971

**RAUL**
REAL MADRID CF
1,380

# GROUP A

**FC BAYERN MUNICH**
(Germany)

**OLYMPIQUE LYONNAIS**
(France)

**CELTIC FC**
(Scotland)

**RSC ANDERLECHT**
(Belgium)

# FC BAYERN MUNICH

**Recent seasons have seen a dominant display from Bayern. They have won the Bundesliga five times in the last seven years (1997, 1999, 2000, 2001, 2003) and the German cup three times in the last six (1998, 2000, 2003). The German giants have also had considerable success in Europe, reaching the Champions League final in 1999 before reigning victorious in 2001. This was the fourth time they have won the European Cup 4 times, as they had a stranglehold over it from 1974–6. Throughout their history, Bayern has won the Bundesliga title on 18 occasions and the Cup on 11. There have been two fine previous eras – the team that won the Bundesliga in 1972, 1973 and 1974 also won the European Cup in 1974, 1975, and 1976. The second era encompassed the 1980–90 seasons when the club won 7 Bundesliga titles in 11 seasons but the bulk of the team was in two losing World Cup finals (1982 and 1986) before the 1990 success. In 1996 Bayern Munich became the fourth club to complete the European treble – European Cup, ECWC and EUFA Cup. The clubs prior to Bayern were Juventus (by 1985) and both Ajax and Barcelona (by 1992).**

## COACH

**OTTMAR HITZFELD** 12.01.49

Hitzfeld's double win with Bayern in 2003 in league and Cup means he is the most be-medalled coach in Bundesliga history. He won them the Bundesliga hat trick (1999, 2000, 2001) as well as the league and cup double in 2000 and 2003. Before he won the European Cup with Bayern in 2001, he coached Dortmund to their 1997 European Cup win. Prior to his success with Dortmund, where he also won two league titles (1995 and 1996) as well as the 1997 European Cup, he coached three Swiss teams Zug (1983– 4), Aarau (1984– 88) and Grasshopper (1988– 91). As a player, Hitzfeld ran out for for Stuttgart in the Bundesliga, and Basle, Lugano and Luzern in his native Swiss League.

## REACTION TO DRAW

**"It's a good draw, but like every other group it is tough. Lyon and Giovanne Elber will want to prove themselves against us, which makes Olympique dangerous for us. I think we are the favourites with Lyon, but after what happened last year we must make sure we reach the second round."** ***Ottmar Hitzfeld***

## SQUAD

**13 MICHAEL BALLACK** 26.09.76

Named 2003 Footballer of the Year after league and cup double win. Joined for £3.9 million, though some say £9 million, from Bayer Leverkusen in May 2002. Was suspended for the World Cup final after scoring the winner in semi v Korea and quarter final v USA. In 2002 he helped Leverkusen achieve runners up positions in Bundesliga, German Cup and Champions League. Other notable goals in 2002 were 17 goals in Bundesliga (in 29 games) to finish 3rd in league lists, scorer of goals in both legs of the World Cup play offs v Ukraine in Nov 2001. He also bagged six goals in the World Cup qualifiers as well as another brace in the 4– 2 win v Liverpool in the Champions League. Signed for Leverkusen in summer 1999 from Kaiserslautern for £2.6 million after winning his first national caps in 1999. Cost Kaiserslautern just £35,000 in summer 1997 from the old GDR top club Chemnitz.

**6 MARTIN DEMICHILIS** 20.12.80
Highly rated Argentine who was part of their World Cup junior winning team. Cost E4.5m from River Plate in summer 2003 where he played three seasons in the first team.

**26 SEBASTIAN DEISLER** 05.01.80
Joined for £6 million in summer 2002 from Hertha Berlin but was not fit until Jan 2003 having damaged knee ligaments. One of those who missed the World Cup through injury – his 3rd serious knee injury in 18 months was sustained against Austria in the final World Cup warm up game in May 2002. Considered the great hope for the future of German football since he made a fine breakthrough in 1999– 2000 following a move to Hertha from relegated Borussia Monchengladbach where he had been playing for five seasons. He cost the Berlin club £1.5 million and after a series of favourable displays at the start of 1999– 2000 was called into the national squad for the Sept and Oct games in Euro2000 qualifiers.

**32 MARKUS FEULNER** 12.02.82
A youth international who became an U21 international in the summer of 2002. Made his debut in 2001– 2 Bundesliga with one game. Now in his sixth season at the club, the midfielder joined from regional club, FC Bamberg.

**15 TOBIAS RAU** 31.12.81
Signed from Wolfsburg for £2.5 million in summer 2003 and is already an international. He made the national team in 2002– 03 and has been a consistent member of the national squad after moving up from the U21 side. Was at Wolfsburg for 2 full seasons, and started to look at home in the left wing back role. He signed for Wolfsburg from Eintracht Braunschweig of Division 3 for £200,000

**23 OWEN HARGREAVES** 20.01.81
Played in the first two games in World Cup until the team formation was changed. Outstanding in suspended Effenberg's place in the Champions League semi final return leg v Real Madrid and almost won man of the match in the final. Has been with the Bayern youth team since 1997 and joined first team squad in 2000. Born in Canada to a Welsh mother from Rhyl and an English father from Bolton hence the British scramble

for him. Invited to play for both Wales U21 and England U21 squads – but Wales claimed they discovered him first. Could have also played for Canada and Germany

**16 JENS JEREMIES** 05.03.74
Despite having just recovered from an injury to his knee, Jeremies went on to play in all seven games for Germany in the World Cup final. He appeared five times as a sub and once from the start including the final when he replaced the suspended Ballack. Another of a growing band from the old GDR, he was with the Dynamo Dresden club in the early part of his career and then moved to Bayern from the other Munich club, 1860, in summer 1998 for just an £800,000 nominal fee. Has a poor scoring record – just 8 Bundesliga goals in 179 games.

**1 OLIVER KAHN** 15.06.69
Named keeper of the tournament after the World Cup despite his costly blunder in the final. Was the hero of the penalty shoot out in 2001 European Cup final with 3 saves and was subsequently elected 2001 German Footballer of the Year – which must have sat nicely next to the 2000 award. Has been Germany's No 1 since Bayern won title in 1999. Was appointed captain since the disaster of the Euro2000 finals. Joined Bayern in summer 1994 from Karlsruhe for £2 million and had settled well after a poor start when injuries and loss of form took their toll.

**5 ROBERT KOVAC** 06.04.74
Played all 3 games for Croatia in 2002 World Cup and became a first choice in central defence for Bayern in 2002. Joined his brother at Bayern in summer 2001 for £5.6 million from Bayer Leverkusen. Niko Kovac left in summer 2003 for Hertha Berlin. The younger of the Croatian brothers, but the more expensive, was born in Berlin of Croatian parents. Robert is a former U21 international for Croatia, and from summer 1999 became a full international, and joined the Leverkusen club from Nurnberg during the 1995-6 season.

**4 SAMMY KUFFOUR** 03.09.76
The Ghanaian international central defender is in his 9th season with the club, after being signed in 1994 from Nurnberg for £850,000 after Ghana won the World Youth Cup. Celebrated his first European game with a goal against Spartak Moscow in the 1994-5 Champions League, just four days after making his first team debut for Bayern. Received his first cap aged just 18 years old.

**25 THOMAS LINKE** 26.12.69
Often more favoured for country than club, Linke played all 7 games in the 2002 World Cup. He signed from Schalke in summer 1998 on a free transfer after helping them win the 1997 UEFA Cup. He spent six seasons at Schalke after joining them from former GDR side, Rot Weiss Erfurt. His finest moment to date must have been taking Bayern's final penalty in the 2001 European Cup final 2001.

# GROUP A
## FC BAYERN MUNICH

**3 BIXENTE LIZARAZU** 09.12.69
Despite having played in all 3 games of France's recent miserable World Cup campaign, Lizarazu has won three major trophies with his country: World Cup 98, Euro2000 and most recently the Confederations Cup in 2001. Has also won three league titles with Bayern 1999– 2001, bagging a fourth in 2003. Was pursued by Manchester United 2001 – but recently there have been doubts about his fitness as he often doesn't train, only plays. Was the subject of an acrimonious move in summer 1997 from Athletic Bilbao in Spain to Bayern. He cost Bayern £2.7 million initially plus another £1.1 million via a FIFA Tribunal.

**14 CLAUDIO PIZARRO** 03.10.78
Peruvian international signed from Werder Bremen for £5.3 million in summer 2001. He scored 15 goals in 30 Bundesliga games for Bayern in 2001– 2 to finish 2nd in the club lists to Elber (17). Added 15 goals in 31 games to the 2003 title win, and was again 2nd to Elber (21). Scored 29 goals in 56 Bundesliga games for Bremen in two seasons. A risky signing for Bremen in summer 1999 for £1.2 million from Peruvian champions Alianza Lima, but settled well. Often away with Peru in their World Cup finals bid.

**2 WILLY SAGNOL** 18.03.77
Was in the France squad for the World Cup but did not play thanks to Lilian Thuram. First capped in Turkey on 15.11.00 as a sub for Thuram, and is now integrated into the national squad after the Bayern 2001 success. Arrived in summer 2000 from Monaco for £5 million to fill the boots of the Liverpool bound Markus Babbel. He won a championship medal in 2000 with Monaco and before that he played for St Etienne.

**20 HASAN SALIHAMIDZIC** 01.01.77
Scorer of crucial goals in the group games of the 1999 Champions League at the Nou Camp and at Old Trafford. Was also a successful penalty taker in 2001 European Cup final. Moved on a free transfer from Hamburg SV in summer 1998. Spent three seasons with HSV where he improved markedly. A key player in the new Bosnia national team, his home club as a teenager was Velez Mostar, one of the cities hit by the troubles.

**24 ROQUE SANTA CRUZ** 16.08.81
Played all 4 games at 2002 World Cup and scored the opener for Paraguay v S Africa. Many people thought Bayern were not up to speed when they signed him from Paraguayan champions Olimpia in summer 1999, however his 3 goals for the host nation in the 1999 Coppa America quickly made them realise he was a real bargain. He was a first team player at just 15, capped at 17, and has made a fine start with Bayern having helped them to 3 championships and the European Cup.

**7 MEHMET SCHOLL** 16.10.70
Played in World Cup warm up games in May 2002 after long term injury, but bravely announced himself not 100% fit for national duty. He then took the summer off to get

fit for the new season. Played in 1999 and 2000 and 2001 title wins in the hole behind the front two strikers or out wide. Played in the last three games of Euro 96 including the final. Not considered for 1998 World Cup by Berti Vogts but back for all three games at Euro2000. He has fulfilled youthful promise and was another from Karlsruhe, arriving in 1992. He had been with Karlsruhe since the age of 13. An attacking midfielder who is of Turkish extraction but is German as regards football nationality. He cost a then German internal record £2.9 million for his move to Bayern.

**11 ZE ROBERTO** 06.07.74
Joined summer 2002 from Bayer Leverkusen for £6.1 million – after a fine season in 2001– 2 with the runners up in three competitions including the Champions League final, where he played left sided midfield. Was disappointed not to make the Brazil 22 for the World Cup though he was not 100% fit at time. Was Leverkusen's big signing of summer 1998 from Flamengo for £4.6 million and played well through 1998– 2002 – he was a first choice in the national side at the turn of the century as well and was in the 1999 Coppa America win. He joined Real in March 1997 when they were about to win the title, then played in only 7 games in 1997– 8 before gaining his release to return to Brazil. Originally Roberto Carlos reserve at left back, but now can play midfield

**21 ALEXANDER ZICKLER** 28.02.74
Six foot three inch Zickler seems to be a sub for both club and country. From the old East Germany, he signed in 1993 from Dynamo Dresden, and cost nearly £1 million. He has won 5 championship medals and 2 league and cup doubles with the club as well as the 2001 Champions League.

# OLYMPIQUE LYONNAIS

**When Lyon retained their French championship in 2003 it was the first time this had been achieved since Marseille's 4-timer 1989-92. The club had threatened a title win with runners up places in 1995 and 2001 but the all round improvement at Lyon climaxed in 2002 when the club won the French championship for the first time in their history. The win was secured in the final match after Lens had lead from week 6 to week 33 of the 34 match programme. Lyon returned to the top Division in 1989 having being promoted as Division 2 champions. They had previously been un-interrupted members of Division 1 from 1950, when the club was established, to 1983. Since 1989, Lyon progressed to runners up in 1994-5 with an excellent youth policy under trainer Jean Tigana. However, Tigana, the famous former French international midfielder, left Lyon after 1994-5 success and moved to Monaco, where he won the 1997 title, and thence to Fulham. The club have been winners of the French Cup in 1961, 1964 and 1973. Now the League Cup in 2001**

# GROUP A
## OLYMPIQUE LYONNAIS

## COACH

**PAUL LE GUEN** 01.03.64
Le Guen took the helm at Lyon after the 2002 title win when the club's coach Jacques Santini replaced Roger Lemerre in the national job. Le Guen came in and succeeded in winning the title in his first season in charge. Le Guen could have been considered a risky choice. Despite being a decent international player, he had been out of work for a year after leaving his only other post - coach to Rennes from 1998-2001. As a player he ran out for Nantes as well as winning, with PSG, the 1996 European Cup Winners' Cup, the 1994 French title, 3 French Cups and 2 League Cups. The midfielder, who won 17 caps in the national team alongside the likes of Ginola, Papin and Cantona, joins a select group of those who have won the championship as a player and then as a coach.

## REACTION TO DRAW

**"It's a group which looks a lot like last year's one with one major favourite and the rest on a par. Last year it was Inter Milan, Ajax and Rosenborg. This year there are two clubs (Celtic and Anderlecht) who don't often make the front page of the newspapers in France but we must be wary. Celtic were UEFA Cup runners-up after eliminating Liverpool while Anderlecht are used to the Champions League. But obviously the favourites are Bayern Munich."** ***Pail Le Guen***

## SQUAD

**31 BRYAN BERGOUGNOUX** 21.01.83
Despite having made his debut in July 2001, this will be his first whole season in the first team squad. Born in Lyon, the player is a graduate from the youth academy.

**23 JEREMY BERTHOD** 24.04.84
A graduate from the youth academy, this defender is enjoying his first season in the senior squad. He has played no first team games prior to the 2003-04 season.

**5 CLAUDIO CACAPA** 29.05.76
Full name Claudio Roberto da Silva, Cacapa joined on loan in Jan 2001 as a replacement for Florent Laville, the club captain, who damaged knee ligaments and was out for the season.Originally a loan signing from Atletico Mineiro, Lyon took up the option to buy him at the end of the 2001 season. After playing for the Brazilian side for four years 1996-2000, he hardly missed a game during Lyon's championship winning seasons of 2002 and 2003. Has won 4 caps for Brazil.

**10 ERIC CARRIERE** 24.05.73
Moved to Lyon in late August 2001 for £8 million from Nantes and took over the playmaker's role from Vikash Dhorasoo. In 2001 he won the French Footballer of the

Year after helping Nantes to the championship. His memorable year continued with his first caps for France in the 2001 Confederations Cup picking up a winners medal. He then won 2002 and 2003 league titles with Lyon. Played for Nantes for six seasons since 1995, prior to which he enjoyed his football in Division 3 for Muret and Auch.

**1 GREGORY COUPET** 31.12.72
The Club captain almost signed for a series Premiership clubs in summer 2003 but he has remained in Lyon. The first choice keeper missed just 5 games in 6 seasons from 1997-2002 and just 3 games in 2003. He joined in summer 1997 from St Etienne where he had played since breaking into the first team aged just 18 years old. Coupet played for France in the 2001 and 2003 Confederations Cup after being in the A side in 2000, and was a former U21 international.

**2 ERIC DEFLANDRE** 02.08.73
Made a £3.6 million move to Lyon in summer 2000 from FC Bruges after Euro2000 where he played in all Belgium's games. Is Belgium's first choice right wing back after having broken through in the 1998 World Cup. Before playing a role in Lyon's two championship wins, Deflandre was at Bruges for five seasons. There he played an important part in their 1996 and 1998 title wins. Previously, he turned out for FC Liege and Germinal Ekeren.

**15 CHRISTOPHE DELMOTTE** 09.06.69
The Belgian born full back joined Lyon in summer 1997 after playing for Lens for well over 150 games from 1991-97. He played 26 games in the 2002 title win but only 18 games in 2003, which suggests that he is becoming a squad man.

**24 VIKASH DHORASOO** 10.10.73
Lyon's diminutive playmaker left in 2001-02 for a loan spell at Bordeaux, where he played all season, but rejoined in summer 2002. Just 5'5" tall, he missed only one game in 2002-03 title win. Born to Mauritian parents, this creative midfielder was considered unlucky not to receive more caps than he did for France. He joined from Le Havre in the summer of 1998 where he spent 5 seasons in the first team in Division 1.

**7 MAMADOU DIARRA** 18.05.81
Diarra joined in summer 2002 from Dutch club Vitesse Arnhem after impressing in the 2002 African nations Cup with semi-finalists Mali. He played 28 of the 38 games in Lyon's 2003 title win. He began his career with the Greek club OFI Crete from 1998-1999 then went to Vitesse who took him for the subsequent 3 seasons 1999-2002.

**3 EDMILSON** 10.07.76
The first World Cup winner ever to play for the French club signed just before the Jan 2002 deadline when he looked more likely to move to Arsenal for £6 million. Unfortunately for the London side, passport problems saw the Brazilian move to Lyon

and he then scored in the UCL for Champions League against them. First capped during the World Cup 2000 qualifiers, the defender previously played for Sao Paulo 1994-2000. He helped the top side to two Paulistas titles in 1998 and 2000.

**9 GIOVANE ELBER** 23.07.72
Arrived in the summer 2003 from Bayern Munich for E4.2m on a 2yr contract to replace Sonny Anderson, who went to Villarreal. The Brazilian was joint Bundesliga top scorer in 2002-03 with 21 goals but became available after Bayern bought Dutchman Roy Makaay. He was top scorer in Bayern's 4 league title wins 1999-2001 and 2003and notched vital goals v Manchester Utd and Real Madrid en route to 2001 European Cup success. Won his first caps for Brazil in the Feb 1998 Concacaf Gold Cup but just missed out on the World Cup 22 back in 1998 and has not really featured since. Bayern saw him as the replacement for Klinsmann at the club and paid Stuttgart just under £5 million - their top buy of the summer of 1997. The Brazilian went to Grasshopper Zurich as a youngster, and then moved to Stuttgart where he scored 41 goals in 87 games.

**4 MICHAEL ESSIEN** 03.12.82
The Ghanaian signed in July 2003 from Bastia for E7m after interesting PSG, Liverpool and Everton. He arrived at Bastia in July 2000 from Liberty FC of Accra and showed a good level of improvement through 66 league games – scored 6 times in 29 games in 2002-03.

**26 GAEL GENEVIER** 26.06.82
Lyon born, academy graduate enjoying first season in the first team squad.

**29 YOHANN GOMEZ** 25.09.81
Born in Lyon and a graduate from the club's juniors, Gomez signed his first pro contract in summer 2002. Is yet to play in the first team before 2003-04

**14 SIDNEY GOVOU** 27.07.79
A graduate from the club's youth academy, Govou comes from nearby Le Puy. Played in the French team that reached the final of the UEFA U21 Championships in May 2002 and since the World Cup has gone into the full national side. The young forward is considered to be one to watch.

**8 JUNINHO (PERNAMBUCANO)** 30.01.75
Signed by Lyon in early summer 2001 for £4 million, the Brazilian was a key member of the 2002 and 2003 title wins and was the club top scorer in the 2003 title win. He bagged 13 goals from midfield, one more than Sonny Anderson. This Juninho played in Brazil's World Cup qualifying shambles alongside Middlesbrough's Juninho, but just failed to make the World Cup squad. He played top flight football in Brazil for Sport Recife from 1993-1995, then from 1995-2001 was with the top club Vasco da Gama.

# GROUP A
## OLYMPIQUE LYONNAIS

**18 PEGGUY LYINDULA** 25.05.79
The French U21 striker moved in late August 2001 from French Cup winners Strasbourg to Lyon. Was bought to replace Steve Marlet when he moved to Fulham for a fee of £6 million after he scored 5 goals in the first 6 matches of Div 2 in 2001-2. He went on to score 11 goals in the 2003 title win. Born in Kinshasa, Zaire-Congo, Lyindula played for Division 2 Niort's juniors until 1998 when Strasbourg came in for him.

**11 FLORENT MALOUDA** 13.06.80
Born in Guyana, he joined Lyon in summer 2003 from Guingamp. Prior to that, the French youth and U21 international played for Chateauroux in their first season in first division in 1998.

**20 PATRICK MULLER** 17.12.76
Costing £5.5 million in summer 2000 from Grasshopper Zurich, the current Swiss international helped Lyon to their 2 league titles. Joined Grasshopper from Juventus in the summer of 1999, but had been back in Switzerland on loan the previous season with Servette, with whom he won the 1999 championship. First capped in 1997, Muller was formerly a forward, but is working his way back through the team - and the Swiss and Lyon now use him now as sweeper.

**30 NICOLAS PUYDEBOIS** 28.02.81
Puydebois is the current French national U21 keeper who has taken over partially in the U21 side from team mate Vercutre. Number three keeper, he played only twice for the first team in the 2002-03 season. Enjoying his first professional contract.

**12 ANTHONY REVEILLERE** 10.11.79
Joined from Valencia in Jan 2003 who had themselves trailed the player for 3 years before signing him. The Spanish club landed him from French top flight club Stade Rennes. The French U21 international joined Rennes in 1996 as a youth team player, and made his first team debut in February 1998. He played some 150 League and Cup games in Rennes first team and was the full back partner of Julien Escude.

**22 ROMAIN SARTRE** 12.11.82
Lyon born, academy graduate enjoying his first season in the first team squad.

**12 REMY VERCOUTRE** 26.06.80
Joined Lyon in summer 2002 as No 2 keeper, he is an U21 international of recent vintage and was back up to Inter Milan's Sebastian Frey in the team that reached the final of the 2002 UEFA U21 championships. Previously with Montpellier, where he played 17 Div 1 games from his Lyon debut in July 2001 to date.

**27 JULIEN VIALE** 13.02.82
Lyon born, academy graduate enjoying his first season in the first team squad.

# CELTIC FC

**This is Celtic's 19th season in the European Cup – in 1967, the club became the first ever British winners of the trophy when the 'Lisbon Lions' beat Inter Milan 2-1 in Portugal. It was an even more remarkable achievement because it was Celtic's first season in the competition. Since that, they have also been runners-up (1970, lost 1-2 to Feyenoord) and twice semi-finalists (1972 and 1974). In total, this is Celtic's 38th European campaign. Since the club's first go, in the 1962-63 season, they've missed out on European football only three times (1978-79, 1990-91 and 1994-95).**

## COACH

**MARTIN O'NEILL** 01.03.52
As a player Martin O'Neill twice won the European Cup, with Nottingham Forest (1979, 1980), the club where he played 264 league games and scored 21 goals between 1971 and 1981. Now as a coach, he is in his second attempt with Celtic (after beating Kaunas and MTK Budapest in the qualifying rounds) at winning the Champions League. In 2001 O'Neill and Celtic fell at the first hurdle although they took nine points (normally enough to qualify) in a group with Juventus, FC Porto and Rosenborg. Last season there was no Champions League football for O'Neill and 'The Bhoys'. They were eliminated in the last qualifying round against Basel. From this setback, O'Neill and Celtic moved forward to make history in the Uefa Cup, reaching their first final in that competition but losing in Seville to FC Porto (3-2 after extra time). With this latest achievement Martin O'Neill has put Celtic back on the European map. Nevertheless, last season was the first since his arrival in July 2000 without any silverware. As Celtic manager, O'Neill - born in Kilrea, Northern Ireland - has won two Scottish league titles (2001, 2002), one Scottish FA Cup (2001) and one Scottish League Cup (2001) completing 'the domestic treble'. O'Neill, who has already had talks with Manchester United about succeeding Sir Alex Ferguson, is tactically very strong and he knows how to motivate his sometimes average players. That was one of his strongest points at Wycombe (1990-95), Norwich City (June-November 1995) and Leicester City, the club he led to promotion to the Premier League and twice to the League Cup. After coaching at Filbert Street (December 1995-June 2000) O'Neill moved to Celtic Park.

## REACTION TO DRAW

**"Bayern are obviously the group favourites, and I see it as a fight between ourselves, Lyon and Anderlecht for the second place. I know Bayern did not reach their normal dizzy heights when they were eliminated in the group stage last season, but they have since signed Roy Makaay, the Golden Boot winner, so I believe they are obvious favourites."** ***Martin O'Neill***

# GROUP A
## CELTIC FC

## SQUAD

**17 DIDIER AGATHE** 16.08.75
The former Montpellier and Raith midfielder joined the club from Hibernian in August 2000. He spent just one season at Raith (1999-00) and scored seven goals in 30 league games there before joining Hibs for a few weeks. The versatile Frenchman missed three months of the 2001-02 season at Celtic through injury, but nevertheless managed 32 appearances and two goals. Last season he made 40 appearances without scoring, but has started this season with goals against MTK and Dundee United – his first goals since February 2002. Agather has played a total of 111 games for Celtic, scoring seven times.

**6 BOBO BALDE** 13.10.75
Guinean international defender Balde cost Celtic a bargain £900,000 from Toulouse in July 2001. Balde, brought up in France, began his career with his hometown club Marseille before spells at Mulhouse and Cannes. Despite missing the start of his debut season with a groin injury, Bobo went on to score six goals in 38 games in 2001-02. Last season, he made more appearances (53) than anyone except Valgaeren, but was sent off in the UEFA Cup Final against Porto. In 95 games for Celtic he has notched 10 goals.

**37 CRAIG BEATTIE** 16.01.84
The 19-year-old striker made his first-team debut as a substitute against Kaunas, in a Champions League qualifier on August 6 this season. Ten days later, he made his league debut as a sub against Dundee United. Beattie signed a new three-year contract with Celtic in the summer after attracting some interest from Spurs.

**2 TOM BOYD** 24.11.65
The veteran defender has spent over ten years at Celtic, since a £750,000 move from Chelsea in February 1992. The 36-year-old (who also used to play for Motherwell) won 72 caps for Scotland, scoring one goal - his last outing for the national team was against Belgium on September 5, 2001. The 36-year-old also had a testimonial against Manchester United at the end of the 2000-01 season. Boyd made 12 appearances in 2001-02 (although he started seven of the final 11) and played just two CIS Cup games last season. In 407 games he has scored just 2 goals.

**40 STEPHEN CRAINEY** 22.06.81
Crainey turned pro in 1997 and is now in his seventh season as a Celtic player. He's been capped four times by Scotland, making his senior debut during manager Berti Vogts' first match in charge - against France on March 27, 2002. His most recent appearance for Scotland was against the Faroe Islands in September last year. Crainey's only goal for the club came in November 2000 during the 5-2 CIS Cup win at Hearts – the player has made 19 appearances in both 2001-02 (13 starts, 6 as sub) and 2002-03 (7 starts, 12 sub). He has scored one goal in 53 games.

# GROUP A
## CELTIC FC

**20 ROBERT DOUGLAS** 24.04.72
Goalkeeper 'Rab' Douglas has kept 56 clean sheets in his 121 appearances for Celtic since taking the number 1 jersey from Jonathan Gould in November 2000, following a £1m move from Dundee. Douglas made his Scotland senior debut against Nigeria on April 17, 2002 and has now won ten caps for his country, seven of them last season. Last season he conceded just 35 goals in 38 games, with 17 clean sheets, and this season he is yet to be beaten in four appearances. Rab has conceded 73 in 121 games.

**12 DAVID FERNANDEZ** 20.01.76
Former Airdrie and Deportivo La Coruna striker Fernandez was signed for £1m in June 2002. The Spanish forward had been signed Airdrie from Depor by Steve Archibald, then got a free transfer to Livingston, where he helped them gain promotion to the SPL in 2000-01. The following season, as Livingston finished third in the SPL, Fernandez scored seven goals (six League, one Scottish Cup). He made his Celtic debut as a sub against Dunfermline on August 3, 2002, and managed one goal (v FK Suduva on October 3, 2002) in 19 appearances last season – although he started only eight games.

**34 MARK FOTHERINGHAM** 22.10.83
At the age of 16, Mark became Celtic's youngest-ever player when he made his debut against St Johnstone in May 2000. The midfielder is in his fifth season as a Celtic professional, although he hasn't played for the senior team since the away game at Kilmarnock on May 20, 2001. He has yet to score for Celtic.

**30 STEVE GUPPY** 29.03.69
Guppy arrived from Leicester for £750,000 in August 2001. It was the third time that manager Martin O'Neill had signed him – he'd also taken Guppy to Wycombe and Leicester. He was a key member of Wycombe's Conference-winning side in 1993, and also won the League Cup with Leicester in 2000. Guppy has one England cap, in a friendly against Belgium in October 1999. Guppy has played 48 games for Celtic without scoring once.

**10 JOHN HARTSON** 05.04.75
Hartson signed from Coventry for £6.5m in August 2001. Celtic was the prolific striker's fifth club in six years – he'd previously been at Luton, Arsenal (£2.5m), West Ham (£3.2m), Wimbledon (£7.5m) and Coventry (£5m) in transfers totaling some £20m. His Coventry move initially threatened to go the same way as previous transfers to Rangers and Tottenham, which both collapsed on medical grounds, but was then renegotiated to a pay-as-you-play deal. Then, after just six months at Highfield Road, he joined Celtic – where he's been hugely successful. Of his 139 career goals, 49 have come in the last two seasons. Hartson has also won 35 caps for Wales and scored 10 goals. He's also scored in each of his last three internationals. He has scored 49 goals in 88 games.

# GROUP A
## CELTIC FC

**21 MAGNUS HEDMAN** 19.03.73

Swedish goalkeeper Hedman signed from Coventry for £1.5m in July 2002, after appearing in all four of Sweden's games at the World Cup. Hedman had spent five seasons at Coventry (four in the Premiership) and made 151 appearances for the Sky Blues. Hedman made his Celtic debut against Dundee United on August 17, 2002, but missed a lot of last season with knee and calf injuries. He did, however, win his 52nd international cap against Tunisia on February 12, 2003. Hedman has played 11 games conceding just four goals.

**14 PAUL LAMBERT** 07.08.69

Scottish Football Writers' Player of the Year for 2001-02, this consistent midfielder played 49 games in 2001-02, scoring five goals, and played 48 games last season, scoring six goals. Lambert has won 38 caps for Scotland and scored his first international goal in an EC qualifier against the Faroes on September 7, 2002. He cost Celtic £2m from Borussia Dortmund in November 1997, where he'd won the Champions League that May. Other previous clubs Lambert's played for include St Mirren and Motherwell. Lambert has scored 16 goals in his 250 appearances.

**7 HENRIK LARSSON** 20.09.71

Since signing for £650,000 from Feyenoord in July 1997, Larsson has scored 31 goals in Europe for Celtic. It's the British record of goals scored by a player for a single club in European competition, beating Ian Rush and Peter Lorimer by one. The Swedish international signed an extension to his contract in June 2001, a deal which will keep him at Celtic until the end of this season. In the 2000-01 season, he picked up the Scottish Football Writers' and Professional Footballers' Association Player of the Year titles, alongside the European Golden Boot award (ahead of Milan's Shevchenko and Lazio's Crespo). Larsson had scored 53 goals in 50 games that season, breaking Charlie Nicholas' 1982-83 post-war club record of 48 goals. He also equalled Brian McClair's SPL record of 35 goals in a season. In 2001-02, Larsson fired 35 goals in 47 games, and last season he hit 44 in 51 – including his 200th Celtic goal in the UEFA Cup final. He has still to break Jimmy McGrory's all-time Celtic goalscoring record – 63 goals during the 1927-28 season. Initially, Larsson retired from international football after the 2002 World Cup (4 games, 3 goals). However, in April 2003, he returned to make an appearance in a European Championships qualifier against Hungary, but has now retired again having won 73 caps for Sweden and scored 24 goals.

**16 ULRIK LAURSEN** 28.02.76

Laursen signed from Hibernian, where he spent two seasons, for £1.5m in July 2002. His arrival has seen competition hotting up in the defensive ranks, with a particularly interesting battle between this new Bhoy and Stephen Crainey, although Laursen has height and aerial ability in his favour. Laursen made his Celtic debut against Dundee United on August 17, 2002.

# GROUP A
## CELTIC FC

**18 NEIL LENNON** 25.06.71
Midfielder who's played 124 games since costing £5.75m from Leicester (where he also played under O'Neill) on December 8, 2000, but has scored only two goals. He last scored in December 2001 and has now gone some 75 games without a goal. Lennon has won a League Cup winners medal for Celtic, after winning English League Cup medals with Leicester in 1997 and 2000. He gained 40 caps for Northern Ireland before retiring from international football in August 2002 following a sectarian death threat.

**4 JACKIE MCNAMARA** 23.10.73
McNamara – who cost £600,000 from Dunfermline in October 1995 - played 30 games in 2001-02, and 27 games last season. His last two goals for the club were both against Dundee United - one on August 17, 2002 and another on August 16, 2003. Jackie won his 18th Scottish cap against Germany on June 7, 2003.

**29 SHAUN MALONEY** 24.01.83
Malaysian striker Maloney is now in his fifth season at Celtic. Made his senior Celtic debut as a sub in the 3-0 league win at Ibrox on April 29, 2001. The following season scored ten goals in 20 games, despite only making five starts, including four in a 8-0 CIS Insurance Cup third round victory over Stirling in November 2001. Last season, Shaun scored five goals in 30 games (20 as sub, including the UEFA Cup final). This season, he has scored twice in four appearances. Maloney has scored 17 goals in 58 appearances.

**35 JOHAN MJALLBY** 09.02.71
Midfielder Mjallby joined Celtic in November 1998, valued at £1.5m in a transfer from AIK Stockholm. He was best known for having scored the winner against England in Euro 2000 qualifier in Stockholm in September 1998. Mjallby went on to play 51 games for Celtic in 2001-02, more than any other outfield player. He scored three goals and was sent off once, in the Rangers derby on April 21, 2002. He missed three months of last season, from September to December 2002, with a knee injury, but made 24 appearances and scored three goals. The same injury has flared up again and will keep him out for the opening weeks of this campaign. Mjallby has played 44 times for Sweden and scored four goals – he started all four games in the 2002 World Cup.

**43 LIAM MILLER** 13.02.81
The 22 year-old Cork-born Rep of Ireland U21 midfielder has been at the club since 1997. Miller made two sub appearances last season (one in the UEFA Cup v FK Suduva, and one in CIS Cup v Inverness CT – both in October 2002). This season he has already played five times, scoring against Kaunas on July 30 – his first goal for the club.

**19 STILIAN PETROV** 05.07.79
The Bulgarian international Petrov signed from CSKA Sofia in August 1999, and the following season was named the first overseas winner of Scotland's Young Player of the Year award. He scored eight goals in both the 2000-01 and 2001-02 seasons from

midfield despite suffering a broken leg in the 2-1 league win at St Johnstone on March 14, 2001 and being out of the team for six months. Last season, he fired 14 goals in 50 games, including six in the final ten matches. Petrov has scored 32 goals in 165 games.

**15 BOBBY PETTA** 06.08.74
Winger Petta (a free transfer from Ipswich in July 1999) has scored only four goals in 80 games for Celtic, and hasn't played for the senior team since November 6, 2002. He was subbed in all of his five appearances last season. The John Barnes signing did score two goals in 27 games in 2001-02, but made only one sub appearance in the last 14 games of that campaign.

**39 JAMIE SMITH** 20.11.80
Midfielder in his sixth season at the club, including a loan to Livingston in 1999-00. He scored one goal in 13 games in 2001-02, and one goal (against St Johnstone in the Scottish Cup on February 23) in 25 games last season. His first goal for the club was struck against Cwmbran in the UEFA Cup in August 1999.

**9 CHRIS SUTTON** 10.03.73
Former Chelsea and Blackburn striker cost a club record £6m in July 2000 and has now played in the CL for three different clubs. He scored once in seven games during Chelsea's 1999-00 CL campaign, and was sent off against Hertha Berlin in November 1999. He scored 14 goals in 35 games in 2000-01, seven goals in 30 games in 2001-02, and 19 goals in 43 games last season. Sutton has been capped once by England, as a sub against Cameroon in November 1997. Sutton's bagged 42 goals in 111 appearances.

**3 MUHAMMED SYLLA** 13.03.77
Sylla - a friend and international team-mate of new Celtic defender Bobo Balde - was born in Ivory Coast, but is a Guinean international. He signed from St Johnstone in the summer of 2001, where he'd fired six goals in 34 league games during his one season there. He'd previously played in France for Le Havre and Le Mans.

**8 ALAN THOMPSON** 22.12.73
The midfielder (£2.75m from Aston Villa) missed the start of last season with an ankle ligament injury, but still scored 12 goals in 45 games, including a blistering run of six goals in the final seven games. He'd played 36 games in 2001-02, scoring nine times, including four goals in his last four appearances of that season. Thompson made his League debut for Celtic in a 3-0 home win against Hibs on September 9, 2000 and was sent off in his Old Firm debut during the 5-1 defeat at Ibrox on November 26, 2000.

**5 JOOS VALGAEREN** 03.03.76
The Belgian defender has played 139 games for Celtic, scoring 10 goals. Along with Balde, he made the most appearances last season – 53 – after missing the World Cup and the last three months of the 2001-02 season due to injury. He scored three goals

last season, and also added five international caps to bring his tally to 18, although he's yet to score for his country. Cost £3.8m from Roda JC Kerkrade in July 2000.

**23 STANISLAV VARGA** 8.10.72
The Slovakian international defender joined Celtic from Sunderland in January. He'd scored one goal (at West Ham in January 2001) in 33 games for Sunderland, who had bought him from Slovan Bratislava for £650,000 in August 2000. Varga was sent off twice in his first season at Sunderland, and then went on-loan to West Brom in the 2001-02 season, making 4 appearances. He then played just three games for Sunderland last season. He made his Celtic debut against Inverness CT in the Scottish Cup quarter-final on March 23, but made only one more appearance last season.

**33 ROSS WALLACE** 23.05.85
The Dundee-born midfielder made his Celtic debut as a sub in a CIS Cup tie v Inverness CT on October 23, 2002. His second first-team game was as a sub v Kaunas in the UCL qualifier on August 6. Wallace signed a new 4-year contract in the summer.

# RSC ANDERLECHT

**The Belgian champions have already played in the Champions League 1993-94, 1994-95, 2000-01 and 2001-02. Now they start for the fifth time in the Champions League, a feat that no Belgian club has bettered. FC Bruges starts for the third time this season while Lierse and Racing Genk have both participated only once.**

## COACH

**HUGO BROOS** 10.04.52
In the 1992-93 season, Broos was the first Belgian to coach a Belgian team in the Champions League. But, in a group with Marseille, Rangers and CSKA Moscow FC Bruges, he didn't impress and only finished third. Ten years later he gets a new chance in the Champions League - this time with Anderlecht. Broos is the only Belgian who has played and coached the two most important clubs in Belgium. He played for Anderlecht from 1971 until 1983 winning 3 league titles, 4 national Cups, 2 Cup Winners Cups and 1 UEFA Cup. From 1983 until 1988 Broos played in the defence of FC Bruges winning 1 league title and 1 national Cup. He played 24 times for Belgium and was present in their most successful World Cup campaign ever in Mexico in 1986. He began his coaching career at RWD Molenbeek (1988-91) before going to FC Bruges where, between 1991 and 1997, he won 2 league titles and 2 national Cups. From 1997 until 2002 he coached Excelsior Mouscron (they lost Belgian Cup final in 2002 against FC Bruges 3-1) before going to Anderlecht.

# GROUP A
## RSC ANDERLECHT

## REACTION TO DRAW

**"Lets not be naive about this. It is a case of Bayern Munich and then the other three – but I think we have a real chance against Celtic and Lyon. I think second place is a possibility but we are used to these matches now, we know what we have to do to survive and I hope that we can do it for our fans."** ***Hugo Broos***

## SQUAD

**10 WALTER BASEGGIO** 19.08.78
In 1991 moved from lower division club SC Clabecq to Anderlecht where he made his debut on August 24th 1996 in the 2-2 draw at home against Lokeren. He scored his first ever Belgian league goal for Anderlecht away to FC Bruges (2-1 defeat on November 8th 1996). Baseggio was excellent in the 2000-2001 and provided several goals for Radzinski and Koller with his long raking passes from midfield.

**5 GLEN DE BOECK** 22.08.71
After 3 seasons with KV Mechelen De Boeck moved in the summer of 1995 to Anderlecht where he established himself as a reliable central defender. Last season's captain played 17 CL games for Anderlecht but missed most of this season because of a hamstring injury he sustained in a friendly away to third division club Oud-Heverlee Leuven (0-4 win on July 11th 2003). He is expected back in the team for the start of the Champions League mid-September.

**33 OLIVIER DESCHACHT** 16.02.81
After Didier Dheedene left in 2001 the left back position was available. Several players got a chance (Ilic, Zewlakow) but it was finally the blond Deschacht who established himself. His good performances in the second half of last season were rewarded with his first cap for Belgium in the friendly at home against Poland (April 30th 2003).

**26 ARUNA DINDANE** 26.11.80
Ivory Coast's dribble wizard joined Anderlecht from ASEC Mimosas Abidjan in 2000. Although he didn't play a lot in the successful Champions League campaign of 2000-01 (coming on 4 times) he managed to put his name in the record books by scoring almost immediately after joining the field against Real Madrid. The second European goal he scored was also against Real Madrid but this time 6 months later in the next campaign.

**12 OLIVIER DOLL** 09.06.73
In 1994 coach Johan Boskamp signed youngster Doll from Seraing. Doll started well in Brussels and took part in the Champions League campaigns of 1994-95 (5 full games). He continued with Anderlecht and besides picking up many yellow cards he also was out sometimes with injuries. In the 2000-01 season he was again present in the Champions League although he didn't play much in that successful campaign (only 3 full

games). In the 2001-02 season he missed out because of a knee injury. Normally a central defender, Doll has recently taken over the position of right back where he had a very good spell in the second half of last season. He continued to perform well in the beginning of this season and that has led to his call up for the European Championships qualifier Belgium v Croatia in September, 6 years after he won his first cap against Turkey.

**15 BESNIK HASI** 25.12.71
Albanian international who made his name in Belgium when he helped take his team Racing Genk back into the first division. After returning from 1860 Munich, where he played for one season, he helped Racing Genk win their first ever Belgian league title. In 2000 he moved to Anderlecht where in his debut season he appeared mostly as a substitute. Has had a very good start this season and can be dangerous from free kicks.

**14 MARC HENDRIKX** 02.07.74
Although right footed, Hendrikx plays mostly as left midfielder. With Racing Genk he won the Belgian Cup in 1998 and the Belgian league title in 1999. In 2001 his mentor at Genk, coach Anthuenis - now the national coach, signed him for Anderlecht.

**22 OLEG IACHTCHOUK** 26.10.77
Came to Brussels in 1996 as a promising talent from Ukrainian club Niva Ternapol. Has only played 69 league games scoring 17 goals since then. Despite being injury prone, Iachtchouk has 22 European appearances for the club scoring 3 goals, the last one away to Sheriff Tiraspol in the 2nd qualifying round of the 2001-02 CL campaign.

**2 ALEKSANDAR ILIC** 26.06.69
Although he has already played 10 CL games for Anderlecht scoring 1 goal (at home against Lokomotiv Moscow) Ilic has never been certain of his place in the team. This season the man with dual nationality (Belgian and Serbian) started on the bench. On the field he is a solid defender who likes to drive forward and is dangerous with the head. Played earlier in Belgium for FC Bruges where he arrived in 1997 from Paniliakos Pirgos (Greece). Ilic previously played for Radnicki Nis (1978-89, 1992-93), Red Star Belgrade (1989-92) and Spanish side Cadiz (1993-94).

**8 NENAD JESTROVIC** 09.05.76
At 21, Jestrovic moved from OFK Belgrade to France. He played one season for Bastia (19 games, 2 goals) before Metz took him on. He didn't perform as expected (8 goals in 44 games) and he was sold to Belgian club Excelsior Mouscron where he really exploded, scoring 20 goals in 25 games. The end of his season, however, was disrupted by a broken leg. Anderlecht bought him in the summer of 2001. Last season the Serbian born forward eventually proved his value scoring 20 goals in the Belgian league in 23 games and helping Anderlecht towards the runners-up spot. In the UEFA cup campaign Jestrovic scored 7 goals in 6 games. Currently suffering from another knee injury, Anderlecht will have to pass the first round if Jestrovic is to play in the Champions League this season.

# GROUP A
## RSC ANDERLECHT

**11 MARTIN KOLAR** 18.09.83
Promising youngster from the Czech Republic who moved from Bohemians Prague to Anderlecht in 2002. A left winger and a good crosser, he played 23 league games last season but has yet to score his first goal for Anderlecht. Bohemians Prague spotted him in 1997 at FC Skodiilky, a club from the lower divisions in the Czech Republic.

**27 VINCENT KOMPANY** 10.04.86
This 17-year-old 1.95m tall central defender, son of a Congolese father and a Belgian mother, is the discovery of the pre-season. Having never played a second in the Belgian league, Kompany made his European debut for Anderlecht on July 30th 2003 in the away game against Rapid Bucharest (2nd qualifying round) as a replacement for injured Glen De Boeck. Some weeks further on he can look forward to his first Champions League campaign since he he's been an ever present in the team since. In the youth teams they even called him 'Desailly'!

**7 GORAN LOVRE** 23.03.82
Anderlecht discovered Lovre in the Yugoslav national under-16 team and at the age of 16 they took him away from Partizan Belgrade. Made his league debut for Anderlecht in January 2002 coming on after 84 mins in the 5-2 home win against La Louvière. But he had to wait for the arrival of new coach Hugo Broos who gave him a chance on November 8th 2002 away to Sint-Truiden. Lovre, physically strong, emerged in the second half of last season when Anderlecht had an unbeaten run of 10 games. Played 15 league games and scored twice last season. Scored his first European goal for Anderlecht in the 3-1 home win over Wisla Krakow in the 3rd qualifying round on August 13th 2003. Sustained a knee ligament injury and is out for several months.

**23 NGALULA MBUYI 'JUNIOR' GABRIEL** 01.06.82
Ngalula Mbuyi, better known as Junior, made his debut for Anderlecht on October 10th 2001 at home against AA Gent. This defensive midfielder took his chance last season as a replacement for injured Yves Vanderhaeghe. On March 23rd 2003 he played an excellent match at home against later champions FC Bruges. Injured a knee in training and is expected back in before the end of the year.

**35 SHERJILL MCDONALD** 20.11.89
Played in the Ajax youth team before moving in 2001 to Anderlecht. Made his name by scoring the qualifying goal (with his hand) for Anderlecht in Oslo against Stabaek in the 1st round of the UEFA Cup last season.

**19 IVICA MORNAR** 12.01.74
Croatian international who played with Hajduk Split against Anderlecht in the autumn of 1994. Mornar played 5 games in that CL campaign that took Hajduk Split into the quarter-finals where they were eliminated by eventual winners Ajax. In August 1995 Mornar moved to Eintracht Frankfurt in Germany. FC Seville (1996-97), CD Orense

(1997-98) and Standard Liège (1998-2001) were his next clubs. He played 5 games in the last CL campaign of Anderlecht scoring the last goal away to AS Rome. Started this season as fourth choice striker but the injury of Nenad Jestrovic gave him an unexpected chance to play. Can be used in midfield as well as in attack.

**24 TRISTAN PEERSMAN** 28.09.70
In the summer of 2000 and after only 16 games in the Belgian league this promising young goalkeeper left Beveren for Anderlecht. Because of injuries Peersman only made his debut for the Belgian runners-up very recently in the first game of this season at home against Antwerp (August 9th 2003, 3-1 win). He is the stand-in for Daniel Zitka.

**18 KI-HYEON SEOL** 18.01.79
South Korean international Seol moved from Antwerp to Anderlecht in 2001 but only had 2 minutes in the Champions League campaign 2001-02 - coming on for Aruna Dindane away to Lokomotiv Moscow on September 11th 2001. Nonetheless he had participated in the qualifying games and scored a goal away to Halmstads BK in Sweden. After having a difficult first season in Brussels he performed much better in his second year under new coach Hugo Broos, who normally plays him on the left wing. When Seol got off the mark, he was top scorer of the Belgian league for some weeks and finally finished the season on 12 goals in 31 league games with a further 8 assists. Most recently Seol scored the winner for Anderlecht in the 2nd qualifying round return leg at home versus Rapid Bucharest. If he hadn't done so Anderlecht would not have been playing European football this season.

**30 HANNU TIHINEN** 01.07.76
Finnish international central defender, discovered in 1997 by HJK Helsinki at Kemin Palloseura. In 2000 he moved to Viking Stavanger in Norway. Had a short spell with West Ham United (8 games between September 2001 and December 2001). After returning to Viking, Anderlecht signed him in the summer of 2002. Played 22 league games last season scoring 3 goals – one a splendid back-heel against Sint-Truiden.

**34 LAMINE TRAORE** 10.06.82
Moved in 1999 from Planète Champion Internationale in Burkina Faso to Anderlecht. He made his debut for the club on February 2nd 2001 away to Charleroi on a snowy pitch. He is always available when necessary and is useful as a central defender to play man-to-man or on the right wing. Made his CL debut at home against Real Madrid (0-2 defeat) on October 16th 2001. Played again against AS Roma two weeks later.

**4 YVES VANDERHAEGHE** 30.01.70
After coming from Excelsior Mouscron in 2000 Yves Vanderhaeghe was a regular as defensive midfielder. Until March 2nd 2003 this hard working man almost played every game for the club. Then he got injured (knee ligaments) at home against Charleroi. Vanderhaeghe, who played already 39 times for Belgium scoring 2 goals, has now

recovered from his knee operation. He is expected back somewhere in October 2003. Already played 17 CL games for Anderlecht.

**25 JAN VAN STEENBERGHE** 04.07.72
After his splendid performance in last seasons Belgian Cup final for La Louvière against Sint-Truiden, Van Steenberghe received an offer from Anderlecht to become their third goalkeeper. Van Steenberghe didn't hesitate and signed in Brussels for two years. Played 12 league games for La Louvière last season.

**17 CHRISTIAN WILHELMSSON** 08.12.79
Swedish midfielder who played and scored for Norwegian club Stabaek against Anderlecht in the 1st round of the UEFA Cup last season. He made such an impression that some months later he was offered a contract by the Belgian runners-up. Is very useful on the right wing and scored his first league goal for Anderlecht on the second day of the new season away to AA Gent (3-1 win).

**9 CLAYTON ZANE** 12.07.77
Australian centre-forward formerly of Molde and Lilleström only played 9 league games last season scoring 2 goals. Finding it difficult to break into the side.

**21 PÄR ZETTERBERG** 14.10.70
Blond midfielder Zetterberg is back for his third spell at Anderlecht, the club he joined from Swedish junior club Falkenberg in 1986. Under national coach Robert Waseige he became the star of the Belgium team and returned to Anderlecht in 1993 to win 3 titles and twice was named Belgian Footballer of the Year (1993 and 1997). In the summer of 2000 he left Brussels again, this time for Olympiakos Piraeus in Greece where he won 3 league titles in 3 seasons. Although injury plagued and a diabetes sufferer, Zetterberg has already proved his value by scoring the important equalising goal in the return leg at home against Rapid Bucharest in the 2nd qualifying round of this campaign.

**6 MICHAL ZEWLAKOW** 22.04.76
Twin brother of forward Marcin Zewlakow, with who he used to play together at Polonia Warszawa, Beveren and most recently Excelsior Mouscron. Michal is a flexible player that can be used as a defender or a midfielder. Was present at the World Cup 2002 in South Korea and Japan for Poland. Followed coach Broos to Anderlecht in August 2002 leaving, for the first time in his life, his twin brother behind.

**1 DANIEL ZITKA** 20.06.75
In November 1999 Czech Republic born Zitka left Tatran Presov for Lokeren in Belgium where he played 60 league games. In the summer of 2002 this 1.9m tall goalkeeper moved to Anderlecht to become the successor to veteran Filip De Wilde. The former national goalkeeper started the season but when he got injured in October 2002 Zitka took his chance. Played 26 league games last season.

# GROUP B

## ARSENAL FC
(England)

## INTERNAZIONALE MILAN
(Italy)

## FC DYNAMO KYIV
(Ukraine)

## FC LOKOMOTIV MOSCOW
(Russia)

# ARSENAL FC

**Arsenal have won the championship 12 times in the 78 successive seasons that they have been in the top division. Last season they set a number of Premiership records despite not winning the title. They were unbeaten in 30 Premiership games before losing at Everton on October 19, 2002. They scored in 55 consecutive Premiership games (a new league record, beating the previous record of 46 games set by Chesterfield between 1929 and 1930) before drawing a blank at Old Trafford on December 7, 2002. They were unbeaten in 23 away league games (another league record) before losing at Everton. In 2001-02 they became the first 'top division' club to go through a whole season unbeaten away from home since Preston achieved it in the first season of the league (1888-89). They equaled the league record of 14 successive wins after their victory over Birmingham on August 18, 2002. This is a new 'top division' record. They have gone 77 Premiership matches without a 0-0 draw. The only blot on their copy book is their discipline record. They have received 50 red cards under Wenger.**

## COACH

**ARSENE WENGER** 22.10.49
Wenger's first game in charge was at Blackburn on October 12, 1996 when Ian Wright scored twice to ensure a winning start for the new boss (2-0). The Arsenal team that day was: Seaman, Dixon, Winterburn, Keown, Bould, Adams, Vieira, Platt, Merson, Wright, Hartson (Parlour).

## REACTION TO DRAW

**"We might not have bought a lot of new players in summer, but we have a great team spirit and a solid foundation among the squad and I believe we have learnt a lot about the Champions League now to go as far as we can."** ***Patrick Vieira***

## SQUAD

**30 JEREMIE ALIADIERE** 30.03.83
Scored 9 goals in Arsenal's FA Youth Cup winning side in 2000-01, equalling the competition's record (Michael Owen also scored 9 in 1996). He also scored twice in the first leg of the 2001 Youth Cup final win over Blackburn. A stylish striker, he is a graduate of the famed Clairefontaine Academy in France. Joined Arsenal in 1999 and turned pro in March 2000. He made his first-team debut as a sub v Grimsby in the Worthington Cup on November 27, 2001 and scored his first goal v West Brom on August 27, 2002. Did not appear after September 1, 2002 last season due to 2 hernia operations.

# GROUP B
## ARSENAL FC

**10 DENNIS BERGKAMP** 18.05.69
Dennis has scored 104 goals in 317 games for Arsenal. Became the 15th Arsenal player to reach 100 goals in the FA Cup v Oxford on January 4, 2003. Scored only 4 goals in 29 Premiership apps last season. Scored only 1 Premiership goal at Highbury last season. Was capped 79 times by Holland, scoring 37 goals – a Dutch record before Patrick Kluivert surpassed it in June 2003. Sent off 3 times for Arsenal (v Sunderland, West Ham and Liverpool). Missed 5 games in September/October 2002 with an Achilles' injury. Signed a new 1-year contract with the club in July 2003.

**23 SOL CAMPBELL** 18.09.74
Suspended for the final 3 Premiership games of last season and the FA Cup final following his red card v Man Utd on April 16. It was his second sending-off of last season (he was also dismissed at Southampton) and the third of his career (his first was for Spurs v Southampton in September 1994). Scored his first goal for Arsenal v Chelsea on Boxing Day 2001. Capped 54 times by England. Scored v Sweden in 2002 World Cup – his only goal for England. Won his 54th cap v Turkey on April 2. Scored 6 goals in 98 games for Arsenal and was included in 2003 PFA Premiership Team of the Year.

**22 GAEL CLICHY** 26.07.85
A left-back signed from Cannes in August 2003. The club have had to pay around £250,000 in compensation to relegated Cannes for Wenger's 18-year-old compatriot, who impressed him with a string of solid performances in pre-season friendlies.

**3 ASHLEY COLE** 20.12.80
Has been capped 19 times by England. Has scored 6 goals in 120 games for Arsenal. Scored once last season, v West Brom on August 27, 2002. Made his senior Arsenal debut v Middlesbrough at the Riverside in the Worthington Cup in November 1999. One red card for Arsenal - in Mallorca on September 11, 2001. Was fined £2,000 and banned for 2 games with immediate effect on January 14, 2003 for using insulting and abusive language towards Paul Durkin in Arsenal's 3-2 defeat at Southampton on November 23, 2002. Included in 2003 PFA Premiership Team of the Year. Underwent a hernia operation on February 27 and missed 7 games as a result.

**18 PASCAL CYGAN** 29.04.74
Signed from Lille for an undisclosed fee in July 2002. He was at Lille for 7 years, was made captain, and helped the team win promotion to the first division in 2000. The subsequent year, Lille won a place in the Champions League. Yet to be capped by France, but he was voted best player in the French first division by France Football magazine in 2000-2001. Played for Lille in both Champions League games v Man Utd in 2001-02. Made his Arsenal debut as a sub at Chelsea on September 1, 2002. Made 31 apps in all comps last season as understudy to Campbell and Keown. Missed 8 games in Dec 02/Jan 03 with a calf injury and the last 4 games of the season with another calf problem. Scored in 2-1 home win v Everton on March 23 – his only goal for Arsenal so far.

# GROUP B
## ARSENAL FC

**17 EDU** 16.05.78
Has scored 6 goals in 62 apps for Arsenal. Scored in League Cup round four win v Grimsby on November 27, 2001 – his first goal for the club. Has suffered a string of injuries since joining from Corinthians in January 2001 and has started only 22 Premiership games to date. Started the first 6 games of last season (all comps) but did not start more than 3 on the trot after that. Scored at both ends in the 2-1 home defeat v Blackburn on October 26, 2002.

**19 GILBERTO** 07.10.76
Was signed from Atletico Mineiro for £4.5m in July 2002. Helped his former club to the 2002 Minas Gerais State Championship and his impressive form earned him a place in the Brazilian team for the World Cup, where he played every minute of every game as Brazil lifted the trophy for the fifth time. Scored on his Gunners debut, in the Community Shield win v Liverpool in August 2002, after coming on as a sub. Scored after 20.07 seconds in Eindhoven on September 25, 2002 – the fastest ever Champions League goal. Yet to score a Premiership goal.

**14 THIERRY HENRY** 17.08.77
Has scored 113 goals in 206 games for Arsenal. Voted PFA Player of the Year and FWA Footballer of the Year for 2003. He is the 11th player to win both awards in the same season. Has scored 32 goals for Arsenal in each of the last 2 seasons. Before scoring v Spurs on November 16, 2002 he had gone 5 appearances without a Premiership goal - his worst run without a Premiership goal since he failed to score in his first 7 league apps for Arsenal back in August/September 1999. Finished as top Premiership scorer in 2001-02 with 24 goals and was one behind 25-goal Golden Boot winner Van Nistelrooy last season. Has scored 82 goals in 136 Premiership games and 26 goals in 49 European games for Arsenal. 46 of his 113 goals have been scored away from Highbury (31 of his 82 Premiership goals have been scored away from Highbury). French international (51 caps, 22 goals). Scored 10 goals in 13 internationals last season, including the only goal of the Confederations Cup final v Cameroon in June. Has missed 4 of his last 7 penalties for Arsenal (v Deportivo, Juventus, Bolton and Chelsea). Scored his 1st ever Premiership header v West Ham on January 19, 2003 (his 74th Premiership goal) – has now scored 2 headers in the Premiership (has also scored 3 headers in Europe for Arsenal). Claimed 20 goal assists last season – a new Premiership record.

**41 CRAIG HOLLOWAY** 10.08.84
A 19-year-old goalkeeper who joined the club in the summer of 2000. In the summer of 2002 he signed his first professional forms with the club. He cemented the deal by joining up with the first-team's pre-season tour of Austria. He was a member of Arsenal's 2001 FA Youth Cup winning side. Last season he was twice an unused sub for the first-team. He was also an unused sub for the first-team in a Worthington Cup tie at Blackburn in 2001-02.

# GROUP B
## ARSENAL FC

**9 FRANCIS JEFFERS** 25.01.81
Joined from Everton for an initial fee of £8m in June 2001. This figure will rise to £10m after appearances. England U-21 international (13 caps, 13 goals). Scored a hat-trick v Albania on September 4, 2001, and a hat-trick v Macedonia on October 15, 2002. Has scored 10 goals in his last 6 U21 internationals. Equalled Alan Shearer's record of 13 England U21 goals in the 1-1 draw with Turkey on April 1 having been released from the senior squad to play. Scored on his England senior debut, v Australia on February 12. Made his Arsenal debut as a sub v Leeds on August 21, 2001. Scored his first Arsenal goal v Bolton on September 22, 2001. Ankle, back and knee injuries have restricted him to just 8 goals in 39 apps for Arsenal. Has made just 4 Premiership starts for Arsenal. Has scored 28 goals in 99 club career apps. Made his Premiership debut at 16 in Everton's 2-0 defeat at Man Utd on Boxing Day 1997. Now on season long loan to Everton.

**57 JUAN** 06.02.82
is a left-back who joined the club from Sao Paulo in the summer of 2001. Brazilian who made his first-team debut in Worthin gton Cup v Grimsby on November 27, 2001, and also started the FA Cup tie v Gillingham on February 16, 2002. Full name: Juan Maldono Duarte. Joined Millwall on a 3-month loan in July 2003.

**25 KANU** 01.08.76
Has scored just 6 goals in each of the last 2 seasons. Has scored 41 goals in 174 games (79 as a sub) for Arsenal. Has scored 29 goals in 109 Premiership appearances. Missed the start of last season with an ankle injury suffered in pre-season and was later troubled with a knee injury. In 1995 he won the Champions League with Ajax at the age of 18, and was an Olympic winner with Nigeria the following summer. Succeeded Mustapha Hadji as African Player of the Year in 1999.

**5 MARTIN KEOWN** 24.07.66
Hasn't scored a Premiership goal since Arsenal's 4-0 win at Leeds in April 2000. His last goals in any competition (2) came in the Champions League v Shakhtar Donetsk at Highbury on September 20, 2000. His last Premiership goal at Highbury was in September 1996 (v Chelsea). Has scored 8 goals in 434 games for Arsenal. Has won 43 caps and scored 2 goals for England. Missed a total of 17 games through hamstring injuries last season. Has made 313 Premiership appearances and 720 club career appearances. Has been sent off 11 times in his career – 1 off the record set by Vinnie Jones, Roy Keane and Patrick Vieira. His last red card came in a FA Cup clash with Liverpool on January 27, 2002.

**12 LAUREN** 19.01.77
Has scored 8 goals in 119 games for Arsenal. Six of his eight goals have been scored at Highbury. The Cameroon international made his Arsenal debut at Sunderland in August 2000. The midfielder turned right back missed the final 3 Premiership games of last season due to ankle ligament damage suffered at Bolton on April 26.

# GROUP B
## ARSENAL FC

**1 JENS LEHMANN** 10.11.69
Was signed from Borussia Dortmund for £1.5m in July 2003. He won the German league title with Dortmund in 2002, and was a member of the Germany World Cup squads in 1998 and 2002, as well as their Euro 2000 squad. He has won 16 caps for Germany and made a combined total of nearly 400 appearances for Schalke and Borussia Dortmund. During his time with these clubs, he made over 50 appearances in European competitions, winning the UEFA Cup with Schalke in 1997 and finishing a runner-up in the same competition with Dortmund in 2002. He played against Arsenal in last season's Champions League. Last season he made 36 apps for Dortmund, but he was sent off twice.

**8 FREDDIE LJUNGBERG** 16.04.77
Signed a new 5-year contract with the club in the summer of 2001. Has scored 44 goals in 184 games for Arsenal. Scored 17 goals in 39 apps in 2001-02. The Swedish international has won 38 caps, scoring 3 goals. He missed the start of Arsenal's last season with a hip injury but returned to action with a goal in the Champion's League win v Borussia Dortmund on September 17, 2002. Has scored 31 goals in 117 Premiership appearances for Arsenal. Picked up the Swedish Player of the Year award in 2002. Missed 14 games between December 2002 and February 2003, first with a virus and then with an Achilles' injury. Scored 9 goals last season, including his first Arsenal hat-trick in the 4-0 final day win at Sunderland.

**15 RAY PARLOUR** 07.03.73
Made his league debut in Arsenal's 2-0 defeat at Liverpool in January 1992. Has won 8 major honours with Arsenal – 4 FA Cups, 2 Premiership titles, 1 League Cup and 1 ECWC. Was sent off 3 times in 2001-02 - at Middlesbrough on the opening day and v Newcastle and Bayer Leverkusen. Hasn't scored since 2002 FA Cup final v Chelsea. Has scored in only 3 of his last 114 Premiership apps. His last 'away' goal was in April 2000 (at Watford). The competitive midfielder has been capped 10 times by England – the last time was in November 2000, v Italy. He has played a total of 430 games for Arsenal, scoring 32 goals. Last season was disrupted with injuries (mainly knee and hamstring).

**21 JERMAINE PENNANT** 15.01.83
Has won 18 England U-21 caps. Earlier last season he had been axed from the squad for breaking a curfew during preparation for the game v Turkey on April 2. Made his Premiership debut as a sub at West Ham on August 24, 2002. Marked his first Premiership start with a 10-minute first-half hat-trick in Arsenal's 6-1 win v Southampton on May 7, 2003. Has now made 14 first-team apps for Arsenal. Was loaned to Watford in 2001-02 (9 appearances, 2 goals) and again last season (14 appearances, 1 goal). Currently on loan to Leeds United.

# GROUP B
## ARSENAL FC

**7 ROBERT PIRES** 29.10.73
Came on as sub in the Champions League defeat v Auxerre on October 22, 2002 – his first appearance since suffering a knee ligament injury in the FA Cup quarter-final replay v Newcastle on March 23, 2002. Scored 8 goals in 51 appearances in 2000-01. Scored 13 goals in 45 apps in 2001-02 and 16 in 42 appearances last season. Has scored 37 goals in 139 games for Arsenal. The French international has been capped 61 timed for his country, scoring 14 goals. He was voted 2001-02 Footballer of the Year by the Football Writers' Association and was included in 2003 PFA Premiership Team of the Year. Scored 16 goals last season including a hat-trick in a 6-1 win v Southampton (his first Arsenal treble) and the only goal of the FA Cup final against the same club. Signed a new contract in August 2003 keeping him at the club until 2006.

**20 PHILIPPE SENDEROS** 14.02.85
Joined the club in the summer of 2003 from Swiss club Servette. Central defender who agreed to join the Gunners in December 2002, but Wenger allowed him to play out the season with Servette. Has established a fine reputation on the continent after leading his country to success at the European Under-17 championship in 2002. He was an imposing presence at the back throughout the tournament and even got forward to score in Switzerland's 3-1 win over the Ukraine. Became a regular at Swiss club Servette last season and has now represented his country at Under-21 level.

**24 RAMI SHAABAN** 30.06.75
Was signed from Djurgaarden of Sweden for an undisclosed fee in August 2002. The goalkeeper was born in Stockholm to a Finnish mother and an Egyptian father. Yet to be called upon by Sweden so could still pledge his international allegiance to Egypt. Was a Swedish Second Division Championship winner with Djurgaardens in 2000, and runner-up in the Swedish top division in 2001. Made his Gunners debut v PSV on November 12, 2002 and made his Premiership debut v Tottenham 4 days later. Came off with a thigh injury v Man Utd on December 7, 2002. Broke his leg in training on Christmas Eve 2002.

**33 GRAHAM STACK** 26.09.81
An excellent shot stopper who was instrumental in Arsenal's FA Youth Cup victory in 2000. Joined Arsenal in the summer of 1998 and turned pro in the summer of 2000.

**26 IGORS STEPANOVS** 21.01.76
Scored his only goal for Arsenal so far on his debut, in 2-1 home Worthington Cup defeat to Ipswich on November 1, 2000. Played 4 times last season. Has now made 31 apps for Arsenal. Latvian international signed for £1m from Skonto Riga in September 2000. Currently on-loan at Beveren.

**13 STUART TAYLOR** 28.11.80
Made his England U-21 debut v Holland on August 14, 2001. Now has 3 caps. Has now

made 30 apps for Arsenal (26 starts). Made his Premiership debut v Man Utd November 25, 2001. Came on as a sub on the final day of 2001-02 v Everton to make his 10th Premiership app of the season and thereby qualify for a winner's medal.

**28 KOLO TOURE** 19.03.81
The Ivory Coast international signed from Asec Mimosas for an undisclosed fee in February 2002, following a successful trial period with the club.
He has been a permanent fixture in the Ivory Coast side since 2000, and featured in the 2002 African Nations Cup. Made his Gunners debut as a sub in the 2002 Community Shield, and made his Premiership debut as a sub v Birmingham on August 18, 2002. Made his first start at Charlton on September 14, 2002. Sent off v PSV on November 12, 2002. He scored his first goal for Arsenal at Chelsea on September 1, 2002. This season Toure has been converted into a centre-back.

**16 GIOVANNI VAN BRONCKHORST** 05.02.75
Was signed from Rangers for £8.5m in June 2001. A Dutch international he has been capped 29 times and scored 3 goals. Scored the 1-0 winner v Argentina on February 12, 2003 after coming on as a sub. He scored 22 goals in 3 seasons at Ibrox. Joined Rangers from Feyenoord in the summer of 1998. Won the domestic treble in his first season at Rangers (1998-99), and also won the double in 1999-00. Scored 6 goals in 2000-01 (3 in Champions League), but missed the second half of the season through injury. Scored at Leicester on January 23, 2002 – his first goal for Arsenal. Sent off at Anfield on December 23, 2001. Missed the final 18 games of 2001-02 after sustaining a serious knee injury v Fulham on February 23, 2002 that also forced him to miss the start of last season. Now on loan to Barcelona.

**4 PATRICK VIEIRA** 23.06.76
Received the 8th red card of his Arsenal career at Chelsea on September 1, 2002. Sent off 7 times in Premiership (a record – level with Roy Keane and Vinnie Jones). Missed a penalty at Sunderland on October 27, 2001. The French international has received 62 caps, scoring 4 goals). Voted France's Player of the Year for 2001. For Arsenal his record stands: 319 games, 23 goals. A knee injury forced him to miss the final 6 games of last season. Included in 2003 PFA Premiership Team of the Year (his 4th consecutive inclusion in the team). Signed a new contract in August 2003 keeping him at the club until 2007.

**29 MORITZ VOLZ** 21.01.83
Made his Arsenal debut in the Worthington Cup v Ipswich on November 1, 2000 at the age of 17 and was a major influence on the FA Youth Cup victories in 2000 and 2001. He scored in the 1st leg of the 2001 final v Blackburn. He is a former captain of the Germany Under-15's. He captained the Germany Under-19 side to the European Under-19 Championship final in the summer of 2002 (they lost to Spain). Was loaned to Wimbledon last season and is currently on-loan at Fulham.

**11 SYLVAIN WILTORD** 10.05.74
Has scored 45 goals in 156 games for Arsenal. Scored 17 goals in 54 appearances in 2001-02 and 13 goals in 54 apps last season. Has been subbed off in 67 of his 111 starts for Arsenal. A French international he has received 55 caps and scored 17 goals. Voted Premiership Player of the Month for August 2002. His last Premiership goal at Highbury was on November 16, 2002. Scored 6 goals in the first 6 Premiership games of last season. Has scored 28 goals in 94 Premiership appearances.

# INTERNAZIONALE MILAN

**In 2002-03 Inter had another fine season of almost winning trophies – they were runners up to Juventus in Serie A, and were unluckily beaten on an away goal by AC Milan in the Champions League semi-final. Inter also threatened to win Serie A in 2001-02 but flopped at the death. They finished 3rd (69pts) to Juventus (71pts) and Roma (70pts) – only winning the dubious title of 'best team for 33 weeks of the season'! Poor Inter have been in the shadow of their rivals AC Milan since their last title wins in 1989 and 1980. In total, Inter have won the title 13 times and the Italian Cup three times - the last in 1982. They were successful in the UEFA Cup in 1991, 1994 and 1998. The other European successes include the European Cup of 1964 and 1965 - on both occasions they went on to win the World Club Cup.**

## COACH

**HECTOR CUPER** 16.11.55
A former Argentine international with 6 caps, he coached Hurucan and Lanus in the Argentine First Division before arriving at Mallorca in 1997. Initially he had much success in the two seasons he had with Mallorca: 1999 European Cup Winners' Cup final, Spanish Cup final, 5th and 3rd in the League, and a Champions League place. Joined Inter in summer 2001 after taking Valencia to the European Cup finals of 2000 and 2001. In his first year in Serie A, Cuper's Inter dominated the season but failed at the final hurdle and secured only third place. There were further near misses in 2002-03 and Cuper had to settle for a Champions League semi final place and the runners up spot in the championship. Cuper is still searching for his first silverware as a manager but his organisation and discipline are already making an impression on Inter.

## REACTION TO DRAW

**"I think we can be reasonably optimistic. I don't know why it is being said that ours is the most difficult of the groups facing the Italian teams. We have to take into consideration that we weren't a top seed and so it could have been**

**worse. We are up against teams who are at a more advanced stage of preparation such as the Russians and Ukrainians, but we are in shape after three months of work."** ***Vice-President Giacinto Facchetti***

## SQUAD

**15 DANIELE ADANI** 10.07.74
One of those jetissoned by bankrupt Fiorentina in summer 2002, a classy defender who just failed to make the World Cup squad after playing friendly international matches in 2002. Began his career in Serie B with Modena from 1991-4, then was snapped up by Lazio, who released him without a first team game in the mid-1990's. Bought in summer 99 from Brescia for £2 million. Won his first cap v England 15.11.00 after being drafted in by his former Fiorentina coach Trappatoni - came on as sub, and has been in squad since.

**25 MATIAS ALMEYDA** 21.02.73
The Argentine midfielder broke his leg v Empoli on 25 Jan 2003 and was out for the rest of the season. Joined from Parma in summer 2002 when out of contract, and played in Argentina's final World Cup game in 2002. Joined Parma in summer 2000 from Lazio with Sergio Conceicao as part of the £34 million swap with Hernan Crespo. Won a championship medal with Lazio 2000 as well as helping his team to the1999 European Cup Winners Cup and European Super Cup. Joined Lazio in the 1997 summer from relegated Seville in the Primera Liga, where he earned much credit for sticking at his job through 5 trainers during a shambles of a season. His first club was River Plate where he spent 5 seasons. There he won championship medals in 1994 and 1995 as well as the Libertadores Cup.

**21 NICOLA BEATI** 13.02.83
Made first team debut in June 2001 v Bologna aged 18 but had to wait until last season to reach first team again. Like Pasquale, he is a graduate from the club's youth team who is in his 5th season with first team squad.

**31 JEREMIE BRECHET** 14.08.79
Joined from Lyon in summer 2003 to cover for the frequently injured Coco after being spotted when he played against Inter in last season's Champions League. Inter beat Paris SG to his signature after the French club seemed certain to sign him. Brechet won league titles with Lyon in 2002 and 2003, the first in the club's history. A French U21 international, the young left back was in the side that finished runners up in the 2002 EuroU21 championships. He received his first senior cap at the 2001 Confederations Cup and is considered one of the stars of the future.

**13 FABIO CANNAVARO** 13.09.73
Joined Inter in summer 2002 from Parma for around £15 million – interestingly, his brother Paolo is now with Parma and is set to take his position. Rated now as the best

Italian defender (ahead of Maldini and Nesta), a key player in 1999 UEFA and Italian Cup wins for Parma. In 1995 he was forced to leave cash-starved Napoli for whom he had played for since 1991. Was in the team that won the 1996 European U21 championship and also went to the Olympics in Atlanta where he was the captain. Is now a fixture in the heart of the national team's defence. He played all 5 games at the 1998 World Cup, was superb at Euro2000 and played in 3 of the 4 games at the 2002 World Cup.

**77 FRANCESCO COCO** 08.01.77
The injury prone Italian starts 2003-04 with further knee ligament damage. Was Paolo Maldini's reserve at Milan and played 5 times in Milan's championship team in 1996 and another 6 in their 1999 success but went on loan for experience at Torino and Vicenza before a move to Barca. Joined Barca in summer 2001 on loan from AC Milan for £4 million and returned to neighbours Inter for around £7.8 million in summer 2002. Member of the Italy team that won the 2000 European U21 championship before being called up to national team after fine start to 2000-1 season. Played last 2 games of 2002 World Cup finals.

**2 IVAN CORDOBA** 11.08.76
Colombian international who began career with Nacional Medellin before playing three seasons with San Lorenzo. Joined Inter midwinter 1999-2000 and settled well, claiming a regular slot at left back and then in central defence since Laurent Blanc left. He reached 100 Serie A games in his penultimate appearance of last season. Scored the winning goal to make Colombia Coppa America winners in 2001.

**9 JULIO RICARDO CRUZ** 10.10.74
Signed to Inter in August 2003 from Bologna to cover for the departed Crespo. Had joined Bologna from Feyenoord in summer 2000 for a club record £8 million and has been their top scorer for the last two seasons. Prior to that move, he was top scorer for Feyenoord in his three seasons (14 goals each time). Feyenoord has signed Cruz from the Argentine champions, River Plate in summer 1997 for $7.5 million after he scored 17 goals in 29 games in the Argentine league 1996-7. First capped in 1997, but did not make squad for World Cup in France.

**5 EMRE (BELOZOGLOU)** 07.09.80
One of the stars of Turkey's 3rd place at the World Cup, he played in 6 of their 7 games at the finals despite an injury hit Serie A season. Cost Inter £1.7 million from Turkish club Galatasaray in summer 2001 and is considered one of the world's most promising midfielders. Played in the Galatasaray squad for 1998 title win in first full season. Also played in 1997, 1999 and 2000 championship triumphs

**12 ALBERTO FONTANA** 23.01.67
Reserve keeper signed from relegated Napoli in summer 2001 on a free transfer as cover for Toldo. Only played one Serie A game in 2001-02 and one in 2002-03.

Although a reserve he has had 5 full seasons as first choice in Serie A, playing a total of 136 games with Cesena, Bari, Atalanta and Napoli and Inter.

**24 CARLOS GAMARRA** 17.02.71
Since joining Inter in summer 2002 from Greek runners up AEK Athens, Gamarra is now playing football in his 7th country. Now on his third spell in Europe, the Paraguayan is on his way to setting a new record for international caps for his country after playing for his country for ten years. Created a fine impression in Portugal a few years ago after joining Benfica from Inter Porto Alegre in summer 1997 but was forced to leave because the club could not afford his wages. Also forced to leave Atletico Madrid 1999-2000 for similar reasons.

**18 KILY GONZALEZ** 04.08.74
Played all 3 games for Argentina in 2002 World Cup finals, but has suffered injury problems since. The former Boca forward was a late summer 1996 signing for Valencia as part of a deal that took Fernando Caceres back to Boca Juniors. - Kily is, who was in the Argentine national squad in 1996-7 for first 2 caps. Valencia paid £2.2 million for Kily and got enormous results. The left-sided winger was a major player in the Spanish team's recent success and helped them to the league title in 2002 and two Champions League finals. He left Valencia to join his old boss Hector Cuper in summer 2003.

**2 THOMAS HELVEG** 24.06.71
Helveg swapped clubs but kept the same home ground when he moved in summer 2003 to Inter from AC Milan. Signed for AC from Udinese by Alberto Zaccheroni for £7 million in 1998 and immediately helped them to the championship in 1999. In 1995 he helped Udinese into Serie A after £500,000 move from Odense where he played 1989-94. The 1994 Danish Footballer of the Year played all 4 games at 2002 World Cup. Formerly a midfielder, Helveg is now more at home as a right wing-back.

**3 MOHAMED KALLON** 06.10.79
Huge talent from Vicenza who was bought in summer 2001 for £2.7 million. Scored collected 10 goals in 29 games at start of 2001-2 when others were injured – but has only played 9 Serie A games since. Originally came to Europe aged 16 with Swiss club Lugano. Went on to play for struggling clubs Bologna, Cagliari, Reggina, and Vicenza, yet still managed to score 25 goals in 83 Serie A games.

**19 GIORGIOS KARAGOUNIS** 06.03.77
Moved to Inter from Panathinaikos in summer 2003. Scorer of fine goal at Old Trafford in 2000-01 - scored again in the 2001-02 Champions League win v Arsenal in Athens. The former U21 international switched to Panathinaikos from the Athens club in 1998. He was the captain at the time of the national U21 side that were runners up in the European U21 championship. Received his first full cap in Aug 1999, the midfielder has now gained a reputation as a freekick specialist.

# GROUP B
## INTERNAZIONALE MILAN

**8 SABRI LAMOUCHI** 09.11.71
Summer 2003 signing from Parma. Joined Parma for £4.3 million in summer 2000 from French champions Monaco where he won a title medal. Signed by Monaco in summer 1998 to replace Man City's Ali Benarbia who went to Bordeaux - but Lamouchi collected ligament damage and missed a third of the season. He made his name in 4 seasons with Auxerre - and was a key player in their 1996 League and Cup double side.

**11 LUCIANO** 03.12.75
Joined from Chievo in summer 2003 on loan with an option to buy. Cost Chievo £750,000 in summer 2001 from Bologna where he had played for three seasons. Was banned worldwide for 6 months after admitting that while at Palmeiras he had adopted a false identity (Eriberto) and birth date (21.01.79).

**30 AKINWUNMI MARTINS OBAFENI** 28.10.84
Nigerian forward who graduated from the youth team. Has done well since the start of the 2002-03 season following injuries to several top forwards (Vieri, Crespo etc) and scored against Bayer Leverkusen and AC Milan in the Champions League. He also played 4 league games in 2002-03, scoring 1 goal.

**23 MARCO MATERAZZI** 19.08.73
The 6'4" central defender signed in summer 2001 from Perugia for £6.3 million after being the club's top scorer with 12 goals (8 pens). After four seasons, he briefly left Perugia to play 27 Premiership games for Everton in 1998-9 before making a £3 million move back to Perugia in summer 1999. Has been an Italian international since he won his first cap in April 2001. Played once at World Cup but was poor in loss v Croatia (sub).

**22 OKAN (BURUK)** 19.10.73
Won 6 titles, 4 Cups and the UEFA Cup at Galatasaray in his 10 years with them. Joined Inter in summer 2001 for £2.3 million. Now a regular in the Turkish national team, Okan was the playmaker in the breakthrough team that won the Euro U18 title in 1992. Received his first full cap against San Marino in 1992 as a teenager but didn't figure for the national team again until Turkey faced Russia in April 1998. He starred in the World Cup play off wins v Austria and scored in both legs (1-0, 5-0) and was in the squad for the finals but did not play due to injury until the game for third place.

**26 GIOVANNI PASQUALE** 05.01.82
This is Pasquale's 2nd season in the first team and has made huge strides in the problem left back role. Has done well in the absence of the frequently injured Coco. A graduate from the club's youth team, he has been in the first team squad for 5 seasons though did not make his debut until 2002-03. Has become first choice in Italy's national U21 side this season.

# GROUP B
## INTERNAZIONALE MILAN

**20 ALVARO RECOBA** 17.03.76
Reputedly the highest paid player in Serie A, the Uruguayan possesses the best left foot in Italy and one of the worst tempers. Signed for Inter in summer 1997 from Nacional of Montevideo on a 4 year contract for around £3.5 million. Was on loan to Venezia in 1998-9 and his 11 goals in 20 games kept them in Serie A.

**1 FRANCESCO TOLDO** 02.12.71
Toldo began his career on the books of AC Milan from 1988-90 but was released without playing a first team game. He came to the fore in Fiorentina's 1993-4 promotion season when they bounced straight back up to Serie A. Missed just 6 games in his last 7 full seasons for Fiorentina before moving to Inter for £18.3 million. This transfer fee was briefly a world record until Buffon made his move to Juventus. Won his first cap for Italy v Croatia on 8.10.95 but has since been overtaken by Buffon in the fight for the number one shirt. At 6'5" he is Serie A's tallest keeper.

**7 ANDY VAN DER MEYDE** 30.09.79
Joined in summer 2003 from Ajax as coach Cuper searched for quality wide players. A huge talent who plays as an orthodox right winger, he was born in Arnhem but was stolen from under the noses of Vitesse by Ajax in 1993. He joined the first team squad in 1997, played a full season on loan with Twente in 1999-2000 then moved straight back into the Ajax first team.

**32 CHRISTIAN VIERI** 12.07.73
Brought up in Australia, the Italian international striker's hero is Allan Border. At the start of 2003-4 he had scored 104 goals in 175 Serie A games. He scored 24 goals in 23 games making him top scorer in Serie A last season. Surprisingly he didn't score in the first group stage of the Champions League 2002-03 despite starting all games. Bagged one goal in the two group stages (v Newcastle) and then notched the winner in first leg of quarter-final. Won a championship medal with Juve in 1996 and was then sold for £10 million to Atletico Madrid - moved back to Italy for £18.9 million in Aug 1998 after a season in Spain where he finished top of the Primera Liga scorers with 24 goals in 24 games. Cost a then world record £32 million from Lazio in summer 1999 – presumably why he wears the number 32 shirt. Scored 5 times at World Cup 1998 and 4 times at 2002 finals to create new Italian record.

**6 CRISTIANO ZANETTI** 10.04.77
Midfielder who spent 1994-6 with Fiorentina before moving to Venezia and Reggiana . He was sold by Reggiana to Inter for £2 million in summer 1998. The U21 international left Inter on swap loan deal with Luigi Di Biagio to Roma but returned in summer 2001. Played at the Olympic Games in Sydney 2000 but is now a full international.

**4 JAVIER ZANETTI** 10.05.73
The captain of Argentina and Inter has just signed a new deal keeping him at the Italian

club until 2007. A summer 1995 signing from the Argentine first Division club, Banfield, for a bargain £1.8 million. He is the current right wing-back in their national team, and was a key player in the 1998 World Cup team. He played all 3 games at the 2002 World Cup finals and as, in fact, only been rested, not dropped, since his first cap immediately after the 1994 World Cup. Hardly misses a game for club and country - nearing 300 Serie A games and won 1998 UEFA Cup with Inter.

# FC DYNAMO KYIV

**Dynamo Kyiv are kicking off their 8th CL campaign – their 7th in succession.In the last three seasons FC Dynamo fell every time at the first hurdle. You have to go back to 1999 when they lost to Bayern Munich to see Kyiv appear in a semi-final of the Champions League. The season before when they were beaten by runners-up Juventus they reached the quarter-final. This great name from the old USSR league was the first Russian team to win a European competition: the Cup Winners Cup in 1975 with a 3-0 win against Hungarian side Ferencvaros Budapest. Further European glory was to follow in the mid-1980s, when Valeriy Lobanovskiy's ambitious dream team finally took shape. A side boasting the 20 best youngsters in Ukraine took the 1985/86 Cup Winners Cup with a 3-0 win against Atletico Madrid. In the 90s, when Lobanovskiy had a third spell at the club, he discovered a brilliant striking partnership in the form of Rebrov and Shevchenko.**

## COACH

**OLEKSIY MYKHALYCHENKO** 30.03.1963
Oleksiy joined Dynamo Kyiv aged 10. The midfielder won the Russian championship 3 times (1985, 1986 and 1990) and the Russian Cup twice (1987 and 1990) before moving to Italy in 1990. With Sampdoria Genoa he won the Italian league title (1991) playing alongside big names like Gianluca Vialli and Roberto Mancini. In 1992 he moved to Scotland and with Rangers he won 5 successive Scottish league titles. He made 44 appearances for the old USSR and CIS before the break up and he was captain of the old country. His biggest achievements were winning a gold medal at the 1988 Olympics in Seoul and playing in the final of the European championships in the same year losing to Holland (2-0) in Munich. In 1997, after working for a year as tv commentator, Mykhalychenko was asked by his mentor Valeriy Lobanovskiy to become his assistant at Dynamo Kyiv. After Lobanovskiy's death on 13 May 2002 Mykhalychenko became his successor. Mykhalychenko had a difficult start losing the title as well as the cup to Shakhtar Donetsk.. To the surprise of many, president Igor Surkis kept his confidence in Mykhalychenko who repaid him by bringing the title and the cup back to FC Dynamo.

# GROUP B
## FC DYNAMO KYIV

## REACTION TO DRAW

**"I welcome the challenge and the chance to show the fact that I believe Ukrainian soccer today has improved and I think that in some respects we are stronger than the Russians. It is a tough group of course but I don't think Arsenal or Inter are necessarily the favourites, I think it's very evenly matched,"** ***President Igor Surkis.***

## SQUAD

**8 VALENTIN BELKEVICH** 27.01.73
Belarus international playmaker nicknamed 'The Master of Passing'. Won 5 league titles and 2 cups in Belarus with Dinamo Minsk before joining FC Dynamo Kyiv in 1996 together with Aleksandr Khatskevich. Won the Ukrainian league title 6 times and 3 Ukrainian cups. Made his international debut for Belarus versus Ukraine in October 1992. Had 45 caps, 9 goals at the end of August 2003. Played 3 CL games last season and scored 1 goal at home versus Feyenoord (2-0 win). He made 24 assists last season when he was named Player of the Year in Ukraine.

**10 FLORIN LUCIAN CERNAT** 10.03.80
Diminutive central or left-sided midfielder, nicknamed 'The Diamond' in Romania because of his enormous value. Product of Otelul Galati where he made his debut as a 18-year-old and was spotted by Dinamo Bucharest. He joined Dynamo Kyiv (Ajax and Bayern Munich were also interested) in the 2000/01 winter break. He was the playmaker for the Romanian national U21 side and became a full international under Gheorghe Hagi. Made his debut for Romania versus Ukraine in spring 2002.

**6 YURIY DMYTRULIN** 10.02.75
He can play as well as full-back, sweeper or as a defensive midfielder. He has played more than 150 league games in Ukraine and 50 European Cup games (3 in the CL last season). Has 37 caps, 1 goal for Ukraine. After playing for Borysfen Boryspil he joined Dynamo. Another product of the club's successful youth system.

**3 SERGIY FEDOROV** 18.02.75
The Ukrainian international centre-back is a product of Dynamo's youth scheme and played 18 months on loan for CSKA Kyiv in 1995-96. Scored the opener in the home game versus Dinamo Zagreb (3-1 win) with a header in the 3rd qualifying round. Has 15 caps for Ukraine, scoring 1 goal.

**32 GORAN GAVRANCIC** 02.08.78
Midfielder from Serbia and Montenegro who developed his football talent and skills in the youth teams of Red Star Belgrade. He joined FC Dynamo in March 2001 from Cukaricki Belgrade. Played 9 times for his national team but is yet to score. Has scored

10 goals in just over 50 league games for Kyiv. Takes the penalties for FC Dynamo.

**17 TIBERIU GHIOANE** 18.06.61
Romanian international playmaker who started his career back home with FC Brasov before being spotted by Rapid Bucharest. Was under-21 international before being promoted into the first team by new coach Georghe Hagi. Can also play as a 'libero'. Joined Dynamo in the summer 2001 and had played 43 league games and scored 4 goals before the start of this season. Played all 6 CL games for Dynamo Kyiv last season.

**4 OLEKSANDR HOLOVKO** 06.01.72
Joined Dynamo in July 1995 from Tavriya Simferopol, the club who won the first ever independent Ukrainian league title in 1992. He is heading for 300 league appearances. He didn't play in the CL last season. Made his debut for Ukraine versus Estonia in April 1995 and had 57 caps before the start of this season.

**14 ANDRII HUSIN** 11.12.72
Out with a thigh injury for 3 months since September 6. Was converted to a midfielder but still has an eye for goal. His total is 32 in 197 league games for FC Dynamo. You can find him normally on the left side or central midfield. Has played for Karpaty Lviv and CSKA Kyiv. Made his international debut for Ukraine as a substitute against Croatia in June 1996 and immediately scored his first goal for his country. Has 45 caps, 5 goals at the start of this season.

**20 OLEH HUSYEV** 25.04.83
Young midfielder who has made progress last season at Arsenal Kyiv before arriving at FC Dynamo. Scored the 3rd goal for his new club in the 3-1 home win against Dinamo Zagreb in the 3rd qualifying round. Has 2 caps for Ukraine but no goals as yet.

**9 BADR EL KADDOURI** 31.01.81
Moroccan international who joined in July 2002 from WAC Marrakech. This midfielder played 2 CL games last season but hasn't made his mark yet in Kyiv with only 4 league games last season.

**2 ALEKSANDR KHATSKEVICH** 19.10.73
Very useful midfielder who played together with Valentin Belkevich at Dinamo Minsk before joining Dynamo Kyiv in July 1996. He is an international for Belarus (34 caps, 4 goals) making his debut in January 1993 versus Ecuador and was elected Belarus Player of the Year in 2000. Played 5 CL games last season scoring 2 goals both at home versus Newcastle United (2-0 win) and versus Feyenoord (also 2-0 win). He has won no fewer than 10 league titles – 6 in Ukraine, 4 in Belarus – and 5 national cups – 3 with Dynamo Kyiv and 2 with Dinamo Minsk. He played at the 1992 European under-21 Championship finals with CIS national team. He was also top scorer in the Ukrainian league 1999/2000 with 20 goals.

**36 JERKO LEKO** 09.04.80
Young midfielder who was spotted by the scouts of Kyiv in Croatia at Dinamo Zagreb where he played first team football since 2000. Leko was a member of the national U21 side, before becoming a full international (10 caps, 1 goal) although he didn't make the final 23 selection for the World Cup 2002 in Japan. Came to Kyiv in 2002 and played 5 CL games last season. Was very satisfied to score the 2nd goal in the home game against his former team Dinamo Zagreb (3-1 win) in the 3rd qualifying round.

**7 OLEKSANDR MELASHCHENKO** 13.12.78
Attacking midfielder who scored 10 goals in 53 league games for Vorskla Poltava and was hot property in the transfer market in the winter of 2000/01. In January 2001 he eventually joined FC Dynamo and scored 10 goals in 15 games in his first season to clinch the title for Dynamo Kyiv. This included a winning goal versus Dnipropetrovsk after 85 mins to win the championship. Was third in 2001 Player of the Year Poll after Andriy Shevchenko and Gennadiy Zubov. In February 2001 he also made his debut for Ukraine versus Georgia. Had 16 caps and 3 goals at the end of August 2003.

**18 ROBERTO ANTONIO NANNI** 20.08.81
Argentine forward who was signed from Velez Sarsfield after the domestic transfer deadline was over which means that he cannot play in the Ukrainian league for FC Dynamo only in the Champions League. Igor Surkis, the president of Dynamo Kyiv, wrote a letter to all clubs and the Professional Football League and asked them to make an exception in order to give Nanni much needed match practice. Eventually the PFL decided to allow Nanni to play in the first half of the 2003/04 season for Dynamo Kyiv's second team in the Ukrainian first division.

**26 ANDRIY NESMACHNYY** 28.02.79
The product of the Olympic Sports School of Simferopol. This left-back joined Dynamo Kyiv in 1996, made his debut one year later and has become a regular since 1999. He was an U21 international before making his international debut versus Bulgaria in April 2000. Has since already played 28 times for Ukraine. Can also be used as defender on the right.

**5 ALESSANDRO MORI NUNES** 10.01.79
Alessandro is a Brazilian right side defender from Rio de Janeiro who joined FC Dynamo this season from Flamengo. Scored his first league goal for Dynamo on August 3rd 2003 in the home game against Dnipropetrovsk (2-1 win).

**22 DENYS ONYSCHENKO** 15.09.78
Son of former Dynamo forward Vladimir, who played in the team of Oleg Blokhin. Denys is a midfielder who joined FC Dynamo this season from Hapoel Tel Aviv to play in the CL. Has already scored twice for Dynamo Kyiv this season, both goals coming at the end of August 2003. One in the cup game away to FC Mykolaiv and one in the league game at home versus Borysfen Boryspil.

# GROUP B
## FC DYNAMO KYIV

**11 GEORGI IVANOV PEEV** 11.03.79
Hard-working right midfielder or forward who joined Dynamo Kyiv in November 2000 from Lokomotiv Sofia. Has already played 7 games in CL for Dynamo (2 in 2001/02, 5 last season). He was an under-21 international for Bulgaria and received first full cap in 1-1 draw versus Ukraine on 18.08.99

**21 VITALIY REVA** 19.11.74
Joined Dynamo Kyiv in 2001 on loan from neighbours CSKA Kyiv. The move was made permanent one year later. Has already played 9 CL games for FC Dynamo. Originally from Dnipropetrovsk, he is known for his penalty-saving qualities. He made his debut in the national team of Ukraine in October 2001 during the World Cup Qualifier versus Poland (1-1) in Chorzow on 06.10.91. Had 9 caps at the beginning of this season.

**15 DIOGO RINCON** 18.04.80
Brazilian forward who's full name is Diogo Augusto Pacheco da Fantoura. He was World under-17 champion with Brazil in 1997 and played in his country for Internacional Porto Alegre. Joined Dynamo Kyiv in July 2002 and played 4 CL games last season. Scored this season the 2nd goal at Dinamo Zagreb (0-2 win) in the 3rd qualifying round.

**35 GORAN SABLIC** 04.08.79
Croatian defender who joined Dynamo in August 2002 after 69 Division One games and 3 goals for Hajduk Split. He made his debut for Hajduk in 1998/99 and won the Croatian cup with them in 2000. He won a bronze medal at 1998 European U18 Championship. Made his debut in the Croatian national team in May 2002 versus Hungary but had only 2 caps at the start of this season.

**16 MAKSIM SHATSKIKH** 30.08.78
International forward for Uzbekistan (14 caps, 9 goals) who joined Dynamo Kyiv in 1999 as a replacement for Andriy Shevchenko who went to AC Milan. Shatskikh was previously playing in Russia for Baltika Kaliningrad in the 2nd division. He is a product of the Tashkent Football School, near the Pakistan border. He started at Dynamo Kyiv with 20 goals in 25 league games becoming Ukrainian top scorer in 1999/2000. Played all 6 games in the CL of last season and scored 3 goals. He scored the 1st goal at home versus Newcastle United (2-0 win) and found the net again in the return game at St James' Park. His other goal was in the home game against Juventus (1-2 defeat).

**1 OLEKSANDR SHOVKOVSKYI** 02.01.75
This 1 m 91 tall national goalkeeper of Ukraine has won 9 league titles and 4 national cups with FC Dynamo where he first made name as a 19 years old in the CL in 1995. He missed the CL campaign 2001/02 because of injury and last season he spent the last 3 games in the first group stage on the substitute bench after a shoulder operation.

**37 ALANDA AYILA YUSSUF** 04.11.84
Nigerian defender who joined Dynamo at the beginning of this season from Union Bank Lagos. Is a young player with a promising future.

# FC LOKOMOTIV MOSCOW

**In 2002 Spartak Moscow lost their league crown to Lokomotiv Moscow, who won their first ever title after 80 years of trying. Loko did it the hard way though – they were level on points with CSKA Moscow at the end of the season and had to win a play-off for the title. It is the Cup that has brought them their other recent success - Loko won the current Russian Cup in 1996 and 1997 and again in 2000 and 2001. They also reached the semi-finals of the European Cup Winners' Cup in both 1998 and 1999 - last two seasons of the competition. In 1998 they lost to Stuttgart, who in turn lost to Chelsea in the final, and in 1999 they lost to eventual winners Lazio. This is their 2nd season in the UCL after their first attempt in 2002-03 when they reached the second group stage, only to succumb to Real Madrid, AC Milan and Borussia Dortmund.**

## COACH

**YURI SYOMIN** 11.05.47
In his 2nd spell as coach to Loko, he was with the club from 1986 to 1990 before taking over the New Zealand national team in 1991 and the Russian national team in 1992-94 and 1996-97. He returned to Loko in 1998 for the recent cup successes and the league win. In a playing career that lasted from 1964-80, Syomin played for 3 of the Moscow clubs - Spartak, Loko and Dynamo as well as two other Super League teams.

## REACTION TO DRAW

**"Arsenal are the favourites. Their game is based on great technical ability and they also improvise a lot. Besides, in Arsene Wenger they have a great coach, a great tactician and so they are always hard to beat. Inter are typically Italian while the matches against Dynamo Kiev will also be interesting – they always are when Russian and Ukrainian teams play each other."** ***Yuri Syomin***

## SQUAD

**32 MIKHAIL ASHVETIA** 10.11.77
Joined the club in 2003 from Alania Valdikavkaz. Was a team mate of Asatiani at Kutaisi, and was in the side that won the 2000 and 2001 national titles, before moving to Alania.

# GROUP B
## FC LOKOMOTIV MOSCOW

**30 MALKHAZ ASATIANI** 04.08.81
A 2003 signing from the Georgian club Torpedo Kutaisi. He broke into the Kutaisi side in 2000, and national honours followed shortly afterwards. Won championship medals in all 3 seasons at Kutaisi, in 2000, 2001 and 2002.

**11 MAKSIM BUZNIKIN** 01.03.77
Was allowed to leave Spartak Moscow for Loko in 2000 and has developed well since then. Had a fine start to his international career (5 goals), but has failed to impress new selectors. Spartak signed him from a junior club, and he was there from 1997-2000 but failed to crack the first team on regular basis.

**16 VADIM EVSEEV** 08.01.76
Has been with the Loko club since 2000 and is in his 4th season with them. Signed from rivals Spartak Moscow where he played from 1993-2000 but only had 4 seasons (all title wins) in the first team squad. The central defender has become a valued member of the Loko first team where he is getting more chances than he did at Spartak.

**41 SERGEI GURENKO** 30.09.72
Rejoined Loko in 2003 after having left them after 5 seasons for AS Roma in summer 99 for £3 million. Not a regular at Roma he went on loan with Piacenza. Played in the semi-final of the 1999 European Cup Winner's Cup when Loko just lost to eventual winners Lazio. Considered one of the best players in the national team.

**5 SERGEI IGNASHEVICH** 14.07.79
Recent U21 and now a full international defender who is in his 2nd season with Loko Called into national squad under coach Valery Gassayev in Aug 2002 and has played virtually every game since despite the change of national coach. Previously played for Kryla Sovietov Samara before making his move in 2001.

**22 ZAUR KHAPOV** 21.10.64
This will be Khapov's 20th season in the top flight, and his 4th season as No 2 at Loko. Spent most of his career with Alania Vladikavkaz from 1991-99 in the side that won the 1995 championship. Also played in the old USSR Super League for Spartak Moscow and the Georgian club Dinamo Tiblisi. Has played over 200 league games – but so often a reserve.

**28 DIMITRI KHOHKLOV** 22.12.75
Returned to Russia in summer 2003 after 4 seasons with the 2003 La Liga runners up Real Sociedad. He played all 3 games at World Cup 2002 and has been a first choice in the Russian national team for the past 6 years since his debut at the age of 20. The former CSKA and Torpedo Moscow midfielder joined PSV in 1997 and had two seasons with them winning a league winner's medal.

# GROUP B
## FC LOKOMOTIV MOSCOW

**77 LEANDRO** 13.08.80
One of several Brazilian Leandros playing in Europe. This forward came from top Brazilian clubs Botafogo (1998-2000) and Corinthians (2000-02) where he was no more than a squad player.

**4 JACOB LEKCHETHO** 24.03.74
Played in World Cup 2002 for South Africa, played once in the finals as sub v Spain. The defender joined in 2001 from Moroka Swallows in S Africa and has impressed in Russia and was a key man in the 2002 title win.

**10 DMITRI LOSKOV** 13.02.74
Captain of the 2002 champions, and scorer of the only goal in the play-off to bring the title to the club. The 2002 Russian Footballer of the Year was one of those players who just turned out each week in an uncomplicated way - then went mad in 2000 and became Russian league top scorer with 15 goals! First played in the old USSR Super League for Rostelmash of Rostov, and was with them from 1991-96, before switching to Loko in 1997.

**8 VLADIMIR MAMINOV** 04.09.74
Scored Loko's first Champions League goal v Anderlecht last season. Has been with Loko ever since he was a teenager in their youth teams, and made his first team debut in 1993. This will be his 11th season in the first team squad.

**9 RUSLAN NIGMATULLIN** 07.10.74
Now back with Loko after leaving in 2001 for spells with CSKA Moscow and Verona in Serie A. Originally from Spartak Moscow, he first joined Loko in 1998 and quickly became the national No 1 choice. He was Russia's keeper in all 3 games at the 2002 World Cup.

**2 GENNADI NIZHEGORODOV** 07.06.77
This is his 4th season with Loko and he has now worked his way into the first team. Originally from Astrakhan, the full-back won caps a couple of years ago when the first choice players from abroad were not available.

**1 SERGEY OVCHINNIKOV** 11.10.70
Originally joined Loko in 1991 and played in the old USSR Super League with the club. Moved to the West in 1997 with Benfica 1997-99, then to Alverca, then to FC Porto from 2000 to early 2002. Returned to Loko in winter 2001-2 to replace the national number one keeper Ruslan Nigmatullin who left for Verona. Recalled to the national squad in summer 2002 and has since held his place.

**52 WINSTON PARKS** 12.10.81
The Costa Rican joined in 2003 from Serie A club Udinese. He spent 3 seasons at

Udinese, where he had been a fringe first teamer and hone on loan at Serie B club Ancona. Has been in his national squad since 2001.

**14 OLEG PASHININ** 12.09.74
Has been with the club for 12 seasons - joined in 1992 and has never been anywhere else. Despite that he has played just over 100 league games, so is very much a squad member rather than first choice. Plays in defence and has now decided to play for his homeland Uzbekhistan after not getting selected by Russia.

**25 RUSLAN PIMENOV** 23.11.81
Was in the Russian World Cup squad, the lively forward played twice at the finals. A graduate from the club's juniors, he is now in his 3rd season in the first team squad.

**17 DIMITRI SENNIKOV** 24.06.76
Capped just before the World Cup, he made the World Cup squad and played once at the finals. Released as a junior by CSKA Moscow, the army team. Joined Loko in 1999, and is now in his 5th season in the first team squad.

**6 NARVIK SIRKHAEV** 16.03.74
Midfielder who joined in summer 2002 from Anji Makhachkala, a provincial club in the Premier League. Was at Anji for 2 seasons 2000 and 2001 and played his part in their rise to 3rd place in the league. Played for Neftchi Baku at home, one of the two best teams in Azerbidjan, but has improved considerably since going to a better league.

**19 NEMANJA VUCICEVIC** 11.08.79
Yugoslavian forward now in his 3rd season at the club. Came from OFK Belgrade club, and is a recent Serbian U21 international

**99 JORGE WAGNER** 17.11.78
Brazilian forward signed in 2003 from leading club Cruzeiro. Had 4 seasons in the Brazilian championship from 1999, first two seasons with Vitoria Bahia, then 2 seasons with Cruzeiro.

# GROUP C

## RC DEPORTIVO CORUNA
(Spain)

## PSV EINDHOVEN
(Netherlands)

## AS MONACO
(France)

## AEK ATHENS
(Greece)

# RC DEPORTIVO CORUNA

**Deportivo finished third in the Primera Liga, behind champions Real Madrid and runners up Real Sociedad. They entered the Champions League at the third qualifying round stage along with their derby rivals Celta Vigo. Depor were the 2000 Spanish league champions - their first championship - and in 2001 and 2002, the club were runners up.**

## COACH

**JAVIER IRUETA** 01.04.48
The coach from summer 1998 at Deportivo has a good reputation for building strong teams with limited resources. Javier Irureta had been with small teams Oviedo, Logrones and Racing Santander and done well with Athletic Bilbao, Real Sociedad. He even took Celta Vigo into Europe. With Depor he has managed to manage some of their errant stars and build a good team spirit. He took the side to their first title in 2000. Irueta is a former Spanish international - he played for Atletico Madrid and Athletic Bilbao and won six caps in midfield for Spain in the early 1970s

## REACTION TO DRAW

**"No one is under the illusion that this is an easy group, but I think we are favourites to qualify. We are left with a slightly bitter sweet taste that we got one of the toughest opponents (Monaco) as the final team in the group, but at least they are a team that lets you play football so that might suit us."**
***President Augusto Cesar Lendoiro***

## SQUAD

**11 JOSE EMILIO AMAVISCA** 19.06.71
The 15-cap Spanish winger joined Depor in summer 2001 from relegated Racing Santander. He won a gold medal in the 1992 Olympics and was signed from Valladolid by Real Madrid in 1994, where he had to compete with Raul for a place in the team. He was in the Real squad during the Champions League success in 1998, but then joined Racing that summer. Didn't make the final 22 for the 1998 World Cup.

**14 JORGE ANDRADE** 09.04.78
The Portuguese player joined in summer 2002 from FC Porto, where he'd spent two seasons. He first made his name with four seasons in Division One with Estrela Amadora. Andrade was injured in the first league game of the season and only returned in February 2003. The 15-cap player made two 2002 World Cup appearances after stepping up from the U21 side.

# GROUP C
## RC DEPORTIVO CORUNA

**15 JOAN CAPDEVILA** 02.03.78
Capdevila, a summer 2000 capture from Atletico Madrid, was originally a midfielder, but now plays at full-back. The £2m signing won his first of two caps in a friendly against Paraguay in October 2002. He won a silver medal in the 2000 Olympics. Depor was his third club in three seasons, starting off in the Espanyol youth side.

**5 CESAR** 02.04.77
Once voted the best young defender in the Primera Liga, Cesar joined from Oviedo (after three seasons there) in summer 1999. His first two seasons at Depor were ravaged by injury. He moved into national team in autumn 1999 but has only won eight caps in four years.

**16 DJALMINHA** 09.12.70
The Brazilian (32 caps) returned to Depor after being away on loan with Austrian champions FK Austria Vienna in 2002-03. He joined the club in 1997 and has since been part of their successes despite occasional ill-discipline. From 1990-97 he was with top Brazilian sides Flamengo, Guarani and Palmeiras.

**23 ALDO DUSCHER** 29.03.79
Duscher is best known as the villain of the David Beckham 'metatarsal saga' before the 2002 World Cup. The Argentine midfielder is in his third season with Depor - he signed from Sporting Lisbon for £6 million and was a key factor in the side that won the 2000 Portuguese championship with Peter Schmeichel.

**10 FRANCISCO JAVIER FRAN** 14.07.69
Fran now holds the club's all-time Primera Liga appearance record with 375 to the start of the 2003-4 season. He joined the first team squad in 1988 and was part of Depor's promotion in 1991 – the playmaker has also played another 110 games in Division 2. Fran has 16 caps for Spain, winning his first in the 1992-3 season, but was overlooked for all international competitions except Euro 2000, where he made a couple of appearances. The midfielder was club captain in the 2000 title victory, but is considered to have suffered a little with the arrival of the Brazilian contingent.

**24 JESUS HECTOR** 11.10.74
Hector had three seasons with Seville, as first choice in both the 1999 and 2001 promotion teams, before joining Depor in summer 2001. The full-back went straight into the first team following Manuel Pablo's unfortunate injury.

**19 ALBERTO LUQUE** 11.03.78
Barcelona-born Luque joined in summer 2002 from Mallorca, after winning his first two caps at the World Cup, and scoring 14 goals for Mallorca in 2001-02. He was in the squad that took silver in the 2000 Olympics after losing on penalties to Cameroon. Luque had joined Mallorca as a junior, and earned his first team squad place in summer

1998. Is now considered a 'super sub', who may be called upon more now that Roy Makaay has gone to Bayern.

**1 JOSE FRANSISCO MOLINA** 08.08.70
Spanish international keeper Molina underwent successful treatment for testicular cancer in January 2003 – he faced chemotherapy similar to Lance Armstrong, the Tour de France winner, and and Bulgaria's Lubo Penev. He'd previously had a lump removed in June 2001. The nine-cap stopper was signed from relegated Atletico Madrid for £5 million in summer 2000, when he was first choice going into Euro2000 - then a nightmare goal against Norway in the first game of the finals meant he was dropped from the side. His first international cap in the warm up to Euro '96 came in exceptional circumstances - he played left wing against Norway because all other outfielders had been used. Molina was an ever present in Atletico's 1996 Championship win - and missed just two games in four seasons before injury forced him to miss seven games in 1999-2000. He's also played for Albacete and Valencia.

**17 PEDRO MUNITIS** 19.06.75
Munitis was released by new Real Madrid coach Carlos Queiroz in August 2003 before joining Deportivo in August 2003 – he'd also been on loan at his former club Racing Santander in 2002-03. The 21-cap winger-midfielder failed to make the last World Cup, but played at Euro2000 and signed for Real Madrid from his hometown club Santander for £6.5 million in summer 2000. Munitis had come right through the ranks at Racing since he was a teenager in the lower leagues in 1993 and has been part of national coach Jose Camacho's plans for the national team since 1999. Won the 2001 title with Real.

**13 GUSTAVO MUNUA** 27.01.78
Uruguayan keeper with eleven caps, who was his country's reserve keeper at the 2002 World Cup finals. Munua joined Depor in summer 2003 from Nacional of Montevideo, where he'd kept goal for six seasons. The goalie won his first national cap in 2000 and is understudy to Fabien Carini.

**4 NOUREDINE NAYBET** 11.03.70
Naybet was the first Moroccan international to reach 100 caps (he now has 127) and played in both the 1994 and 1998 World Cups. He then almost joined Manchester Utd in August 1999, but has now completed eight seasons with Depor, and played almost 200 Primera Liga games. Ironically, it was his goal that beat Man Utd in the 2001/2 Champions League season. The defender could have played for France, and has played there for Nantes (1993/4). He then moved to Sporting Lisbon and Porto, who sold him in summer 1996 for the bargain price of £1.3 million.

**2 MANUEL PABLO** 25.01.76
The right-back played just ten games last season, after breaking his leg and missing months of football. Pablo arrived on a Bosman free from Las Palmas - at the same time

as former team mate Turu Flores, on a contract until 2005, but with a buy-out clause of £40m. He played 13 games in a row for Spain, overtaking Real Madrid's Michel Salgado, but has not played for national side since his recovery. He played 36 out of 38 games in Depor's 2000 title win.

**7 WALTER PANDIANI** 27.04.76
Pandiani returned in summer 2003 from a season's loan at Mallorca, where he was top scorer in 2002-03 with 13 goals. The 26-cap Uruguayan centre-forward was exchanged for Alberto Luque. Last summer, Pandiani just failed to make the Uruguay 2002 World Cup squad. He spent three seasons in Penarol's first team before moving to Deportivo in 2000.

**3 ENRIQUE ROMERO** 23.06.71
Romero made three appearances at the 2002 World Cup, winning his seventh caps against Portugal in September 2003. The left-footed defender joined in summer 1998 from the excellent Mallorca side for £2.4 million, where he had his best season after being offloaded by Valencia. He now has over 300 Primera Liga games under his belt.

**12 LIONEL SCALONI** 16.05.78
Argentine midfielder Scaloni won the 1997 World Junior Cup with his country, and joined Depor that summer from Estudiantes, after having previously played for Newells Old Boys. This is his seventh season with the side, and his 32 Primera Liga games last year were his best seasonal return for the club.

**8 SERGIO** 10.10.76
Sergio moved from Espanyol to Deportivo in mid-August 2001 for $14.92 million on an eight-year contract, to help his former club with their $26m debt. The 10-cap star made his national debut in March 2001 – he's a product of the Espanyol youth team, making his first team debut at the start of 1997-8. Sergio now has over 100 Primera Liga games under his belt.

**6 MAURO SILVA** 12.01.68
Mauro Silva has now played well over 300 Primera Liga games – he is in his 12th season with Depor after moving from Brazilian club Bragantino. The Brazilian World Cup winning midfielder played in all seven World Cup games in the USA, and won further success in the 1997 Copa America. He is still troubled by injuries, but regarded highly at the club as an example to his fellow South Americans in terms of loyalty and attitude.

**25 JACQUES SONGO'O** 17.03.64
The Cameroon international keeper (64 caps) retired a couple of seasons ago but has returned to replace the departed Junami. Songo'o first joined Depor in 1996 from French side Metz (he also played for Toulon and Le Mans). He captained Cameroon at the 1998 World Cup and was also captain of their African Nations winning teams of

1998 and 2000 – his international career took off late because Thomas N'kono and Joseph Antoine Bell (both also national captains) had been keeping him out of the side.

**9 DIEGO TRISTAN** 05.01.76
The striker cost £10 million from Mallorca in summer 2000, though certain reports suggest £13 million. His first season for Depor saw 19 goals in 29 games. He was top scorer in the Primera Liga with 21 goals in the 2001-02 season, only his second in the top flight. Tristan then managed nine goals in 28 games after suffering injury the following year. He made two appearances at the 2002 World Cup, and is now established in the national side with 14 caps. His two goals at Old Trafford helped Depor beat Manchester United in the Champions League group stage. Has also played for Betis and Mallorca's B teams.

**21 JUAN CARLOS VALERON** 17.06.75
The 31-cap Canaries-born midfielder played in four of Spain's five 2002 World Cup games. He joined Depor in summer 2000 for £5 million after his side Atletico was relegated. Valeron played in the Spanish U21 team that won the 1998 European U21 championship - and played the first two games of Euro2000. He gained his first full cap after a fine first season with Atletico, who he'd joined for £4m from Mallorca. His first side was his hometown club, Division Two's Las Palmas.

**18 VICTOR** 23.02.76
Victor signed from Racing Santander in summer 1999, costing a then club record £5.5 million. The winger's breakthrough season was in the Real Madrid 1997 title win, playing 34 times in 1996/97, but was then replaced by Savio. Victor didn't get a cap for Spain until the match against England at Villa Park in August 2000. He gained four more caps, his last against Mexico in November 2001. He had an infamous punch-up with his own team mate Djalminha in winter 2000-1.

# PSV EINDHOVEN

**On 25th May 1988 PSV beat Benfica of Portugal on penalties to win the European Cup. In the last 30 years they have mostly been in the shadows of fellow Dutch team Ajax, but impressively have been the home to Romario, Ronaldo, Gullit and Koeman at various times. Knocked out at the first round stage last season including a heavy home defeat at the hands of Arsenal, they will hope to improve this time round, with an experienced team that has, despite rumours to the contrary, managed to retain the services of both Mark Van Bommel and Dutch top scorer and Player of the Year Mateja Kezman. Group C rivals Monaco and AEK Athens will provide stiff but not overwhelming opposition so qualification is a distinct possibility.**

# GROUP C
## PSV EINDHOVEN

## COACH

**GUUS HIDDINK** 08.11.46
Hiddink enhanced his reputation in the summer of 2002 by guiding South Kora to the World Cup semi-final. His services were much in demand after the event but he opted to return to PSV where he had enjoyed success in the late 1980s. He won the Dutch title three times in a row, a similar run of victories in the Dutch Cup and the European Cup in 1988. Hiddink left in 1990 for Fenerbahce before taking over at Valencia a year later. In 1995 he was appointed Dutch national coach and he took the team to the World Cup semis in 1998. He followed this with stints at Real Madrid (winning the World Club Championship) and Betis Seville before moving to Korea.

## REACTION TO DRAW

**"I know Depor from my Spanish period and strange things can happen over there. The same about AEK, so they will be tough away matches. Monaco is just a good team with a beautiful stadium, but no scary atmosphere. Everyone in the squad is looking forward to the Champions League and of course we want to reach the second round. We are up for it and ambitious."** ***Guus Hiddink***

## SQUAD

**30 KASPER BOGELUND** 08.10.80
Arrived at PSV in summer 1999, Danish defender Bogelund played five league games in his first two seasons (1999-2001) and 44 games in the next two seasons. Had not scored a league goal in his first four seasons with the club, but played in all six group games in the 2002/03 Champions League. Bogelund is an international defender with seven caps – he played twice as a substitute at the 2002 FIFA World Cup.

**5 WILFRED BOUMA** 15.06.78
Defender Bouma debuted for PSV v Willem II Tilburg, aged just 16 in October 1994. After playing for the national Olympic and U21 teams, he made a full international debut on September 2, 2000 against Ireland and now has seven caps for Holland. Has played in all six group games in the past two Champions League seasons and has a total of 18 games (one goal) in the competition.

**20 JURGEN COLIN** 20.01.81
Defender Colin returned to PSV in summer 2003 after two loan spells – he played seven games for KRC Genk in their 2001/02 Belgian championship win, and then played all 34 Eredivisie games last season for NAC Breda. The Dutchman debuted for PSV in the 2001/02 season with four league games.

# GROUP C
## PSV EINDHOVEN

**25 JOHN DE JONG** 08.03.77
Dutch midfielder whose former clubs include FC Den Haag, ADO Den Haag, FC Utrecht, SC Heerenveen (loan). De Jong joined PSV in summer 2000 from FC Utrecht and played 28 games (three goals) in the 2000/01 championship win. He was away on loan at SC Heerenveen (nine goals in 26 games) in 2002/03 so missed out on a further title medal. De Jong has ten Champions League games under his belt, but just one goal.

**4 ERNEST FABER** 27.08.71
This is the Dutch defender's 14th season as a professional - he was a PSV junior and made his club debut in 1992/93 season after returning from loan at NEC and Sparta Rotterdam. Faber is the only survivor still at the club from the PSV team that played on the first night of Champions League football on November 25, 1992 (sub v FC Porto). This is his sixth Champions League season – he's played 24 games (1 goal). Faber has played 246 league games (6 goals), has four championship medals (1997, 2000, 2001, 2003) and one international cap (v Mexico in 1998).

**9 MATEJA KEZMAN** 12.04.79
The Serbian forward (26 caps, 10 goals) was the Eredivisie top scorer in 2002/03 season with 35 goals in 33 games, the best return since Marco van Basten scored 37 goals for AFC Ajax in the 1985/86 season. His league total is 74 goals in 93 league games since joining from FK Partizan in summer 2000. He was the Yugoslav league top scorer with 28 goals in 1999-00. Has played all 18 UCL games in the past three seasons (three goals). Kezman's other former clubs are FK Zemun, FK Radnicki Pirot, FK Sartid 1913 Smederovo and FK Loznica.

**10 LEANDRO DO BONFIM** 08.01.84
Brazilian midfielder, played in the first three group games of last season's Champions League. He joined PSV in July 2002 on a four-year contract and played 14 games (1 goal) in the 2002/03 championship win.

**29 KEVIN HOFLAND** 07.06.79
Joined PSV in summer 1999 from SC Fortuna Sittard (59 league games, one goal). Hofland has played 13 Champions League games, with his one goal so far being the winner v S.S.Lazio in 2001/02. Six International caps for Holland.

**22 JORDI HOOGSTRATE** 02.06.83
The Dutch U21 international midfielder signed for PSV in summer 2003 after last season's 42 league games (two goals) for his previous club FC Groningen, where he was a team mate of Arjen Robben.

**3 YOUNG-PYO LEE** 23.04.77
South Korean international (58 caps) who played five games at the 2002 FIFA World Cup before following his former national coach Guus Hiddink to PSV in January 2003.

The defender played 15 Eredivisie games for PSV (no goals) in their 2002/03 championship success.

**16 THEO LUCIUS** 19.12.76
The Dutch defender joined PSV in summer 1998 from FC Den Bosch. Won championship medals in 2001 and 2003, but was on loan at FC Utrecht for the club's 2000 success. Now has played 19 games (1 goal) in four Champions League campaigns.

**24 MARCO AURELIO PEREIRA ALVES MARQUINHO** 20.02.82
The Brazilian midfielder (his only other club was Sao Paolo FC) has been with PSV since 2000, but has only played three league games (no goals) in three seasons.

**2 ANDRE OOIJER** 11.07.74
Defender Ooijer signed for PSV in January 1998 from Roda JC, after making his league debut for FC Volendam in 1994/95. Once a junior for AFC Ajax, Ooijer has scored a goal in each of his nine seasons in Dutch football. This is his fourth Champions League season – he's scored twice in 13 games, including a goal on his CL debut v HJK Helsinki in 1998. Has eight international caps, making his debut v Brazil on 05.06.99.

**7 JI SUNG PARK** 25.02.81
South Korean midfielder Park joined PSV in December 2002 and played eight games in the 2002/03 championship success. Previously played for three seasons for Kyoto Purple Sanga. Has 43 international caps – and played all seven games at the 2002 FIFA World Cup for the co-host nation. Rejoined his former national coach Guus Hiddink at PSV.

**11 ARJEN ROBBEN** 23.01.1984
Signed by PSV in summer 2002 from FC Groningen where Robben had played in midfield for two seasons in their first team from the age of 16. Was PSV's second top scorer with 12 goals in 33 league games in the 2002/03 championship win, and has a contract until 2007. Robben had previously played 46 Eredivisie games for Groningen (eight goals) from 2000-2002. The Dutchman won first international cap on April 30, 2003 v Portugal at Eindhoven (sub). Played four Champions League games, one goal.

**19 DENNIS ROMMEDAHL** 22.07.78
Joined PSV in summer 1996 from Lyngby FC, Rommedahl has missed one league game in the past two seasons, and scored a personal best 12 goals in 2001/02. The Danish forward has played in 25 of the last 30 Champions League games for the club, scoring just two goals.

**6 MARK VAN BOMMEL** 22.04.77
The Dutch midfielder joined PSV form SC Fortuna Sittard in summer 1999 and has won championship medals in three of his four seasons. The international has won 20 caps after his debut v Cyprus on October 7, 2000. Van Bommel is in his fifth Champions League season – he's played 17 games and hit two goals.

**13 REMCO VAN DER SCHAAF** 28.02.79

Midfielder Van Der Schaaf joined PSV in summer 2002 from SBV Vitesse on a five-year contract. He played for Vitesse from 1997-2002 but was on loan for part of the 1999-2000 season at SC Fortuna Sittard. Managed 17 games (no goals) in last season's championship campaign, and played four Champions League games (one goal v BV Borussia Dortmund).

**1 ROB VAN DIJK** 15.01.69

The Dutch goalkeeper joined PSV in summer 2003. Van Dijk was reserve to his international team-mate Ed de Goey at Feyenoord, playing four league games. In 1996, he moved to RKC for seven seasons, missing just five league games in his first five seasons. Has played 216 Eredivisie games in total.

**8 JAN VENNEGOR OF HESSELINK** 07.11.78

This is the Dutchman's third season with PSV after five seasons with FC Twente Enschede (1996-2001) where he scored 59 goals in 142 Eredivisie games. Jan scored 22 league goals in his first season at PSV in 2001/02, but only eight goals in 32 games in 2002/03. Has yet to score a Champions League goal in nine games. His surname is an amalgam of two farms (Vennegor & Hesselink) in the Enschede region. He won his first international cap on October 11, 2000 against Portugal – he has two caps with no goals to date.

**14 JOHANN VOGEL** 08.03.77

Swiss midfielder Vogel has now won six championship medals (three each with both Grasshopper-Club (1995, 1996, 1998) and PSV (2000, 2001, 2003). He signed for PSV after seven seasons with Grasshopper-Club (1992-1999), and this is also his seventh Champions League season - played 31 games, no goals. He's been a Swiss international since the age of 18, and has won 58 caps (2 goals).

**23 RONALD WATERREUS** 25.08.70

Dutch goalkeeper (6 caps) who joined PSV in summer 1994 from Roda JC and has won four championship medals and played 252 league games for the club. Waterreus also played 65 league games for Roda JC from 1992-1994. This year marks his seventh Champions League campaign - he has played 29 games in the competition.

# AS MONACO

**Monaco secured a fine second place in the 2002-03 championship behind Lyon. But the club had a scare in June 2003 when they were almost 'relegated' after mounting debts threatened but rescue came in the form of a local businessmen and the Royal Family. Monaco suffered from their Championship wins in 1997 and 2000, with many of the team leaving for new pastures - despite the lure of Champions League football. The club has won seven championships (the most**

**recent in 2000), the French Cup on five occasions (most recent in 1991) and the League Cup in 2003. The 1988 Championship win was masterminded by Glenn Hoddle, who is still a revered figure in the Principality, and Mark Hateley - who played less often because of injury but was club top scorer. The club reached the final of the 1992 Cup Winners Cup, where they lost 2-0 to Bremen. They have twice reached the semi-finals of the Champions League - in 1994 when they lost to AC Milan after taking the suspended Marseille's place, and again in 1998 when they beat Manchester United in the quarter-finals thanks to an away goal from Trezeguet, before losing to Juventus in the semi.**

## COACH

**DIDIER DESCHAMPS** 15.10.68
The Frenchman has been coach since 2001 in his first role but nearly lost his job in 2001-02 when the club were 15th. However, in 2002-03, Monaco were second in the league and won the League Cup which vindicated everything Deschamps had done. Marcello Lippi, his old Juventus boss, always said he'd be a good coach.

## REACTION TO DRAW

**"It's interesting. La Coruna and PSV are used to the Champions League and know how to play these matches, while AEK have more experience in the UEFA Cup. I hope we'll be successful, and least for sure it will be a very enriching experience, whatever the outcome."** ***Didier Deschamps***

## SQUAD

**24 EMMANUEL ADEBAYOR** 26.02.84
Teenage striker Adebayor made his Division I debut for Monaco in November 2001, then went to Metz, where he helped them back to the top flight in 2002-03, as club top scorer with 13 goals. Adebayor, who has seven caps for his country Togo, then returned to Monaco from Metz in summer 2003. He has played a dozen top flight games so far.

**7 LUIS BERNARDI** 27.09.77
The Argentine midfielder is in his third season at Monaco after joining from Marseille where he had played for one year. Originally from the Newells Old Boys side, he moved to France in 2000 and is now looking to establish himself in midfield following the departure of fellow Argentine playmaker Marcelo Gallardo.

**16 ANDRE BIANCARELLI** 12.03.70
Reserve keeper joined in summer 2000 from Metz. Had just 17 D1 games before this season - three seasons with Bastia, then five with Metz – but was reserve at both clubs. He made his first division debut when at Bastia in March 1993.

# GROUP C
## AS MONACO

**26 SOULEYMANE CAMARA** 22.12.82
The Senegalese player was born in Dakar, but is a graduate of the Monaco youth academy. Camara has won 14 caps and went to the 2002 World Cup, but did not play in the finals. He made his first team debut in July 2001, and he has now played some 50 league games.

**37 SEBASTIAN CAROLE** 08.09.82
A midfielder from the club's youth academy, this is Carole's second season in the first team squad. He made his debut in March 2002 and has played around ten league games in total.

**14 EDOUARD CISSE** 30.03.78
Not to be confused with the international who plays for Auxerre, Cisse used to play for Paris-SG in midfield but has subsequently been on loan at West Ham among other clubs. Cisse has played over 100 Division 1 games since his debut for PSG in 1997. He is now on loan at Monaco.

**24 HASSAN EL FAKIRI** 18.04.77
The Moroccan-born player was brought up as a Norwegian national, and has two caps for his country. El Fakiri arrived in Monaco in summer 2000 from Brann Bergen - where he had been for a season, but didn't make his debut until 2002. He made 15 appearances in the 2002/3 season.

**3 PATRICE EVRA** 15.05.81
The Senegal-born left back had trials for PSG and Nice before signing for Monaco. Evra had a fine first season in the first team in 2002-03, only missing two league games and winning a League Cup medal. He was named in the French U21 squad for the Euro U21 championship qualifiers in September 2003.

**8 LUDOVIC GIULY** 10.07.76
Giuly is Monaco's playmaker, scoring 11 goals from midfield in the side that finished runners-up to Lyon in 2003. This made him the equal third top scorer in the French League lists in the 2002/3 season. The 5'4" right-sided player arrived from Lyon in January 1998 for a then-record £4.2 million. Giuly's excellent season culminated in the 2003 Confederations Cup final win in June. He first made the French full squad in 2000, and was capped against the Scots in March that year. Giuly developed through the Lyon youth system, and was brought through into their first team aged 18. He's now played nine seasons of Division 1 football.

**32 GAEL GIVET** 09.10.81
Givet played played 23 league games last season in his most productive season yet for Monaco. From the club's youth academy, he made his first team debut in 2000 and has subsequently made the French U21 squad for Euro2004 U21 championship

qualifiers in September 2003. Givet also came on as substitute in the League Cup final win 2003.

**4 HUGO IBARRA** 01.04.74
Arrived at Monaco in summer 2003 from FC Porto, who won the Portuguese league, Cup and UEFA Cup in 2002-03. He came from Boca Juniors in summer 2001 where he'd won three titles, the South American Libertadores Cup in 2000 and the World Club Cup. Ibarra now has eight caps.

**9 FERNANDO MORIENTES** 05.04.76
The Spanish striker lost his place up front at Real Madrid to Ronaldo in the 2002/3 season, and moved to Monaco in August 2003 after turning down Premiership interest. Real had signed him as their major summer capture of 1997 from Zaragoza (£4.2m) where he'd scored 15 goals each season. Morientes subsequently played in the Champions League final victories of 2000 and 2002. The forward was also runner up to Diego Tristan (along with Kluivert) in the 2001-2 Primera Liga with 18 goals. Morientes has 28 caps for Spain, including five at the 2002 World Cup, where he scored three goals. National coach Jose Antonio Camacho has since admitted that he was wrong to leave the English-style striker out of his Euro 2000 line up.

**18 SHABANI 'CHRIS' NONDA** 06.03.77
Nonda could be out all season with the knee injury he picked up in a collision with Jose Pierre-Fanfan (his team mate last season) on 24.08.03 versus Paris SG. He was the league top scorer in 2002-03 wth 26 goals. The striker moved from Rennes to the French champions Monaco for a club record and French internal record of £14.8 million, to replace David Trezeguet (who went to Juventus). The 23-cap Congo striker was also top scorer in the Swiss league with FC Zurich (aged 21) with 24 goals in 1998. Nonda was born in Burundi, but opted to play for Congo/Zaire which is his parents' birthplace.

**6 JAROSLAV PLASIL** 05.01.82
The Czech U21 international midfielder joined Monaco as a youth from Hradec Kralove, and went out on loan last season to Paris-based Division 2 club Creteil. Plasil has played about ten first team games at Monaco since July 2001.

**1 STEPHANE PORATO** 19.09.73
Porato returned to his former club Monaco from Marseille in summer 2000 for £2.8 million after Barthez left for Manchester United. He had originally moved to Marseille in summer 1998 to get more opportunities, after playing just 19 games in four seasons in his first spell with Monaco. He won his only cap in a friendly against Croatia at the Stade de France on 13.11.99 thanks to an injury for Barthez. Porato took over at Marseille from Andy Kopke as club number one keeper in October 1998. Played in France A team in 1999 and 2000, after being an U21 international – Porato was in the full national squad as reserve to Barthez during 1999 and part of 2000.

# GROUP C
## AS MONACO

**9 DADO PRSO** 05.11.74
The Croatian forward won his first cap in November 2002, and now has four. Born at Zadar, near Split, he joined Monaco in 1996 from D3 club Saint-Raphael, a resort just up the road. Prso scored 12 times in the 2002-03 league season as target man in tandem with 26-goal Nonda. He made his first team debut in 1998, and scored 13 goals in 1998-9 when on loan at D2 club Ajaccio. He then was backup striker to the Trezeguet-Simone pairing in the 2000 title win.

**27 JULIEN RODRIGUEZ** 11.06.78
One of Monaco's juniors, Rodriguez made the first of some 80 appearances in January 1999 for the first team as a defender. The next year, he made the national U21 squad and is now considered a regular first-teamer.

**19 SEBASTIAN SQUILLACI** 11.08.80
Like Evra, Squillaci was introduced into the Monaco first team at the start of 2002-03 by Deschamps and missed just three league games – he also scored in the League Cup final win. From Toulon, he played for the local team and also went on loan to Ajaccio.

**29 TONY MARIO SYLVA** 17.05.75
Senegal's World Cup keeper in 2002 played five games at the competition, but now has more international caps (24) than Division 1 games (20). This is his sixth season at the club – he played for Epinal in Division 2 a couple of seasons ago when on loan, and has recently been on loan at Ajaccio to get first team experience.

**30 FLAVIO ROMA** 21.06.74
Rome-born keeper Roma took over as number one choice goalie in 2002 from international stoppers Porato and Sylva. He joined Monaco in summer 2001, after being a Lazio junior, and only playing in Serie A for Piacenza in 1999-2000. Roma does have plenty of Serie B experience with Piacenza, Chievo, Foggia and Venezia, but has certainly taken his chances at Monaco.

**25 JEROME ROTHEN** 31.03.78
Rothen arrived at Monaco after spells with Caen in Division 2 and Troyes, via the French School of Excellence. He came into the national squad in 2003 when coach Santini opted to rest top players. Rothen had a fine first season, topping the league goal 'assists' this past season with 13 decisive passes. He was first choice in the French team for the 2003 Confederations Cup win but was injured for the group games, and has three caps in total.

**15 VASSILIOS ZYKOS** 01.06.74
The Greek international midfielder signed for Monaco in 2002 from AEK Athens, and is a midfield ballwinner who should benefit from the departure of playmaker Marcelo Gallardo. Zykos has 15 caps for his country and has played 200 games in the top Greek League for Xanthi (1993-98) and for AEK (1998-2002).

# AEK ATHENS

**Athletiki Enosis Konstantinopoulos Athens was formed in the Greek capital in 1924 by a group of immigrants from Constantinople. AEK has won the National Championship 11 times (the last time in 1994) and the National Cup 13 times (last time in 2002). Their best European run was in the 1976/77 UEFA Cup when they fell to eventual winners Juventus in the semi-finals. Recently the club have been troubled by administrative and financial problems but nevertheless AEK have qualified for the CL three times. AEK Athens are holders of a strange record in the 11-year-history of the competition. They are the only team to have played 12 games without even winning once. Last season they set down another record by drawing 6 games in succession. Even Real Madrid were unable to beat them. This season AEK they will have to play their home games at the Panathinaikos stadium because their stadium is being rebuilt for the 2004 Olympics.**

## COACH

**DUSAN BAJEVIC** 10.12.48
The forward Bajevic (40 caps, 36 goals for Yugoslavia) moved in 1977 from his home town club Velez Mostar (now Bosnia-Herzegovina) to AEK Athens where he won 2 Greek championships (1978, 79) and 1 Greek Cup (1979) in 4 seasons before returning home in 1981. Seven years later Bajevic, now a coach, arrived for the second time at AEK Athens. It was the start of a new era for the club with 4 title wins (1989, 1992, 1993, 1994) and 1 cup (1996). But then Bajevic moved to neighbours and rivals Olympiakos. There he continued to win trophies: 3 successive Greek championships (1997, 1998 and 1999) and 1 national Cup (1999). After all the success Bajevic had a row with the board and left Olympiakos in 2000 to take over at PAOK Saloniki where his biggest achievement was to win the national cup win in 2001 against his former club Olympiakos (4-2). Since July 1st 2002 Bajevic has been back with his first Greek love AEK Athens.

## REACTION TO DRAW

**"You don't expect it to be easy in this competition and what is certain is that it won't be. But we will be competitive, we have players used to the big occasion and we will relish the challenge. Personally I would like to see all three Greek teams get through this stage – and I think they can"** ***Dusan Bajevic.***

## SQUAD

**19 KOFI AMPONSAH** 23.04.78
Young defender from Ghana who joined the club this summer from PAOK Saloniki

where he won the Greek cup 2001 under coach Bajevic in the 4-2 win against Olympiakos. Two years later it was Bajevic who urged him to come and play for AEK.

**2 VASSILIOS BORBOKIS** 12.02.69
Very experienced right-sided defender who began his career at Apollon Kalamarias in 1986. He first joined AEK in 1993 winning the league title in 1994 and the national cup in 1996 (both under current coach Bajevic). In 1997 he moved to England to play for Sheffield United in 1997 (55 games, 5 goals in the league) then to Derby County (16 games). He returned to Greece in December 1999 with PAOK Saloniki where again he played under Bajevic and won the Cup in 2001 against Olympiakos (4-2) scoring a goal. In the summer of 2002 this very committed and highly respected player joined AEK Athens for a second spell. Played 3 CL games last season.

**31 GRIGORIOS GEORGATOS** 31.10.72
Left-sided midfielder who made his debut in the Greek top flight at Panahaiki in 1991before being transferred to Olympiakos in December 1995. There he won 3 successive league titles (1997, 1998, 1999), 1 cup (1999) and he made his CL debut against FC Porto (1-0 defeat). It was also against FC Porto, in the return match that he scored his first CL goal. In the summer 1999 Georgatos moved to Inter (28 games, 2 goals) but a year later he was back at Olympiakos to win another league title. Was signed by Inter but after 38 games and 3 goals he joined AEK Athens in the summer of 2002. Played 4 CL games for AEK last season. He is very fast and delivers a wicked cross with his left foot.

**16 NIKOLAOS GEORGEAS** 27.12.76
Joined Kalamata in 1996 after one season with Pas Giannena. In January 2001 he was transferred to AEK. The defender hopes to play more games this season in the CL because last season he didn't come off the substitute bench.

**22 DIONISIOS HIOTIS** 04.06.77
Started in the AEK amateur team in 1995 and was sent on loan to Ethnikos Piraeus (1998/99) and Proodeftiki (1999/2000) to gain first team experience. He returned to AEK in 2000 where he became first choice in the 2001/02 season. Played all 6 CL games last season.

**30 ILIJA IVIC** 17.02.71
Yugoslav international forward who began his career with Proleter before moving to Red Star Belgrade in the summer of 1991 just after their European Cup success. He moved to Greece in 1994 after winning 3 successive league titles with Olympiakos (1997, 1998, 1999). Then he moved to Italy where he played for Torino (only 19 league games). In 2000 he returned to Greece first to play for Aris Saloniki and since January 2002 he has been at AEK with his old Olympiakos coach Bajevic. Ivic played 5 CL games last season and scored 9 times in the national league.

# GROUP C
## AEK ATHENS

**33 MIHALIS KAPSIS** 18.10.73
Central defender who began his career at Aris Nikeas (1990-92) before moving to Ethnikos Piraeus in 1993. In January 1998 he joined AEK Athens where he has played more than 150 league games. He was also present in every CL game last season.

**17 MIHALIS KASAPIS** 06.06.71
Experienced left-side defender and one of the leaders in the team who joined AEK Athens when he was 22 years old (in 1993) from Levadiakos. Won the Greek championship in 1994 and played all 6 CL games in the 1994/95 season. Last season he played 5 CL games but sat on the bench for the last group stage match to AS Roma. Kasapis has played more than 35 times for Greece. After being out of the national team for 13 months he was recalled by to play in the match Beckham scored his famous free kick to secure England's place World Cup 2002.

**21 KOSTAS KATSOURANIS** 21.06.79
Midfielder who played for Panahaiki (94 league games, 14 goals in 6 seasons) before moving to AEK Athens in July 2002. Katsouranis played every minute of last seasons CL campaign and scored his only goal in the Bernabeu stadium against Real Madrid. He plays in the role of defensive midfielder but he can easily go forward and join the attack. Scored the first goal in the 3rd qualifying round home game against Grasshoppers Zurich (3-1 win).

**20 SOTIRIOS KONSTANTINIDIS** 19.04.77
Has represented Greece U-16, U-18, U-21 levels and has 3 senior caps. After 5 years with Iraklis he signed for AEK in the summer 1999. Has played more than 175 league games in Greece and scored more than 30 league goals but didn't play at all in the CL last season although he appeared on the substitute bench.

**5 NIKOLAOS KOSTENOGLOU** 03.10.70
Experienced central defender joined AEK Athens in 1994 after 6 years at Xanthi. Has played more than 300 league games in his 9 seasons at the club but has only 1 cap for the Greek national team. Played all 6 CL games last season.

**8 MICHEL KREEK** 16.10.71
Skilful Dutch midfielder who started his career at Ajax in 1988 where he won three championship medals and one UEFA Cup in 1992 under Louis Van Gaal. In 1994 he moved to Italy to play for Padova and Perugia all together scoring 13 goals in 85 serie A appearances. In 1997 he went back home to play for Vitesse Arnhem. Joined AEK Athens in the summer of 2002 but doesn't have a regular place in the team, although he sometimes gets a chance as libero. Played once for the Dutch national team.

**23 VASSILIOS LAKIS** 10.09.76
Undoubtedly the fastest Greek player. Lakis moved from 2nd division side Naousa to Paniliakos before he became in 1998 a record signing for AEK. Is a Greek international

(42 caps, 7 goals) who made his debut on 20.08.99 in a 3-0 win versus El Salvador in Kavala. Played 6 CL games last season and scored the equaliser at home against Racing Genk (1-1).

**12 SOTIRIS LIBEROPOULOS** 26.06.77
The club's third choice goalkeeper behind Hiotis and Mihailidis. Played for Kalamata before joining AEK Athens.

**33 NIKOLAOS LYBEROPOULOS** 04.08.75
Last summer's big Greek transfer. Last season's top scorer with 16 goals moved from Panathinaikos to AEK as a replacement for Demis Nikolaidis who left the club for Atletico Madrid. The Greek international forward (39 caps, 8 goals) scored 72 goals in 86 league games for Panathinaikos. Scored once already in the 3rd qualifying round home game against Grasshoppers Zurich (3-1 win).

**7 CHRISTOS MALADENIS** 23.05.74
Joined AEK Athens in 1995 from Xanthi one year after his team mate Kostenoglou made the same move. Played 4 CL games last season and scored a goal in the home game against Real Madrid (3-3). Can play on any position in midfield.

**1 CHRYSOSTOMOS MIHAILIDIS** 15.01.75
6'3" tall reserve goalkeeper who joined AEK Athens in 1997 from 4th division club Eordaikos Ptolemaidas. He spent 2001/02 season on loan to Ethnikos Asteras. Has played little more than 25 top flight games but is a loyal club man.

**18 EVAGGELOS MORAS** 26.08.81
Young central defender who joined AEK Athens this summer from Proodeftiki. Was bought as cover up for the first team. Made his debut in Europe during the third qualifying round game away to Grasshoppers Zurich (1-0 defeat) coming on after 87 minutes for Maladenis.

**88 DIMITRIOS NALITZIS** 25.01.76
He started his career at Panionios before moving to Ethnikos in 1998. One season later he joined PAOK Saloniki to become top scorer in Greece with 25 goals in the 1999/2000 season. He also won the Greek cup with PAOK in 2001 coming on and scoring a goal in the 4-2 win against Olympiakos. Then he headed for Italy but he didn't succeed at Udinese nor at Perugia. In 2001/02 he played on loan for Sporting Clube de Portugal (Lisbon) and joined AEK in August 2002. Played 3 CL games last season without scoring a goal but in the national league he netted 9 goals. Has 6 caps for Greece.

**9 YANNIS OKKAS** 11.02.77
Centre forward who came in the summer break from PAOK Saloniki on a Bosman ruling together with Ghanese defender Kofi Amponsah. Has played under Bajevic

before at PAOK when they won the Greek cup in 2001 against Olympiakos (4-2). Okkas is an international for Cyprus where he used to play his club football for Anorthosis Famagusta.

**3 MILEN PETKOV** 19.01.74
Bulgarian international right-sided midfielder who joined CSKA Sofia in 1995 after 4 seasons with Dobrudzha, the club he made his debut for aged 17. He left Sofia for Athens in January 2000. Although he is a regular with his national team, he is not always first choice at AEK. Last season he played 3 CL games but in total only 58 minutes. Is very fast but sometimes unpredictable on his right wing.

**14 IVAN RUSEV** 10.05.79
Bulgarian midfielder who joined AEK Athens in the summer of 2002 from Athinaikos. He is not a regular in the team but he gets his chances to play in cup games. Scored a goal in the cup very recently against Doxa Dramas (3-0 win).

**39 GRIGORIOS TOSKAS** 08.01.83
Young midfielder from the reserves who may only play if a number of players get injured or suspended. Has a promising future and can also operate as defender.

**10 VASSILIOS TSARTAS** 12.11.72
He is the most creative player of AEK, the team he joined in 1992 from Naousa. In his first 2 seasons he won 2 Greek championships (1993, 1994) and he played in all 6 CL games in 1994/95. After becoming the Greek league top scorer back in 1995/96 with 26 goals in 33 games he left for Spain to play for FC Seville. Tsartas played 139 league games and scored 43 goals but was unable to stop them being relegated twice. He returned to AEK in the summer 2000. Scored 10 league goals last season.

**6 THEODOROS ZAGORAKIS** 27.10.71
Greek national team captain and central midfielder who moved in 1992 from his home-town Kavala to PAOK Saloniki. He joined the Greek squad after the 1994 World Cup and has played in all 34 internationals from the autumn of 1994 until 1999. After PAOK Saloniki beat Arsenal in the first round of the 1997/98 UEFA Cup English clubs started chasing him. He finally joined Leicester City in February 1998 for a bargain fee of £750.000. Played 50 league games at Filbert Street and scored 3 goals before returning home on a Bosman in the summer of 2000 to play for AEK. Played 5 CL games last season.

# GROUP D

**JUVENTUS FC**
(Italy)

**GALATASARAY**
(Turkey)

**REAL SOCIEDAD**
(Spain)

**FC OLYMPIAKOS PIRAEUS**
(Greece)

# JUVENTUS FC

**Each of the two gold stars on the Juve shirt represents 10 Scudettas or Serie A championships. In fact Turin's finest have won the title no less than 27 times. As Italian champions they encountered a strange campaign in last year's Champions League . Breezing through the first stage with an impressive 13 points they struggled in the second being out played by Man United 3-0 at the Stadio del Alpe and qualifying only on goal difference. After a 1—1 home draw they played superbly against Barcelona in the Nou Camp and were superior in both legs against Madrid in the semis. Glory beckoned, but was met with a lacklustre and negative performance in the final. A pedigree outfit that could well add to their 3 European Cups in the near future.**

## COACH

**MARCELLO LIPPI** 01.04.48
Lippi returned to the club in summer 2001 to replace Carlo Ancelotti and immediately landed the 2001-02 Scudetto. He had spent time at Inter Milan – but was sacked after the club failed to qualify for the UCL in August 2000. He was at Juventus from 1994-99 during which the club won 3 championships – 1995, 1997, 1998, one Italian Cup in 1995, and the treble of the European Cup, Super Cup and World Club Cup in 1996. A former B international player for Italy, he played some 240 games with Sampdoria from 1972-81 before becoming their youth coach in 1984 and moving on from there.

## REACTION TO DRAW

**"We are up against three tough opponents that are very similar in character. We'll meet some familiar faces in Olympiakos and our former player Darko Kovacevic (Real Sociedad). But it is a draw that we can live with and I wouldn't say that we are unhappy with it. We have good players and we have a good squad so we are confident again,"** ***Vice president Roberto Bettega.***

## SQUAD

**18 STEPHEN APPIAH** 24.12.80
Summer 2003 signing from Brescia Calcio, and had previously played for Udinese Calcio and Parma AC. Won 2002 Italian Cup medal with Parma AC, and to the start of 2003/04 season had played 95 Serie A games with 7 goals – all last season for Brescia. Despite his 18 caps for Ghana, this will be the midfielder's debut season in the Champions League.

**15 ALESSANDRO BIRINDELLI** 12.11.74
Joined Juventus in summer 1997 from then Serie B club Empoli FC, for whom he had

played since their Serie C1 days. Played 118 league games for Empoli. Has won 3 Serie A winners medals in 1998, 2002 and 2003. Won first international cap on 20.11.02 v Turkey and has picked up a total of 4 caps to date. This will be the Italian defender's 6th Champions League season and so far has played 45 games and scored 3 goals in the competition.

**1 GIANLUIGI BUFFON** 28.01.78
Joined Juventus in 2001 from Parma AC for world record fee for a goalkeeper and has won Serie A championship in both his seasons with the club. Played 168 Serie A games for Parma AC from 1995-2001, making debut aged 17, and won UEFA Cup, Italian Cup, and Italian Super Cup in 1999. Played 31 Champions League games by the start of 2003/04 campaign, including 15 games last season. Has won 38 international caps after coming through the U21 system, winning a 1996 UEFA U21 championship medal.

**16 MAURO GERMAN CAMORANESI** 04.10.78
Opted to play for Italy in Februay 2003 after not being selected for Argentina – and has since picked two caps. The midfielder won 2003/04 Serie A winners medal in his first season with Juventus after joining from Hellas-Verona FC. Has also played for Argentine club CA Banfield and Cruz Azul in the Mexican league. Has been in Italy since 2000, and played first CL season in 2002/03 with 13 games and one goal under his belt.

**12 ANTONIO CHIMENTI** 30.06.70
The Italian keeper joined Juventus in summer 2002 from US Lecce and played 10 league and cup games for the club in 2002/03 including 2 Champions League games. Spent first 10 seasons of career in the lower leagues, made Serie A debut when at AS Roma on 21.09.97. Played 32 Serie A games for AS Roma 1997-1999 and 98 Serie A games in 3 seasons with US Lecce.

**8 ANTONIO CONTE** 31.07.69
Longest serving current Juventus player who signed in November 1991 from his hometown club US Lecce. Has won 5 Serie A medals, a 1993 UEFA Cup and 1996 Champions League honours. Has played 279 Serie A games for the club before 2003/04 plus a further 75 Serie A games for US Lecce (1985-1991). His 20 international caps to 01.07.03 include 2 games at the 1994 FIFA World Cup and 3 games at Euro2000.

**26 EDGAR DAVIDS** 13.03.73
Picked up by Juventus in December 1997 after just 19 league games in the previous 17 months for AC Milan. Originally with AFC Ajax before playing in Italy, he won 3 championship medals with the Dutch side in 1994, 1995 and 1996, as well as the Champions League and Toyota Intercontinental Cup in 1995. Now has six domestic championship medals after 3 successful seasons with Juventus in 1998, 2002 and 2003. This is his 9th Champions League season and has played 65 games, scoring 3 goals. A Dutch international, the midfielder has 54 caps despite having had operations on both eyes due to acute glaucoma.

# GROUP D
## JUVENTUS FC

**10 ALESSANDRO DEL PIERO** 09.11.74
Joined Juventus in summer 1993 after just 14 Serie B games for Padova Calcio and one goal. Before 2003/04 season he had scored 100 Serie A goals in 246 games with 16 goals in both the past two seasons (2001/02 and 2002/03). Has 5 Serie A winners medals in 1995, 1998, 1998, 2002 and 2003, and has won the 1996 Champions League and Toyota Intercontinental Cup medals. Enters the 2003/04 campaign with 29 goals in 60 Champions League games – making him third in the scoring lists equal with Patrick Kluivert and behind Raul (43) and Ruud van Nistelrooy (30). First international cap was won in March 1995 v Estonia. Has won 58 caps.

**20 MARCO DI VAIO** 15.07.76
Joined Juventus in summer 2002 just before the Champions League deadline from Parma AC and won a championship medal in first season with 7 goals in 26 games. His 20 goals for Parma AC in 2001/02 had alerted Juventus – he scored 41 league goals in 83 games for Parma AC. Born in Rome, he played for S.S. Lazio but came to the fore with Salernitana Sport in their 1998 promotion to Serie A. In his first Champions League season in 2002/03 he scored 4 goals in 11 games. The Italian forward has 7 international caps to 01.07.03.

**2 CIRO FERRARA** 11.02.67
Has the most honours of all current Italian players with 18 major medals including 7 Serie A championships, the 1996 Champions League and 1989 UEFA Cup. Joined Juventus in 1994 after 10 seasons with SSC Napoli where he played alongside Diego Maradona in the 1990 Serie A success. In 20th season of Serie A football and so far has made 479 appearances and scored 26 goals. The 2003 final was Ferrara's 50th Champions League game throughout which he has scored just one goal. The Italian defender has picked up 49 international caps since 1987.

**6 SALVATORE FRESI** 16.01.73
Played 9 Serie A games and scored 1 goal in the 2002/03 championship winning season - his first season with Juventus. The Italian defender made his Serie A debut on 27.08.95 for Internazionale FC, and was in their 1998 UEFA Cup winning squad. He played one Champions League game for Internazionale FC in 1998/99 and 3 games in 2002/03.

**13 MARK IULIANO** 12.08.73
Signed by Juventus in summer 1996 from Serie B club Salernitana Sport after 123 games in the lower leagues. The defender has won 4 Serie A winners' medals in 1997, 1998, 2002 and 2003 scoring his first goal for the club to clinch the 1997 success. Played all six games at Euro2000, but only one game against South Korea at the 2002 FIFA World Cup. Has 19 international caps since debut v Wales on 05.09.98. This will be his 7th Champions League season, having already played 46 games in the competition.

# GROUP D
## JUVENTUS FC

**23 NICOLA LEGROTTAGLIE** 20.10.78
Made a Juventus player in summer 2003 from Chievo Verona, and immediately won his first career medal on 03.08.03 in the Italian Super Cup. Missed just 4 Serie A games for Chievo last season and won first international cap on 20.11.02 v Turkey. The Italian defender has 5 caps to date.

**14 ENZO MARESCA** 10.02.80
The Italian midfielder signed for Juventus after playing for Cagliari Calcio, West Bromwich Albion, Bologna FC and Piacenza FC.

**9 FABRIZIO MICCOLI** 27.06.79
Was signed by Juventus in summer 2002 after he signed 15 goals for Serie B club Ternana – and was loaned to AC Perugia for 2002/03 where he impressed. Scored 9 league goals for Perugia last season, and was called into the international squad in February 2003 and now has 4 caps.

**22 ANTONIO MIRANTE** 08.07.83
Young Italian Goalkeeper used as backup to Buffon.

**4 PAOLO MONTERO** 03.09.71
Only the second Uruguayan to play for Juventus after Raul Banfi in 1941/42. Joined from Atalanta BC in summer 1996, and has won 4 Serie A championships in 1997, 1998, 2002 and 2003. This will be his 6th Champions League campaign, having already played 46 games and scored 4 goals in the competition. Has won 48 international caps, including all 3 games at the 2002 FIFA World Cup.

**11 PAVEL NEDVED** 30.08.72
Elected the Czech Republic Player of the Decade in May 2003, and has 4-times been Czech Footballer of Year. Joined S.S.Lazio from AC Sparta after the Euro96 final, and moved to Juventus in summer 2001, winning Serie A medals in his first two seasons with them to add to the 2000 title with S.S.Lazio. Also won 1994 and 1995 Czech championship medals with AC Sparta. Scored the last ever Cup Winners' Cup final goal against RCD Mallorca. Has played 44 Champions League games and scored 9 goals in 4 previous seasons, but missed the 2003 final through suspension.

**7 GIANLUCA PESSOTTO** 11.08.70
Scored the Champions League winner in 1995/96 in his first season with Juventus, following a move from Torino Calcio. Has played 59 Champions League games without scoring. The Italian defender won 22 caps from 1996-2002, including 3 games at 1998 FIFA World Cup and 5 games at Euro2000. Pessotto is the proud owner of 4 Serie A winners medals with the club in 1997, 1998, 2002 and 2003.

# GROUP D
## JUVENTUS FC

**3 ALESSIO TACCHINARDI** 23.07.75
Joined Juventus in summer 1994 from Atalanta BC and has won 5 Serie A medals with them – in 1995, 1997, 1998, 2002 and 2003. Made his Atalanta debut on 24.01.93 aged 17, and spent two seasons there before his move. Won Champions League in 1996, and has played 7 Champions League seasons before 2003/04, appearing in 59 games – scoring 3 goals. The Italian midfielder has 11 international caps.

**21 LILIAN THURAM** 01.01.72
Signed by Juventus in summer 2001 from Parma AC and has won Serie A in both seasons with the club. Won UEFA Cup, Italian Cup and Italian Super Cup in 1999 at Parma AC. Also played for AS Monaco from 1990-1996 and Parma AC from 1996-2001. Has played in the Champions League for all his 3 clubs, and before 2003/04 had appeared in 35 Champions League games, scoring once. The French defender has won 89 international caps including the hat trick of success at 1998 FIFA World Cup, Euro2000 and 2003 FIFA Confederations Cup.

**17 DAVID TREZEGUET** 15.10.77
Joined Juventus from AS Monaco in summer 2000 after scoring the Euro2000 winner. Injury curtailed his season in 2002/03 but nevertheless has scored 47 Serie A goals in 76 games. Has 2 championship medals with AS Monaco (1997, 2000) and 2 with Juventus (2002, 2003). The striker has scored 22 goals in 43 appearances and is the proud owner of winners' medals following his involvement in 1998 FIFA World Cup and Euro2000.

**5 IGOR TUDOR** 16.04.78
Joined Juventus in summer 1998 aged 20 having already played for three seasons for NK Hajduk. This will be the midfielder's 5th Champions League campaign, having played 28 games and scored 4 goals in the competition. He scored the winning goal against RC Deportivo to ensure qualification from last season's knock out stages. Has won 29 international caps, playing 3 games in the 1998 FIFA World Cup finals, but missed the 2002 finals through injury.

**25 MARCELO ZALAYETA** 05.12.78
Has been with Juventus since November 1997 but was loaned to Empoli FC in 1997/98 and Sevilla FC from 1999-2001. Had roles in 3 Serie A championship wins in 1998, 2002 and 2003. In his first Champions League season in 2002/03, he scored 2 goal in 9 games. The Uruguayan has picked up 24 international caps.

**19 GIANLUCA ZAMBROTTA** 19.02.77
Joined Juventus in summer 1999 from AS Bari after 3 seasons in Serie B and CI with hometown Como, and two seasons in Serie A with AS Bari. Won Serie A championship medals in 2002 and 2003, and has 30 caps including 4 games at both Euro2000 and the 2002 FIFA World Cup. The Italian midfielder who can operate down either flank has played 22 Champions League games in past two seasons.

# GALATASARAY SK

**Galatasaray, the oldest and most successful team in Turkey have turned themselves into a force to be reckoned with. Winning the UEFA Cup in 2000, they overcame favourites Arsenal in Copenhagen (4-1 on penalties following a goalless draw) was undoubtedly the highlight in their history. The win over Real Madrid in Monaco (2-1 following a golden goal) in the European Super Cup was a superb after-party. Since their foundation in Istanbul in 1905 Galatasaray have won a record 15 league titles (the last one in 2002 and significantly one more than city rivals Fenerbahçe) and a record 13 Turkish Cups (most recently in 2000). The first to win the championship 3 times in a row (1971-72-73), a feat they then surpassed between 1997 and 2000 with 4 successive triumphs. Only 2nd in the Turkish league last season behind champions Besiktas, Galatasaray had to knock out Bulgarian champions CSKA Sofia in the 3rd qualifying round in order to participate in the Champions for the 9th time. Only Manchester United and FC Porto, share that record.**

## COACH

**FATIH TERIM** 14.09.53
Fatih Terim has played a very important role in Turkish football. As head coach he led Turkey to the European Championships for the first time in 1996. After 6 years with the national team, Terim went back to club football and after Ankaragücü (1988/89) and Göztepe Izmir (1989/90) he became the boss at Galatasaray. He didn't disappoint and has since won 4 league titles, 2 national cups, 2 doubles and the UEFA Cup. In the summer 2000 he moved to Fiorentina but 6 months later, in December 2000, he was sacked. He then joined AC Milan in July 2001 but that adventure didn't last long either. By the end of November 2001 Terim had left San Siro and in July 2002 he went back to Galatasaray where he is still to bag any silverware.

## REACTION TO DRAW

**"They are very strong opponents and Juventus is one of the group favourites...but I think we can get out of this group in second place at least. There are powerful teams in this group. We want to succeed this year after failing to do so last season,"** ***striker Hakan Sukur***

## SQUAD

**4 ORHAN AK** 29.09.77
Defender who was transferred this summer from Kocaelispor to strengthen the squad for the Champions League.

# GROUP D
## GALATASARAY SK

**18 AYHAN AKMAN** 23.02.77
Gaziantepspor spotted this highly promising midfielder at Inegölspor before he joined Besiktas in 1998. Made his debut for Turkey on 18.02.98 away to Israel (0-4 win) and was in the squad for Euro 2000 but didn't play. Played 3 CL games for Besiktas in 2000/01 season before moving across Istanbul in 2001 to Galatasaray. Has played 10 CL games for this club.

**20 VOLKAN ARSLAN** 29.08.78
Defensive midfielder. Born in Hannover where he also starred in the Hannover youth team. Moved to Turkey to play for Adanaspor then Kocaelispor. Joined Galatasaray in 2003.

**14 ELVIR BALJIC** 08.07.74
Bosnian midfielder who can also play up front. Started his career at FK Sarajevo before he fled the War and moved to Bursaspor in Turkey in 1995. In 3 seasons he scored 42 goals in 87 games. Fenerbahçe was his next stop and his 19 goals in 26 league games attracted the interest of John Toshack and Real Madrid. He signed for Real in 1999 and was in the squad in their CL 2000 winning campaign but didn't play in the final against Valencia. Was loaned back to Fenerbahçe in 2000/01 winning the Turkish title. In the next season he played 1 CL game for Real Madrid and 10 league games on loan to Rayo Vallecano before joining Galatasaray in the summer 2002. 4 CL games last season, but no goals.

**8 JOAO BATISTA** 04.03.75
Brazilian midfielder from Uniao Sao Joao. He arrived in Turkey at Premier Division side Gaziantepspor where he had made big impression before moving to Galatasaray in 2001/02. Played 16 league games scoring 1 goal in his first season at the club. Last season he was present in 5 CL games only missing the away game at FC Bruges (3-1 defeat).

**7 GÖKTAN BERKANT** 12.12.80
Born in Munich he joined Bayern as an 8-years-old. He was a member of the side who won the German Youth Championship in 1997. Played 22 times for Bayern Munich in the Bundesliga and once in the CL in 1998 coming on as a substitute at home against Manchester United. He scored 33 times in 43 matches for Turkey at youth level. Was also loaned out to Borussia Mönchengladbach and Arminia Bielefeld but both teams were relegated. In 2001 he moved to Galatasaray where he took up a role on the left side of central midfield. Played 6 CL games in 2001/02 but none last season.

**61 MEHMET BOLUKBASI** 24.08.78
The club's 2nd goalkeeper. He was signed in 1997 from third division team Akçaabatspor. Made his debut for Galatasaray in 1998/99 when he made 2 league appearances. Played also 1 CL game on 20.10.99 at home against Chelsea (0-5 defeat) after Taffarel had been sent off in the previous game at Stamford Bridge 3 weeks earlier. But as the result shows it was not one of his best experiences.

# GROUP D
## GALATASARAY SK

**5 FRANK DE BOER** 15.05.70
Dutch international central defender (103 caps before this season) who left Barcelona this summer for a 2-year-contract by the Bosphorus. Galatasaray will be his third club after starting his career at Ajax where he won the Champions League, the UEFA Cup, the Intercontinental Cup, the European Super Cup, 5 league titles and 2 national Cups. His 5 years at FC Barcelona since January 1999 were less successful with only 1 league title and suffering a lot of criticism in his last season.

**22 ABDULLAH ERCAN** 08.12.71
Turkish international midfielder (70 caps) who played in the Turkish top flight for Trabzonspor before joining Fenerbahçe in 1999. Made 30 league appearances and scored 1 goal in the 2001/02 season when Fenerbahçe won their 14th league title. Played 5 CL games in the following season but couldn't prevent his team from finishing the first group stage without a single point. Moved to city rivals Galatasaray this summer.

**12 AYKUT ERCETIN** 14.09.82
Joined Galatasaray this summer to become the third goalkeeper. He comes from German runner-up VfB Stuttgart where he played in the youth teams.

**33 MURAT ERDOGAN** 01.08.76
Is born on the same day as Hasan Sas. Murat is a 27-years-old midfielder who played for Gaziantepspor and Istanbulspor before moving to Galatasaray this summer.

**6 ARIF ERDEM** 02.01.72
Right-winger who joined Galatasaray in 1991 from Zeytinburnuspor. Arif, who also played for Turkey at Euro 96 and at Euro 2000, got a lucrative offer from Real Sociedad in the summer 2000 but his stay in San Sebastian didn't last longer than 3 months. He returned to Galatasaray where he instantly felt at home again. 35 CL games overall, 2 goals (5 games and 1 goal last season). Played 4 games (all as a sub) at the World Cup 2002 including the semi-final.

**19 CIHAN HASPOLATLI** 04.01.80
Right-sided central midfielder who is one of the great young domestic talents. He played for Kocaelispor before joining Galatasaray in the summer 2002. Played 3 CL games last season and scored 1 goal in the last game of the first group stage at Nou Camp against Barcelona (3-1 defeat).

**9 ÜMIT KARAN** 01.10.76
Striker who made name at Gençlerbirligi when he scored 18 goals in 33 games in the 1999/2000 season. Signed for Galatasaray in 2001 and started with 7 goals in 28 league games. Has played 13 CL games for the club but only 2 last season. Made his debut for Turkey on 04.04.99 coming on as a 89th minute sub versus Northern Ireland in Belfast. 6 caps before the start of this season.

# GROUP D
## GALATASARAY SK

**3 BÜLENT KORKMAZ** 24.11.68
He was a key defender in the Turkish World Cup side 2002 that finished third. He played 6 of 7 games and was rested for the other. He is the club captain and has won 7 championship medals. He has been with the club since his schooldays and has come through the ranks to be a full international of considerable standing. Played 44 games in 8 CL campaigns but scored only 1 goal in this famous competition on 25.10.2000 away to Monaco (4-2 defeat).

**21 ALI LUKUNKU** 14.04.76
Forward who started at Norcep Grenoble before moving to French 2nd division side Valence (1995-97). The Kinshasa born Frenchman then went to Monaco where he didn't get into the first team (1997-99) before joining Standard Liège in Belgium. Joined Galatasaray in the beginning of 2003 but had a difficult start at the club. The return of Sükür could make it hard for him to break into the first team.

**1 ALI FARYD CAMILO MONDRAGON** 21.06.71
Colombian international goalkeeper who was an unused sub at 1994 World Cup but played all 3 games at France 1998. Started his career at Deportivo Cali and then played for Independiente Santa Fé in Colombia before moving abroad to Cerro Porteno in Paraguay. In Argentina he played for Argentinos Juniors and Independiente. He had a brief spell in Spain with Real Zaragoza using a Greek passport but was implicated in the false passports row of Spring 2001 when he was playing at Metz in France. Was loaned out to Galatasaray in the summer 2001 to replace Brazilian Taffarel. Played all 18 CL games of Galatasaray since then without missing a single minute.

**2 ERDOGAN ÖMER** 03.05.77
Defender who joined Galatasaray this summer from Turkish Super League club Diyarbakirspor. Provides cover for the first choice players.

**67 ERGUN PENBE** 17.05.72
Was spotted by Galatasaray playing for Gençlerbirligi in 1994. The left-sided midfielder has played 32 CL games for the club but scored only once in the 2000/01 campaign at home against Sturm Graz. Played for Turkey at Euro 2000 and in the World Cup 2002. 39 caps before the start of this season. His unusually high squad number is actually the frequency of a local radio station.

**24 OVIDIU PETRE** 22.03.82
Romanian international midfielder who was signed on transfer deadline from National Bucharest. He moved to Ajax in January 2003 but failed to obtain a work permit in Holland. He was signed together with another Romanian, the 23-year-old striker Florin Bratu from Rapid Bucharest who will be ineligible for the CL because he played against Anderlecht in the 2nd qualifying round defeat by Anderlecht.

# GROUP D
## GALATASARAY SK

**17 FABIO PINTO** 09.10.80
Brazilian right-sided midfielder who played for Internacional Porto Alegre before he moved to Spain in 1998 to play for Real Oviedo. It was not a complete success since he only started twice and didn't get more than 17 appearances in his first season. Played 14 league games in his second season but the lack of any appearances in his third made him decide to return to Brazil. In the summer 2002 he came back to Europe to play for Galatasaray. 4 CL games, 1 goal last season in the away game at FC Bruges (3-1 defeat).

**29 CESAR PRATES** 08.02.75
Brazilian right-sided defender who joined Galatasaray this summer from Portugal where he played for Sporting Lisbon (all 6 CL games in 2000/01 season). Was impressive during the Amsterdam Tournament 2003 in the beginning of August where he scored with a splendid free kick and was named 'Man of the Match' against Liverpool (2-1 win). Also scored from a free kick in the 3rd qualifying round away game against CSKA Sofia (3-0 win).

**55 SABRI SARIOGLU** 26.07.84
Diminutive midfielder who came through from the youth squad in 2003 and played in the 3rd qualifying round at CSKA Sofia (0-3 win) scoring a goal on his European debut.

**11 HASAN SAS** 01.08.76
The bald-headed forward who operates on the left side of the field is famous for his high speed dribbling. Made his league debut for Ankaragücü in 1995 before joining Galatasaray in 1998. Has played 38 CL games for the club and scored 3 goals versus Milan AC, Real Madrid and Lokomotiv Moscow (5 CL games and 1 goal last season). Played for Turkey at Euro 2000 and in the successful World Cup where they finished third. 25 caps before the start of this season.

**10 HAKAN SÜKÜR** 01.09.71
Star of Turkish football who played 84 times for the national side and scored a record 38 goals before the start of this season. Came back to Galatasaray this summer after having left the club following the UEFA Cup win. He had a spell in Italy with Internazionale and Parma and last season joined Blackburn Rovers but broke his leg at the beginning of the season. He joined Galatasaray for the first time in 1992 after 2 seasons with Bursaspor (54 games, 11 goals). Before he played for Sakaryspor from 1987 to 1990 (44 games, 15 goals in 3 seasons). At Galatasaray he won 6 league titles, 4 national Cups and the UEFA Cup. He scored 174 goals in 239 league appearances. He was 3 times Turkish top scorer in 1997 (38 goals), in 1998 (32 goals) and in 1999 (19 goals). He played 28 CL games and scored 7 goals in his first spell at the club.

**30 SEBASTIAN GABRIEL TAMAS** 09.11.83
Young Romanian central defender who was spotted by Galatasaray at Dinamo Bucharest. He moved to Istanbul this summer and is considered one for the future.

**57 HAKAN ÜNSAL** 14.05.73
The victim of the Rivaldo dive in World Cup 2002 is a left-sided midfielder or defender. He joined Galatasaray for the first time in 1996 from Karabükspor. He promptly gained a first team spot in Gala's 1997 championship win and was called up to the national squad as a result. Played for Turkey at Euro 2000 (quarter-finalists) and in the World Cup 2002 (4 games) finishing third. Was present in Gala's big European performances. Moved to England in February 2002 but couldn't settle at Blackburn Rovers (8 games in the Premiership). Has returned Galatasaray for a second spell. Scored 2 goals in the CL (against Rangers and Monaco in September and October 2000) and was also twice sent off in the CL (away to Sparta Prague in October 1997 and away to Barcelona in December 2001). Played all 6 CL games last season and has played 33 CL games overall.

**23 SUAT USTA** 03.08.81
Tall young defender who was born in Turkey but played for Dutch 2nd division club Maastricht VV and then in the youth of PSV Eindhoven before joining Galatasaray in 2003. He was noticed following his bright performances in the Turkish National youth team.

# REAL SOCIEDAD

**Only inexperience and arguably the rub of the green due to some unfortunate refereeing decisions prevented Sociedad from surprising the football world and beating real Madrid to the 2002-03 La Liga title. Bearing in mind that the previous season they narrowly avoided relegation, coming second, just two points behind Real represents a highly successful campaign and a justified first entry into the Champions League. In the first half of last season Sociedad were invincible with Sheffield Wednesday reject Darko Kovacevic leading the line and Russian midfielder Valerie Karpin rejoining the club from Celta Vigo, scoring 16 goals. The outstanding Spanish defender was Lopez and the team fielded two ex-Liverpool players Sander Westerweld and Bjorn Tore Kvarme. A well organised and disciplined side whose compact home ground, the Anoute, will be filled to its 32,000 capacity to provide an intimidating welcome for any visiting team. Could be dark horses.**

## COACH

**RAYNALD DENOUEIX** 14.05.48
Defender Denoueix, born in Rouen, played for Nantes between 1966 and 1978 where he won the French league title three times (1966, 1973 and 1977). From 1982 until 1997 he was responsible for Nantes' youth development programme before taking over the first team in the summer of 1997 from Jean-Claude Suaudeau. Denoueix led Nantes to the French Cup twice (1999 and 2000) before surprisingly winning the league

title in 2001. He took Nantes to the second group stage of the Champions League the next year in a group with Lazio, Galatasaray and PSV Eindhoven but was sacked in the middle of the season for the poor domestic performances and results of the club. In the summer of 2002, after a half-season holiday, Denoueix was asked to become the coach of struggling Real Sociedad. The Basque club hoped to profit from his ability to bring players through from their famed youth scheme. Denoueix performed beyond everybody's expectations. Real's astonishing league performances and their second place behind Real Madrid led them straight into the Champions League 2003/04, where they'll make their first-ever appearance.

## REACTION TO DRAW

**"In principle we are optimistic because before we were picked out this group was shaping up as the best we could hope for. We will approach it with our customary humility and are determined to enjoy the experience of being in what is a new competition for us,"** ***President Jose Luis Astiazaran.***

## SQUAD

**18 BITTOR ALKIZA** 26.10.70
Started his career in La Liga with Real Sociedad on September 1st 1991 against FC Barcelona (2-0 defeat). Joined Athletic Club Bilbao in 1994, where he was used as defensive midfielder. Came back this summer to San Sebastian. Alkiza has already played in the Champions League with Athletic Club Bilbao in the autumn of 1998 (four games, no goals) also against Galatasaray and Juventus, two teams he will meet again now with Real Sociedad.

**3 AGUSTIN ARANZABAL ALKORTA** 15.03.73
Left-back Aranzabal has a long tradition with Real Sociedad. His father used to play in the first team in the 1970s and Agustin has recently overtaken his dad, with more than 270 appearances. Fans hope he can equal his exceptional performances of last season in 33 league games.

**12 XABIER PRETO ARGARATE** 29.08.83
Young midfielder who joined Real Sociedad from Lizeo Santo Tomas.

**24 JAVIER GARRIDO BEHOBIDE** 15.03.85
18-year-old defender, an option for the future as he still plays in the youth team at Sociedad.

**17 IGOR GABILONDO DEL CAMPO** 10.02.79
Powerful, tall midfielder who is very good in the air, left-footed and the cover for De Pedro on the wing. Joined Real Sociedad as a youth player coming from Anorga. 29 games, one goal last season.

# GROUP D
## REAL SOCIEDAD

**19 LEE CHUN-SOO** 09.07.81
South Korean international winger who arrived this summer from Ulsan Hyundai (18 games, eight goals last season). He is one of the young sensations of Korean football who played all seven games at the World Cup 2002, with his country finishing fourth. He had already had trials in France with Lille and in Italy with Brescia, but Real Sociedad is his first club in Europe. Will normally be used by coach Denoueix as a substitute but he has the talent, the confidence and the technical skills to make it in Spain.

**11 MIKEL ARANBURU EIZAGIRRE** 18.02.79
Before the arrival of coach Denoueix, Aranburu spent most of the time on the bench. Under the French coach he's a regular at the heart of midfield. He is a disciplined and hard-working player who protects the defence and provides cover for gifted Xabi Alonso. Played 35 games last season and scored two goals.

**10 FRANCISCO JAVIER DE PEDRO FALQUE** 04.08.73
He got into the first team squad in 1991 but many substitute appearances in his early days hindered his progress. Has played more than 250 league games for the Basque club and operates usually down the flanks, mostly on the left. Made his debut for Spain under Camacho, playing in his first three games, but Bilbao's Joseba Echeverria was preferred. Was recalled in March 2002 (after four years) to Spain's World Cup squad and did not disappoint in his four games. Had two excellent seasons with Real Sociedad. De Pedro has a wonderful touch, he's a superb deliverer of corners and free-kicks and his crosses are a gift for the aerial ability of striker Kovacevic. Played 30 league games last season and scored seven goals.

**1 ALBERTO LOPEZ FERNANDEZ** 20.05.69
Alberto is the club's second goalkeeper and the stand-in if anything happens to Dutchman Westerveld. He is reliable, secure - some critics say unspectacular. Played one game last season but has already more than 300 first team appearances to his name since making his debut for Real Sociedad in April 1993.

**21 OSCAR DE PAULA GAMERO** 31.05.75
Played at CD Badajos (Spanish second division) before joining Real Sociedad in 1995. He used to score a lot of goals as a substitute but forward De Paula didn't have many opportunities to play last season (only 12 games without scoring a goal). He is dangerous on the break.

**7 IGOR JAUREGI IRAOLA** 29.04.74
Former coach Roberto Olabe recalled Jauregi from second division team Eibar two years ago when he took over from John Toshack. Jauregi used to play as centre-back but moved into the position of defensive midfielder when Aranbura got injured. 37 games, one goal last season.

**15 NIHAT KAHVECI** 23.11.79
This diminutive Turkish international is the perfect foil for Kovacevic up front and a deadly finisher having scored 23 goals (in 36 games) last season in La Liga, where he was a revelation. He arrived in Spain in January 2002 from Besiktas for a club record fee of £3.4 million. Kahveci is exceptionally quick and he buzzes all along the front line, an excellent weapon for the fast-pressing game coach Denoueix likes to play. Besides his nose for goals he also has great technical skills. He made his debut for Besiktas at 17.

**8 VALERI KARPIN** 02.02.69
Russian winger Karpin symbolised Real Sociedad's resurgence. With his spirit, work rate and never-say-die attitude, Karpin was for many the buy of last season, coming back from Celta Vigo on a free transfer after six years away. 37 league games last season and scored eight goals.

**9 DARKO KOVACEVIC** 18.11.73
International for Serbia and Montenegro who left Red Star Belgrade and the former Yugoslavia in January 1996 to play in England for Sheffield Wednesday. After 16 Premiership appearances and four goals, Kovacevic moved to Spain to play three seasons for Real Sociedad (98 league games, 41 goals). His next stop was Italy in summer 1999 for Juventus and then Lazio (August 2001). Darko has played already in the Champions League for Juventus and Lazio but scored only one goal for 'The Old Lady', against Hamburg on October 24th 2000, the game in which both his team-mates Zinedine Zidane and Edgar Davids were sent off. He returned to Sociedad on loan from Lazio. He is a real fighter, a superb finisher (scored 20 goals in 37 games last season) offering strength and touch, he is unparalleled in the air and can also be used as a target man.

**2 BJORN TORE KVARME** 17.06.72
Central defender who is strong in the air but is occasionally caught out on the ground. Started his professional career at Rosenborg in 1991. He left the club from Trondheim in 1997 for Liverpool but two years later he was on the move again to France, this time to play for Saint Etienne, another club with a European tradition. After two seasons with 'les Verts' John Toshack brought this one-time Norwegian international to Real Sociedad. Last season he took the place of Jauregi when the centre-back moved to midfield.

**5 ZUHAITZ GURRUTXAGA LOIOLA** 23.11.80
Gurrutxaga is a pacy centre-back but he is not first choice for coach Denoueix. He spent most of last season on the substitute bench. Normally very aggressive in his actions to block the forwards of the opponents, he joined Real Sociedad as a youth player from Elgoibar. Made his debut in the first team in January 2000 against Atletico Madrid.

**23 SERGIO BORIS GONZALEZ MONTEAGUDO** 26.05.80
Boris has great potential. He can be used as centre-back or as a defensive midfielder. In

the summer of 2002, he became the first non-Basque Spaniard for 35 years at Real Sociedad when he signed from Real Oviedo, the team where he spent most of his youth after being spotted at Real Aviles Industrial. Played 25 games last season.

**16 MIKEL ALONSO OLANO** 16.05.80
The older brother by about 18 months of Sociedad's young promising talent Xabi Alonso. Played nine games last season and scored one goal.

**4 XABI ALONSO OLANO** 25.11.81
Son of Periko Alonso, who was the central midfield lynchpin in the Real Sociedad side that won two successive titles (1981 and 1982 - the only championship victories in the club's 93-year history). Xabi Alonso is Real Sociedad's great young hope in central midfield. Made his debut in January 2001 after John Toshack wanted him to rescue the side that was lingering at the foot of the table. He had been playing on loan for Basque second division team Eibar. It turned out to be an excellent move - Sociedad escaped the drop and Alonso started his rise to prominence. At 21 he shows wonderful vision, great passing ability, superb distribution and leadership qualities. Played 34 league games last season, scoring three goals. In April, earlier this year, he was rewarded with his first cap for Spain against Ecuador. Barcelona, Real Madrid and Manchester United are already interested in the biggest talent of Real Sociedad, who can become one of the stars of future Champions League competitions.

**22 LIONEL POTILLON** 10.02.74
French central or left-sided defender who was recently signed from Paris SG, where he'd played since 2001. Youth product of Louhans-Cuiseaux. Joined Saint-Etienne in 1993. In his eight years with 'Les Verts' he was twice relegated to the second division as well in 1996 as in 2001, but to compensate he won the title in the French second division in 1999.

**14 AITOR LOPEZ REKARTE** 18.08.75
28-year-old Lopez Rekarte used to play as a right-sided midfielder but he has converted to the full-back position. He's an extra weapon if Sociedad want to go forward because he is always willing to get up and down the field. He has excellent crossing ability and can supply the forwards whenever necessary. Joined Real Sociedad as a youth player in 1989, coming from Mondragon. Was European champion with the Spanish under-21 team.

**20 JOSE JAVIER BARKERO SALUDES** 27.04.79
Young midfielder who played in the youth teams of Real Sociedad after being spotted at UD Aretxabaleta. Was also loaned to Eibar to get some first team experience. Was World Champion with the Spanish under-20 team. Played 12 games last season.

**6 GABRIEL FRANCISCO SCHURRER** 16.08.71
Very experienced Argentine centre-back, who also has a Spanish passport. Together with Norwegian Kvarme, it will be difficult to beat the Basque club in the air. Schurrer

previously played in Spain for Racing Santander, Deportivo La Coruna and Las Palmas. He joined Real Sociedad from the club on the Isles in the summer of 2002 on a free transfer. Played in Argentina for Lanus (1990-96).

**13 MIKEL SAIZAR SOROA** 18.01.83
Third goalkeeper whose club of origin is Real Union. Still a youth player.

**25 SANDER WESTERVELD** 23.10.74
Dutch goalkeeper who played for Twente (1990-96) and Vitesse Arnhem (more than 100 league appearances) before moving abroad in 1999. With Liverpool he won the UEFA Cup, the League Cup and the FA Cup (all in 2001). He was the most used player in that 'treble cup' campaign and added in August of the same year the European Super Cup after beating Bayern Munich in Monaco (3-2). But after a mistake in the away game against Bolton Wanderers, Westerveld fell from grace at Anfield Road. Coach Houiller preferred Polish goalkeeper Jerzy Dudek so Westerveld opted to continue his career at Real Sociedad. In the Basque country, traditionally a goalkeeping hotbed, Westerveld found himself the subject of much debate. Commentators didn't appreciate having a foreigner as their goalkeeper - Westerveld answered on the field with some superb performances and leading Real Sociedad to the runners-up spot in La Liga.

# FC OLYMPIAKOS PIRAEUS

**This will be Olympiakos 39th season in Europe and their 7th successive year in the Champions League. Last season they were crowned champions for a record 32 times. Olympiakos endured a ten-year spell without winning the league between 1987 and 1997 but the championship drought came to an end in 1996/97, when they won the first of seven consecutive league titles. Regarded the best – if not the most famous – club in Greece, they have won more league titles than city rivals Panathinaikos (18) and AEK (11) and they also hold the record of Cup wins (20). On the international scene Olympiakos have never got further than a European quarter final: in 1992/93 they lost to Atletico Madrid and in 1998/99 Juventus them from advancing further in the Champions League.**

## COACH

**OLEG PROTASSOV** 04.02.64
Ukraine born Protassov started his playing career at Dnipropetrovsk before joining Dynamo Kyiv. In 1990 he went to Greece where he played for Olympiakos until 1994. After a short spell in Japan he came back to Greece where he finished his playing career at Veria and Proodeftiki. He was capped 69 times for the old USSR team and scored 25 goals. He also played the final of the European Championships in 1988 that the USSR

lost to Holland (2-0). He started his coaching career at Veria and in February 2003 he took over at Olympiakos after they had gone through 4 coaches in 7 months. He brought back the team's confidence and Olympiakos won their 7th league title in a row.

## REACTION TO DRAW

**"God owed us something. That's why we got Juventus. We have something to settle with them. They scored against us late in the game to knock us out in 1999. I am looking forward to playing them," *Olympiakos player Andreas Niniadis.***

## SQUAD

**31 DIMITRIOS ELEFTHEROPOULOS** 07.08.76
Probably the best Greek goalkeeper who joined Olympiakos from Proodeftiki. With Greece he was a 1995 European Under-18 Championship bronze medallist and a 1998 European Under-21 Championship runner-up. As a youngster he won the league title in 1997 but he missed the next season because of a serious knee injury. However from the summer 1998 he was back as first choice. Missed only 1 match of the last 32 CL games for Olympiakos in the last 5 seasons although since the summer 2002 Katergiannakis has been threatening his place in goal. Made his debut for Greece in 1-0 friendly versus Belgium on 05.02.99 and has won 12 caps since.

**32 GEORGIOS ANATOLAKIS** 16.03.74
Strong central defender made his debut for Iraklis in 1992 and played 134 league games before joining Olympiakos in 1996. Has been present in the 7 consecutive title wins and all the CL campaigns (5 games last season). Has 10 caps for Greece making his debut versus Portugal in Lisbon on 27.03.96

**18 PARASKEVAS ANTZAS** 18.08.76
6'4" tall central defender who can play as libero and as a defensive midfielder. Was a bronze medallist at the 1995 European Under-18 Championship and a runner-up in the Under-21 side at the 1998 European Championship with Greece. Had played 68 league games for Xanthi before joining Olympiakos in 1998. Missed the 2001/02 CL season through injury but played all 6 CL games last season.

**16 JURAI BUCEK** 15.09.73
Slovakian international goalkeeper who joined Olympiakos this summer from Skoda Xanthi where he played 165 league games since making his debut on 31 August 1997. In Slovakia he played in goal for Hemlon Humene and won the Slovakian Cup in 1996.

**7 NERI ALBERTO CASTILLO** 13.06.84
Was spotted by Olympiakos at Danubio (Uruguay) and joined them as a 16-years-old. Made his league debut on 8 April 2001 and has played 27 league games and scored 3

goals before the start of this season. No CL games last season.

**9 LAMBROS CHOUTOS** 07.12.79
Born in Athens and a youth player at Panathinaikos before he moved to Italy as a teenager. He made his Serie A debut at 16 in AS Roma's 4-1 win versus Naples on 20.04.96. He returned to Athens in 2000 and joined Olympiakos. Scored 10 league goals in 19 league games in 2000 and 2001 but missed the next (2001/02) season through injury. Has played 5 CL games (only 2 last season) and scored 1 goal at home against Manchester United on 23 October 2002 (2-3 defeat). Made his debut for Greece versus Moldova in Larisa on 16.12.99. Scored his first goal for Greece in his 2nd cap versus Romania on 29.03.2000.

**11 PREDRAG DJORDJEVIC** 04.08.72
Hard-working left-sided Serbian midfielder who started his career at Red Star Belgrade before moving to Greek club Paniliakos when the war started. Joined Olympiakos together with Giannakopoulos who has left now for Bolton Wanderers. Has played 36 CL games for Olympiakos and scored 8 goals. His best performance was last season with 4 goals in 6 CL games (3 goals in the first game at home versus Bayer Leverkusen) but that couldn't prevent Olympiakos finishing last in their group. Has 13 caps for Yugoslavia. Is married to a Greek girl and has become a Greek citizen. Scored 14 league goals last season.

**8 GEORGIOS GEORGIADIS** 08.03.72
Greek international midfielder (53 caps) who joined Olympiakos this summer from PAOK Saloniki where he played 105 league games and scored 42 goals (14 last season) since 1999. Made his league debut for Doxa Dramas on 16.09.90 and moved to Panathinaikos in 1993 where he played 176 league games scoring 60 goals. In the 1997/98 season he scored 21 league goals in the league and Newcastle United signed him but his Premiership experience didn't go further than 10 games without a goal. He returned to Greece after one year abroad.

**20 PANAGIOTIS GONIAS** 06.10.71
Experienced midfielder signed this summer after a good season at Iraklis (29 games, 6 goals). It will be his second spell at the club after a first period from 1993 to 1996. He made his league debut on 4 March 1990 for Levadiakos where Olympiakos spotted him in 1993. From 1996 onwards he played for Iraklis (1996/98), 11 games for Sporting Gijon in the Spanish 2nd division scoring 1 goal (1998/99), for Panaliakos (1999/2000), for Panionios (2000/02) and again for Iraklis (2002/03). Had played 199 league games scoring 32 goals in the Greek top flight before the start of this season.

**10 GIOVANNI** 04.02.72
After having 3 good seasons with Santos, Brazilian Giovanni Silva de Oliveira traded Pele's No 10 shirt for the playmaker's role at Barcelona in the summer 1996 at a cost of £5 million. He scored 4 times in the 9 CL games for Barcelona but was not part of

Louis Van Gaal's plans. When Jari Litmanen arrived at the Nou Camp Giovanni moved for £4 million to Olympiakos. He had a splendid start in Greece scoring 2 goals in his first CL game for Olympiakos against Real Madrid. He is technically brilliant and has superb vision. Before the start of this season he had already played 20 CL games and scored 7 goals (5 games and no goals last season). Giovanni played in the opening game at 1998 World Cup Finals between Brazil and Scotland (2-1 win). He has 19 caps and 6 goals for Brazil.

**1 PANTELIS KAFES** 24.06.78
Midfielder who joined Olympiakos this summer from PAOK Saloniki where he played 146 league games and scored 29 goals since making his debut on 16.02.97. Won the Greek Cup in 2001 with PAOK against Olympiakos (4-2) and will play wearing the number 1 despite not being in goal. His first club of origin was AU Pontion. He has 15 caps for Greece, 1 goal.

**5 CHRISTIAN KAREMBEU** 03.12.70
French World Champion 1998 who was born in Lifou (New Caledonia). Started his career at Nantes where he won the French Championship in 1995 before moving to Sampdoria Genoa (1995-97). Found to his dismay that the club had sold him to Barcelona but with UEFA's help he transferred in January 1998 to Real Madrid. There he played an important role in the run to the CL win in Amsterdam in 1998 scoring 3 goals. In 2000 he won the CL again in Paris against Valencia and in the same year he became European Champion with France although he stayed on the substitute bench in both finals. He moved to the Premier League in 2000 but after one season at Middlesbrough he joined Olympiakos in the summer 2001. There he played all 12 CL games since. Is married to Slovakian Supermodel and Miss Wonderbra Adriana Sklenarikova.

**22 THEOFANIS KATERGIANNAKIS** 16.02.74
This 6'3" tall goalkeeper made his Greek league debut with Aris Saloniki in 1994 and continued to play for Aris until the summer 2002 (130 league games in total). Then he joined Olympiakos as a free agent. He is a serious contender for Eleftheropoulos' place in the team since he made his debut for Greece in November 1999 versus Bulgaria. He has 6 caps for Greece.

**19 ATHANASSIOS KOSTULAS** 24.03.76
International defender who is cover for the first choice players. Started his career at Olympiakos Volou where he was spotted by Kalamata in 1994. There he played 135 league games before joining Olympiakos in the summer 1999. Didn't play in the CL last season.

**44 EFTHIMIOS KOULOUCHERIS** 10.03.81
Young defender who has only played 5 league games in the Greek top flight. Will have

to wait for his chance and will be used as a cover.

**21 MARCIN KUZBA** 15.04.77
Polish striker who had a splendid season with Wisla Krakow winning the national championship and scoring 21 goals in 27 league games. Olympiakos is not his first experience abroad as he has already played in France (with Auxerre in 1998/99 and with 2nd division side Saint-Etienne in 2001/02) and in Switzerland (with Lausanne Sports from 1999 until 2001). His first club in Poland was Gornik Zabrze where he played 83 league games and scored 31 goals between 1995 and 1997.

**14 DIMITRIOS MAVROGENIDIS** 23.12.76
Right-sided defender who made his league debut aged 17 for Aris Saloniki. Like Eleftheropoulos and Antzas he took a bronze medal with Greece at the 1995 European under-18 Championship and he was a runner-up at the 1998 European Under-21 Championship. Made his debut for the Greek national team as a sub versus Georgia on 14.10.98 in Euro 2000 qualifier and has been in the national squad ever since. Joined Olympiakos in 1997, has won 6 league titles and 1 cup (1999) and played 27 CL games (but only 2 last season) scoring 2 goals.

**4 ANDREAS NINIADIS** 18.02.71
Midfielder or forward originally from AU Pontion where he was spotted by Ethnikos, the club he made his debut for in the Greek league in 1994. In 1997 he moved to Olympiakos to boost the CL squad. Scored a goal in the last 2 CL campaigns against Lille in 2001 and against Maccabi Haifa last season. Married on the same day in June 2002 as his team mate Stylianos Venetidis.

**30 ANASTASIOS PANTOS** 05.05.76
New signing from Proodeftiki where he played 52 league games and scored 1 goal since making his league debut in 1998. Is a defender who can also operate in midfield.

**2 CHRISTOS PATSATZOGLOU** 19.03.79
One of the most talented players in Greece who is physically very strong and technically gifted. Is a full-back who can also take up a role in midfield if necessary. He played under former Olympiakos coach Matsurakis at Xanthi where he was brought into top flight football at the age of 17. In the summer 2000 he moved to Olympiakos after 87 league appearances for Xanthi and went straight into the national team making his senior debut in September 2000 versus Germany. Had 16 caps at the start of this season. Played all 18 CL games in the last 3 CL campaigns of the club.

**6 IEROKLIS STOLTIDIS** 02.02.75
Midfielder who played 238 league games and scored 33 goals since making his debut in December 1992 for Iraklis. Has 6 caps for Greece and scored 1 goal for

the national team. Joined Olympiakos this summer and should take up a role in central midfield.

**23 ALEXANDROS TATSIS** 28.08.79
Forward who was signed this summer from Proodeftiki where he played 46 league games scoring 16 goals since 2001 (21 league games, 6 goals last season). Started his career in the 2nd division with PAS Giannina in 1996. In 1999 he moved for one season to Panargiakos before returning to PAS Giannina.

**25 SPYROS VALLAS** 26.08.81
Young defender who made his league debut for Xanthi on 28 May 2000. In the next 3 seasons he played 53 games and scored 4 goals before joining Olympiakos this summer.

**3 STYLIANOS VENETIDIS** 19.11.76
A left-back who joined Olympiakos in the summer 2001 after 163 league games and 3 goals for PAOK Saloniki. He also won the Greek Cup 2001 with PAOK against Olympiakos (4-2). Made his debut for the Greek national team on 20.08.99 in Kavala versus El Salvador (3-0). Had 32 caps for Greece at the start of this season. Has played 10 CL games for the club and didn't miss a minute in the 6 CL games of last season.

# GROUP E

**MANCHESTER UNITED**
(England)

**PANATHINAIKOS**
(Greece)

**GLASGOW RANGERS FC**
(Scotland)

**VFB STUTTGART**
(Germany)

# MANCHESTER UNITED FC

**After an indifferent start to the 2002-03 Season, many believed that the bedrock of the team that had won 7 Premiership Titles was coming apart at the seams. The low point was a 3-1 defeat to local rivals Manchester City. Thereafter, United were invincible in the League but still had to rely on rivals Arsenal, blowing a 5 point lead to regain the Premiership. In Europe, United disappointed their fans after cruising through the group stages. Two defeats in thrilling matches with Real Madrid heralded a quarter-final exit. Summer transfers saw the departures of David Beckham and Seba Veron. New arrivals include Kleberson, Christian Ronaldo, Tim Howard and Eric Djemba-Djemba.**

## COACH

**SIR ALEX FERGUSON** 31.12.41
The most successful British manager ever appeared to be bowing out at the top when he announced his retirement plans in 2001 but the challenge of winning back the Premiership and the Champions League ultimately proved to be irresistible. Ferguson made his name in Scotland, where despite being sacked at St Mirren, he went on to build success at unfashionable Aberdeen, breaking the stranglehold of the two Glasgow clubs and taking Aberdeen to domestic and European success. It took him over five years to get things right at Old Trafford, but by the 1990s the Red had monopolised English football. Many believe that Coach Carlos Querioz was the dominant influence behind United's domestic success last campaign. We wait with interest to see if there is a re-match between Real Madrid (where Querioz is now coach) and United in this season's Champions League.

## REACTION TO DRAW

**"(Rangers manager) Alex McLeish is an old player of mine at Aberdeen and has done a geat job at Rangers. It's a great draw. We have been to Panathinaikos before and and were lucky in March 2001 when we got a 1-1 draw and could have been slaughtered. We have not played Stuttgart – but we have experience of German football. You're not expecting an easy ride and it won't be, but I am optimistic of reaching the later stages which is where Manchester United belongs."** ***Alex Ferguson***

## SQUAD

**1 FABIEN BARTHEZ** 28.06.71
Has won 2 Premiership titles with Man Utd. Started 46 games last season, conceding 46 goals and keeping15 clean sheets. Has played 139 games for United (50 clean sheets

and 136 goals conceded). Has saved Premiership penalties from Muzzy Izzet (November 17, 2001) and Steed Malbranque (October 19, 2002) – used delaying tactics for both. Won his 59th France cap in the 1-0 Confederations Cup final win v Cameroon on June 29.06.2003. A 1998 World Cup and Euro 2000 winner, Barthez has lost his place in the Manchester United team to new signing, Tim Howard.

**12 DAVID BELLION** 27.11.82
Was signed on July 1, 2003 after his contract at Sunderland had expired. Joined Sunderland from Cannes on a free transfer in the summer of 2001. The French forward is highly rated despite starting only 5 Premiership games for Sunderland and scoring just one goal in a 1-0 home win v Aston Villa on September 28, 2002. Was dogged by a persistent heel injury last season.

**6 WES BROWN** 16.03.79
Has now won 3 Premiership winners medals with Utd. Signed a new 4-year contract with United in July 2001, keeping him at Old Trafford until 2005. Scored v Juventus on February 19, 2002 – his first goal for United (in his 111th app). A member of England's 2002 World Cup squad but did not make an appearance. Won his 7th cap as a 2nd half sub v Australia on February 12. Still only 23 but has already suffered a number of serious of injuries; he missed the whole of the 1999-00 season with a cruciate knee ligament injury and was out for 4 months of season 2001-02 with another knee injury (December 2001-March 2002). Missed another 3 months after breaking his right ankle after 5 minutes of the Champions League qualifier v Zalaegerszeg in Budapest on August 14, 2002. Missed 4 games in March 2003 with a hamstring injury and ruptured the anterior cruciate ligament in his left knee at Everton on the final day of last season.

**8 NICKY BUTT** 21.01.75
Has won 6 Premiership winners medals with Man Utd. Won his 28th England cap v Croatia on August 20 2003. Has not scored since March 16, 2002 in a 5-3 win at West Ham. Has made 354 appearances for Man Utd, scoring 24 goals. Sent off 5 times for United. Now in his 12th season as a United professional. Missed 25 games between October 2002 and January 2003 with an ankle injury.

**13 ROY CARROLL** 30.09.77
Cost £2.5m from Wigan in July 2001, signing a 4-year contract. Has won13 caps for Northern Ireland. Made his Man Utd debut at Villa Park on August 26, 2001 and his European debut v Lille on October 31, 2001. Made 14 starts last season (6 clean sheets), appearing in 4 different competitions. Has played 26 games for Man Utd (12 clean sheets, 19 goals conceded). Made his 10th Premiership appearance of last season in the final day win at Everton, thus qualifying for a winner's medal.

**19 ERIC DJEMBA-DJEMBA** 04.05.81
Signed from Nantes for an initial £3.5m in July 2003. An additional £700,000 will be paid

depending on appearances. Has signed a 5-year contract. Part of the famous Nantes youth academy whose most famous products are Marcel Desailly and Didier Deschamps. As a Cameroon international he won the 2002 African Nations Cup and also played in the 1-0 defeat to France in the final of the 2003 Confederations Cup. Was a member of Cameroon's 2002 World Cup squad, but didn't play in any of their 3 games. Played in the Champions League in both phases in 2001-02 and he started in the 5-1 hiding at Old Trafford in February 2002 – where he reportedly caught Alex Ferguson's eye. Scored 1 goal in 28 league games for Nantes last season, picking up 11 yellow cards and 1 red. Made his Man Utd debut as sub in the Community Shield victory v Arsenal.

**5 RIO FERDINAND** 07.11.78

Joined from Leeds in July 2002 for a British record fee that could rise to £33m. Won his first Premiership title (and first major honour) last season. Not scored a club goal since April 21, 2001 (for Leeds at West Ham) – 93 club appearances without a goal. Ended a run of 95 Premiership games without a yellow card when he was booked v Sunderland on New Year's Day (his first yellow card in the Premiership since December 1999, for West Ham v Derby). An England international with 33 caps, he scored 1 goal for England, in the 3-0 World Cup 2nd round win v Denmark in June 2002. Missed the Euro 2004 qualifiers in October 2002 after undergoing knee surgery; he also missed the home qualifier v Slovakia on June 11 with another knee problem. Missed 16 games for United at various stages of last season due to ankle, knee and then thigh injuries.

**24 DARREN FLETCHER** 01.02.84

Made an impressive first team debut in the 1-1 Champions League draw with Basle on March 12, 2003. Made his 2nd app v Deportivo on March 18. He joined Man Utd as a trainee in July 2000 and turned professional in February 2001. A creative central midfield player, he is a Scotland U-21 international. Born in Edinburgh, his first-team debut was delayed by a twice-fractured foot and an ankle injury.

**21 DIEGO FORLAN** 19.05.79

Was signed from Independiente for £7.5m in January 2002 when United beat Middlesbrough to his signature. Scored his first United goal from the spot in 5-2 win v Maccabi Haifa on September 18, 2002 – his 27th appearance (20 as a sub). Scored v Villa on October 26, 2002 – his first Premiership goal, in 24 appearances (15 as a sub). Has now scored 9 goals in 64 appearances for Man Utd (42 as a sub). Began his career at Penarol. Made his debut for Independiente in 1998 as a 19-year-old. In December 2001 he ended the Apertura (the first of two leagues in Argentina's footballing season) as second highest goalscorer, netting 12 times in the 18-game season as Independiente finished mid-table. Scored 36 goals in 77 league games for Independiente. The Uruguayan international marked his only appearance at the 2002 World Cup by scoring a spectacular long range volley in the 3-3 draw with Senegal.

# GROUP E
## MANCHESTER UNITED FC

**25 QUINTON FORTUNE** 21.05.77
Is now in his 5th season at the club. Signed a new 3-year contract in May 2003. Has made 59 appearances for United scoring 7 goals. Joined United for £1.5m from Atletico Madrid in August 1999. The South African international missed the start of last season with a knee ligament injury (came on as a sub in UCL v Olympiakos on October 1, 2002 for his first app of last season). Missed another 3 months after fracturing a leg v Liverpool on December 1, 2002. Has yet to win a Premiership title winners' medal because he has not yet played the required 10 games in a season.

**11 RYAN GIGGS** 29.11.73
Celebrating his 12th year at the club, Giggs is United's longest serving player. Signed a new five-year contract in April 2001. He has now won 8 Premiership winners medals with United, equalling the most top flight League titles won by a player in England (Alan Hansen and Phil Neal also won 8 – all with Liverpool). Has won 13 major honours with United - Champions League (1), Premiership (8), FA Cup (3) and League Cup (1). Has played 545 games for United, scoring 113 goals. Made his 500th United appearances at Fulham on October 19, 2002 and is now 3rd in the list of all-time Man Utd appearances behind Bobby Charlton (759) and Bill Foulkes (682). Of his last 25 Premiership goals, 23 have been scored away from Old Trafford. Scored 14 goals last season – his best season since 1993-94, when he netted 17. Has won 40 caps for Wales for whom he has scored 8 goals.

**14 TIM HOWARD** 06.03.79
A US international goalkeeper signed from New York-New Jersey MetroStars in a £2.3m deal in July 2003 (4-year contract). Was ever-present at the Confederations Cup this summer. Did not make the 2002 US World Cup squad; Friedel, Keller and Meola were chosen ahead of him. Born in New Brunswick (New Jersey) he made his debut for the 'Metros' in 1998 at the age of 18 and was twice named in the MLS Best XI. Kept 15 clean sheets in 85 MLS appearances. Was diagnosed with Tourette's Syndrome at the age of 10 and his subsequent work in helping others with the disorder earned him the 2001 MLS New York Life Humanitarian of the Year award (he insists the condition does not affect him during games). Trained with AC Milan for a short spell in November 1998. Made his United debut in the Community Shield v Arsenal last Sunday, saving penalties from Van Bronckhorst and Pires in the shoot-out victory. Appears to have captured a permanent starting position in United's first XI.

**16 ROY KEANE** 10.08.71
Returned as a sub at Blackburn on December 22, 2002 after being out for 4 months following a hip operation. Has won 7 Premiership winners medals with Man Utd (4 as captain). Has been sent off 10 times for Man Utd (11 times in his career). Sent off 7 times in Premiership (a record – level with Vieira and Vinnie Jones). His last goal was in April 2002 (in Champions League game at Leverkusen). His last Premiership goal came at home to Blackburn on January 19, 2002. Has played 394 games for Man Utd, scoring

46 goals. Signed a new 4-year contract in March 2002. Voted both the Football Writers' and PFA Player of the Year in 1999-2000. Won 58 caps for Rep of Ireland, scoring 9 goals. Was sent home from the 2002 World Cup following a fierce verbal attack on manager Mick McCarthy in a team meeting prior to Ireland's opening game. Has now quit international football.

**15 KLEBERSON** 19.06.79
Was finally signed from Atletico Paranaense on August 12, 2003 for £5.93m after he was granted a work permit. A Brazilian League title winner in 2002, the midfielder started the 2002 World Cup finals on the bench but ended up making 5 appearances (2 as sub), starting the last 3 games in the place of Juninho, including the final triumph v Germany. The first Brazilian to play for Man Utd.

**38 MARK LYNCH** 02.09.81
The Manchester-born defender signed as a trainee in July 1998 and turned professional in August 1999. Made his first-team debut v Deportivo on March 18, 2003 – scored an own goal in a 2-0 defeat. Has also been an unused sub for 2 first-team games – the final Premiership game of season 2001-02, at home to Charlton, and the Champions League game at Maccabi Haifa on October 29, 2002.

**40 DANNY NARDIELLO** 22.10.82
The son of former Coventry winger Donato Nardiello has been a prolific striker at youth level for United. He turned pro in October 1999, only 5 months after starting his scholarship with the Reds. He made his first-team debut on November 5, 2001, when he came on as sub for Bojan Djordjic in the Worthington Cup 3rd round tie at Arsenal. Made 2 appearances last season, as a sub at Maccabi Haifa in the Champions League on October 29, 2002, and started the Worthington Cup tie at home to Leicester on November 5, 2002.

**2 GARY NEVILLE** 18.02.75
Has won 6 Premiership winners medals with United. In May 2001 he signed a new 6-year contract - keeping him at Old Trafford until 2007. Has won 57 caps but missed the 2002 World Cup after breaking the fifth metatarsal of his left foot against Bayer Leverkusen on April 24, 2002. Now in his 12th season with United, Neville has played 393 games and scored 4 goals. Scored v Basle on March 12, 2002 – his first goal since 2-0 home Premiership win v Villa on January 20, 2001. Has never scored an 'away' goal for Man Utd.

**3 PHIL NEVILLE** 21.01.77
Has now won 6 Premiership winners medals with United. In May 2001 he signed a new 6-year contract, keeping him at Old Trafford until 2007. An England international with 41 caps. Now in his 10th season with United, he has played 310 games, scoring 7 goals. Scored twice last season, both at home (v Southampton in the Premiership and v West Ham in the FA Cup).

# GROUP E
## MANCHESTER UNITED FC

**22 JOHN O'SHEA** 30.04.81
Signed professional terms with United in August 1998 and made his first team debut just over a year later, away to Aston Villa in a Worthington Cup defeat. Joined Bournemouth on loan in January 2000. After 11 starts and 1 goal (v Millwall) he returned to Old Trafford in March 2000. Embarked on another loan spell in season 2000-01, this time with Royal Antwerp. Won his first senior Rep of Ireland cap on August 14, 2001, when he came on as an 84th min sub v Croatia. Won his 6th and 7th caps v Albania and Georgia in June 2003. Has made 69 first-team appearances for Man Utd (0 goals). Started 42 games last season – at full-back, centre-half and in midfield. Won his first Premiership title last season. Signed a new 4-year contract in March 2002.

**26 DANNY PUGH** 19.10.82
The midfielder signed as a trainee in July 1999 and turned pro a year later. Made his senior debut as sub in the 5-2 Champions League win v Maccabi Haifa on September 18, 2002. Made his Premiership debut as a sub v Tottenham on September 21, 2002. First start was the 2-0 Worthington Cup round 4 win at Burnley on December 3, 2002, and his second start v Deportivo on March 18. Has made 5 first-team appearances for Man Utd (2 starts).

**19 RICARDO** 30.12.71
The goalkeeper was signed from Real Valladolid for £1.5m on August 30 2002. Was a member of Spain's 2002 World Cup squad but did not make an appearance. Joined Valladolid from Atletico Madrid in 1998. Was an ever present as Valladolid finished 12th in Spain's Primera Liga in 2001-02; only Athletic Bilbao conceded more goals that season (66 compared to Valladolid's 58). Won his first cap for Spain as a sub in the 1-0 friendly win v Mexico in November 2001. Made his United debut as a sub v Maccabi Haifa on September 18, 2002, and made his full debut at Maccabi Haifa on October 29, 2002, conceding 3 goals and conceding a penalty. Has given away a penalty in 3 of his 5 United appearances. Made his Premiership debut as a half-time sub for Barthez v Blackburn on April 19 2003 and his first act was to concede a penalty (he saved it from Dunn).

**23 KIERAN RICHARDSON** 21.10.84
The London-born midfielder made his debut as sub for Veron in the 3-2 Champions League win v Olympiakos on October 23, 2002 (was on for 3 minutes), and made his full debut at Maccabi Haifa on October 29, 2002. Scored his first senior goal in the 2-0 Worthington Cup win v Leicester on November 5, 2002. Has scored 1 goal in 9 games for Man Utd. Scored in both legs of the FA Youth Cup semi-final last season – a 1-1 draw at Charlton and a 2-0 home win on April 9. Also scored in 1st leg of final v Middlesbrough (Man Utd went on to win it).

**7 CRISTIANO RONALDO** 05.02.85
Is the first Portuguese player to sign for Man Utd. He joined from Sporting Lisbon in a 5-year deal worth a total of £12.24m on August 12, 2003. An 18-year-old striker, he can play anywhere across the forward line. Impressed in Sporting's 3-1 pre-season win

v Man Utd on August 6 in a friendly to mark the opening of their new home stadium. Finished 3rd in the Portuguese League with Sporting last season. Helped Portugal U20's win the 2003 Toulon Tournament in June and is also an U21 international; he scored in the 4-2 European Championship qualifier win v England on March 28, 2003.

**18 PAUL SCHOLES** 16.11.74
Has now won 6 Premiership winners medals. In July 2001 he signed a new contract with the club keeping him at Old Trafford until June 2006. Has 57 England caps scoring 13 goals. Scored 20 goals last season - his best ever tally for Man Utd. Has scored 101 goals in 376 games for Man Utd. Scored in 6 consecutive games in January 2003. Scored 6 goals in United's final 6 Premiership games last season. The only United player included in the 2003 PFA Premiership Team of the Year.

**27 MIKAEL SILVESTRE** 09.08.77
Has won 3 Premiership winners medals with Utd. Scored v Leeds on March 5 – his first Premiership goal since a 2-0 home win v Leicester on March 17, 2001. Has made 191 appearances for United, scoring 4 goals. Cost £4m from Inter Milan in September 1999. A French international he has made 22 appearances for his national side and scored 2 goals. Agreed a new contract in December 2002 that will keep him at the club until at least 2007. Scored United's first goal of this season in the 1-1 Community Shield draw with Arsenal.

**20 OLE GUNNAR SOLSKJAER** 26.02.73
Has won 5 Premiership winners medals with United. Scored 25 goals in 47 appearances in 2001-02 – his best scoring season since arriving at Old Trafford from Molde in July 1996. Has scored 114 goals in 311 games, 121 of which have been as a sub for Man Utd. Has scored 16 goals in the last 28 Premiership away games. A Norwegian international he has won 58 caps and scored 21 goals.

**17 MICHAEL STEWART** 26.02.81
Made his debut as a sub in the League Cup 3rd round tie at Watford in October 2000. Has made 14 appearances for Man Utd without scoring. Signed a new 4-year contract in March 2002. Made his senior Scotland debut as a sub v Nigeria on April 17, 2002. Went on a season-long loan to Forest in July 2003.

**39 PAUL TIERNEY** 15.09.82
A full-back who was born in nearby Salford. Was an unused sub for the first 4 games of last season. Yet to make his first-team debut for Man Utd. He started his three-year scholarship in July 1999 and turned professional 12 months later. Rep of Ireland U-21 international who has made 22 appearances and scored 1 goal for his country.

**43 MADS TIMM** 31.10.84
A Danish-born attacking midfielder or striker who made his first-team debut as a sub in the Champions League game at Maccabi Haifa on October 29, 2002. He arrived at

United in July 2001. He has represented his country at youth level. He was a member of the United side that won the FA Youth Cup last season.

**10 RUUD VAN NISTELROOY** 01.07.76
Officially completed his then-club record £19m move from PSV Eindhoven on July 1, 2001, almost exactly 12 months to the day after his original move to Old Trafford had collapsed due to a knee injury. Voted 2002 PFA Player of the Year, the Dutch international has been capped 25 times and scored 11 goals. Scored 36 goals (7 pens) in 49 in 2001-02, becoming the first Utd player to score 30 goals in all comps in a season since Brian McClair in 1987-88. Set a new Premiership record of scoring in 8 successive games between December 12, 2001 and January 19, 2002 of last season. Top scorer in the CL in the last 2 seasons (scored a competition-record 12 last season). Has scored 22 goals in 23 Champions League games for Man Utd. Scored 43 goals in his last 41 appearances at Old Trafford. Has scored 80 goals (19 pens) in 102 games for Man Utd.

**30 BEN WILLIAMS** 27.08.82
A goalkeeper who was an unused sub in the opening 5 games of last season. Is a former England Schoolboy international. Yet to make his first-team debut for Man Utd. Manchester-born. He signed as a trainee in August 1999. He made the step up to the reserves in 2001-02 as cover and competition for Carroll and Van der Gouw. Went on a 1-month loan at Coventry in November 2002, but didn't play for the Sky Blues. Was also on-loan at Chesterfield last season (made 14 appearances).

# PANATHINAIKOS FC

**The Greek club won their 18th title in 1996 but haven't captured the title since. They have been challengers but ultimately have not been able to stop Olympiakos' current run of seven straight championships – they have been second on four occasions, and third three times. In 2002-03, the club lost to their rivals only on goal difference. There has been much English influence through the years at Panathinaikos - the club was created from an English-organised team called Panhellenic. The club's trainers have included Sir Alf Ramsey, Ronnie Allen and Burnley's Les Shannon. Panathinaikos have missed out on Europe's top prize - their best effort was at Wembley in 1971, when they reached the European Cup final, only to lose to Ajax 2-0. The side was coached by Ferenc Puskas - still the only Greek team to reach a European final.**

## COACH

**ITZHAK SHUM** 01.09.45
Former Israeli international played for 22 years notching up 78 caps and scoring 9 goals.

Began coaching career at Kfar-Sabo, becoming boss of the Israel Olympic Team 1992-2000. Moved onto Maccabi Haifa in 2002 before taking up his current appointment in July 2003 where he hopes to lead the Athens outfit to their first league title since 1996.

## REACTION TO DRAW

**"I love playing against Manchester United ... everyone wants to do that. It's going to be a big game and I cannot forget the match at Old Trafford last year with Maccabi Haifa. All opponents are strong teams but we have to win points if we want to go further in the competition."** ***Itzhak Shum***

## SQUAD

**6 AGGELOS BASINAS** 07.08.72
The Croatian forward was the top scorer while playing for Dinamo Zagreb in his national league in 1992/93 (22) and then again in 1993/94 (29) before undergoing brain surgery after signing for Padova Calcio. He left to join Valencia where he played just one game (6 mins) during the Spanish outfit's run to the Champions League 1999/2000 final. Joined Panathinaikos in June 2000 and has since played 19 Champions League games and scored 2 goals. Has been capped 52 times for his country and scored 15 goals. He played all 7 games in the 1998 FIFA World Cup when his country came third.

**26 KOSTAS CHALKIAS** 30.05.74
The Greek keeper returned to the club in July 2003 after 2 seasons with Iraklis FC. A graduate from the Panathinaikos academy he was in the first team squad from 1995-2001 but was loaned out three times to GC Apollon. He played 4 Champions League games in 2000/01. Chalkias has won 4 international caps.

**10 JOEL EPALLE** 20.02.78
The Cameroon forward joined from Aris FC in July 2003. He registered with Panathinaikos FC in 1997/98 but has been playing for 3 other Greek clubs on loan. He has won 29 caps for his country and featured in the Cameroon squad at 2003 FIFA Confederations Cup, where he played v USA. He also was in the Cameroon squad at 2002 FIFA World Cup but failed to play a game.

**30 PANAGIOTIS FYSSAS** 12.06.73
Joined in January 1999 from neighbouring Athens club, Panionios GS. Was at Panionios GC from 1990-99 playing 117 Division 1 games (9 goals) and 34 games (no goals) in Division 2. The Greek defender has played 23 Champions League games in the two seasons 2000-02. He won 1st cap on 18.11.1998 v Albania and now has 21 caps to his name.

**21 XENOFONTAS GITAS** 22.06.79
The Greek midfielder made his debut for PAS Iannina in 1997 when the club were in

3rd division. He eventually helped them into the first division. The former Greek U21 international midfielder then signed for Panathanaikos in January 2003.

**8 GIANNIS GOUMAS** 24.05.75
Graduated from the club's youth academy to the first team squad in 1995. Has won championship medals in 1994/95 when he played 2 games and 1995/96 when he played 8 games. Has played 26 games and scored 3 goals in the previous 4 Champions League competitions. Has won 20 caps since receiving his first v Finland on 03.02.99.

**2 RENE HENRIKSEN** 27.08.69
The Danish defender moved to Panathinaikos in 1999 after playing 347 games and 14 goals for AB Kobenhavn in 10 years for the club. Has played 24 Champions League games (no goals) for the club in 2 seasons 2000-02. He won his first international cap on 25.03.98 v Scotland and played all 3 games at EURO2000 as well as all 4 games at the 2002 FIFA World Cup. In total he has 53 caps, playing in 48 of the last 49 internationals.

**27 PANTELIS KONSTADINIDIS** 16.08.75
The Greek international midfielder with 19 caps signed for the club in July 2002. Having been released by AEK without a league game, he played for Kavala FC (1994-96), GC Apollon (1996-98) and was at PAOK from 1998.

**19 MICHALIS KONSTADINOU** 19.02.78
Aged just 19 years old, Konstadinous was Cypriot league top scorer in 1996/97 with 17 goals for Paralimni FC. He then joined the Greek team Iraklis FC who he played for 1997-2001, appearing in 119 league games and scoring 60 goals. He joined Panathinaikos in July 2001 and played all 14 games and scored 6 goals in the club's 2001/02 Champions League campaign. The Cypriot striker won his first cap in 1997 v Latvia and now has 37 caps and has scored 17 goals for his country.

**33 STEFANOS KOTSOLIS** 05.06.79
Elevated from the club's youth academy to first team squad in 1997 aged 18, the Greek keeper made his debut in 1998/99 season but only played one league game in each of first 4 seasons 1998-2002. Has played for Greece at U21 level.

**16 SOTIRIS KYRGIAKOS** 03.07.79
A graduate from the club's youth academy, the Greek defender played for two other teams on loan (Agios Nikoloas and OFI Crete) before returning in 2001. He played in 12 Champions League games in 2001/02. An international at youth and U21 level, he is now a full international and has received 11 caps since his first senior team debut v Romania on 21.08.02.

# GROUP E
## PANATHINAIKOS FC

**4 SILVIO MARIC** 20.03.75
The Croatian forward joined the Greek side in June 2003. Prior to the move he played for NK Croatia/Dinamo from 1992-98 before joining Newcastle United for 23 league games where he failed to score. After the disappointing period in the English Premiership he moved on to FC Porto in 2001 before returning back toNK Croatia/Dinamo between 2001-2003. He won championship medals with NK Croatia/Dinamo in 1993, 1996, 1997, 1998 and 2003 and played 6 Champions League games for them in 1998/9. The Croatian has won 19 international caps.

**35 JAN MICHAELSEN** 28.11.70
Born in France when father Allan, who also played for Denmark, was playing for FC Nantes-Atlantique. The Danish midfielder played 141 games (20 games) for former club AB Kobenhavn before moving to Panathinaikos in July 2001. He since played 10 UCL games (no goals) for the club in 2001/02. Has 18 international caps and was in 2002 FIFA World Cup squad but did not play in finals.

**3 NASIEF MORRIS** 16.04.81
The young South African defender first played for Santos before moving to Aris FC. The former U21 international played there for two seasons before signing in July 2003 for Panathinaikos.

**20 MARKUS MUNCH** 07.09.72
The German midfielder played 49 games for FC Bayern (1990-97) & 60 league games (6 goals) for Besiktas JK (1999-2001) before joining Borussia Monchengladbach, the team he joined Panathinaikos from. Munch signed in a swap deal with Jonas Kolkka in July 2003. He got his first taste of Champions League when he played all 6 group games for Besiktas JK in 2000/01 (no goals).

**1 ANTONIS NIKOPOLIDIS** 14.10.71
The Greek goalkeeper joined the club from Anagennisi Arta in 1989 at the age of 18 in 1989. He then had to wait until 1995 for his first team debut and was not first choice until two years later. Has played 23 games in the Champions League since 2000 including all 14 games in 2001/02

**23 EMMANUEL OLISADEBE** 22.12.78
Nigerian born but brought up in Poland, the striker joined Panathinaikos during 2000/01 winter break. Previously he played for KP Polonia from 1997 before being spotted by former Poland national coach Jerzy Engel in Nigeria. He gained Polish citizenship in 2000 and scored 2 goals in 10 Champions League appearances in 2001/02 season. Olisadebe received his first cap on 16.08.00 v Romania and has since scored 11 goals in 24 internationals. He played all 3 games at 2002 FIFA World Cup, scoring in final game v USA.

# GROUP E
## PANATHINAIKOS FC

**11 DIMITRIS PAPADOPOULOS** 20.09.81
The Greek forward joined in July 2003 from Burnley FC after 18 months in England. He played 40 games for Burnley FC in 2002/03, 32 of which were as a sub but still managed to score 6 goals. A former U21 international, the Kazakhstan born player gained his first full cap v Ireland on 20.11.02.

**18 LUCIAN SANMARTEAN** 13.03.80
The Romanian midfielder joined the club in July 2003 from FC Gloria where he had featured in the first team squad from 1998-2003. Since progressing from the national U21 squad, he has won 3 caps for his country.

**22 MILTIADIS SAPANIS** 28.01.76
The former U18 & U21 Greek midfield international played 72 league games and scored 12 goals for Paniliakos between 1997-2001 before signing for Panathinaikos in June 2001.

**5 GIORGOS SEITARIDIS** 04.06.81
The Greek international has won 10 caps for his country. He signed in January 2001 after over 2 seasons with PAS Iannina. He has scored one goal in the nine Champions League games played.

**31 ALEXANDROS TZORVAS** 12.08.82
Yet to start a Champions League match this 21-year-old goalkeeper is a product of the Panathinaikos Youth Academy. Recently spent lengthy loan spell at Agios Nikolas. Highly regarded but unlikely to make an impact this season.

**9 KRZYSZTOF WARZYCHA** 17.11.64
The forward joined the club in 1989 from the Polish team KS Ruch Chorzow. He scored 36 goals in 45 between games for them between 1987-89 before leaving for Greece. He was also Polish league top scorer in 1987/88 with 24 goals. He now has dual nationality since being granted Greek citizenship in 1998. He is the club's highest ever goal scorer, and won 4 championship medals in 1990, 1991, 1995, 1996. He has been the Greek league top scorer three times in 1993/94 (24), 1994/95 (29) and 1997/98 (32). In 4 previous Champions League campaigns he has played 26 games and scored 8 goals. Wazycha has scored 9 goals in 50 international games for Poland.

**14 RAIMONDAS ZUTAUTAS** 04.09.72
On leaving Lithuania, the midfielder played for FC Alania Vladikavkaz (1996-99) before signing for Maccabi Haifa (1999-2003). He joined Panathinaikos in July 2003 to once again team up with coach Yitzhak Shum. Played 4 Champions League games in 2002/03 for Maccabi Haifa and managed a goal against Manchester United on 29.10.02. Has won 41 international caps for his country.

# GLASGOW RANGERS FC

**Last season Glasgow Rangers won their 50th league title (a world record), and their first since 1999-00. They also achieved the 'treble' for the seventh time. They have won 105 major trophies - 50 league titles, 31 Scottish Cups, 23 Scottish League Cups and one Cup Winners' Cup, beating Dynamo Moscow 3-2 in the 1972 final.**

## COACH

**ALEX MCLEISH** 21.01.59
Joined Rangers as manager in Dec 2001, guiding them in the first season to the Scottish FA and League Cup Double. Last season went one better adding the Scottish League title. Will now join Europe's elite in Man Utd's group. Widely tipped as possible successor to Sir Alex. Extensive career in Scotland. Played 18 years for Aberdeen securing a Cup Winners Cup medal under Fergie in 1983. Began managerial career as player boss of Motherwell moving onto Hibs in 1998. Considered a young coach who will go far.

## REACTION TO DRAW

**"It's the Scottish champions versus the English champions and so is a mini play-off for the British title. But our fans will relish the challenge of going abroad to Greece and Germany – and even further abroad to Manchester. This will be a bigger game than Liverpool v Celtic last season in terms of interest and emotion. There will be a lot of noise in the build-up but I think all British clubs are good friends. I would settle for second place in the group as long as we beat United."** ***Chairman John McClelland***

## SQUAD

**23 MIKEL ARTETA** 26.03.82
Signed from Barcelona for £5.8m in July 2002. Spanish striker who spent one-and-a-half seasons on-loan at Paris St Germain before joining Rangers. Scored only five goals for Rangers last season (four in Scottish Premier League & one in Scottish Cup). Arteta has scored 11 goals in 41 games for Rangers – he played four games (no goals) for PSG in the 2000-01 Champions League and played for PSG against Rangers in 2001-02 UEFA Cup.

**7 SHOTA ARVELADZE** 22.02.73
Georgian international signed from Ajax for £2m in September 2001. Scored 16 goals last season (15 in SPL and one in Scottish Cup). Was the third top scorer last season. Scored 17 goals in 2001-02 and a total of 35 goals in 73 games for Rangers. Played three games (no goals) for Ajax in the 1998-99 Champions League.

# GROUP E
## GLASGOW RANGERS

**18 MICHAEL BALL** 02.10.79
Defender signed from Everton for £6.5m in August 2001. One cap for England (in Eriksson's first game in charge, against Spain in February 2001). Ball missed the whole of last season with a serious knee injury. Played in the opening five games of this season – his first Rangers appearances since December 2001. Scored one goal in 16 games for Rangers, in the UEFA Cup v Dynamo Moscow in October 2001. He will be making his Champions League debut this season.

**25 HENNING BERG** 01.09.69
Berg joined the club in August 2003. He was a free agent after being released by Blackburn in the summer and has signed a one-year contract with the club. He spent almost three years at Blackburn, having joined them from Manchester United for £1.75m in December 2000 after a loan spell. Berg made 103 appearances for Man Utd, scoring three goals in just over three years. Berg has got three English Premier League title medals, in 1995 with Blackburn and in 1999 and 2000 with Man Utd. He scored seven goals in 296 games for Rovers (including both spells) and one goal in 19 appearances for Blackburn last season. Berg missed more than three months of last season after rupturing an Achilles at the end of October 2002. In January 2003 he turned down the chance to become the player/manager of Brann Bergen although he had announced that he would return to Norway when his Blackburn contract expired at the end of last season. However, he decided to move to Scotland. A Norwegian international with 96 caps and international goals, Berg won his 96th cap v Scotland on August 20. He has played 29 Champions League games in his career (one goal). Played for Blackburn in the 1995-96 season, and then three seasons for Man Utd. However, he wasn't part of the squad that won the Cup in 1999.

**30 CHRIS BURKE** 02.12.83
A Glasgow-born midfielder who has come up through the ranks at Ibrox. Burke made his first-team debut as a sub v Kilmarnock in March 2002, scoring in a 5-0 win. Made his full debut at Dunfermline in May 2002. He then made his third first-team appearance as a sub v Hibernian on August 23, scoring in a 5-2 win. So, he has scored two goals in three games for Rangers. Burke will be making his Champions League debut this season.

**20 NUNO CAPUCHO** 21.02.72
Portuguese international striker signed from Porto for £670,000 in June 2003. He's signed a two-year contract. Capucho played six seasons at Porto. He was from the Vitoria Guimaraes club originally, and was a leading figure in Porto's 1998 and 1999 championship wins. Nuno was a member of the 1991 Junior World Cup winning team, whom Sporting amazingly let go after a spell from 1992 to 1995. He then rediscovered his form with Guimaraes, won his first caps, and moved to Porto. He is often the sub for Figo in the national set up, and made one sub appearance in the 2002 World Cup (v Poland). He was also a member of Portugal's Euro 2000 squad, where they reached the semi-finals. Capucho scored at Dundee United on August 31 – his first goal for

Rangers. He played in Porto's UEFA Cup final win over Celtic last season. Last season Porto won the League and Cup double, as well as the UEFA Cup. He didn't play too much for Porto last season as Deco was the main man up front. This led to his decision to leave and sign for Rangers. Capucho has scored two goals in 35 Champions League games for Porto in four seasons (1997-98, 1998-99, 1999-00 and 2001-02).

**14 RONALD DE BOER** 15.05.70
Veteran Dutch international – the twin brother of Frank de Boer - signed from Barcelona for £4.5m in August 2000. De Boer was top scorer last season with 20 goals (16 in Scottish Premier League, one in Scottish Cup, one in CIS Cup and two in UEFA Cup). In total, he's scored 38 goals in 113 games for Rangers. De Boer has won 67 caps and scored 13 goals for Holland. Played at Euro 2000, but not in the semi-final defeat on penalties to Italy. Also played at USA 94, Euro 96 and at France 98. He's played 54 Champions League games in his career (five goals), including six games for Rangers (one goal) in the 2000-01 season. Won Champions League with Ajax in 1995 (was also a runner-up with them in 1996). Won five Dutch league titles and two Dutch Cups with Ajax, and well as the 1995 World Club Cup. Was Dutch Player of the Year for 1994 and 1996.

**4 EMERSON** 12.04.72
Brazilian midfielder signed from Atletico Madrid on August 29, 2003. It was thought he was off to Wolves, but in the end the deal fell through. Emerson spent one-and-a-half seasons at Middlesbrough. He was a member of their side that lost the 1997 FA Cup and League Cup finals, and was relegated from the Premiership all in the same season. He's played in the Champions League for both FC Porto and Deportivo. He reached the quarter-final with Deportivo in 2000-01 (lost to Leeds) and has scored two goals in 23 Champions League games in his career. Emerson spent only a season at Atletico and scored two goals in 29 Primera Liga games for them last season. Made his Rangers debut as a sub at Dundee United on August 31.

**27 STEPHEN HUGHES** 14.11.82
Motherwell-born midfielder who has come up through the youth ranks at Ibrox. Has scored two goals in 46 games for Rangers; 21 of those 46 games have been as a sub. Hughes scored one goal (at Hearts on December 1, 2002) in 16 games last season. His other goal for Rangers came in a 2-2 draw v Hibs in August 2001. Current Scotland Under-21 international, who won seven Under-21 caps last season. Will be making his Champions League debut this season.

**15 ZURA KHIZANISHVILI** 06.11.81
Georgian international defender signed from Dundee in June 2003. He's signed a two-year contract. Khizanishvili was at Dundee for just over two years. The former Lokomotiv Tbilisi player played 25 games for Dundee last season (no goals) and was sent off at home to Rangers in November 2002. He has yet to score a goal in Scottish club football. Will be making his Champions League debut this season.

# GROUP E
## GLASGOW RANGERS

**1 STEFAN KLOS** 16.08.71
German goalkeeper signed from Borussia Dortmund for £700,000 in December 1998. Has never been capped at senior international level. Klos has now played 220 games for Rangers. He's also played 36 Champions League games in his career (32 for Dortmund, and four for Rangers, in the 2000-01 season). Klos was a member of Dortmund's 1997 Champions League winning side and played for Dortmund v Rangers in the 1995-96 Champions League.

**26 PETER LOVENKRANDS** 29.01.80
Danish international striker (eight caps, no goals) signed from AB Copenhagen for £1.3m in June 2000. He made one sub appearance for Denmark at the 2002 World Cup (v Senegal). Lovenkrands has scored 21 goals in 78 games for Rangers including 12 goals last season (nine in Scottish Premier League, one in Scottish Cup and two in CIS Cup). He scored in the CIS Cup final v Celtic. Didn't play in Rangers' 2000-01 Champions League campaign, so he'll be making his Champions League debut this season.

**12 ROBERT MALCOLM** 12.11.80
Glasgow-born defender who has come up through the youth ranks at Ibrox. Malcolm has scored two goals in 58 games for Rangers. He made his Rangers debut over three years ago (back in April 2000). He scored one goal in 34 appearances for Rangers last season – by far his most successful term to date at the club. He last scored on November 2, 2002 (at Dundee). The former Scotland Under-21 international (one cap) will be making his Champions League debut this season.

**22 ALLAN MCGREGOR** 31.01.82
Current back-up goalkeeper to Klos, McGregor has come up through the youth ranks at Ibrox. He's made three appearances for Rangers, all in the 2001-02 season. His last appearance was back in May 2002, in a 1-1 draw at Dunfermline - he's conceded only one goal in his three games.

**10 MICHAEL MOLS** 17.12.70
Dutch international striker signed from FC Utrecht for £4m in July 1999 – Mols has six caps without scoring for Holland. Has scored 40 goals in 107 games for Rangers. He missed most of his first season at the club after suffering a cruciate knee injury in the Champions League at Bayern Munich in November 1999. It put him out of action for 10 months. Mols was sent off in a Champions League qualifier v Fenerbahce in August 2001. Last season he scored 14 goals (13 in Scottish Premier League and one in Scottish Cup). He's scored four goals in ten Champions League appearances for Rangers.

**3 CRAIG MOORE** 12.12.75
Now in his second spell at the club – he was previously there from 1993 to 1998. Then had a six-month spell at Crystal Palace before rejoining Rangers in April 1999. Moore is an Australian international who played in their 3-1 win over England at Upton Park in

February 2003. He hasn't scored since January 25 (in Scottish Cup at Arbroath) but hit a total of four goals last season. He's scored one goal (v Valencia in October 1999) in 11 Champions League games for Rangers during three seasons of Champions League football (1995-96, 1996-97 and 1999-00).

**8 CHRISTIAN NERLINGER** 21.03.73
Former German international midfielder signed from Borussia Dortmund for £1.8m in June 2001. Six caps, no goals for Germany and last capped in 1999. Nerlinger has hit four goals in only 18 games for the club since joining (he has been tormented by many injuries). He last scored for Rangers back in March 2002 (two in the Scottish Cup v Partick). Last season he played only three times. He's scored three goals in 23 Champions League games in his career (three goals in 17 games for Munich and no goals in six games for Dortmund). Reached the Champions League semi-final v Bayern Munich in 1994-95 (lost to Ajax).

**9 EGIL OSTENSTAD** 02.01.72
Signed on a free transfer in August 2003, the Norwegian international striker had joined Blackburn from Southampton in August 1999 as part of the deal that saw Kevin Davies move in the opposite direction. He didn't score in 2001-02 (made just seven appearances) but scored twice last season. However, he hasn't scored since October 6, 2002 (at home to Spurs). Now he's gone 20 club games without a goal. Ostenstad scored 13 goals in 81 games for Rovers, and 46 goals total in English football. He injured knee ligaments in the 1-0 win v Man City on March 1 and hasn't played since. Scored 2 goals in 25 appearances for Rovers last season. Will be making his Champions League debut this season.

**2 FERNANDO RICKSEN** 27.07.76
Dutch international defender signed from AZ Alkmaar for £3.75m in July 2000. Ricksen has nine goals in 136 games for Rangers. Capped 12 times by Holland, he made his international debut v Spain in November 2000 and was capped eight times last season. He won the Dutch Second Division title with Fortuna Sittard in 1995 and with AZ Alkmaar in 1998. He hasn't scored since December 1, 2002 (two in a 4-0 win at Hearts). Was sent off at home to Dundee United on December 14, 2002. Was also sent off in a UEFA Cup tie v PSG in November 2001, and at Celtic twice (in the Scottish Premier League in February 2001 and in April 2002). So he's been sent off four times in his Rangers career. Ricksen has played in 46 of Rangers' 50 games last season, including one Champions League game for Rangers in the 2000-01 season.

**21 MAURICE ROSS** 03.02.81
The Scottish international defender has come up through the youth ranks at Ibrox. He won his 11th Scottish cap v Norway on August 20 - all of his caps has come under Berti Vogts, since his debut v South Korea in May 2002. Ross has scored one goal in 60 games for Rangers. That goal was in a 2-0 win at Livingston in September 2002. He'll be making his Champions League debut this season.

**19 STEVEN THOMPSON** 14.10.78
A Scottish international striker who joined the club from Dundee United in January 2003. Thompson has scored two goals in 16 games for Rangers. He's started only one of those 16 games (v Motherwell on March 19). He hit nine goals for Dundee United last season before his move. In total he's won ten caps (two goals) for Scotland, scoring v Hong Kong in May 2002 and v Canada in October 2002. He made his debut in Berti Vogts' first game in charge (in a 5-0 defeat in France in March 2002).

**16 PAOLO VANOLI** 12.08.72
Italian international left-back signed from Bologna on a free transfer in August 2003. He's signed a two-year contract, and has effectively replaced Arthur Numan. His contract at Bologna had expired and he moved on a Bosman. Has played in Europe for Parma against Rangers (in a Champions League qualifier in 1999 – Rangers won 2-1 on aggregate). Vanoli was previously with Parma and Fiorentina. He was hardly a regular at Bologna last season. He featured in only six Serie A games last term. He played for Italy in two Euro 2000 warm-up games, scoring in a friendly at home to Belgium in November 1999.

# VFB STUTTGART

**Stuttgart finished as runners up to Bayern in 2002-03. In the last few seasons, Stuttgart have struggled to keep afloat but the current side – an interesting blend of youth and experience - has shown marked improvement. After two fourth place finishes in 1997 and 1998, Stuttgart were in relegation trouble in 1999 and 2001. In 2000-01 they finished one place from the drop but returned to eighth place in 2001-02. Stuttgart were the 1992 champions, the fourth time they had won the title after 1950, 1952 and 1984. In 1997 they won the DFB Cup for the third time, but for the first time in 41 years. They beat the rank outsiders Energie Cottbus (then from Division 3) 2-0 in the final. This is Stuttgart's first ever time in the Champions League. Stuttgart were last remembered in major European thoughts as the team that lost to Chelsea 1-0 in the 1998 Cup Winners' Cup final in Stockholm. Prior to that they had amazingly lost to Leeds in the first round of the 1992-3 European Cup. Having won the tie 3-0 and 1-4 on away goals, they found that they had fielded one too many foreigners (teams were only allowed three at one time in those days) and had to play a replay. Leeds won that tie 2-1 in Barcelona, and coach Christoph Daum never lived down his error.**

## COACH

**FELIX MAGATH** 26.07.53
Magath, the son of a German mother and a Puerto Rican father, has revitalised the club

by adopting a youth policy. Has agreed another two-year deal in summer 2003 after being linked to Schalke and Austria Vienna. Magath has been at Stuttgart since February 2001 after beginning his coaching career in 1989. He coached Saarbrucken, Bayer Uerdingen, Hamburg, Nurnberg, Werder Bremen and Eintracht Frankfurt without conspicuous success. Magath was a fine midfield player with Hamburg in the Keegan era – he played in the Hamburg side that won the 1983 European Cup and 1977 Cup Winners' Cup, and won 43 caps for Germany from 1977-86. He played in the Hamburg team that lost to Forest in the 1980 European Cup final and played in 1982 World Cup semi-final and the 1986 World Cup final (lost to Argentina). Magath won three Bundesliga titles, all with Hamburg, and played 305 games, scoring 50 goals.

## REACTION TO DRAW

**"I'm really pleased Felix Magath and his young team have been given the chance to compete against some good clubs. I'm a real fan of British football so I'm particularly looking forward to meeting Manchester United and Glasgow Rangers. I'm sure our team is up to the job and perhaps we'll even deliver a couple of surprises,"** ***President Erwin Staudt***

## SQUAD

**11 IOANNIS AMANATIDIS** 03.12.81
Another huge talent who has come through last season to full international honours (2 caps so far). Amanatidis is a Greek national who made his debut in a round of November 2002 friendlies, but the Germans are also keen. He had always played in Germany, first for a junior club, SC Stuttgart, then for the VFB Stuttgart club, and made real progress last season on loan at Division 2 club Gruether Furth. This is his second Bundesliga season.

**10 KRASMIR BALAKOV** 29.03.66
The Bulgarian with 91 caps is now in his 21st season of senior football in Bulgaria with Etar, Portugal with Sporting and Stuttgart – he debuted in the Bulgarian top flight in 1982. Voted in the past as the best overseas player in the Bundesliga, he is the free-kick expert and playmaker. Balakov retired internationally after the 1998 World Cup - he was one of the Bulgarian stars of the semi-final team in 1994 and was in many critics 'team of the tournament'. In 1994 he played as left-sided midfielder, he plays a more central role these days. It's his eighth season at the club, signed from Sporting Lisbon, and he has maintained a good scoring record for a midfielder.

**31 DIEGO BENAGLIO** 08.09.83
The Swiss keeper is in his second season at Stuttgart but has yet to play in the Bundesliga. Benaglio arrived from Grasshoppers in summer 2002 and is a Swiss youth international.

# GROUP E
## VFB STUTTGART

**5 MARCELO BORDON** 07.01.76
Brazilian central defender came to Stuttgart in January 1999 from top Brazilian club Sao Paulo for £3.5 million and this is his fifth season in Germany. Recently passed the 100 Bundesliga games mark.

**35 SERGE BRANCO** 11.10.80
The Cameroon player (16 caps) was with Eintracht Frankfurt last season but left on a free transfer. Branco is an Olympic gold medallist after playing in the Sydney 2000 final v Spain which was won on penalties. Branco joined Eintracht in summer 2000 from another Eintracht, the Braunschweig club in Division 2 for just £300,000. Originally came from Cameroon Division 1 club Boufang.

**16 BRADLEY CARNELL** 22.01.77
The South African midfielder with 25 caps is in his fifth season with the club - he came from the famous Soweto club Kaiser Chiefs in 1998. Carnell is approaching 100 games in Stuttgart colours. He played all three games for SA in the 2002 World Cup.

**18 CAUCAU** 27.03.81
Caucau signed in summer 2003 from Nurnberg on a free transfer. He played 44 Bundesliga games for Nurnberg (scoring eight goals). He then moved to Stuttgart once Nurnberg were relegated.

**14 EMMANUEL CENTURION** 25.08.82
Centurion signed for Stuttgart in summer 2003 from Argentine club Velez Sarsfield. He'd spent two seasons in the Velez first team (2001-03) in midfield after coming through their youth academy.

**29 STEFFAN DANGELMAYR** 09.09.78
Dangelmayr has been with the club since the age of 11 in 1989 and is another plucked from the reserve pool by coach Magath. He made his first team debut in 2003. He had played just 5 first team games before the 2003-04 season.

**18 SEAN DUNDEE** 07.12.72
A Durban-born South African forward bought in summer 1999 for £1.5 million from Liverpool without really kicking a ball for them. Dundee cost Liverpool £2 million the previous summer from Karlsruhe, who were relegated from the Bundesliga. Previously played for neighbours Stuttgart Kickers. In his first spell in Germany Dundee had an excellent return of 36 goals in 85 games -which attracted Liverpool - he now has 55 goals in 153 games.

**21 THOMAS ERNST** 23.12.67
The 35-year-old keeper has been a squad player wherever he has played. Ernst played in the Bundesliga back in 1987 for Eintracht Frankfurt, then had only four more games

in seven seasons, so left for Bochum where only one of his six seasons was as first choice. This is his third season now at Stuttgart.

**9 ION GANEA** 19.08.73
The 35-cap Romanian star was the player who took the last minute penalty to send England out of Euro2000 – he'd come on as a sub 15 mins earlier. Ganea joined Stuttgart in summer 1999 from Rapid Bucharest for £1.3 million, he has scored 15 goals for Romania though his Bundesliga goals are scarcer. Was the Romanian League top scorer with 28 goals in his last season in 1998-9 and his club won the championship. Ganea also played in a couple of Romanian Division 1 clubs, Barsov, Universitatea Craiova and Gloria Bistrita before his breakthrough season with Rapid.

**12 HEIKO GERBER** 11.07.72
Gerber moved from relegated Nurnberg in summer 1999 to Stuttgart for £500,000. From the old GDR, Gerber joined Nurnberg for £150,000 in summer 1998 from Arminia Bielefeld. This is his fifth season with Stuttgart in midfield.

**16 HORST HELDT** 09.12.69
Heldt came from Eintracht Frankfurt in January 2003 on a free after a short spell in Austria with Sturm Graz. He joined Eintracht from 1860 Munich in summer 1999 for just £1 million, which seemed a bargain as he was in the national squad at the start of the 1999-2000 season. A tenacious and consistent midfielder, twice capped, he has played over 200 Bundesliga games for Cologne and 1860. Heldt was with Cologne for several seasons, then switched to 1860 in 1995 and had four seasons with the Munich club.

**23 DIRK HEINEN** 03.12.70
Heinen is a good Bundesliga keeper but is, as yet, uncapped. He has made eight Champions League appearances. The keeper returned to Germany in summer 2003 from Turkish club Denizlispor, who had a fine run in last season's UEFA Cup. He was signed by the Turks in summer 2002 on a free transfer from Eintracht Frankfurt, who were then under the control of Felix Magath. Heinen played over 150 Bundesliga games for Bayer Leverkusen and in 2000 moved to Einracht Frankfurt. He was at Leverkusen from 1992-2000.

**1 TIMO HILDEBRAND** 05.04.79
Currently first choice in the side when fit, Hildebrand was the recent German U21 international keeper. The goalie has been in the youth set up at Stuttgart since the age of 15 and deputised for Austrian national keeper Franz Wohlfarht in 1999-2000 season; he's now number one at Stuttgart as Wohlfahrt went back to FK Austria Vienna. This is his fourth season as first choice in between the Stuttgart sticks.

**2 ANDREAS HINKEL** 26.03.82
First capped in spring 2003, Hinkel has three caps for Germany. The right-back has

already played some 70 Bundesliga games. Has been with the club since the age of 10 and is now enjoying his fifth season in the first team squad.

**15 ALIAKSANDR HLEB** 01.05.81
Another young find, Hleb is a Belarus international with 13 caps. The 2002 Belarus Footballer of the Year and Young Player of the Year in 2001, Hleb has been awarded Man of the Match for Stuttgart in several recent games. This is his fourth season at Stuttgart, and he has just passed 50 Bundesliga games. He joined in 2000 from the Belarus champions BATE Borisov.

**22 KEVIN KURANYI** 02.03.82
Kuranyi has three caps for his country and was in the national squad for the September 2003 qualifiers for Euro 2004. The young sensation of the 2002-03 season first received recognition in the full German side for the Euro2004 qualifier v Lithuania on 29.03.03 (sub). He scored 15 Bundesliga goals and plenty of assists last season in 32 games. Made his club debut at the start of 2001-02 and played four games (scoring one goal) but then returned to the reserves. He restarted his senior career at the start of 2002-03 with fine results.

**21 PHILIPP LAHM** 11.11.83
The Bayern Munich junior has been on loan at Stuttgart since July 2003. Lahm was immediately called into the first team squad and made his Bundesliga debut in August 2003.

**4 RUI MANUEL MARQUES** 03.09.77
Marques has been in Germany since 1999 when he played in Ulm's season in the Bundesliga and played so well that he stayed after Ulm's relegation. He moved to Hertha Berlin in 2000, then almost immediately back to the region with Stuttgart, where he is in his fourth season in the first team squad. Born in Portugal, he's opted for Angola as his country, winning four caps, and was a former Benfica junior until his 1999 move to Germany.

**6 FERNANDO MEIRA** 05.06.78
First choice for Portugal since the 2002 World Cup, Meira was injured for the finals but has now reached 17 caps. This is Meira's third season with Stuttgart - he joined from Benfica in summer 2001 and has sewn up the central defensive role but can also play defensive midfield. He made the Portuguese national team in place of Jorge Costa, and made strides at Benfica after joining them from Vitoria Guimaraes.

**7 SILVIO MEISSNER** 19.01.73
A midfield ball winner in his fourth season with Stuttgart since signing from Bundesliga club, Arminia Bielefeld. He spent his career in the old GDR set up, with Chemie Halle, before Bielefeld, and is now nearing 200 Bundesliga games.

**25 MICHAEL MUTZEL** 27.09.79

Mutzel joined on a free from Eintracht Frankfurt (now Division 2) in summer 2002. He is registered as an amateur and is another known to coach Magath from his time with Eintracht where he spent three years.

**24 MICHAEL RUNDIO** 21.01.83

Current youth international - Rundio played v England in February 2003. Like Dangelmayer, he has played in 2003 since being brought through by coach Magath. He arrived in 2002 from local regional side Geislingen, and has been promoted from the reserves since the winter break in January 2003.

**17 JOCHEN SEITZ** 11.10.76

Former Hamburg SV and Unterhaching right winger in the Bundesliga - now in his third season with Stuttgart. Seitz played in the Hamburg first team in 1996-97 when coach Magath was also in charge there. Just reached 100 Bundesliga games and playing the best football of his career.

**14 THOMAS SCHNEIDER** 24.11.72

Schneider joined the club in 1983, aged 11, has played around 150 first team games, and is the longest serving player on the current Stuttgart staff. It's his seventh season as a regular in the side, though he has been a sub recently.

**20 ZVONMIR SOLDO** 02.11.67

The Croatian utility player has 61 caps. He was with the Croatian squad at the 1998 World Cup, either as defender, wing back or defensive midfield - his national coach Blazevic has him in the squad because of his versatility. He was outstanding in the team that finished third in France. Soldo then retired from internationals after the two games he played at the 2002 World Cup finals. This is his eighth season at the Stuttgart club, he joined from Croatian champions Croatia (Dinamo) Zagreb, where he had spent most of his earlier career, leaving after their 1996 league and cup double win.

**19 IMRE SZABICS** 22.03.81

The Hungarian youth international signed in summer 2003 on a free transfer from former Austrian champions Sturm. He has three full caps for his country and was in the squad for the September 2003 Euro 2004 qualifiers. Szabics has made seven Champions League appearances in 2000/1.

**13 CHRISTIAN TIFFERT** 18.02.82

A current German U21 international midfielder alongside Thomas Hitzlsperger (Aston Villa) in central midfield. This is Tiffert's fourth season in the Stuttgart first team squad – he's now passed 50 first team games, since arriving in summer 2000 from Division 2 club Tennis Borussia Berlin. Another youngster making fine progress with the club.

**8 JENS TODT** 05.01.70
Todt is currently on loan at Austrian club Sturm Graz - will stay there and sign full contract. He came from Werder Bremen in summer 1999 on a free transfer and is now out of contract. The player was capped by Germany in an excellent season with Freiburg back in 1994-5, but has not approached that form since. Played for Freiburg when they came into the Bundesliga for the first time in 1993. He then had three seasons at Bremen - after three seasons from 1993-6 in the Bundesliga with Freiburg, and now is now in his fourth season with Stuttgart, so has passed 200 career games in the Bundesliga.

**8 JURICA VRANJES** 30.01.80
The 12-cap Croatian midfielder arrived in summer 2003 from Bayer Leverkusen on a free transfer after a season or two dogged by injuries. Vranjes played twice at the 2002 World Cup finals, and is the squad for Euro2004. He originally joined Leverkusen with Marko Babic for a combined £3.5 million from the Croatian third-placed team Osijek in January 2000, and made his first team debut in spring 2000. Vranjes has played 16 Champions League games to date.

**3 TIMO WENZEL** 30.11.77
Has been with the club since 1994, and was formerly with nearby SSV Ulm. Made first team squad in 1999, and then made first team debut in 2000. This is the left-back's fourth season in the first team squad.

# GROUP F

**REAL MADRID CF**
(Spain)

**FC PORTO**
(Portugal)

**OLYMPIQUE DE MARSEILLE**
(France)

**PARTIZAN BELGRADE**
(Russia)

# REAL MADRID

**Seasoned pundit Ron Atkinson described the first hour of Real Madrid's 3-1 home win over Man Utd as "the finest hour of European club football I have ever seen". With world class players including Zidane, Figo, Raul and now Ronaldo surely retaining the trophy won in 2002 for the 9th time was a foregone conclusion. A poor display however in both legs of the semis against Juventus meant a season of disappointment. Winning the Primera Liga was neither a consolation for the fans nor enough to save Vicente del Bosque's job. The much vaunted arrival of David Beckham and equally as significant the appointment of Carlos Querioz as coach should see Los Merengues reach, at least, the final.**

## COACH

**CARLOS QUERIOZ** 01.03.53
This former Sporting Lisbon and Portuguese international entered European club management as assistant to Sir Alex at Old Trafford. Sir Alex spotted his emerging talent as coach of South Africa at the World Cup 2002. Now coach of Real Madrid he has reached the pinnacle of management within a very short time. This season will demonstrate whether his team is able to continue playing with the verve and flair expected by supporters, but coupled with the solid defence necessary to win everything in their path

## REACTION TO DRAW

**"In theory there are more difficult groups than ours, so we are moderately pleased with the draw. It has to be said, though, that Porto had a great season last time and that Partisan have showed that they are in good form by knocking out Newcastle United in the qualifiers. The Milan, Ajax, Celta Vigo and Bruges group certainly looks to be tougher than ours in theory. But we know too that as long as we play to our potential we should qualify," *Real director Emilio Butragueno.***

## SQUAD

**23 DAVID BECKHAM** 02.05.75
England captain Beckham signed for Real Madrid from Manchester United for £25m in July 2003. He became the second most expensive British player ever (after Rio Ferdinand). Beckham has won 60 caps for his country, 24 as captain, and has scored 11 goals. The midfielder started all five World Cup games (scoring once, a penalty v Argentina) and then scored in all four of his European Championship qualifiers last

season – the first player to score in four consecutive competitive England fixtures since Gary Lineker in 1986. Beckham has won six Premierships, two FA Cups and 1 European Cup with Man Utd, where he played 394 games and scored 85 goals – including 11 goals in 52 games last season. Finished runner-up to Luis Figo in the 2001 World Player of the Year awards.

**15 RAUL BRAVO** 14.04.81
The Spanish defender made nine appearances (one goal) last season and went on loan to Leeds from February to the end of last season. He played six times, but only once under Peter Reid. He has eight caps for Spain.

**30 BORJA** 14.01.81
The Orense-born defender made just one appearance as a sub last season in the Spanish Cup.

**19 ESTEBAN CAMBIASSO** 18.08.80
The Argentinian midfielder played 39 games (no goals) last season although played much less in the second half of the season. He first joined Real as a teenager from Argentinos Juniors (Maradona's first club) in 1996 - and played for the B team for two seasons. He went back to Argentina on loan to play for top clubs Independiente 1998-2000 (four goals in 39 games) and River Plate 2000-2002 (12 goals in 2001-02 season) and then returned in summer 2002.

**3 ROBERTO CARLOS** 10.02.73
The small but competitive Brazilian left-back played 55 games last season (seven goals). He also won his 95th cap for Brazil against Portugal on March 29 (1-2) but was sent off for arguing and pushing the ref, and was subsequently banned for three international matches. Like Ronaldo, didn't play in the Confederations Cup. Alongside three European Cup winner's medals, Roberto Carlos has a 2002 World Cup winner's medal – he played in six of their seven games and missed only the Costa Rica game when rested. He also played in the 1998 final – he's played regularly for his country since the 1994 World Cup. The full-back joined from Inter Milan in summer 1996 for £3m. He played just the one season with Inter after arriving from Palmeiras. Despite his reputation following the 'Goal of the Season' v France at Le Tournoi, he's not a great scorer - he has never scored more than six league goals in a season. Has 13 Champions League goals to date.

**1 IKER CASILLAS** 20.05.81
Casillas made more appearances than anyone but Roberto Carlos last season, playing 55 times in goal. He has also played in 19 of Spain's last 21 internationals, and has now collected 28 caps for his country. Played a major part in the 2002 Champions League final after Cesar's injury and kept out three goalbound shots in the last minute, and then played all five Spanish games at the World Cup as injury also took care of Valencia's

Canizares. Casillas came to prominence with amazing displays in goal in the run to the 2000 European Cup win after making his debut just a few weeks earlier thanks to Bodo Illgner's injury. He turned 19 just 4 days before the 2000 European Cup win.

**20 ALBERT CELADES** 29.09.75

Celades made only 13 appearances for the first team last season, scoring two goals. Of his 10 starts, six were in the Spanish Cup and four were in the Champions League. Moved from Celta in summer 2000 on a Bosman transfer, and became another of the select band to have played for Barcelona and Real – there are 15 major moves in history between the two clubs. Celades' breakthrough season was at Barcelona under Louis van Gaal in 1997-98 when he played 36 of 38 league games in the 1998 title win. He was then capped just before the World Cup, and went on to play twice at France 98 before suffering injuries the following season and moving to Celta Vigo for one year. Has also won the 2001 title with Real, and won five caps for his country.

**16 FLAVIO CONCEICAO** 12.06.74

The Brazilian defensive central midfielder has 44 caps for his country, and joined Real in the summer of 2000 from the champions Deportivo for £16.5m, and won the 2001 title despite a persistent groin injury. He missed the start of last season through injury, but returned in early December 2002. Conceicao got into his national side in 1995 and won the Copa America in 1997 and 1999 – his last appearance for Brazil was in September 2000. Scored 1 goal in 32 games for Real last season.

**10 LUIS FIGO** 04.11.72

The 2001 FIFA World Player of the Year has 93 caps and 28 goals for Portugal and was once the most expensive striker in the world. He was acquired for £36.4m from Barcelona in 2000 (who paid £1.9m for him in 1995 from Sporting Lisbon, where he debuted aged 17). The right midfielder scored 12 goals in 51 games for Real last season, but none in his last 12 appearances.

**14 JM GUTI** 31.10.76

Jose Guttierrez Hernandez is another who has come through the youth teams at Real, a local lad from Madrid who plays in left midfield and was a key member of the Spanish national side that won the 1998 European U21 championship. He won his first senior cap in June 1999, but has won only eight more, the last as a sub against Ecuador on April 30. Only Casillas and Roberto Carlos played more games than Guti last season - he made 54 appearances (13 goals). Whilst winning the 2001 title with Real, he was second top scorer with 14 goals. However, Guti missed both the 2000 and 2002 Champions League finals.

**6 IVAN HELGUERA** 28.03.75

The Spanish utility player (defence or midfield) scored six goals in 50 games (49 starts) for Real last season. He also played all five games for Spain in the World Cup, and now has 35 caps and three international goals. His breakthrough season was the one season (1998-99) he played for Espanyol - he made the full national team and then in summer 1999 moved to Real for £4.75m.

**17 OSCAR MINAMBRES** 01.02.81
Made 24 first team appearances last season but didn't score. The Madrid-born defender was first choice only in the absence of Michel Salgado last season, but has three seasons' experience with the B team and is highly rated within the club. Plays in wing back positions but appeared all over the place last season.

**22 FRANSISCO PAVON** 09.01.80
Pavon, a defender from the B team, had his first season in the first team squad in 2001-02, then played 38 games last season, although he started only one of the final 14 games of last season.

**18 JAVIER GARCIA PORTILLO** 30.03.82
Left footed striker Portillo – a graduate of the Madrid youth team – signed with Real in 1994 aged 12 and scored an astonishing 354 goals at all junior levels for the side. He announced himself with a stunner from 35 yards in the Champions League game with Panathinaikos in March 2002, and scored a crucial last-minute equaliser against Dortmund in the Champions League group stage 2 last season. Hit 14 goals in only 24 games last season.

**7 RAUL** 27.06.77
The all-time Champions League top scorer has 43 goals in the competition to date. Raul is also Spain's all-time top scorer (63 caps, 32 goals) and the fourth highest scoring Real player ever. He's hit 217 (155 league) goals in Madrid, and is now behind only Di Stefano (307), Santillana (290) and Puskas (236). Was Spanish league top scorer in 1998-99 (25 goals) and 2000-01 (24 goals). Drafted into the senior side from the C team by Valdano in 1994-95 aged just 17, Raul quickly became the sensation of Spanish football. Last season he scored 25 goals in 47 matches. At the age of 26, he has already won three championship medals and three European Cup medals and World Club Cup medals. Just like Butragueno before him, Raul's career will haunt Atletico president Jesus Gil - Raul was working his way through the youth teams at Atletico when Gil decided to release him and shut down the youth team, so Raul went to Real, where some rename the club 'Raul Madrid' after him!

**11 RONALDO** 22.09.76
Brazil's World Player of the Year 1996, 1997 and 2002 joined Real in August 2002 for around £29.8m from Inter Milan. His first season saw 30 goals in 44 games, including a hat-trick in the Champions League at Old Trafford and 15 goals in his final 15 appearances of last season. He was joint top scorer with Nihat in the Primera Liga last season with 23 goals, after having top scored for Barcelona in his only season for them

(34 goals, 37 games in 1996-97). Ronaldo's former clubs include Cruzeiro (1993-94), PSV (1994-95), Barcelona and Inter (1997-2002). However, he was out for over two years from 1999 to late 2001 with knee ligament damage, returning to score seven goals in ten games for Inter then winning the World Cup with Brazil (he scored eight goals in the Finals). Has 69 caps and 47 international goals.

**29 RUBEN** 29.01.82
The defender made six appearances last year without scoring a goal, all but one in the Spanish Cup.

**25 CARLOS SANCHEZ** 19.01.78
The number three keeper at Real didn't appear for the first-team last season. Sanchez last played in the Primera Liga in 2001-02 v Mallorca on December 23, 2001 – he'd spent one season in the C team (1999-2000) and two seasons in the B team (2000-02).

**13 CESAR SANCHEZ 0**2.09.71
Spanish goalkeeper Sanchez (one cap) joined from Real in summer 2000 for a £2.3m fee from Valladolid, where he'd spent nine seasons (the last six as first choice keeper). He took over from Iker Casillas as first choice in 2001-02 (March 2, 2002) but was injured in the Champions League final win over Bayer Leverkusen (2-1) and missed the World Cup. Made just seven appearances last season, one of which was in the Champions League, but now has over 200 Primera Liga games under his belt.

**2 MICHEL SALGADO** 22.10.75
Started nine consecutive internationals for Spain last season although he wasn't in the 2002 World Cup squad. He also made 52 appearances for Real, scoring one goal. The £8m signing from Celta (summer 1999) was Spain's first choice right back at Euro 2000 after being in the team that won the 1998 European U21 Championship. Last season, Real players wore black armbands against Seville on April 27 as mark of respect for his mother, who had sadly died. Has won 26 caps.

**21 SANTIAGO SOLARI** 07.10.76
Solari can play in defence or midfield, and 34 of his 44 games (1 goal) for Real last season were as substitute. The Argentine international (12 caps) started just one game in 2003 (in the Champions League at Lokomotiv Moscow on March 18) although he started the 2002 final. Solari joined Real for £2.25m from Atletico when the latter side suffered a shock relegation in 2000. He refused to join Inter Milan in January 2003 as part of the Ronaldo deal – Solari said he wanted to stay and fight for his place, so Inter are still owed a player. The player has also won two titles at River Plate and the 2001 Primera Liga with Real.

**12 JORGE TOTE** 23.11.78
A Madrid-born forward who is basically still in the B team. Hit six goals in six games last

season, including a hat-trick in a Spanish Cup game v San Sebastian. He also scored in the Champions League v Genk. Made just one Primera Liga appearance last season (he started v Recreativo on May 10).

**5 ZINEDINE ZIDANE** 23.06.72
The French midfielder joined from Juventus for a world record £47.2m in summer 2001, and has taken over the No. 5 shirt worn by the now retired former captain Manuel Sanchis, the club's longest ever serving player. Won both 1998 and 2000 World and European Footballer of Year awards. Zidane has 82 caps for France, with 22 goals, including two goals in the World Cup win of 1998 – he was injured for the opening two games of the 2002 World Cup. He scored 12 goals in 50 games last season. Zidane was originally a summer 1996 signing from the 1996 UEFA Cup finalists Bordeaux and cost Juve what is now an absolute bargain £3.2m after playing every game at Euro 96. He made his Division 1 debut in France at the age of 17, and played four seasons for both Cannes and Bordeaux before moving to Italy. Zidane was the first ever goalscorer at the new Stade de France (v Spain 1998).

# FC PORTO

**Together with Manchester United and Galatasaray, Futebol Clube do Porto has made the most appearances in the Champions League. In the 12th season of this famous competition all three start their 9th campaign. While Manchester United (Champions League 1999) and Galatasaray (UEFA Cup 2000) have enjoyed European glory some years ago, the triumph of FC Porto in Europe is somewhat more recent with The 'Dragons' becoming UEFA Cup winners in May 2003 after beating Celtic in Seville (3-2 after extra time). 2002/03 was undoubtedly a season to remember for Porto after they secured their 18th league title and won their first UEFA Cup. They also captured their 12th national Cup with a 1-0 win over Uniao Leiria in June 2003. FC did win the Champion Clubs' Cup in 1987 against Bayern Munich (2-1) but in the CL they have not yet to progress further than the semi-final in 1994 which they lost to Barcelona. In 1997 and 2000 they lost to Manchester United and Bayern Munich in the quarter-finals.**

## COACH

**JOSE MOURINHO** 26.01.63
Jose Mourinho was born on 26 January 1963 in Setubal only 30 metres away from the Stadium of Div 1 club Vitoria. When he was 15 years old he was already sure that he was to become a coach one day. Two years later helped his father, who was a coach at Setubal, scout opponents. Mourinho arrived at Sporting Lisbon as a member of Bobby Robson's

staff. When Robson was sacked, Mourinho followed him first to FC Porto and then to Barcelona where he stayed as assistant under Louis Van Gaal. He learned a lot from both of them but seemingly not enough as his first job as head coach of Benfica lasted just 9 games. His next stop at Uniao Leiria went better and FC Porto promptly signed him up.

## REACTION TO GROUP

**"We have raised ourselves up a level after winning the UEFA Cup last season and I have every confidence in my team but you cannot take anything for granted. Matches against Real Madrid are always special and I would like to think we have improved enough to beat them this time,"** ***manager Jose Mourinho***

## SQUAD

**15 DIMITRI ALENITCHEV** 20.10.72
Attacking midfielder who was voted Russian Footballer of the Year while playing for Spartak Moscow in their championship winning season of 1997. In the summer 1998 he moved to AS Roma where he settled in well. Despite being a crowd favourite he was not given many chances in the first team. Moved to Perugia and then joined Porto in the summer 2000. Scored Porto's 2nd goal in the UEFA Cup final against Celtic.

**29 HUGO ALMEIDA** 23.05.84
The Portuguese forward was signed from Naval. Provides cover in case first team strikers bet injured. Normally plays in the youth team or the reserves.

**99 VITOR BAIA** 15.10.69
Vitor Baia arrived at FC Porto for the first time in 1988. He won 5 league titles at the club and almost immediately became Portugal's number one before moving in summer 1996 to Barcelona for £4.8 million along with Bobby Robson. Got injured and was out for a long time because of a knee operation. Had a nightmare 1997/98 season with Barcelona. The only senior game he played in was the CL return game with Dynamo Kyiv where he let in 4 goals and was dropped by Louis Van Gaal. Went back to Porto in January 1999 and promptly won his 6th title in 1999. Reached the semi-finals with Portugal at Euro 2000 but the World Cup 2002 was less successful with a surprising first round exit. Has 80 caps for Portugal but is not certain of his place under new national coach Luiz Felipe Scolari. Although completely fit he was omitted for a friendly versus Italy in February 2003. Winning the UEFA Cup last season undoubtedly was a moral boost in an injury-plagued career.

**17 JOSE BOSINGWA** 24.08.82
Star of the Portuguese U21-team who was signed from neighbours Boavista as a replacement for Nuno Capucho who left the club for Glasgow Rangers. Originally from Congo this midfielder made 7 CL appearances in 2001/02 with Boavista) and was a UEFA Cup semi-finalist with Boavista against Celtic last April.

# GROUP F
## FC PORTO

**4 RICARDO CARVALHO** 18.05.78
Plays in central defence in tandem with Jorge Costa. Is a product of the club's youth academy after joining from Amarante. Was loaned to Leça in 1997/98 to gain Div I experience and subsequently to Vitoria Setubal (1998/99), Santa Clara (1999/2000) and Alverca (2000/01). The elegant yet competitive centre-back is considered one of the most promising players in the country and has played for Portugal at all youth levels.

**2 JORGE COSTA** 14.10.71
Skipper and central defender who played in the club's first CL campaign 11 years ago. Has played up to 40 CL games since but only scored one goal at home against Sparta Prague (2-2) on 15.03.2000. Has great commitment and leadership qualities as well plenty of international experience (played at Euro 96, Euro 2000 and the World Cup 2002 with Portugal) but these days is short on pace. Had a short spell in the Premiership at Charlton Athletic in a loan deal just before World Cup 2002. Winner of the triple (league title, national Cup and UEFA Cup) last season.

**5 RICARDO COSTA** 16.05.81
The young central defender came on in the UEFA Cup final against Celtic after 9 minutes for the injured Costinha. He is the star of the Portuguese Under-21 team and was promoted to the first squad in 2001/02.

**6 COSTINHA** 01.12.74
Francisco Jose Rodrigues da Costa was born in Lisbon and moved from Div 2B club Oriental to Nacional (also in Div 2B) in 1996. Joined Monaco in 1997 where he played 4 seasons (84 league games and scored 3 goals). Played in the CL with Monaco in 1997/98 and scored a goal against Rangers. Arrived at FC Porto in the summer 2001 and played in 10 CL games in 2001/02. The Portuguese international sustained an injury in the UEFA Cup final in Seville and was replaced after 9 minutes by Ricardo Costa.

**10 DECO** 27.08.77
Brazilian born Anderson Luis de Sousa is the gifted playmaker of FC Porto, the club he joined in the beginning of 1999 after 12 games and 2 goals for Salgueiros. He arrived in Portugal in 1997 from Corinthians Alagoano and started in Alverca's second team in regional football. Was recently granted Portuguese citizenship and immediately scored a goal (a splendid free-kick) for Portugal in his debut against Brazil. Has played 23 CL games and scored 5 goals for Porto in the CL campaigns of1999/2000 and 2001/02. Scored 10 league goals last season.

**11 DERLEI** 14.07.75
The two-goal hero of the UEFA Cup final was also the match winner in the Portuguese Cup final against Uniao Leiria when he scored the game's only goal. Vanderlei Fernandes Silva was once with top Brazilian sides Guarani and Sao Paulo before moving to Portugal. The striker scored 21 goals for Uniao Leiria and was second in the top

scorer's chart behind Jardel in 2001/02. Moved to Porto in the summer 2002 and is being used there on the left side of attack.

**3 PEDRO EMANUEL** 11.02.75
Pedro Emanuel dos Santos Martins Silva, born in Angola, is a centre-back who is very strong in the air and provides cover for Jorge Costa or Ricardo Carvalho. He caused a storm in the city when he left Boavista to join the neighbours FC Porto in the summer 2002 after commenting that Boavista was 'yesterday's club'. Played in the UEFA Cup final against Celtic last season coming on as a 71st minute substitute for Jorge Costa.

**25 RICARDO FERNANDES** 21.04.78
The diminutive playmaker arrived at Porto this summer from Sporting Lisbon to strengthen the squad. Can replace Deco should he be unavailable for selection.

**20 MARCO FERREIRA** 12.03.78
Promising right-winger who made his debut for Portugal in October 2002 in a friendly against Tunisia in Lisbon. Played in the UEFA Cup final against Celtic coming on as a sub for Nuno Capucho after 98 minutes. Left his former club Vitoria Setubal during the winter break 2002/03. His full name is Julio Castanheira Afonso Alves Marco Ferreira.

**22 PAULO FERREIRA** 18.01.79
Right-back who just like Nuno Valente made his debut for Portugal in the friendly against England in September 2002. Arrived at FC Porto from Vitoria Setubal in the summer 2002. He showed excellent form last season and played the full 120 minutes in the UEFA Cup final against Celtic.

**9 EDGARAS JANKAUSKAS** 12.03.75
The Lithuanian international forward (33 caps) played in Russia for CSKA Moscow and Torpedo Moscow before he was spotted by FC Bruges in 1997. Left Belgium for a Spanish adventure with Real Sociedad but didn't make it over there and was loaned to Benfica. FC Porto took him on in the summer 2002. Has come off the bench to score some vital goals. Very dangerous in the air from corners and set pieces. Scored 9 goals in the league last season.

**18 MANICHE** 11.11.77
Tiny, dynamic and skilful, this midfielder joined Porto from Benfica in the summer 2002. He was a revelation in the run to the triple win and hopes to do as well in the Champions League. He is full of confidence after scoring 7 league goals last season.

**77 BENNI MCCARTHY** 12.11.77
Benedict joined Porto this summer from Celta Vigo as a replacement for Premiership bound Helder Postiga (Tottenham). Played for the club in 2000/01 on loan and scored 12 goals. Is a South African international forward who played all 3 games for his country

in the World Cup 1998 in France and in the World Cup 2002 in South Korea. Scored the first ever goal for South Africa at the World Cup finals in 1998 in Toulouse against Denmark (1-1) and also scored a goal in the WC 2002 in South Korea against Spain (2-3 defeat). Has played in the CL before with Ajax in 1998/99 including one against his current club FC Porto.

**23 PEDRO MENDES** 26.02.79
Twenty-four-year-old midfielder who joined Porto this summer from Vitoria Guimaraes to strengthen the squad. Recruited mainly as cover for the midfield.

**28 BRUNO SANTOS MORAES** 07.07.84
Young Brazilian forward who is considered a star of the future. Could have a taste of first team football this season and possibly even the Champions League.

**13 SIMOES NUNO** 25.01.74
Stand-in for Vitor Baia joined the club in summer 2002 from Deportivo La Coruna where he was the reserve goalkeeper in 2001/02. Played 3 CL games in that season at home against Lille (1-1) and Bayer Leverkusen (1-3 defeat) and away to Olympiakos (1-1). Left Portugal's Vitoria Guimaraes in 1996 for Deportivo but after playing only 1 game in each of his first 2 seasons he was loaned out for 2 seasons to Merida (1998/2000) and then to Osasuna (2000/01).

**14 CESAR PEIXOTO** 12.05.80
The speedy left-winger and former Portuguese Under-21 star is not a regular in the team. Was an unused sub in the UEFA Cup final in Seville last May. Joined FC Porto in the summer 2002 from Belenenses. Critics say that he is recently making more progress after a difficult start at the club.

**7 CARLOS SECRETARIO** 12.05.70
Enterprising right-back who played his first CL game for FC Porto on 24.11.93 at home against Werder Bremen. Played 32 CL games overall in 5 CL campaigns with the club and scored 2 goals both in the first season against Anderlecht and Werder Bremen. Was sent off in his last CL game at home against Panathinaikos on 12.03.2002. Moved to Real Madrid in 1996 but flopped in the Spanish capital and came back to FC Porto. Has 35 caps for Portugal but persistent knee trouble has restricted his first team appearances lately. The arrival of Paulo Ferreira in 2002 has also reduced his playing opportunities.

**19 SERGINHO** 01.05.78
Brazilian forward Elisergio da Silva came from neighbours Boavista, the club he joined in the summer 2001 after playing in Brazil for Vitoria de Baia, Rio Branco and Corinthians Alagoano. Played 5 CL games for Boavista in 2001/02 mainly as a sub but made appearances against Liverpool and Manchester United.

**30 MARIO SILVA** 24.04.77
Born in Oporto and a product of the Boavista youth system this left-back or left-sided midfielder made his debut for Boavista on 29.10.1995. He won the national Cup in 1997 and the Portuguese Supercup. Left Boavista in 2000 after 87 league games to join Nantes in France. Mario Fernando Magalhaes da Silva (his full name) had 20 league games and became French champion with the club in 2001. In the summer of the same year he returned home but this time to play for FC Porto where he is normally second choice.

**66 MOREIRA TIAGO** 04.07.74
Defensive midfielder who also played under Mourinho at Uniao Leiria. He joined Porto in the summer 2002. Mourinho appreciates his tactical awareness and hard working unlike many of the club's fans.

**8 NUNO VALENTE** 12.09.74
Adventurous left-back who made his debut for Portugal in September 2002 in a friendly against England. Is a good dribbler, can deliver a perfect cross and is technically polished but can be drawn out of his defensive position easily. Played at Mourinho's former club Uniao Leiria before joining Porto in the summer 2002.

# OLYMPIQUE DE MARSEILLE

**In 1993 Marseille were the first winners of the new competition to replace the European Cup. But their 1993 1-0 success over AC Milan brought problems. President Bernard Tapie was accused of match fixing, found guilty and jailed, and the club stripped of their titles. Though the offences were in league football, UEFA concurred. In 1994-96, Marseille were in Division 2 and although they progressed to runners up in 1999, further financial overspending caused further problems at the turn of the century. The arrival of Alain Perrin meant a clearout of overpaid players, and he restructured the club on the solid principles he employed at Troyes. Marseille were third in 2002-03 and went into the CL draw in the third qualifying round, where they beat Austria Vienna 1-0 over two legs. Their last Champions League outing in 1999-2000 saw them reach the second group stage. Marseille were champions in 1937, 1948, 1971, 1972 and then won four in a row in 1989, 1990, 1991 and 1992. 1989 was a double winning year with their 10th and last French Cup win to date.**

## COACH

**ALAIN PERRIN** 07.10.56
Former youth team and reserve coach at former playing club AS Nancy, he went to Troyes in 1993 and took them from the regional leagues into the first division. After nine

years at Troyes he moved to the bigger club Marseille in 2002 and took the club to third place in his first season and into the Champions League – Troyes, in the meantime, went down. Perrin was the sixth coach appointed in two years at Marseille!

## REACTION TO DRAW

**"Real Madrid are the greatest team in the world and we don't always get the chance to greet Zizou so it will be special playing against him. I think our supporters have been spoilt by this draw to be honest!"** ***Coach Alain Perrin***

## SQUAD

**16 FREDERIC CARRASCO** 30.12.81
Reserve keeper, who played for his home town club Avignon (Division 3) then went to Crystal Palace before his first team debut last season at Marseille.

**5 PHILIPPE CRISTANVAL** 31.08.78
Had thigh injury for much of 2002-03 and returned to France from Barcelona. First cap for 30 minutes v South Africa in October 2000, replaced Frank Leboeuf - was in the national U21 side and was in the training squad for Euro2000 though only for experience. Made the World Cup squad 2002 but did not play in the finals. Was strongly linked with Bayern Munich in summer 2000 - to go with Willy Sagnol - but the deal fell away. First choice in Monaco's 2000 title win after making debut in 1998. Was in the famous U18 French team that won the European title in 1996, with Anelka, Henry, Trezeguet and others. Has made 20 Champions League appearances.

**6 MANUEL DOS SANTOS** 28.03.74
Fourth season with the club, with extensive Division 1 experience with Monaco and Montpellier. Dos Santos (from the Cape Verde Islands) played for Monaco 1995-97, then Montpellier 1997-2000 and onto Marseille and has played over 200 Division 1 games.

**11 DIDIER DROGBA** 11.03.78
Drogba (who has 11 caps for Ivory Coast) was the big signing of the summer 2003 transfer market, coming in for e7m from Guingamp, the little team from Brittany in the top flight. Was third in the golden boot competition last season for Guingamp with 17 goals, hence the interest. Drogba played for Le Mans when they were in Division 2, then had his breakthrough season 2002-03 at Guingamp.

**21 JOHNNY ECKER** 16.01.73
Played in D2 and D3 for Nimes from 1993-99, and then made his name at Lille with a tight-knit team that achieved fine results at the turn of the century. He was a late starter in Division 1 in 2000, aged 27. Ecker played all six games in the Manchester United Champions League group in 2001-02 and so impressed Marseille that they came in for him.

# GROUP F
## OLYMPIQUE DE MARSEILLE

**6 BRAHIM HEMDANI** 15.03.78
A French/Algerian who is in his third season at Marseille. Hemdani has had decent experience with Cannes and Strasbourg in the top flight and is approaching 150 career games. He made his Division 1 debut in 1997 with Cannes.

**15 PASCAL JOHANSEN** 28.04.79
The former U21 international is in his second season with the club. He arrived from Strasbourg. Johansen has played some 70 Division 1 games to date.

**20 STEVE MARLET** 10.01.74
Marlet's unhappy spell at Fulham ended just before the Champions League deadline with a loan move and an option to buy. He'll be playing in the Champions League for his third club after Auxerre and Lyon. He has played 15 games in the competition and scored six goals so far. French international (18 caps) who was in the September 2003 qualifiers for Euro2004. Marlet joined Auxerre in 1996 from Red Star Paris (Division 2) after the double win and stayed for four years then was a key player in Lyon's championship runners up team.

**12 ABDOULAYE MEITE** 06.10.80
The central defender has been developed quietly by the club and is around the 50-game mark. Meite is from Paris and played for Red Star in Division 2 until moving to Marseille in summer 2000.

**18 CAMEL MERIEM** 18.10.79
A deadline transfer, on loan for the season from Bordeaux, Meriem is a former U21 international who made the Division 1 grade with Sochaux and moved to Bordeaux in summer 2002. He only missed one league game for Bordeaux in 2002-03.

**7 SYLVAIN N'DIAYE** 25.06.76
The Senegalese (nine caps) player joined the club in summer 2003 from Lille and like Ecker he played in the Lille Champions League ties in the Man United group in 2001-02, making five appearances. Also a member of the Senegal World Cup squad but did not play at the finals. Has been in the 1st Division since 1997 with Bordeaux, Martigues, Toulouse and Lille and is approaching 100 league games.

**8 SEBASTIAN PEREZ** 24.11.73
A Blackburn Rovers player in 1999, Perez then played a season of Champions League football for both Marseille (1999-00) and Galatasaray (2001-02). He'd arrived at Blackburn from St Etienne and Bastia, then returned to Bastia and went to Marseille in 1999. He was at Marseille 1999-2000, then went for two years to Galatasaray and is now back at Marseille for a second spell. Perez has now played 200 Division 1 games in France and 20 Champions League games, scoring two goals.

# GROUP F
## OLYMPIQUE DE MARSEILLE

**23 HABIB BEYE** 19.10.77
A deadline transfer in August 2003 from Strasbourg, Beye had been at Strasbourg through over 100 Division 1 games in five seasons since 1998 when he had arrived from Paris SG. He was born in France but has opted to play for Senegal, and now has six caps.

**29 FABIO CELESTINI** 31.10.75
The 22-cap Swiss midfielder came across from Troyes in summer 2002 with coach Perrin. He was Perrin's captain at Troyes and now is his captain at Marseille. Born at Lausanne of Italian parents, he played for Lausanne Sports in the Swiss league until 2000 when Perrin came in for him for Troyes.

**10 FERNANDAO** 18.03.78
A Brazilian who has been with the club since summer 2001 when he signed from Goias, a top flight Brazilian club, and has quietly made his way to 50 first team games at the end of last season. Fernandao is 6'3", and appears to be playing as a target man rather than a heavy scorer.

**11 AHMED (MIDO) HOSSAM** 23.02.83
Hossam - also known as Mido - joined Marseille in summer 2003 from Ajax for _6m after a major fallout with Ajax coach Ronald Koeman, who disciplined him in February 2003 after he returned late from an international midweek match, and was immediately sent on loan to Celta Vigo. Koeman said he wouldn't pick him again. Ajax club top scorer with 18 in all competitions until his departure, he joined Ajax in summer 2001 from top flight Belgian club Ghent, where he was top scorer in his only season with 11 goals. Mido is a huge talent who was given his chance as soon as Koeman arrived, hitting 12 goals in 24 league games in the 2002 double win (including 10 goals in last 13 games. Mido cost Ajax £3 million. First capped aged 17, he now has 29 caps for Egypt. His first club was the African champion club Zamalek, where he starred in the junior teams from 1991-2000. Has made eight Champions League appearances.

**1 VEDRAN RUNJE** 10.02.76
The Croatian (one cap) is in his third season with the club and is proving a good buy - he arrived from Belgian club Standard Liege along with Van Buyten. Runje played for his home town club Hajduk Split from 1995-97 then moved to Standard for four seasons.

**22 DIMITRI SYTCHEV** 26.10.83
Another troublesome teenage international, the Russian with 12 caps refused to play under Oleg Romantsev at Spartak Moscow last season, and went on strike. He came to Marseille in January 2003 and has ben a bit of a hero, though needs goals to substantiate his promise. Sytchev was capped as a teenager by Russia in 2002 and scored once in the World Cup that year.

**14 STEPHAN VACHOUSEK** 26.07.79
The Czech player joined the club in summer 2003 from Slavia Prague and had previously played for Teplice. He was in the midfield in the team that won the 2002 European U21 championship with a win v France in the final. He moved on to full national honours last season.

**4 DANIEL VAN BUYTEN** 07.02.78
A fine central defender in his third season with the club – big clubs including Man Utd had a long look at him in summer 2003. Van Buyten arrived in summer 2001 from Standard Liege along with the keeper Runje. He'd had four seasons of top flight Belgian football – two each with Charleroi and then Standard. He came into the national side after Euro2000, played all four games at 2002 World Cup, and in current Euro2004 squad for the qualifiers. Now has 21 caps.

# PARTIZAN BELGRADE

**Since the break up of the former Yugoslavia, Partizan have been the most consistent of the teams left in what is basically Serbia and Montenegro. Partizan are the current champions - and have retained the title they won in 2002. Since the war in the early 1990s, they were also champions in 1993, 1994, 1996, and 1997 and 1999. Partizan have won the Cup on nine occasions – the last in 2001. In all, Partizan have won the championship 18 times from their foundation in 1945. The team was originally the army team, founded at the end of World War II, but recent events have left them disclaiming any involvement with the army. Partizan's best European achievement was to beat Manchester United in the semi-final of the 1966 European Cup, and losing narrowly 2-1 to Real Madrid in the final. They also saw off Newcastle to qualify this season.**

## COACH

**LOTHAR MATTHAUS** 12.03.61
The legendary German international midfielder-sweeper has been with the club since last winter and guided it to the 2002-03 title with the aim of European progress. Matthaus arrived without a great coaching reputation following his disappointing stint at Rapid Vienna, whom he failed to lift out of the doldrums. He replaced Ljubisa Tumbakovic who won Partizan nine championships and six cups. Matthaus won his 150th and final cap at Euro2000 in the defeat by Portugal, and then went to the NY/NJ Metrostars and into coaching with Rapid Vienna. He won six league titles with Bayern and the 1990 World Cup, and was subbed off in the closing seconds of the 1999 Champions League final v Manchester United - before the deluge.

# GROUP F
## PARTIZAN BELGRADE

## REACTION TO DRAW

**"All three are great teams and all of them have won the European Cup. But if we give it our best shot, who knows, we might be in with a chance. Let's face it matches against Real Madrid are special. They come around once every 100 years or so – by that I mean it will be a match of outstanding importance. I think if we hit top form we could be a real surprise to a lot of teams at the top level in Europe,"** ***coach Lothar Matthaeus***

## SQUAD

**25 BRANIMIR BAJIC** 19.10.79
A defender who came to the club as a junior from FK Radnik, Bajic has had four seasons in the first team squad.

**23 BOJAN BRNOVIC** 10.02.79
First season with club.

**11 DAMIR CAKAR** 28.06.73
A workhorse in midfield, he is back with the club for a second spell since 2001 and has won the 2002 and 2003 championships with them. 6'3", he was originally with Partizan then left to play in France with Chateauroux and in Holland with Vitesse Arnhem. First returned to the country to play for Sutjeska Niksic, where he was capped (he now has three caps), so Partizan took him back.

**2 MILIVOJE CIRKOVIC** 14.04.77
Key defender, he is an international with seven caps from the era just after Euro2000 when experiments were made. Has won three championship medals and came from a junior club in Belgrade.

**9 ANDRIJA DELIBASIC** 24.04.81
Very promising young forward – played for the national U21 side v England at Hull on 02.06.03. From the club's youth academy and highly rated.

**14 NENAD DJORDJEVIC** 07.08.79
Summer 2003 signing from the Belgrade club, FC Obilic, who were run by the war-lord Arkan. He had five seasons with Obilic. Was an international with Obilic, and sub v England at Leicester. Djordjevic usually operates in a wing-back role and strengthens the 2003 Champions League squad as a current international with six caps.

**10 LJUBINKO DRULOVIC** 11.09.68
Returned home in 2003 after six championships with FC Porto but had failed to gain a regular place in the past 18 months. Drulovic has been in the national squad 1996-2002,

but was especially potent at Euro2000 where his left-sided play gave Yugoslavia much success. He made the 1998 World Cup squad - did not play in finals, and now has 37 caps. Was a January 1994 signing from fellow Division 1 club Gil Vicente and made an immediate impact. Originally joined Gil Vicente in 1992 from the Yugoslav first Division club Red Belgrade. Although he has a useful scoring record, he now operates deeper in midfield and so goals are increasingly rare.

**4 IGOR DULJAJ** 29.10.79
Current international squad – started against England at Leicester last June – and has been in the national squad since Euro2000 with increasing effect. The midfielder has 22 caps. and has been with the youth section since the age of 11 in 1990. He made the first team in 1998 so has won three championship medals and two cups with the club to date.

**22 SASA ILIC** 30.12.77
Goalscorer who plays behind the front two, Ilic is the team's captain and major influence. The goals are starting to arrive from this 16-cap international, and he was the league top scorer with 22 goals in 1999. From the youth team and now has five years in the first team. He has 1998 Cup medal, and 1999, 2002, 2003 titles.

**17 IVICA ILIEV** 27.10.79
Forward from the youth team and was with the club's youth set up for three seasons, until promotion in 1999. Iliev is in line for more national honours (he has four caps) but the national team is filled by Milosevic, Kovacevic and Mijatovic with Kezman in the wings.

**DRAGOLJUB JEREMIC** 09.08.78
Capped three times in January 2001 on a winter tour. Jeremic is a defender who came from the same club as keeper Radkovic and has been in the squad that won the 2002 and 2003 titles.

**30 IVICA KRALJ** 26.03.73
Has returned in summer 2003 to his first senior club from PSV on a free transfer. Did not play for PSV last season. Was at Partizan from 1987 for 11 years until after the World Cup 1998, but was only on bench duty at his next clubs FC Porto and PSV and was twice loaned out. Was Yugoslavia's number one keeper at France98 and Euro2000, and says his move back home could herald a return to the national team – he is stuck on 45 caps. Won three championships with the club in his first spell at Partizan.

**15 NIKOLA MALBASA** 12.09.77
Played a part in the 2003 title success in his first season with the club. He joined from provincial Premiership club Hajduk Kula. Made the national team in spring 2003 and was a sub against England at Leicester. Now has four caps.

# GROUP F
## PARTIZAN BELGRADE

**28 ALBERT NADJ** 29.10.74
The second season back with the club, he's been away in Spain with Betis Seville and Oviedo. Nadj helped in the 2003 title win and can play midfield, defence or wing-back. He won two national titles with Partizan up to 1996, then went to the Primera Liga with Betis from 1996-99 and Oviedo 1999-2002. He played at Euro2000 and was a first choice when in Spain for Yugoslavia. He's now won 36 caps.

**19 AJAZDIN NUHI** 10.10.79
Squad member, from the youth academy.

**5 DEJAN OGNJANOVIC** 21.06.78
Third season with the club, he won titles in both previous years (2002 and 2003). Arrived from Buducnost Podgorica. He won two caps in January 2001.

**15 DORDE PANTIC** 27.01.80
Huge reserve keeper – Pantic is nearly 6'6" tall. In his fourth season at club. Came from a junior club in Belgrade.

**1 RADOVAN RADAKOVIC** 06.02.71
Keeper who was capped twice in 2002 World Cup qualifiers, but not again since. The former club number one, he arrived from Radnicki Kragujevac, a provincial Premiership club, about five years ago. He may have to stand down for Kralj, but has won two titles in the past two seasons.

**6 DZENAN RADONCIC** 02.08.83
First season in first team squad – youth international.

**26 TOMASZ RZASA** 11.03.73
Joined summer 2003 from Feyenoord. Rzasa is from Poland's 2002 World Cup squad. He's now playing in another country after winning championship medals with Grasshopper in the Swiss League and with Feyenoord – he played in the Champions League for both sides. He joined the latter club in June 1999 and played once at the 2002 World Cup (sub). He made his name at home with Sokol Pniewy from 1991-95 when they came from Division 3 to Division 1 in successive seasons. Then moved to Grasshoppers in Switzerland from 1995 to 1997, where he was first capped with their champions and also went on loan to Lugano and Young Boys. Played midfield in Poland and Switzerland and scored 40 goals in 117 league games. He has 11 caps.

**24 BRANKO SAVIC** 08.08.72
This is the first season of the defender's second spell at the club - he originally joined in summer 1997 from rival Division 1 club Proleter Zrenjanin. Savic left in 2000 to play in Israel with Stojanoski for Beitar Jerusalem, returned in summer 2002 and won a

championship medal. He had won a 1998 Cup medal and the 1999 championship in his first spell in central defence.

**7 MILAN STOJANOSKI** 16.09.73
This is the second season of his second spell with the club. Originally bought from Proleter Zrenjanin, a provincial Premiership team, he spent two seasons in Israel with Beitar Jerusalem, before returning to Partizan in summer 2002. A 17-cap Macedonian international, he played as a sub v England at Southampton.

**16 TARIBO WEST** 26.03.74
Formerly with Derby County on loan, the 42-cap Nigerian star then went to Kaiserslautern on loan and on to Partizan, two weeks after Matthaus' arrival. Nigerian World Cup player and African Nations champion, West was found by Guy Roux at Auxerre, then went to Inter and AC Milan before Derby. Played 18 games for Derby in 2000-01 and helped to keep them in the Premiership.

**21 BOJAN ZAVISIC** 09.08.79
From the club's youth academy, was a squad player in the 2002 and 2003 title wins.

# GROUP G

**CHELSEA FC**
(England)

**SS LAZIO**
(Italy)

**AC SPARTA PRAGUE**
(Czech Republic)

**BESIKTAS JK**
(Turkey)

# CHELSEA FC

**Can unlimited funds buy success? At the time of writing new owner Roman Abromavich has spent in excess of £100 million with a promise of more to come in January. The glittering array of talent, consisting of a combination of European flair in Mutu, Crespo, Geremi and Makelele and English stars of tomorrow with Glenn Johnson, Joe Cole, Wayne Bridge and Frank Lampard make expectations high. We predict Adrian Mutu, scorer of 15 goals in Serie A to become Europe's Golden Boot in 2003-04.**

## COACH

**CLAUDIO RANIERI** 20.10.51
Formerly manager of Atletico Madrid, this amiable and softly spoken Italian arrived at Chelsea after a 6 months absence from the game. His early months were dogged by his inability to speak English to either his players or the media. Then last season, fans complained that his team tinkering and squad rotation cost many points, although vitally a 4-0 home win against Liverpool on the last day of the season insured Champions League football – probably a key factor in Mr Abramovich's decision to buy the club. With so much money pumped into the club, Ranieri has plenty of pressure to deliver success soon. His only victory to date has been the Spanish Copa del Rey in 1999. Roman born played for Roma and now Roman owned!

## REACTION TO DRAW

**"We're going to have to go back to Istanbul, which we have happy memories of. We won 5-0 there against Galatasaray and although it's a tough group we're confident. Lazio are the only (European) team to have beaten us in Europe at Stamford Bridge, so we owe them one and that will probably be the star two-legged tie of the round. We're looking forward to it,"** ***Chairman Ken Bates.***

**31 MARCO AMBROSIO** 30.05.73
Goalkeeper signed from Serie A club Chievo on a free transfer in July 2003. The 30-year-old was Chievo's number two - the Italian's appearances for the club were mainly restricted to cup matches. Last season, he played eight Serie A matches for Chievo. Ambrosio was signed on the recommendation of goalkeeping coach Giorgio Pellizzaro.

**3 CELESTINE BABAYARO** 29.08.78
Babayaro has played 178 games for Chelsea, scoring seven goals (three of which were scored in Europe). The defender scored against Boro on November 16, 2002 – his first goal since the 3-1 home Champions League win against Feyenoord in November 1999, and his first Premiership goal since May 1999, against Derby (won 2-1 at home). He

played two games for Nigeria at the 2002 World Cup, then missed eight games for Chelsea in September/October 2002 with a calf injury and some games earlier this year with a thigh strain and a heavy cold. Scored one goal in 24 games last season.

**18 WAYNE BRIDGE** 05.08.80
England full back (12 caps) Bridge signed from Southampton in a £7m deal in July 2003. The deal involved Graeme Le Saux moving the other way. Bridge started 113 consecutive Premiership games for Southampton, including every Premiership game in 2000-01 and 2001-02 - a record of consecutive Premiership appearances for an outfield player (David James holds the record with 159). He played a total of 174 games for Southampton, scoring two goals - his Premiership debut was as a sub against Liverpool at the Dell in August 1998. Bridge's international debut came against Holland in February 2002 and he made two sub appearances in the 2002 World Cup (v Argentina and Nigeria). Named in 2001-02 PFA Premiership Team of the Season.

**39 CARLTON COLE** 12.10.83
Striker Cole scored one goal in seven games whilst on loan at Wolves from November 2002 to January 2003. Carlton made his England U21 debut as a sub v Turkey at St James' Park on April 1, 2003 - he made his Chelsea debut as a sub v Everton a year earlier. His first start was at Middlesbrough on April 27, 2002 after Hasselbaink picked up an injury in the warm-up – Cole then scored in the 2-0 win. He also scored twice on his Worthington Cup debut v Gillingham on November 6, 2002. In total, he's scored seven times in 19 games for Chelsea. Currently on loan to Charlton.

**10 JOE COLE** 08.11.81
Cole was signed from West Ham for £6.6m in August 2003. He is still only 21 but had already made 150 appearances for the east London side, scoring 13 goals. Cole captained West Ham at Boro on December 7, 2002, becoming the club's youngest captain since Bobby Moore. Cole has won ten caps, scoring one goal for England (v Serbia on June 3). He made one appearance as a sub in the 2002 World Cup against Sweden, then returned to the U21 side, for whom he has eight caps. He started 40 of West Ham's 42 games last season and scored five goals, equalling his best tally for a season set in 2000-01. Cole hasn't scored in domestic football since January 11.

**21 HERNAN CRESPO** 05.07.75
Chelsea coach Ranieri described Crespo as 'a lion' on capture of his signature for Chelsea. Nine goals in a mere 12 Serie A games for Inter Milan last season were more than enough to confirm his pedigree. Strong, fast and with good looks, instant stardom is guaranteed. Born in Florida, Argentina Crespo is an Argentine international and joins fellow countryman Veron at the Blues. Previous clubs include Parma and Lazio.

**23 CARLO CUDICINI** 06.09.73
Italian keeper Cudicini made 40 starts in 2001-02, conceding 39 goals and keeping 19

clean sheets. Carlo has now played 120 games for Chelsea (123 goals conceded, 47 clean sheets), including 62 in succession up to December 2002. He saved three penalties in 2001-02 and then saved penalties from Wayne Rooney (December 4, 2002) and Thierry Henry (March 8, 2003) last season - in total he's saved five of the last nine pens he's faced. His father Fabio played in goal for Roma and AC Milan - he was in the Milan team that won the 1968 Serie A title and ECWC plus the 1969 European Cup and World Club Cup.

**21 ENRIQUE DE LUCAS** 17.08.78

Former Spanish Under-21 international De Lucas (prefers to be known as 'Quique') was signed from Espanyol on a free transfer in July 2002; he was virtually a league ever-present for Espanyol in 2001-02, scoring seven goals, including two against Real Madrid, one home and one away. His first and only goal for Chelsea was during the UEFA Cup first leg v Viking on September 19, 2002. He made 31 appearances last season.

**6 MARCEL DESAILLY** 07.09.68

Club captain Desailly has played 197 games for Chelsea, scoring seven goals. The French international defender has won a record 108 caps (3 goals) – he started all three of France's 2002 World Cup games and won his most recent cap in the 2003 Confederations Cup final win over Cameroon. Desailly has won the European Cup with two different clubs - Marseille in 1993 and AC Milan in 1994 – and was the first to do so in consecutive seasons. His third consecutive final came in 1995. Desailly signed a one-year extension to his contract in August 2003, keeping him at the club until 2005.

**11 DAMIEN DUFF** 02.03.79

Republic of Ireland international Duff signed from Blackburn for a club record £17m in July 2003. The fee was the fourth highest involving a British or Irish player (after Ferdinand, Beckham and Ferdinand again). Duff has scored 35 goals in 223 games for Rovers and four goals in 37 games for his country. He started all four games in the 2002 World Cup. Last season he hit 11 goals in 31 Rovers games including goals in five consecutive Premiership appearances.

**32 MIKAEL FORSSELL** 15.03.81

Finnish international striker Forssell (24 caps, 9 goals) has scored 12 goals in 51 games for Chelsea (12 starts plus 39 as a sub). All nine of his goals in 2001-02 were scored after coming on as sub – he made only four starts that season. He spent the whole of season 2000-01 on loan at Crystal Palace, scoring 15 goals in 49 apps and helping them reach the League Cup semi-finals. Last season he went on loan to Borussia Monchengladbach, scoring seven goals in 16 Bundesliga games. This season he is on loan at Birmingham City.

**13 WILLIAM GALLAS** 17.08.77

Gallas (a former French Under-21 international) was signed from Marseille for £6.2m in May 2001. The defender made his senior international debut in a Euro 2004 qualifier v Slovenia on October 12, 2002 and won his tenth cap in the 2003 Confederations Cup final win over Cameroon. His Chelsea debut was as a sub v Newcastle on August 19, 2001. He made 48 appearances last season, scoring four times – in total he's scored six goals in 89 games – although he's yet to score an 'away' Premiership goal for Chelsea. He and Lampard were the only players to appear in every Chelsea game last season. Included in the 2003 PFA Premiership Team of the Year.

**14 GEREMI** 20.12.78
The Cameroon international signed from Real Madrid for £6.9m in July 2003 on a five-year contract. He was on-loan at Middlesbrough last season from Real Madrid after a move to Chelsea in the summer of 2002 broke down. Geremi played in all three of Cameroon's 2002 World Cup games and scored in Cameroon's pre-World Cup friendly draw with England in Kobe (2-2). Previously, he captained Cameroon's 2000 Olympic gold-winning team in Sydney and was an African Nations Cup winner with Cameroon in 2000 and 2002. Whilst at Real, he won the Spanish League with Real in 2000-01 and was an unused sub in Real Madrid's 2000 Champions League final win v Valencia. Scored 7 goals in 34 games for Boro last season.

**30 JESPER GRONKJAER** 12.08.77
Gronkjaer signed from Ajax for £7.8m in December 2000 and has since scored eight goals in 72 games for Chelsea, including five in 39 last season. The Danish international (37 caps, 3 goals) appeared in all four of their 2002 World Cup games (3 starts, 1 as a sub). Gronkjaer was out for almost six months of 2001-02 (September to March) with a knee injury that required surgery.

**22 EIDUR GUDJOHNSEN** 15.09.78
The club's second top scorer in 2001-02 with 23 goals (14 in the Premiership, three in each of the FA Cup, the League Cup the UEFA Cup) in 47 games. The Icelandic international has scored 47 goals in 129 games for Chelsea after signing from Bolton (73 apps, 27 goals) for £4m in July 2000. He made his Chelsea debut as a sub in 2000 Charity Shield v Man Utd. 20 of his 44 games last season were as a sub (he finished 90 minutes on only 13 occasions).

**9 JIMMY FLOYD HASSELBAINK** 27.03.72
The Dutch forward (who played under Ranieri at Atletico Madrid) won the Golden Boot in 2000-01 with 23 Premiership goals. He was Chelsea's top scorer again in 2001-02 with 29 goals in 48 games (again scoring 23 in the Premiership, one behind Golden Boot winner Thierry Henry). This was the best return by a Chelsea player in a season since Kerry Dixon netted 36 goals in all comps in 1984-85. However, last season was the first time in seven seasons he's failed to score 20 goals in a campaign (15 goals in 44 games). In total, he has scored 112 times in 220 games in English football, and 70 goals in 133 games for Chelsea. Hasselbaink has won 23 caps for his country, scoring nine goals.

# GROUP G
## CHELSEA FC

**29 ROBERT HUTH** 18.08.84
Huth is a Berlin-born defender who made his debut in the final Premiership game of 2001-02, as a sub in the 3-1 home defeat against Aston Villa. Huth came to Chelsea as a 16-year-old in August 2000 from German club FC Union Berlin – he made his full debut for Chelsea in the first leg v Viking on September 19, 2002 and started four games in succession.

**2 GLEN JOHNSON** 23.08.84
Johnson was signed from West Ham for £6m in July 2003 - the most expensive teenage signing in the club's history, surpassing Babayaro's £2.25m transfer back in 1997. An English defender loaned to Millwall last season, he made eight appearances for the First Division club between October 19, 2002 and December 7, 2002. His Premiership debut then came as sub in the 4-2 defeat at Charlton on January 22. He made his England U21 debut as sub in the 1-1 draw with Turkey at St James' Park on April 1 (he now has two caps). He started the final 14 West Ham games of last season.

**36 JOE KEENAN** 14.10.82
Left-back/midfielder Keenan is a former England U18 international born in Southampton who turned pro in October 1999. He came on as a substitute at Villa on February 9, 2002 to make his first-team debut. Keenan broke his leg playing for the reserves last season, but the departure of Jon Harley has enhanced his opportunities.

**8 FRANK LAMPARD** 21.06.78
England international midfielder Lampard signed from West Ham for £11m in June 2001. He and Gallas were the only players to have appeared in every Chelsea game last season – he scored eight times in 48 games. The season before, he appeared more times than any other Chelsea player, scoring seven goals in 53 games. Has won 11 England caps but wasn't included in the 2002 World Cup squad. Before this season Lampard has hit 54 goals in 300 senior club appearances, including 15 goals in 102 games for Chelsea.

**36 JURGEN MACHO** 24.08.77
Goalkeeper Macho signed from Sunderland on a free transfer in July 2003. He played 16 games last season for the north-eastern club in place of the injured Sorensen. He'd joined Sunderland on a free from Austrian second division side First Vienna in July 2000. In all, Macho played 27 games for Sunderland. He also made his Austrian international debut as a substitute in friendly v Norway on November 20, 2002.

**4 CLAUDE MAKELELE** 18.02.73
Joined Chelsea at the beginning of the season after going on strike against Real Madrid. The French defensive midfielder appeared 42 times for the Galacticos last season, but didn't score once. He joined the club in summer 2000 from Celta Vigo for £9m, after hawking himself around Premiership clubs for £11m. The 24-cap player played for

France in the pre-1998 World Cup warm up games, but just failed to make the final 22, and wasn't considered again until Didier Deschamps retired in autumn 2000. Makelele made his name as captain of the French national U21 side and a key player in the Nantes team that won the 1995 title with Loko, Ouedec, Karembeu, Pedros and co, then moved to Marseille in 1997. The Zaire-born midfielder moved again in summer 1998 from Marseille to Celta for £1m.

**15 MARIO MELCHIOT** 04.11.76
Melchiot has made 132 appearances for Chelsea, scoring three goals (two of which have been against Man Utd). He hasn't scored since March 6, 2002. The Dutch international (10 caps – won his 10th cap as a sub in friendly v Portugal on April 30). Was 'sent off' in semi-final, 2nd leg at Tottenham on January 23, 2002 – the referee mistakenly banished Hasselbaink – and banned for three matches as a result.

**7 ADRIAN MUTU** 08.01.79
Mutu was signed from Parma for £15.8m in August 2003. He scored 17 goals in 30 Serie A games for Parma last season. The Romanian international striker made his name at Dinamo Bucharest, scoring 18 league goals in 1999-00. This earned a move to Inter Milan, but he failed to score in 10 Serie A games for the club, so in 2000 he moved to Hellas Verona for two seasons. In 2001-02 he scored 12 Serie A goals in a relegated side.

**28 FELIPE OLIVERA** 27.05.84
19-year-old Portuguese forward Olivera signed from Porto in October 2001 for an undisclosed fee. The Portugal U19 international is yet to score a first-team goal. He made his Chelsea debut as substitute in the 2-1 UEFA Cup win v Viking Stavanger on September 19, 2002 and then made his Premiership debut, also as a sub, in the 3-0 win at Man City on October 19, 2002. He made a total of five substitute appearances last season.

**17 EMMANUEL PETIT** 22.09.70
Petit was a member of Arsenal's 1997-98 League and Cup double winning side – the defensive midfielder made 118 appearances (11 goals) for Arsenal in his three seasons at the club (1997-00). His first goal for Chelsea came at home to Derby on March 30, 2002. The French international (63 caps, six goals) played in the first two of France's 2002 World Cup games – he was suspended for the third. Petit won his 63rd cap v Czech Republic on February 12, 2003, but was subsequently left out of the squad for Euro 2004 qualifiers with calf and groin injuries and didn't play in the Confederations Cup. The midfielder has scored only three goals in 69 games for Chelsea.

**40 LENNY PIDGELEY** 07.02.84
19-year-old English keeper who was on the bench for six games in October and November 2002, and for two games in December 2002. Pidgeley was a regular for the reserves last season, saving a penalty v Ipswich in August 2002. The former youth international (U16 and U17 levels) signed a new pro contract with the club in March 2002.

# GROUP G
## CHELSEA FC

**12 MARIO STANIC** 10.04.72
Stanic scored twice on his Premiership debut, in a 4-2 win against West Ham at Stamford Bridge on the opening day of 2000-01, then scored at St Mary's, Southampton on August 25, 2001 – his first goal for a year. The former Croatian defender (49 caps, seven goals) announced his international retirement in May 2003. Stanic cost £5.6m from Parma in June 2000, where he scored 25 goals in 109 games for Parma, with whom he won the Super Cup, UEFA Cup (1999) and the Italian Cup. Mario has scored 10 goals in 75 games for Chelsea. He missed several matches last season with injuries including a stomach strain, a knee problem, an Achilles problem, and then a fever.

**26 JOHN TERRY** 07.12.80
Terry has played 119 games for Chelsea, scoring 12 goals. The England centre back made his senior debut (as 17-year-old) as a sub in 4-1 Worthington Cup win against Aston Villa in October 1998. After making nine England U21 appearances, Terry made his senior debut as a sub v Serbia & Montenegro on June 3. Has had a number of disciplinary problems – he was fined two weeks' wages, along with Jody Morris, on January 8, 2002 for being on licensed premises two days before a game. In August 2002 he was cleared of assaulting the doorman of a London nightclub in January 2002. Terry has scored four goals from the back in his last ten appearances either side of the summer break.

**20 JUAN SEBASTIAN VERON** 09.03.75
The Argentine midfielder was signed from Man Utd (where he scored 11 goals in 82 games) for an initial fee of £12.5m in August 2003 - the fee will rise to £15m, depending upon the club's success over the length of his four-year deal. Completed his then-British transfer record £28.1m move from Lazio to Man Utd on July 12, 2001 – he was the first South American to play for Man Utd. Veron's previous clubs include Boca Juniors, Sampdoria and Parma; his first club was Estudiantes, who he joined at the age of five. Veron won the Italian Cup and UEFA Cup with Parma in 1999, before moving to Sven Goran Eriksson's Lazio side for around £20m in 1999. In his first season with Lazio, he won the Italian League and Cup 'double' and was also in the side that beat Man Utd in the 1999 European Super Cup. He then won last year's Premiership with United. The Argentine played all three 2002 World Cup games. Veron scored six goals last season – four in the Champions League, but hadn't scored since December 14, 2002 until he netted in Chelsea's early season win at Anfield.

**24 BOUDEWIJN ZENDEN** 15.08.76
Scored on his Chelsea debut, v Newcastle on August 19, 2001 (the opening day of last season). Completed 90 minutes only 3 times in 2001-02, and again only 3 times last season. Has lost his No. 11 shirt to Duff. Signed from Barcelona for £7.5m in August 2001. Is a black belt in karate. Turned down a move to Newcastle to come to Chelsea. Dutch international (45 caps, 6 goals). Started all 9 internationals last season. Won his

45th cap v Belarus on June 7. In 1999-00 he reached the Champions League semi-final with Barcelona, beating Chelsea along the way (in the quarter-final). Has scored 4 goals in 59 games for Chelsea. Hasn't scored since August 23, 2002 (at home to Man Utd). Before 2001-02 he had played in the previous 3 seasons in the Champions League with Barcelona. Missed 10 games earlier last season with an ankle injury. Started only 12 games last season. Is now on loan with Middlesbrough.

# SS LAZIO

**The Biancocleleste finished a troubled year financially in 4th place in Serie A, reaching the semis of both the Italian Cup and the UEFA Cup. Still playing at the 80,000+ seater Olympic Stadium in Rome (which they share with Roma) the team is packed with experience but is rapidly ageing following the departure of 10 stars in the close season including Diego Simeone to Athletico Madrid and Gaizka Mendieta to Middlesbrough. Arrivals include Luciano Zauro from Atalanta, Sergio Conceicao and former Ipswich goalkeeper Matteo Sereni. Under new coach Roberto Mancicni a breath of fresh air has relieved the immediate monetary troubles and the team will be tough to beat - especially at home**

## COACH

**ROBERTO MANCINI** 27.11.64
After a short spell in his first coaching job at Fiorentina, Lazio president Sergio Cragnotti convinced Mancini to come back to Rome to become coach of Lazio. Cragnotti held Mancini in high esteem as the latter had played for the club and won the Italian league title, two Italian Cups and the last-ever Cup Winners' Cup (1999). Earlier at Sampdoria Genoa, where he formed a splendid attacking partnership with Gianluca Vialli, Mancini had already won one league title, four Italian Cups and the 1990 Cup Winners' Cup. Besides that, he lost the Champions Cup Final in 1992 at Wembley against Barcelona. 38-year-old Mancini certainly knows how to motivate his players. They were able to reach that important fourth place in Serie A and they got to the semi-final of the Uefa Cup during a season in which their financial crises hit them very hard (most of the players didn't receive any salary for five months).

## REACTION TO DRAW

**"We are very happy. For us the match with Chelsea will be a great occasion especially as we will be up against two great former players in Hernan Crespo and Juan Veron. The other teams in the group also merit respect ... but we are capable of qualifying,"** ***managing director Luca Baraldi.***

# GROUP G
## SS LAZIO

## SQUAD

**4 DEMETRIO ALBERTINI** 23.08.71
As a youngster Albertini always played for Milan, the club he made his debut for on January 15th 1989 (4-0 win against Como) and he only left in 1990-91 to gain some first team experience at Padova in Serie B (28 games, five goals). Back at San Siro, he appeared in the first ever Champions League game for Milan against Goteborg on November 25th 1992 (4-0 win) and played in the first three Champions League finals with 'the Rossoneri' - winning only in 1994 in Athens against Barcelona (4-0). Midfielder Albertini won five Italian league titles with Milan and played 79 times for the Squadra Azzurra losing the World Cup Final in 1994 to Brazil after penalties (3-2) although he scored from the spot for Italy. Played last season in Spain for Atletico Madrid (28 games, two goals). First season at Lazio, where he will probably also take the penalties.

**15 FABRIZIO CASAZZA** 16.09.70
The reserve goalkeeper from promoted side Sampdoria Genoa left the club of his birthplace this summer to become third choice at Lazio. Played five games in Serie B for Sampdoria last season. Casazza has played for Verona (1994-96, Serie B), Torino (1996-99, Serie B), Venezia (1999-2000, Serie A) and Sampdoria Genoa (2001-03, Serie B).

**2 FRANCESCO COLLONESE** 10.08.71
Defender whose biggest achievement was winning the UEFA Cup in 1998 with Internazionale in Paris against Lazio, the club he subsequently joined in the summer of 2000. Colonnese began his Serie A career in August 1993 with Cremonese. He also played for AS Roma (1994-95) and Naples (1995-97). Having no playing opportunities at AS Roma at the start of the 1997/98 season, he left in October 1997 for Internazionale. Collonese has layed only 12 league games for Lazio in Serie A in the last three seasons (four in 2000/01, eight in 2001/02 and none last season).

**9 BERNARDO CORRADI** 30.03.76
Tall striker Corradi left top division club Cagliari in 2000 for Serie B newcomers Chievo. With that team he clinched immediately promotion (36 games, scoring 12 goals) to Serie A and obtained a Uefa Cup ticket in his first season in the top flight (scoring ten goals in 32 games). That was enough for Internazionale to give him a contract but without even playing one game for the 'nerazzuri' he was moved on to Lazio in September 2002. Corradi made his debut in Serie A for Cagliari in Rome against Lazio on August 30th 1999 and he scored the first goal at home against Benfica in the third qualifying round (3-1 win). 32 league games, ten goals last season.

**24 FERNANDO COUTO** 02.08.69
Very talented but sometimes hot tempered Portuguese international central defender who left FC Porto in 1994 (after three Portuguese league titles and three Portuguese cup wins) to play in Italy for Parma. In his two seasons at Parma he won the UEFA Cup

in 1995. With FC Barcelona, the team he joined in 1996, he won the Cup Winners' Cup (1997) and twice the Spanish Cup (1997 and 1998). In 1998 Couto went back to Italy, this time to play for Lazio. In his first season he won the Cup Winners' Cup again (against Mallorca in 1999) and, in his second season, the Italian double. Since then, there have been no more trophies for this defender with a good head, although he has now amassed more than 80 Portuguese caps. 15 games in Serie A last season, no goals.

**6 OUSMANE DABO** 08.02.77
18-year-old midfielder Dabo made his debut in the French league on October 27th 1995 for Rennes at home against Nice (1-0 win). After three seasons he left the club at the same time as Mickael Silvestre for Internazionale. But Dabo's path to the team was blocked by too many famous players - he was loaned to Vicenza just after New Year (1999). Since then, the promising talent has always been on the move with little success. He went back to Inter in the summer of 1999 and his next clubs were Parma (1999-2000), Monaco (2000-February 2001), Vicenza (Feb 2001-June 2001) and Atalanta Bergamo since July 2001. Last season he played 31 games and scored four goals in Serie A for the relegated club. This summer he came to Lazio, along with left-back Luciano Zauri.

**19 GIUSEPPE FAVALLI** 08.01.72
A youth product of Cremonese, the club he made his debut for in Serie A on August 27th 1989 away to Internazionale (2-1 defeat). After 94 games in the first team of Cremonese (59 in Serie A, 35 in Serie B) Favalli joined Lazio in the summer of 1992. In Rome he has been a regular in defence playing between 20 and 30 games a season (26 last season, one goal). With Lazio he won the Italian Cup in 1998, the Cup Winners' Cup in 1999 and the Italian double in 2000. He also played twice for the Squadra Azzurra in the autumn of 1994.

**14 STEFANO FIORI** 17.04.75
Right-winger Stefano Fiori arrived at Lazio in the summer of 2001 coming from Udinese. But it was with Parma that he earlier made the headlines, winning two Uefa Cups (in 1995 and 1999) and one Italian Cup (in 1999 against Fiorentina). In the autumn of 1997, he also played in the Champions League with Parma (five games – two starts and three substitute appearances) but that campaign in a group with Borussia Dortmund, Galatasaray and Sparta Prague didn't go beyond the first group stage. Fiore also played for Cosenza (Serie B until 1994), Padova (Serie A in 1995/96) and Chievo (Serie B in 1996/97) on loan while awaiting first team chances. He has more than 25 caps for Italy and he will have to work hard to keep his place this season because of the return of Sergio Conceiçao. He scored in the third qualifying round at home against Benfica. 33 league games, six goals last season.

**16 GIULIANO GIANNICHEDDA** 21.09.74
Played for third division club Sora when Udinese bought him in 1995. After six seasons, 151 league games, two goals and often being the best in his position, he moved to Lazio in the summer of 2001. Although he doesn't score goals he's a very useful player,

working hard in midfield for Lazio and always plays with his heart. 28 games in 2001-02, 25 games last season.

**17 GUERINO GOTTARDI** 18.12.70
Swiss-born midfielder who started his career at home town club Young Boys Bern. In 1991 he joined Neuchatel Xamax where he played for four successive seasons (119 league games, eight goals). In 1995 Gottardi tried his luck abroad with Lazio. Until 1999 he had a regular place in the team playing around 20 league games a season. From then onwards his appearances diminished with only one game in Serie A last season.

**21 SIMONE INZAGHI** 05.04.76
The younger brother of Milan striker Filippo is the only forward aside Dutchman Marco Van Basten to score four goals in one Champions League match. He achieved that performance on March 14th 2000 for Lazio in the 5-1 home win over Olympique Marseille. Van Basten needed 29 minutes to do it, Inzaghi 54 minutes (between 17th min and 71st min). Inzaghi played for Carpi (C1), Novara (C2), Lumezzane (C2) and Brescello (C1) in the lower division of Italian football before making his debut for Piacenza at home against Lazio (1-1) on September 13th 1998. After 30 games and 15 goals for Piacenza he joined Lazio in the summer of 1999. Scored 20 goals in 73 league games for Lazio since then (four goals in 18 games last season).

**20 FABIO LIVERANI** 29.04.76
Midfielder Liverani joined Lazio in September 2001 from Perugia where he made his debut in Serie A on October 1st 2000 at home versus Lecce (1-1). In his first season of top flight football he also made his debut in the Italian national team at home against South Africa (1-0 win) on April 25th 2001. Played 47 games for Lazio, scoring two goals (26 games and two goals in 2001-02, 21 last season without scoring). Perugia found him at fourth division club Viterbese, where he'd played first team football since December 1996.

**8 CLAUDIO JAVIER LOPEZ** 17.07.74
Argentine international forward who made his name in European club football with Valencia in the Champions League, scoring some wonderful goals and reaching the final in Paris in 2000 (a 3-0 defeat against Real Madrid). 'The Flea' moved to Lazio in 2000 – they wanted to get their hands on the Champions League after winning the Italian double. But Lopez started struggling with injuries and Lazio failed in Europe. Nevertheless, Claudio Lopez was Lazio's topscorer last season with 15 goals in 34 games. He's played 12 games for Lazio in the Champions League scoring six goals (adding to his 16 CL games and five goals for Valencia). Claudio Lopez played in Argentina for Estudiantes (youth teams until 1992) and Racing Club (1992-96) and he won a silver medal at the Atlanta Olympics in 1996.

**11 SINISA MIHAJLOVIC** 20.02.69
This international defender for Serbia and Montenegro (more than 60 caps) starts his

12th season in Serie A and his sixth for Lazio, the club he signed for in the summer of 1998 after spending four seasons at Sampdoria Genoa. Mihajlovic, who scores regularly from free-kicks (as he did in the Champions League third qualifying round at home against Benfica in August) made his name in 1991 when he won the Champions Cup and the Intercontinental Cup with Red Star Belgrade. In 1992, he left Crvena Zvezda for AS Roma. He won the double with Lazio in 2000. 21 league games, one goal last season.

**18 ROBERTO MUZZI** 21.09.71
One of Lazio's most recent signings, coming from Udinese where he played since 1999. Scored 39 goals in 103 league games for Udinese (five in 28 games last season). Right-winger Muzzi started his professional career at AS Roma, making his debut on February 11th 1990 at home against Inter (1-1). In November 1993, he was loaned to second division team Pisa. Back at AS Roma he had few chances to play so he moved to Cagliari one year later (November 1994) where he scored 48 goals in 108 games in Serie A. Won the Italian Cup with AS Roma in 1991 and, now in his thirties, Muzzi will feature in the Champions League for the first time this season.

**23 PAOLO NEGRO** 16.04.72
Experienced defender who began his career in the Italian top flight with Bologna on October 28th 1990 away to Genoa (0-0). Played one season for Brescia (1992/93) before joining Lazio in the summer of 1993. In his ten seasons at Lazio (247 games and 19 goals) he has managed to score at least once every season (19 games, one goal last season).

**22 MASSIMO ODDO** 14.06.76
Originally in the youth teams of Milan, this defender, who usually plays on the right wing, spent four seasons in the Italian third division (C1) with four different teams (Fiorenzuola, Monza, Prato, Lecco) and two seasons in the Serie B, again for two different clubs (Monza where he also played before and Naples) before moving to Serie A club Verona in 2000. There he impressed so much that in 2002, he got a transfer to Lazio. Played 19 games in Serie A last season for Lazio.

**53 SERGIO CONCEICAO** 15.11.74
Is back at Lazio, where he played between 1998 and 2000 (63 games, seven goals) and won an Italian double. Got to the semi-final of Euro 2000 with Portugal, scoring a hat trick versus Germany in Rotterdam. Moved to Parma in summer of 2000 with Matias Almeyda as part of the £34 million move of Hernan Crespo in the other direction - but one year later the Portuguese winger was off to Internazionale where he didn't really perform as demanded by coach Hector Cuper. Played all three games in a disappointing World Cup campaign for Portugal in 2002 in South Korea. He's also won two league titles in two seasons with FC Porto in 1997 and 1998.

**1 ANGELO PERUZZI** 16.02.70
This experienced goalkeeper made his debut in Serie A on December 13th 1987 for

neighbours AS Roma. It was his only game of the season. In 1989 he defended Verona's goal for one season and after another spell on the substitutes' bench of the 'giallorosso', Peruzzi moved in 1991 to Juventus. With that club he became a regular goalkeeper for the Squadra Azzurra and he won three Scudettos, one Italian Cup, one Uefa Cup (1993), the Champions League and the Intercontinental Cup (both in 1996). In 1997 and 1998 Peruzzi reached the final of the Champions League again but lost to Borussia Dortmund (3-1) and Real Madrid (1-0). In 1999 Peruzzi left for Internazionale and although he played a full season for the 'nerazzurri' in the summer of 2000, he went back to the city where it all began - this time to play for Lazio. 30 games in Serie A last season (conceding 28 goals).

**3 CESAR APARECIDO RODRIGUEZ** 24.10.74
Brazilian defender who can also play in midfield (on the left) if necessary and who is able to score a goal as he did in Porto, in the return leg of the third qualifying round against Benfica. It proved to be the winner. Cesar arrived at Lazio halfway through the 2001-02 season from Sao Caetano. His original club in Brazil was Juve Sao Paulo. 26 games, three goals in Serie A last season.

**33 MATTEO SERENI** 11.02.75
Sereni was playing for Ipswich in England when he made his name in Italy. It was finally Brescia who gave him a chance to play in Serie A again. Sereni had earlier spells in the Italian top flight with Sampdoria Genoa (10 games between 1995 and 1997), with Piacenza (34 games in 1997/98) and Empoli (30 games in 1998/99). After two seasons with Sampdoria Genoa in Serie B, Sereni moved abroad. Joined Lazio in the summer as back up for Peruzzi. 23 league games last season for Brescia.

**31 JAAP STAM** 17.07.72
Dutch international Stam made his name as a defender in his first season at Willem II in 1995. After the winter break, he joined PSV Eindhoven where he progressed and became a more complete central defender. In the summer of 1998 Alex Ferguson brought him to Manchester United where he won three Premierships, one FA Cup, one Champions League and one Intercontinental Cup. After the publication of his biography - in which he criticised the coach - Stam had to leave Old Trafford in August 2001. He moved to Lazio where he had a difficult start because of a UEFA ban for allegedly using nandrolone. Played 28 games in Serie A last season.

**19 DEJAN STANKOVIC** 11.09.78
Serbia and Montenegro international Stankovic is the creative force of Lazio. He is the man with the ideas, he is a good dribbler and has a tremendous shot. He starts his third Champions League campaign with Lazio, the club he signed for in 1998, coming from Red Star Belgrade. Has already won the Cup Winners' Cup, the European Super Cup (both in 1999) and the Italian double in 2000. He made his European debut with Red Star Belgrade at 16, beating the record held by Dragan Dzajic. 29 games in Serie A last season, six goals.

**5 LUCIANO ZAURI** 20.01.78
New signing Zauri is a product of Atalanta Bergamo, relegated to Serie B last season. As left back, Zauri has already played five times for the Squadra Azzurra, making his debut on September 5th 2001 at home against Morocco (1-0 win). Not being able to play first team football at Atalanta, Zauri took up with Chievo in Serie B in 1997/98. 32 league games for Atalanta last season.

# AC SPARTA PRAGUE

**The club name 'Sparta' comes from the Greek team whose feats gained admiration around the time the Czech club was founded in 1894. The club's strip was brought back from England after a visit to Arsenal in 1906. Number one team in the Czech Prepublic, Sparta have won 29 titles as well as the championship last season. This impressive record includes 8 of the 10 national titles since 1994. The club's best result in Europe was when they reached the semi-final of the European Cup Winners Cup in 1972-3. Since then they have reached the second group stage of the Champions League twice in 1999-00 and 2001-02. Their success hasn't gone unchecked though. There was a fallow period without a win from 1967-84 for 17 seasons and from 1954-84 they only won 2 titles after the arrival of Communism as the army teams dominated.**

## COACH

**JIRI KOTRBA** 28.02.58
A former player with Ceske Budejovice and Bohemians Prague, Kotrba coached Ceske Budejovice, Viktoria Zizkov and Jablonec until he joined Marila Pribram in 1998. There he gained a fine reputation for organising the provincial club and only left for Sparta at the start of this season.

## REACTION TO DRAW

**I am looking forward to playing Lazio and Chelsea too where former Lazio team mate Juan Sebastian Veron is playing. It's a good draw, tough, but I pleased we have the chance to test ourselves against some of the best players around. That's what the Champions League is, it's the best players,"** ***Captain Karel Poborsky.***

## SQUAD

**29 JAROMIR BLAZEK** 29.12.72
Former international keeper who played in the Champions League from 1999-2001. This is his 5th season at Sparta, prior to which he played for Prague rivals Bohemians and

Slavia. In 2001-02 he went out on loan to Pribram. Has played nearly 200 top flight league games, and was back in the national squad in June 2003 as back up to Peter Cech.

**17 PETER CECH** 20.05.82
There is widespread belief that this keeper will be the best since the great Ivo Viktor was the world's greatest in the late 1960's and early 1970's. He gained his first full cap in 2002 Cyprus Cup in February. He is in his first season with the club after joining from Premier side Chemel Blsany. Forced his way into the side at the start of the season and went 11 league and Champions League games - over 1,039 minutes. The 6'5" tall keeper was in the World Junior U20 Cup team for the Czechs in summer 2001 and is already an U21 international.

**5 JAN FLACHBART** 03.03.78
Signed from the neighbouring Bohemians club, after three seasons in their first team. A former U21 international, Flachbart has now been with the club for 5 years. He played a small role in the 1999 title win before growing increasingly influential in 2000. In the following season he was away on loan at Jablonec. Flachbart has now played 100 league and nine Champions League games for Sparta.

**27 IGOR GLUSCEVIC** 30.03.74
The much-travelled striker has come to rest at Sparta in summer 2003. He started off his career at the Yugoslav club Vojvodina, where he played from 1994-96 before setting off on his travels via Extremadura and FC Seville (Spain), Aris Salonica (Greece) and the past 2 seasons have seen him with Utrecht. He scored 20 league goals in 2 seasons at Utrecht from 2001-03 - his best return to date.

**13 VLADIMIR GLUSEVIC** 20.10.79
Younger brother of Igor, Vladimir, a native of Serbia and Montenegro helped his local side Mogren Budva to promotion in 2001 only to see them relegated in the following season. Trialist for Dutch side SC Heerenveen. Joined Sparta this summer. Yet to play Champions League football.

**2 ZDENEK GRYGERA** 14.05.80
Played in final of 2000 European U21 championship v Italy and then went straight into the national squad for the World Cup qualifiers for the 2002 finals. Joined Sparta in summer 2000 from fellow Division One club Drnovice, for whom he made a first team debut in 1998. Much is expected of this young full back, who had a long term injury last season, but still won a 2001 title medal. Pulled a hamstring in the first leg of World Cup play-offs v Belgium then was injured on return at the 2002 Cyprus Cup in February.

**22 JIRI HOMOLA** 02.07.80
A defender who joined in summer 2003 from Jablonec where he played in the first team from 1999-2003. The U21 international was once with Sparta's rivals Slavia Prague.

# GROUP G
## AC SPARTA PRAGUE

**16 TOMAS HUBSCHMANN** 09.04.81
Having joined Sparta at 16, Hubschmann is now enjoying his third season in the first team. Won his first caps for his country when he played both games against the Belgians in the World Cup play-offs in Nov 2001 and has been in the squad ever since

**20 JIRI JAROSIK** 27.10.77
Very promising former Czech U21 international who played in the final of the 2000 EuroU21 championship, and gained his first cap on 16.08.00 against Slovenia. Has now established himself in the national midfield in place of Radek Bejb. Has been at Sparta for the last 6 seasons, but was away 1997-99 on loan at Liberec. At 6'3" and having just been upgraded from the U21 and Olympic teams, Jarosik is definitely one to watch.

**11 PATRICK JEZEK** 28.12.76
Returned to the country in summer 2003 after spells in Austria and Germany. The midfielder first played for Viktoria Pilzen in the Czech league, before he left to play Tirol Innsbruck in Austria in 1997. There he won three titles before Tirol were stripped of the title in 2002 for dodgy financial dealings, after which he was transferred to Bundesliga Division 2 club, Karslruhe.

**17 PETR JOHANA** 01.11.76
Enjoying his first season at Sparta, the central defender is also in the current national squad. He joined in summer 2003 from Slovan Liberec where he had been a key player in the surprise 2002 league title win.

**9 MAREK KINCL** 03.04.73
The tall forward joined Sparts in summer 2000 from Viktoria Zivkov, where he was their top scorer in 1999-2000 with 16 goals. He replaced Lokvenc who went to Kaiserslautern. The 6'3" striker won a championship winner's medal in 2001 and 2003 when he scored 50 league goals. Kincl played in 12 Champions League games in 2001-02.

**1 PETR KOUBA** 28.01.69
The Czech keeper played all 6 games including the final at Euro96 but has suffered from injury problems ever since. This is the second season of his second spell at Sparta. He played with the club from 1991-96 when he helped them win 4 national titles. Rated one of the best keepers in Europe, he was transferred to Deportivo but serious shoulder and knee injuries meant he hardly played for the Spanish club. His rehab included loan spells at Kaiserslautern, Viktoria Zizkov and Jablonec before he was returned to Sparta in summer 2002.

**15 RADOSLAV KOVAC** 27.11.79
Signed in summer 2003 from Sigma Olomouc. Joined them in 1995 and went on to play over 100 league games for them. Sparta have had their eyes on him ever since he played in the national U21 team that won the 2002 European U21 championship in Switzerland.

# GROUP G
## AC SPARTA PRAGUE

**12 PAVEL KRMAS** 03.03.80
The 6'4" midfielder joined the club in 2001 from Hradecv Kralove, a regional Premier Division club. Krmas played for Kralov since 1995 and was then loaned back there by Sparta for the 2002-03 season. Has since rejoined Sparta after summer 2003.

**3 VLADIMIR LABANT** 08.06.74
The left-sided defender started his career playing in Slovakia for Kosice and Dukla Banska Bystrica. Labant came over to the Czech Republic in 1997 to play for Slavia Prague. Then he moved to Sparta for the 2000 and 2001 title wins before going to West Ham. Following that brief spell at the London side in 2002-03, the Slovakian international is now back with Sparta.

**10 RATISLAV MICHALIK** 14. 01.74
The Slovak international has played his football in the Czech Republic since 1994, when he left the army team, Dukla Banska Bystrica. Has been out on loan from Sparta since 1997 - first at Slovan Liberec and then at Pribram. Hauled back in by Sparta from 2001 after 4 years away and has since played well, earning a place in the Slovak national squad from autumn 2001.

**20 JIRI NEMEC** 15.05.66
The captain of the national side has returned to his former club this season at the end of a marvellous career. Nemec played for Sparta from 1990-93 after joining from the army side Dukla Prague. After that spell, he spent 10 seasons from 1993 to 2002 in the Bundesliga as captain of Schalke, helping them to win the 1997 UEFA Cup as well as the German Cup in 2001 and 2002 honours. He returned home to the Czech Republic to play for Chenmel Blsany in 2002 but his form was so excellent he joined Sparta in 2003.

**4 PAVEL PERGL** 14.11.77
The midfielder was with Sparta from 1987-97 before he went to the provinces to play Premier football with Chmel Blsany, Drnovice and Pribram. In summer 2003 he was reunited with Kortba at Sparta, after playing for him at Pribram.

**19 MARTIN PETRAS** 02.11.79
Summer 2002 signing from Jablonec where he played from 2000-02. The Slovakia international is much improved and played in both Euro2004 qualifiers v England.

**8 KAREL POBORSKY** 30.03.72
The all time caps record holder for the new Czech Republic returned home in summer 2002 from Lazio. He scored his first international goal - a lob against Portugal at Euro 96. That goal inspired Manchester Utd to buy the midfielder from 1996 champions Slavia Prague for £3.5 million where he played a part in the team that won the 1997 Championship and reached the European Cup semi-final. He then moved in December 1998 to Benfica for £2 million where he enjoyed two good seasons before joining Lazio.

**18 MIRKO POLEDICA** 11.09.78
The Serbian 6'3" defender arriving at Sparta in summer 2003 from the Polish club Lech Poznan where he had spent just one season.

**6 JIRI ROSICKY** 11.11.77
Originally played with Sparta until 1998. Went to Atletico Madrid for what turned out to be 2 seasons in their B team. Then moved to the Austrian Premier Division club Bregenz, 2000-03 and after 100 games, came back to Sparta in summer 2003.

**14 LIBOR SIONKO** 01.02.77
The Czech international midfielder joined Sparta in summer 1999 from Banik Ostrava where he played over 100 games before the move. Capped first in April 1999 v Poland, Sionko featured in the championship winning side in 2000 and 2001 and 2003. He has played all 12 group games in the Champions League.

**30 MICHAL SPIT** 09.04.75
Spit has been Sparta's reserve keeper for the last 15 years. He has been loaned out twice, playing Div 1 football for Jablonec and Pribram. In summer 2001 he thought he had a chance of joining the first team when two international keepers left the side. He was even given the No 1 jersey but then Peter Cech was brought in.

**26 MARTIN ZABONCAK** 21.07.75
Played some 150 Premier Division games for Brno (1995-2001) and Slovan Liberec (2002-03) before joining Sparta in summer 2003 to give the squad some depth.

**7 LUKAS ZELENKA** 05.10.79
First joined the club at the age of 6 but at 18 he was signed by Belgian club, Anderlecht. The move did not work out and he was loaned to Westerlo, a mid-table side in 1999, and eventually came back to Sparta in summer 2001 after four years in Belgium. The former U21 international, who captained the team that won the European U21 championship in 2002, played 10 of Sparta's 12 Champion League games in 2001-02.

# BESIKTAS JK

**After winning their first title in 8 years last season, Besiktas Jimnasti Külübü have their first automatic entrance into the Champions League. Twice before they reached the 1st group stage after eliminating Slovenian champions Maribor (in 1997) and Russian runners-up Lokomotiv Moscow (in 2000). In 1997 they started well with 6 points from 9 in their first 3 games but 3 successive defeats (in Goteborg, at home versus Bayern Munich and away to Paris Saint-Germain) finished their hopes. In 2000 they did even worse taking only 4 points out of a**

**possible 18. They lost twice against Milan (4-1 in San Siro and 0-2 at home), they were blown away in Barcelona's Nou Camp (5-0) and at Elland Road they registered one of the (two) heaviest defeats ever in the competition (6-0). Nevertheless 3 weeks later they managed to keep Leeds United at a goalless draw (0-0) in Istanbul but their only performance to be proud of was 3-0 versus Barcelona preventing Louis Van Gaal's team from reaching the 2nd group stage. The ŒBlack Eagles, have have won 12 league titles and 5 Turkish cups but their best performance in Europe was reaching the quarter-finals. In 1986/87 they bowed out against Dynamo Kiev in the Champions Clubs, Cup, last season they were eliminated in the Uefa Cup by Lazio.**

## COACH

**MIRCEA LUCESCU** 29.07.45
Midfielder Lucescu won six Romanian league titles and six Romanian national cups with Dinamo Bucharest, his home town club. He played 74 times for the Romanian national team. In 1977 he started the season as player-coach at Corvinul Hunedoara. He stopped playing in 1981, but continued as a coach and in the same year he also took charge of the Romanian team, which he led to the 1984 European championships in France. In 1986 he went back to Dinamo Bucharest and after reaching the semi-final of the Cup Winners' Cup in 1990 (beaten by Anderlecht) he left Romania for Italy where he successively coached Pisa (1990-91), Brescia (1991-96) and Reggiana (1996-97). In 1997 it was time for a brief return to Romania with Rapid Bucharest. Struggling Internazionale asked him at the end of 1998 to take over from Simoni, but after being eliminated by Man Utd in the quarter-final of the CL (March 1999) his stay in Milan came to an abrupt halt. He went back to coach Rapid Bucharest for a second time (1999-2000) before moving to Galatasaray on July 1st 2000. He immediately won the European Super Cup in Monaco against Real Madrid (2-1 after a golden goal from Jardel) but in the league finished runners-up behind Fenerbahçe. In 2002, Galatasaray won their 15th Turkish league title but Lucescu, sometimes criticised for his defensive play, was still ambitious and moved to neighbours Besiktas. In his first season with his second Turkish club he won the Turkish league title again.

## REACTION TO DRAW

**"Lazio beat us in the UEFA Cup last year so it would be good to get revenge for that. You have to admit it is a difficult draw but I would like to think we can get through it,"** ***chairman Yildirim Demiroren.***

## SQUAD

**2 EMRE ASIK** 13.12.73
The defender joined BJK from Galatasaray SK in summer 2003. His senior league debut was in 1999 with Istanbulspor then he joined Galatasaray in 2000 where he made 19

Champions League appearances in three seasons. Has played 20 games for the Turkish national team, including two appearances at the 2002 World Cup.

**23 UMIT ATALAY** 03.01.84
Turkish U21 midfielder from the BJK youth academy. First season in the first team squad.

**14 UMIT AYDIN** 16.01.80
From Istanbul, midfielder Aydin made his first team debut for Adanaspor (20 games, three goals last season) then was signed by BJK in summer 2003.

**1 OSCAR EDUARDO CORDOBA** 03.02.70
Colombian goalkeeper Cordoba joined Besiktas in summer 2002 from Boca Juniors, where he'd been since 1997. Cordoba won a 2002-03 Turkish championship in his first season with Besiktas - he also won three titles in his five years at Boca. He played all three of Colombia's games at the 1994 World Cup and has 70 international caps.

**17 KAAN DOBRA** 14.03.72
Also listed as Roman Dabrowski, the Polish utility man has been playing in Turkey since 1999, when he joined Kocaelispor. He moved to BJK in summer 2002 and played 24 games (scoring one goal) in the 2002-03 title win. First capped by Poland at the age of 30 in 2002-03, he has two caps now.

**7 AHMET DURSUN** 25.01.78
Born in Gelsenkirchen, Germany, played his early football with SG Wattenscheid, then moved to BJK from Kocaelispor in summer 1999. Scored 21 in 30 games in 1999/2000. The forward made six CL appearances, hitting two goals, in 2000/01, and last season he struck eight goals in 23 games (the second highest scorer). Has three international caps.

**20 FEDERICO GIUNTI** 06.08.71
The Italian midfielder made 126 appearances in Serie A1996-2002. Previously with AC Citta di Castello, Perugia AC, Parma AC, AC Milan and Brescia Calcio. Played six games in Milan's 1999 Serie A title win, 12 games for Milan in the Champions League between 1999 and 2001 and one Champions League game for Parma in 1997-98. Giunti joined from Brescia Calcio in 2002, winning a championship medal in his first season. Won one cap for Italy in November 1996 during the 2-1 defeat to Bosnia-Herzgovena at Sarajevo.

**5 RONALDO GUIARO** 18.02.74
Brazilian defender Guiaro moved to Besiktas in 2001 from SL Benfica after five seasons with the Portuguese club, where he'd played six Champions League group games in 1998-99. He missed just one game out of 34 in Besiktas' 2002-03 championship success

**AHMED HASSAN** 02.05.75
Egyptian midfielder Hassan (93 caps) hit 13 league goals in 27 games for Genclerbirligi

in 2002-03 from midfield, which earned him a move in summer 2003 to Besiktas. He's played in Turkey since 1998 and has played in four African Nations Cups.

**3 TAYFUR HAVUTCU** 23.04.70
Midfielder Havutcu played all six Champions League group games for the club in both 1997-98 and 2000-01, scoring one goal in the latter season. He signed in 1997 from Kocaelispor. The German-born player became a full Turkish international in 1995, and played three games at both Euro 2000 and the 2002 World Cup. Has won 45 caps in total.

**SINAN KALOLU** 10.06.81
Signed in summer 2003 from Altay Izmir, Kalolu is a Turkish Under-21 international striker who spent ten years at Altay and scored 10 league goals in 28 games in 2002/03.

**OKAN KOC** 22.01.82
Midfielder Koc was signed by Besiktas in June 2003 for a substantial fee plus three players on a three year contract. He was first noticed by Dardanelspor AS, but joined Genclerbirligi in January 2002 after AFC Ajax & Galatasaray SK had shown interest. He played for the Turkish Under-21 side in 2002-03.

**RAMAZAN KURSUNLU** 07.07.81
Turkish goalkeeper in the national Under-21 squad 2002/03. Joined from Altay Izmir in summer 2003. From the Altay youth academy - he was first team keeper for three seasons.

**26 ILHAN MANSIZ** 10.08.75
Born at Kempten, striker Mansiz played in Germany, before signing in summer 2001 and becoming equal top scorer in the Turkish league with 21 goals in his first season. He followed that with seven goals in 23 games in last season's title win. Played in all seven games at 2002 FIFA World Cup, scoring three goals. Mansiz has 18 caps for Turkey.

**67 TUMER METIN** 14.10.74
Signed from Samsunspor in summer 2001 after 11 goals in 2000/01 from midfield. He appeared 22 times last season and scored three goals. Metin has played twice for Turkey.

**79 HAKAN HASAN HACIBEKTASOGLU** 23.04.84
Turkish defender from the BJK youth academy – his first season in the first team squad.

**21 SERDAR OZKAN** 01.01.87
Turkish U21 midfielder from the BJK youth academy, his first season in the first team squad.

**9 DANIEL GABRIEL PANCU** 17.08.77
Romanian forward (15 caps) Pancu joined the club in summer 2002 from Rapid Bucuresti. Pancu had previously played under Besiktas coach Mircea Lucescu at Rapid, where he won a 1999 championship medal.

# GROUP G
## BESIKTAS JK

**6 YASIN SULUN** 17.12.77
From the BJK youth academy (he debuted for the senior team in 1998) Sulun played 23 games in midfield during the 2002-03 championship win. Sulun managed five Champions League appearances with no goals in the 2000/01 campaign.

**41 SERDAR TOPRAKTEPE** 25.08.76
Turkish midfielder (two caps) in his second spell at the club, returning in 2002 from Kocaelispor. Played six Champions League group games, scoring no goals in 1997-98, then moved to Kocaelispor in 1999.

**19 IBRAHIM UZELMEZ** 10.03.74
Turkish midfielder joined in summer 2000 from Gazientepspor. Last season he played 25 games and scored one goal. Winning his first cap against Italy in November 2002, Uzelmez played four games at the 2003 FIFA Confederations Cup and has nine caps so far.

**10 SERGEN YALCIN** 05.10.72
Yalcin began his career in the in BJK youth team before leaving to play for Fenerbahce SK, Siirt Jetpaspor, Trabzonspor and Galatasaray SK. The Turkish midfielder rejoined the club in summer 2002 from Gala and was club top scorer with 11 goals in 28 games in the 2002/03 championship win. He's played eight Champions League games for Gala, scoring two goals, in 2001/02 under coach Lucescu. He has 36 caps.

**4 AHMET YILDIRIM** 25.04.74
Has played for all the top three Istanbul clubs – the midfielder joined Besiktas from Gala in 2001, where he'd played eight Champions League games in the previous two seasons without scoring. Yildirim has eight caps for Turkey.

**22 YASIN NUVIT YILDIZ** 30.09.80
The Turkish goalkeeper came from the club's youth academy – he took no part in last season's title win as he was the number three keeper.

**30 CARLOS ANTONIO ZAGO** 18.05.69
The Brazilian defender (52 caps) added a Turkish championship medal in 2002-03 to his Serie A championship medal with AS Roma in 2000-01 and three Brazilian championships with Sao Paulo in 1991, 1993 & 1994. Zago played five Champions League games for AS Roma.

**55 GORKHAN ZAN** 07.09.81
Turkish U21 international defender Zan spent three seasons in the Dardanelspor AS first team squad, played 26 league games last season and scored five goals.

**25 SERKAN ZEYBEKOGLU** 01.01.83
Turkish midfielder from BJK youth academy, this is his first season in the first team squad.

# GROUP H

**AC MILAN**
(Italy)

**CELTA VIGO**
(Spain)

**AFC AJAX**
(Netherlands)

**FC BRUGES**
(Belgium)

# AC MILAN

**Remarkable as it may seem, AC Milan qualified in 4th place from Serie A and ended the previous season 14 points behind their rivals and ground sharers Inter. Reached the group stages on away goals following a defeat to little known Liberec Club. In the groups they came out top in both stages, beating Real Madrid at the San Siro on the way. In the semis, the battle of Milan provided to be two unique contests. Quite who was at home in the first leg, we shall never really know as the fans boycotted any suggestion of ticket re-allocation, selecting their preferred end of the San Siro as allegiance dictated. A drab final at Old Trafford was won on pens to record their 6th European title. Write them off at your peril!**

## COACH

**CARLOS ANCELOTTI** 10.05.59
Ancelotti was a stylish midfielder with Parma, Roma and Milan and won 26 caps for Italy from 1981-90 and was in the Milan team that won the European Cup in 1989 and 1990 with the three Dutchmen Van Basten, Rijkaard and Gullit. He began coaching in 1995 with Serie B club Reggiana then moved to Parma as coach from 1996-98. Then switched to Juventus to replace Marcello Lippi from 1998-2001 but despite two third places in three years he lost his job. He took over at Milan after nine games of 2001-2002 season upon the departure of the Turk Fatih Terim. Last year he guided his side to a Champions League victory – a feat he would no doubt love to repeat.

## REACTION TO DRAW

**"I'd give the group seven out of ten for. These days in the Champions League you can't really talk about easy or difficult opponents -- they are all testing challenges. But we have beaten both Ajax and Bruges in seasons we have gone on to win the European Cup, so, I am hoping history will repeat itself. Celta Vigo? They are very dangerous for us. The Spanish league is so competitive so we must treat them with great care," *director Umberto Gandini.***

## SQUAD

**77 CHRISTIAN ABBIATI** 08.07.77
Abbiati became the first Milan keeper to play for Italy for 42 years when he gained his first cap on 30.04.03 v Switzerland. He's a former UEFA U21 champion in 2000, who went to Euro2000 and the 2002 FIFA World Cup as reserve. The keeper has played 16 Champions League games before 2003/04 including five games in 2002/03 – he was considered club first choice for four seasons 1998-2002, but Dida took over the role for 2002/03.

# GROUP H
## AC MILAN

**23 MASIMO AMBROSINI** 29.05.77
The Italian midfielder has been with AC Milan since 1995, but was away on loan in 1997/98 season at Vicenza Calcio. An 87th min sub in 2003 Champions League final, he'd played 11 games (no goals) in the campaign. His competition tally reads 22 games without scoring. Ambrosini has 11 international caps including a sub appearance in the EURO2000 final.

**18 MARCO BORRIELLO** 18.06.82
The striker signed for AC Milan in 1998, but has been out on loan to gain experience until 2002. Borriello played 12 Serie games (two goals) in 2002/03 but is yet to appear in the Champions League. He is an Italian U21 international.

**32 CHRISTIAN BROCCHI** 30.01.76
The Italian midfielder played seven games in his first Champions league season last year. Brocchi has been on the club books since 1994, but has been away with Serie A clubs FC Hellas-Verona and neighbours Internazionale FC. His Serie A debut for AC Milan came in 2001/02 season.

**2 MARCOS EVANGELISTA DE MORAES MARCOS CAFU** 07.06.70
The Brazilian defender was the first to appear in three consecutive FIFA World Cup finals – 1994 (won), 1998 (lost), 2002 (won) – and was captain of the 2002 winners. Cafu signed for AC Milan in summer 2003 on two-year contact after being out of contract at AS Roma, for whom he had played since 1997. Cafu played for Sao Paulo FC (98 games 1989-94), Real Zaragoza (16 games in 1994/95) & SE Palmeiras (1995-97) before his six years at AS Roma. Cafu won a Brazilian championship medal in 1991 and both the Libertadores Cup and Intercontinental Cup in 1992 & 1993 with FC Sao Paulo. Won Serie A in 2001. He then had two Champions League seasons with AS Roma with 10 games (two goals) in 2001/02 and 12 in 2002/03 (no goals).

**19 ALESSANDRO COSTACURTA** 24.04.66
The veteran defender has been in the first team squad since 1985; he was on loan at Monza in Serie C1 in 1986/87 and made his Milan debut on 25.10.87. Costacurta has won 19 medals with the club including six championships; played in 1989 and 1990 European Cup wins, but was suspended for both the Champions League & FIFA World Cup finals in 1994. The Italian international (59 caps) started the 2003 Champions League final – it was his 48th game in the competition. He's played over 400 Serie A games, but hasn't scored a goal since the 1991/92 season.

**12 NELSON DE JESUS SILVA DIDA** 07.10.73
The Brazilian keeper made three saves in the Champions League final penalty shoot out (from Trezeguet, Zalayeta, Montero). He played 12 games in the 2002/03 competition to add to his six games in 2000/01, recovering from a hand injury in the semi-final v Internazionale FC to make the final. His first full season for AC Milan was 2002/03 with

# GROUP H
## AC MILAN

30 Serie A games played – Dida joined the club in 1998 but has been on loan at FC Lugano & Corinthians. He was reserve keeper at 1998 and 2002 FIFA World Cups – and now has 58 caps.

**1 VALERIO FIORI** 27.04.69
Italian goalkeeper Fiori has been with AC Milan since summer 1999 but had played one Serie A game for the club in his first four seasons – on 24.05.03 v former club Piacenza FC, a few days before the 2003 Champions League final. Played 228 Serie A games for his previous clubs – S.S.Lazio (1986-93), Cagliari Calcio (1993-96), AC Cesena (1996/97), Fiorentina AC (1997/98) and Piacenza FC (1998/99). Rated number three keeper at the club behind Dida and Abbiati.

**8 IVAN GENNARO GATTUSO** 09.01.78
Gattuso played eight Serie A games for AC Perugia in 1996/97, then played 40 league games (seven goals) for Rangers FC from summer 1997 to November 1999. The Italian midfielder returned to his home country with Salernitana Sport in November 1998 before joining AC Milan in summer 1999. He's a former U21 international (and UEFA U21 champion in 2000), he has 19 full caps and played twice at the 2002 FIFA World Cup. Last season's Champions League final was his 25th game in the competition without scoring.

**9 FILIPPO INZAGHI** 09.08.73
The Italian striker has played for Piacenza FC, US Leffe, FC Hellas-Verona, Piacenza FC, Parma AC, Atalanta BC and Juventus FC. Inzaghi joined Milan in summer 2001 after four seasons in Turin. He was second top scorer in last season's Champions League (10 goals, 14 games) and has also scored 17 goals in the competition for Juventus in 26 games. His Serie A debut was for Parma AC in 1994/95 and his career league tally reads 110 goals in 218 games. Inzaghi also has 15 goals in 45 international appearances.

**30 RICARDO IZECSON SANTOS LEITE KAKA** 22.04.82
Brazilian midfielder Kaka (10 caps) joined Milan in August 2003 after playing three seasons for Sao Paulo's first team, who had developed him through their academy. He played 18 minutes against Costa Rica in the 2002 FIFA World Cup finals, and is the Olympic team captain. Also played all five games at the FIFA Confederations Cup in July 2003.

**4 KAKHABER KALADZE** 27.02.78
Georgian Kaladze joined Milan in 2001 from FC Dynamo Kyiv. The 35-cap defender won the league and cup double in all four seasons at his first club FC Dinamo Tiblisi, and a championship all four seasons at FC Dynamo Kyiv (plus three Cup medals). He's had four seasons in the Champions League before 2003/04 with 37 games and three goals. The player missed a penalty in 2003 final shoot out.

# GROUP H
## AC MILAN

**24 MARTIN LAURSEN** 26.07.77
Laursen had his first season in the competition last year, with seven Champions League games for AC Milan in 2002/03. He joined the club in summer 2001 after three seasons with Hellas-Verona, who had signed him after only 35 games for Silkeborg IF. The Danish defender played all four games at 2002 FIFA World Cup, and has 27 caps.

**3 PAOLO MALDINI** 26.06.68
Maldini made his club debut on 20.01.85 v Udinese Calcio – he's now in his 20th season in the Milan first team. The Italian defender has played a club record 505 Serie A games to the start of 2003/04 – he's won six national titles and four European Cup medals (1989, 1990, 1994 and 2003). Also, Paolo has won an Italian record 126 international caps from 1988-2002 including four FIFA World Cups and three European Championship finals. His father, Cesare Maldini, lifted the 1963 European Cup for AC Milan at Wembley. Paolo's career total of 65 Champions League games includes all 17 in the victorious campaign last season. He's scored one goal in the competition (on 02.03.94 v SV Werder Bremen).

**13 ALESSANDRO NESTA** 19.03.76
Italian defender Nesta joined Milan just before the August 2002 Champions League deadline. He played 14 games without scoring in last year's competition, although he did convert a penalty in the final shoot out. He'd previously played 21 European Cup games without scoring for Lazio, his only other club, where he'd spent ten years, was club captain and had played 193 Serie A games (one goal) while winning the 2000 Championship, the 1998 and 2000 Italian Cup and 1999 Cup-Winners' Cup medals. A former UEFA U21 champion in 1996, he now has 53 international caps and was in the 'Team of the Tournament' at Euro 2000.

**16 GIUSEPPE PANCARO** 26.08.71
The Italian defender (13 caps) joined AC Milan in summer 2003. Pancaro has played in Serie A for Cagliari Calcio (1992-97) and S.S.Lazio (1997-2003) in over 250 league games. His medals include the 2000 championship, 1998 & 2000 Italian Cup, and the 1999 Cup Winners' Cup medals with S.S. Lazio. Pancaro has made 26 UCL appearances without scoring in three seasons (1999-2002) with Lazio.

**21 ANDREA PIRLO** 19.05.79
Italian midfielder who crossed the city from Internazionale to AC Milan in summer 2001. Played five Champions League games for Internazionale in 1998/99 and 12 without scoring for Milan in 2002/03. Eight of his nine league goals last season came from the penalty spot, but he was subbed off during the 2003 final and missed the shoot out. Pirlo, a former national U21 playmaker, won his first four international caps in 2002/03.

**5 FERNANDO REDONDO** 06.06.69
Argentine midfielder (29 caps) who signed from Real Madrid CF in 2000 but did not play in his first two seasons due to knee ligament injuries. Redondo played eight Serie

A games last season. He's won the Champions League as captain in 1998 & 2000 with Real and also has 1995 and 1997 Primera Liga championship medals. The player hasn't scored in 42 Champions League games, of which five were for AC Milan in 2002/03.

**11 VITOR BORBA FERREIRA RIVALDO** 19.04.72
The Brazilian played 12 games in last year's Champions League, scoring two goals. Rivaldo was top scorer in the competition with 10 goals in 1999/2000. He also played 43 games for FC Barcelona, scoring 22 goals. He joined AC Milan from FC Barcelona in summer 2002 after the FIFA World Cup, which he won with Brazil after playing all seven games (five goals) in the finals and has 69 international caps (33 goals). Rivaldo also had one season with RC Deportivo scoring 21 goals in 41 league games in 1996/97 and collected 76 league goals in five seasons with FC Barcelona in 157 games.

**25 JOSE VITOR ROQUE JUNIOR** 31.08.76
Roque Junior joined AC Milan in 2000 from SE Palmeiras. The 24-cap Brazilian defender's only Champions League appearance last season was as a sub in the final after injury. He also played only four Serie A games. Roque Junior played seven Champions League games (no goals) in 2000/01 and won the 2002 FIFA World Cup after playing six games and scoring one goal. Now on loan at Leeds United.

**10 RUI MANUEL COSTA** 29.03.72
The Portuguese midfielder played for Benfica 1991-94, then made 215 Serie A appearances for Fiorentina AC before joining AC Milan in 2001. His first Milan season in 2001/02 was interrupted by ankle injury. Last season was Rui Costa's second in the competition – he played 12 games (one goal) in 1999/2000 for Fiorentina AC, and appeared in 16 of the 17 games (no goals) in Milan's 2002/03 success. He has 79 international caps for Portugal.

**20 CLARENCE SEEDORF** 01.04.76
Dutch midfielder Seedorf became the first player to win the Champions League with three different clubs last season. The 2003 title was added to his successes with AFC Ajax (1995) and Real Madrid CF (1998). Seedorf crossed the city from Internazionale FC in summer 2002. The Dutchman has 65 caps and has now played 11 Champions League games (no goals) for AFC Ajax, 25 games (three goals) for Real Madrid CF, and 14 games (one goal) for AC Milan. He was the youngest player at 16 years in 1992 to have played first team for AFC Ajax.

**27 SERGIO CLAUDIO DOS SANTOS SERGINHO** 27.06.71
The Brazilian midfielder Serginho scored the opening penalty for the club in the 2003 Champions League final. He was in the Brazil squad that won the 1999 Copa America, and joined AC Milan (93 Serie A appearances) from FC Sao Paulo. His career tally reads 26 Champions League games and two goals in three campaigns. Serginho has 11 international caps.

**7 ANDRIY SHEVCHENKO** 29.09.76
Ukrainian forward awarded his country's top honour ('Merited Master of Sport') for scoring the decisive penalty in the 2003 Champions League final penalty shoot out, the first footballer to win the award since 1986. The prolific striker has hit 24 goals in 48 Champions League games (14 goals in 20 games for FC Dynamo Kyiv, 10 goals in 28 games for AC Milan). Shevchenko played for FC Dynamo Kyiv from 1995-99, then was Serie A top scorer with 24 goals in his first season with AC Milan in 1999/2000. He now has 48 international caps and 21 goals, as well as four Ukrainian Footballer of the Year awards.

**14 DARIO SIMIC** 12.11.75
The Croatian defender was a product of the NK Dinamo football academy - he won five championship medals with NK Dinamo, before a move to Milan's rivals Internazionale FC in January 1999 – he crossed the city in summer 2002. Simic played 12 games (no goals) in last season's victory, he has also played in the competition for NK Croatia/Dinamo (ten games, one goal). The 57-cap defender was in Croatia's third-placed team at the 1998 FIFA World Cup.

**15 JON DAHL TOMASSON** 29.08.76
The Danish forward joined AC Milan in summer 2002 after helping Feyenoord to a UEFA Cup where he won the Man of the Match with a goal and two assists in a 3-2 win v BV Borussia Dortmund. Tomasson was injured for last season's Champions League final, but played 10 games (scoring three goals) in earlier rounds. The striker has also played in the competition for Newcastle United FC (five games, no goals in 1997/98) and Feyenoord (15 games, seven goals). The Dane was twice top scorer for SC Heerenveen (1995-97) and also helped Feyenoord to the 1999 championship. He has 51 caps (25 goals) and scored four goals in the group stages of the 2002 FIFA World Cup finals.

# CELTA VIGO

**Real Club Celta de Vigo are debutants in this season's Champions League after beating Slavia Prague in the third qualifying round (3-0 win at home, 2-0 defeat in Prague). Finished 4th in la Liga ahead of Valencia and Barcelona. Since 1997/98 Celta have always finished in the Spanish top 7 (consecutively 6th, 5th, 7th, 6th, 5th, 4th) but they have never won a league title nor a national cup. The highlight of their history came between 1999 and 2001 when they were consecutive quarter-finalists in the UEFA Cup for three years.**

## COACH

**MIGUEL ANGEL LOTINA** 18.06.57
Lotina arrived at Celta de Vigo in the summer 2002. Before coming to Vigo he managed

to keep Osasuna in the top flight. He secured 4th place for Celta with a brand of football that was effective if unspectacular, and at times, unattractive to watch.

## REACTION TO DRAW

**"It is a great day because it is the first time we have been in a draw as important as this, although we have ended up in an extremely strong group. Milan and Ajax are two great clubs with great players. Of course it is going to be tough, but we will not just be there to lie down for the big teams,"** ***President Horacio Gomez.***

## SQUAD

**8 LOPEZ RUANO ANGEL** 10.03.81
Right-winger who played in the Spanish U21 team and was spotted by Celta at Las Palmas in 2002. Is a hard working player who scored 1 goal in almost 100 games in La Liga. 13 league games for Celta last season.

**6 EDUARDO BERIZZO** 13.11.69
Argentine left-sided defender who is competing with his fellow countryman Caceres for a place in the team. Is 1m84 tall and 9 months younger than Caceres. Has played 13 times for Argentina.

**3 SYLVINHO MENDES DE CAMPOS** 12.04.74
Brazilian international defender who has played 6 times for his country (the last time in 2001). Normally plays on the left wing. Joined Celta in 2001 from Arsenal. Played in Brazil for Corinthians. Once believed to be a contender for Roberto Carlos' place in the national team.

**24 CATANHA** 06.03.72
Henrique Guedes da Silva is a 31-year-old Brazilian central forward. Born in Recife, the 'Red Crab' hasn't really sparkled in recent months. Has played 140 league games and scored 61 goals in Lla Liga and won 3 caps for Brazil. Arrived at Celta in 2000 from Malaga where he played since 1998. Before he was at Leganes (1997/98), Salamanca (1996/97) and Belenenses in Portugal (1995/96). His most famous club in Brazil was Fluminense.

**1 PABLO CAVALLERO** 13.04.74
Was Argentina's goalkeeper at the World Cup 2002. Was the reserve in 1998 in France to Mallorca's Roa. At home he played for Velez Sarsfield but was reserve to Jose Luis Chilavert, so moved in 1998 to Union Santa Fe where he made the national squad. He came to Europe in 1999 signing for Espanyol but he left the Barcelona-based club one year later in the summer 2000. Immediately after his £4 million move to Celta he broke his leg but has since recovered. Usually he plays in la Liga and the Spanish Cup while Pinto is Celta's goalkeeper for the Champions League.

# GROUP H
## CELTA VIGO

**2 JUAN VELASCO DAMAS** 15.05.75
Right-sided defender who can also play in midfield. This Spanish international (5 caps) is likely to start on the substitute bench in the Champions League. Has played more than 120 league games in Spain but only scored 1 goal.

**5 GIOVANELLA EVERTON** 13.09.70
Brazilian midfielder who usually warms the bench. Has played 180 league games and scored 4 goals. Played in Brazil for Internacional Porto Alegre (1993), in Portugal for Estoril (1993/94), Tirsense (1994/95), Belenenses (1995/96) and in Spain for Salamanca (from 1996 onwards) before arriving at Celta in 1999.

**21 JANDRO CASTRO FERNANDEZ** 27.02.79
Forward who was loaned to Albacete last season and has rejoined Celta for this CL campaign. He can play on the left side and will probably appear as a sub for Gustavo Lopez, who runs out of fuel after 60 or 70 minutes.

**15 PABLO ANDRES CONTRERAS FICA** 11.09.78
Tall central defender and Chilean international. First season at Celta since moving from Sporting Lisbon. Played for Monaco in the French league. Was approached by Lazio this summer but preferred to move to Spain.

**14 JUANFRAN GARCIA** 17.07.76
A full-back but can also play on the left midfield. Spanish international who played at the World Cup 2002. Played 3 games but missed a penalty in the shoot-out against Republic of Ireland and subsequently didn't play in the quarter-final against South Korea. Moved to Celta from Valencia in summer 1999. Improved a lot in the north west of Spain. Joined Valencia in the summer 1997 from 2nd division club Levante (for whom Johan Cruyff once played). Won Spanish Cup with Valencia in 1999.

**23 SERGIO FERNANDEZ GONZALEZ** 23.05.77
Blond right-sided defender who joined Celta in 1999 from Sporting Gijon. Was out in 2000 after tearing his knee ligaments. Played only 33 games over the last 2 seasons. He is very strong with the head, technically skilful but a bit slow. Is vulnerable to injury.

**16 JOSE IGNACIO** 28.09.73
Spanish central defensive midfielder. Played for Valencia and was relegated with Real Zaragoza in 2002 before joining Celta. He is the best friend of the coach. Has played up to 300 league games in Spain and has never been sent off.

**11 GUSTAVO LOPEZ** 13.04.73
Tiny Argentine forward who doesn't score as much as his fellow countryman Claudio who plays at Lazio. The Lopez of Celta is very fast, a good dribbler and he has a lot of experience. Was called up for the first time for Argentina in 1996 and moved from

Independiente, his club back home, to Real Zaragoza in the same year. Joined Celta in the summer 1999 for around £4 million. He is left footed but can also play on the right wing. He has a very impressive acceleration but is physically weak. An hour play is more than enough for him. Sometimes hot tempered and favourite of the female Celta fans.

**22 PETER BERNARD LUCCIN** 09.04.79
French midfielder who started his career as a 17-years-old at Cannes away to Montpellier (1-0 win) on 24.08.96. After 13 Div 1 games he moved to Bordeaux in January 1997. He played 41 league games for les 'Girondins' before he joined Marseille in the summer 1998. He scored his first of only 3 league goals ever in France for Marseille against Auxerre (1-0 win) on 22.05.99. In the summer 2000 he was transferred to ambitious Paris Saint-Germain where he played alongside Nicolas Anelka but one year later he moved to Celta. Luccin played in the CL before with Marseille in 1999/2000 (12 games) and PSG in 2000/01 (10 games and 1 goal in the 7-2 win against Rosenborg). So this is the start of his third CL campaign with a third different club.

**9 SAVO MILOSEVIC** 02.09.73
With 5 goals, this Serbian was joint top scorer at Euro 2000. In the opening game of Celta's CL campaign he will return back to a stadium (Bruges) where he scored in the crazy Euro 2000 first round match Yugoslavia-Spain that finished 3-4. Despite doubts about his knee Celta agreed to loan him from Parma after he played 24 league games and scored 12 goals for Espanyol Barcelona. Before his arrival in Italy Milosevic had played for Real Zaragoza, Aston Villa and the club where it all started: Partizan Belgrade.

**10 ALEXANDRE MOSTOVOI** 22.08.68
Russian international who scored the first goal in the 3rd qualifying round home win against Slavia Prague (3-0) but also made the headlines in the return leg after being sent off. Will be suspended for Celta's opener at FC Bruges in Belgium. Mostovoi is the most experienced player in the team. A central midfielder and playmaker who can change games with his wonderful technique and splendid free-kicks. Was playing at Spartak Moscow when he was first spotted. In 1991 he moved to Benfica and later to Caen in France. Joined Celta after being relegated with Strasbourg in 1996. The form of Mostovoi will probably decide how far Celta will go in this competition.

**20 JESULI ANTONIO MORA NIETO** 24.01.78
Spanish attacking midfielder Jesuli is technically very skilful, has a terrific shot and is a good dribbler – which is why most Celta fans adore him. Can be outstanding on his day and he is said to be the joker in the dressing room. Joined Celta from FC Seville in 2000.

**7 VAGNER ROGERIO NUNES** 19.03.73
Central midfielder with a good work ethic. Is the best friend of Roberto Carlos who tried to introduce him at Real Madrid. Is not afraid of tackling and so receives a lot of yellow cards. Started only 4 times last season. Joined Celta in 2000 from AS Roma.

**17 SEBASTIAN MENDEZ PARDINAS** 07.04.77
Argentine defender who is not first choice at Celta but is always available to take up a defensive role in the team. Has only played 18 league games since arriving in Spain.

**13 JOSE MANUEL PINTO** 08.11.75
Originally playing for Betis Sevilla he joined Celta in 1998. He is Celta's goalkeeper for the CL and surprisingly also their captain. Critics say that he is more reliable than Cavallero.

**12 MANOLO SANCHEZ** 27.11.76
Midfielder who was loaned to Numancia last season to gain more first team experience. Still has a lot of progress to make if he wants to get into the team.

**19 LUIS EDU SCHMIDT** 01.01.79
Brazilian right-sided midfielder with good technical skills. Edu has already played more than 100 league games in Spain scoring 25 goals - about a goal every 4 games. Joined Celta in 2000 from Sao Paulo.

**4 FERNANDO CACERES ZAYA** 07.02.69
Argentine central or left-sided defender who will have to compete with Berizzo for a place in the first team. Despite being smaller than his fellow countryman he has played more internationals (23 caps versus 13).

# AFC AJAX

**Always noted for their stylish play and the nurturing of home talent, Ajax is rapidly becoming known for its latest crop of youngsters with the likes of Hatem Trablesi (much coveted by Man Utd) at left-back, Rafael Van de Vaert (coveted by most of Europe) and Steven Pienaar all well on the way to establishing themselves as serios players. Particularly watch out for a young Romanian forward, Nicolae Mitea who at just 18 may not be seen much this season but is a great prospect. In a tough group including Celta Vigo and AC Milan, if they can qualify, they will go far, and as in 1995 could surprise everyone and reach the final. Playing at the magnificent Amsterdam Arena, a must for all football fans, Ajax under the tutelage of Ronal Koeman, were last season, beaten into second place in the Dutch League by PSV Windhaven**

## COACH

**RONALD KOEMAN** 21.03.63
Born in Zaandam, he played for FC Groningen, Ajax, PSV Eindhoven, Barcelona and Feyenoord. Caps for Holland: 78 (14 goals) – European Champions with Holland in

1988. Honours as a coach include the Dutch league title, Dutch domestic cup and the Dutch Super Cup with Ajax two seasons ago.

## REACTION TO DRAW

**"We have been given the chance to settle things," after his team were drawn against Milan who beat them in the quarter-finals last season. "The other two teams I don't know so well, but it won't be easy. They are all good teams, Club Bruges eliminated Borussia Dortmund and that says something."** ***Ajax Amsterdam captain Rafael van der Vaart***

**15 MAXWELL SCHERRER CABELINO ANDRADE** 27.08.81
The Brazilian midfielder signed for Ajax in summer 2001 from a youth tournament. He played 24 league games without scoring during the league and cup double success in his first season with the club. Then he played 30 league games (four goals) in 2002/03. Andrade also played in 12 of the 14 Champions League games (no goals) for the club in 2002/03.

**21 MAARTEN STEKELEN BERG** 22.09.82
The Dutch keeper was one of four used in last season's Champions League. The Under-21 international made three appearances in the competition. From the Ajax youth academy, he joined in 1996 from VV Schoten. He made his League debut in August 2002, and played nine league games in 2002/03.

**28 NOURDIN BOUKHARI** 30.06.80
A summer 2002 signing from relegated Sparta Rotterdam, after 13 goals in 76 games in three seasons at Sparta. The forward had been recommended by former Ajax star Aron Winter, who was on loan at Sparta. Born in Rotterdam, he opted to play for Morocco and has 11 caps. Four Champions League games (no goals) in 2002/03, he also played 22 league games (six goals) last season.

**31 SANDER BOSCHKER** 20.10.70
The Dutch keeper joined in summer 2003 from FC Twente on a two-year contract. He played 356 league games for FC Twente after his debut in 1989, including a major role in the 2001 Dutch Cup win for FC Twente v PSV – he saved three penalties in the shootout. Had missed just four league games in the past seven seasons for FC Twente before his move to Ajax.

**17 WAMBERTO DE JESUS SOUSA CAMPOS** 13.12.74
The Brazilian forward is in his 13th season in European football – he was with FC Seraing (1991-96) from the age of 17, and then Standard Liege from 1996-98. Campos signed for Ajax from Standard in summer 1998. He played 31 league games (nine goals) in the 2001-2 league and cup double success, but then broke his metatarsal bone in

2002/03 and played only four league games. Four Champions League games in 1998/99, two Champions League games in 2002/03 – but he's yet to score for Ajax in the competition.

**16 NIGEL DE JONG** 30.11.84
The Dutch defender is the son of Jerry de Jong, the ex-Ajax and PSV player who won three caps for Holland and played under Sir Bobby Robson at PSV. The younger De Jong made his League debut on 19.11.02 v AZ Alkmaar (6-2) and his Champions League debut on 22.10.02 v Rosenborg BK. He played a total of ten games in the competition, including one goal at Highbury in 2002/03, as well as playing 17 league games in 2002/03. Still a teenager, he is a Dutch youth & Under-21 international.

**4 JULIEN ESCUDE** 17.08.79
The French defender joined Ajax in summer 2003 from Stade Rennes. Escude is the brother of Grand Slam finalist and Davis Cup tennis player Nicolas Escude. Julien played for AS Cannes in 1998/99, then had four seasons and 103 Division 1 games (one goal) for Rennes. Played in 2002 UEFA Under-21 championship final loss to Czech Republic on penalties.

**6 TOMAS GALASEK 15.01.73**
The Czech midfielder with 25 caps joined Ajax in summer 2000 from Willem II when coach Co Adriaanse moved clubs. He started his career at FC Banik Ostrava then moved to Holland in 1996 with Willem II after 121 games (nine goals) in Czech league. He scored a silver goal penalty v Grazer AK in the Champions League third qualifying round. Five Champions League games (no goals) for Willem II in 1999/2000, 13 Champions League games (no goals) for Ajax in 2002/03.

**23 ZDENEK GRYGERA** 14.05.80
The Czech midfielder joined Ajax in summer 2003 from AC Sparta on a four-year contract. He played 12 Champions League games without scoring for AC Sparta from 2000-02 – after joining them in 2000, he won championship medals in 2001 and 2003. Grygera played in the winning Czech team at 2002 UEFA Under-21 championships, and has 16 full caps.

**12 JOHN HEITINGA** 15.11.83
The defender is from the Ajax youth academy (under former UCL winning captain Danny Blind). The Dutchman played 15 league games in the 2001/02 league and cup double win but only managed one league game in 2002/03 due to injury.

**9 ZLATAN IBRAHIMOVIC** 03.10.81
The Swedish striker joined Ajax from Malmo in summer 2001 for a Swedish record fee – he then played 24 league games and hit six goals in the Ajax league and cup double win in 2001/02. His former clubs also include FBK Balkan, BK Flagg. He scored 13

league goals in 25 games in 2002/03 and 13 Champions League games (five goals) in 2002/03. Two games (as sub) at 2002 FIFA World Cup – Ibrahimovic has 16 caps for Sweden but is of Bosnian parentage.

**20 JARI LITMANEN** 20.02.71
The Finnish star returned to Ajax in summer 2002, having played for the club also from 1992-99. His other clubs include FC Reipas Lahti, HJK Helsinki, MyPa, FC Barcelona and Liverpool FC. His Champions League record includes 32 games (18 goals) for Ajax 1994-99, the 1995 victory, a goal in the 1996 final, eight games (no goals) for FC Barcelona (1999-2000) and seven games (three goals) for Liverpool FC (2001/02). In total, before the 2003/04 season he's hit 22 goals in 54 games in seven seasons in the competition and was top scorer in 1995/96 with nine. Five times Finland Footballer of the Year, Litmanen has 84 caps.

**1 BOGDAN LOBONT** 19.01.78
The Romanian goalkeeper (25 caps) signed from FC Rapid in January 2000, after winning a championship medal in 1999. He played just one league game for Ajax in 2000/01 season and then was loaned to FC Dinamo Bucuresti in 2001/02 where he won a championship medal. 17 league games for Ajax last season as well as six Champions League games – he was the fourth goalkeeper used by Ajax in the 2002/03 competition.

**26 ANTHONY OBADAI** 06.08.82
The Ghanaian midfielder made the first team squad in 2001/02 but played no league games. He then spent 2002-3 on loan at partner club Germinal Beerschot in the Belgian top division, where he played 29 games and scored two goals. Obadai was then recalled to the Ajax first team squad from summer 2003.

**5 JOHN O'BRIEN** 29.08.77
Joined Ajax in 1997/98 but went on loan to Utrecht (19 games, two goals) in 1998/99. The American defender previously played for California Flyers Soccer, and didn't make his Ajax debut until September 1999. He made 27 appearances in league games in 2001/02 League and Cup double win, and played all five USA games at 2002 FIFA World Cup – he now has 23 caps. Five Champions League games (no goals) in 2002/03.

**3 PETRI PASANEN** 24.09.80
Finnish defender Pasanen signed from FC Lahti in summer 2000 after 57 Finnish league games. He only managed one league game in 2001/02 championship win due to injury, but played eight Champions League games last season including a goal v Valencia. He won his first international cap on 15.11.2000 and has won 14 caps in total.

**8 STEVEN PIENAAR** 17.03.82
The South African midfielder was signed from the club's South African partner team,

AFC Ajax Cape Town, before joining the Ajax youth academy and making his first team debut on 12.01.02. Pienaar played eight games in the 2001/02 championship success, and 31 league games (five goals) in 2003/04. His South African international debut came just before the 2002 FIFA World Cup; he was in the squad for the finals but did not play, and has seven caps to 01.07.03. Played 12 Champions League games (two goals) in 2002/03.

**11 VICTOR SIKORA** 11.04.78
The Dutch forward has played for DVV Roda Deventer, Go Ahead Eagles Deventer and SBV Vitesse. He signed for Ajax from Vitesse in July 2002, he'd played there for 18 months under current Ajax coach Ronald Koeman. Also, he had played five seasons for Go Ahead eagles, the first two seasons in Eredivisie 3. Seasons 1999-2002 with Vitesse saw 84 games and 20 goals as well as his first caps for Holland. He now has six caps. Played four Champions League games (no goals) in 2002/03.

**19 WESLEY SONCK** 09.08.78
The Belgian forward played at Nonove, RWD Molenbeek, Germinal Ekeren, Germinal Beershot Antwerp and KRC Genk before joining Ajax in summer 2003 on a five-year contract from Genk. Sonck was the 2001 Belgian Player of the Year, and the Belgian league top scorer in 2001/02 with 30 goals in 32 games during their championship win, and co-top scorer in 2002/03 with 22 goals in 29 games – in all, he scored 65 league goals in 93 games for Genk. His Champions League form for Genk was six games and two goals in 2002/03, the only goals the club have scored in the competition. Sonck has 26 international caps (ten goals).

**18 WESLEY SNEIJDER** 09.06.84
The Dutch midfielder was added to Ajax's Champions League squad in January 2003. He played 17 league games, scoring four goals, in his first season in 2002/03 after progressing from the youth academy. He made his full international debut as a sub against Portugal on 30.04.03, and has already played in the Netherlands age group teams. His Champions League debut came against Arsenal on 26.02.03 – he played three games (no goals) in last season's competition. Sneijder signed a new four-year contract in May 2003.

**2 HATEM TRABELSI** 25.01.77
Tunisian defender who previously played for Club Sportif Sfaxien, Trabelsi helped Ajax to the League and Cup double in first season in 2001/02. He's played in two FIFA World Cup finals – one game in 1998 v England, all three games in 2002. Played all 14 Champions League games for Ajax in 2002/03 without scoring and has 37 international caps.

**14 JELLE VAN DAMME** 18.10.83
Belgian defender who signed in summer 2001; he played seven games for Ajax feeder club Germinal Beershot in 2001/02. This was followed by 11 league games (no goals)

in 2002/03 but he became a full international and played seven Champions League games as well. First cap on 29.03.03 v Croatia, second cap on 20.08.03 v Holland.

**27 CEDRIC VAN DER GUN** 05.05.79
The Dutch striker (a former youth and Under-21 international) came into the Ajax first team squad in 1997, played 33 league games (nine goals) in the 2001/02 season, then only managed two league games in his other three seasons. He was on loan at Willem II in 2002/03 with 30 league games and six goals there.

**10 RAFAEL VAN DER VAART** 11.02.83
The Dutch midfielder is a product of the Ajax youth academy – he was spotted playing in a caravan park. Van der Vaart made his first team debut in 19.04.2000, then scored 14 league goals in 20 games in the following season's league and cup double win. He was club top scorer with 18 league goals in 21 games in 2002/03; he started 2003/04 season with a record of 39 league goals in 69 games for the club. Six Champions League games (two goals) in 2002/03. Won his first cap against Andorra on 16.10.01 and has eight caps to 01.07.03.

**22 ABUBAKARI YAKUBU** 13.10.81
A Ghanaian youth international, coached in the Ajax youth academy, the midfielder made his first team debut aged 17 on the same day as Van der Vaart. Yakubu played 21 league games in the 2001/02 league and cup double win and nine Champions League games (no goals) in 2002/03. Had not scored a league goal in 4 seasons before 2003/04.

# FC BRUGES

**FC Bruges start their 12th Champions League/European Cup campaign, as Belgian Champions. An impressive record in Europe boasts 175 matches with 84 wins, 30 draws and 61 defeats. New season arrivals include two Croatians, a goalkeeper Tomislav Butina from Dinamo and a striker, Josep Simic**

## COACH

**TROND SOLLIED** 29.04.59
As a player-coach (and later coach) of Bodo Glimt between 1992-97, Sollied won the league title and Cup in Norway. He then moved to Rosenborg where he won two league titles as assistant-coach and later head coach. Between 1998-2000, he guaranteed Belgian team AA Gent a place in the UEFA Cup before making the switch to FC Bruges. Since then he has won the Belgian Cup (2002) and the league title in 2003 as well as marshalling two successive qualifications for the Champions League.

# GROUP H
## FC BRUGES

## REACTION TO DRAW

**"We will come up against three Belgian internationals playing for Ajax (Jelle Van Damme, Tom Soetaers and Wesley Sonck) that we know very well and that might work in our favour. I think we have a good chance of finishing second and qualifying, but Milan, Celta and Ajax are very good teams. It won't be easy,"** ***midfielder Timmy Simmons.***

## SQUAD

**13 TOMISLAV BUTINA** 30.03.74
After seven league titles and six national Cups with Dinamo Zagreb, Butina arrived this summer in Bruges to fill in the gap between first choice goalkeeper Dany Verlinden and the youngster Stijn Stijnen. Making his official debut for FC Bruges in Dortmund he made a mistake after two minutes, letting the ball slip away from his foot so Amoroso could score easily. But Butina went from 'zero to hero' in the penalty shoot-out by saving the spot kicks from Amoroso and Bergdolmo. Butina came to FC Bruges on advice of Robert Spehar and Mario Stanic, former Croatian players of the club.

**10 NASTJA CEH** 26.01.78
After a very difficult first season in Bruges, nobody expected anything from this Slovenian midfielder but Ceh proved his critics wrong. He scored an important equaliser from a free kick against Shakhtar Donetsk in August 2002 and he played a vital role in the run towards the first Belgian league title in five years for FC Bruges. Last season he played 25 league games, nine goals and four Champions League games.

**6 PHILIPPE CLEMENT** 22.03.74
Clement moved from Belgian cup holders Racing Genk to Coventry City in the summer of 1998 but never made much impact in the Premier League. With FC Bruges, Clement returned to the spotlight, winning the Belgian Cup in 2002 and the Belgian league in 2003. He missed the World Cup in 2002 because of a hamstring injury. This summer he almost went to the Bundesliga to join 1860 Munich but finally decided to stay in Bruges. Unusually, he is the only Belgian player in the team with any foreign experience. Last season he played 28 league games, scoring four goals and five Champions League games.

**25 HANS CORNELIS** 05.01.82
Hans Cornelis started this season in the first match against Racing Genk (1-0 win) in the right-back position in place of the crocked Olivier De Cock. He only made one appearance last season, but his performances this term suggest he may be too good to warm to the bench .

**2 OLIVIER DE COCK** 09.11.75
Right-back Olivier De Cock is one of the few youngsters who made it through all the

youth teams of FC Bruges straight into the first team. He made his debut on November 29th 1996 away to AA Gent. Since then he has made more than 150 appearances in the first team, scoring ten goals. Last season he played every minute in six Champions League games for Bruges, and in October 2002 he won his first cap for Belgium, away to Andorra. He's not afraid to leave his defensive position to join the attack and he can cause danger with his free kicks. Last season he played 30 league games, scoring four goals in the Belgian league and six in the Champions League.

**8 GAETAN ENGLEBERT** 11.06.76
Just like Timmy Simons, his colleague in midfield, Englebert signed a long term contract with the club until 2008. Englebert started his career with FC Liège (1987-95) and Tilleur-Liège (1995-97) before tasting First Division football at Sint-Truiden (1997-99). In 1999 he moved on to FC Bruges. In 2001 he made his debut for the Belgian national team in the qualifying home game against San Marino (February 28th 2001) that ended in a sensational 10-1 victory. In 2002 he won his first trophy with FC Bruges, the Belgian Cup and last season he won his first Belgian league title as well as playing all six games in the Champions League, scoring one goal against FC Barcelona. During the summer break he underwent an ankle operation but he was back for the important away game in Dortmund.

**17 KAREL GERAERTS** 05.01.82
In 1998, youngster Karel Geraerts left the youth set-up of Racing Genk for FC Bruges. Last season he played seven games in the first team in midfield and proved that he is an option for the future, especially as a defensive midfielder.

**17 IVAN GVOZDENOVIC** 19.08.78
This Serbia and Montenegro international was spotted by FC Bruges at Red Star Belgrade where he'd played since 1998 captaining the team that won three league titles and two national Cups. Gvozdenovic was bought for the left-back position as competition for Peter Van Der Heyden, but he can also operate on the right wing or in midfield.

**21 SEBASTIEN HERMANS** 03.05.83
A young midfielder who can play on both wings. Played no league games last season. Scored a goal in the first team in a Cup game against fourth division team Aarschot (12-2 win) in the 2001/02 season.

**19 RUNE LANGE** 24.06.77
This Norwegian forward scored the important penalty at home against Shakhtar Donetsk which gave FC Bruges a Champions League spot last season but in the competition itself Lange played only two games without making any impact. Suffering from a back injury, Lange only managed to play 12 league games last season scoring four goals.

**26 BIRGER MAERTENS** 28.06.80
From the beginning of 2002 Maertens took his place in central defence. The new season started well with the qualification for the Champions League but then everything went wrong for Maertens. He made the mistake that led the Lokomotiv Moscow goal which eliminated FC Bruges from the Champions League. Then at home against VfB Stuttgart, Maertens took his first of three red cards in ten days. He was also sent off away to Sint-Truiden and at home in the top game against Anderlecht. Despite this poor end to 2002, Maertens came back in 2003 with renewed confidence.

**11 SANDY MARTENS** 23.12.73
The former AA Gent player had such a wonderful season last year that in February 2003, after an absence of three and a half years, he was called up again to play for the national team in the friendly game against Algeria. Martens impressed in the Belgian league and in the Champions League home game against Galatasaray when he scored. Last season he scored 13 goals in 29 league games.

**18 ANDRES MENDOZA** 26.04.78
Peruvian international Andrès Mendoza has his fans in Bruges but also his critics. He can score some incredible goals and then miss the easy ones. On two recent occasions, however, Mendoza presence in the team proved crucial. On May 9th 2002 his three goals won FC Bruges the Belgian Cup making him the first player to score a hat trick in a Cup final in Belgian professional football. He also scored the important away goal in Dortmund from a free kick and the decisive penalty that put FC Bruges through to the Champions League.

**4 DAVID ROZENAHL** 05.07.80
Rozenahl was spotted by FC Bruges playing for Sigma Olomouc two seasons ago. The young Czech Republic central defender played for the Under-21 Czech team that took the European title in Switzerland in 2002. A strong defender who is good with his head, he did an excellent job against his national team-mate Jan Koller in the third qualifying round games against Borussia Dortmund. Unfortunately, he was also sent off in Dortmund after picking up a second yellow card.

**9 BENGT SAETERNES** 01.01.75
Came to FC Bruges a year ago just before the transfer deadline closed. In his first season at FC Bruges he scored seven goals in ten league games. He also managed to score a cracker at home against Galatasaray in the Champions League. The tall, right-footed and very fast forward played in Norway for Viking Stavanger, Odd Grenland (2nd division) and Bodo Glimt, where he got himself a reputation after notching 72 goals in 126 games.

**16 SERGEI SEREBRENNIKOV** 01.09.76
Serebrennikov won three league titles, two national Cups and played in the Champions

League for Dinamo Kiev before coming to FC Bruges in the summer of 2002. He was noticed in the friendlies FC Bruges played against the Ukrainian team in the 2001/02 season. Serebrennikov even scored against FC Bruges in one of those games. In his first season in Belgium, he played 17 games and scored one goal. He also played three times for FC Bruges in the Champions League last season.

**28 JOSIP SIMIC** 16.09.77
This centre-forward was loaned to Aris Saloniki in Greece last season. Simic has played 41 league games for FC Bruges, scoring seven goals, between 2000 and 2002. He came to FC Bruges from Dinamo Zagreb in 2000.

**3 TIMMY SIMONS** 11.12.76
Winner of the Belgian Golden Boot Award in 2002 (best Belgian Professional Footballer of the year) Timmy Simons received offers from Schalke 04 and Aston Villa. But the directors' board of the club reacted by giving their most valuable player a long-term contract. Simons stayed in Bruges and after winning his first Belgian Cup in 2002, he won his first Belgian league title last season. Since arriving at FC Bruges from Lommel in 2000, Simons has played already more than 100 successive league games. He is yet to miss a minute of play! Takes the spot kicks for Bruges.

**24 TIM SMOLDERS** 26.08.80
Smolders is normally a substitute. When he enters the field he can play just behind the forwards or in the centre of attack. He is a very tall player and some fans compare his style of play with former FC Bruges-legend Jan Ceulemans. Played 22 league games last season scoring three goals but only played one minute in the Champions League, coming on for Gert Verheyen at home against Galatasaray.

**15 MAREK SPILAR** 11.02.75
Spilar, a tough defender, was noticed by FC Bruges when he played a friendly with Slovakia against Belgium in Brussels on April 17th 2002. He made a good start in Bruges but received an ankle injury after six games. He hasn't been back in the team since and is now recovering from a bacterial infection in the same ankle. Hopes to be back by October. Has played before in the Champions League with FC Kosice in a group that included Manchester United, Feyenoord and Juventus.

**23 STIJN STIJNEN** 07.04.81
Stijnen, now the third goalkeeper after Butina and Verlinden, made his debut for FC Bruges last season on April 18th 2003 away to Racing Genk (0-3 win) when Verlinden was out with a minor injury. He also played the next game at Lierse (1-1 draw). In those two games he showed the reason why youth team boss Hans rates him so highly.

**14 ALIN STOICA** 10.12.79
Stoica, who originally - like his father - played for Steaua Bucharest, was adored at the

Romanian club but was forced to leave after falling out with the club's board. Played for Anderlecht since 1996 but left the Belgian capital for FC Bruges where he scored on his home debut v KV Mechelen (4-0) on August 31st 2002. Stoica scored four more goals in the league but he played only 19 games and he didn't really make the expected impact in Bruges' run towards the title. In the Champions League he also failed to reach the heights he did for Anderlecht, where he scored four times in 15 Champions League games.

**5 PETER VAN DER HEYDEN** 16.07.76
Since arriving at FC Bruges from Eendracht Alost Peter Van Der Heyden has established himself at left-back. His performances won him his first cap for the Belgian national team against the Czech Republic in 2001 and later on a place in the Belgian squad for the World Cup 2002. Coming in to the team in place for the Nico Van Kerckhoven, he scored his first ever goal for the Belgian national team, the equaliser against Japan (2-2). In 2002 he also won the Belgian Cup with FC Bruges (3-1 against Mouscron) and last season he won his first Belgian league title.

**22 BIRGER VAN DE VEN** 30.04.82
Was noticed by FC Bruges in 2001 when he was playing fot KV Mechelen, the team where he made his debut in the First Division. In his first season in Bruges he played five league games as a substitute. Last season he didn't get into the first team at all. Can be used on the left as defender or midfielder.

**7 GERT VERHEYEN** 20.09.70
After four seasons with Anderlecht, Verheyen was transferred to FC Bruges in He played all six European games that season and scored a goal, the winner against CSKA Moscow (2-1 on April 7th 1993). Last season Verheyen participated for the second time in the Champions League, playing all six games again and scoring at home against Galatasaray (3-1 win) on October 23rd 2002. After the World Cup 2002 Verheyen retired from the national team (50 caps, 10 goals) to fully concentrate on FC Bruges. Playing on the right wing just behind the forwards, he scored the important second goal in the third qualifying round home game against Borussia Dortmund.

**1 DANY VERLINDEN** 15.08.63
Played in the third qualifying round at home against Borussia Dortmund on August 13th 2003, his 70th European Cup game and maybe his last for FC Bruges after letting the ball slip out of his hands for Amoroso to score 2-1. Three more conceded goals at home versus Cup holders La Louvière ten days later (the match finished in a 3-3 draw) meant he lost his place to Tomislav Butina for the return in Dortmund. Verlinden, who came to FC Bruges from Lierse in 1988, is likely to retire after this season and he should take up a new job at the club as goalkeeping coach. He'd played 12 Champions League games for FC Bruges until the start of this season (six in 1992-93 and six in 2002-03).

# CHAMPIONS LEAGUE HISTORY 1992-2003

A COMPLETE
TEAM-BY-TEAM GUIDE
TO EVERY CHAMPIONS
LEAGUE GAME

BY CHRIS RHYS

## AALBORG BK

**1995-1996**
**GROUP STAGE 1**
**27.09.95 v FC Porto (a) Lost 0-2**
Gill, Simonsen, Boye, Kristensen, Jessen, Thomsen (Thomasberg 17), Facius, Pedersen (Madsen 63), Henrik Rasmussen, Andersen, Peter Rasmussen (Gronkjaer 79)

**18.10.95 v FC Nantes Atlantique (a) Lost 1-3**
Gill, Simonsen, Boye, Madsen (Gronkjaer 70), Jessen (Kruger 87), Thorst, Facius (Thomasberg 82), Pedersen, Henrik Rasmussen, Andersen, Peter Rasmussen. Scorer: Andersen 46

**25.10.95 v Panathinaikos FC (h) Won 2-1**
Gill, Boye, Jessen, Thorst, Simonsen, Facius, Thomasberg, Pedersen (Madsen 23), Henrik Rasmussen, Andersen, Peter Rasmussen (Gronkjaer 84). Scorers: Andersen 7, Madsen 89

**01.11.95 v FC Nantes Atlantique (h) Lost 0-2**
Gill, Boye, Thorst, Simonsen, Jessen, Facius (Thomsen 71), Madsen (Hjermitslev 82), Thomasberg, Henrik Rasmussen, Andersen (Gronkjaer 46), Peter Rasmussen. Sent off: Boye 66

**22.11.95 v Panathinaikos FC (a) Lost 0-2**
Gill, Kruger, Kristensen (Hjermitslev 82), Jessen, Simonsen, Madsen (Gronkjaer 61), Facius, Pedersen, Henrik Rasmussen, Andersen, Peter Rasmussen. Sent off: Pedersen 89

**06.12.95 v FC Porto (h) Drawn 2-2**
Winde, Kruger, Thomsen, Kristensen, Jessen, Madsen (Pedersen 82), Facius, Thomasberg, Gronkjaer (Nielsen 79), Henrik Rasmussen (Hjermitslev 65), Andersen
Scorers: Andersen 11, Madsen 69

| SEASONS | PLAYED | WON | DRAWN | LOST | FOR | AGAINST |
|---|---|---|---|---|---|---|
| 1 | 6 | 1 | 1 | 4 | 5 | 12 |

## AEK ATHENS

**1994-1995**
**GROUP STAGE 1**
**14.09.94 v SV Austria Salzburg (a) Drawn 0-0**
Atmatsidis, Agorogiannis, Karagianis, Manolas, Sabanadzovic, Vlachos, Saravakos (Kopitsis 70), Savevski, Kostis, Tsartas, Kassapis

**28.09.94 v AFC Ajax (h)** **Lost 1-2**
Atmatsidis, Agorogiannis, Karagianis (Mirtsekis 75), Manolas, Kassapis, Vlachos, Saravakos, Savevski, Kopitsis, Tsartas (Dimitriadis 62), Kostis. Scorer: Savevski 30

**19.10.94 v Milan AC (h)** **Drawn 0-0**
Atmatsidis, Kopitsis (Agorogiannis 78), Papadopoulos, Manolas, Sabanadzovic, Vlachos, Saravakos, Savevski, Kostis (Ketsbaia 62), Tsartas, Kassapis

**02.11.94 v Milan AC (a)** **Lost 1-2**
Atmatsidis, Kopitsis (Agorogiannis 74), Karagianis, Manolas, Sabanadzovic, Vlachos, Saravakos, Savevski, Kostis, Tsartas (Ketsbaia 76), Kassapis. Scorer: Savevski 16. Sent off: Manolas 87

**23.11.94 v SV Austria Salzburg (h)** **Lost 1-3**
Atmatsidis, Agorogiannis (Kopitsis 46), Karagianis (Borbokis 70), Kuotoulas, Sabanadzovic, Vlachos, Saravakos, Ketsbaia, Kostis, Tsartas, Kassapis. Scorer: Vlachos 28

**07.12.94 v AFC Ajax (a)** **Lost 0-2**
Atmatsidis, Agorogiannis, Papadopoulos, Kuotoulas (Kopitsis 46), Stamatis, Vlachos, Saravakos, Borbokis, Kostis (Ketsbaia 66), Tsartas, Kassapis

## 2002-2003
### GROUP STAGE 1

**17.09.02 v KRC Genk (a)** **Drawn 0-0**
Chiotis, Borbokis, (Petkov 53), Kostenoglou, Wright, Kassapis, Kapsis, Zagorakis, Katsouranis, Tsartas (Maladenis 90), Nalitzis (Lakis 64), Nikolaidis

**25.09.02 v AS Roma (h)** **Drawn 0-0**
Chiotis, Lakis, Kostenoglou, Wright, Kassapis (Georgatos 46), Kapsis, Zagorakis, Katsouranis, Tsartas (Petkov 85), Ivic (Nalitzis 64), Nikolaidis

**02.10.02 v Real Madrid CF (h)** **Drawn 3-3**
Chiotis, Lakis, Kostenoglou, Wright, Kassapis, Kapsis, Zagorakis (Centeno 84), Katsouranis, Petkov (Maladenis 16), Tsartas (Ivic 84), Nikolaidis
Scorers: Tsartas 6, Maladenis 25, Nikolaidis 28

**22.10.02 v Real Madrid CF (a)** **Drawn 2-2**
Chiotis, Lakis, Kostenoglou, Wright, Kassapis, Kapsis, Zagorakis, Katsouranis, Georgatos (Centeno 69), Tsartas (Maladenis 54), Nikolaidis (Ivic 54)
Scorers: Katsouranis 74, Centeno 89

**30.10.02 v KRC Genk (h)** **Drawn 1-1**
Chiotis, Borbokis (Centeno 86), Kostenoglou, Wright, Kassapis, Kapsis, Lakis, Katsouranis, Georgatos (Maladenis 78), Tsartas (Ivic 64), Nikolaidis Scorer: Lakis 30

**12.11.02 v AS Roma (a)** **Drawn 1-1**
Chiotis, Borbokis, Wright, Kapsis (Kostenoglou 46), Georgatos, Lakis (Tsartas 61), Zagorakis, Katsouranis, Centeno, Nalitzis (Ivic 46), Nikolaidis Scorer: Centeno 90

| SEASONS | PLAYED | WON | DRAWN | LOST | FOR | AGAINST |
|---|---|---|---|---|---|---|
| 2 | 12 | 0 | 8 | 4 | 10 | 16 |

## AIK SOLNA (STOCKHOLM)

**1999-2000**
**GROUP STAGE 1**
**14.09.99 v FC Barcelona (h)** **Lost 1-2**
Asper, Nordin, Ola Andersson, Brundin, Novakovic (Mattiasson 86), Tjernstrom (Bergh 77), Andreas Andersson, Lagerlof, Ljung, Kjolo, Kaamark (Corneliusson 86). Scorer: Novakovic 72

**22.09.99 v Arsenal FC (a)** **Lost 1-3**
Asper, Nordin, Ola Andersson (Corneliusson 88), Brundin, Gustafsson, Novakovic (Aslund 82), Tjernstrom, Andreas Andersson, Lagerlof, Ljung, Kaamark (Kjolo 46). Scorer: Nordin 53

**29.09.99 v AC Fiorentina (h)** **Drawn 0-0**
Asper, Nordin, Ola Andersson (Corneliusson 55), Brundin, Gustafsson, Novakovic, Tjernstrom, Andreas Andersson, Lagerlof, Ljung, Kjolo
**19.10.99 v AC Fiorentina (a)** **Lost 0-3**
Asper, Nordin, Ola Andersson, Brundin, Gustafsson, Novakovic (Hoch 46), Tjernstrom, Mattiasson (Johansson 82), Lagerlof (Corneliusson 58), Ljung, Kjolo

**27.10.99 v FC Barcelona (a)** **Lost 0-5**
Asper, Nordin (Ola Andersson 46), Corneliusson, Brundin, Gustafsson, Novakovic, Tjernstrom (Lagerlof 75), Ljung, Kjolo, Kaamark, Hoch (Mattiasson 46)

**02.11.99 v Arsenal FC (h)** **Lost 2-3**
Asper (Baxter 72), Nordin, Corneliusson (Aslund 72), Ola Andersson, Gustafsson, Novakovic, Tjernstrom, Andreas Andersson, Lagerlof, Kjolo, Kaamark.
Scorer: Andreas Andersson 41, 68

| SEASONS | PLAYED | WON | DRAWN | LOST | FOR | AGAINST |
|---|---|---|---|---|---|---|
| 1 | 6 | 0 | 1 | 5 | 4 | 16 |

## RSC ANDERLECHT

**1993-1994**
**GROUP STAGE 1**
**24.11.93 v Milan AC (h) Drawn 0-0**
De Wilde, Crasson, Rutjes, Albert, De Wolf, Walem, Zetterberg, Bosman, Haagdoren, Bruno Versavel, Boffin (Van Baekel 89)

**01.12.93 v SV Werder Bremen (a) Lost 3-5**
De Wilde, Crasson, Rutjes, Albert, Emmers, Walem, Zetterberg (Kooiman 56), Bosman (Nilis 68), Haagdoren, Bruno Versavel, Boffin. Scorers: Albert 16, Boffin 18, 33

**02.03.94 v FC Porto (h) Won 1-0**
De Wilde, Suray (Crasson 46), Nwanu, Albert, Emmers, Walem, Bruno Versavel (Kooiman 88), Bosman, Nilis, Degryse, Boffin. Scorer: Nilis 85

**16.03.94 v FC Porto (a) Lost 0-1**
De Wilde, Crasson, Nwanu, Rutjes, Emmers (Haagdoren 73), Walem, Bruno Versavel (Bosman 46), Suray, Nilis, Degryse, Boffin

**30.03.94 v Milan AC (a) Drawn 0-0**
De Wilde, Crasson, Nwanu, Suray, Emmers, Walem, Haagdoren, Bosman, Nilis, Degryse, Boffin

**13.04.94 v SV Werder Bremen (h) Lost 1-2**
De Wilde, Crasson, Nwanu, Marchoul (Michel De Wolf 46), Emmers (Peiremans 70), Walem, Bruno Versavel, Bosman, Nilis, Haagdoren, Boffin. Scorer: Bosman 45

**1994-1995**
**GROUP STAGE 1**
**14.09.94 v Steaua Bucaresti (h) Drawn 0-0**
De Wilde, Crasson, Rutjes, Emmers, Doll, Walem, Weber, Boffin (Suray 87), Haagdoren (Preko 72), Bosman, Degryse

**28.09.94 v SL Benfica (a) Lost 1-3**
De Wilde, Crasson, Rutjes, Nwanu, Doll, Walem, Weber, Boffin, Haagdoren, Bosman, Degryse. Scorer: Paulo Madeira og 86

**19.10.94 v HNK Hajduk Split (a)** **Lost 1-2**
De Wilde, Crasson, Rutjes, Suray, Nwanu, Walem, Zetterberg, Peiremans, Boffin, Weber, Bosman. Scorer: Weber 87

**02.11.94 v HNK Hajduk Split (h)** **Drawn 0-0**
De Wilde, Crasson, Rutjes, Suray, Doll, Walem, Zetterberg, Peiremans (Haagdoren 73), Boffin, Weber, Bosman

**23.11.94 v Steaua Bucaresti (a)** **Drawn 1-1**
De Wilde, Crasson, Rutjes, Babayaro, Doll, Walem, Haagdoren (Peiremans 65), Zetterberg, Boffin, Bosman, Degryse. Scorer: Bosman 44. Sent off: Babayaro 37

**07.12.94 v SL Benfica (h)** **Drawn 1-1**
De Wilde, Crasson, Rutjes, Emmers (Haagdoren 68), Doll, Walem, Preko, Boffin, Zetterberg (Peiremans 88), Bosman, Degryse. Scorer: Rutjes 48

**2000-2001**
**GROUP STAGE 1**
**13.09.00 v Manchester United FC (a)** **Lost 1-5**
De Wilde, Vanderhaeghe, De Boeck, Staelens, Goor (Ilic 58), Koller, Dheedene, Baseggio, Radzinski (Youla 59), Van Diemen (Oyen 46), Crasson. Scorer: Koller 55

**19.09.00 v PSV Eindhoven (h)** **Won 1-0**
De Wilde, Vanderhaeghe, De Boeck, Staelens, Goor, Koller, Dheedene, Baseggio, Radzinski (Dindane 73), Crasson, Iachtchouk (Stoica 58). Scorer: Dheedene 80

**26.09.00 v FC Dynamo Kyiv (a)** **Lost 0-4**
De Wilde, Vanderhaeghe, De Boeck (Stoica 59), Staelens, Goor (Youla 81), Koller, Dheedene, Baseggio, Radzinski, Van Diemen, Crasson (Iachtchouk 63)

**18.10.00 v FC Dynamo Kyiv (h)** **Won 4-2**
De Wilde, Vanderhaeghe, De Boeck, Staelens, Goor, Koller, Dheedene, Baseggio, Stoica (Dindane 87), Radzinski, Crasson. Scorers: Vaschuk og 10, Radzinski 38, 41, Stoica 45

**24.10.00 v Manchester United (h)** **Won 2-1**
De Wilde, Vanderhaeghe, De Boeck, Staelens, Goor, Koller, Dheedene, Baseggio, Stoica (Oyen 81), Radzinski (Dindane 90), Crasson. Scorer: Radzinski 15, 34

**08.11.00 v PSV Eindhoven (a)** **Won 3-2**
De Wilde, Vanderhaeghe, De Boeck, Staelens, Goor, Koller, Dheedene, Baseggio, Stoica (Hasi 55), Radzinski (Youla 84), Crasson. Scorers: Crasson 9, Koller 37, Youla 90

**GROUP STAGE 2**

**22.11.00 v SS Lazio (h) Won 1-0**
De Wilde, Crasson, Doll, Ilic, Dheedene, Baseggio, Hasi, Goor, Stoica, Radzinski (Van Diemen 90), Koller. Scorer: Radzinski 83

**05.12.00 v Real Madrid CF (a) Lost 1-4**
De Wilde, Crasson, De Boeck, Doll, Dheedene, Van Diemen, Vanderhaeghe (Stoica 59), Goor, Hasi (Ilic 62), Radzinski, Koller. Scorer: Stoica 89

**13.02.01 v Leeds United AFC (a) Lost 1-2**
Milojevic, Crasson, De Boeck, Ilic, Dheedene, Vanderhaeghe, Stoica, Baseggio, Goor, Radzinski, Koller (no subs). Scorer: Stoica 65

**21.02.01 v Leeds United AFC (h) Lost 1-4**
Milojevic, Crasson, De Boeck, Ilic (Dindane 39), Dheedene, Vanderhaeghe, Stoica, Baseggio, Goor, Radzinski, Koller. Scorer: Koller 76

**06.03.01 v SS Lazio (a) Lost 1-2**
Milojevic, Crasson (Van Demen 82), De Boeck, Doll, Ilic, Vanderhaeghe, Dheedene, Hasi, Goor, Radzinski, Koller (Stoica 45). Scorer: Stoica 49

**14.03.01 v Real Madrid CF (h) Won 2-0**
Milojevic - Van Diemen, Doll, De Boeck, Ilic, Hasi (Vanderhaeghe 79), Stoica (Dindane 83), Baseggio, Goor, Radzinski, Youla (Koller 70). Scorers: Dindane 83, Goor 90

**2001-2002**

**GROUP STAGE 1**

**11.09.01 v FC Lokomotiv Moscow (a) Drawn 1-1**
De Wilde, Pirard, De Boeck, Crasson, Ilic, Dindane (Seol 88), Hasi, Vandenhaeghe, Hendrikx, De Bilde (Stoica 77), Mornar (Van Houdt 90). Scorer: Hendrikx 15

**19.09.01 v AS Roma (h) Drawn 0-0**
De Wilde, Crasson, De Boeck, Van Houdt, Hendrikx, Dindane, Hasi, Baseggio (El Said 88), Vandenhaeghe, Stoica (Thompson 78), Mornar (De Bilde 67)

**26.09.01 v Real Madrid CF (a) Lost 1-4**
De Wilde, Crasson, De Boeck, Van Houdt, Ilic, Dindane, Hasi (De Bilde 59), Baseggio (El Said 66), Vandenhaeghe, Hendrikx, Stoica (Thompson 71). Scorer: Dindane 33

**16.10.01 v Real Madrid CF (h) Lost 0-2**
De Wilde, Crasson, De Boeck, Traore, Hendrikx, Dindane, Hasi, Baseggio (El Said 46), Vandenhaeghe, Iachtchouk (Thompson 79), Mornar

**24.10.01 v FC Lokomotiv Moscow (h) Lost 1-5**
De Wilde, Crasson, De Boeck, Ilic, Hendrikx, Dindane (Jestrovic 64), Hasi, El Said (De Bilde 46), Vandenhaeghe, Iachtchouk (Karaca 52), Mornar. Scorer: Ilic 2

**30.10.01 v AS Roma (a) Drew 1-1**
De Wilde, Crasson (Van Houdt 46), De Boeck, Traore, Ilic, Baseggio, Vandenhaeghe, Stoica, Hendrikx (Oyen 46), Iachtchouk, Mornar (Jestrovic 76). Scorer: Mornar 11

| SEASONS | PLAYED | WON | DRAWN | LOST | FOR | AGAINST |
|---|---|---|---|---|---|---|
| 4 | 30 | 7 | 9 | 14 | 31 | 55 |

## AFC AJAX

### 1994–1995
### GROUP STAGE 1

**14.09.94 v Milan AC (h) Won 2-0**
Van der Sar, Reiziger, Blind, Rijkaard, F De Boer, R De Boer, Finidi, Davids (Seedorf 89), Kluivert (Van Vossen 76), Litmanen, Overmars. Scorers: R De Boer 50, Litmanen 64

**28.09.94 v AEK Athens (a) Won 2-1**
Van der Sar, Reiziger, Blind, Seedorf, F De Boer, R De Boer (Kreek 76), Finidi, Davids, Kluivert, Litmanen, Overmars (Van Vossen 63). Scorers: Litmanen 33, Kluivert 65

**19.10.94 v SV Austria Salzburg (a) Drawn 0-0**
Van der Sar, Reiziger, Blind, Rijkaard, F De Boer, Overmars (Kreek 46), Seedorf, R De Boer, Kluivert (Kanu 67), Litmanen, Van Vossen

**02.11.94 v SV Austria Salzburg (h) Drawn 1-1**
Van der Sar, Reiziger, Seedorf, Rijkaard, F De Boer, R De Boer, Finidi, Davids, Kluivert (Kanu 57), Litmanen, Overmars (Van Vossen 46). Scorer: Litmanen 85

**23.11.94 v Milan AC (a) Won 2-0**
Van der Sar, Reiziger, Blind, Rijkaard, F De Boer, Finidi, Seedorf, Davids (Overmars 81), R De Boer, Litmanen, Van Vossen (Kanu 36). Scorers: Litmanen 2, Baresi og 66

**07.12.94 v AEK Athens (h) Won 2-0**
Van der Sar, Reiziger, Blind, Rijkaard, F De Boer, Finidi (Van Vossen 76), Seedorf, Oulida, R De Boer, Litmanen (Kluivert 76), Overmars. Scorer: Oulida 8, 78

**QUARTER FINAL**

**01.03.95 v HNK Hajduk Split (a) Drawn 0-0**

Van der Sar, Reiziger, Blind, Rijkaard, F De Boer, Finidi, Seedorf, Davids, Kluivert (Bogarde 77), Litmanen, Overmars (Van Vossen 58)

**15.03.95 v HNK Hajduk Split (h) Won 3-0**

Van der Sar, Reiziger, Blind, Rijkaard, F De Boer, Finidi, Seedorf (Bogarde 76), Kanu (Kluivert 72), R De Boer, Litmanen, Overmars. Scorers: Kanu 38, F De Boer 42, 73

**SEMI FINAL**

**05.04.95 v FC Bayern Munchen (a) Drawn 0-0**

Van der Sar, Reiziger, Blind, Rijkaard, F De Boer, R De Boer (Bogarde 75), Finidi, Seedorf, Kanu (Kluivert 63), Litmanen, Overmars

**19.04.95 v FC Bayern Munchen (h) Won 5-2**

Van der Sar, Reiziger, Blind, Rijkaard, Bogarde, R De Boer, Finidi (Davids 87), Seedorf, Kanu (Kluivert 67), Litmanen, Overmars. Scorers: Litmanen 11, 47, Finidi 41, R De Boer 44, Overmars 88

**FINAL**

**24.05.95 v Milan AC (n) Won 1-0**

Van der Sar, Reiziger, Blind, Rijkaard, F De Boer, Finidi, Seedorf (Kanu 53), Davids, R De Boer, Litmanen (Kluivert 70), Overmars. Scorer: Kluivert 84

**1995-1996**

**GROUP STAGE 1**

**13.09.95 v Real Madrid CF (h) Won 1-0**

Van der Sar, Reiziger, F De Boer, Bogarde, Finidi, R De Boer (Tuhuteru 87), Davids, Reuser (Wooter 46), Litmanen, Kanu (Musampa 69), Overmars. Scorer: Overmars 14

**27.09.95 v Ferencvarosi TC (a) Won 5-1**

Van der Sar, Reiziger, Blind, F De Boer, Bogarde, Finidi, R De Boer, Davids, Litmanen, Kanu (Kluivert 57), Overmars. Scorers: Litmanen 57, 79, 87 pen, Kluivert 67, F De Boer 84

**18.10.95 v Grasshopper-Club (h) Won 3-0**

Van der Sar, Reiziger, Blind (Scholten 73), F De Boer, Bogarde, Finidi, R De Boer (Kanu 62), Davids, Litmanen, Kluivert, Overmars. Scorers: Kluivert 12, 68, Finidi 87

**01.11.95 v Grasshopper-Club (a) Drawn 0-0**

Van der Sar, Reiziger, F De Boer, Bogarde, Blind, R De Boer (Kanu 59), Finidi, Davids, Litmanen, Kluivert, Overmars (Reuser 74)

**22.11.95 v Real Madrid CF (a) Won 2-0**
Van der Sar, Reiziger, Bogarde, Blind, Musampa (Reuser 89), R De Boer, Finidi, Davids, Litmanen, Kluivert, Overmars. Scorers: Litmanen 64, Kluivert 76

**06.12.95 v Ferencvarosi TC (h) Won 4-0**
Van der Sar, Reiziger, F De Boer, Bogarde, Scholten, R De Boer, Finidi (Wooter 77), Davids (Musampa 46), Litmanen (Reuser 77), Kluivert, Overmars. Scorers: Overmars 17, R De Boer 22, Litmanen 62, 66

**QUARTER FINAL**
**06.03.96 v BV Borussia Dortmund (a) Won 2-0**
Van der Sar, Reiziger (Scholten 84), Silooy, Bogarde, Blind, R De Boer, Finidi, Davids, Kanu, Kluivert, Wooter (Musampa 46). Scorers: Davids 8, Kluivert 83

**20.03.96 v BV Borussia Dortmund (h) Won 1-0**
Van der Sar, Silooy, F De Boer, Bogarde, Scholten, R De Boer, Musampa, Wooter, Davids, Kanu, Litmanen (Landzaat 87). Scorer: Musampa 75

**SEMI FINAL**
**03.04.96 v Panathinaikos FC (h) Lost 0-1**
Van der Sar, Reiziger, Blind, Bogarde, F De Boer, R De Boer, Finidi, Davids, Kanu, Kluivert, Litmanen (Musampa 76)

**17.04.96 v Panathinaikos FC (a) Won 3-0**
Van der Sar, Reiziger, F De Boer, Silooy (Wooter 74), Blind, R De Boer, Finidi, Davids (Scholten 86), Bogarde, Kanu, Litmanen. Scorers: Litmanen 4, 77, Wooter 86

**FINAL**
**23.05.96 v Juventus FC (n) Drawn 1-1 Lost 4-2pens**
Van der Sar, Silooy, F De Boer (Scholten 69), Blind, R De Boer (Wooter 91), Finidi, Davids, Bogarde, Musampa (Kluivert 46), Kanu, Litmanen. Scorer: Litmanen 41. Penalty scorers: Litmanen, Scholten Missed: Davids, Silooy

**1996-1997**
**GROUP STAGE 1**
**11.09.96 v AJ Auxerre (a) Won 1-0**
Van der Sar, Marcio Santos, Melchiot (Willems 80), F De Boer, Bogarde, Mariano Juan, Litmanen (Reuser 90), Musampa, Babangida, R De Boer, Overmars (Turpijn 72). Scorer: Litmanen 4

**25.09.96 v Grasshopper-Club (h) Lost 0-1**
Van der Sar, Marcio Santos, Blind, F De Boer, Bogarde, Mariano Juan (Melchiot 68), Litmanen (Wooter 46), Musampa, Babangida (Scholten 75), R De Boer, Overmars

**16.10.96 v Rangers FC (h) Won 4-1**
Van der Sar, Marcio Santos, Veldman, F De Boer, Bogarde, R De Boer, Dani (Wooter 79), Scholten, Babangida, Reuser (R Witschge 42), Overmars. Scorers: Dani 25, 41, Babangida 83, Wooter 90

**30.10.96 v Rangers FC (a) Won 1-0**
Van der Sar, Veldman, Marcio Santos, Melchiot, Scholten, F De Boer (Wooter 70), R De Boer, R Witschge, Babangida (Dani 72), Kluivert, Overmars (Turpijn 79). Scorer: Scholten 39

**20.11.96 v AJ Auxerre (h) Lost 1-2**
Van der Sar, Veldman (Splinter 23), Melchiot, Bogarde, R De Boer, Scholten, Wooter, (Dani 64), Willems, Babangida, Kluivert, Overmars. Scorer: Babangida 44

**04.12.96 v Grasshopper-Club (a) Won 1-0**
Van der Sar, Veldman (Melchiot 41), F De Boer, Splinter, Musampa, Scholten, Reuser (Litmanen 63), R De Boer, Babangida (Wooter 83), Kluivert, Overmars. Scorer: Kluivert 32

**QUARTER FINAL**
**05.03.97 v Club Atletico de Madrid (h) Drawn 1-1**
Van der Sar, Melchiot (Veldman 83), Blind, F De Boer, R De Boer, Witschge, Litmanen, Musampa (Scholten 46), Babangida (Wooter 70), Kluivert, Overmars. Scorer: Kluivert 53

**19.03.97 v Club Atletico de Madrid (a) Won 3-2 after extra-time**
Van der Sar, Melchiot, Blind (Veldman 46), F De Boer, Witschge, Litmanen (Dani 80), Musampa (Wooter 87), Scholten, Babangida, R De Boer, Overmars.. Scorers: R De Boer 49, Dani 99, Babangida 120

**SEMI FINAL**
**09.04.97 v Juventus FC (h) Lost 1-2**
Van der Sar, Melchiot, Blind, F De Boer, Scholten (Wooter 46), Witschge (Dani 70), Litmanen, Musampa (Bogarde 72), Babangida, R De Boer, Overmars. Scorer: Litmanen 66

**23.04.97 v Juventus FC (a) Lost 1-4**
Van der Sar, Melchiot, Blind, F De Boer, Scholten (Musampa 56), Witschge (Dani 83), Litmanen, Bogarde, Babangida, R De Boer, Overmars. Scorer: Melchiot 75

**1998-1999**
**GROUP STAGE 1**
**16.09.98 v NK Croatia (Dinamo) Zagreb (a) Drawn 0-0**
Van der Sar, Tobiasen, Blind, Oliseh, F De Boer, R Witschge, Litmanen, Dani (R De Boer 63), Babangida (Kinkladze 77), B McCarthy, Hoekstra (Gronkjaer 71)

**30.09.98 v FC Porto (h) Won 2-1**
Van der Sar, Tobiasen, Rudy, Oliseh, F De Boer, R De Boer, Litmanen, R Witschge (Dani 65), Babangida (Gronkjaer 90), Arveladze (Sibon 79), Hoekstra. Scorers: Rudy 57, Litmanen 86 pen

**21.10.98 v Olympiakos Piraeus FC (a) Lost 0-1**
Van der Sar, Tobiasen, Rudy, Oliseh, F De Boer, R De Boer, Litmanen, R Witschge, Wamberto (Dani 46), Arveladze (B McCarthy 79), Gronkjaer (Kinkladze 46)

**04.11.98 v Olympiakos Piraeus FC (h) Won 2-0**
Van der Sar, Tobiasen (Dani 38), Oliseh, F De Boer, Sier, R De Boer, Litmanen (Gorre 40), R Witschge, Wamberto, Arveladze (B McCarthy 27), Hoekstra. Scorers: R Witschge 33, Gorre 88

**25.11.98 v NK Croatia (Dinamo) Zagreb (h) Lost 0-1**
Van der Sar, Mensah, Blind, F De Boer, Sier (Melchiot 42), R De Boer, Dani, R Witschge, Wamberto (Babangida 73), Hose (B McCarthy 64), Hoekstra

**09.12.98 v FC Porto (a) Lost 0-3**
Van der Sar, Mensah, Blind, F De Boer, Rudy (B McCarthy 72), Oliseh, Gorre (Dani 46), Hoekstra, Wamberto, Gronkjaer (Babangida 74), R De Boer

**2002-2003**
**GROUP STAGE 1**
**17.09.02 v Olympique Lyonnais (h) Won 2-1**
Stekelenberg, Trabelsi, Chivu, Yakubu, O'Brien, Galasek (Van Halst 57), Litmanen, Maxwell, Sikora (Pienaar 68), Zlatan (Bergdolmo 81), Van der Meyde. Scorer: Zlatan 11, 34. Sent off: Yakubu 85

**25.09.02 v Internazionale FC (a) Lost 0-1**
Stekelenberg (Timmer 23), Trabelsi, Pasanen (Hossam 80), Chivu, Van Damme, Galasek, Litmanen, Maxwell, Van der Meyde (Pienaar 78), Zlatan, Sikora

**02.10.02 v Rosenborg BK (a) Drawn 0-0**
Didulica, Trabelsi, Bergdolmo, Chivu, Van Damme, Galasek, Van Halst (Winter 69), Wamberto, Witschge (Maxwell 79), Zlatan (Van der Meyde 69), Hossam

**22.10.02 v Rosenborg BK (h) Drawn 1-1**
Timmer, Trabelsi, Bergdolmo, Chivu, Van Damme, Galasek, Litmanen, Witschge (De Jong 83), Van der Meyde, Zlatan (Hossam 71), Boukhari. Scorer: Zlatan 41. Sent off: Van Damme 84

**30.10.02 v Olympique Lyonnais (a) Won 2-0**
Didulica, Trabelsi, Bergdolmo, Chivu, De Jong, Maxwell, Galasek, Pienaar, Sikora (Yakubu 65), Zlatan (Van der Meyde 77), Hossam (Van der Vaart 55). Scorers: Pienaar 7, Van der Vaart 90. Sent off: Chivu 62

**12.11.02 v Internazionale FC (h) Lost 1-2**
Didulica, Trabelsi, Bergdolmo, De Jong, Van Damme (Witschge 58), Galasek (Yakubu 71), Pienaar (Wamberto 58), Maxwell, Van der Meyde, Hossam, Van der Vaart. Scorer: Van der Vaart 90

**27.11.02 v Valencia CF (a) Drawn 1-1**
Didulica, Trabelsi, Bergdolmo, Chivu, Maxwell, Galasek, Pienaar (De Jong 71), Van der Vaart, Van der Meyde, Litmanen (Zlatan 59), Hossam (Boukhari 85). Scorer: Zlatan 88

**10.12.02 v AS Roma (h) Won 2-1**
Stekelenberg, Trabelsi (Yakubu 33), Bergdolmo, Pasanen, Maxwell, Van der Meyde (Boukhari 80), Pienaar, De Jong, Witschge, Zlatan, Hossam (Litmanen 57)
Scorers: Zlatan 11, Litmanen 66

**18.02.03 v Arsenal FC (a) Drawn 1-1**
Lobont, Trabelsi, Chivu, Pasanen, Van Damme (Witschge 76), Pienaar (Yakubu 90), Galasek, De Jong, Maxwell, Van der Meyde, Zlatan (Boukhari 79). Scorer: De Jong 17

**26.02.03 v Arsenal FC (h) Drawn 0-0**
Lobont, Trabelsi, Chivu, Pasanen, Witschge, Pienaar (Sneijder 90), Galasek (Yakubu 71), De Jong, Maxwell, Van der Meyde, Zlatan (Hossam 84)

**11.03.03 v Valencia CF (h) Drawn 1-1**
Lobont, Trabelsi, Chivu, Pasanen, O'Brien, Pienaar, Galasek, De Jong (Van der Meyde 46), Maxwell, Van der Vaart, Zlatan. Scorer: Pasanen 57

**19.03.03 v AS Roma (a) Drawn 1-1**
Lobont, Trabelsi, Chivu, Pasanen, O'Brien (Van Damme 90), Pienaar (Yakubu 90), Galasek, Van der Vaart, Maxwell, Van der Meyde (Sikora 72), Zlatan (Witschge 89). Scorer: Van der Meyde 1

**QUARTER FINAL**

**08.04.03 v AC Milan (h) Drawn 0-0**
Lobont, Trabelsi, Chivu, Pasanen (De Jong 74), O'Brien, Pienaar, Galasek (Sneijder 67), Yakubu, Maxwell, Van der Vaart, Zlatan (Litmanen 73)

**23.04.03 v AC Milan (a) Lost 2-3**
Lobont, Trabelsi, Chivu, Pasanen, Van Damme (Litmanen 46), Pienaar (De Jong 84),

Sneijder, Yakubu, O'Brien, Van der Meyde (Bergdolmo 89), Zlatan. Scorers: Litmanen 63, Pienaar 78

| SEASONS | PLAYED | WON | DRAWN | LOST | FOR | AGAINST |
|---|---|---|---|---|---|---|
| 5 | 52 | 25 | 16 | 11 | 72 | 39 |

## ARSENAL FC

**1998-1999**
**GROUP STAGE 1**
**16.09.98 v RC Lens (a) Drawn 1-1**
Seaman, Dixon, Keown, Adams, Winterburn, Petit (Hughes 73), Vieira, Parlour, Bergkamp (Garde 90), Anelka, Overmars. Scorer: Overmars 51

**30.09.98 v Panathinaikos FC (h) Won 2-1**
Seaman, Dixon, Keown, Adams, Winterburn, Garde (Vivas 78), Vieira, Petit, Overmars, Bergkamp, Anelka. Scorers: Adams 64, Keown 72

**21.10.98 v FC Dynamo Kyiv (h) Drawn 1-1**
Seaman, Dixon, Keown, Adams, Winterburn, Garde, Parlour, Hughes, Overmars, Bergkamp, Anelka (Vivas 85). Scorer: Bergkamp 74

**04.11.98 v FC Dynamo Kyiv (a) Lost 1-3**
Seaman, Dixon, Keown, Bould (Grimandi 45), Winterburn, Parlour, Vieira, Petit, Vivas (Garde 85), Boa Morte (Hughes 68), Wreh. Scorer: Hughes 83

**26.11.98 v RC Lens (h) Lost 0-1**
Seaman, Dixon, Keown, Adams (Bould 46), Winterburn, Parlour, Garde (Vivas 70), Hughes, Overmars, Wreh (Boa Morte 70), Anelka. Sent off: Parlour 90

**09.12.98 v Panathinaikos FC (a) Won 3-1**
Seaman, Grondin, Vivas, Bould, Upson, Grimandi, Mendez (Black 78), Boa Morte, Vernazza, Anelka, Wreh. Scorers: Asanovic og 65, Anelka 80, Boa Morte 86

**1999-2000**
**GROUP STAGE 1**
**14.09.99 v AC Fiorentina (a) Drawn 0-0**
Manninger, Winterburn, Vieira, Keown, Adams, Ljungberg, Suker (Kanu 61), Bergkamp (Henry 82), Overmars, Grimandi, Luzhny
**22.09.99 v AIK Solna (h) Won 3-1**
Manninger, Dixon, Winterburn, Vieira, Keown, Adams, Ljungberg (Henry 69), Suker,

Bergkamp, Overmars (Kanu 69), Grimandi (Silvinho 56). Scorers: Ljungberg 28, Henry 90, Suker 90

**29.09.99 v FC Barcelona (a) Drawn 1-1**
Manninger, Dixon, Winterburn, Vieira, Keown, Adams, Bergkamp (Suker 73), Overmars (Ljungberg 80), Parlour (Henry 73), Grimandi, Kanu. Scorer: Kanu 81. Sent off: Grimandi 80

**19.10.99 v FC Barcelona (h) Lost 2-4**
Seaman, Dixon, Winterburn, Vieira, Keown (Upson 74), Adams, Ljungberg (Henry 77), Bergkamp, Overmars, Parlour, Kanu (Suker 77). Scorers: Bergkamp 44, Overmars 85

**27.10.99 v AC Fiorentina (h) Lost 0-1**
Seaman, Dixon (Suker 74), Winterburn, Vieira, Keown, Adams, Bergkamp, Overmars, Parlour (Ljungberg 57), Petit (Vivas 60), Kanu

**02.11.99 v AIK Solna (a) Won 3-2**
Manninger, Dixon, Winterburn, Vieira, Ljungberg, Suker (Hughes 78), Overmars, Petit (Malz 78), Luzhny (Vivas 78), Kanu, Upson. Scorers: Overmars 17, 52, Suker 56

**2000-2001**
**GROUP STAGE 1**
**12.09.00 v AC Sparta Praha (a) Won 1-0**
Seaman, Dixon, Vieira, Keown, Pires, Ljungberg (Vivas 80), Henry (Wiltord 77), Silvinho, Grimandi, Luzhny, Kanu. Scorer: Silvinho 33

**20.09.00 v FC Shakhtar Donetsk (h) Won 3-2**
Seaman, Dixon, Vieira, Keown, Pires (Wiltord 34), Ljungberg (Bergkamp 66), Henry, Silvinho, Grimandi, Luzhny, Kanu. Scorers: Wiltord 45, Keown 85, 90

**27.09.00 v SS Lazio (h) Won 2-0**
Seaman, Vieira, Keown, Adams, Ljungberg, Bergkamp (Vivas 79), Henry (Wiltord 84), Parlour, Silvinho, Luzhny, Kanu. Scorer: Ljungberg 43, 56

**17.10.00 v SS Lazio (a) Drawn 1-1**
Lukic, Dixon, Vieira, Keown, Ljungberg (Wiltord 74), Henry, Parlour (Pires 60), Silvinho, Grimandi (Lauren 69), Luzhny, Kanu. Scorer: Pires 88

**25.10.00 v AC Sparta Praha (h) Won 4-2**
Seaman, Dixon, Vieira, Pires (Bergkamp 63), Lauren, Henry (Wiltord 70), Parlour, Silvinho (Cole 46), Luzhny, Vivas, Kanu. Scorers: Parlour 5, Lauren 8, Dixon 35, Kanu 51
**07.11.00 v FC Shakhtar Donetsk (a) Lost 0-3**
Taylor, Dixon, Keown, Wiltord, Lauren, Henry (Ljungberg 62), Parlour (Vernazza 72),

Upson, Vivas, Kanu, Cole

**GROUP STAGE 2**

**22.11.00 v FC Spartak Moscow (a) Lost 1-4**

Manninger, Keown, Adams, Pires (Lauren 70), Ljungberg, Henry, Parlour, Silvinho, Luzhny, Vivas, Kanu (Wiltord 66). Scorer: Silvinho 2

**05.12.00 v FC Bayern Munchen (h) Drawn 2-2**

Manninger, Vieira, Keown, Adams, Pires (Wiltord 77), Ljungberg, Henry, Grimandi, Luzhny (Lauren 82), Kanu, Cole. Scorers: Henry 4, Kanu 55

**13.02.01 v Olmpique Lyonnais (a) Won 1-0**

Seaman, Dixon, Vieira, Adams, Pires (Ljungberg 69), Lauren, Henry, Parlour, Grimandi, Kanu (Vivas 90), Cole. Scorer: Henry 59

**21.02.01 v Olympique Lyonnais (h) Drawn 1-1**

Seaman, Dixon, Vieira, Pires (Lauren 80), Ljungberg, Bergkamp (Wiltord 71), Henry (Kanu 83), Parlour, Grimandi, Luzhny, Cole. Scorer: Bergkamp 33

**06.03.01 v FC Spartak Moscow (h) Won 1-0**

Seaman, Dixon, Vieira, Adams, Pires (Wiltord 71), Ljungberg, Bergkamp (Kanu 71), Lauren, Henry (Vivas 90), Grimandi, Cole. Scorer: Henry 82

**14.03.01 v FC Bayern Munchen (a) Lost 0-1**

Seaman, Dixon, Vieira, Adams, Pires (Silvinho 76), Ljungberg (Parlour 61), Lauren, Henry, Grimandi, Kanu (Wiltord 61), Cole

**QUARTER FINAL**

**04.04.01 v Valencia CF (h) Won 2-1**

Seaman, Dixon, Vieira, Keown, Adams, Pires, Ljungberg (Wiltord 46), Henry, Parlour, Kanu (Lauren 84), Cole. Scorers: Henry 58, Parlour 60

**17.04.01 v Valencia CF (a) Lost 0-1**

Seaman, Dixon, Vieira, Keown, Adams, Pires (Kanu 77), Wiltord, Lauren, Henry, Parlour (Ljungberg 46), Cole

**2001-2002**

**GROUP STAGE 1**

**11.09.01 v RCD Mallorca (a) Lost 0-1**

Seaman, Lauren, Campbell, Keown, Cole, Pires (Parlour 79), Vieira, Ljungberg (Jeffers 71), Van Bronckhorst, Wiltord (Kanu 72), Henry. Sent off: Cole 11

**19.09.01 v FC Schalke 04 (h) Won 3-2**

Seaman, Lauren, Keown, Grimandi, Van Bronckhorst, Pires (Inamoto 76), Vieira,

Parlour, Ljungberg, Wiltord (Bergkamp 72), Henry (Upson 90). Scorers: Ljungberg 33, Henry 36, 47pen

**26.09.01 v Panathinaikos FC (a) Lost 0-1**
Seaman, Lauren, Keown, Upson, Cole, Pires, Vieira, Parlour (Van Bronckhorst 58), Ljungberg (Kanu 68), Wiltord (Jeffers 68), Henry

**16.10.01 v Panathinaikos FC (h) Won 2-1**
Wright, Lauren, Campbell, Upson, Cole, Pires (Parlour 71), Ljungberg, Vieira, Van Bronckhorst, Wiltord (Bergkamp 71), Henry (Grimandi 90). Scorers: Henry 23, 52pen

**24.10.01 v RCD Mallorca (h) Won 3-1**
Wright, Lauren, Campbell, Keown, Van Bronckhorst, Pires, Grimandi (Parlour 84), Vieira, Ljungberg (Kanu 79), Bergkamp (Wiltord 72), Henry. Scorers: Pires 61, Bergkamp 63, Henry 90

**30.10.01 v FC Schalke 04 (a) Lost 1-3**
Wright, Luzhny, Campbell (Keown 68), Upson (Stepanovs 66), Cole, Pires, Parlour, Grimandi, Edu, Wiltord, Kanu (Pennant 78). Scorer: Wiltord 71. Sent off: Luzhny 17

**GROUP STAGE 2**

**21.11.01 v RC Deportivo La Coruna (a) Lost 0-2**
Wright (Taylor 46), Lauren, Campbell, Upson, Cole, Pires, Ljungberg, Vieira, Van Bronckhorst (Edu 78), Wiltord (Kanu 73), Henry

**04.12.01 v Juventus FC (h) Won 3-1**
Taylor, Lauren, Campbell, Upson, Cole (Keown 90), Ljungberg, Vieira, Parlour, Pires, Kanu (Bergkamp 69), Henry (Grimandi 84). Scorers: Ljungberg 21, 88, Henry 28

**19.02.02 v Bayer 04 Leverkusen (a) Drawn 1-1**
Seaman, Lauren, Campbell, Stepanovs, Van Bronckhorst, Wiltord (Grimandi 71), Vieira, Parlour, Pires, Kanu (Edu 76), Henry. Scorer: Pires 56. Sent off: Parlour 68

**27.02.02 v Bayer 04 Leverkusen (h) Won 4-1**
Seaman, Dixon, Campbell, Stepanovs, Lauren (Inamoto 84), Wiltord (Pennant 90), Grimandi (Edu), Vieira, Pires, Bergkamp, Henry. Scorers: Pires 5, Henry 7, Vieira 48, Bergkamp 83

**12.03.02 v RC Deportivo la Coruna (h) Lost 0-2**
Seaman, Lauren, Campbell, Stepanovs,Luzhny, Wiltord (Kanu 64), Grimandi (Ljungberg 64), Vieira, Pires, Bergkamp, Henry

**20.03.02 v Juventus FC (a) Lost 0-1**
Seaman, Dixon Campbell, Luzhny, Lauren (Cole 82), Ljungberg, Vieira, Edu (Wiltord

79), Pires, Kanu, Henry

**2002-2003**
**GROUP STAGE 1**
**17.09.02 v BV Borussia Dortmund (h) Won 2-0**
Seaman, Luhzny (Lauren 74), Campbell, Keown, Cole, Ljungberg (Cygan 84), Vieira, Gilberto, Wiltord (Toure 90), Bergkamp, Henry. Scorers: Bergkamp 62, Ljungberg 77

**25.09.02 v PSV Eindhoven (a) Won 4-0**
Seaman, Lauren, Campbell, Keown (Cygan 10), Cole, Ljungberg (Toure 86), Vieira, Gilberto, Wiltord, Bergkamp (Kanu 80), Henry. Scorers: Gilberto 1, Ljungberg 66, Henry 81, 90

**02.10.02 v AJ Auxerre (a) Won 1-0**
Seaman, Lauren, Campbell, Cygan, Cole, Toure (Edu 60), Vieira, Gilberto, Wiltord (Luhzny 84), Kanu, Henry (Pennant 58). Scorer: Gilberto 46

**22.10.02 v AJ Auxerre (h) Lost 1-2**
Seaman, Lauren (Toure 77), Campbell, Cygan, Cole, Ljungberg, Vieira, Gilberto (Pires 72), Wiltord, Kanu, Henry. Scorer: Kanu 53

**30.10.02 v BV Borussia Dortmund (a) Lost 1-2**
Seaman, Lauren, Campbell, Cygan, Cole, Ljungberg. Pires (Toure 67), Vieira, Gilberto (Edu 80), Wiltord (Kanu 72), Henry. Scorer: Henry 18

**12.11.02 v PSV Eindhoven (h) Drawn 0-0**
Shaaban, Luhnzy, Stepanovs, Cygan, Van Bronckhorst, Toure, Vieira (Gilberto 78), Edu, Pires, Jeffers (Wiltord 70), Henry (Bergkamp 84). Sent off: Toure 84

**GROUP STAGE 2**
**27.11.02 v AS Roma (a) Won 3-1**
Shaaban, Luhzny, Campbell, Cygan, Cole, Ljungberg (Edu 90), Vieira, Gilberto, Pires (Van Bronckhorst 79), Wiltord (Keown 85), Henry . Scorer: Henry 6, 70, 75

**10.12.02 v Valencia CF (h) Drawn 0-0**
Seaman, Lauren, Keown, Cygan, Cole, Ljungberg (Wiltord 79), Vieira (Parlour 38), Gilberto, Pires (Kanu 83), Bergkamp, Henry

**18.02.03 v AFC Ajax (h) Drawn 1-1**
Seaman (Taylor 46), Lauren, Campbell, Cygan, Cole, Wiltord, Vieira, Gilberto (Jeffers 72), Pires, Bergkamp (Kanu 85), Henry. Scorer: Wiltord 5
**26.02.03 v AFC Ajax (a) Drawn 0-0**
Seaman, Lauren, Keown, Campbell, Cole, Wiltord (Jeffers 79), Vieira, Gilberto, Pires

(Van Bronckhorst 87), Bergkamp (Parlour 79), Henry

**11.03.03 v AS Roma (h)** **Drawn 1-1**
Seaman, Lauren (Kanu 88), Keown, Cygan, Van Bronckhorst, Wiltord (Ljungberg 73), Vieira, Gilberto, Pires, Bergkamp (Jeffers 73), Henry. Scorer: Vieira 12

**19.03.03 v Valencia CF (a)** **Lost 1-2**
Taylor, Lauren, Campbell, Cygan, Toure (Kanu 86), Ljungberg, Vieira, Gilberto, Pires, Wiltord (Jeffers 76), Henry. Scorer: Henry 48

| SEASONS | PLAYED | WON | DRAWN | LOST | FOR | AGAINST |
|---|---|---|---|---|---|---|
| 5 | 50 | 20 | 13 | 16 | 68 | 61 |

## ATHLETIC CLUB BILBAO

**1998-1999**
**GROUP STAGE 1**
**16.09.98 v Rosenborg BK (h)** **Drawn 1-1**
Imanol Exteberria, Alkorta, Roberto Rios (Lacruz 46), Carlos Garcia, Larrazabal, Imaz, Jose Mari (Urrutia 74), Joseba Exteberria, Ezquerro, Guerrero (Urzaiz 68), Javi Gonzalez. Scorer: Joseba Exteberria 6

**30.09.98 v Galatasaray SK (a)** **Lost 1-2**
Imanol Exteberria, Alkorta, Roberto Rios, Carlos Garcia, Larrazabal, Joseba Exteberria (Javi Gonzalez 71), Imaz, Alkiza, Urzaiz (Lacruz 80), Ezquerro, Urrutia (Guerrero 85). Scorer: Urzaiz 17

**21.10.98 v Juventus FC (h)** **Drawn 0-0**
Imanol Exteberria, Lacruz, Alkorta (Roberto Rios 5), Carlos Garcia, Larrazabal, Alkiza, Guerrero (Ezquerro 58), Imaz, Urrutia (Jorge Perez 86), Urzaiz, Joseba Exteberria

**04.11.98 v Juventus FC (a)** **Drawn 1-1**
Imanol Exteberria, Lasa (Jorge Perez 72), Carlos Garcia, Roberto Rios, Larrazabal, Imaz (Lacruz 57), Ferreira, Alkiza, Guerrero, Joseba Exteberria, Ezquerro (Urzaiz 67). Scorer: Guerrero 45. Sent off: Lacruz 85

**25.11.98 v Rosenborg BK (a)** **Lost 1-2**
Imanol Exteberria, Felipe, Roberto Rios, Ferreira, Larrazabal (Carlos Garcia 46), Imaz, Urrutia (Urzaiz 46), Guerrero (Jorge Perez 61), Alkiza, Joseba Exteberria, Ezquerro. Scorer: Jorge Perez 90
**09.12.98 v Galatasaray SK (h)** **Won 1-0**
Imanol Exteberria, Larrainzar, Felipe, Carlos Garcia, Larrazabal, Javi Gonzalez (Joseba Exteberria

77), Ferreira, Nagore (Cesar 84), Jorge Perez (Lasa 74), Guerrero, Ezquerro Scorer: Guerrero 44

| SEASONS | PLAYED | WON | DRAWN | LOST | FOR | AGAINST |
|---|---|---|---|---|---|---|
| 1 | 8 | 4 | 2 | 2 | 15 | 8 |

## ATLETICO MADRID

**1996-1997**
**GROUP STAGE 1**
**11.09.96 v Steaua Bucaresti (h) Won 4-0**
Molina, Geli, Santi, Solozabal, Toni, Aquilera (Lopez 69), Bejbl, Simeone, Kiko (Juan Carlos 63), Pantic, Esnaider (Biagini 84). Scorers: Esnaider 33, 46, Simeone 64, 85

**25.09.96 v Widzew Lodz (a) Won 4-1**
Molina, Toni, Solozabal, Geli, Simeone (Pablo 77), Santi, Pantic, Bejbl, Aquilera (Lopez 74), Esnaider, Kiko (Roberto 81). Scorers: Pantic 25, Simeone 32, 58, Kiko 60

**16.10.96 v BV Borussia Dortmund (h) Lost 0-1**
Molina, Geli, Santi, Solozabal, Toni, Aquilera (Lopez 78), Bejbl (Juan Carlos 75), Simeone, Kiko, Pantic, Esnaider

**30.10.96 v BV Borussia Dortmund (a) Won 2-1**
Molina, Geli (Lopez 59), Santi, Solozabal, Toni, Roberto, Pantic (Aquilera 83), Vizcaino, Bejbl, Esnaider (Pablo 79), Kiko. Scorers: Roberto 37, Pantic 42

**20.11.96 v Steaua Buharesti (a) Drawn 1-1**
Molina, Geli, Lopez, Pablo, Solozabal, Caminero, Bejbl, Simeone (Aquilera 88), Esnaider (Juan Carlos 82), Pantic (Vizcaino 72), Kiko. Scorer: Pantic 24

**04.12.96 v Widzew Lodz (h) Won 1-0**
Molina, Geli, Pablo, Santi, Toni, Caminero (Aquilera 46), Vizcaino (Bejbl 46), Pantic, Simeone (Lopez 85), Esnaider, Kiko. Scorer: Pantic 83

**QUARTER FINAL**
**05.03.97 v AFC Ajax (a) Drawn 1-1**
Molina, Geli (Vizcaino 87), Santi, Solozabal, Toni, Bejbl, Aguilera, Pantic (Paunovic 75), Simeone, Caminero, Esnaider. Scorer: Esnaider 8

**19.03.97 v AFC Ajax (h) Lost 2-3 after extra-time**
Molina, Aguilera, Santi, Solozabal, Geli, Caminero, Bejbl, Simeone (Lopez 112), Pantic,

Esnaider (Biagini 110), Kiko. Scorers: Kiko 29, Pantic 105 pen

| SEASONS | PLAYED | WON | DRAWN | LOST | FOR | AGAINST |
|---|---|---|---|---|---|---|
| 1 | 8 | 4 | 2 | 2 | 15 | 8 |

## AJ AUXERRE

**1996–1997**
**GROUP STAGE 1**
**11.09.96 v AFC Ajax (h) Lost 0-1**
Charbonnier, Goma, West, Zelic, Rabarivony, Lamouchi, Henna, Saib, Tastaout (Sibierski 78), Laslandes (Marlet 80), Diomede

**25.09.96 v Rangers FC (a) Won 2-1**
Charbonnier, Goma, Danjou, West, Rabarivony, Lamouchi, Henna, Violeau, Saib, Deniaud (Sibierski 86), Diomede. Scorer: Deniaud 55, 69

**16.10.96 v Grasshopper-Club (h) Won 1-0**
Charbonnier, Goma, Danjou, West, Rabarivony, Violeau, Henna, Saib, Lamouchi (Sibierski 83), Deniaud, Diomede. Scorer: Deniaud 42

**30.10.96 v Grasshopper-Club (a) Lost 1-3**
Charbonnier, Goma, Danjou, West, Assati, Sibierski, Henna, Saib, Violeau, Marlet, Diomede (Tasfaout 66). Scorer: Danjou 48

**20.11.96 v AFC Ajax (a) Won 2-1**
Charbonnier, Silvestre, Danjou, West, Assati (Jay 70), Violeau, Henna, Saib, Marlet, Laslandes (Tasfaout 46), Diomede (Lepaul 86). Scorers: Diomede 11, Marlet 57

**04.12.96 v Rangers FC (h) Won 2-1**
Charbonnier, Goma, Silvestre, Danjou, Rabarivony, Saib, Violeau, Assati, Marlet, Laslandes, Lepaul (Sibierski 77). Scorers: Laslandes 20, Marlet 32

**QUARTER FINAL**
**05.03.97 v BV Borussia Dortmund (a) Lost 1-3**
Charbonnier, Goma, Silvestre, Danjou, West, Henna (Sibierski 46), Violeau, Lamouchi, Saib, Laslandes, Diomede. Scorer: Lamouchi 75

**19.03.97 v BV Borussia Dortmund (h) Lost 0-1**
Charbonnier, Goma, Silvestre, Danjou, West (Zelic 86), Violeau, Lamouchi, Saib,

Sibierski (Lepaul 80), Laslandes, Diomede

**2002-2003**
**GROUP STAGE 1**
**17.09.02 v PSV Eindhoven (h) Drawn 0-0**
Cool, Radet, Mexes, Boumsong, Jaures, Tainio, Lachuer, Faye, Fadiga, B Mwaruwari (Gonzalez 84), Kapo

**25.09.02 v BV Borussia Dortmund (a) Lost 1-2**
Cool, Radet, Mexes, Boumsong, Jaures, Tainio, Lachuer, Faye, Fadiga, B Mwaruwari, Kapo. Scorer: Benjani Mwaruwari 83

**02.10.02 v Arsenal FC (h) Lost 0-1**
Cool, Radet, Mexes, Boumsong, Jaures, Tainio (Sirieix 90), Lachuer (Gonzalez 74), Faye, Fadiga, B Mwaruwari, Kapo

**22.10.02 v Arsenal FC (a) Won 2-1**
Cool, Radet, Mexes, Boumsong, Jaures, Tainio, Lachuer, Faye, Fadiga, B Mwaruwari, Kapo. Scorers: Kapo 8, Fadiga 27

**30.10.02 v PSV Eindhoven (a) Lost 0-3**
Cool, Radet, Mexes, Boumsong, Jaures, Mathis, Lachuer (Sirieix 81), Faye, Fadiga (Gonzalez 87), B Mwaruwari (Grichting 27), Kapo. Sent off: Mexes 26, Kapo 51

**12.11.02 v BV Borussia Dortmund (h) Won 1-0**
Cool, Radet, Grichting, Boumsong, Jaures, Tainio (B Mwaruwari 46), Lachuer, Faye, Fadiga, Mathis, Cisse. Scorer: B Mwaruwari 76

| SEASONS | PLAYED | WON | DRAWN | LOST | FOR | AGAINST |
|---|---|---|---|---|---|---|
| 2 | 14 | 6 | 3 | 5 | 19 | 15 |

## FC BARCELONA

**1993-1994**
**GROUP STAGE 1**
**24.11.93 v Galatasaray SK (a) Drawn 0-0**
Zubizarreta, Ferrer, Guardiola, Ronald Koeman, Nadal, Bakero, Juan Carlos (Amor 74), Eusebio, Michael Laudrup, Romario, Sergi

**08.12.93 v AS Monaco (h) Won 2-0**
Zubizarreta, Ferrer, Guardiola (Ivan 80), Ronald Koeman, Sergi, Bakero, Goicoechea,

Stoichkov, Michael Laudrup, Amor, Beguiristain (Nadal 61). Scorers: Beguiristain 16, 27

**02.03.94 v FC Spartak Moscow (a) Drawn 2-2**
Zubizarreta, Ferrer, Nadal, Ronald Koeman, Sergi, Bakero (Goicoechea 72), Ivan, Stoichkov, Amor, Romario, Beguiristain (Eusebio 82). Scorers: Stoichkov 10, Romario 67

**16.03.94 v FC Spartak Moscow (h) Won 5-1**
Zubizarreta, Ferrer, Guardiola, Ronald Koeman (Beguiristain 86), Nadal, Bakero (Goicoechea 65), Ivan, Stoichkov, Amor, Romario, Sergi. Scorers: Stoichkov 34, Amor 75, Koeman 78, 80, Romario 86 pen

**30.03.94 v Galatasaray SK (h) Won 3-0**
Zubizarreta, Ferrer, Nadal, Ronald Koeman, Sergi, Ivan, Quique Estebaranz (Goicoechea 66), Amor, Michael Laudrup, Romario, Beguiristain (Eusebio 56). Scorers: Amor 21, Koeman 69 pen, Eusebio 75

**13.04.94 v AS Monaco (a) Won 1-0**
Zubizarreta, Ferrer, Guardiola, Ronald Koeman, Nadal, Bakero (Juan Carlos 60), Ivan, Stoichkov, Amor (Eusebio 74), Romario, Sergi. Scorer: Stoichkov 13

**SEMI FINAL**
**27.04.94 v FC Porto (h) Won 3-0**
Zubizarreta, Ferrer, Guardiola, Ronald Koeman, Nadal, Bakero, Sergi (Goicoechea 74), Stoichkov, Amor, Romario, Beguiristain (Ivan 41). Scorers: Stoichkov 11, 36, Koeman 72

**FINAL**
**18.05.94 v Milan AC (n) Lost 0-4**
Zubizarreta, Ferrer, Guardiola, Ronald Koeman, Nadal, Bakero, Sergi (Quique Estebaranz 72), Stoichkov, Amor, Romario, Beguiristain (Eusebio 52)

**1994–1995**
**GROUP STAGE 1**
**14.09.94 v Galatasaray SK (h) Won 2-1**
Busquets, Abelardo, Guardiola, Koeman, Sergi, Eusebio, Ivan, Stoichkov, Amor (Jordi Cruyff 70), Romario, Beguiristain (Luis Martinez 60). Scorers: Koeman 30, Amor 50

**28.09.94 v IFK Goteborg (a) Lost 1-2**
Busquets, Ferrer, Abelardo, Koeman, Nadal, Sergi, Bakero, Luis Martinez (Amor 81), Stoichkov, Jordi Cruyff, Hagi (Ivan 68). Scorer: Stoichkov 10
**19.10.94 v Manchester United FC (a) Drawn 2-2**
Busquets, Abelardo, Guardiola, Koeman, Sergi, Bakero, Luis Martinez (Eusebio 46),

Stoichkov, Nadal, Romario, Beguiristain (Jordi Cruyff 67). Scorers: Romario 33, Bakero 49

**02.11.94 v Manchester United (h) Won 4-0**
Busquets, Ferrer, Guardiola, Koeman, Abelardo, Bakero (Sanchez Jara 70), Amor, Stoichkov, Jordi Cruyff (Ivan 63), Romario, Sergi. Scorers: Stoichkov 9, 59, Romario 45, Ferrer 88

**23.11.94 v Galatasaray SK (a) Lost 1-2**
Busquets, Ferrer, Guardiola (Abelardo 59), Koeman, Nadal, Bakero (Beguiristain 69), Eusebio, Stoichkov, Amor, Romario, Sergi. Scorer: Romario 15

**07.12.94 v IFK Goteborg (h) Drawn 1-1**
Busquets, Nadal, Guardiola, Koeman, Sergi, Bakero, Eusebio, Stoichkov, Amor (Jordi Cruyff 85), Romario, Beguiristain (Abelardo 71). Scorer: Bakero 81

**QUARTER FINAL**
**01.03.95 v Paris Saint-Germain (h) Drawn 1-1**
Busquets, Ferrer, Guardiola (Amor 19), Koeman, Sergi, Bakero, Korneev, Jose Mari, Ivan, Stoichkov, Beguiristain (Eskurza 75). Scorer: Lama og 48

**15.03.95 v Paris Saint-Germain (a) Lost 1-2**
Busquets, Ferrer, Koeman, Nadal, Sergi, Bakero, Ivan, Eusebio, Stoichkov, Hagi (Abelardo 72), Beguiristain (Jose Mari 58). Scorer: Bakero 4

**1997-1998**
**GROUP STAGE 1**
**17.09.97 v Newcastle United FC (a) Lost 2-3**
Hesp, Celades, Reiziger, Nadal, Sergi, Figo, De La Pena, Luis Enrique, Amunike (Ciric 46), Rivaldo, Anderson (Dugarry 56). Scorers: Luis Enrique 73, Figo 89

**01.10.97 v PSV Eindhoven (h) Drawn 2-2**
Hesp, Celades, Reiziger, Nadal (Guardiola 59), Sergi, Luis Enrique, Figo, De La Pena, Rivaldo, Ciric (Pizzi 73), Anderson (Dugarry 16). Scorer: Luis Enrique 61, 74

**22.10.97 v FC Dynamo Kyiv (a) Lost 0-3**
Hesp, Ferrer, Reiziger, Fernando Couto, Sergi, Luis Enrique, Oscar (Busquets 63), Roger, Figo (Ciric 82), Dugarry (Pizzi 80), Rivaldo. Sent off: Hesp 62

**05.11.97 v FC Dynamo Kyiv (h) Lost 0-4**
Vitor Baia, Celades, Reiziger, Fernando Couto, Sergi, Ferrer, Oscar (Nadal 71), Rivaldo, Ciric, Giovanni (Amor 53), Figo. Sent off: Sergi 47
**27.11.97 v Newcastle United FC (h) Won 1-0**
Hesp, Ferrer, Abelardo, Fernando Couto, Reiziger, Celades, Giovanni (Nadal 80),

Guardiola (Amor 65), Ciric, Anderson (Pizzi 56), Rivaldo. Scorer: Giovanni 17

**10.12.97 v PSV Eindhoven (a) Drawn 2-2**
Hesp, Ferrer, Abelardo, Reiziger, Roger, Celades (Amor 88), Guardiola (Fernando Couto 50), Giovanni (Ciric 77), Figo, Anderson, Rivaldo. Scorers: Abelardo 32, Giovanni 67

**1998-1999**
**GROUP STAGE 1**
**16.09.98 v Manchester United FC (a) Drawn 3-3**
Hesp, Luis Enrique, Abelardo, Reiziger, Sergi, Giovanni (Xavi 68), Cocu, Rivaldo, Figo, Anderson, Zenden. Scorers: Anderson 47, Giovanni 60 pen, Luis Enrique 71 pen

**30.09.98 v Brondby IF (h) Won 2-0**
Hesp, Okunowo (Zenden 78), Abelardo, Cocu (Reiziger 67), Sergi, Giovanni (Xavi 46), Roger, Luis Enrique, Rivaldo, Figo, Anderson. Scorer: Anderson 44, 85

**21.10.98 v FC Bayern Munchen (a) Lost 0-1**
Hesp, Reiziger, Abelardo, Okunowo, Cocu, Luis Enrique (Zenden 78), Giovanni, Xavi (Oscar 87), Figo, Anderson, Rivaldo

**04.11.98 v FC Bayern Munchen (h) Lost 1-2**
Hesp, Okunowo, Abelardo, Celades, Sergi, Giovanni, Xavi, Cocu, Figo, Anderson, Rivaldo. Scorer: Giovanni 29 pen

**25.11.98 v Manchester United FC (h) Drawn 3-3**
Hesp, Celades, Okunowo, Reiziger, Sergi, Giovanni, Xavi, Rivaldo, Figo, Anderson, Zenden. Scorers: Anderson 1, Rivaldo 57, 73

**09.12.98 v Brondby IF (a) Won 2-0**
Hesp, Celades, Okunowo, Reiziger, Xavi, Guardiola, Sergi, Figo, Rivaldo (Roger 64), Anderson (Giovanni 70), Cocu (Cuadrado 89). Scorers: Figo 5, Rivaldo 35. Sent off: Guardiola 42

**1999-2000**
**GROUP STAGE 1**
**14.09.99 v AIK Solna (a) Won 2-1**
Hesp, R De Boer, Figo, Cocu, Kluivert (Dani 74), Litmanen, Rivaldo, Sergi, Bogarde (Abelardo 27), F De Boer, Xavi (Gabri 79). Scorers: Abelardo 86, Dani 90

**22.09.99 v AC Fiorentina (h) Won 4-2**
Hesp, Reizgier, Guardiola (Xavi 79), R De Boer, Figo, Cocu (Zenden 76), Kluivert (Dani 60), Rivaldo, Sergi, Bogarde, Luis Enrique. Scorers: Figo 7, Luis Enrique 10, Rivaldo 68 pen, 70
**29.09.99 v Arsenal FC (h) Drawn 1-1**
Hesp, Reizgier (R De Boer 70), Guardiola, Figo, Cocu, Rivaldo, Sergi, Bogarde, Dani,

Luis Enrique (Litmanen 77), F De Boer. Scorer: Luis Enrique 16

**19.10.99 v Arsenal FC (a) Won 4-2**
Arnau, Reizgier, Guardiola (Dehu 90), Abelardo, Figo, Cocu (Zenden 90), Kluivert, Rivaldo, Sergi, Bogarde, Luis Enrique (Gabri 71). Scorers: Rivaldo 15 pen, Luis Enrique 16, Figo 56, Cocu 70

**27.10.99 v AIK Solna (h) Won 5-0**
Arnau, Dehu, Abelardo (Rieziger 81), R De Boer, Kluivert, Litmanen (Mario 60), Simao Sabrosa, Zenden, Xavi, Gabri, Puyol (Nano 46). Scorers: Kluivert 15, 33, Zenden 43, Gabri 53, Dehu 56

**02.11.99 v AC Fiorentina (a) Drew 3-3**
Arnau, Dehu, Guardiola (Xavi 46), R De Boer (Puyol 46), Figo, Cocu, Kluivert, Rivaldo, Bogarde, Luis Enrique, Zenden. Scorers: Figo 20, Rivaldo 43, 74

**GROUP STAGE 2**

**23.11.99 v Hertha BSC Berlin (a) Drawn 1-1**
Hesp, Reiziger, Dehu, Guardiola, R De Boer (Simao Sabrosa 69), Figo, Cocu, Kluivert (Dani 72), Luis Enrique, F De Boer, Zenden. Scorer: Luis Enrique 14

**08.12.99 v AC Sparta Praha (h) Won 5-0**
Arnau, Reiziger (Xavi 84), Dehu, Guardiola, Figo (Simao Sabrosa 76), Cocu, Kluivert, Rivaldo, Luis Enrique (R De Boer 76), F De Boer, Zenden. Scorers: Kluivert 44, 63, Luis Enrique 45, 76, Guardiola 60

**01.03.00 v FC Porto (h) Won 4-2**
Hesp, Guardiola, Abelardo, Figo (R De Boer 86), Cocu, Kluivert, Rivaldo, Luis Enrique, F De Boer, Zenden (Dehu 52), Puyol (Reiziger 46). Scorers: Rivaldo 16, 89, F De Boer 23, Kluivert 45

**07.03.00 v FC Porto (a) Won 2-0**
Hesp, Guardiola, Abelardo, R De Boer, Figo (Xavi 90), Cocu (Gabri 46), Kluivert, Rivaldo (Dani 75), Bogarde, F De Boer, Puyol. Scorers: Abelardo 37, Rivaldo 59

**15.03.00 v Hertha BSC Berlin (h) Won 3-1**
Hesp, Abelardo (Dehu 53), R De Boer (Litmanen 71), Figo (Simao Sabrosa 46), Kluivert, Rivaldo, Bogarde, F De Boer, Xavi, Gabri, Puyol. Scorers: Xavi 11, Gabri 49, Kluivert 83

**21.03.00 v AC Sparta Praha (a) Won 2-1**
Hesp, Reiziger, Dehu, Guardiola (Xavi 60), Cocu (Litmanen 75), Rivaldo (R De Boer 46), Bogarde, Dani, Simao Sabrosa, F De Boer, Gabri. Scorer: Gabri 52, 89

**QUARTER FINAL**
**05.04.00 v Chelsea FC (a) Lost 1-3**
Hesp, Abelardo, Figo, Cocu, Kluivert (Dani 71), Rivaldo, Bogarde, F De Boer, Xavi, Gabri, Puyol (Litmanen 46). Scorer: Figo 64

**18.04.00 v Chelsea FC (h) Won 5-1 after extra-time**
Hesp, Reiziger (Sergi 105), Guardiola, Figo, Cocu, Kluivert, Rivaldo, F De Boer, Zenden (Dani 72), Gabri, Puyol (Abelardo 86). Scorers: Rivaldo 24, 99 pen, Figo 45, Dani 83, Kluivert 104

**SEMI FINAL**
**02.05.00 v Valencia CF (a) Lost 1-4**
Hesp, Reiziger, Guardiola, Cocu, Kluivert, Rivaldo, Dani (Litmanen 61), F De Boer, Zenden (Simao Sabrosa 75), Gabri, Puyol (Bogarde 46). Scorer: Pellegrino og 27

**10.05.00 v Valencia CF (h) Won 2-1**
Hesp, Reiziger, Guardiola (Sergi 69), Abelardo (Litmanen 76), Figo, Cocu, Kluivert, Rivaldo, F De Boer, Zenden (Simao Sabrosa 63), Xavi. Scorers: F De Boer 78, Cocu 90

**2000-2001**
**GROUP STAGE 1**
**13.09.00 v Leeds United AFC (h) Won 4-0**
Dutruel, De Boer, Abelardo, Cocu (Petit 54), Kluivert, Rivaldo (Alfonso 73), Overmars, Sergi, Gerard, Dani (De La Pena 65), Simao Sabrosa. Scorers: Rivaldo 10, De Boer 20, Kluivert 75, 84

**19.09.00 v Besiktas JK (a) Lost 0-3**
Dutruel, De Boer, Abelardo, De La Pena, Kluivert (Dani 74), Rivaldo, Overmars, Sergi (Alfonso 65), Gerard, Petit, Simao Sabrosa (Zenden 77)

**26.09.00 v Milan AC (h) Lost 0-2**
Dutruel, Reiziger, De Boer, Abelardo (Dani 80), De La Pena (Luis Enrique 46), Cocu, Kluivert, Rivaldo, Sergi, Gerard (Overmars 64), Simao Sabrosa

**18.10.00 v Milan AC (a) Drawn 3-3**
Dutruel, Abelardo, Alfonso (Dani 62), Cocu (De Boer 46), Rivaldo, Sergi, Xavi, Petit (Reiziger 25), Simao Sabrosa, Luis Enrique, Puyol. Scorers: Rivaldo 19, 43, 68

**24.10.00 v Leeds United AFC (a) Drawn 1-1**
Dutruel, Reiziger (Gerard 66), Abelardo, Alfonso, Cocu, Rivaldo, Sergi, Xavi, Simao Sabrosa, Luis Enrique (Dani 66), Puyol. Scorer: Rivaldo 90

**08.11.00 v Besiktas JK (h) Won 5-0**
Arnau, Abelardo, Cocu, Rivaldo, Sergi, Xavi (Gabri 83), Petit, Dani (Kluivert 64), Simao Sabrosa (Gerard 64), Luis Enrique, Puyol. Scorers: Cocu 11, Luis Enrique 17, 49, Rivaldo 81 pen, Gabri 88

**2001-2002**
**GROUP STAGE 1**
**10.10.01 v Olympique Lyonnais (h) Won 2-0**
Bonano, Gabri, Puyol, F de Boer, Coco, Luis Enrique (Motta 90), Xavi, Cocu, Geovanni (Saviola 46), Kluivert, Rivaldo (Reiziger 87). Scorers: Kluivert 79, Rivaldo 87pen .
*played 10 October after 11 Sept atrocities

**18.09.01 v Fenerbahce SK (a) Won 3-0**
Bonano, Puyol (Gabri 69), Christinval, Andersson, Sergi, Fabio, Xavi, Cocu, Geovanni (Saviola 56), Kluivert, Luis Enrique (F de Boer 60). Scorers: Kluivert 25, Andersson 28, Saviola 66

**25.09.01 v Bayer 04 Leverkusen (a) Lost 1-2**
Bonano, Puyol (Gabri 72), Christinval, Andersson, Sergi, Fabio (Gerard 78), Xavi, Cocu, Geovanni (Saviola 55), Kluivert, Luis Enrique. Scorer: Luis Enrique 22

**17.10.01 v Bayer 04 Leverkusen (h) Won 2-1**
Bonano, Puyol, Christinval, F de Boer, Coco, Luis Enrique, Xavi (Gerard 48), Cocu, Saviola (Geovanni 78), Kluivert, Rivaldo (Gabri 74). Scorer: Kluivert 12, Luis Enrique 38

**23.10.01 v Olympique Lyonnais (a) Won 3-2**
Bonano, Puyol, Christinval, F de Boer, Coco (Reiziger 58), Luis Enrique (Gerard 73), Xavi, Gabri, Cocu, Kluivert, Rivaldo (Geovanni 87). Scorers: Kluivert 8, Rivaldo 18, Gerard 90

**31.01.01 v Fenerbahce SK (h) Won 1-0**
Reina, Puyol, F de Boer, Reiziger, Overmars (Alfonso 81), Xavi, Gabri, Gerard, Saviola (Dani 74), Rivaldo, Geovanni (Fabio 59). Scorer: Rivaldo 90

**GROUP STAGE 2**
**20.11.01 v Liverpool FC (a) Won 3-1**
Bonano, Christinval, F de Boer, Andersson, Coco, Gabri (Fabio 58), Xavi, Cocu, Luis Enrique (Overmars 17), Kluivert (Reiziger 89), Rivaldo. Scorers: Kluivert 41, Fabio 65, Overmars 84
**05.12.01 v Galatasaray SK (h) Drawn 2-2**
Bonano, Puyol, Christinval, Andersson, Coco, Fabio (Gerard 46), Xavi (Overmars 46), Cocu, Saviola, Kluivert, Rivaldo. Scorer: Saviola 49, 66

**20.02.02 v AS Roma (h) Drawn 1-1**
Reina, Puyol, Christinval, F de Boer, Sergi (Xavi 74), Luis Enrique, Motta (Fabio 68), Cocu, Saviola (Overmars 57), Kluivert, Rivaldo. Scorer: Kluivert 82

**26.02.02 v AS Roma (a) Lost 0-3**
Reina, Puyol, Christinval, F de Boer, Sergi (Xavi 78), L Enrique (Fabio 82), Gerard, Motta (Overmars 65), Cocu, Rivaldo, Kluivert

**13.03.02 v Liverpool FC (h) Drawn 0-0**
Bonano, Puyol, Christinval, F de Boer, Coco, L Enrique (Gerard 77), Motta, Cocu, Rivaldo, Kluivert, Saviola (Geovanni 88)

**19.03.02 v Galatasaray SK (a) Won 1-0**
Bonano, Puyol, Christinval, Abelardo, Coco, L Enrique (Reiziger 89), Fabio, Xavi, Gabri, Overmars, Kluivert (Motta 84) Scorer: L Enrique 67

**QUARTER FINAL**
**03.04.02 v Panathinaikos FC (a) Lost 0-1**
Bonano, Puyol, F de Boer, Abelardo, Coco (Reiziger 68), Fabio (Rivaldo 72), Motta, Gabri, Cocu (Xavi 54), Overmars, Kluivert

**09.04.02 v Panathinaikos FC (h) Won 3-1**
Bonano (Reina 84), Puyol, F de Boer, Abelardo, Coco (Kluivert 45), L Enrique, Xavi, Cocu, Rivaldo, Overmars (Gabri 75), Saviola. Scorers: L Enrique 21, 59, Saviola 61

**SEMI FINAL**
**23.04.02 v Real Madrid CF (h) Lost 0-2**
Bonano, Reiziger (Giovanni 59), F de Boer, Abelardo, Fabio, L Enrique, Motta (Gabri 82), Cocu, Kluivert, Overmars, Saviola

**01.05.02 v Real Madrid CF (a) Drawn 1-1**
Bonano, Puyol, F de Boer, Abelardo, Coco (Overmars 46), L Enrique, Fabio (Geovanni 67), Xavi, Cocu (Sergi 75), Kluivert, Saviola. Scorer: Helguera 48 og

**2002-2003**
**GROUP STAGE 1**
**18.09.02 v Club Brugge KV (h) Won 3-2**
Victor Valdes, Puyol, F de Boer, Fernando Navarro, Mendieta (F Rochemback 76), Xavi, Cocu, Motta, L Enrique (Riquelme 73), Saviola, Kluivert. Scorers: L Enrique 5, Mendieta 40, Saviola 43
**24.09.02 v Galatasaray SK (a) Won 2-0**
Victor Valdes, Puyol, F de Boer, Fernando Navarro, Mendieta, Xavi, Cocu, Motta, L Enrique, Saviola (Geovanni 83), Kluivert (Gerard 90). Scorers: Kluivert 27, L Enrique 59

**01.10.02 v FC Lokomotiv Moskva (a) Won 3-1**
Victor Valdes, Puyol, F de Boer, Fernando Navarro, Mendieta, Xavi, Cocu, Motta, L Enrique (Geovanni 61), Saviola (F Rochemback 86), Kluivert (Gerard 75). Scorers: Kluivert 29, Saviola 32, 49

**23.10.02 v FC Lokomotiv Moskva (h) Won 1-0**
Bonano, Puyol, F de Boer, Fernando Navarro, Mendieta (F Rochemback 66), Xavi, Cocu, Gabri, Riquelme, Saviola, Kluivert. Scorer: F de Boer 76

**29.10.02 v Club Brugge KV (a) Won 1-0**
Enke, Puyol, Dani Tortolero, Fernando Navarro, F Rochemback, Gerard, Iniesta, Gabri (David Sanchez 89), Riquelme, Dani, Geovanni (Sergio Garcia 62). Scorer: Riquelme 64

**13.11.02 v Galatasaray SK (h) Won 3-1**
Enke, Reiziger, Puyol (Dani Tortolero 61), F de Boer (Oleguer 86), Fernando Navarro, Mendieta, Gerard, Motta, Dani, Geovanni (Kliuvert 79), Saviola. Scorers: Dani 10, Gerard 44, Geovanni 56

**GROUP STAGE 2**

**27.11.02 v Bayer 04 Leverkusen (a) Won 2-1**
Bonano, Puyol, Reiziger, Cocu, Fernando Navarro, Mendieta (Saviola 46), Gabri (Riquelme 46), Xavi, F Rochemback, Motta (Overmars 75), Kluivert. Scorers: Saviola 48, Overmars 88

**11.12.02 v Newcastle United FC (h) Won 3-1**
Bonano, Reiziger (Christinval 14), Puyol, F de Boer: Motta, Xavi, Cocu (Mendieta 16), Riquelme, Overmars, Kluivert, Dani (Saviola 78). Scorers: Dani 7, Kluivert 35, Motta 58

**18.02.03 v FC Internazionale (h) Won 3-0**
Bonano, Reiziger, Puyol, F de Boer, Gabri: Motta (Mendieta 73), Xavi, Cocu, Overmars (Fabio 71), Kluivert, Saviola (L Enrique 81). Scorers: Saviola 7, Cocu 29, Kluivert 67

**26.02.03 v FC Internazionale (a) Drawn 0-0**
Bonano, Reiziger, Puyol (Andersson 78), F de Boer, Gabri, Motta, Xavi, Cocu (Mendieta 59), Fabio (Riquelme 67), Kluivert, Saviola

**11.03.03 v Bayer 04 Leverkusen (h) Won 2-0**
Bonano, Reiziger, Andersson, F de Boer (Oleguer 62), Gabri, Overmars (Iniesta 68), Xavi, Mendieta, Riquelme, Kluivert, Saviola (Motta 46). Scorers: Saviola 17, F de Boer 49

**19.03.03 v Newcastle United FC (a) Won 2-0**
Victor Valdes, Reiziger, Andersson, F de Boer, Gabri, Fabio R, Xavi (Gerard 46), Mendieta (Iniesta 68), Motta, Kluivert (Sergio Garcia 70) Riquelme. Scorers: Kluivert 60, Motta 74

**QUARTER FINAL**
**09.04.03 v Juventus FC (a) Drawn 1-1**
Bonano, Gabri, Puyol, F de Boer, Reiziger, Overmars (Luis Enrique 83), Xavi (Gerard 74), Motta, Riquelme (Mendieta 63), Kluivert, Saviola. Scorer: Saviola 78

**22.04.03 v Juventus FC (h) Lost 1-2**
Bonano, Puyol, Andersson (Mendieta 61), F de Boer, Reiziger (Gerard 91), Overmars (Riquelme 85), Luis Enrique, Xavi, Motta, Kluivert, Saviola. Scorer: Xavi 66

| SEASONS | PLAYED | WON | DRAWN | LOST | FOR | AGAINST |
|---|---|---|---|---|---|---|
| 8 | 80 | 42 | 20 | 18 | 155 | 99 |

## BAYER 04 LEVERKUSEN

**1997-1998**
**GROUP STAGE 1**
**17.09.97 v K Lierse SK (h) Won 1-0**
Heinen, Worns, Nowotny (Emerson 90), Happe, Ramelow, Lehnhoff, Niko Kovac (Robert Kovac 86), Beinlich, Heintze, Kirsten (Paulo Rink 73), Meijer. Scorer: Beinlich 40 pen. Sent off: Beinlich 77

**01.10.97 v AS Monaco (a) Lost 0-4**
Heinen, Robert Kovac, Lottner, Happe, Lehnhoff (Rydlewicz 61), Niko Kovac, Emerson, Zivkovic (Paulo Rink 61), Heintze, Meijer, Feldhoff (Frydek 84)

**22.10.97 v Sporting Clube de Portugal (a) Won 2-0**
Heinen, Worns, Lottner, Happe, Lehnhoff, Emerson (Zivkovic 86), Ramelow, Beinlich, Heintze, Kirsten (Frydek 86), Meijer. Scorers: Beinlich 70, Emerson 82

**05.11.97 v Sporting Clube de Portugal (h) Won 4-1**
Heinen, Worns, Happe, Robert Kovac, Lehnhoff, Emerson, Ramelow, Niko Kovac (Frydek 57), Heintze, Kirsten (Paulo Rink 46), Meijer (Feldhoff 87). Scorers: Emerson 16, 73, Paulo Rink 84, Frydek 90

**26.11.97 v K Lierse SK (a) Won 2-0**
Heinen, Worns, Happe, Robert Kovac, Lehnhoff (Zivkovic 82), Emerson, Ramelow, Beinlich, Heintze, Kirsten (Niko Kovac 90), Meijer (Paulo Rink 40). Scorers: Emerson 54, Kirsten 66. Sent off: Happe 72

**10.12.97 v AS Monaco (h) Drawn 2-2**
Heinen, Worns, Nowotny, Robert Kovac, Lehnhoff, Niko Kovac (Zivkovic 61), Ramelow,

Beinlich, Heintze, Kirsten (Paulo Rink 86), Meijer. Scorers: Beinlich 29, Meijer 57

**QUARTER FINAL**

**04.03.98 v Real Madrid CF (h) Drawn 1-1**

Heinen, Ramelow, Worns, Nowotny, Zivkovic, Heintze, Lehnhoff (Feldhoff 71), Emerson (Lottner 87), Beinlich, Kirsten, Paulo Rink. Scorer: Beinlich 18

**18.03.98 v Real Madrid CF (a) Lost 0-3**

Heinen, Worns, Nowotny, Happe, Heintze, Zivkovic, Emerson, Ramelow, Lehnhoff (Paulo Rink 51), Beinlich (Meijer 81), Kirsten

**1999-2000**

**GROUP STAGE 1**

**14.09.99 v SS Lazio (h) Drawn 1-1**

Matysek, Kovac, Nowotny, Ze Roberto, Emerson, Reichenberger (Ponte 82), Hejduk, Gresko (Beinlich 67), Schneider, Neuville (Brdaric 73), Ramelow. Scorer: Neuville 14

**22.09.99 v NK Maribor (a) Won 2-0**

Matysek, Kovac, Nowotny (Ponte 70), Zivkovic, Kirsten, Emerson, Gresko, Beinlich, Schneider, Neuville (Brdaric 82), Ramelow. Scorers: Zivkovic 82, Kirsten 90

**29.09.99 v FC Dynamo Kyiv (h) Drawn 1-1**

Matysek, Kovac, Reeb, Nowotny, Ponte (Reichenberger 85), Kirsten, Emerson, Beinlich, Schneider, Neuville (Hejduk 46), Ramelow. Scorer: Kirsten 52

**19.10.99 v FC Dynamo Kyiv (a) Lost 2-4**

Matysek, Reeb, Nowotny, Zivkovic, Kirsten, Emerson, Hejduk (Ponte 77), Beinlich, Schneider, Neuville, Ramelow. Scorers: Kirsten 12, Neuville 49

**27.10.99 v SS Lazio (a) Drawn 1-1**

Matysek, Reeb (Hejduk 67), Nowotny, Zivkovic, Kirsten (Mamic 88), Emerson, Gresko (Happe 25), Beinlich, Schneider, Neuville, Ramelow. Scorer: Kirsten 44

**02.11.99 v NK Maribor (h) Drawn 0-0**

Matysek, Reeb (Brdaric 46), Nowotny, Zivkovic, Emerson, Reichenberger (Ponte 46), Hejduk, Beinlich, Schneider (Hoffmann 76), Neuville, Ramelow

**2000-2001**

**GROUP STAGE 1**

**12.09.00 v FC Spartak Moscow (a) Lost 0-2**

Zuberbuhler, Kovac, Nowotny, Zivkovic, Ze Roberto (Brdaric 61), Rink, Ballack, Vranjes, Ojigwe (Schneider 62), Neuville, Ramelow

**20.09.00 v Sporting Clube de Portugal (h) Won 3-2**
Zuberbuhler, Kovac, Nowotny, Zivkovic, Rink, Ballack, Ojigwe (Brdaric 46), Gresko (Neuendorf 68), Schneider (Vranjes 90), Neuville, Ramelow. Scorers: Ramelow 65, Brdaric 73, Neuville 77

**27.09.00 v Real Madrid CF (h) Lost 2-3**
Zuberbuhler, Kovac, Reeb, Nowotny, Zivkovic, Ze Roberto (Gresko 79), Rink, Ballack, Schneider (Brdaric 79), Neuville, Ramelow. Scorers: Schneider 27, Ballack 44

**17.10.00 v Real Madrid CF (a) Lost 3-5**
Zuberbuhler, Kovac, Reeb, Nowotny, Zivkovic, Ze Roberto, Kirsten, Ballack, Brdaric (Schneider 87), Neuville (Robson 70), Ramelow (Rink 70). Scorers: Brdaric 20, Kirsten 55, Rink 77

**25.10.00 v FC Spartak Moscow (h) Won 1-0**
Matysek, Reeb, Nowotny, Zivkovic, Ze Roberto (Vranjes 81), Kirsten, Rink (Ojigwe 46), Ballack (Brdaric 76), Hoffmann, Neuville, Ramelow. Scorer: Ballack 52

**07.11.00 v Sporting Clube de Portugal (a) Drawn 0-0**
Zuberbuhler, Kovac, Zivkovic, Robson (Neuveille 71), Ze Roberto, Rink, Hoffmann, Vranjes, Ojigwe, Hejduk (Brdaric 72), Schneider (Neuendorf 75)

**2001-2002**
**GROUP STAGE 1**
**10.10.01* v Fenerbahce SK (h) Won 2-1**
Butt, Schneider, Nowotny, Lucio, Placente, Ballack, Ramelow, Basturk, Ze Roberto (Vranjes 90), Kirsten (Sebescen 86), Neuville (Berbatov 68). Scorers: Lucio 36, Ballack 55
* played 10 October after 11 Sept atrocities

**18.09.01 v Olympique Lyonnais (a) Won 1-0**
Butt, Sebescen, Nowotny, Lucio, Placente, Schneider, Ballack, Ramelow, Basturk (Zivkovic 80), Kirsten (Ojigwe 80), Neuville (Brdaric 85). Scorer: Kirsten 75

**25.09.01 v FC Barcelona (h) Won 2-1**
Butt, Nowotny, Lucio, Placente, Sebescen (Basturk 46), Schneider, Ballack, Ramelow, Ze Roberto (Zivkovic 83), Kirsten (Ojigwe 75), Neuville. Scorers: Basturk 52, Neuville 69

**16.10.01 v FC Barcelona (a) Lost 1-2**
Butt, Schneider, Nowotny (Zivkovic 46), Lucio, Placente, Basturk, Ballack, Ramelow (Brdaric 76), Ze Roberto, Kirsten (Sebescen 75), Neuville. Scorer: Ramelow 32

**23.10.01 v Fenerbahce SK (a) Won 2-1**
Butt, Sebescen, Nowotny, Zivkovic,Schneider, Ballack, Ramelow, Ze Roberto, Basturk

(Vranjes 89), Kirsten (Brdaric 68), Neuville (Ojigwe 83). Scorers: Schneider 21, Kirsten 34

**31.10.01 v Olympique Lyonnais (h) Lost 2-4**
Butt, Zivkovic, Lucio, Placente, Sebescen, Schneider, Ojigwe (Basturk 46), Vranjes, Ze Roberto, Neuville, Berbatov (Daun 72). Scorers: Sebescen 45, Berbatov 52

**GROUP STAGE 2**

**21.10.01* v Juventus FC (a) Lost 0-4**
Butt, Sebescen, Nowotny, Lucio, Placente (Zivkovic 66), Ballack, Ramelow, Basturk (Schneider 52), Ze Roberto, Kirsten (Vranjes 75), Neuville
*postponed to 29.11.01 (fogx2 on 21 and 28 Nov)

**04.12.01 v Deportivo La Coruna (h) Won 3-0**
Butt, Zivkovic, Nowotny, Lucio, Placente, Schneider, Ballack (Vranjes 87), Ramelow, Ze Roberto, Kirsten (Basturk 76), Neuville (Berbatov 86). Scorers: Ze Roberto 64, Neuville 67, Ballack 79

**19.02.02 v Arsenal FC (h) Drawn 1-1**
Butt, Zivkovic, Nowotny (Vranjes 61), Lucio, Placente (Berbatov 75), Schneider, Ballack, Basturk, Ze Roberto, Kirsten, Neuville. Scorer: Kirsten 90

**27.02.02 v Arsenal FC (a) Lost 1-4**
Butt, Zivkovic (Sebescen 74), Nowotny, Lucio, Placente, Schneider (Basturk 46), Ballack, Ramelow, Ze Roberto, Kirsten (Berbatov 46), Neuville. Scorer: Sebescen 86

**12.03.02 v Juventus FC (h) Won 3-1**
Butt, Sebescen, Nowotny (Vranjes 12), Lucio, Placente, Schneider, Ramelow, Basturk (Kleine 90), Ze Roberto, Berbatov (Babic 83), Brdaric. Scorers: Butt 24pen, Brdaric 73, Babic 90

**20.03.02 v Deportivo (a) Won 3-1**
Butt, Sebescen, Nowotny, Lucio, Placente, Schneider (Zivkovic 90), Ramelow, Ballack, Basturk (Vranjes 88), Ze Roberto, Brdaric (Neuville 64). Scorers: Ballack 34, Schneider 54, Neuville 86

**QUARTER FINAL**

**03.04.02 v Liverpool FC (a) Lost 0-1**
Butt, Sebescen, Ramelow, Lucio, Placente, Schneider, Ballack, Basturk, Ze Roberto, Berbatov (Zivkovic 65), Neuville (Kirsten 74)

**09.04.02 v Liverpool FC (h) Won 4-2**
Butt, Sebescen (Neuville 46), Nowotny, Lucio, Placente, Schneider, Ballack, Basturk,

Ze Roberto, Kirsten (Berbatov 46), Brdaric (Zivkovic 70). Scorers: Ballack 18, 64, Berbatov 68, Lucio 84

**SEMI FINAL**

**24.04.02 v Manchester United FC (a) Drawn 2-2**

Butt, Zivkovic, Nowotny (Sebescen 46), Lucio, Placente, Schneider, Ballack, Ramelow, Basturk (Vranjes 77), Ze Roberto, Berbatov (Neuville 72). Scorers: Ballack 62, Neuville 75

**30.04.02 v Manchester United FC (h) Drawn 1-1**

Butt, Zivkovic, Nowotny (Sebescen 10), Lucio, Placente, Schneider, Ballack, Ramelow, Basturk (Vranjes 79), Ze Roberto, Neuville (Berbatov 85). Scorer: Neuville 45

**FINAL**

**15.05.02 v Real Madrid CF (n) Lost 1-2**

Butt, Sebescen (Kirsten 65), Zivkovic, Lucio (Babic 90), Placente, Schneider, Ballack, Ramelow, Basturk, Brdaric (Berbatov 39), Neuville. Scorer: Lucio 14

**2002-2003**

**GROUP STAGE 1 1**

**18.09.02 v Olympiakos FC (a) Lost 2-6**

Juric, Balitsch (Ojigwe 71) , Kleine (Brdaric 51), Lucio, Zivkovic, Schneider, Ramelow, Vranjes, Simak, Basturk, Neuville. Scorer: Schneider 22, 78pen

**24.09.02 v Manchester United FC (h) Lost 1-2**

Juric, Lucio, Ramelow, Zivkovic, Schneider, Balitsch (Franca 81), Ojigwe (Simak 64), Basturk, Brdaric, Babic, Neuville (Berbatov 22). Scorer: Berbatov 52

**01.10.02 v Maccabi Haifa (a) Won 2-0**

Butt, Lucio, Ramelow, Zivkovic, Schneider (Bierofka 85), Balitsch, Ojigwe, Basturk, Brdaric (Berbatov 70), Babic (Vranjes 77), Neuville. Scorer: Babic 31, 64

**23.10.02 v Maccabi Hiafa (h) Won 2-1**

Butt, Sebescen, Juan, Lucio, Placente, Schneider, Ramelow, Basturk, Brdaric (Neuville 46), Babic, Franca (Simak 60). Scorers: Babic 45, Juan 67

**29.10.02 v Olympiakos FC (h) Won 2-0**

Butt, Zivkovic, Lucio, Juan (Ojigwe 46), Placente, Schneider, Balitsch, Basturk, Babic, Neuville (Simak 62), Berbatov (Brdaric 90). Scorers: Juan 14, Schneider 90pen

**13.11.02 v Manchester United FC (a) Lost 0-2**

Butt, Sebescen, Ramelow, Kleine, Zivkovic, Bierofka (Dogan 78), Balitsch (Preuss 81), Simak, Babic, Brdaric, Berbatov (Franca 62)

**GROUP STAGE 2**

**27.11.02 v FC Barcelona (h) Lost 1-2**
Butt, Zivkovic, Lucio, Ramelow, Placente, Schneider, Balitsch, Basturk, Babic (Bierofka 66), Berbatov (Simak 83), Brdaric (Neuville 55). Scorer: Berbatov 39

**10.12.02 v Internazionale FC (a) Lost 2-3**
Butt, Zivkovic, Lucio, Juan, Kleine, Placente, Schneider, Balitsch (Bierofka 78), Basturk (Simak 83), Berbatov (Franca 75), Neuville. Scorers: Zivkovic 63, Franca 89

**18.02.03 v Newcastle United FC (h) Lost 1-3**
Butt, Preuss (Schneider 46), Cris (Callsen-Bracker 72), Kleine, Ojigwe, Brdaric, Basturk, Balitsch (Kaluzny 76), Simak, Neuville, Franca. Scorer: Franca 26

**26.02.03 v Newcastle United FC (a) Lost 1-3**
Butt, Preuss, Cris (Zivkovic 29), Kleine, Placente, Ramelow (Babic 46), Basturk, Kaluzny, Simak, Neuville (Brdaric 61), Franca. Scorer: Babic 73

**11.03.03 v FC Barcelona (a) Lost 0-2**
Butt, Cris, Kleine, Ojigwe, Basturk (Schneider 74), Balitsch, Babic (Dogan 33), Kaluzny, Simak, Berbatov (Brdaric 58), Franca

**19.03.03 v Internazionale FC (h) Lost 0-2**
Butt, Kaluzny, Kleine, Ojigwem, Placente, Brdaric (Neuville 46), Basturk (Schneider 46), Ramelow, Simak (Cris 62), Bierofka, Franca

| SEASONS | PLAYED | WON | DRAWN | LOST | FOR | AGAINST |
|---|---|---|---|---|---|---|
| 5 | 49 | 18 | 10 | 21 | 71 | 84 |

## FC BASEL

**17.09.02 v Spartak Moscow (h) Won 2-0**
Zuberbuhler, Haas, Quennoz, M Yakin, Atouba, Barberis, Cantaluppi, Esposito, H Yakan (Savic 87), Rossi (Tum 75), Gimenez. Scorers: H Yakin 50, Rossi 55

**25.09.02 v Liverpool FC (a) Drawn 1-1**
Zuberbuhler, Haas, Quennoz, M Yakin, Atouba, Barberis, Cantaluppi, Esposito, H Yakan (Duruz 67), Rossi (Tum 74), Gimenez. Scorer: Rossi 43

**02.10.02 v Valencia CF (a) Lost 2-6**
Zuberbuhler, Haas, Quennoz (Ergic 62), M Yakin, Atouba, Barberis, Cantaluppi, Esposito (Duruz 79), H Yakan, Rossi, Gimenez (Varela 46). Scorers: Rossi 46, H Yakin 90

**22.10.02 v Valencia CF (h) Drawn 2-2**
Zuberbuhler, Haas, Zwyssig, M Yakin, Duruz, Varela (Rossi 65), Cantaluppi, Esposito (Koumantarakis 85), Ergic, H Yakin, Gimenez (Tum 60). Scorer: Ergic 32, 90

**05.11.02 v FC Spartak Moskva (a) Won 2-0**
Zuberbuhler, Haas, Zwyssig, M Yakin, Duruz, Ergic, Cantaluppi, Esposito (Atouba 16), H Yakin, Rossi (Gimenez 67), Tum. Scorers: Rossi 18, Gimenez 89

**12.11.02 v Liverpool FC (h) Drawn 3-3**
Zuberbuhler, Haas, Zwyssig, M Yakin, Atouba, Ergic, Cantaluppi, Esposito, H Yakin (Koumantarakis 90), Rossi (Tum 76), Gimenez (Barberis 66). Scorers: Rossi 2, Gimenez 22, Atouba 29

**26.11.02 v Manchester United FC (h) Lost 1-3**
Zuberbuhler, Haas, Zwyssig, M Yakin, Atouba, Ergic (Barberis 83), Cantaluppi, Chipperfield (Tum 73), H Yakin, Rossi (Duruz 84), Gimenez. Scorer: Gimenez 1

**11.12.02 v Juventus FC (h) Lost 0-4**
Zuberbuhler, Barberis, Zwyssig, M Yakin, Atouba, Esposito, Cantaluppi, Chipperfield (Duruz 65), H Yakin (Tum 77), Rossi, Gimenez (Varela 46)

**19.02.03 v RC Deportivo (h) Won 1-0**
Zuberbuhler, Haas, Zwyssig, M Yakin, Atouba, Barberis, Cantaluppi, Chipperfield (Duruz 70), H Yakin (Varela 85), Gimenez, Rossi (Huggel 51). Scorer: H Yakin 30

**25.02.03 v RC Deportivo (a) Lost 0-1**
Zuberbuhler, Haas, Zwyssig, Quennoz, Atouba, Barberis (Tum 73), Huggel, Chipperfield, H Yakin, Varela (Rossi 57), Gimenez

**12.03.03 v Manchester United FC (a) Drawn 1-1**
Zuberbuhler, Haas, Zwyssig, M Yakin, Atouba, Barberis, Cantaluppi, Chipperfield, H Yakin, Rossi (Huggel 63), Gimenez (Tum 77). Scorer: Gimenez 14

**18.03.03 v Juventus FC (a) Won 2-1**
Zuberbuhler, Haas, Zwyssig, M Yakin, Atouba, Barberis (Huggel 56), Cantaluppi, Chipperfield, H Yakin (Varela 79), Rossi (Tum 72), Gimenez. Scorers: Cantaluppi 38, Gimenez 90

| SEASONS | PLAYED | WON | DRAWN | LOST | FOR | AGAINST |
|---|---|---|---|---|---|---|
| 1 | 12 | 4 | 4 | 4 | 17 | 22 |

## FC BAYERN MUNCHEN

**1994-1995**
**GROUP STAGE 1**
**14.09.94 v Paris Saint-Germain (a) Lost 0-2**
Kahn, Jorginho, Kreuzer, Matthaus, Helmer, Ziege, Scholl (Hamann 47), Schupp, Nerlinger, Sutter, Witeczek (Mazinho 57)

**28.09.94 v FC Dynamo Kyiv (h) Won 1-0**
Kahn, Jorginho, Babbel, Matthaus, Helmer, Ziege, Scholl (Hamann 61), Schupp, Nerlinger, Sutter, Witeczek (Papin 46). Scorer: Scholl 9

**19.10.94 v FC Spartak Moscow (a) Drawn 1-1**
Kahn, Jorginho, Kreuzer, Matthaus, Babbel, Ziege, Scholl, Frey, Nerlinger, Zickler, Sutter (Sternkopf 64). Scorer: Babbel 90

**02.11.94 v FC Spartak Moscow (h) Drawn 2-2**
Kahn, Jorginho, Kreuzer, Matthaus, Kuffour, Ziege, Scholl (Frey 54), Schupp (Hamann 64), Nerlinger, Zickler, Witeczek. Scorers: Nerlinger 28, Kuffour 36

**23.11.94 v Paris Saint-Germain (h) Lost 0-1**
Kahn, Jorginho, Frey, Matthaus, Babbel, Helmer, Scholl, Schupp (Hamann 62), Nerlinger, Papin (Zickler 69), Sutter

**07.12.94 v FC Dynamo Kyiv (a) Won 4-1**
Scheuer, Babbel, Kreuzer, Matthaus (Frey 72), Helmer, Ziege, Jorginho, Hamann, Nerlinger, Papin, Sutter (Scholl 77). Scorers: Nerlinger 45, Papin 57, 82, Scholl 86

**QUARTER FINAL**
**01.03.95 v IFK Goteborg (h) Drawn 0-0**
Scheuer, Frey (Kreuzer 70), Babbel, Helmer, Ziege, Nerlinger, Zickler, Schupp (Sternkopf 63), Scholl, Kostadinov, Witeczek

**15.03.95 v IFK Goteborg (a) Drawn 2-2**
Scheuer, Babbel, Kreuzer, Helmer, Ziege, Nerlinger, Zickler (Kuffour 82), Frey, Scholl, Kostadinov (Gospodarek 20), Witeczek (Schupp 61). Scorers: Zickler 63, Nerlinger 72. Sent off: Scheuer 20

**SEMI FINAL**
**05.04.95 v AFC Ajax (h) Drawn 0-0**

Gospodarek, Babbel, Kuffour, Helmer (Grimm 88), Ziege, Hamann, Schupp, Scholl, Nerlinger, Sutter, Zickler

**19.04.95 v AFC Ajax (a) Lost 2-5**
Scheuer, Babbel, Kuffour, Helmer (Kreuzer 41), Ziege, Frey, Schupp, Scholl, Nerlinger, Zickler (Sutter 71), Witeczek. Scorers: Witeczek 36, Scholl 75 pen

**1997-1998**
**GROUP STAGE 1**
**17.09.97 v Besiktas JK (h) Won 2-0**
Kahn, Babbel, Matthaus, Helmer, Hamann, Basler (Lizarazu 88), Strunz, Scholl, Tarnat, Rizzitelli (Fink 52), Elber (Jancker 82). Scorers: Helmer 3, Basler 70

**01.10.97 v IFK Goteborg (a) Won 3-1**
Kahn, Babbel, Helmer, Kuffour, Hamann, Strunz (Fink 38), Scholl (Basler 77), Nerlinger, Tarnat, Elber, Jancker. Scorers: Jancker 2, Hamann 35, Elber 90

**22.10.97 v Paris Saint-Germain (h) Won 5-1**
Kahn, Babbel, Helmer, Kuffour, Basler (Zickler 74), Hamann (Fink 72), Scholl, Nerlinger, Tarnat, Elber, Jancker (Rizzitelli 76). Scorers: Elber 4, 73, Jancker 21, 47, Helmer 51

**05.11.97 v Paris Saint-Gemian (a) Lost 1-3**
Kahn, Babbel, Helmer (Basler 71), Kuffour, Scholl (Zickler 87), Fink, Hamann, Nerlinger, Tarnat, Elber, Jancker. Scorer: Babbel 29

**26.11.97 v Besiktas JK (a) Won 2-0**
Kahn, Kuffour, Matthaus, Helmer, Scholl (Zickler 81), Fink (Babbel 87), Hamann, Nerlinger, Tarnat, Elber, Jancker (Rizzitelli 83). Scorers: Jancker 5, Helmer 31

**10.12.97 v IFK Goteborg (h) Lost 0-1**
Kahn, Babbel, Matthaus, Helmer (Nerlinger 21), Zickler (Gerster 57), Hamann, Scholl, Fink, Tarnat, Jancker, Rizzitelli (Elber 57)

**QUARTER FINAL**
**04.03.98 v BV Borussia Dortmund (h) Drawn 0-0**
Kahn, Matthaus (Fink 75), Babbel, Helmer, Basler, Nerlinger, Scholl (Strunz 71), Hamann, Tarnat, Elber, Jancker

**18.03.98 v BV Borussia Dortmund (a) Lost 0-1 after extra-time**
Kahn, Matthaus (Lizarazu 110), Scholl, Babbel, Kuffour, Tarnat, Hamann, Fink, Nerlinger (Strunz 110), Elber (Zickler 101), Jancker

# CHAMPIONS LEAGUE HISTORY

**1998-1999**
**GROUP STAGE 1**
**16.09.98 v Brondby IF (a) Lost 1-2**
Kahn, Babbel, Matthaus, Helmer, Strunz (Jeremies 73), Fink, Lizarazu, Basler (Zickler 73), Effenberg, Elber, Jancker (Salihamidzic 76). Scorer: Babbel 76

**30.09.98 v Manchester United FC (h) Drawn 2-2**
Kahn, Babbel, Matthaus, Linke, Strunz (Jeremies 73), Effenberg, Jeremies (Fink 82), Lizarazu, Jancker (Daei 63), Elber, Salihamidzic (Goktan Berkant 63). Scorers: Elber 11, Sheringham og 90

**21.10.98 v FC Barcelona (h) Won 1-0**
Kahn, Babbel (Linke 80), Jeremies, Kuffour, Tarnat, Fink, Effenberg, Lizarazu, Basler, Elber (Jancker 89), Salihamidzic (Zickler 80). Scorer: Effenberg 46

**04.11.98 v FC Barcelona (a) Won 2-1**
Kahn, Babbel, Matthaus, Kuffour, Tarnat (Strunz 75), Effenberg, Lizarazu, Fink, Basler (Salihamidzic 64), Elber, Zickler (Daei 64). Scorers: Giavanni og 29, Zickler 48

**25.11.98 v Brondby IF (h) Won 2-0**
Kahn, Babbel, Matthaus, Kuffour, Strunz, Jeremies (Fink 70), Tarnat, Lizarazu, Basler, Elber (Salihamidzic 84), Zickler (Jancker 46). Scorers: Jancker 51, Basler 57

**09.12.98 v Manchester United FC (a) Drawn 1-1**
Kahn, Matthaus (Linke 61), Strunz, Babbel, Kuffour, Lizarazu, Zickler (Basler 82), Effenberg, Jeremies, Elber (Jancker 82), Salihamidzic. Scorer: Salihamidzic 56

**QUARTER FINAL**
**03.03.99 v 1 FC Kaiserslautern (h) Won 2-0**
Kahn, Matthaus (Tarnat 46), Babbel, Linke, Strunz (Zickler 75), Effenberg, Jeremies, Lizarazu, Basler (Salihamidzic 83), Elber, Jancker. Scorers: Elber 31, Effenberg 35

**17.03.99 v 1 FC Kaiserslautern (a) Won 4-0**
Kahn, Linke, Matthaus, Kuffour, Babbel, Jeremies (Fink 46), Effenberg (Scholl 46), Lizarazu, Basler (Salihamidzic 72), Zickler, Jancker. Scorers: Effenberg 8 pen, Jancker 22, 39, Basler 56

**SEMI FINAL**
**07.04.99 v FC Dynamo Kyiv (a) Drawn 3-3**
Kahn, Babbel, Matthaus, Kuffour, Strunz, Jeremies, Scholl (Zickler 72), Tarnat, Effenberg, Jancker (Daei 90), Salihamidzic. Scorers: Tarnat 45, Effenberg 78, Jancker 88

**21.04.99 v FC Dynamo Kyiv (h) Won 1-0**

Kahn, Linke, Matthaus, Kuffour, Babbel, Jeremies, Effenberg, Tarnat (Fink 84), Basler, Jancker (Salihamidzic 75), Zickler (Daei 75). Scorer: Basler 35

**FINAL**

**26.05.99 v Manchester United FC (n) Lost 1-2**

Kahn, Linke, Matthaus (Fink 80), Kuffour, Babbel, Jeremies, Effenberg, Tarnat, Basler (Salihamidzic 90), Jancker, Zickler (Scholl 71). Scorer: Basler 6

**1999-2000**

**GROUP STAGE 1**

**15.09.99 v PSV Eindhoven (h) Won 2-1**

Kahn, Lizarazu, Kuffour, Andersson, Scholl (Salihamidzic 87), Strunz, Matthaus, Effenberg, Paulo Sergio (Zickler 79), Jeremies, Santa Cruz (Jancker 68). Scorer: Paulo Sergio 11, 69

**21.09.99 v Rangers FC (a) Drawn 1-1**

Wessels, Lizarazu (Jancker 46), Kuffour, Scholl, Elber (Santa Cruz 73), Matthaus (Zickler 81), Effenberg, Jeremies, Tarnat, Salihamidzic, Linke. Scorer: Tarnat 90

**28.09.99 v Valencia CF (h) Drawn 1-1**

Wessels, Kuffour, Scholl, Elber (Jancker 62), Matthaus, Effenberg, Jeremies, Tarnat, Salihamidzic, Zickler (Santa Cruz 46), Linke. Scorer: Elber 6

**20.10.99 v Valencia CF (a) Drawn 1-1**

Kahn, Babbel, Lizarazu, Kuffour, Elber (Jancker 81), Matthaus, Effenberg, Paulo Sergio (Santa Cruz 90), Jeremies, Zickler (Salihamidzic 75), Linke. Scorer: Effenberg 18 pen

**26.10.99 v PSV Eindhoven (a) Lost 1-2**

Wessels, Babbel (Salihamidzic 68), Lizarazu, Andersson, Elber, Matthaus, Effenberg, Paulo Sergio (Santz Cruz 26), Jeremies, Zickler (Jancker 75), Linke. Scorer: Santa Cruz 51. Sent off: Jeremies 90

**03.11.99 v Rangers FC (h) Won 1-0**

Kahn, Babbel, Lizarazu, Scholl (Paulo Sergio 66), Strunz, Elber, Matthaus, Effenberg (Tarnat 74), Fink, Santz Cruz (Salihamidzic 66), Linke. Scorer: Strunz 33 pen

**GROUP STAGE 2**

**24.11.99 v Rosenborg BK (a) Drawn 1-1**

Kahn, Babbel, Kuffour, Andersson, Scholl (Zickler 82), Effenberg, Paulo Sergio (Santa Cruz 79), Fink, Tarnat, Jancker, Salihamidzic. Scorer: Jancker 10

**07.12.99 v FC Dynamo Kyiv (h) Won 2-1**

Kahn, Babbel, Kuffour, Matthaus, Paulo Sergio (Wiesinger 90), Fink, Tarnat, Jancker,

Salihamidzic, Santa Cruz (Zickler 75), Linke. Scorers: Jancker 6, Paulo Sergio 80

**29.02.00 v Real Madrid CF (a) Won 4-2**
Kahn, Babbel (Linke 62), Lizarazu, Kuffour, Scholl (Tarnat 86), Elber (Santa Cruz 86), Matthaus, Effenberg, Paulo Sergio, Fink, Salihamidzic. Scorers: Scholl 21, Effenberg 24, Fink 39, Paulo Sergio 66

**08.03.00 v Real Madrid CF (h) Won 4-1**
Kahn, Lizarazu, Kuffour, Scholl (Wiesinger 88), Elber (Zickler 74), Matthaus (Andersson 90), Effenberg, Paulo Sergio, Fink, Salihamidzic, Linke. Scorers: Scholl 4, Elber 30, Zickler 79, 90

**14.03.00 v Rosenborg BK (h) Won 2-1**
Kahn, Babbel, Kuffour, Andersson, Scholl (Salihamidzic 75), Paulo Sergio (Santa Cruz 84), Jeremies, Fink, Tarnat, Jancker (Elber 75), Zickler. Scorers: Scholl 11, Paulo Sergio 39 pen

**22.03.00 v FC Dynamo Kyiv (a) Lost 0-2**
Wessels, Kuffour, Andersson, Wiesinger, Wojciechowski, Fink, Tarnat, Salihamidzic, Zickler (Di Salvo 35), Santa Cruz (Johansson 77), Linke (Jarolim 77)

**QUARTER FINAL**
**04.04.00 v FC Porto (a) Drawn 1-1**
Kahn, Babbel, Lizarazu, Kuffour, Andersson, Scholl (Fink 87), Elber (Jancker 73), Effenberg, Paulo Sergio, Jeremies, Salihamidzic (Santa Cruz 80). Scorer: Paulo Sergio 80

**19.04.00 v FC Porto (h) Won 2-1**
Kahn, Babbel, Andersson, Scholl, Elber (Jancker 90), Paulo Sergio, Jeremies, Fink, Tarnat (Kuffour 81), Santa Cruz (Salihamidzic 68), Linke. Scorers: Paulo Sergio 15, Linke 90

**SEMI FINAL**
**03.05.00 v Real Madrid CF (a) Lost 0-2**
Kahn, Babbel, Lizarazu, Scholl, Elber (Jancker 78), Paulo Sergio, Jeremies, Fink, Tarnat (Wiesinger 46), Salihamidzic (Santa Cruz 78), Linke

**09.05.00 v Real Madrid CF (h) Won 2-1**
Kahn, Babbel (Salihamidzic 60), Lizarazu, Kuffour, Andersson, Scholl, Elber, Effenberg, Paulo Sergio, Jeremies (Fink 59), Jancker (Santa Cruz 79). Scorers: Jancker 12, Elber 54

**2000-2001**
**GROUP STAGE 1**
**13.09.00 v Helsingborgs IF (a) Won 3-1**

Kahn (Wessels 67), Sagnol, Lizarazu, Kuffour, Andersson, Wiesinger, Scholl (Strunz 65), Sforza, Fink, Jancker, Salihamidzic (Hargreaves 83). Scorers: Scholl 7, Salihamidzic 48, Jancker 55. Sent off: Kuffour 38

**19.09.00 v Rosenborg BK (h) Won 3-1**
Kahn, Sagnol, Lizarazu (Tarnat 44), Andersson (Santa Cruz 46, Elber 73), Wiesinger, Scholl, Sforza, Fink, Jancker, Salihamidzic, Linke. Scorers: Jancker 73, Elber 77, Linke 80

**26.09.00 v Paris Saint-Germain (a) Lost 0-1**
Kahn, Sagnol (Strunz 77), Andersson, Wiesinger (Santa Cruz 77), Scholl, Sforza, Fink, Tarnat, Jancker (Elber 83), Salihamidzic, Linke

**18.10.00 v Paris Saint-Germain (h) Won 2-0**
Kahn, Tarnat, Andersson, Scholl, Sforza, Fink, Tarnat, Jancker (Elber 58), Salihamidzic, Santa Cruz (Paulo Sergio 76), Linke (Jeremies 29). Scorers: Salihamidzic 3, Paulo Sergio 89

**24.10.00 v Helsingborgs IF (h) Drawn 0-0**
Kahn, Sagnol, Scholl, Sforza, Jeremies (Zickler 84), Fink, Tarnat, Jancker (Elber 67), Salihamidzic, Santa Cruz (Paulo Sergio 67), Linke

**08.11.00 v Rosenborg BK (a) Drawn 1-1**
Wessels, Sagnol, Kuffour, Wiesinger (Elber 74), Sforza, Effenberg (Jeremies 63), Fink, Tarnat, Jancker, Salihamidzic (Scholl 63), Zickler. Scorer: Jeremies 88

**GROUP STAGE 2**

**22.11.00 v Olympique Lyonnais (h) Won 1-0**
Kahn, Kuffour, Sforza, Linke, Fink, Effenberg, Jeremies, Tarnat (Lizarazu 75), P Sergio, Elber (Jancker 75), Zickler. Scorer: Jeremies 55

**05.12.00 v Arsenal FC (a) Drawn 2-2**
Kahn, Sagnol (P Sergio 46), Kuffour, Sforza, Linke, Tarnat, Salihamidzic, Effenberg, Jeremies, Scholl (Zickler 83), Elber. Scorers: Tarnat 56, Scholl 66

**13.02.01 v FC Spartak Moscow (h) Won 1-0**
Kahn, Kuffour, Jeremies, Linke, Salihamidzic, Effenberg, Fink, Lizarazu (Tarnat 90), Scholl (Sagnol 84), Elber, P Sergio (Jancker 65). Scorer: Elber 79

**21.02.01 v FC Spartak Moscow (a) Won 3-0**
Kahn, Sagnol, Kuffour, Andersson, Linke, Lizarazu, Salihamidzic, Effenberg, Fink (Hargreaves 90), Scholl (Paulo Sergio 82), Elber (Jancker 82). Scorers: Scholl 17, 75pen, P Sergio 87

**06.03.01 v Olympique Lyonnais (a) Lost 0-3**
Kahn, Sagnol, Kuffour (Jancker 46), Andersson, Linke, Tarnat, Salihamidzic (Scholl 71),

Effenberg, Jeremies, Paulo Sergio, Elber

**14.03.01 v Arsenal FC (h) Won 1-0**
Kahn, Kuffour, Andersson, Linke, Lizarazu, Salihamidzic, Fink, Jeremies, Scholl (Wiesinger 90), Jancker, Elber (Tarnat 90). Scorers: Elber 10

**QUARTER FINAL**
**03.04.01 v Manchester United FC (a) Won 1-0**
Kahn, Kuffour, Andersson, Linke, Salihamidzic, Jeremies, Effenberg, Lizarazu, Jancker (Zickler 69), Elber, Scholl (Paulo Sergio 77). Scorer: Paulo Sergio 86

**18.04.01 v Manchester United FC (h) Won 2-1**
Kahn, Kuffour, Andersson, Linke, Sagnol, Jeremies, Effenberg, Tarnat, Jancker (Zickler 35), Elber (Santa Cruz 64), Scholl (Paulo Sergio 88). Scorers: Elber 5, Scholl 40

**SEMI FINAL**
**01.05.01 v Real Madrid CF (a) Won 1-0**
Kahn, Sagnol, Kuffour, Andersson, Linke, Lizarazu, Salihamidzic, Jeremies, Effenberg, Elber (Jancker 74), Scholl (Paulo Sergio 72). Scorers: Elber 55

**09.05.01 v Real Madrid CF (h) Won 2-1**
Kahn, Sagnol, Kuffour, Andersson, Linke, Lizarazu, Salihamidzic, Jeremies (Sforza 70), Hargreaves, Elber (Zickler 86), Scholl (Santa Cruz 59). Scorers: Elber 8, Jeremies 34

**FINAL**
**23.05.01 v Valencia (n) Drawn 1-1**
Kahn, Sagnol (Jancker 46), Kuffour, Andersson, Linke, Lizarazu, Salihamidzic, Effenberg, Hargreaves, Scholl (P Sergio 108), Elber (Zickler 100). Scorer: Effenberg 50pen. (Bayern won 5-4 on pens after extra-time – scorers: Salihamidzic, Zickler, Effenberg, Lizarazu, Linke. Missed: Paulo Sergio, Andersson)

**2001-2002**
**GROUP STAGE 1**
**10.10.01 v Feyenoord (a) Drawn 2-2**
Kahn, Sagnol, Kuffour, R Kovac, Lizarazu, Salihamidzic, Fink (Sforza 84), Thiam (Hargreaves 46), P Sergio, Elber (Santa Cruz 78), Pizarro. Scorer: Elber 13, 50
* played 10 Oct after 11 Sept atrocities

**18.09.01 v AC Sparta Praha (h) Drawn 0-0**
Kahn, Sagnol, Kuffour, R Kovac, Lizarazu, N Kovac (P Sergio 46), Fink, Sforza, Salihamidzic, Elber (Pizarro 72), Jancker

**25.09.01 v FC Spartak Moscow (a) Won 3-1**

Kahn, Sagnol, Kuffour, R Kovac, Lizarazu, Salihamidzic (P Sergio 82), Fink (Hargreaves 87), Thiam, N Kovac, Elber, Santa Cruz (Pizarro 79). Scorers: Salihamidzic 16, Elber 41, 74

**17.10.01 v FC Spartak Moscow (h) Won 5-1**
Kahn - Sagnol, Kuffour, R Kovac (Linke 85), Lizarazu - Salihamidzic, Fink, Hargreaves, P Sergio (Zickler 78) - Elber (Santa Cruz 65), Pizarro. Scorers: Pizarro 7, 22, Elber 34, 52, Zickler 90

**23.10.01 v Feyenoord (h) Won 3-1**
Kahn, Sagnol, Kuffour, R Kovac, Lizarazu (Tarnat 46), Salihamidzic, Fink (Thiam 84), Hargreaves, P Sergio (Zickler 69), Santa Cruz, Pizarro. Scorers: Kuffour 12, Santa Cruz 30,90

**31.10.01 v AC Sparta Praha (a) Won 1-0**
Wessels, Linke, Kuffour, R Kovac, Tarnat, Thiam, Sforza, Hargreaves (P Sergio 46), Feulner, Zickler (Fink 84), Pizarro (Santa Cruz 72). Scorer: Novotny 41og

**GROUP STAGE 2**

**20.11.01 v Manchester United FC (h) Drawn 1-1**
Kahn, Sagnol, Kuffour, R Kovac, Lizarazu, Salihamidzic (Zickler 73), Effenberg (Sforza 67), Hargreaves, Paulo Sergio, Elber (Jancker 67), Pizarro. Scorer: Paulo Sergio 87

**05.12.01 v FC Nantes Atlantique (a) Won 1-0**
Wessels, Sagnol, Kuffour, R Kovac, Lizarazu, N Kovac, Fink, Hargreaves (Sforza 68), Paulo Sergio, Pizarro (Elber 71), Jancker (Zickler 83). Scorer: Paulo Sergio 65

**20.02.02 v Boavista FC (a) Drawn 0-0**
Kahn, Sagnol, Kuffour, R Kovac, Lizarazu, Scholl (Feulner 82), Fink, Effenberg, Jeremies, Santa Cruz (Jancker 90), Elber (Pizzaro 72)

**26.02.02 v Boavista FC (h) Won 1-0**
Kahn, Sagnol, Kuffour, R Kovac, Lizarazu, Scholl ( P Sergio 76), Hargreaves, Jeremies (Pizarro 61), Effenberg, Santa Cruz, Elber (Fink 83). Scorer: Santa Cruz 81

**13.03.02 v Manchester Utd (a) Drawn 0-0**
Kahn, Kuffour, R Kovac, Linke, Lizarazu, P Sergio (Elber 83), Hargreaves, Jeremies (Fink 73), Effenberg, Santa Cruz (Zickler 77), Pizarro

**19.03.02 v FC Nantes Atlantique (a) Won 2-1**
Kahn, Kuffour, Linke, Tarnat, Scholl, Hargreaves, Jeremies, Effenberg (Salihamidzic 46), Fink, Santa Cruz (Zickler 72), P Sergio, Pizarro (Feulner 85). Scorers: Jeremies 58, Pizarro 87

**QUARTER FINAL**

**02.04.02 v Real Madrid CF (h) Won 2-1**
Kahn, Sagnol (Salihamidzic 63), R Kovac, Kuffour, Lizarazu, Hargreaves, Effenberg, Jeremies (N Kovac 83), P Sergio (Pizarro 63), Elber, Santa Cruz. Scorers: Effenberg 82, Pizarro 88

**10.04.02 v Real Madrid CF (a) Lost 0-2**
Kahn, Kuffour (Pizarro 74), Linke, R Kovac, Lizarazu, Hargreaves, Effenberg, Jeremies (Fink 84), Salihamidzic, Elber, Santa Cruz. Sent off: Salihamidzic 90

**2002-2003**

**GROUP STAGE 1**

**18.09.02 v RC Deportivo La Coruna (h) Lost 2-3**
Kahn, Sagnol (Hargreaves 46), Kuffour, Linke, Tarnat, Salihamidzic, Jeremies (N Kovac 78), Ballack, Ze Roberto (Zickler 84), Elber, Pizarro. Scorers: Salihamidzic 57, Elber 64

**24.09.02 v RC Lens (a) Drawn 1-1**
Kahn, R Kovac, Linke, Tarnat (Kuffour 77), Salihamidzic, Jeremies, Hargreaves, Ballack, Ze Roberto, Elber (Zickler 73), Pizarro. Scorer: Linke 23

**01.10.02 v AC Milan (h) Lost 1-2**
Kahn, Hargreaves, R Kovac, Linke, Tarnat (Zickler 84), Salihamidzic, Jeremies, Ballack, Ze Roberto, Elber, Pizarro. Scorer: Pizarro 54

**23.10.02 v AC Milan (a) Lost 1-2**
Kahn (Wessels 51), Sagnol, Kuffour, R Kovac, Tarnat, Salihamidzic (Scholl 70), Jeremies, Ballack, Ze Roberto, Elber, Pizarro (Santa Cruz 72). Scorer: Tarnat 23

**29.10.02 v RC Deportivo La Coruna (a) Lost 1-2**
Wessels, Sagnol, Kuffour, R Kovac, Tarnat (Lizarazu 60), Salihamidzic (Santa Cruz 46), Jeremies, Ballack (Fink 52), Ze Roberto, Elber, Scholl. Scorer: Santa Cruz 77

**13.11.02 v RC Lens (h) Drawn 3-3**
Wessels, R Kovac, Linke, Lizarazu, Salihamidzic, N Kovac, Fink, Feulner (Lahn 90), Scholl (Schweinsteiger 76): Zickler, Pizarro (Elber 46). Scorers: N Kovac 6, Salihamidzic 19, Feulner 87

## SL BENFICA

| SEASONS | PLAYED | WON | DRAWN | LOST | FOR | AGAINST |
|---|---|---|---|---|---|---|
| 7 | 82 | 39 | 25 | 18 | 124 | 86 |

**1994-1995**
**GROUP STAGE 1**
**14.09.94 v HNK Hajduk Split (a) Drawn 0-0**
Preud-homme, Veloso, da Silva Paulao, Helder, Dimas, Nelo, Vitor Paneira (Kenedy 86), Abel Xavier, Tavares, Caniggia (Cesar Brito 89), Isaias

**28.09.94 v RSC Anderlecht (h) Won 3-1**
Preud-homme, Abel Xavier (Veloso 77), Paulo Madeira, Helder, Dimas, Tavares, Vitor Paneira, Joao Pinto (Kenedy 89), Nelo, Caniggia, Isaias. Scorers: Caniggia 27, 41, Tavares 72

**19.10.94 v Steaua Bucaresti (h) Won 2-1**
Preud-homme, Veloso (Cesar Brito 79), Mozer, Helder, Dimas, Tavares, Vitor Paneira, Nelo (Kenedy 80), Joao Pinto, Caniggia, Isaias. Scorers: Caniggia 43 pen, Joao Pinto 60

**02.11.94 v Steaua Bucaresti (a) Drawn 1-1**
Preud-homme, Veloso, Mozer, Paulo Madeira, Abel Xavier, Dimas, Vitor Paneira (Tavares 85), Helder, Nelo, Joao Pinto, Isaias. Scorer: Helder 63

**23.11.94 v HNK Hajduk Split (h) Won 2-1**
Preud-homme, Paulo Madeira, Mozer, Helder, Abel Xavier, Dimas, Tavares (Kenedy 78), Joao Pinto, Nelo, Caniggia, Isaias (Vitor Paneira). Scorers: Isaias 32, Joao Pinto 75

**07.12.94 v RSC Anderlecht (a) Drawn 1-1**
Preud-homme, Veloso, William, Helder, Dimas, Tavares, Vitor Paneira (Paulo Bento 67), Joao Pinto, Nelo (Kenedy 67), Caniggia, Edilson. Scorer: Edilson 83

**01.03.95 v Milan AC (a) Lost 0-2**
Preud-homme, Veloso, Mozer, William, Dimas, Paulo Bento, Vitor Paneira, Joao Pinto, Abel Xavier, Caniggia, Tavares (Kenedy 22, Isaias 81)

**15.03.95 v Milan AC (h) Drawn 0-0**
Preud-homme, Veloso, Paulo Pereira, William (Helder 89), Dimas, Paulo Bento, Vitor Paneira, Joao Pinto, Nelo, Caniggia, Edilson (Isaias 59)

**1998-1999**
**GROUP STAGE 1**
**16.09.98 v 1 FC Kaiserslautern (a) Lost 0-1**
Preud-homme, Tahar, Ronaldo Guiaro, Paulo Madeira, Bruno Basto, Calado, Thomas, Joao Manuel Pinto (Poborsky 65), Pembridge, Pringle, Deane (Hugo Leal 76, Sousa 90)

**30.09.98 v PSV Eindhoven (h) Won 2-1**
Preud-homme, Sousa, Andrade, Ronaldo Guiaro, Bruno Basto, Thomas (Kandaurov

60), Hugo Leal, Pembridge, Poborsky (Deane 77), Nuno Gomes (Pringle 77), Joao Manuel Pinto. Scorers: Nuno Gomes 47, Joao Manuel Pinto 76

**21.10.98 v HJK Helsinki (a) Lost 0-2**
Preud-homme, Sousa, Paulo Madeira, Ronaldo Guiaro, Thomas, Hugo Leal, Minto, Kandaurov (Calado 84), Pembridge, Nuno Gomes (Poborsky 61), Pringle (Porfirio 75)

**04.11.98 v HJK Helsinki (h) Drawn 2-2**
Preud-homme, Andrade (Porfirio 46), Paulo Madeira, Ronaldo Guiaro, Minto, Calado, Hugo Leal, Pembridge, Poborsky (Pringle 82), Joao Manuel Pinto, Nuno Gomes. Scorers: Nuno Gomes 76, Calado 80

**26.11.98 v 1 FC Kaiserslautern (h) Won 2-1**
Ovchinnikov, Tahar, Paulo Madeira, Ronaldo Guiaro, Calado, Hugo Leal, Pembridge, Poborsky, Minto, Nuno Gomes, Joao Manuel Pinto. Scorers: Nuno Gomes 30, Joao Manuel Pinto 70

**09.12.98 v PSV Eindhoven (a) Drawn 2-2**
Ovchinnikov, Tahar, Andrade, Ronaldo Guiaro, Minto, Thomas (Calado 69), Hugo Leal, Pembridge (Bruno Basto 88), Poborsky (Pringle 82), Nuno Gomes, Joao Manuel Pinto. Scorer: Nuno Gomes 47 pen, 65

| SEASONS | PLAYED | WON | DRAWN | LOST | FOR | AGAINST |
|---|---|---|---|---|---|---|
| 2 | 14 | 5 | 6 | 3 | 17 | 16 |

## BESIKTAS JK

**1997-1998**
**GROUP STAGE 1**
**17.09.97 v FC Bayern Munchen (a) Lost 0-2**
Fevzi, Rahim, Erkan, Alpay, Recep, Serdar (Emre Eren 78), Yankov, Mehmet (Letchkov 72), Tayfur, Oktay, Amkoachi (Mustafa Ozturk 80)

**01.10.97 v Paris Saint-Germain (h) Won 3-1**
Fevzi, Recep, Alpay, Erkan, Mehmet, Yankov, Serdar (Mutlu 86), Tayfur, Amokachi (Letchkov 86), Oktay (Ertegrul74). Scorers: Oktay 5, 42, Ertegrul 83

**22.10.97 v IFK Goteborg (h) Won 1-0**
Mrmic, Recep, Rahim, Erkan, Mehmet, Ertegrul, Serdar, Tayfur, Amokachi (Letchkov 84), Yankov, Oktay. Scorer: Oktay 6

**05.11.97 v IFK Goteborg (a) Lost 1-2**
Mrmic, Recep, Ertegrul, Rahim (Salih 60), Alpay, Serdar (Fevzi 69), Mehmet (Yusuf 57),

Tayfur, Yankov, Letchkov, Oktay. Scorer: Oktay 47. Sent off: Mrmic 69

**26.11.97 v FC Bayern Munich (h) Lost 0-2**
Fevzi, Recep (Emre Eran 59), Erkan, Alpay, Ertegrul, Serdar (Osman 80), Yankov, Letchkov, Tayfur, Hikmet (Amokachi 62), Oktay

**10.12.97 v Paris Saint-Germain (a) Lost 1-2**
Mrmic, Rahim, Recep, Tayfur, Alpay, Serdar (Letchkov 66), Erkan, Yankov, Mehmet, Oktay (Ertegrul 71), Amokachi (Osman 77). Scorer: Mehmet 37

**2000-2001**
**GROUP STAGE 1**
**13.09.00 v Milan AC (a) Lost 1-4**
Shorunmu, Kahran, Tayfur, Halilagic (Khlestov 70), Ahmet Dursun, Munch, Umit, Erman, Ibrahim (Bayram 76), Nouma, Yasin (Mehmet 61). Scorer: Tayfur 20 pen

**19.09.00 v FC Barcelona (h) Won 3-0**
Shorunmu, Kahran, Tayfur, Ahmet Dursun (Yasin 81), Nihat, Munch, Umit, Khlestov, Erman (Rahim 90), Ibrahim, Nouma (Fazli 88). Scorers: Ahmet Dursun 38, 75, Nouma 87

**26.09.00 v Leeds United AFC (a) Lost 0-6**
Shorunmu, Kahran, Tayfur, Ahmet Dursun, Nihat, Munch, Umit, Khlestov, Erman (Rahim 82), Ibrahim (Mehmet 72), Nouma (Fazli 72)

**18.10.00 v Leeds United AFC (h) Drawn 0-0**
Shorunmu, Kahran, Tayfur, Ali Eren (Murat 63), Ahmet Dursun (Akman Ayhan 81), Nihat, Mehmet (Ibrahim 81), Munch, Umit, Khlestov, Yasin

**24.10.00 v Milan AC (h) Lost 0-2**
Shorunmu, Kahran, Tayfur, Ali Eren (Erman 46), Ahmet Dursun, Nihat, Mehmet (Akman Ayhan 72), Munch, Umit, Khlestov (Ibrahim 46), Yasin

**08.11.00 v FC Barcelona (a) Lost 0-5**
Fevzi, Tayfur, Ali Eren (Erman 21), Ahmet Dursun, Nihat, Mehmet (Ilhan 85), Munch, Umit, Akman Ayhan, Ibrahim (Bayram 78), Yasin

| SEASONS | PLAYED | WON | DRAWN | LOST | FOR | AGAINST |
|---|---|---|---|---|---|---|
| 2 | 12 | 3 | 1 | 8 | 10 | 26 |

## BLACKBURN ROVERS FC

**1995-1996**
**GROUP STAGE 1**
**13.09.95 v FC Spartak Moscow (h) Lost 0-1**
Flowers, Berg, Le Saux, Hendry, Pearce, Sherwood, Ripley (Makel 46), Batty, Atkins (Sutton 73), Shearer, Newell

**27.09.95 v Rosenborg BK (a) Lost 1-2**
Flowers, Berg, Kenna, Hendry, Pearce, Sherwood (Warhurst 84), Batty, Sutton, Makel (Ripley 46), Shearer, Newell. Scorer: Newell 63

**18.10.95 v Legia Warzawa (a) Lost 0-1**
Flowers, Berg, Kenna, Hendry, Pearce, Sherwood, Warhurst (Newell 81), Batty, Holmes, Sutton, Shearer

**01.11.95 v Legia Warszawa (h) Drawn 0-0**
Flowers, Berg, Kenna, Hendry, Pearce, Sherwood, Ripley, Batty, Warhurst (Le Saux 62), Newell (Sutton 74), Shearer

**22.11.95 v FC Spartak Moscow (a) Lost 0-3**
Flowers, Kenna, Le Saux (Holmes 57), Hendry, Berg, Sherwood, Ripley (Sutton 77), Batty, Warhurst, Newell, Shearer. Sent off: Hendry 75

**06.12.95 v Rosenborg BK (h) Won 4-1**
Flowers, Berg, Kenna, Marker, Sherwood, Ripley, Warhurst, Holmes (Gallacher 73), Sutton, Newell, Shearer. Scorers: Shearer 16 pen, Newell 31, 37, 40. Sent off: Warhurst 51

| SEASONS | PLAYED | WON | DRAWN | LOST | FOR | AGAINST |
|---|---|---|---|---|---|---|
| 1 | 6 | 0 | 1 | 4 | 5 | 8 |

## BOAVISTA FC

**1999-2000**
**GROUP STAGE 1**
**14.09.99 v Rosenborg BK (h) Lost 0-3**
William Andem, Paulo Sousa, Rui Bento, Pedro Emanuel, Timofte (Formoso 9), Luis Manuel (Emanuel 46), Gilmar (Whelliton 54), Litos, Jorge Couto, Augustine, Mario Silva

**22.09.99 v BV Borussia Dortmund (a) Lost 1-3**
William Andem, Paulo Sousa, Rui Bento, Pedro Emanuel, Luis Manuel (Formoso 45), Cesar, Litos, Rogerio (Martelinho 64), Jorge Silva, Augustine (Gilmar 71), Mario Silva. Scorer: Rui Bento 44

**29.09.99 v Feyenoord (h) Drawn 1-1**
William Andem, Paulo Sousa, Rui Bento, Pedro Emanuel (Formoso 79), Cesar (Gilmar 46), Emanuel, Litos, Rogerio, Jorge Couto, Jorge Silva, Augustine (Douala 68), Mario Silva. Scorer: Mario Silva 87. Sent off: William Andem 90

**19.10.99 v Feyenoord (a) Drawn 1-1**
Ricardo, Paulo Sousa, Rui Bento, Pedro Emanuel, Timofte (Rogerio 90), Luis Emanuel (Sergio 75), Emanuel, Litos, Jorge Couto, Jorge Silva, Augustine (Martelinho 81). Scorer: Timofte 83 pen

**27.10.99 v Rosenborg BK (a) Lost 0-2**
Ricardo, Paulo Sousa, Rui Bento, Pedro Emanuel, Timofte, Luis Emanuel (Augustine 71), Litos, Jorge Couto, Jorge Silva, Nilton, Whelliton (Gilmar 84)

**02.11.99 v BV Borussia Dortmund (h) Won 1-0**
Ricardo, Paulo Sousa, Sergio, Pedro Emanuel, Luis Emanuel (Carlos Alberto 90), Emanuel, Litos, Douala (Ricardo Silva 69), Jorge Silva, Nilton, Whelliton (Rogerio 62). Scorer: Pedro Emanuel 16. Sent off: Nilton 65

**2001-2002**
**GROUP STAGE 1**
**11.09.01 v Liverpool FC (a) Drawn 1-1**
Ricardo, Nuno Frechaut, Pedro Emanuel, Turra, Erivan, Petit, Glauber, Sanchez (Pedro Santos 59), Alexandre, E Silva (Serginho 79), Duda (J Silva 84). Scorer: E Silva 3

**19.09.01 v FC Dynamo Kyiv (h) Won 3-1**
Ricardo, Nuno Frechaut, Pedro Emanuel, Turra, Erivan, Petit, Glauber, Sanchez, Alexandre (Pedro Santos 76), E Silva (Marcio Santos 87), Duda (Bosingwa 84). Scorers: Sanchez 4, E Silva 11, Duda 30

**26.09.01 v BV Borussia Dortmund (h) Won 2-1**
Ricardo, Nuno Frechaut, Pedro Emanuel, Turra, Erivan, Petit, Glauber (Gouveia 76), Sanchez, Alexandre (Bosingwa 81), E Silva (Serginho 76), Duda. Scorers: E Silva 23, Sanchez 39

**16.10.01 v BV Borussia Dortmund (a) Lost 1-2**
Ricardo, Rui Oscar, Pedro Emanuel, Turra, Erivan, Nuno Frechaut, Marcio Santos (Martelinho 59), Sanchez, Alexandre (E Silva 70), Bosingwa (Petit 48), Duda. Scorer: Alexandre (Goulart) 33

**24.10.01 v Liverpool FC (h) Drawn 1-1**
Ricardo, Rui Oscar (Martelinho 26), Pedro Emanuel, Turra, Erivan, Nuno Frechaut, Petit, Sanchez, Alexandre (Marcio 56), E Silva, Duda (Bosingwa 56). Scorer: E Silva 59

**30.10.01 v FC Dynamo Kyiv (a) Lost 0-1**
Ricardo, Nuno Frechaut, Pedro Emanuel (Serginho 81), Loja, Erivan, Bosingwa, Petit, Sanchez, Duda, E Silva (Marcio 54), Alexandre

**GROUP STAGE 2**

**20.11.01 v FC Nantes Atlantique (h) Won 1-0**
Ricardo, Rui Oscar (Martelinho 20), Turra, Loja, Erivan, Nuno Frechaut, Bosingwa (P Santos 59), Sanchez, Alexandre (J Silva 63), E Silva, Duda. Scorer: Sanchez 24

**05.12.01 v Manchester United FC (a) Lost 0-3**
Ricardo, J Silva (Martelinho 63), Pedro Emanuel, Turra, Erivan, Nuno Frechaut, Petit, Sanchez (P Santos 69), Alexandre, E Silva (Marcio 58) , Duda

**20.02.02 v FC Bayern Munchen (h) Drawn 0-0**
Ricardo, Pedro Emanuel, Turra, Loja, Nuno Frechaut, J Silva, Avelos, Sanchez (Alexandre 72), Marcio (E Silva 57), Martelinho, Serginho (Duda 55)

**26.02.02 v FC Bayern Munchen (a) Lost 0-1**
Ricardo, Bosingwa, Pedro Emanuel, Loja, Erivan, J Silva, Avelos, Sanchez (Rui Lima 78) J Couto (Duda 66), E Silva (Alexandre 46), Martelinho

**13.03.02 v FC Nantes Atlantique (a) Drawn 1-1**
Ricardo, Rui Oscar, Pedro Emanuel, Turra, Erivan, Petit, J Silva, Rui Lima (Martelinho 46), P Santos (Sanchez 46), Alexandre (M Santos 62), Duda. Scorer: Martelinho 78

**20.03.02 v Manchester United FC (h) Lost 0-3**
Ricardo, Nuno Frechaut, Pedro Emanuel, Turra, Loja, Petit, J Silva (Martelinho 34), E Silva (Alexandre 21, Marcio 59), Sanchez, Duda, Serginho

| SEASONS | PLAYED | WON | DRAWN | LOST | FOR | AGAINST |
|---|---|---|---|---|---|---|
| 2 | 18 | 4 | 6 | 8 | 14 | 25 |

## BORDEAUX (FC GIRONDINS DE BORDEAUX)

**1999-2000**

**GROUP STAGE 1**

**15.09.99 v AC Sparta Praha (a) Drawn 0-0**
Rame, Saveljic, Rouviere, Micoud, Laslandes, Wiltord, Grenet, Martins (Batlles 90), Diabate, Afanou, Alicarte

**21.09.99 v Willem II (h) Won 3-2**
Rame, Saveljic, Bonnissel, Rouviere, Micoud, Laslandes, Wiltord (Feindouno 73), Grenet, Martins (Batlles 63), Diabate, Afanou. Scorers: Victoria og 17, Laslandes 22, Feindouno 82

**28.09.99 v FC Spartak Moscow (h) Won 2-1**
Rame, Saveljic, Bonnissel, Pavon, Micoud, Laslandes, Wiltord (Feindouno 87), Grenet, Martins (Batlles 72), Diabate, Afanou. Scorers: Wiltord 9, Micoud 56

**20.10.99 v FC Spartak Moscow (a) Won 2-1**
Rame, Bonnissel, Pavon, Micoud, Laslandes, Wiltord (Batlles 87), Grenet, Martins (Rouviere 76), Diabate, Afanou, Alicarte. Scorers: Micoud 21, Wiltord 76

**26.10.99 v AC Sparta Praha (h) Drawn 0-0**
Rame, Jemmali, Saveljic, Bonnissel, Rouviere, Pavon, Laslandes, Wiltord (Zanotti 90), Martins (Micoud 76), Diabate (Batlles 66), Alicarte

**03.11.99 v Willem II (a) Drawn 0-0**
Rame, Jemmali, Bonnissel, Rouviere, Micoud, Wiltord, Martins (Grenet 83), Diabate, Batlles (Feindouno 68), Afanou, Alicarte

**GROUP STAGE 2**

**23.11.99 v Valencia CF (a) Lost 0-3**
Rame, Saveljic, Pavon, Micoud, Laslandes, Wiltord, Grenet, Martins (Ziani 58), Diabate (Rouviere 86), Afanou, Alicarte

**08.12.99 v AC Fiorentina (h) Drawn 0-0**
Rame, Saveljic, Pavon, Micoud, Laslandes, Wiltord, Grenet, Martins (Rouviere 85), Diabate, Afanou, Alicarte

**01.03.00 v Manchester United FC (a) Lost 0-2**
Rame, Bonnissel, Pavon, Micoud, Laslandes, Wiltord, Grenet, Martins (Ziani 65), Diabate, Afanou, Alicarte

**07.03.00 v Manchester United (h) Lost 1-2**
Rame, Saveljic, Bonnissel, Pavon, Micoud, Laslandes, Ziani (Rouviere 60), Wiltord (Feindouno 82), Grenet, Batlles (Diabate 9), Afanou. Scorer: Pavon 9. Sent off: Laslandes 23

**15.03.00 v Valencia CF (h) Lost 1-4**
Rame, Saveljic, Bonnissel, Pavon, Micoud (Rouviere 77), Ziani, Wiltord, Grenet, Diabate (Afanou 50), Alicarte, Feindouno (Colucci 62). Scorer: Wiltord 54. Sent off: Saveljic 47

**21.03.00 v AC Fiorentina (a) Drawn 3-3**
Rame, Bonnissel, Rouviere (Colucci 73), Pavon, Micoud (Zanotti 80), Laslandes, Ziani (Sahnoun 59), Wiltord, Diabate, Batlles, Alicarte. Scorers: Wiltord 5, Zanotti 87, Batlles 90. Sent off: Alicarte 46

| SEASONS | PLAYED | WON | DRAWN | LOST | FOR | AGAINST |
|---|---|---|---|---|---|---|
| 1 | 12 | 3 | 5 | 4 | 12 | 18 |

## BV BORUSSIA DORTMUND

**1995-1996**
**GROUP STAGE 1**
**13.09.95 v Juventus FC (h) Lost 1-3**
Klos, Kohler, Julio Cesar, Sammer, Reinhardt, Freund, Reuter, Zorc (Ruben Sosa 46), Moller, Tretschock (Tanko 46), Herrlich (Ricken 73). Scorer: Moller 1

**27.09.95 v Rangers FC (a) Drawn 2-2**
Klos, Kohler, Freund, Julio Cesar (Scmidt 53), Kree, Sammer, Reuter, Zorc, Moller (Tretschock 84), Ricken (Berger 80), Herrlich. Scorers: Herrlich 19, Kree 68

**18.10.95 v Steaua Bucaresti (h) Won 1-0**
Klos, Kohler, Freund, Julio Cesar, Sammer, Reinhardt, Reuter, Berger (Tretschock 89), Ricken (Kutowski 88), Herrlich, Tanko (Zorc 46). Scorer: Ricken 58

**01.11.95 v Steaua Bucaresti (a) Drawn 0-0**
Klos, Kohler, Freund, Julio Cesar, Sammer, Kree, Berger (Reinhardt 87), Zorc, Moller, Ricken, Ruben Sosa (Tretschock 74)

**22.11.95 v Juventus FC (a) Won 2-1**
Klos, Kree, Schmidt, Freund, Kohler, Sammer, Reuter, Zorc, Moller (Ruben Sosa 89), Ricken (Berger 67), Herrlich (Riedle 75). Scorers: Zorc 29, Ricken 65

**06.12.95 v Rangers FC (h) Drawn 2-2**
Klos, Franck, Freund, Kree, Wolters, Zorc, Moller, Berger, Reinhardt (Ruben Sosa 82), Herrlich, Riedle (Kutowski 64). Scorers: Moller 17, Riedle 48

**QUARTER FINAL**
**06.03.96 v AFC Ajax (h) Lost 0-2**
Klos, Kohler, Schmidt (Herrlich 46), Freund, Julio Cesar, Sammer, Reuter, Ricken (Zorc 76), Riedle, Berger, Reinhardt

**20.03.96 v AFC Ajax (a) Lost 0-1**
Klos, Kohler, Freund, Julio Cesar, Kree, Tretschock (Reinhardt 63), Wolters (Moller 61), Zorc, Ricken, Chapuisat (Ruben Sosa 80), Riedle

**1996-1997**
**GROUP STAGE 1**
**11.09.96 v Widzew Lodz (h) Won 2-1**
Klos, Kohler, Sammer, Julio Cesar, Reuter, Lambert (Feiersinger 24), Zorc, Heinrich, Herrlich (Tretschock 77), Moller, Chapuisat (But 90). Scorer: Herrlich 45, 68

**25.09.96 v Steaua Bucaresti (a) Won 3-0**
Klos, Kohler, Reuter, Julio Cesar, Lambert, Feiersinger, Moller (But 86), Heinrich (Tretschock 85), Zorc, Herrlich, Ricken (Chapuisat 75). Scorers: Ricken 6, Heinrich 37, Chapuisat 77

**16.10.96 v Clube Atletico de Madrid (a) Won 1-0**
Klos, Reuter, Kohler, Feiersinger, Julio Cesar (Kree 67), Heinrich, Zorc, Lambert, Tretschock (Herrlich 86), Ricken (Kirovski 71), Chapuisat. Scorer: Reuter 51

**30.10.96 v Clube Atletico de Madrid (h) Lost 1-2**
Klos, Pedersen (Kirovski 82), Reuter, Julio Cesar, Zorc, Lambert, Mller, Reinhardt, Chapuisat, Herrlich, Tretschock (Ricken 67). Scorer: Herrlich 17

**20.11.96 v Widzew Lodz (a) Drawn 2-2**
Klos, Kohler, Sammer, Heinrich, Reuter, Tretschock (Chapuisat 28), Lambert, Reinhardt (Kree 90), Ricken (Tanko 82), Herrlich, Moller. Scorers: Lambert 14, Kohler 65

**04.12.96 v Steaua Bucaresti (h) Won 5-3**
Klos, Kohler, Sammer, Kree, Heinrich (Pedersen 67), Lambert, Zorc, Reinhardt, Tretschock, Riedle (Tanko 64), Chapuisat. Scorers: Chapuisat 13, 22, Tretschock 43, Riedle 63, Zorc 65

**QUARTER FINAL**
**05.03.97 v AJ Auxerre (h) Won 3-1**
Klos, Reuter, Kree (Schneider 35), Feiersinger, Heinrich, Ricken (Tretschock 89), Lambert, Moller, Paulo Sousa, Riedle, Chapuisat (Tanko 80). Scorers: Riedle 12, Schneider 54, Moller 82. Sent off: Reuter 82

**19.03.97 v AJ Auxerre (a) Won 1-0**
Klos, Sammer, Kohler, Kree, Heinrich, Ricken (Feiersinger 80), Lambert, Paulo Sousa (Herrlich 82), Moller, Riedle, Chapuisat (Zorc 81). Scorer: Violeau og 59

**SEMI FINAL**
**09.04.97 v Manchester United FC (h) Won 1-0**
Klos, Reuter, Feiersinger, Kree, Ricken (Freund 90), Lambert, Paulo Sousa, Moller, Heinrich, Herrlich (Zorc 90), Tretschock (Reinhardt 85). Scorer: Pallister og 75

**23.04.97 v Manchester United FC (a) Won 1-0**
Klos, Kohler, Feiersinger, Kree, Reuter (Tretschock 24), Ricken (Zorc 61), Lambert, Moller, Heinrich, Riedle (Herrlich 73), Chapuisat. Scorer: Ricken 8

**FINAL**
**28.05.97 v Juventus FC (n) Won 3-1**
Klos, Kohler, Sammer, Kree, Reuter, Lambert, Paulo Sousa, Moller (Zorc 88), Heinrich, Riedle, Chapuisat (Ricken 70). Scorers: Riedle 29, 34, Ricken 71

**1997-1998**
**GROUP STAGE 1**
**17.09.97 v Galatasaray SK (a) Won 1-0**
Klos, Reinhardt, Kohler (Kree 46), Julio Cesar, Feiersinger, Lambert, Freund (But 46), Zorc, Heinrich, Herrlich, Chapuisat. Scorer: Chapuisat 74

**01.10.97 v AC Sparta Praha (h) Won 4-1**
Klos, Kohler, Sammer, Heinrich, Reuter, Feiersinger (Zorc 76), Paulo Sousa (Lambert 81), Moller, Reinhardt, Herrlich (Booth 84), Chapuisat. Scorers: Herrlich 20, Chapuisat 59, 75, Heinrich 69

**22.10.97 v Parma AC (a) Lost 0-1**
Klos, Kohler, Feiersinger (Zorc 89), Julio Cesar, Reuter, Freund (Herrlich 80), Paulo Sousa, Heinrich, Moller, Chapuisat, But

**05.11.97 v Parma AC (h) Won 2-0**
Klos, Reuter, Feiersinger, Julio Cesar, Timm (Kirovski 46), Lambert, Paulo Sousa (Freund 79), But, Heinrich, Moller, Chapuisat (Booth 54). Scorer: Moller 50, 75

**27.11.97 v Galatasaray SK (h) Won 4-1**
Klos, Reuter, Feiersinger, Julio Cesar, Freund, Paulo Sousa (Timm 79), But (Kirovski 46), Heinrich, Moller (Zorc 46), Herrlich, Chapuisat. Scorers: But 22, Herrlich 34, Zorc 48, 86 pen

**10.12.97 v AC Sparta Praha (a) Won 3-0**
Klos, Reuter, Feiersinger, Kree, Freund, But (Timm 80), Ricken (Mehnert 67), Reinhardt, Moller (Booth 62), Herrlich, Kirovski. Scorers: Moller 29, Kirovski 47, Booth 71

**QUARTER FINAL**

**04.03.98 v FC Bayern Munchen (a) Drawn 0-0**
Klos, Feiersinger, Kohler, Julio Cesar, Heinrich, Ricken, Freund, Moller, But, Chapuisat (Zorc 88), Decheiver (Herrlich 64)

**18.03.98 v FC Bayern Munchen (h) Won 1-0 after extra-time**
Klos, Reuter (Zorc 105), Kohler, Feiersinger, Julio Cesar, Heinrich, Freund (Ricken 78), Moller, But, Chapuisat, Decheiver (Schneider 119). Scorer: Chapuisat 109

**SEMI FINAL**

**01.04.98 v Real Madrid CF (a) Lost 0-2**
Klos, Reuter, Julio Cesar, Binz, Kree, Reinhardt, Ricken (Zorc 81), Freund, But, Herrlich (Decheiver 47), Chapuisat

**14.04.98 v Real Madrid CF (h) Drawn 0-0**
Klos, Ricken (Timm 77), Reuter, Binz, Kree (Zorc 11), Heinrich, Moller, Feiersinger, But, Tanko (Decheiver 71), Chapuisat

**1999-2000**

**GROUP STAGE 1**

**14.09.99 v Feyenoord (a) Drawn 1-1**
Lehmann, Stevic (Feiersinger 66), Reuter, Nerlinger, Moller, Reina, Nijhuis (Barbarez 77), Dede, Ricken, Bobic (Herrlich 90), Evanilson. Scorer: Bobic 71

**22.09.99 v Boavista FC (h) Won 3-1**
Lehmann, Kohler, Reuter, Nerlinger, Moller, Reina (Nijhuis 88), Dede, Ricken, Addo (Stevic 79), Bobic (Herrlich 73), Evanilson. Scorers: Moller 40, Bobic 53, 65

**29.09.99 v Rosenborg BK (a) Drawn 2-2**
Lehmann, Stevic (Nijhuis 74), Kohler, Reuter, Nerlinger, Herrlich (Addo 70), Reina, Barbarez, Dede, Ricken, Evanilson (Baumann 46). Scorers: Barbarez 11, Kohler 22

**19.10.99 v Rosenborg BK (h) Lost 0-3**
Lehmann, Worns (Bobic 46), Kohler, Reuter, Nerlinger (Addo 61), Moller, Reina, Barbarez, Dede, Ricken, Evanilson (Kapetanovic 83). Sent off: Ricken 69

**27.10.99 v Feyenoord (h) Drawn 1-1**
Lehmann, Stevic, Kohler, Reuter, Nerlinger, Moller, Reina, Dede, Addo, Bobic (Barbarez 74), Evanilson. Scorer: Addo 45

**02.11.99 v Boavista FC (a) Lost 0-1**
Lehmann, Worns (Barbarez 76), Stevic, Kohler, Reuter, Nerlinger (Herrlich 46), Reina (Evanilson 62), Dede, Ricken, Addo, Bobic

**2001-2002**
**GROUP STAGE 1**
**11.09.01 v FC Dynamo Kyiv (a) Drawn 2-2**
Lehmann, Evanilson, Worns, Kohler, DedeReuter, Ricken, Oliseh (Stevic 53), Rosicky (Sorensen 84), Koller, Amoroso (Bobic 88). Scorers: Koller 56, Amoroso 74

**19.09.01 v Liverpool FC (h) Drawn 0-0**
Lehmann, Evanilson, Worns, Kohler, Dede, Reuter, Stevic, Rosicky, Sorensen, Koller, Amoroso (Ricken 87)

**26.09.01 v Boavista FC (a) Lost 1-2**
Lehmann, Reuter, Worns, Kohler (Ricken 73), Evanilson, Stevic (Herrlich 83), Rosicky, Sorensen (Bobic 46), Dede, Koller, Amoroso. Scorer: Amoroso 76. Sent off: Amoroso 90

**16.10.01 v Boavista FC (h) Won 2-1**
Lehmann, Reuter, Metzelder, Worns, Evanilson, Stevic, Rosicky (Kohler 90), Sorensen (Oliseh 76), Dede, Koller, Ricken (Madouni 90). Scorers: Ricken 50, Koller 68

**24.10.01 v FC Dynamo Kyiv (h) Won 1-0**
Lehmann, Reuter, Metzelder, Worns, Evanilson, Oliseh, Rosicky, Sorensen (Bugri 83), Dede, Koller, Ricken (Madouni 90). Scorer: Rosicky 34

**30.10.01 v Liverpool FC (a) Lost 0-2**
Lehmann, Evanilson, Reuter, Worns, Metzelder, Dede, Ricken, Oliseh (Bobic 68), Rosicky, Koller, Sorensen

**2002-2003**
**GROUP STAGE 1**
**17.09.02 v Arsenal FC (a) Lost 0-2**
Lehmann, Evanilson, Metzelder, Madouni, Dede, Fernandez (Herrlich 72), Frings, Kehl, Heinrich, Koller, Ewerthon (Reina 72)

**25.09.02 v AJ Auxerre (h) Won 2-1**
Lehmann, Evanilson, Metzelder, Worns, Heinrich, Reuter, Frings (Ricken 74), Kehl, Rosicky (Amoroso 66), Koller, Ewerthon (Dede 84). Scorers: Koller 6, Amoroso 78

**02.10.02 v PSV Eindhoven (a) Won 3-1**
Lehmann, Worns, Metzelder, Madouni, Dede, Reuter (Ricken 90), Frings, Rosicky (Kehl 79), Heinrich, Koller, Ewerthon (Amoroso 65). Scorers: Koller 21, Rosicky 69, Amoroso 90

**22.10.02 v PSV Eindhoven (h) Drawn 1-1**
Lehmann, Evanilson, Worns, Madouni, Dede, Reuter (Frings 78), Rosicky, Kehl, Ricken (Amoroso 72), Koller, Ewerthon. Scorer: Koller 10

**30.10.02 v Arsenal FC (h) Won 2-1**
Lehmann, Evanilson, Worns, Metzelder, Dede, Frings, Rosicky (Madouni 90), Kehl (Reuter 68), Ricken (Heinrich 84), Koller, Ewerthon. Scorers: Gilberto 38og, Rosicky 62pen

**12.11.02 v AJ Auxerre (a) Lost 0-1**
Lehmann, Heinrich (Demel 26), Kehl, Madouni, Dede, Reuter, Frings, Leandro (Reina 81), Ricken, Koller, Ewerthon (Amoroso 65)

**GROUP STAGE 2**

**26.11.02 v FC Lokomotiv Moskva (a) Won 2-1**
Lehmann, Frings, Worns, Metzelder, Dede, Reuter, Rosicky (Reina 90), Kehl (Madouni 89), Heinrich, Koller, Ewerthon (Ricken 82). Scorers: Frings 33, Koller 43

**11.12.02 v AC Milan (h) Lost 0-1**
Lehmann, Heinrich (Evanilson 73), Worns, Metzelder, Dede, Frings,Kehl (Reina 83) Rosicky, Amoroso, Koller, Ewerthon (Ricken 64)

**19.02.03 v Real Madrid CF (a) Lost 1-2**
Lehmann, Evanilson (Ricken 83), Worns, Metzelder, Dede, Frings, Reuter (Kehl 76), Rosicky, Amoroso (Reina 67), Koller, Ewerthon. Scorer: Koller 30

**25.02.03 v Real Madrid CF (h) Drawn 1-1**
Lehmann, Madouni, Worns, Metzelder, Dede (Amoroso 90), Evanilson (Ricken 80), Frings, Reuter, Kehl, Koller, Ewerthon (Reina 87). Scorer: Koller 23

**12.03.03 v FC Lokomotiv Moscow (h) Won 3-0**
Lehmann, Evanilson, Worns, Metzelder, Dede (Madouni 20), Frings, Reuter, Kehl, Amoroso (Herrlich 83), Koller (Ricken 70), Ewerthon. Scorers: Frings 38, Koller 58, Amoroso 66

**18.02.03 v AC Milan (a) Won 1-0**
Lehmann, Evanilson, Worns, Metzelder, Dede (Madouni 83), Frings, Reuter (Ricken 50), Kehl, Amoroso, Koller, Ewerthon (Odonkor 74). Scorer: Koller 80

| SEASONS | PLAYED | WON | DRAWN | LOST | FOR | AGAINST |
|---|---|---|---|---|---|---|
| 6 | 53 | 26 | 13 | 14 | 75 | 54 |

## BRONDBY IF

**1998-1999**
**GROUP STAGE 1**
**16.09.98 v FC Bayern Munchen (h) Won 2-1**
Mogens Krogh, Colding, Rasmussen, Per Nielsen, Brian Jensen, Bjur, Daugaard (Mikkel Jensen 73), Ravn, Faxe, Sand (Bo Hansen 56), Lindrup (Soren Krogh 76). Scorers: Helmer og 87, Ravn 90

**30.09.98 v FC Barcelona (a) Lost 0-2**
Mogens Krogh, Skarbalius, Rasmussen, Per Nielsen, Brian Jensen, Ravn (Mikkel Jensen 12), Faxe (Bo Hansen 65), Daugaard, Bjur (Soren Krogh 78), Sand, Lindrup

**21.10.98 v Manchester United (h) Lost 2-6**
Mogens Krogh, Colding, Rasmussen, Per Nielsen (Mikkel Jensen 31), Brian Jensen (Vragel Da Silva 27), Bjur, Daugaard, Ravn, Lindrup, Sand, Bo Hansen (Bagger 67). Scorers: Daugaard 35, Sand 90

**04.11.98 v Manchester United (a) Lost 0-5**
Emeka Andersen, Colding, Rasmussen, Per Nielsen, Skarbalius, Bjur (Soren Krogh 74), Faxe, Daugaard, Ravn, Bagger (Thygesen 68), Sand (Bo Hansen 77)

**25.11.98 v FC Bayern Munchen (a) Lost 0-2**
Emeka Andersen, Colding, Rasmussen, Per Nielsen (Vragel Da Silva 68), Skarbalius, Bjur, Faxe, Daugaard, Bagger (Lindrup 65), Sand, Bo Hansen (Christensen 70)

**09.12.98 v FC Barcelona (h) Lost 0-2**
Mogens Krogh, Colding, Rasmussen, Per Nielsen, Skarbalius, Daugaard (Christensen 70), Faxe (Thygesen 80), Bjur, Sand, Bagger (Lindrup 74), Bo Hansen

| SEASONS | PLAYED | WON | DRAWN | LOST | FOR | AGAINST |
|---|---|---|---|---|---|---|
| 1 | 6 | 1 | 0 | 5 | 4 | 18 |

## CLUB BRUGGE KV

**2002-2003**
**GROUP STAGE 1**
**18.09.02 v FC Barcelona (a) Lost 2-3**
Verlinden, De Cock, Spilar, Maertens, Van der Heyden (Stoica 56), Engelbert, Serebrennikov (Lesnjak 46), Simons, Martens (Ceh 71), Verheyen, Mendoza. Scorers: Simons 22pen, Engelbert 85

**24.09.02 v FC Lokomotiv Moskva (h) Drawn 0-0**
Verlinden, De Cock, Spilar (Clement 61), Maertens, Van der Heyden, Engelbert, Serebrennikov, Simons, Verheyen, Mendoza (Stoica 66), Lange

**01.10.02 v Galatasaray SK (a) Drawn 0-0**
Verlinden, De Cock, Clement, Maertens, Van der Heyden, Engelbert, Serebrennikov, Simons, Stoica (Ceh 87), Verheyen (Martens 90), Lange (Mendoza 54)

**23.10.02 v Galatasaray SK (h) Won 3-1**
Verlinden, De Cock, Clement, Maertens, Van der Heyden, Engelbert, Stoica (Spilar 84), Simons, Ceh (Saeternes 64), Verheyen (Smolders 90), Martens. Scorers: Maertens 45, Verheyen 72, Saeternes 90

**29.10.02 v FC Barcelona (h) Lost 0-1**
Verlinden, De Cock, Clement (Spilar 68) Maertens, Van der Heyden (Ristic 68), Engelbert, Stoica, Simons, Lesnjak (Saeternes 80), Verheyen, Martens

**13.11.02 v FC Lokomotiv Moskva (a) Lost 0-2**
Verlinden, De Cock, Clement, Maertens, Van der Heyden, Engelbert, Stoica (Ceh 84), Simons, Martens, Verheyen, Mendoza (Lesnjak 72)

| SEASONS | PLAYED | WON | DRAWN | LOST | FOR | AGAINST |
|---|---|---|---|---|---|---|
| 1 | 6 | 1 | 2 | 3 | 5 | 7 |

## CHELSEA FC

**1999-2000**
**GROUP STAGE 1**
**15.09.99 v Milan AC (h) Drawn 0-0**
De Goey, Petrescu, Babayaro, Leboeuf (Hogh 81), Desailly, Deschamps, Poyet (Le Saux 80), Wise, Ferrer, Flo (Sutton 85), Zola

**21.09.99 v Hertha BSC Berlin (a) Lost 1-2**
De Goey, Petrescu, Babayaro, Leboeuf, Desailly, Deschamps, Wise, Le Saux (Morris 71), Ferrer (Ambrosetti 64), Flo (Sutton 64), Zola. Scorer: Leboeuf 86 pen

**28.09.99 v Galatasaray SK (h) Won 1-0**
De Goey, Petrescu, Babayaro, Leboeuf, Desailly (Hogh 63), Sutton (Flo 85), Wise, Ferrer, Ambrosetti (Poyet 53), Morris, Zola. Scorer: Petrescu 55

**20.10.99 v Galatasaray SK (a)** **Won 5-0**
De Goey, Babayaro, Leboeuf, Desailly, Deschamps (Wise 67), Poyet (Petrescu 67), Le Saux, Ferrer, Flo, Morris, Zola (Ambrosetti 76). Scorers: Flo 32, 49, Zola 54, Wise 79, Ambrosetti 88

**26.10.99 v Milan AC (a)** **Drawn 1-1**
De Goey, Petrescu (Morris 46), Babayaro, Leboeuf, Desailly, Deschamps, Poyet (Di Matteo 75), Wise, Ferrer, Flo, Zola (Ambrosetti 81). Scorer: Wise 77

**03.11.99 v Hertha BSC Berlin (h)** **Won 2-0**
De Goey, Petrescu, Babayaro, Hogh (Leboeuf 66), Desailly (Lambourde 86), Deschamps, Sutton, Wise, Ferrer, Flo, Zola (Poyet 64). Scorers: Deschamps 11, Ferrer 44. Sent off: Sutton 90

**GROUP STAGE 2**

**24.11.99 v Feyenoord (h)** **Won 3-1**
De Goey, Petrescu, Babayaro, Leboeuf, Desailly, Deschamps (Dalla Bona 88), Poyet (Di Matteo 88), Wise, Ferrer, Flo, Zola. Scorers: Babayaro 45, Flo 67, 86

**07.12.99 v SS Lazio (a)** **Drawn 0-0**
De Goey, Petrescu, Babayaro, Leboeuf, Desailly, Deschamps (Di Matteo 75), Poyet, Wise, Ferrer, Flo, Zola

**29.02.00 v Olympique de Marseille (a)** **Lost 0-1**
De Goey, Petrescu, Leboeuf, Desailly, Deschamps (Di Matteo 62), Poyet, Wise, Ferrer (Morris 81), Flo (Sutton 81), Zola, Harley

**08.03.00 v Olympique de Marseille (h)** **Won 1-0**
De Goey, Babayaro, Leboeuf, Desailly, Deschamps (Di Matteo 79), Poyet, Wise, Ferrer, Flo, Morris, Zola (Harley 79). Scorer: Wise 27

**14.03.00 v Feyenoord (a)** **Won 3-1**
De Goey, Petrescu, Babayaro, Leboeuf, Desailly, Deschamps, Poyet (Morris 77), Wise, Di Matteo, Flo, Zola (Ambrosetti 90). Scorers: Zola 39, Wise 64, Flo 69

**22.03.00 v SS Lazio (h)** **Lost 1-2**
De Goey, Petrescu, Babayaro (Harley 74), Leboeuf (Hogh 62), Desailly, Deschamps, Poyet, Di Matteo (Morris 74), Ferrer, Flo, Zola. Scorer: Poyet 45

**QUARTER FINAL**

**05.04.00 v FC Barcelona (h)** **Won 3-1**
De Goey, Petrescu (Di Matteo 71), Babayaro, Desailly, Deschamps, Wise, Ferrer, Flo (Sutton 87), Morris, Zola, Thome. Scorers: Zola 30, Flo 34, 38

**18.04.00 v FC Barcelona (a)** **Lost 1-5 after extra-time**
De Goey, Babayaro, Leboeuf, Desailly, Deschamps (Petrescu 102), Wise, Di Matteo, Ferrer (Lambourde 46), Flo, Morris, Zola (Poyet 106). Scorer: Flo 60. Sent off: Babayaro 98

| SEASONS | PLAYED | WON | DRAWN | LOST | FOR | AGAINST |
|---|---|---|---|---|---|---|
| 1 | 14 | 7 | 3 | 4 | 22 | 14 |

## CLUB BRUGGE KV (FC BRUGES)

**1992-1993**
**GROUP STAGE 1**
**25.11.92 v CSKA Moscow (h)** **Won 1-0**
Verlinden, Disztl, Van der Elst, Verheyen, Borkelmans, Cossey, Plovie, Verspaille (Creve 78), Staelens, Dziubinski, Amokachi (Querter 89). Scorer: Amokachi 17

**09.12.92 v Olympique de Marseille (a)** **Lost 0-3**
Verlinden, Disztl, Van der Elst, Verheyen, Borkelmans, Van der Heyden, Plovie, Verspaille, Staelens, Dziubinski (Cossey 46), Amokachi

**03.03.93 v Rangers FC (h)** **Drawn 1-1**
Verlinden, Cossey, Van der Elst, Verheyen, Borkelmans, Dziubinski, Creve (Verspaille 79), Querter, Staelens, Booy, Amokachi. Scorer: Dziubinski 44

**17.03.93 v Rangers FC (a)** **Lost 1-2**
Verlinden, Disztl, Van der Elst, Verheyen, Borkelmans, Van der Heyden, Creve, Cossey, Staelens (Dzuibinski 76), Schaessens, Amokachi. Scorer: Staelens 52

**07.04.93 v CSKA Moscow (a)** **Won 2-1**
Verlinden, Cossey, Van der Elst, Verheyen, Borkelmans, Van der Heyden, Creve, Dzuibinski (Booy 46), Staelens, Schaessens, Amokachi (Vanmaele 88). Scorers: Schaessens 44, Verheyen 84

**21.04.93 v Olympique de Marseille (h)** **Lost 0-1**
Verlinden, Disztl, Cossey, Verheyen, Borkelmans, Vanmaele (Renier 86), Creve, Schaessens, Staelens, Dzuibinski, Amokachi

| SEASONS | PLAYED | WON | DRAWN | LOST | FOR | AGAINST |
|---|---|---|---|---|---|---|
| 1 | 6 | 2 | 1 | 3 | 5 | 8 |

## CELTIC FC

**2001-2002**
**GROUP STAGE 1**
**10.10.01* v Rosenborg BK (h) Won 1-0**
Douglas, Balde, Valgaeren, Mjallby, Thompson (Guppy 66), Agathe, Lennon, Lambert, Petrov, Sutton, Larsson. Scorer: Thompson 21
*played 10 October after 11 Sept atrocities

**18.09.01 v Juventus FC (a) Lost 2-3**
Douglas, Balde, Valgaeren, Mjallby, Thompson (Petta 58), Agathe, Lennon, Lambert, Petrov, Sutton, Larsson. Scorers: Petrov 67, Larsson 85pen

**25.09.01 v FC Porto (h) Won 1-0**
Douglas, Balde, Valgaeren, Mjallby, Agathe, Lennon, Lambert, Petrov (McNamara 89), Petta (Thompson 69), Sutton, Larsson. Scorer: Larsson 36

**16.10.01 v FC Porto (a) Lost 0-3**
Douglas, Balde, Valgaeren, Mjallby, Thompson (Moravcik 56), Agathe, Lennon, Lambert, Petrov (Sylla 67), Larsson, Hartson (Maloney 88)

**23.10.01 v Rosenborg BK (a) Lost 0-2**
Douglas, Balde, Valgaeren, Mjallby, Thompson (Hartson 79), Agathe, Lennon, Lambert, Petrov (Moravcik 68), Sutton, Larsson

**31.10.01 v Juventus FC (h) Won 4-3**
Douglas, Balde, Valgaeren, Mjallby, Agathe, Lennon, Lambert, Moravcik (Petrov 65), Petta, Sutton, Larsson. Scorers: Valgaeren 24, Sutton 45, 64, Larsson 57pen

| SEASONS | PLAYED | WON | DRAWN | LOST | FOR | AGAINST |
|---|---|---|---|---|---|---|
| 1 | 6 | 3 | 0 | 3 | 8 | 11 |

## NK CROATIA/DYNAMO ZAGREB

**1998-1999**
**GROUP STAGE 1**
**16.09.98 v AFC Ajax (h) Drawn 0-0**
Ladic, Juric, Tokic, Dario Simic, Rukavina (Saric 57), Prosinecki, Cvitanovic, Jelicic (Sokota 79), Mujcin, Viduka (Mikic 68), Maric

**30.09.98 v Olympiakos Piraeus FC (a) Lost 0-2**
Ladic, Tokic, Juric, Dario Simic, Rukavina, Jurcic, Cvitanovic, Jelicic (Sokota 74), Mujcin (Sabic 46), Viduka (Josip Simic 81), Maric

**21.10.98 v FC Porto (a) Lost 0-3**
Ladic, Tokic, Juric, Dario Simic, Rukavina, Jurcic, Krznar, Jelicic (Mujcin 46), Saric (Sabic 46), Maric (Viduka 58), Sokota

**04.11.98 v FC Porto (h) Won 3-1**
Ladic, Tokic, Juric, Dario Simic, Rukavina, Jelicic, Saric (Cvitanovic 75), Mujcin, Krznar (Biscan 46), Maric (Josip Simic 55), Mikic. Scorers: Mikic 7, Rukavina 37, Mujcin 61

**25.11.98 v AFC Ajax (a) Won 1-0**
Ladic, Tokic, Juric, Dario Simic, Rukavina (Sabic 81), Jelicic, Cvitanovic, Saric (Josip Simic 54), Krznar (Jurcic 46), Maric, Biscan. Scorer: Josip Simic 68

**09.12.98 v Olympiakos Piraeus FC (h) Drawn 1-1**
Ladic, Dario Simic, Juric, Tokic, Saric, Jelicic, Rukavina, Mujcin, Biscan (Josip Simic 69), Maric, Mikic (Abramovic 82). Scorer: Jelicic 35

**1999-2000**
**GROUP STAGE 1**
**14.09.99 v Manchester United FC (a) Drawn 0-0**
Ladic, Tokic, Juric, Mujcin (Mumlek 70), Rukavina (Sokota 89), Saric, Simic (Mikic 67), Cvitanovic, Tomas, Biscan, Jurcic

**22.09.99 v Olympique de Marseille (h) Lost 1-2**
Ladic, Tokic (Mumlek 46), Juric, Mujcin, Rukavina (Jelicic 76), Saric, Simic, Cvitanovic (Sokota 46), Tomas, Biscan, Jurcic. Scorer: Sokota 64

**29.09.99 v SK Sturm Graz (h) Won 3-0**
Ladic, Juric, Mujcin (Prosinecki 66), Rukavina (Tokic 74), Saric, Simic, Cvitanovic, Tomas, Biscan, Jurcic, Sokota (Mikic 79). Scorers: Rukavina 28, Sokota 34, 58 pen

**19.10.99 v SK Sturm Graz (a) Lost 0-1**
Ladic (Butina 12), Juric, Prosinecki, Mujcin, Rukavina, Saric, Simic (Mikic 46), Tomas (Cvitanovic 46), Biscan, Jurcic, Sokota

**27.10.99 v Manchester United FC (h) Lost 1-2**
Butina, Tokic, Sedloski, Juric (Prosinecki 36), Mujcin, Rukavina, Mikic (Simic 54), Saric, Cvitanovic (Mumlek 69), Tomas, Sokota. Scorer: Prosinecki 90

**02.11.99 v Olympique de Marseille (a) Drawn 2-2**
Butina, Tokic, Prosinecki (Jelicic 70), Mujcin (Mumlek 68), Rukavina, Saric, Simic, Cvitanovic, Tomas, Jurcic, Sokota (Mikic 62). Scorers: Mujcin 42, Mikic 84

| SEASONS | PLAYED | WON | DRAWN | LOST | FOR | AGAINST |
|---|---|---|---|---|---|---|
| 2 | 12 | 3 | 4 | 5 | 12 | 14 |

## CSKA MOSCOW

**1992-1993**
**GROUP STAGE 1**
**25.11.92 v Club Brugge KV (a) Lost 0-1**
Kharine (Guteev 46), Goutchine, Kolotovkine, Bystrov, Malioukov, Kolesnikov, Machkarine, Grichine (Karsakov 32), Sergejev, Bushmanov, Faizouline

**09.12.92 v Rangers FC (h) Lost 0-1**
Guteev, Goutchine (Ivanov 66), Kolotovkine, Bystrov, Fokin, Malioukov, Minko (Grichine 59), Karsakov, Sergejev, Bushmanov, Faizouline

**03.03.93 v Olympique de Marseille (h) Drawn 1-1**
Plotnikov, Mamtchour, Kolotovkine, Bystrov, Malioukov, Antonovich, Minko (Karsakov 71), Ivanov (Doudnik 46), Sergejev, Bushmanov, Faizouline. Scorer: Faizouline 55

**17.03.93 v Olympique de Marseille (a) Lost 0-6**
Guteev, Mamtchour, Kolotovkine, Bystrov, Malioukov, Antonovich, Minko, Machkarine (Karsakov 40), Sergejev, Bushmanov (Grichine 46), Faizouline

**07.04.93 v Club Brugge KV (h) Lost 1-2**
Plotnikov, Goutchine, Kolotovkine, Machkarine, Malioukov, Bushmanov, Minko, Karsakov (Mamtchour 71), Ivanov (Antonovich 32), Sergejev, Faizouline. Scorer: Sergejev 19

**21.04.93 v Rangers FC (a) Drawn 0-0**
Plotnikov, Goutchine, Mamtchour, Machkarine, Malioukov, Bushmanov, Minko, Karsakov, Antonovich, Sergejev, Faizouline (Doudnik 62)

| SEASONS | PLAYED | WON | DRAWN | LOST | FOR | AGAINST |
|---|---|---|---|---|---|---|
| 1 | 6 | 0 | 2 | 4 | 2 | 11 |

## RC DEPORTIVO LA CORUNA

**2000-2001**
**GROUP STAGE 1**
**13.09.00 v Panathinaikos FC (a) Drawn 1-1**
Molina, Manuel Pablo, Romero, Naybet, Mauro Silva, Diego Tristan (Cesar Sampaio 86), Fran, Emerson (Valeron 72), Pandiani, Victor (Scaloni 81), Donato. Scorer: Naybet 84

**19.09.00 v Hamburger SV (h) Won 2-1**
Molina, Manuel Pablo, Romero, Naybet, Mauro Silva, Diego Tristan (Turu Flores 66), Fran, Emerson (Valeron 63), Pandiani, Victor (Scaloni 82), Donato. Scorers: Pandiani 44, Scaloni 90

**26.09.00 v Juventus FC (a) Drawn 0-0**
Molina, Manuel Pablo, Romero, Naybet, Mauro Silva, Fran (Fernando 69), Turu Flores (Emerson 57), Scaloni (Victor 80), Cesar Sampaio, Pandiani, Donato

**18.10.00 v Juventus FC (h) Drawn 1-1**
Molina, Manuel Pablo, Romero, Naybet, Djalminha, Turu Flores (Fernando 66), Emerson, Cesar Sampaio, Pandiani (Diego Tristan 76), Victor (Scaloni 87), Donato. Scorer: Victor 12

**24.10.00 v Panathinaikos FC (h) Won 1-0**
Molina, Manuel Pablo, Romero, Naybet, Djalminha (Diego Tristan 82), Turu Flores (Fernando 61), Emerson, Cesar Sampaio, Pandiani, Victor (Scaloni 62), Donato. Scorer: Pandiani 82

**08.11.00 v Hamburger SV (a) Drawn 1-1**
Molina, Manuel Pablo, Cesar, Scaloni, Emerson (Ramis 76), Capdevlia, Pandiani (Makaay 46), Donato (Cesar Sampaio 46), Valeron, Helder, Fernando. Scorer: Makaay 58

**GROUP STAGE 2**
**21.11.00 v Paris Saint-Germain (a) Won 3-1**
Molina, Manuel Pablo, Naybet, Donato (Helder 89), Capdevilla, Victor, Mauro Silva, Emerson, Valeron (Scaloni 61), D Tristan (Makaay 62), Turu Flores. Scorers: Naybet 64, Turu Flores 70, Makaay 90

**06.12.00 v Milan AC (h) Lost 0-1**
Molina, Manuel Pablo, Naybet, Donato, Romero, Victor (Fernando 69), Mauro Silva, Emerson (Scaloni 80), Djalminha, D Tristan, Turu Flores (Makaay 58)

**14.02.01 v Galatasaray SK (a) Lost 0-1**
Molina, Manuel Pablo, Naybet, Donato, Romero, Scaloni (Victor 55), Mauro Silva, Valeron, Djalminha (Pandiani 78), D Tristan (Makaay 59), Pandiani

**20.02.01 v Galatasaray SK (h) Won 2-0**
Songo'o, Manuel Pablo, Naybet, Donato, Romero, Victor (Scaloni 82), Mauro Silva, Valeron, Djalminha (Pandiani 74), Fran (Makaay 61), D Tristan. Scorers: Victor 40, Djalminha 73pen

**07.03.01 v Paris Saint-Germain (h) Won 4-3**
Molina, Manuel Pablo, Naybet, Donato, Romero, Victor (Scaloni 62), Mauro Silva, Emerson (Pandiani 46), Djalminha, Fran (D Tristan 59), Makaay (Scaloni 85). Scorers: Pandiani 57, 76, 84 D Tristan 60

**13.03.01 v Milan AC (a) Drawn 1-1**
Molina, Manuel Pablo, Naybet, Donato, Romero, Victor, Mauro Silva (Helder 23), Emerson, Djalminha, Fran (Capdevilla 64), Makaay (Pandiani 81). Scorer: Djalminha 74pen

**QUARTER FINAL**

**04.04.01 v Leeds United AFC (a) Lost 0-3**
Molina, Manuel Pablo, Naybet, Cesar, Romero, Scaloni (Tristan 71), Duscher (Valeron 54), Emerson, Djalminha, Fran (Pandiani 71), Makaay

**17.04.01 v Leeds United AFC (h) Won 2-0**
Molina, Manuel Pablo, Naybet, Cesar, Romero, Victor (D Tristan 62), Mauro Silva, Djalminha (Valeron 69), Fran, Pandiani (Turi Flores 79), Makaay. Scorers: Djalminha 9, D Tristan 73pen

**2001-2002**

**GROUP STAGE 1**

**10.10.01* v Lille OSC (a) Drawn 1-1**
Molina, Hector, Naybet, Donato, Romero, Victor (Scaloni 71), Duscher, Valeron (Sergio 79), Emerson, Fran (Amavisca 64), Pandiani. Scorer: Valeron 49
* played 10 October after 11 Sept atrocities

**18.09.01 v Olympiakos Piraeus FC (h) Drawn 2-2**
Molina, Manuel Pablo, Naybet, Donato, Romero, Victor (Scaloni 37), Mauro Silva, Sergio (Valeron 84), Fran, Pandiani, D Tristan (Makaay 70). Scorers: Fran 22, Valeron 90

**25.09.01 v Manchester United FC (h) Won 2-1**
Molina, Manuel Pablo, Naybet, Donato, Romero, Makaay (Pandiani 61), Mauro Silva, Sergio, Emerson (Valeron 46), Fran, D Tristan. Scorers: Pandiani 86, Naybet 90

**17.10.01 v Manchester United FC (a) Won 3-2**
Molina (Nuno 46), Hector, Naybet, Donato, Romero (Capdevila 79), Victor, Sergio, Valeron, Duscher, Amavisca, D Tristan (Pandiani 82). Scorers: Sergio 37, D Tristan 39, 60

**23.10.01 v Lille OSC (h) Drawn 1-1**
Nuno, Hector, Naybet, Donato, Capdevila, Victor, Valeron (Djalminha 70), Emerson, (Sergio 60), Duscher, Amavisca, D Tristan (Pandiani 76). Scorer: D Tristan 14pen

**31.10.01 v Olympiakos Piraeus FC (a) Drawn 1-1**
Nuno, Hector (Amavisca 53), Helder, Cesar (Donato 40), Capdevila, Emerson, Mauro Silva (Pandiani 63), Djalminha, Scaloni, Makaay, Jose Manuel. Scorer: Capdevila 84

**GROUP STAGE 2**
**21.11.01 v Arsenal FC (h) Won 2-0**
Molina, Scaloni, Naybet, Donato, Romero, Victor, Valeron (Djalminha 73), Mauro Silva, Emerson, Makaay (Pandiani 49), D Tristan (Amavisca 29). Scorers: Makaay 9, D Tristan 25

**04.12.01 v Bayer 04 Leverkusen (a) Lost 0-3**
Molina, Hector, Naybet, Donato, Romero, Scaloni (Djalminha 71), Valeron (D Tristan 76), Mauro Silva, Emerson, Fran (Amavisca 59), Makaay

**19.02.02 v Juventus FC (a) Drawn 0-0**
Molina, Hector, Naybet, Cesar, Romero, Scaloni, Valeron (Duscher 68), Mauro Silva, Sergio, Amavisca (Capdevila 90), D Tristan (Pandiani 81)

**27.02.02 v Juventus FC (h) Won 2-0**
Molina, Scaloni, Naybet, Cesar (Capdevila 86), Romero, Victor (Duscher 61), Sergio, Mauro Silva, Valeron (Djalminha 70), Fran, D Tristan. Scorers: Tristan 8, Djalminha 77

**12.03.02 v Arsenal (a) Won 2-0**
Molina, Scaloni, Naybet, Cesar, Romero, Victor, Sergio, Mauro Silva, Valeron (Duscher 80), Fran (Capdevila 71), D Tristan (Makaay 85). Scorers: Valeron 30, Naybet 40

**20.03.02 v Bayer 04 Leverkusen (h) Lost 1-3**
Nuno, Hector (Tristan 67), Naybet, Cesar, Capdevila, Amavisca, Djalminha, Mauro Silva, Duscher (Valeron 60), Makaay, Pandiani (Sergio 60). Scorer: Tristan 75

**QUARTER FINAL**
**02.04.02 v Manchester United FC (h) Lost 0-2**
Molina, Scaloni, Naybet, Cesar, Romero, Victor (Duscher 87), Mauro Silva, Sergio, Valeron (Djalminha 68), Fran (Makaay 60), Tristan

**10.04.02 v Manchester United FC (a) Lost 2-3**
Molina, Scaloni, Naybet, Hector, Romero, Victor (Makaay 51), Duscher, Valeron, Djalminha, Fran (Capdevilla 63), Tristan (Pandiani 72). Scorers: Blanc 45og, Djalminha 90. Sent off: Scaloni 59, Duscher 75

**18.09.02 v FC Bayern Munchen (a) Won 3-2**
Juanmi, Hector, Naybet, Donato, Romero, Victor (Acuna 71), Mauro Silva, Valeron, Sergio, Fran (Capdevila 67), Makaay (Luque 86) Scorer: Makaay 12, 45, 77

**24.09.02 v AC Milan (h) Lost 0-4**
Juanmi, Scaloni, Naybet, Cesar, Romero, Victor, Acuna (Duscher 62), Mauro Silva (Donato 79), Sergio, Fran (D Tristan 62), Makaay

**01.10.02 v RC Lens (h) Won 3-1**
Juanmi, Hector (Sergio 46), Naybet, Cesar, Romero, Scaloni, Duscher (Capdevila 70), Mauro Silva, Fran, D Tristan (Luque 76), Makaay. Scorers: Makaay 49, Capdevila 79. Cesar 84

**23.10.02 v RC Lens (a) Lost 1-3**
Juanmi, Hector, Naybet, Donato, Romero, Victor (Scaloni 65), Sergio, Mauro Silva, Fran, Capdevila, Makaay (D Tristan 70) Scorer: Makaay 15

**29.10.02 v FC Bayern Munchen (h) Won 2-1**
Juanmi, Scaloni, Naybet, Cesar, Romero, Victor (D Tristan 84), Mauro Silva, Sergio, Fran (Acuna 66), Capdevila, Makaay (Donato 90). Scorers: Victor 54, Makaay 89

**13.02.02 v AC Milan (a) Won 2-1**
Juanmi, Scaloni, Hector, Romero, Capdevila, Mauro Silva, Sergio, Fran (Acuna 65), D Tristan, Makaay, Luque (Amavisca 56)
Scorers: D Tristan 58, Makaay 70

**26.11.02 v Juventus FC (h) Drawn 2-2**
Juanmi, Scaloni, Hector, Romero, Capdevila, Mauro Silva, Sergio, Duscher, Fran (Amavisca 77), D Tristan (Luque 64), Makaay (Victor 62). Scorers: D Tristan 9, Makaay 11

**11.12.02 v Manchester United FC (a) Lost 0-2**
Juanmi, Scaloni, Cesar, Romero, Capdevila, Victor (Luque 76), Mauro Silva, Sergio, Valeron (Acuna 65), Amavisca (D Tristan 46), Makaay

**19.02.03 v FC Basel (a) Lost 0-1**
Juanmi, Hector, Naybet, J Andrade, Romero, Scaloni, Donato (D Tristan 46), Duscher, Sergio (Acuna 82), Luque (Amavisca 64), Makaay

**25.02.03 v FC Basel (h) Won 1-0**
Juanmi, Hector, Naybet, J Andrade, Romero, Scaloni, Duscher, Sergio, Fran (Amavisca 59), D Tristan (Valeron 69), Makaay (Luque 79)
Scorer: D Tristan 4

**12.03.02 v Juventus FC (a) Lost 2-3**
Juanmi, Hector, Naybet, Cesar (J Andrade 71), Romero, Scaloni, Duscher, Mauro Silva, Fran (Capdevila 46), D Tristan (Valeron 66), Makaay. Scorers: D Tristan 34, Makaay 52

**18.03.02 v Manchester United FC (h) Won 2-0**
Dani Mallo, Manuel Pablo, Cesar, J Andrade (Djorovic 64), Capdevila, Victor (Hector 78), Acuna, Duscher, Fran (Scaloni 52), Valeron, Luque. Scorers: Victor 32, Lynch 47og

| SEASONS | PLAYED | WON | DRAWN | LOST | FOR | AGAINST |
|---|---|---|---|---|---|---|
| 3 | 40 | 17 | 11 | 12 | 55 | 53 |

## FC DYNAMO KYIV

**1994–1995**
**GROUP STAGE 1**
**14.09.94 v FC Spartak Moscow (h) Won 3-2**
Shovkovsky, Luzhny, Vashchuk, Lezhentsev, Shmatovalenko (Khomin 65), Kovalets, Kossovsky, Skatchenko (Rebrov 54), Mikhailenko, Leonenko, Prizetko. Scorers: Leonenko 48, 76, Rebrov 8

**28.09.94 v FC Bayern Munchen (a) Lost 0-1**
Shovkovsky, Luzhny, Vashchuk, Lezhentsev, Shmatovalenko, Kovalets, Mizin, Kosovsky, Mikhailenko, Leonenko (Rebrov 67), Prizetko. Sent off: Mizin 32

**19.10.94 v Paris Saint-Germain (h) Lost 1-2**
Shovkovsky, Luzhny, Vashchuk, Khomin, Shmatovalenko, Kovalets, Lezhentsev, Kosovsky (Prizetko 84), Mikhailenko, Leonenko, Rebrov (Dzhishkariani 70). Scorer: Leonenko 33 pen

**02.11.94 v Paris Saint-Germain (a) Lost 0-1**
Shovkovsky, Luzhny, Vashchuk, Lezhentsev, Shmatovalenko, Kovalets, Kosovsky, Skatchenko, Prizetko, Rebrov (Dzhishkariani 71), Mikhailenko

**23.11.94 v FC Spartak Moscow (a) Lost 0-1**
Shovkovsky, Luzhny, Vashchuk, Khomin, Sharan, Kovalets, Lezhentsev, Rebrov (Skatchenko 56), Mikhailenko (Mizin 64), Leonenko, Shkapenko. Sent off: Vashchuk 86

**07.12.94 v FC Bayern Munchen (h) Lost 1-4**
Shovkovsky, Luzhny, Lezhentsev, Khomin, Mikhailenko, Kovalets, Kosovsky (Prizetko 68), Skatchenko, Shevchenko, Leonenko (Mizin 61), Shkapenko. Scorer: Shevchenko 37

**1995–1996**
**GROUP STAGE 1**
**13.09.95 v Panathinaikos FC (h) Won 1-0**
Shovkovsky, Luzhny (Shmatovalenko 71), Holovko, Bezhenar, Dmitrulin, Kalitvintsev, Kossovsky, Maksimov (Mizin 84), Pokhlebaev, Shevchenko, Rebrov. Scorer: Kosovskii 61
*FC Dynamo disqualified and suspended for earlier financial irregularities*

**1997-1998**
**GROUP STAGE 1**
**17.09.97 v PSV Eindhoven (a) Won 3-1**
Shovkovsky, Vashtchuk, Kossovsky, Holovko, Khatskevitch (Belkevitch 56), Dmitrulin, Kalitvintsev, Maksimov (Mikhailenko 77), Husin (Bezhenar 72), Shevchenko, Rebrov. Scorers: Maksimov 33, Rebrov 47, Shevchenko 90

**01.10.97 v Newcastle United FC (h) Drawn 2-2**
Shovkovsky, Luzhny (Bezhenar 42), Vashtchuk, Dmitrulin, Belkevitch (Mikhailenko 68), Khatskevitch (Radchenko 74), Holovko, Husin, Kossovsky, Shevchenko, Rebrov. Scorers: Rebrov 4, Shevchenko 28

**22.10.97 v FC Barcelona (h) Won 3-0**
Shovkovsky, Luzhny (Volosianko 62), Vashtchuk, Holovko, Dmitrulin, Maksimov (Mikhailenko 83), Kalitvintsev, Husin, Kossovsky, Shevchenko, Rebrov. Scorers: Rebrov 6, Maksimov 32, Kalitvintsev 65

**05.11.97 v FC Barcelona (a) Won 4-0**
Shovkovsky, Luzhny (Volosianko 59), Vashtchuk, Holovko, Dmitrulin, Khatskevitch, Kalitvintsev (Maksimov 46), Husin (Mikhailenko 60), Kossovsky, Shevchenko, Rebrov. Scorers: Shevchenko 9, 32, 44 pen, Rebrov 79

**27.11.97 v PSV Eindhoven (h) Drawn 1-1**
Shovkovsky, Luzhny (Volosianko 87), Vashtchuk, Dmitrulin, Khatskevitch, Kalitvintsev, Holovko, Kossovsky, Maksimov (Bezhenar 83), Shevchenko, Rebrov. Scorer: Rebrov 19

**10.12.97 v Newcastle United FC (a) Lost 0-2**
Shovkovsky, Luzhny, Bezhenar, Dmitrulin, Mikhailenko (Radchenko 79), Volosianko (Venglinski 79), Kalitvintsev, Husin, Kossovsky, Shevchenko, Rebrov

**QUARTER FINAL**
**04.03.98 v Juventus FC (a) Drawn 1-1**
Shovkovsky, Luzhny (Volosianko 46), Bezhenar, Holovko, Dmitrulin (Radchenko 68), Husin, Kossovsky, Gerassimenko (Mikhailenko 68), Kalitvintsev, Shevchenko, Rebrov. Scorer: Husin 56

**18.03.98 v Juventus FC (h) Lost 1-4**
Shovkovsky, Dmitrulin, Bezhenar, Holovko, Kossovsky, Khatskevitch (Radchenko 63), Husin, Gerasimenko, Kalitvintsev (Kardash 38), Shevchenko, Rebrov. Scorer: Rebrov 54

**1998-1999**

**GROUP STAGE 1**

**16.09.98 v Panathinaikos FC (a) Lost 1-2**

Shovkovsky, Luzhny, Vaschuk, Dmitrulin, Gerassimenko (Kalitvintsev 77), Holovko, Husin, Kaladze, Bialkevich (Konovalov 74), Rebrov, Shevchenko. Scorer: Rebrov 31

**30.09.98 v RC Lens (h) Drawn 1-1**

Shovkovsky, Luzhny, Vaschuk, Holovko, Dmitrulin (Kiriukhin 84), Husin, Kaladze, Kossovsky, Shevchenko, Rebrov, Gerassimenko (Kalitvintsev 78). Scorer: Shevchenko 61

**21.10.98 v Arsenal FC (a) Drawn 1-1**

Shovkovsky, Luzhny, Dmitrulin, Holovko, Vaschuk, Kossovsky, Bialkevich, Husin (Kardash 82), Kaladze, Shevchenko, Rebrov. Scorer: Rebrov 90

**04.11.98 v Arsenal FC (h) Won 3-1**

Shovkovsky, Luzhny, Dmitrulin, Holovko, Vaschuk, Kossovsky, Bialkevich (Kalitvinstev 90), Kardash, Husin, Shevchenko, Rebrov. Scorers: Rebrov 27 pen, Holovko 62, Shevchenko 72

**26.11.98 v Panathinaikos FC (h) Won 2-1**

Shovkovsky, Luzhny, Holovko, Federov, Dmitrulin, Kardash (Mykhailenko 88), Husin, Khatskevitch, Kossovsky (Bialkevich 46), Shevchenko, Rebrov. Scorers: Rebrov 72, Basinas og 80

**09.12.98 v RC Lens (a) Won 3-1**

Shovkovsky, Luzhny, Vaschuk, Holovko, Dmitrulin (Kossovsky 46), Husin, Kaladze (Kiriukhin 67), Khatskevitch, Kardash (Bialkevich 51), Shevchenko, Rebrov. Scorers: Kaladze 60, Vaschuk 75, Shevchenko 85

**QUARTER FINAL**

**03.03.99 v Real Madrid CF (a) . Drawn 1-1**

Shovkovsky, Luzhny (Kiriukhin 89), Holovko, Vaschuk, Kaladze, Bialkevich (Kardash 81), Husin, Khatskevitch, Kossovsky (Kormiltsev 84), Shevchenko, Rebrov. Scorer: Shevchenko 55

**17.03.99 v Real Madrid CF (h) Won 2-0**

Shovkovsky, Luzhny, Holovko, Vaschuk, Kaladze, Kardash (Bialkevich 46), Husin, Khatskevitch, Kossovsky (Yashkin 87), Shevchenko, Rebrov. Scorer: Shevchenko 63, 79

**SEMI FINAL**

**07.04.99 v FC Bayern Munchen (h) Drawn 3-3**

Shovkovsky, Luzhny, Holovko, Vaschuk, Kaladze, Bialkevich, Husin, Khatskevitch (Kiriukhin 81), Kossovsky, Shevchenko, Rebrov. Scorers: Shevchenko 16, 43, Kossovsky 50

**21.04.99 v FC Bayern Munchen (a) Lost 0-1**
Shovkovsky, Luzhny, Holovko, Vaschuk, Kaladze, Bialkevich, Husin (Kardash 82), Khatskevitch, Kossovsky, Shevchenko, Rebrov

**1999-2000**
**GROUP STAGE 1**
**14.09.99 v NK Maribor (h) Lost 0-1**
Shovkovsky, Gerassimenko (Konovalov 70), Holovko, Vaschuk, Dmitrulin, Kaladze, Kossovsky, Rebrov, Husin, Shatskikh (Venhlinsky 66), Kormiltsev (Fedorov 60)

**22.09.99 v SS Lazio (a) Lost 1-2**
Shovkovsky, Gerassimenko (Kossovsky 46), Holovko, Vaschuk, Dmitrulin, Kaladze, Rebrov, Husin, Shatskikh (Venhlinsky 83), Fedorov, Kormiltsev (Konovalov 46). Scorer: Rebrov 68 pen

**29.09.99 v Bayer 04 Leverkusen (a) Drawn 1-1**
Shovkovsky, Holovko, Vaschuk, Dmitrulin (Kormiltsev 74), Kaladze, Kossovsky, Rebrov, Husin, Shatskikh, Konovalov (Gerassimenko 59), Mamedov (Fedorov 81). Scorer: Husin 71

**19.10.99 v Bayer 04 Leverkusen (h) Won 4-2**
Shovkovsky, Gerassimenko (Bialkevich 46), Holovko, Vaschuk, Dmitrulin (Iachkin 59), Kaladze, Kossovsky, Rebrov, Husin, Shatskikh, Mamedov. Scorers: Kossovsky 4, Shatskikh 36, Holovko 61, Vaschuk 89

**27.10.99 v NK Maribor (a) Won 2-1**
Shovkovsky, Holovko, Vaschuk, Dmitrulin, Kaladze, Kossovsky, Rebrov, Husin, Iachkin (Bialkevich 6), Shatskikh, Mamedov. Scorer: Rebrov 37, 84 pen

**02.11.99 v SS Lazio (h) Lost 0-1**
Shovkovsky, Holovko, Vaschuk, Dmitrulin, Kaladze, Bialkevich, Kossovsky, Rebrov, Husin, Fedorov (Shatskikh 46), Mamedov

**GROUP STAGE 2**
**24.11.99 v Real Madrid CF (h) Lost 1-2**
Shovkovsky, Khatskevitch, Holovko, Vaschuk, Dmitrulin, Bialkevich, Rebrov, Husin, Iachkin, Konovalov (Shatskikh 46), Mamedov. Scorer: Rebrov 86 pen

**07.12.99 v FC Bayern Munchen (a) Lost 1-2**
Shovkovsky, Khatskevitch (Gerassimenko 48), Holovko, Vaschuk, Dmitrulin, Kaladze, Bialkevich, Rebrov, Husin, Iachkin, Kardash (Venhlinsky 46). Scorer: Rebrov 50

**29.02.00 v Rosenborg BK (h) Won 2-1**
Shovkovsky, Khatskevitch, Gerassimenko, Holovko, Kaladze, Bialkevich, Rebrov, Husin, Mamedov (Fedrorov 86), Nesmachny, Demetradze (Shatskikh 87). Scorers: Khatskevitch 9, Rebrov 29

**08.03.00 v Rosenborg BK (a) Won 2-1**
Shovkovsky, Khatskevitch, Gerassimenko, Kaladze, Bialkevich, Rebrov, Husin, Shatskikh (Demetradze 46), Fedrorov, Mamedov, Nesmachny (Kormiltsev 67). Scorer: Rebrov 32, 67

**14.03.00 v Real Madrid CF (a) Drawn 2-2**
Shovkovsky, Khatskevitch, Gerassimenko, Holovko, Bialkevich, Rebrov (Kostyuk 78), Husin, Shatskikh (Karsdash 46), Mamedov, Nesmachny, Demetradze. Scorers: Khatskevitch 42, Hierro og 56

**22.03.00 v FC Bayern Munchen (h) Won 2-0**
Shovkovsky, Khatskevitch (Kardash 85), Gerassimenko, Holovko, Kaladze, Bialkevich, Rebrov (Shatskikh 85), Husin, Mamedov, Nesmachny (Yashkin 36), Demetradze. Scorers: Kaladze 34, Demetradze 72

**2000-2001**
**GROUP STAGE 1**
**13.09.00 v PSV Eindhoven (a) Lost 1-2**
Shovkovsky, Khatskevitch (Kuzmichev 74), Holovko, Vaschuk, Dmitrulin, Kaladze, Bialkevich, Shatskikh (Serebrennikov 74), Demetradze, Husin (Moroz 82, Nesmachny. Scorer: Shatskikh 6

**19.09.00 v Manchester United FC (h) Drawn 0-0**
Shovkovsky, Khatskevitch, Holovko, Vaschuk, Dmitrulin (Bodnar 83), Kaladze, Bialkevich, Shatskikh, Demetradze (Kuzmichev 68), Husin (Fedorov 87), Nesmachny

**26.09.00 v RSC Anderlecht (h) Won 4-0**
Shovkovsky, Holovko, Vaschuk, Dmitrulin, Kaladze (Kuzmichev 66), Bialkevich, Shatskikh, Demetradze, Husin, Fedorov (Bodnar 46), Nesmachny. Scorers: Husin 52, Shatskikh 82, Demetradze 89, 90

**18.10.00 v RSC Anderlecht (a) Lost 2-4**
Shovkovsky, Khatskevitch, Holovko, Vaschuk (Gerasimenko 56), Kaladze, Bialkevich, Demetradze (Serebrennikov 77), Husin, Yashkin (Kuzmichev 51), Bodnar, Nesmachny. Scorers: Kaladze 1, Bialkevich 87

**24.10.00 v PSV Eindhoven (h) Lost 0-1**
Shovkovsky, Khatskevitch, Holovko, Vaschuk (Fedorov 19), Dmitrulin, Kaladze (Kuzmichev 54), Bialkevich, Shatskikh, Demetradze (Yashkin 74), Husin, Nesmachny

**08.11.00 v Manchester United FC (a) Lost 0-1**
Shovkovsky, Khatskevitch, Gerasimenko (Kuzmichev 62), Holovko (Fedorov 76), Vaschuk, Kaladze, Bialkevich, Shatskikh (Demetradze 67), Bodnar, Nesmachny, Lysytskyy

**2001-2002**
**GROUP STAGE 1**
**11.09.01 v BV Borussia Dortmund (h) Drawn 1-1**
Filimonov, Nesmachnyi, Holovko (Federov 24), Vaschuk, Ghioane, Gavrancic, Khatskevich (Bodnar 64), Bialkevich, Serebrennikov (Cernat 46), Melaschenko, Idahor. Scorer: Melaschenko 15

**19.09.01 v Boavista FC (a) Lost 1-3**
Filimonov, Federov, Holovko, Vaschuk, Nesmachnyi, Gavrancic, Khatskevich (Idahor 57), Bialkevich, Cernat, Ghioane, Melaschenko. Scorer: Ghioane 5

**26.09.01 v Liverpool FC (a) Lost 0-1**
Filimonov, Federov, Holovko, Vaschuk, Nesmachnyi, Gavrancic, Idahor, Bialkevich (Serebrennikov 81), Cernat (Peev 69), Ghioane, Melaschenko

**16.10.01 v Liverpool FC (h) Lost 1-2**
Rewa, Gavrancic, Holovko, Vaschuk, Nesmachnyi, Ghioane, Katskevich, Bialkevich, Bodnar (Husin 59), Cernat, Melaschenko (Idahor 79). Scorer: Ghioane 59

**24.10.01 v BV Borussia Dortmund (a) Lost 0-1**
Rewa, Gavrancic (Bodnar 62), Federov, Vaschuk, Nesmachnyi, Ghioane, Katskevich, Bialkevich, Husin, Idahor (Cernet 53), Melaschenko

**30.10.01 v Boavista FC (h) Won 1-0**
Rewa, Federov (Gavrancic 60), Vaschuk, Nesmachnyi, Ghioane, Peev (Cernat 76), Katskevich, Bialkevich, Husin, Shatskikh (Serebrennikov 90), Melaschenko. Scorer: Melaschenko 49

**2002-2003**
**GROUP STAGE 1**
**18.09.02 v Newcastle United FC (h) Won 2-0**
Reva, Sablic, Nesmachnyi, Ghioane, Peev, Cernat, Khatskevich (Gavrancic 75), Husin, Leko, Shatskikh, Leandro (Melaschenko 56). Scorers: Shatskikh 17, Khatskevich 62

**24.09.02 v Juventus FC (a) Lost 0-5**
Reva, Sablic, Nesmachnyi, Ghioane, Peev, Cernat, Khatskevich (Melaschenko 71), Gavrancic, Husin, Leko, Shatskikh

**01.10.02 v Feyenoord (a) Drawn 0-0**
Reva, Bodnar, Nesmachnyi, Ghioane, Peev, Cernat (Rincon 84), Khatskevich (Leko 63), Gavrancic, Husin, Shatskikh, Melaschenko

**23.10.02 v Feyenoord (h) Won 2-0**
Reva, Dmytrullin (Sablic 77), Ghioane, Gavrancic, Peev, Khatskevich, Belkevich, Husin, Rincon (Nesmachnyi 57), El Kaddouri, Shatskikh. Scorers: Khatskevich 16, Belkevich 47

**29.10.02 v Newcastle United FC (a) Lost 1-2**
Reva, Dmytrullin, Ghioane, Gavrancic, Peev, Belkevich, Husin, Nesmachnyi, Leko (Rincon 71), El Kaddouri (Cernat 77), Shatskikh. Scorer: Shatskikh 47

**13.11.02 v Juventus FC (h) Lost 1-2**
Reva, Dmytrullin, Ghioane, Gavrancic, Bodnar, Khatskevich (Leko 59), Belkevich, Husin, Rincon (Cernat 67), Nesmachnyi, El Kaddouri, Shatskikh. Scorer: Shatskikh 50

| SEASONS | PLAYED | WON | DRAWN | LOST | FOR | AGAINST |
|---|---|---|---|---|---|---|
| 7 | 54 | 17 | 12 | 25 | 73 | 76 |

## FENERBAHCE SK

**1996-1997**
**GROUP STAGE 1**
**11.09.96 v SK Rapid Wien (a) Drawn 1-1**
Rustu, Ilker, Uche Okechukwu, Hogh, Halil Ibrahim, Bulent Uygun, Okocha, Kemalettin, Tayfun, Bolic, Tarik (Tuncay 79). Scorer: Bolic 30

**25.09.96 v Juventus FC (h) Lost 0-1**
Rustu, Ilker, Uche Okechukwu, Hogh, Halil Ibrahim, Bulent Uygun, Okocha, Kemalettin, Tuncay (Erol 81), Bolic, Tarik (Benhur 88)

**16.10.96 v Manchester United FC (h) Lost 0-2**
Rustu, Ilker, Uche Okechukwu, Hogh, Halil Ibrahim, Bulent Uygun (Erol 65), Okocha, Kemalettin, Tuncay (Tarik 84), Bolic, Kostadinov (Aygun 84)

**30.10.96 v Manchester United FC (a) Won 1-0**
Rustu, Ilker, Saffet, Uche Okechukwu, Erol, Tuncay (Mustafa Dogan 72), Kemalettin, Hogh (Bulent Uygun 79), Kostadinov, Okocha, Bolic (Tarik 82). Scorer: Bolic 78

**20.11.96 v SK Rapid Wien (h) Won 1-0**
Rustu Recber, Ilker Yagcioglu, Uche Okechukwu, Saffet Akbas, Erol Bulut, Hogh, Kemalettin Senturk, Tuncay Akgun (Mustafa Dogan 52), Bolic, Okocha, Kostadinov (Tarik Dasgun 90). Scorer: Hogh 76

**04.12.96 v Juventus FC (a) Lost 0-2**
Rustu, Ilker (Mustafa Dogan 84), Uche Okechukwu, Saffet, Erol Bulut, Hogh (Aygun 87), Kemalettin, Okocha, Tuncay (Tarik 72), Bolic, Kostadinov

**2001-2002**
**GROUP STAGE 1**
**10.10.01* v Bayer 04 Leverkusen (a) Lost 1-2**
Rustu, Mirkovic, Johnson, Ogun (Serhat 79), Umit Ozat, Meric, Lazetic (Ali Gunes 79), Aki Akdeniz, Abdullah, Revivo (Hakan Bayraktar 64), Rapajic. Scorer: Revivo 6. Sent off: Johnson 37
*played 10 October after 11 Sept atrocities

**18.09.01 v FC Barcelona (h) Lost 0-3**
Rustu, Mirkovic, Johnson, Ogun (Meric 75), Umit Ozat, Mustafa Dogon, Lazetic (Ali Gunes 79), Abdullah, Revivo, Rapajic (Ceyhun 70), Serhat (Oktay 56)

**25.09.01 v Olympique Lyonnais (h) Lost 0-1**
Rustu, Mirkovic, Johnson, Ogun, Meric, Lazetic (Ceyhun 82), Mustafa Dogon, Ali Gunes (Serhat 73), Abdullah, Revivo, Rapajic (K Andersson 46)

**17.10.01 v Olympique Lyonnais (a) Lost 1-3**
Rustu, Umit Ozat, Mustafa Dogon (Deniz 24), Meric, Lazetic (Ali Gunes 73), Ali Akdeniz, Yusuf, Abdullah, Revivo (Rapajic 73), Oktay. Scorer: Oktay 35

**23.10.01 v Bayer 04 Leverkusen (h) Lost 1-2**
Rustu, Mustafa Dogon, Johnson, Meric, Deniz, Lazetic (Hakan Bayraktar 65), Ali Akdeniz (Rapajic 77), Yusuf (Ogun 52), Ali Gunes, Revivo, Oktay. Scorer: Oktay 40

**31.10.01 v FC Barcelona (a) Lost 0-1**
Rustu, Mustafa Dogon, Johnson, Umit Ozat, Meric, Lazetic, Ali Akdeniz, Ali Gunes (Ceyhun 89), Abdullah (Hakan Bayraktar 77), Rapajic (Yusuf 79), Serhat

| SEASONS | PLAYED | WON | DRAWN | LOST | FOR | AGAINST |
|---|---|---|---|---|---|---|
| 2 | 12 | 2 | 1 | 9 | 6 | 18 |

## FERENCVAROSI TC

**1995-1996**
**GROUP STAGE 1**
**13.09.95 v Grasshopper-Club (a) Won 3-0**
Hajdu, Simon, Telek, Szucs, Milovanovics, Vincze, Nyilas, Lisztes, Zavadszky (Nagy 77), Kopunovics, Fatusi. Scorers: Lisztes 61, Vincze 81, 90

**27.09.95 v AFC Ajax (h) Lost 1-5**
Hajdu, Simon, Telek, Kouznetsov (Keller 79), Kecskes, Vincze, Nyilas, Lisztes, Zavadszky, Kuntics, Kopunovics. Scorer: Nyilas 59 pen

**18.10.95 v Real Madrid CF (a) Lost 1-6**
Hajdu, Telek, Keller, Szucs, Milovanovics (Hrutka 56), Vincze (Albert 46), Nyilas, Kecskes, Lisztes, Kuntics (Nagy 68), Kopunovics. Scorer: Kopunovics 63

**01.11.95 v Real Madrid CF (h) Drawn 1-1**
Hajdu, Hrutka, Telek, Kouznetsov, Paling, Keller, Albert (Nagy 46), Nyilas, Lisztes, Kuntics (Vincze 90), Kopunovics (Zavadszky 79). Scorer: Albert 36

**22.11.95 v Grasshopper-Club (h) Drawn 3-3**
Hajdu, Hrutka, Keller, Kouznetsov, Szucs, Kecskes (Vinncze 65), Albert (Nagy 65), Nyilas, Lisztes, Kuntics, Kopunovics (Zavadszky 83). Scorers: Albert 20, Lisztes 24, Nyilas 85 pen

**06.12.95 v AFC Ajax (a) Lost 0-4**
Hajdu, Hrutka, Kouznetsov, Szucs, Keller, Paling (Nagy 90), Albert, Nyilas, Lisztes, Kuntics (Kopunovics 66), Vincze

| SEASONS | PLAYED | WON | DRAWN | LOST | FOR | AGAINST |
|---|---|---|---|---|---|---|
| 1 | 6 | 1 | 2 | 3 | 9 | 19 |

## FEYENOORD

**1997-1998**
**GROUP STAGE 1**
**17.09.97 v Juventus FC (a) Lost 1-5**
Dudek, Van Gobbel, Fraser, Picun (Connolly 70), Graff, Bosvelt, Korneev (Boateng 46), Van Gastel, Van Bronckhorst, Cruz, Sanchez. Scorer: Van Gastel 58 pen

**01.10.97 v 1 FC Kosice (h) Won 2-0**
Dudek, Van Gobbel (Boateng 61), Fraser, Van Gastel, Picun, Graff, Bosvelt (Connolly 89), Sanchez (Van Wonderen 80), Korneev, Van Bronckhorst, Cruz. Scorers: Van Gastel 26 pen, Cruz 35

**22.10.97 v Manchester United FC (a) Lost 1-2**
Dudek, Picun, Van Gobbel, Van Wonderen, Van Gastel, Schuiteman, Graff, Bosvelt, Connolly (Vos 73), Sanchez (Boateng 76), Van Bronckhorst (Korneev 38). Scorer: Vos 83

**05.11.97 v Manchester United FC (h) Lost 1-3**
Dudek, Van Gobbel, Van Gastel, Graff (Claeys 27), Van Wonderen, Boateng, Schuiteman, Korneev, Bosvelt (Zwijnenberg 83), Van Bronckhorst, Cruz (Vos 77). Scorer: Korneev 88

**27.11.97 v Juventus FC (h) Won 2-0**
Dudek, Zwijnenberg, Van Gobbel, Van Wonderen, Claeys, Boateng, Van Gastel, Sanchez (Bosvelt 66), Van Bronckhorst, Cruz, Vos. Scorer: Cruz 67, 88

**10.12.97 v 1 FC Kosice (a) Won 1-0**
Dudek, Zwijnenberg, Van Gobbel, Van Wonderen, Boateng, Bosvelt, Van Gastel, Van Bronckhorst, Sanchez (Korneev 69), Connolly (Nelisse 46, Schuiteman 87), Vos. Scorer: Van Bronckhorst 81

**1999-2000**
**GROUP STAGE 1**
**14.09.99 v BV Borussia Dortmund (h) Drawn 1-1**
Dudek, Rzasa (De Visser 46), Van Gastel, Bosvelt, Kalou, Van Wonderen, Cruz, Tomasson, Van Vossen (Samardzic 82), Konterman, Paauwe. Scorer: Van Wonderen 67

**22.09.99 v Rosenborg BK (a) Drawn 2-2**
Dudek, Van Gastel, Bosvelt, Kalou, Van Wonderen, Cruz, Tomasson, Konterman, Paauwe, De Visser, Van Gobbel. Scorers: Tomasson 12, Kalou 22

**29.09.99 v Boavista FC (a) Drawn 1-1**
Dudek, Van Gastel, Bosvelt, Kalou, Van Wonderen, Cruz (Van Vossen 58), Tomasson, Konterman, Paauwe, De Visser, Van Gobbel. Scorer: Bosvelt 62

**19.10.99 v Boavista FC (h) Drawn 1-1**
Dudek, Van Gastel, Bosvelt, Kalou, Cruz, Tomasson, Van Vossen (Samardzic 46), Konterman, Paauwe (Somalia 70), De Visser, Van Gobbel. Scorer: Tomasson 76

**27.10.99 v BV Borussia Dortmund (a) Drawn 1-1**
Dudek, Rzasa, Bosvelt, Kalou, Tomasson, Konterman, Paauwe (Van Vossen 58), De Visser, De Haan, Van Gobbel (Korneev 78), Somalia (Cairo 58). Scorer: Van Vossen 72

**02.11.99 v Rosenborg BK (h) Won 1-0**
Dudek, Rzasa, Kalou, Van Wonderen (Paauwe 72), Tomasson, Samardzic (Van Vossen 89), Konterman, Korneev (Somalia 75), De Visser, De Haan, Van Gobbel. Scorer: Somalia 86

**GROUP STAGE 2**
**24.11.99 v Chelsea FC (a) Lost 1-3**
Dudek, Van Gastel, Bosvelt, Kalou, Van Wonderen, Tomasson (Cruz 58), Van Vossen (Samardzic 60), Konterman, De Visser, Van Gobbel, Somalia. Scorer: Cruz 90

**07.12.99 v Olympique de Marseille (h) Won 3-0**
Dudek, Gyan, Rzasa, Van Gastel, Bosvelt, Kalou, Van Wonderen, Cruz, Van Vossen (De Visser 37), Konterman, Paauwe. Scorers: Cruz 72, 90, Bosvelt 83. Sent off: Van Wonderen 7

**29.02.00 v SS Lazio (a) Won 2-1**
Dudek, Rzasa, Van Gastel (Gyan 82), Bosvelt, Kalou (Tomasson 46), Cruz, Konterman, Paauwe, De Visser (Samardzic 75), De Haan, Van Gobbel. Scorer: Tomasson 78, 84

**08.03.00 v SS Lazio (h) Drawn 0-0**
Dudek, Rzasa, Van Gastel, Bosvelt, Van Wonderen, Cruz, Tomasson, Konterman, Paauwe (Kalou 66), De Visser, Van Gobbel

**14.03.00 v Chelsea FC (h) Lost 1-3**
Dudek, Rzasa, Van Gastel, Bosvelt, Van Wonderen, Cruz, Tomasson, Konterman, Paauwe (Kalou 46), De Visser (Samardzic 69), Van Gobbel. Scorer: Kalou 59

**22.03.00 v Olympique de Marseille (a) Drawn 0-0**
Dudek, Rzasa, Van Gastel (Somalia 75), Bosvelt, Kalou, Van Wonderen, Cruz, Tomasson, Konterman, De Visser (Van Vossen 65), Van Gobbel (Korneev 80)

**2001-2002**
**GROUP STAGE 1**
**10.10.01 v FC Bayern Munchen (h) Drawn 2-2**
Zoetebier, Collen, Van Wonderen, De Haan, Rzasa (Van Haaren 65), Emerton, Bosvelt, Paauwe, Kalou (Ono 77), Tomasson, Van Hoojdonk. Scorers: Van Hoojdonk 38, Tomasson 45

**18.09.01 v FC Spartak Moscow (a) Drawn 2-2**
Zoetebier, Van Gobbel, De Haan, Rzasa, Emerton, Bosvelt, Paauwe, Van Gastel (De Visser 67), Kalou (Collen 71), Tomasson, Van Hoojdonk. Scorers: Bosvelt 12, Tomasson 59

**25.09.01 v AC Sparta Praha (a) Lost 0-4**
Zoetebier, Van Gobbel, De Haan, Rzasa, Emerton, Bosvelt, Paauwe, Van Gastel (Leonardo 80), Kalou, Tomasson, Van Hoojdonk. Sent off: Van Gobbel 37

**17.10.01 v AC Sparta Praha (h) Lost 0-2**
Timmer, Collen (L Dos Santos 62), Van Wonderen, De Haan, Rzasa, Emerton, Bosvelt, Paauwe, Leonardo (Kalou 46), Ono, Van Hoojdonk. Sent off: Van Hoojdonk 67, De Haan 74

**23.10.01 v FC Bayern Munchen (a) Lost 1-3**
Zoetebier, Collen, Van Gobbel (Gyan 46), Van Wonderen, Rzasa, Emerton, Bosvelt, Paauwe, Van Gastel (Smolarek 80), Elmander, Ono. Scorer: Elmander 25

**31.10.01 v FC Spartak Moscow (h) Won 2-1**
Zoetebier, Collen (Van Gastel 64), Gyan, De Haan, Rzasa, Emerton, Bosvelt, Paauwe, Ono, Elmander (Smolarek 88), Tomasson. Scorers: Tomasson 5, Elmander 18

**18.09.02 v Juventus FC (h) Drawn 1-1**
Zoetebier, Gyan (Bombarada 70), Pauwe, Van Wonderen, Van Haaren, Song, Emerton, Ono, Pardo (Kalou 55), Buffel, Van Hooijdonk. Scorer: Van Hooijdonck 75

**24.09.02 v Newcastle United FC (a) Won 1-0**
Zoetebier, Emerton, Pauwe, Van Wonderen, Rzasa, Song, Bosvelt, Ono, Pardo (Lurling 82), Buffel, Van Hooijdonk. Scorer: Pardo 4

**01.10.02 v FC Dynamo Kyiv (h) Drawn 0-0**
Zoetebier, Emerton, Pauwe, De Haan, Rzasa, Song, Bosvelt, Ono, Pardo (Van Persie 55), Buffel (Kalou 66), Van Hooijdonk

**23.10.02 v FC Dynamo Kyiv (a) Lost 0-2**
Zoetebier, Emerton (Bombarda 62), Pauwe, Loovens, Van Haaren (Rzasa 56), Song, Van Wonderen, Ono, Van Persie (Lurling 39), Buffel, Kalou

**29.10.02 v Juventus FC (a) Lost 0-2**
Zoetebier (Lodewijks 46), Emerton, Pauwe, Van Wonderen, Rzasa, Song, Bosvelt, Ono, Lurling, Buffel, Bombarda

**13.11.02 v Newcastle United FC (h) Lost 2-3**
Lodewijks, Gyan, Pauwe, Van Wonderen, Rzasa, Song (Bombarda 52), Bosvelt, Emerton, Lurling, Buffel, Kalou. Scorers: Bombarda 65, Lurling 71

| SEASONS | PLAYED | WON | DRAWN | LOST | FOR | AGAINST |
|---|---|---|---|---|---|---|
| 4 | 30 | 8 | 11 | 10 | 33 | 45 |

## AC FIORENTINA

**1999-2000**
**GROUP STAGE 1**
**14.09.99 v Arsenal FC (h) Drawn 0-0**
Toldo, Repka, Padalino, Mijatovic, Batistuta, Rui Costa, Cois, Di Livio, Heinrich, Chiesa, Pierini (Adani 84)

**22.09.99 v FC Barcelona (a) Lost 2-4**
Toldo, Repka, Adani, Padalino, Mijatovic (Balbo 86), Batistuta (Amor 77), Rui Costa, Cois, Di Livio, Heinrich, Amoruso (Chiesa 56). Scorers: Batistuta 50, Chiesa 79

**29.09.99 v AIK Solna (a) Drawn 0-0**
Toldo, Repka, Padalino, Mijatovic (Balbo 72), Batistuta, Rui Costa, Cois (Rossitto 90), Di Livio (Bressan 61), Heinrich, Chiesa, Pierini

**19.10.99 v AIK Solna (h) Won 3-0**
Toldo, Repka, Firicano, Mijatovic (Amoruso 53), Batistuta, Rui Costa, Cois (Okon 71), Di Livio, Heinrich, Chiesa (Balbo 82), Pierini. Scorers: Batistuta 5, Chiesa 32, Balbo 86

**27.10.99 v Arsenal FC (a) Won 1-0**
Toldo, Repka, Firicano, Batistuta, Rui Costa, Rossitto, Cois (Adani 46), Di Livio, Heinrich, Chiesa, Pierini. Scorer: Batistuta 75

**02.11.99 v FC Barcelona (h) Drawn 3-3**
Toldo, Adani, Firicano, Rui Costa, Rossitto (Amor 90), Di Livio, Heinrich, Balbo, Chiesa (Okon 34), Bressan, Pierini. Scorers: Bressan 14, Balbo 56, 69

**GROUP STAGE 2**

**23.11.99 v Manchester United FC (h) Won 2-0**
Toldo, Repka, Torricelli, Firicano, Batistuta, Rui Costa, Cois, Di Livio (Rossitto 67), Heinrich, Balbo (Brassan 79), Pierini (Adani 79). Scorers: Batistuta 24, Balbo 52

**08.12.99 v Girondins de Bordeaux (a) Drawn 0-0**
Toldo, Repka, Torricelli, Firicano, Rui Costa, Di Livio, Heinrich, Balbo, Chiesa (Bressan 70), Pierini, Amoroso (Rossitto 70)

**01.03.00 v Valencia CF (h) Won 1-0**
Toldo, Repka, Torricelli, Adani, Mijatovic, Batistuta, Rui Costa, Cois (Amoroso 83), Di Livio (Rossitto 73), Heinrich, Pierini (Tarozzi 80). Scorer: Mijatovic 20 pen

**07.03.00 v Valencia CF (a) Lost 0-2**
Taglialatela, Repka, Torricelli (Tarozzi 77), Adani, Mijatovic (Balbo 57), Batistuta, Rui Costa, Cois, Di Livio, Heinrich (Amoroso 53), Pierini

**15.03.00 v Manchester United FC (a) Lost 1-3**
Toldo, Repka, Torricelli (Tarozzi 76), Adani, Mijatovic (Chiesa 63), Batistuta, Rui Costa, Rossitto, Di Livio (Amoroso 76), Heinrich, Pierini. Scorer: Batistuta 16. Sent off: Rossitto 62

**21.03.00 v Girondins de Bordeaux (h) Drawn 3-3**
Toldo, Repka, Torricelli, Firicano, Batistuta (Balbo 80), Rui Costa, Cois (Okon 73), Di Livio, Chiesa, Bressan (Amoroso 38), Pierini. Scorers: Chiesa 47 pen, Batistuta 61, Rui Costa 64

| SEASONS | PLAYED | WON | DRAWN | LOST | FOR | AGAINST |
|---|---|---|---|---|---|---|
| 1 | 12 | 4 | 5 | 3 | 16 | 15 |

## GALATASARAY SK

**1993-1994**
**GROUP STAGE 1**
**08.12.93 v FC Spartak Moscow (a) Drawn 0-0**
Hayrettin, Stumpf, Bulent Korkmaz, Yusuf Tepekule, Mert (Erdal 85), Tugay, Ugur, Hamza, Hakan Sukur, Suat, Arif

**24.11.93 v FC Barcelona (h) Drawn 0-0**
Hayrettin, Bulent Korkmaz, Gotz (Yusuf Altintas 28), Stumpf, Yusuf Tepekule, Ugur (Arif 60), Tugay, Suat, Hamza, Hakan Sukur, Kubilay Turkyilmaz

**02.03.94 v AS Monaco (a) Lost 0-3**
Hayrettin, Mert, Bulent Korkmaz, Soner (Hamza 60), Gotz, Tugay, Ugur, Yusuf Tepekule, Hakan Sukur, Erdal, Arif (Okan 84)

**16.03.94 v AS Monaco (h) Lost 0-2**
Hayrettin, Mert, Bulent Korkmaz, Yusuf Tepekule, Gotz, Tugay (Mustafa Kocabey 69), Ugur, Hamza, Hakan Sukur, Suat (Okan 78), Arif

**30.03.94 v Barcelona (a) Lost 0-3**
Hayrettin, Mert (Arif 46), Bulent Korkmaz, Yusuf Tepekule, Gotz, Tugay, Ugur, Hamza, Hakan Sukur, Suat (Kubilay Turkyilmaz 78), Erdal

**13.04.94 v FC Spartak Moscow (h) Lost 1-2**
Hayrettin, Cihat, Mert, Yusuf Tepekule, Gotz, Tugay, Ugur, Hamza Hamzaoglu, Benhur, Suat, Kubilay Turkyilmaz, (Erdal 40, Stumpf 46). Scorer: Cihat 87

**1994-1995**
**GROUP STAGE 1**
**14.09.94 v FC Barcelona (a) Lost 1-2**
Stauce, Mapeza, Bulent Korkmaz, Sedat, Mert, Tugay, Ergun (Cihat 55), Saffet Sancakli (Arif 72), Hakan Sukur, Hamza, Kubilay Turkyilmaz. Scorer: K Turkyilmaz 14

**28.09.94 v Manchester United FC (h) Drawn 0-0**
Stauce, Mapeza, Bulent Korkmaz, Sedat, Mert, Tugay (Arif 46), Yusuf Tepekule, Saffet Sancakli (Osman 75), Hakan Sukur, Hamza, Kubilay Turkyilmaz

**19.10.94 v IFK Goteborg (a) Lost 0-1**
Stauce, Mapeza, Bulent Korkmaz, Sedat, Mert (Osman 81), Yusuf Tepekule, Arif, Hamza, Hakan Sukur, Suat, Kubilay Turkyilmaz (Saffet Sancakli 72)

**02.11.94 v IFK Goteborg (h) Lost 0-1**
Stauce, Mapeza, Bulent Korkmaz, Sedat, Mert, Yusuf Tepekule (Tugay 46), Arif Erdem, Saffet Sancakli, Hakan Sukur, Suat, Hamza (Kubilay Turkyilmaz 66)

**23.11.94 v FC Barcelona (h) Won 2-1**
Stauce, Mapeza, Bulent Korkmaz, Sedat, Mert, Ergun, Arif, Yusuf Tepekule (Tugay 46), Hakan Sukur, Suat, Hamza (Okan 58). Scorers: Hakan Sukur 72, Arif 88

**07.12.94 v Manchester United (a) Lost 0-4**
Stauce, Ergun, Bulent Korkmaz, Sedat, Mert, Tugay (Yusuf Tepekule 63), Arif, Hamza (Ugur 46), Hakan Sukur, Suat, Kubilay Turkyilmaz

**1997-1998**
**GROUP STAGE 1**
**17.09.97 v BV Borussia Dortmund (h) Lost 0-1**
Volkan, Fatih, Bulent Korkmaz, Hakan Unsal, Umit Devala (Arif 67), Tugay, Popescu, Hagi, Ergun, Ilie, Hakan Sukur

**01.10.97 v Parma AC (a) Lost 0-2**
Volkan, Fatih, Bulent Korkmaz, Filipescu, Popescu, Umit Devala (Mehmet 79), Tugay, Ergun (Ilie 46), Hakan Unsal, Arif (Osman 62), Hakan Sukur

**22.10.97 v AC Sparta Praha (a) Lost 0-3**
Volkan, Umit Devala, Fatih, Vedat, Popescu, Hagi (Hakan Sukur 46), Filipescu, Tugay, Hakan Unsal, Arif, Ilie (Bulent Korkmaz 69). Sent off: Vedat 40, Hakan Unsal 67

**05.11.97 v AC Sparta Praha (h) Won 2-0**
Volkan, Umit Devala (Arif 75), Fatih, Bulent Korkmaz, Hagi (Emre 89), Ergun, Popescu, Tugay, Osman, Hakan Sukur (Adnan 83), Ilie. Scorer: Tugay 58, 86

**27.11.97 v BV Borussia Dortmund (a) Lost 1-4**
Volkan, Filipescu, Fatih, Bulent Korkmaz, Popescu, Tugay, Ergun, Emre Belozoglu (Osman 37), Hakan Sukur, Umit Devala (Okan 46). Scorer: Ergun 87

**10.12.97 v Parma AC (h) Drawn 1-1**
Volkan, Filipescu (Osman 85), Fatih, Bulent Korkmaz, Popescu, Ilie, Tugay, Ergun, Hagi, Hakan Sukur, Umit Devala (Arif 69). Scorer: Ilie 52

**1998-1999**
**GROUP STAGE 1**
**16.09.98 v Juventus FC (a) Drawn 2-2**
Taffarel, Umit Davala, Vedat, Popescu, Hakan Unsal, Okan, Filipescu, Tugay (Arif 79), Hasan Sas (Ergun 82), Hakan Sukur, Hagi. Scorers: Hakan Sukur 44, Umit Davala 63

**30.09.98 v Athletic Club Bilbao (h) Won 2-1**
Taffarel, Umit Davala (Arif 70), Vedat (Bulent Korkmaz 75), Popescu, Hakan Unsal, Okan, Filipescu (Fatih 33), Tugay, Hasan Sas, Hakan Sukur, Hagi. Scorers: Okan 16, Hagi 90

**21.10.98 v Rosenborg BK (a) Lost 0-3**
Taffarel, Fatih, Popescu, Vedat, Okan (Emre Belozoglu 87), Umit Davala (Tolunay 75), Ergun, Hagi, Hakan Unsal, Hasan Sas (Arif 87), Hakan Sukur

**04.11.98 v Rosenborg BK (h) Won 3-0**
Taffarel, Fatih, Popescu, Filipescu, Okan (Ufuk 84), Tugay, Ergun (Arif 46), Hakan Unsal, Hagi (Umit Davala 79), Hasan Sas, Hakan Sukur. Scorers: Hakan Sukur 55, 74, Arif 66

**02.12.98 v Juventus FC (h) Drawn 1-1**
Taffarel, Fatih Akyel, Popescu, Filipescu, Okan Buruk, Umit Davala, Tolunay Kafkas (Arif Erdem 77), Hasan Sas (Suat Kaya 77), Hakan Unsal (Vedat Inceefe 90), Hagi, Hakan Sukur. Scorer: Suat 90

**09.12.98 v Athletic Club Bilbao (a) Lost 0-1**
Taffarel, Fatih Akyel, Popescu, Filipescu, Arif Erdem, Okan Buruk, Tolunay Kafkas (Burak Akdis 66), Suat Kaya (Vedat Inceefe 66), Umit Davala, Hagi, Hasan Sas (Emre Belozoglu 80)

**1999-2000**
**GROUP STAGE 1**
**15.09.99 v Hertha BSC Berlin (h) Drawn 2-2**
Taffarel, Bruno (Tugay 46), Popescu, Arif (Marcio 67), Okan (Fatih 46), Suat Kaya, Hakan Sukur, Hagi, Umit Davala, Hakan Unsal, Capone. Scorers: Hakan Sukur 24, Hagi 86 pen

**21.09.99 v Milan AC (a) Lost 1-2**
Taffarel, Bruno (Okan 46), Popescu, Suat Kaya, Hakan Sukur, Hagi (Arif 46), Fatih (Ergun 49), Ahmet, Umit Davala, Hakan Unsal, Capone. Scorer: Umit Davala 50

**28.09.99 v Chelsea FC (a) Lost 0-1**
Taffarel, Popescu, Arif (Mehmet 34), Okan (Emre Belozoglu 72), Hakan Sukur, Hagi (Hasan Sas 73), Fatih Umit Davala, Hakan Unsal, Capone, Ergun. Sent off: Taffarel 33

**20.10.99 v Chelsea FC (h) Lost 0-5**
Mehmet, Popescu, Emre Belozoglu, Arif, Okan, Hakan Sukur (Saffet 65), Hagi (Hasan Sas 46), Fatih (Umit Davala 46), Tugay, Hakan Unsal, Capone

**26.10.99 v Hertha BSC Berlin (a) Won 4-1**
Taffarel, Popescu, Emre Belozoglu, Arif (Emrah 87), Okan, Suat, Hakan Sukur, Fatih (Ergun 46), Ahmet, Hasan Sas (Tugay 71), Capone. Scorers: Hakan Sukur 48, 66, Tugay 81, Okan 90

**03.11.99 v Milan AC (h) Won 3-2**
Taffarel, Popescu (Ergun 70), Emre Belozoglu, Arif (Marcio 77), Okan, Hakan Sukur, Hagi (Hasan Sas 66), Ahmet, Umit Davala, Hakan Unsal, Capone. Scorers: Capone 27, Hakan Sukur 87, Umit Davala 90 pen

**2000-2001**
**GROUP STAGE 1**
**12.09.00 v AS Monaco (h) Won 3-2**
Taffarel, Bulent Korkmaz, Popescu, Emre Belozoglu, Okan (Akin Bulent 18), Suat, Jardel (Marcio 90), Hagi, Umit Davala (Hasan Sas 66), Capone, Hakan Unsal. Scorers: Jardel 16, Hagi 29, Capone 80. Sent off: Hagi 69

**20.09.00 v SK Sturm Graz (a) Lost 0-3**
Taffarel, Bulent Korkmaz, Popescu, Ahmet (Marcio 46), Suat, Jardel, Hasan Sas (Ergun 46), Umit Davala (Faruk 70), Akin Bulent, Capone, Hakan Unsal. Sent off: Suat 69

**27.09.00 v Rangers FC (h) Won 3-2**
Taffarel, Bulent Korkmaz, Popescu, Emre Belozoglu (Faruk 76), Jardel, Hasan Sas (Ahmet 90), Fatih, Umit Davala, Akin Bulent, Hakan Unsal, Ergun. Scorers: Akin Bulent 51, Hakan Unsal 57, Jardel 70

**17.10.00 v Rangers FC (a) Drawn 0-0**
Taffarel, Bulent Korkmaz, Popescu, Jardel (Marcio 87), Hagi (Okan 72), Hasan Sas, Fatih, Umit Davala, Akin Bulent, Hakan Unsal, Ergun

**25.10.00 v AS Monaco (a) Lost 2-4**
Inan Kerem, Bulent Korkmaz, Popescu, Okan, Suat (Marcio 85), Jardel, Hagi (Akin Bulent 42), Umit Davala (Hasan Sas 61), Capone, Hakan Unsal, Ergun. Scorers: Hakan Unsal 57, Bulent Korkmaz 63

**07.11.00 v SK Sturm Graz (h) Drawn 2-2**
Inan Kerem, Bulent Korkmaz, Popescu, Emre Belozoglu, Okan, Jardel (Marcio 90), Hagi (Serkan 67), Hasan Sas (Faruk 86), Fatih, Hakan Unsal, Ergun. Scorers: Ergun 30 pen, Jardel 75. Sent off: Emre Belozoglu 79

**GROUP STAGE 2**
**21.11.00 v Milan AC (a) Drawn 2-2**
Inan Kerem, Fatih (Emre Asik 77), Bulent Korkmaz, Popescu (Capone 69), Vedat, Ergun, Hagi, Okan, Suat (Umit Davala 80), Jardel , Hasan Sas. Scorers: Jardel 39, Hasan Sas 41

**06.12.00 v Paris Saint-Germain (h) Won 1-0**
Taffarel, Fatih, Bulent Korkmaz, Hakan Unsal (Vedat 73), Capone, Ergun, Emre Belozoglu (Umit Davala 34), Okan, Suat (Faruk 80), Jardel, Hasan Sas. Scorer: Umit Davala 51pen

**14.02.01 v RC Deportivo La Coruna (h) Won 1-0**
Taffarel, Fatih, Bulent Korkmaz, Popescu, Hakan Unsal (Ergun 26), Emre Belozoglu, Umit Davala (Okan 64), Hagi, Suat (Arif 80), Jardel , Hasan Sas. Scorer: Suat 11

**20.02.01 v RC Deportivo La Coruna (a) Lost 0-2**
Taffarel, Fatih, Capone, Popescu, Vedat, Ergun, Okan, Hagi (Serkan 80), Suat (Ahmet 46), Akin Bulent, Jardel (Arif 80). Sent off: Vedat 58

**07.03.01 v Milan AC (h) Won 2-0**
Taffarel, Capone, Bulent Korkmaz (Emre Asik 76), Popescu, Ahmet, Emre Belozoglu, Umit Davala (Arif 85), Okan, Hagi, Suat, Jardel (Faruk 88), Hasan Sas. Scorers: Hagi 20, Jardel 86

**13.03.01 v Paris Saint-Germain (a) Lost 0-2**
Taffarel, Capone, Ergun, Popescu (Fatih 56), Ahmet (Faruk 46), Emre Belozoglu, Umit Davala, Suat (Akin Bulent 46), Serkan, Emre Asik, Jardel

**QUARTER FINAL**
**03.04.01 v Real Madrid CF (h) Won 3-2**
Taffarel, Capone (Fatih 46), Bulent Korkmaz, Popescu, Umit Davala, Suat (Akin Bulent 46), Hagi, Okan, Ergun, Jardel, Hasan Sas. Scorers: Umit 47pen, Hasan Sas 66, Jardel 75

**18.04.01 v Real Madrid CF (a) Lost 0-3**
Taffarel, Fatih, Bulent Korkmaz, Emre Asik, Umit Davala, Suat (Akin Bulent 46), Okan, Emre Belozoglu, Hagi, Jardel, Hasan Sas (Arif 67)

**2001-2002**
**GROUP STAGE 1**
**11.09.01 v SS Lazio (h) Won 1-0**
Mondragon, Emre Asik, Bulent Korkmaz, Capone (Perez 72), Hakan Unsal, Umit Davala, Suat (Berkant 88), Ergun, Hasan Sas, Arif (Sergen 63), Umit Karan. Scorer: Umit Karan 79

**19.09.01 v PSV Eindhoven (a) Lost 1-3**
Mondragon, Emre Asik, Bulent Korkmaz, Capone, Hakan Unsal (Victoria 61), Sergen, Suat (Akin Bulent 59), Berkant (Arif 68), Ergun, Hasan Sas, Umit Karan. Scorer: Umit Karan 68

**26.09.01 v FC Nantes Atlantique (a) Won 1-0**
Mondragon, Emre Asik, Capone, Perez, Hakan Unsal, Suat (Fleurquin 67), Akin Bulent, Ergun, Hasan Sas, Arif (Sergen 57), Serkan (Umit Karan 77). Scorer: Sergen 79

**16.10.01 v FC Nantes Atlantique (h) Drawn 0-0**
Mondragon, Perez, Ergun, Emre Asik, Hakan Unsal, Vedat, Sergen, Akin Bulent (Suat 65), Hasan Sas, Arif (Fleurquin 75), Serkan (Umit Karan 59)

**24.10.01 v SS Lazio (a) Lost 0-1**
Mondragon, Perez, Vedat (Suat 16), A Emre,Victoria (Serkan 81), Fleurquin, Akin Bulent, Ergun, Hasan Sas, Sergen, Umit Karan (Arif 64)

**30.10.01 v PSV Eindhoven (h) Won 2-0**
Mondragon, Perez, Ergun, Emre Asik,Victoria, Fleurquin, Sergen (Ayhan 73), Akin Bulent, Hasan Sas, Arif (Suat 81), Umit Karan (Serkan 70). Scorer: Sergen 26, Arif 50

**GROUP PHASE 2**

**20.11.01 v AS Roma (h) Drawn 1-1**
Mondragon, Capone, Bulent Korkmaz, Emre Asik, Hakan Unsal, Perez, Akin Bulent (Fleurquin 46), Ayhan, Hasan Sas, Sergen, Umit Karan (Arif 88). Scorer: Perez 22

**05.12.01 v FC Barcelona (a) Drawn 2-2**
Mondragon, Capone, Bulent Korkmaz, Emre Asik, Hakan Unsal, Perez, Ergun, Akin Bulent (Sergen 85), Fleurquin, Ayhan (Suat 51), Umit Karan. Scorers: Umit Karan 5, Fleurquin 41. Sent off: Capone 62, Hakan Unsal 90

**20.02.02 v Liverpool FC (a) Drawn 0-0**
Mondragon, Perez, Bulent Korkmaz, Emre Asik, Viktoria, Ergun, Berkant, Fleurquin, Akin Bulent, Hasan Sas (Murat 80, Niculescu 90), Umit Karan

**26.02.02 v Liverpool FC (h) Drawn 1-1**
Mondragon, Perez, Bulent Korkmaz, Viktoria, Ergun, Berkant, Fleurquin, Ayhan, Hasan Sas, Arif, Niculescu (Serken 80). Scorer: Niculescu 71

**13.03.02 v AS Roma (a) Drawn 1-1**
Mondragon, Perez (Capone 84), Bulent Korkmaz, Emre Asik, Viktoria, Ergun, Berkant, Fleurquin, Ayhan, Hasan Sas, Umit Karan (Niculescu 89). Scorer: Umit Karan 45

**19.03.02 v FC Barcelona (h) Lost 0-1**
Mondragon, Perez (Capone 79), Bulent Korkmaz, Emre Asik, Ergun, Berkant, Fleurquin, Ayhan (Niculescu 62), Hasan Sas, Umit Karan, Arif (Suat 74)

**2002-2003**

**GROUP STAGE 1**

**18.09.02 v Lokomotiv Moscow (a) Won 2-0**
Mondragon, Umit Davala, K Bulent, Almaguer, Hakan Unsal, Ayhan (Fabio Pinto 46), Batista, Felipe, Ergun, Arif (Emre Asik 84), Hasan Sas (Sarr 70). Scorers: Sarr 72, Arif 81

**24.09.02 v FC Barcelona (h) Lost 0-2**
Mondragon, Sarr (Hasan Sas 46), K Bulent, Almaguer, Hakan Unsal, Umit Davala, Batista, Felipe, Ergun (Umit Karan 80), Arif, Christian (Suat 70)

**01.10.02 v Club Brugge KV (h) Drawn 0-0**
Mondragon, K Bulent (Vedat 83), Emre Asik, Hakan Unsal, Umit Davala, Batista, Felipe (Ayhan 70), Suat, Hasan Sas (Baljic 46), Umit Karan, Arif

**23.10.02 v Club Brugge KV (a) Lost 1-3**
Mondragon, Mehmet Polat (Felipe 46), K Bulent, Emre Asik, Hakan Unsal, Umit Davala, Fabio Pinto, Cihan, Ergun, Arif (Ayhan 55), Baljic. Scorer: Fabio Pinto 56

**29.10.02 v FC Lokomotiv Moskva (h) Lost 1-2**
Mondragon, K Bulent, Emre Asik, Hakan Unsal, Umit Davala, Cihan (Felipe 70), Fabio Pinto, Ergun, Arif (Batista 46), Baljic (Hasan Sas 46), Christian. Scorer: Hasan Sas 73

**13.11.02 v FC Barcelona (a) Lost 1-3**
Mondragon, Sarr, K Bulent, Almaguer, Hakan Unsal, Fabio Pinto, Batista (Ayhan 61), Cihan (Suat 46), Ergun, Hasan Sas, Baljic (Christian 75). Scorer: Cihan 20

| SEASONS | PLAYED | WON | DRAWN | LOST | FOR | AGAINST |
|---|---|---|---|---|---|---|
| 8 | 58 | 16 | 17 | 25 | 60 | 95 |

## KRC GENK

**2002-2003**
**GROUP STAGE 1**
**17.09.02 v AEK Athens (h) Drawn 0-0**
Moons, Vanbeuren, Tomasic, Zakora, Ingrao, Besilja, Thijs, Skoko, Daerden, Sonck, Dagano

**25.09.02 v Real Madrid CF (a) Lost 0-6**
Moons, Vanbeuren (Seylo 61), Tomasic, Zakora, Roumani, Besilja (Suzuki 83), Warnfor, Skoko, Daerden, Sonck, Dagano (De Camargo 79)

**02.10.02 v AS Roma (h) Lost 0-1**
Moons, Warnfor, Tomasic, Zakora, Roumani, Besilja (Scholten 12), Thijs, Skoko, Daerden (Seylo 68), Sonck, Dagano. Sent off: Moons 10

**22.10.02 v AS Roma (a) Drawn 0-0**
Scholten, Warnfor, Tomasic, Zakora, Roumani, Besilja, Thijs, Skoko, Daerden (Suzuki 77), Sonck, Dagano

**30.10.02 v AEK Athens (a) Drawn 1-1**
Moons, Warnfor, Tomasic, Zakora, Roumani, Besilja (Chatelle 90), Thijs, Skoko, Daerden, Sonck, Suzuki (Seylo 90). Scorer: Sonck 22

**12.11.02 v Real Madrid CF (h) Drawn 1-1**
Moons, Ingrao (Suzuki 60), Tomasic, Zakora, Roumani, Besilja, Thijs, Skoko, Seylo, Sonck, Vandenbergh (Chatelle 69)
Scorer: Sonck 86

| SEASONS | PLAYED | WON | DRAWN | LOST | FOR | AGAINST |
|---|---|---|---|---|---|---|
| 1 | 6 | 0 | 4 | 2 | 2 | 9 |

## IFK GOTEBORG

**1992-1993**
**GROUP STAGE 1**
**25.11.92 v Milan AC (a) Lost 0-4**
T Ravelli, Johansson, Pedersen, Svensson, Kaamark, Eriksson, Rehn (Leksell 68), Mild, Nilsson, Andersson, Ekstrom

**09.12.92 v FC Porto (h) Won 1-0**
T Ravelli, Johansson, Kaamark, Svensson, Nilsson, Eriksson, Rehn, Mild, Bengtsson (Lindqvist 72), Andersson, Ekstrom. Scorer: Eriksson 87

**03.03.93 v PSV Eindhoven (a) Won 3-1**
T Ravelli, Johansson, Bjorklund, Svensson, Kaamark, Eriksson, Rehn, Mild, Nilsson, Martinsson (Andersson 67), Ekstrom (Lindqvist 89). Scorers: Nilsson 19, Ekstrom 34, 44

**17.03.93 v PSV Eindhoven (h) Won 3-0**
T Ravelli, Johansson, Bjorklund, Svensson, Kaamark, Eriksson (Andersson 57), Rehn, Mild, Nilsson, Martinsson, Ekstrom. Scorers: Nilsson 1, Ekstrom 44, Martinsson 47

**07.04.93 v Milan AC (h) Lost 0-1**
T Ravelli, Johansson, Bjorklund, Svensson, Kaamark, Eriksson, Rehn, Mild, Nilsson, Martinsson, Ekstrom

**21.04.93 v FC Porto (a) Lost 0-2**
T Ravelli, Johansson, Bjorklund (Olsson 65), Kaamark, Nilsson, Lindqvist, Rehn, Mild, Bengtsson, Martinsson (Eriksson 55), Ekstrom

**1994-1995**
**GROUP STAGE 1**
**14.09.94 v Manchester United FC (a) Lost 2-4**
T Ravelli, Kaamark, Johansson, Bjorklund, Nilsson, Martinsson, Erlingmark, Lindqvist, Blomqvist, Olsson (Rehn 44), Pettersson. Scorers: Pettersson 26, Rehn 49

**28.09.94 v FC Barcelona (h) Won 2-1**
T Ravelli, Kaamark, Olsson (Johansson 63), Bjorklund, Nilsson, Martinsson (Wahlstedt 68), Rehn, Lindqvist, Blomqvist, Erlingmark, Pettersson. Scorers: Erlingmark 73, Blomqvist 88

**19.10.94 v Galatasaray SK (h) Won 1-0**
T Ravelli, Kaamark, Johansson, Bjorklund, Nilsson, Martinsson (Wahlstedt 74), Rehn, Lindqvist, Blomqvist (Andersson 89), Erlingmark, Pettersson. Scorer: Erlingmark 76

**02.11.94 v Galatasaray SK (a) Won 1-0**
T Ravelli, Kaamark, Johansson, Bjorklund, Nilsson, Erlingmark, Rehn, Lindqvist, Andersson, Martinsson (Wahlstedt 75), Blomqvist (Gustavsson 88). Scorer: Erlingmark 85

**23.11.94 v Manchester United FC (h) Won 3-1**
T Ravelli, Kaamark, Johansson, Bjorklund, Nilsson, Martinsson (Wahlstedt 49), Erlingmark, Lindqvist, Blomqvist, Rehn, Pettersson (Andersson 79). Scorers: Blomqvist 11, Erlingmark 65, Kaamark 72 pen

**07.12.94 v FC Barcelona (a) Drawn 1-1**
T Ravelli, Kaamark, Johansson, Bjorklund, Nilsson, Martinsson (Wahlstedt 69), Erlingmark, Lindqvist, Blomqvist, Rehn, Pettersson. Scorer: Rehn 89

**QUARTER FINAL**

**01.03.95 v FC Bayern Munchen (a) Drawn 0-0**
T Ravelli, Kaamark, Olsson, Johansson, Nilsson, Martinsson, Erlingmark, Lindqvist, Eriksson, Rehn (Lilienberg 62), Pettersson (Andersson 87)

**15.03.95 v FC Bayern Munchen (h) Drawn 2-2**
T Ravelli, Kaamark, Johansson, Bjorklund, Nilsson (Lilienberg 77), Martinsson, Rehn, Lindqvist, Blomqvist, Erlingmark, Pettersson (Wahlstedt 69). Scorers: Lilienberg 79, Martinsson 89

**1996-1997**

**GROUP STAGE 1**

**11.09.96 v Rosenborg BK (h) Lost 2-3**
T Ravelli, Magnus Johansson, Lucic, Olsson (Wahlstedt 72), Nilsson, Landberg, Alexandersson (Martinsson 83), Lindqvist, Blomqvist, Erlingmark, Andersson. Scorer: Erlingmark 19, 49

**25.09.96 v FC Porto (a) Lost 1-2**
T Ravelli, Landberg, Lucic, Olsson, Nilsson, Alexandersson, Erlingmark, Lindqvist, Blomqvist, Andersson, Pettersson (Martinsson 83). Scorer: Jorge Costa og 72

**16.10.96 v Milan AC (h) Won 2-1**
T Ravelli, Landberg (Johansson 78), Lucic, Olsson, Nilsson, Alexandersson, Erlingmark, Lindqvist, Blomqvist, Andersson, Pettersson (Wahlstedt 74). Scorers: Wahlstedt 75, Alexandersson 85

**30.10.96 v Milan AC (a) Lost 2-4**
T Ravelli, Landberg, Lucic, Olsson, Nilsson, Alexandersson (Eriksson 75), Erlingmark, Lindqvist, Blomqvist, Andersson (Martinsson 81), Pettersson. Scorers: Blomqvist 27, Andersson 32

**20.11.96 v Rosenborg BK (a) Lost 0-1**
T Ravelli, Landberg (Martinsson 86), Lucic, Olsson, Nilsson, Alexandersson, Erlingmark, Lindqvist, Eriksson, Andersson, Pettersson (Wahlstedt 86). Sent off: Alexandersson 66

**04.12.96 v FC Porto (h) Lost 0-2**
T Ravelli, Landberg (Johansson 18, Wahlstedt 83), Lucic, Olsson, Nilsson, Eriksson (Lillenberg 75), Erlingmark, Lindqvist, Blomqvist, Andersson, Pettersson

**1997-1998**
**GROUP STAGE 1**
**17.09.97 v Paris Saint-Germain (a) Lost 0-3**
T Ravelli, Magnusson, Lucic, Erlingmark, Nilsson, Landberg (Karlsson 57), Pettersson, Alexandersson, Eriksson, Ekstrom (Tetteh 57), Robert Andersson

**01.10.97 v FC Bayern Munchen (h) Lost 1-3**
T Ravelli, Johansson, Erlingmark, Lucic, Nilsson, Alexandersson, Pettersson, Lindqvist, Karlsson, Tetteh (Martinsson 85), Robert Andersson (Eriksson 58). Scorer: Lucic 86

**22.10.97 v Besiktas JK (a) Lost 0-1**
T Ravelli, Johansson, Lucic, Erlingmark, Nilsson, Eriksson (Ekstrom 79), Lindqvist, Martinsson (Karlsson 62), Pettersson, Alexandersson, Robert Andersson (Tetteh 69)

**05.11.97 v Besiktas JK (h) Won 2-1**
T Ravelli, Johansson, Lucic, Nilsson, Magnusson, Alexandersson, Pettersson, Lindqvist, Karlsson (Tetteh 85), Robert Andersson (Eriksson 73), Ekstrom (Jarelov 77). Scorers: Pettersson 18 pen, Robert Andersson 23. Sent off: Ravelli 76

**26.11.97 v Paris Saint-Germain (h) Lost 0-1**
Jarelov, Magnusson, Erlingmark, Lucic, Nilsson, Alexandersson, Pettersson, Lindqvist (Eriksson 85), Karlsson, Ekstrom (Martinsson 89), Robert Andersson

**10.12.97 v FC Bayern Munchen (a) Won 1-0**
T Ravelli, Magnusson, Johansson, Lucic, Nilsson, Eriksson, Erlingmark, Karlsson, Martinsson (Svensson 90), Ekstrom (Lundstrom 72), Robert Andersson (Tetteh 82). Scorer: Babbel og 51

| SEASONS | PLAYED | WON | DRAWN | LOST | FOR | AGAINST |
|---|---|---|---|---|---|---|
| 4 | 26 | 10 | 3 | 13 | 30 | 39 |

## GRASSHOPPER-CLUB (ZURICH)

**1995-1996**
**GROUP STAGE 1**
**13.09.95 v Ferencvarosi TC (h) Lost 0-3**
Zuberbuhler, Vogel, Gren, Vega, Thuler (De Napoli 67), Koller, Geiger, Massimo Lombardo, Yakin, Magnin (Viscaal 67), Comisetti (Ali Ibrahim 57)

**27.09.95 v Real Madrid CF (a) Lost 0-2**
Zuberbuhler, Nemstsoudis, Vega, Koller, Thuler, Geiger, Massimo Lombardo, Yakin, Duke (De Napoli 57), Vogel (Viscaal 76), Comisetti (Magnin 66)

**18.10.95 v AFC Ajax (a) Lost 0-3**
Zuberbuhler, Gamperle, Gren, Vega, Vogel, Koller, Geiger, Massimo Lombardo, Viscaal, Magnin, Rzasa (Semeter 73)

**01.11.95 v AFC Ajax (h) Drawn 0-0**
Foletti, Haas, Gren, Vega, Thuler, Koller, Geiger, Massimo Lombardo, Comisetti (Semeter 81), Ali Ibrahim (Viscaal 87), Magnin (De Napoli 67)

**22.11.95 v Ferencvarosi TC (a) Drawn 3-3**
Foletti, Haas, Gren, Vega, Gamperle, Koller, Geiger, Massimo Lombardo, Comisetti, Subiat, Ali Ibrahim (Magnin 88). Scorers: Subiat 21, Comisetti 47, Ali Ibrahim 64

**06.12.95 v Real Madrid CF (h) Lost 0-2**
Foletti, Haas, Gren, Vega, Gamperle, Koller, Geiger, Massimo Lombardo, Comisetti (Semeter 75), Subiat (Magnin 67), Ali Ibrahim (De Napoli 82)

**1996-1997**
**GROUP STAGE 1**
**11.09.96 v Rangers FC (h) Won 3-0**
Zuberbuhler, Gamperle, Haas, Gren, Thuler, Magnin (Massimo Lombardo 73), Vogel, Esposito (Koller 88), Yakin, Moldovan, Turkyilmaz (Rzasa 85). Scorers: Yakin 18, Turkyilmaz 28, 79

**25.09.96 v AFC Ajax (a) Won 1-0**
Zuberbuhler, Gamperle, Haas, Gren, Thuler, Massimo Lombardo (Koller 89), Yakin, Esposito, Vogel, Moldovan (Smiljanic 90), Magnin (Comisetti 78). Scorer: Yakin 60

**16.10.96 v AJ Auxerre (a) Lost 0-1**
Zuberbuhler, Haas, Smiljanic, Gren, Thuler (Magnin 81), Massimo Lombardo, Vogel, Comisetti (Berger 30), Turkyilmaz, Esposito (Subiat 75), Moldovan

**30.10.96 v AJ Auxerre (h) Won 3-1**
Zuberbuhler, Haas, Smiljanic, Gren, Thuler, Massimo Lombardo (Gamperle 90), Yakin, Esposito (Magnin 85), Vogel (Comisetti 79), Moldovan, Turkyilmaz. Scorers: Moldovan 17, 29 pen, Gren 59

**20.11.96 v Rangers FC (a) Lost 1-2**
Zuberbuhler, Haas, Gren, Smiljanic, Thuler, Massimo Lombardo, Esposito, Vogel (Subiat 80), Comisetti (Berger 64), Magnin, Turkyilmaz. Scorer: Berger 77

**04.12.96 v AFC Ajax (h) Lost 0-1**
Zuberbuhler, Nemtsoudis, Smiljanic, Gren, Thuler, Massimo Lombardo, Yakin, Esposito (Comisetti 22), Vogel (Magnin 66), Subiat, Moldovan

| SEASONS | PLAYED | WON | DRAWN | LOST | FOR | AGAINST |
|---|---|---|---|---|---|---|
| 2 | 12 | 3 | 2 | 7 | 11 | 18 |

## HNK HAJDUK SPLIT

**1994-1995**
**GROUP STAGE 1**
**14.09.94 v SL Benfica (h) Drawn 0-0**
Gabric, Butorovic, Person, Hibic, Stimac, Andrijasevic (Racunica 74), Vulic, Rapajic, Mornar (Erceg 57), Asanovic, Mestrovic. Sent off: Stimac 89

**28.09.94 v Steaua Bucaresti (a) Won 1-0**
Gabric, Butorovic, Prazenica, Hibic, Person, Pralja, Vulic, Rapajic (Vukas 90), Erceg (Vucevic 78), Asanovic, Mestrovic. Scorer: Asanovic 88

**19.10.94 v RSC Anderlecht (h) Won 2-1**
Gabric, Butorovic, Pralja, Hibic, Person, Andrijasevic, Vulic, Rapajic, Erceg (Vukas 86), Asanovic, Mornar (Vucevic 56). Scorers: Pralja 33, Butorovic 86

**02.11.94 v RSC Anderlecht (a) Drawn 0-0**
Gabric, Butorovic, Vuica, Hibic, Stimac, Pralja, Vulic, Rapajic (Erceg 84), Mestrovic (Andrijasevic 81), Asanovic, Mornar

**23.11.94 v SL Benfica (a) Lost 1-2**
Gabric, Butorovic, Person (Vucevic 55), Hibic, Vuica, Andrijasevic, Vulic, Pralja, Mestrovic, Asanovic, Mornar (Erceg 63). Scorer: Andrijasevic 69

**07.12.94 v Steaua Bucaresti (h) Lost 1-4**
Slavica, Butorovic, Person, Hibic, Stimac (Racunica 46), Andrijasevic, Vulic, Pralja, Erceg, Asanovic, Vucevic (Vukas 46). Scorer: Andrijasevic 48

**QUARTER FINAL**
**01.03.95 v AFC Ajax (h) Drawn 0-0**
Gabric, Butorovic, Prazenica, Person, Stimac, Andrijasevic, Vulic (Vuica 46), Pralja, Rapajc, Asanovic, Mornar (Seferovic 70)

**15.03.95 v AFC Ajax (a) Lost 0-3**
Gabric, Person, Prazenica, Hibic, Stimac, Vuica, Jurcec (Rapajc 67), Pralja, Erceg (Vulic 51), Asanovic, Mestrovic

| SEASONS | PLAYED | WON | DRAWN | LOST | FOR | AGAINST |
|---|---|---|---|---|---|---|
| 1 | 8 | 2 | 3 | 3 | 5 | 10 |

## HAMBURGER SV

**2000-2001**
**GROUP STAGE 1**
**13.09.00 v Juventus FC (h) Drawn 4-4**
Butt, Panadic, Hertzsch, Hoogma, Groth (Tofting 27), Kovac, Barbarez, Mahdavikia, Yeboah, Hollerbach (Ketelaer 46), Cardoso (Prager 66). Scorers: Yeboah 17, Mahdavikia 65, Butt 72 pen, Kovac 82

**19.09.00 v RC Deportivo La Coruna (a) Lost 1-2**
Butt, Panadic, Hertzsch, Hoogma, Kovac, Tofting, Barbarez (Fischer 87), Mahdavikia, Yeboah (Cardoso 46), Hollerbach, Ketelaer (Prager 46). Scorer: Barbarez 53

**26.09.00 v Panathinaikos FC (h) Lost 0-1**
Butt, Kientz (Katelaer 46), Panadic, Hoogma, Heinz (Yeboah 64), Kovac, Tofting, Barbarez, Mahdavikia, Hollerbach, Cardoso (Prager 4)

**18.10.00 v Panathiniakos FC (a) Drawn 0-0**
Butt, Panadic, Hertzsch, Hoogma, Groth (prager 62), Heinz, Kovac, Tofting, Barbarez, Yeboah (Bester 78), Hollerbach (Ketelaer 71)

**24.10.00 v Juventus FC (a) Won 3-1**
Butt, Kientz (Mahdavikia 50), Panadic, Hertzsch, Hoogma, Kovac (Maul 17), Tofting, Barbarez, Yeboah, Prager, Ketelaer (Heinz). Scorers: Prager 24, Yeboah 48, Panadic 62

**08.11.00 v RC Deportivo La Coruna (h) Drawn 1-1**
Butt, Kientz (Ketelaer 66), Panadic, Hoogma, Kovac (Hertzsch 17), Tofting, Barbarez, Mahdavikia, Yeboah (Bester 55), Hollerbach, Prager. Scorer: Mahdavikia 10

| SEASONS | PLAYED | WON | DRAWN | LOST | FOR | AGAINST |
|---|---|---|---|---|---|---|
| 1 | 6 | 1 | 3 | 2 | 9 | 9 |

## SC HEERENVEEN

**2000-2001**
**GROUP STAGE 1**
**12.09.00 v Olympique Lyonnais (a) Lost 1-3**
Vonk, Venema, Hansma, G De Nooijer, Radomski, Nurmela, Talan (Ebbinge 83), Jensen (Tuhuteru 39), Lurling, Houttuin, Van Gessel (Huizingh 72). Scorer: Talan 35

**20.09.00 v Valencia CF (h) Lost 0-1**
Vonk, Venema, Hansma, G De Nooijer, Radomski, Nurmela, Talan, Jensen (Denneboom 82), Lurling, Huizingh, Ebbinge

**27.09.00 v Olympiakos Piraeus FC (a) Lost 0-2**
Vonk, Venema, Hansma, G De Nooijer, Radomski, Nurmela, Talan (Houttuin 44), Denneboom 81), Jensen, Lurling (Tuhuteru 83), Huizingh, Ebbinge

**17.10.00 v Olympiakos Piraeus FC (h) Won 1-0**
Vonk, Venema, Klompe, G De Nooijer, Radomski, Nurmela, Talan, Jensen, Lurling, Huizingh, Nwankpa (Van Gessel 31). Scorer: Jensen 83

**25.10.00 v Olympique Lyonnais (h) Lost 0-2**
Vonk, Venema, Klompe, Hansma, G De Nooijer, Radomski (Van Gessel 25, Denneboom 71), Nurmela, Talan (Kolk 68), Jensen, Lurling, Huizingh

**07.11.00 v Valencia CF (a)** **Drawn 1-1**
Vonk, Venema, Hansma, G De Nooijer, Nurmela, Talan (Wijngaarde 72), Jensen (Holm 63), Lurling, Huizingh, Van Gessel, Ebbinge. Scorer: Venema 37. Sent off: Ebbinge 60

| SEASONS | PLAYED | WON | DRAWN | LOST | FOR | AGAINST |
|---|---|---|---|---|---|---|
| 1 | 6 | 1 | 1 | 4 | 3 | 9 |

## HERTHA BSC BERLIN

**1999-2000**
**GROUP STAGE 1**
**15.09.99 v Galatasaray SK (a)** **Drawn 2-2**
Kiraly, Herzog, Konstantinidis, Wosz (Thom 50), Daei, Preetz, Dardai, Schmidt, Hartmann, Deisler, Helmer (Veit 17, Neuendorf 46). Scorers: Preetz 12, Wosz 13. Sent off: Konstantinidis 84

**21.09.99 v Chelsea FC (h)** **Won 2-1**
Kiraly, Herzog, Van Burik, Wosz, Daei, Preetz, Sanneh (Veit 66), Dardai (Halmer 80), Schmidt, Tretschok (Michalke 12), Deisler. Scorer: Daei 3, 70

**28.09.99 v Milan AC (a)** **Drawn 1-1**
Kiraly, Herzog, Van Burik, Wosz (Neuendorf 82), Daei, Preetz, Dardai, Schmidt, Michalke, Deisler, Helmer. Scorer: Daei 69

**20.10.99 v Milan AC (h)** **Won 1-0**
Kiraly, Van Burik, Sverrisson, Wosz, Daei (Aracic 70), Rekdal, Preetz, Dardai (Sanneh 87), Michalke, Deisler, Helmer. Scorer: Wosz 41

**26.10.99 v Galatasaray SK (h)** **Lost 1-4**
Kiraly, Van Burik, Sverrisson, Wosz, Daei, Rekdal (Neuendorf 81), Preetz (Aracic 74), Schmidt, Michalke, Deisler, Helmer (Herzog 14). Scorer: Rekdal 35 pen

**03.11.99 v Chelsea FC (a)** **Lost 0-2**
Kiraly, Van Burik, Sverrisson, Wosz (Konstantinidis 46), Daei, Rekdal, Preetz (Aracic 46), Sanneh, Michalke, Deisler, Helmer (Schmidt 58)

**GROUP STAGE 2**
**23.11.99 v FC Barcelona (h)** **Drawn 1-1**
Kiraly, Van Burik, Konstantinidis, Sverrisson, Wosz, Daei, Preetz, Schmidt, Michalke (Herzog 87), Thom, Rehmer (Veit 72). Scorer: Michalke 33

**08.12.99 v FC Porto (a)** **Lost 0-1**
Kiraly, Herzog, Van Burik, Konstantinidis (Daei 82), Sverrisson, Wosz, Preetz, Schmidt, Neuendorf (Thom 64), Michalke, Rehmer (Hartmann 46)

**01.03.00 v AC Sparta Praha (h)** **Drawn 1-1**
Fielder, Herzog, Van Burik, Sverrisson, Wosz (Roy 88), Daei, Preetz, Veit, Schmidt, Hartmann, Deisler. Scorer: Veit 45

**07.03.00 v AC Sparta Praha (a)** **Lost 0-1**
Fielder, Herzog, Konstantinidis, Daei, Rekdal (Sanneh 90), Roy (Preetz 79), Schmidt, Hartmann, Alves, Michalke (Veit 21), Rehmer

**15.03.00 v FC Barcelona (a)** **Lost 1-3**
Kiraly, Herzog, Van Burik (Wosz 56), Sverrisson, Preetz, Covic, Schmidt (Sanneh 78), Hartmann, Alves, Michalke, Rehmer (Neuendorf 59). Scorer: Alves 7

**21.03.00 v FC Porto (h)** **Lost 0-1**
Kiraly, Herzog, Van Burik (Konstantinidis 46), Sverrisson, Daei, Covic, Roy, Sanneh, Alves (Aaracic 56), Michalke, Deisler (Dardai 46)

| SEASONS | PLAYED | WON | DRAWN | LOST | FOR | AGAINST |
|---|---|---|---|---|---|---|
| 1 | 12 | 2 | 4 | 6 | 10 | 18 |

## HJK HELSINKI

**1998–1999**
**GROUP STAGE 1**
**16.09.98 v PSV Eindhoven (a)** **Lost 1-2**
Koivistoinen, Ilola, Nylund, Saastamoinen, Tihinen, Vasara (Juvaja 68), Riihilahti, Lehkosuo, Piracaia, Kuqi (Kanerva 85), Kottila (Kopteff 68). Scorer: Kottila 32

**30.09.98 v 1 FC Kaiserslautern (h)** **Drawn 0-0**
Viander, Tihinen, Kanerva, Saastamoinen, Nylund, Riihilahti, Wiss, Ilola (Lehtola 83), Lehkosuo, Kuqi (Luiz Antonio Moraes 76), Piracaia (Vasara 67)

**21.10.98 v SL Benfica (h)** **Won 2-0**
Viander, Tihinen, Kanerva, Saastamoinen, Nylund, Vasara (Riihilahti 31), Ilola, Lehkosuo, Piracaia, Kuqi (Luiz Antonio Moraes 64), Kottila (Kopteff 80). Scorers: Lehkosuo 20 pen, Kottila 70

**04.11.98 v SL Benfica (a) Drawn 2-2**
Koivistoinen, Tihinen, Kanerva, Saastamoinen, Nylund, Kuqi (Kopteff 88), Ilola, Lehkosuo, Riihilahti, Kottila (Luiz Antonio Moraes 81), Piracaia (Forssell 60). Scorers: Minto og 3, Luiz Antonio Moraes 85

**26.11.98 v PSV Eindhoven (h) Lost 1-3**
Koivistoinen, Turpeinen, Kanerva (Luiz Antonio Moraes 46), Saastamoinen, Nylund, Riihilahti, Tihinen (Forssell 83), Lehkosuo, Kuqi (Kopteff 72), Kottila, Piracaia. Scorer: Lehkosuo 70 pen

**09.12.98 v 1 FC Kaiserslautern (a) Lost 2-5**
Viander, Tihinen, Saastamoinen, Nylund, Turpeinen, Kuqi (Luiz Antonio Moraes 59), Ilola, Riihilahti, Lehkosuo, Kottila (Forssell 83), Piracaia (Kopteff 66). Scorers: Ilola 29, Luiz Antonio Moraes 68

| SEASONS | PLAYED | WON | DRAWN | LOST | FOR | AGAINST |
|---|---|---|---|---|---|---|
| 1 | 6 | 1 | 2 | 3 | 8 | 12 |

## HELSINGBORGS IF

**2000-2001**
**GROUP STAGE 1**
**13.09.00 v FC Bayern Munchen (h) Lost 1-3**
Sven Andersson, Ola Nilsson, Roland Nilsson, Matovac, Bjorn Johansen, Ulrik Jansson (Jesper Jansson 77), Alvaro, Persson, Hansson, Stig Johansen (Eklund 61), Christoffer Andersson (Prica 73). Scorer: B Johansen 90

**19.09.00 v Paris Saint-Germain (a) Lost 1-4**
Sven Andersson, Ola Nilsson, Roland Nilsson, Matovac, Bjorn Johansen (Eklund 82), Ulrik Jansson, Alvaro, Persson, Stig Johansen (Prica 82), Christoffer Andersson (Michael Hansson 72), Jesper Jansson. Scorer: B Johansen 45

**26.09.00 v Rosenborg BK (a) Lost 1-6**
Sven Andersson, Ola Nilsson, Matovac, Bjorn Johansen, Ulrik Jansson (Stig Johansen 36), Alvaro (Prica 70), Eklund, Persson, Michael Hansson, Lindberg (Christoffer Andersson 59), Jesper Jansson. Scorer: Prica 90

**18.10.00 v Rosenborg BK (h) Won 2-0**
Sven Andersson, Ola Nilsson, Roland Nilsson, Matovac, Bjorn Johansen, Ulrik Jansson (Wahlstedt 74), Eklund (Alvaro 60), Persson, Stig Johansen, Prica (Christoffer Andersson 84), Jesper Jansson. Scorers: Jesper Jansson 32, Alvaro 77

**24.10.00 v FC Bayern Munchen (a) Drawn 0-0**
Sven Andersson, Ola Nilsson, Roland Nilsson, Matovac, Bjorn Johansen, Ulrik Jansson, Alvaro (Eklund 81), Persson (Prica 72), Stig Johansen (Michael Hansson 81), Christoffer Andersson, Jesper Jansson

**08.11.00 v Paris Saint-Germain (h) Drawn 1-1**
Sven Andersson, Ola Nilsson, Roland Nilsson, Matovac, Ulrik Jansson (Eklund 46), Alvaro (Lindstrom 76), Persson, Michael Hansson (Wahlstedt 66), Stig Johansen, Prica, Jesper Jansson. Scorer: Persson 71

| SEASONS | PLAYED | WON | DRAWN | LOST | FOR | AGAINST |
|---|---|---|---|---|---|---|
| 1 | 6 | 1 | 2 | 3 | 6 | 14 |

## INTERNAZIONALE FC (MILAN)

**1998-1999**
**GROUP STAGE 1**
**16.09.98 v Real Madrid CF (a) Lost 0-2**
Pagliuca, Javier Zanetti, Fresi, Bergomi, Galante, Milanese, Winter (Ventola 81), Simeone, Cauet (Silvestre 46), Zamorano, Ronaldo (Pirlo 75). Sent off: Fresi 42

**30.09.98 v SK Sturm Graz (h) Won 1-0**
Pagliuca, Silvestre, Bergomi, Galante, Moriero (Pirlo 73), Cauet (Zamorano 65), Winter, Simeone, Javier Zanetti, Ventola, Djorkaeff. Scorer: Djorkaeff 90

**21.10.98 v FC Spartak Moscow (h) Won 2-1**
Pagliuca, Silvestre, Simeone, Galante, West, Cauet, Paulo Sousa, Winter, Djorkaeff (Pirlo 34), Ventola (Zamorano 83), Ronaldo (Ze Elias 74). Scorers: Ventola 32, Ronaldo 59

**04.11.98 v FC Spartak Moscow (a) Drawn 1-1**
Pagliuca, Colonnese, Bergomi (Pirlo 76), Galante, Javier Zanetti, Moriero (Silvestre 90), Paulo Sousa, Simeone, Cauet, Zamorano, Ronaldo (Ventola 66). Scorer: Simeone 89

**25.11.98 v Real Madrid CF (h) Won 3-1**
Pagliuca, Colonnese, Bergomi, Galante, West, Moriero (Javier Zanetti 57), Paulo Sousa (Cauet 75), Simeone, Winter, Zamorano (Roberto Baggio 68), Ronaldo. Scorers: Zamorano 51, Roberto Baggio 86, 90

**09.12.98 v SK Sturm Graz (a) Won 2-0**
Pagliuca, Colonnese, Bergomi, Galante, Silvestre, Javier Zanetti, Winter, Ze Elias (Recoba 82), Simeone, Djorkaeff (Roberto Baggio 70), Ronaldo (Zamorano 61). Scorers: Zanetti 64, Roberto Baggio 80

**QUARTER FINAL**

**03.03.99 v Manchester United FC (a) Lost 0-2**

Pagliuca, Colonnese, Bergomi, Galante, Javier Zanetti, Winter, Simeone, Cauet, Djorkaeff, Roberto Baggio (Pirlo 80), Zamorano (Ventola 69)

**17.03.99 v Manchester United FC (h) Drawn 1-1**

Pagliuca, Colonnese, West, Bergomi (Moriero 69), Silvestre, Javier Zanetti, Simeone (Ze Elias 32), Cauet, Roberto Baggio, Ronaldo (Ventola 60), Zamorano. Scorer: Ventola 63

**2002-2003**

**GROUP STAGE 1**

**17.09.02 v Rosenborg BK (a) Drawn 2-2**

Toldo, Cordoba, Cannavaro, Materazzi, Coco, Zanetti, Dalmat (Emre 63), Almeyda, Morfeo (Recoba 77), Crespo (Adani 88), Vieri. Sent off: Cannavaro (2 cards). Scorers: Crespo 33, 79

**25.09.02 v AFC Ajax (h) Won 1-0**

Toldo, Cordoba, Materazzi, Pasquale, Zanetti, Okan (S Conceicao 69), Dalmat, Di Biagio (Almeyda 65), Emre (Recoba 52), Crespo, Vieri
Scorer: Crespo 75

**02.10.02 v Olympique Lyonnais (h) Lost 1-2**

Toldo, Cordoba, Cannavaro, Materazzi, Coco (Pasquale 86), Zanetti, Dalmat (Morfeo 61), Di Biagio (S Conceicao 69), Almeyda, Crespo, Vieri. Scorer: Cannavaro 73

**22.10.02 v Olympique Lyonnais (a) Drawn 3-3**

Toldo, Cordoba, Materazzi, Coco, Zanetti, Emre, S Conceicao (Adani 72), Di Biagio (Almeyda 24), Morfeo, Crespo (Recoba 78), Vieri. Scoer: Cacapa 31og, Crespo 56, 66

**30.10.02 v Rosenborg BK (h) Won 3-0**

Toldo, Cannavaro, Materazzi, Coco (Pasquale 87), Zanetti, Emre, Di Biagio, S Conceicao, Recoba, Crespo (Almeyda 75), Vieri. Scorers: Recoba 31, Saarinen 52og, Crespo 72

**12.11.02 v AFC Ajax (a) Won 2-1**

Toldo, Cordoba, Materazzi, Coco, Zanetti, Di Biagio, S Conceicao (Adani 72), Almeyda, Morfeo (Emre 90), Crespo (Recoba 65), Vieri. Scorer: Crespo 50,52

**GROUP STAGE 2**

**27.11.02 v Newcastle United FC (a) Won 4-1**

Toldo, Cannavaro, Materazzi, Pasquale, Zanetti, Okan (Dalmat 66), Almeyda, Morfeo, Emre, Crespo (Recoba 81), Vieri. Scorers: Morfeo 2, Almeyda 35, Crespo 45, Rocoba 81

**10.12.02 v Bayer 04 Leverkusen (h) Won 3-2**
Toldo, Cordoba, Gamarra, Pasquale, Zanetti, Di Biagio (Beati 71), Almeyda, Emre, Crespo (Kallon 88), Recoba, Vieri (S Conceicao 74). Scorer: Di Biagio 15, 27, Butt 0og

**18.02.03 v FC Barcelona (a) Lost 0-3**
Toldo, Cannavaro, Gamarra, Cordoba, J Zanetti, Dalmat, Di Biagio (Okan 59), C Zanetti, Morfeo (Kallon 66), Vieri, Recoba. Off: Recoba 80

**26.02.03 v FC Barcelona (h) Drawn 0-0**
Toldo, Cannavaro, Gamarra, Pasquale, J Zanetti, Dalmat (Martins 61), Guly (S Conceicao 78), C Zanetti, Morfeo, Kallon, Vieri

**11.03.03 v Newcastle United FC (h) Drawn 2-2**
Toldo, Cannavaro, Cordoba, Coco, J Zanetti,S Conceicao, Di Biagio, Okan, Emre (Pasquale 76), Guly (Martins 46), Vieri. Scorers: Vieri 47, Cordoba 61

**19.03.03 v Bayer 04 Leverkusen (a) Won 2-0**
Toldo, Cannavaro, Cordoba, Coco, J Zanetti,S Conceicao (Guly 83), Di Biagio, Okan (C Zanetti 19), Emre, Morfeo (Pasquale 75), Martins. Scorers: Martins 36, Emre 90

**QUARTER FINAL**

**09.04.03 v Valencia CF (h) Won 1-0**
Toldo, J Zanetti, Cordoba, Materazzi, Coco (Pasquale 31), S Conceicao (Okan 65), C Zanetti, Di Biagio, Emre, Vieri, Crespo (Cannavaro 83). Scorer: Vieri 14. Sent off: Emre 57

**22.04.03 v Valenica CF (a) Lost 1-2**
Toldo, J Zanetti, Cordoba, Materazzi, Gamarra, Pasquale (Adani 46), Dalmat, C Zanetti, Di Biagio (Okan 75), Vieri (Recoba 32), Crespo. Scorer: Vieri 5

**07.05.03 v AC Milan (a) Drawn 0-0**
Toldo, Cordoba, Cannavaro, Materazzi, Coco (Pasquale 84), J Zanetti, Di Biagio, S Conceicao (Guly 66), Emre, Crespo, Recoba (Kallon 72)

**13.05.03 v AC Milan (h) Drawn 1-1**
Toldo, J Zanetti, Cannavaro, Materazzi, Cordoba, S Conceicao, Di Biagio (Dalmat 46),C Zanetti, Emre, Crespo (Kallon 71), Recoba (Martins 46). Scorer: Martins 83

| SEASONS | PLAYED | WON | DRAWN | LOST | FOR | AGAINST |
|---|---|---|---|---|---|---|
| 2 | 24 | 11 | 8 | 5 | 36 | 27 |

## JUVENTUS FC

### 1995-1996

### GROUP STAGE 1

13.09.95 v BV Borussia Dortmund (a) Won 3-1
Peruzzi, Ferrara, Pessotto, Porrini, Torricelli, Paulo Sousa, Di Livio, Jugovic, Conte (Marocchi 87), Padovano, Del Piero (Deschamps 90). Scorers: Padovano 12, Del Piero 37, Conte 69

**27.09.95 v Steaua Bucaresti (h) Won 3-0**
Peruzzi, Ferrara, Pessotto, Tacchinardi (Vierchowod 81), Torricelli, Paulo Sousa, Di Livio, Deschamps, Vialli, Del Piero (Padovano 72), Ravanelli (Conte 67). Scorers: Di Livio 35, Del Piero 40, Ravanelli 49

**18.10.95 v Rangers FC (h) Won 4-1**
Peruzzi, Ferrara, Vierchowod, Porrini (Carrera 78), Torricelli, Paulo Sousa, Di Livio (Marocchi 65), Deschamps, Conte (Tacchinardi 83), Del Piero, Ravanelli. Scorers: Moore og 15, Conte 17, Del Piero 23, Ravanelli 76

**01.11.95 v Rangers FC (a) Won 4-0**
Peruzzi, Torricelli, Pessotto, Carrera, Porrini (Ferrara 79), Paulo Sousa, Di Livio, Tacchinardi (Marocchi 74), Conte, Vialli (Ravanelli 70), Del Piero. Scorers: Del Piero 16, Torricelli 65, Ravanelli 88, Marocchi 90

**22.11.95 v BV Borussia Dortmund (h) Lost 1-2**
Peruzzi, Porrini, Carrera, Vierchowod, Pessotto, Tacchinardi (Fusi 82), Di Livio, Marocchi, Jugovic (Sorin 46), Vialli (Del Piero 66), Padovano. Scorer: Del Piero 90

**06.12.95 v Steaua Bucaresti (a) Drawn 0-0**
Rampulla, Ferrara, Pessotto, Porrini, Carrera, Torricelli, Deschamps, Conte, Marocchi (Lombardo 66), Jugovic, Ravanelli (Del Piero 46)

### QUARTER FINAL

**06.03.96 v Real Madrid CF (a) Lost 0-1**
Peruzzi, Ferrara, Carrera (Pessotto 77), Vierchowod, Toricelli, Paulo Sousa (Jugovic 66), Lombardo (Padovano 46), Conte, Deschamps, Ravanelli, Del Piero

**20.03.96 v Real Madrid CF (h) Won 2-0**
Peruzzi, Torricelli, Vierchowod, Porrini, Pessotto, Jugovic (Di Livio 46), Deschamps, Conte, Del Piero (Marocchi 88), Vialli, Padovano (Lombardo 74). Scorers: Del Piero 17, Padovano 54. Sent off: Torricelli 79

**SEMI FINAL**

**03.04.96 v FC Nantes Atlantique (h) Won 2-0**

Peruzzi, Ferrara, Vierchowod (Marocchi 62), Porrini, Pessotto, Paulo Sousa (Carrera 81), Di Livio (Lombardo 75), Jugovic, Del Piero, Vialli, Padovano. Scorers: Vialli 49, Jugovic 66

**17.04.96 v FC Nantes Atlantique (a) Lost 2-3**

Peruzzi, Ferrara, Vierchowod, Carrera, Pessotto, Conte, Di Livio, Deschamps, Del Piero (Paulo Sousa 46), Vialli (Jugovic 79), Ravanelli (Padovano 45). Scorers: Vialli 17, Paulo Sousa 50

**FINAL**

**23.05.96 v AFC Ajax (n) Drawn 1-1 Won 4-2pens**

Peruzzi, Torricelli, Vierchowod, Ferrara, Pessotto, Conte (Jugovic 44), Paulo Sousa, (Di Livio 57), Deschamps, Ravanelli (Padovano 78), Del Piero, Vialli. Scorer: Ravanelli 13. Penalty scorers: Ferrara, Pessotto, Padovano, Jugovic

**1996-1997**

**GROUP STAGE 1**

**11.09.96 v Manchester United FC (h) Won 1-0**

Peruzzi, Porrini, Ferrara, Montero (Juliano 90), Pessotto, Conte, Zidane (Di Livio 78), Deschamps, Boksic, Vieri (Nicola Amoruso 73), Del Piero. Scorer: Boksic 34

**25.09.96 v Fenerbahce SK (a) Won 1-0**

Rampulla, Porrini, Ferrara, Montero, Pessotto, Conte, Zidane (Di Livio 71), Deschamps, Boksic, Vieri (Padovano 59), Del Piero (Tacchinardi 83). Scorer: Boksic 22

**16.10.96 v SK Rapid Wien (a) Drawn 1-1**

Rampulla, Porrini, Ferrara, Montero, Torricelli, Di Livio, Tacchinardi (Lombardo 70), Deschamps (Pessotto 84), Jugovic, Vieri (Padovano 63), Boksic. Scorer: Vieri 9

**30.10.96 v SK Rapid Wien (h) Won 5-0**

Peruzzi, Torrichelli, Ferrara, Montero, Pessotto (Porrini 70), Di Livio (Lombardo 64), Deschamps, Jugovic, Del Piero, Boksic (Padovano 64), Zidane. Scorers: Boksic 5, 59, Montero 26, Del Piero 29, 75

**20.11.96 v Manchester United FC (a) Won 1-0**

Peruzzi, Torrichelli (Juliano 83), Ferrara, Montero, Porrini, Di Livio (Tacchinardi 81), Deschamps, Zidane, Jugovic, Del Piero, Boksic. Scorer: Del Piero 36

**04.12.96 v Fenerbahce SK (h) Won 2-0**

Peruzzi, Torrichelli, Porrini, Montero, Juliano, Di Livio, Tacchinardi, Zidane (Ferrara 77), Lombardo, Padovano (Trotta 85), Del Piero (Nicola Amoruso 46). Scorers: Padovano 42, Amoruso 85

**QUARTER FINAL**

**05.03.97 v Rosenborg BK (a) Drawn 1-1**

Peruzzi, Torrichelli, Ferrara, Montero, Juliano, Di Livio, Deschamps (Tacchinardi 83), Jugovic, Zidane, Padovano (Nicola Amoruso 59), Vieri. Scorer: Vieri 53

**19.03.97 v Rosenborg BK (h) Won 2-0**

Peruzzi, Porrini, Ferrara, Montero, Juliano, Di Livio (Lombardo 78), Deschamps, Jugovic, Zidane (Tacchinardi 82), Nicola Amoruso, Vieri (Boksic 44). Scorers: Zidane 28, Amoruso 90 pen

**SEMI FINAL**

**09.04.97 v AFC Ajax (a) Won 2-1**

Peruzzi, Porrini, Ferrara, Montero, Pessotto, Di Livio (Tacchinardi 69), Deschamps, Jugovic (Lombaro 85), Zidane, Nicola Amoruso, Vieri. Scorers: Amoruso 14, Vieri 41

**23.04.97 v AFC Ajax (h) Won 4-1**

Peruzzi, Ferrara, Tacchinardi, Montero, Juliano, Lombardo, Deschamps, Zidane (Conte 84), Di Livio, Vieri (Nicola Amoruso 69), Boksic. Scorers: Lombardo 35, Vieri 36, Amoruso 78, Zidane 79

**FINAL**

**28.05.97 v BV Borussia Dortmund (n) Lost 1-3**

Peruzzi, Porrini (Del Piero 46), Ferrara, Montero, Juliano, Di Livio, Deschamps, Zidane, Jugovic, Vieri (Nicola Amoruso 73), Boksic (Tacchinardi 87). Scorer: Del Piero 64

**1997-1998**

**GROUP STAGE 1**

**17.09.97 v Feyenoord (h) Won 5-1**

Peruzzi, Birindelli, Ferrara, Montero, Dimas, Conte, Deschamps, Zidane (Pessotto 72), Di Livio, F Inzaghi (Fonseca 82), Del Piero (Tacchinardi 60). Scorers: Del Piero 3, 11 pen, F Inzaghi 34, Zidane 67, Birindelli 81. Sent off: Di Livio 57

**01.10.97 v Manchester United FC (a) Lost 2-3**

Peruzzi, Birindelli, Ferrara, Montero, Dimas, Pecchia (Juliano 69), Deschamps, Tacchinardi (Pessotto 19), Zidane, F Inzaghi, Del Piero (Amoruso 78). Scorers: Del Piero 1, Zidane 90. Sent off: Deschamps 66

**22.10.97 v 1 FC Kosice (a) Won 1-0**

Peruzzi (Rampulla 38), Pessotto, Birindelli, Juliano, Dimas, Di Livio (Pecchia 33), Tacchinardi, Conte, Zidane, F Inzaghi, Del Piero. Scorer: Del Piero 34

**05.11.97 v 1 FC Kosice (h) Won 3-2**

Peruzzi, Birindelli, Ferrara, Tacchinardi, Juliano, Conte, Deschamps, Zidane (Amoruso 58), Pecchia (Torricelli 70), F Inzaghi (Fonseca 58), Del Piero. Scorers: Del Piero 43, Amoruso 59, Fonseca 61

**27.11.97 v Feyenoord (a) Lost 0-2**
Peruzzi, Birindelli, Ferrara, Juliano (Dimas 74), Pessotto, Di Livio, Deschamps (Torricelli 43), Tacchinardi, Zidane, Amoruso, Del Piero (Fonseca 69)

**10.12.97 v Manchester United FC (h) Won 1-0**
Peruzzi, Birindelli (Dimas 76), Ferrara, Juliano, Torricelli, Di Livio, Conte (Montero 65), Tacchinardi (Pecchia 46), Zidane, Fonseca, F Inzaghi. Scorer: F Inzaghi 84

**QUARTER FINAL**
**04.03.96 v FC Dynamo Kyiv (h) Drawn 1-1**
Peruzzi, Birindelli (Conte 63), Juliano, Montero, Torricelli (Dimas 62), Di Livio, Deschamps, Davids, Zidane, Del Piero, F Inzaghi. Scorer: F Inzaghi 70

**18.03.98 v FC Dynamo Kyiv (a) Won 4-1**
Peruzzi, Birindelli (Dimas 7), Juliano, Montero, Pessotto, Conte, Deschamps, Davids, Zidane, Del Piero, F Inzaghi (Tacchinardi 79). Scorers: F Inzaghi 28, 65, 73, Del Piero 88

**SEMI FINAL**
**01.04.98 v AS Monaco (h) Won 4-1**
Peruzzi, Torricelli (Conte 46), Juliano, Montero, Pessotto (Birindelli 46), Di Livio (Tacchinardi 66), Deschamps, Davids, Zidane, Del Piero, F Inzaghi. Scorers: Del Piero 34, 48 pen, 62 pen, Zidane 88

**14.04.98 v AS Monaco (a) Lost 2-3**
Peruzzi, Torricelli, Birindelli, Juliano, Dimas, Conte, Tacchinardi, Pessotto, Zidane (Pecchia 59), Del Piero, F Inzaghi (Amoruso 6). Scorers: Amoruso 14, Del Piero 74

**FINAL**
**23.05.98 v Real Madrid CF (n) Lost 0-1**
Peruzzi, Torricelli, Juliano, Montero, Di Livio (Tacchinardi 46), Deschamps (Conte 77), Davids, Pessotto (Fonseca 71), Zidane, Del Piero, F Inzaghi

**1998-1999**
**GROUP STAGE 1**
**16.09.98 v Galatasaray SK (h) Drawn 2-2**
Peruzzi, Birindelli, Tudor, Tacchinardi, Pessotto (Blanchard 68), Di Livio, Deschamps, Davids, Fonseca (Rampulla 32), Inzaghi (Zidane 62), Del Piero. Scorers: F Inzaghi 17, Birindelli 68. Sent off: Peruzzi 32

**30.09.98 v Rosenborg BK (a) Drawn 1-1**
Rampulla, Birindelli, Tudor, Montero, Mirkovic (Pessotto 77), Tacchinardi, Deschamps, Davids, Del Piero, F Inzaghi (Fonseca 61), Zidane (Zalayeta 79). Scorer: F Inzaghi 27

**21.10.98 v Athletic Club Bilbao (a) Drawn 0-0**
Rampulla, Birindelli, Montero, Tudor, Pessotto (Juliano 29), Di Livio, Deschamps, Davids (Tacchinardi 77), Zidane, F Inzaghi, Del Piero (Fonseca 81)

**04.11.98 v Athletic Club Bilbao (h) Drawn 1-1**
Peruzzi, Tudor (Blanchard 46), Juliano, Montero, Di Livio (Perrotta 84), Davids, Tacchinardi, Pessotto (Amoruso 55), Zidane, F Inzaghi, Del Piero. Scorer: Lasa og 68

**02.12.98 v Galatasaray SK (a) Drawn 1-1**
Peruzzi (Rampulla 59), Birindelli, Ferrara, Juliano, Montero, Conte, Deschamps, Blanchard, Pessotto (Amoruso 66), Zidane, F Inzaghi (Tudor 81). Scorer: Amoruso 78

**09.12.98 v Rosenborg BK (h) Won 2-0**
Peruzzi, Birindelli, Tudor, Montero, Pessotto (Davids 65), Conte (Di Livio 88), Deschamps, Tacchinardi, Zidane, Amoruso (Juliano 68), F Inzaghi. Scorers: F Inzaghi 16, Amoruso 36

**QUARTER FINAL**
**03.03.99 v Olympiakos Piraeus FC (h) Won 2-1**
Peruzzi, Mirkovic, Juliano, Montero, Di Livio (Tacchinardi 90), Davids, Deschamps, Conte, Zidane, F Inzaghi, Fonseca (Birindelli 82). Scorers: F Inzaghi 38, Conte 79

**17.03.99 v Olympiakos Piraeus FC (a) Drawn 1-1**
Rampulla, Mirkovic (Birindelli 83), Juliano, Montero, Di Livio, Davids, Deschamps, Conte, Zidane (Tacchinardi 90), F Inzaghi, Esnaider (Amoruso 69). Scorer: Conte 85

**SEMI FINAL**
**07.04.99 v Manchester United FC (a) Drawn 1-1**
Peruzzi, Mirkovic, Juliano, Montero (Ferrara 68), Pessotto, Di Livio (Tacchinardi 77), Davids, Deschamps, Conte, Zidane, F Inzaghi (Esnaider 88). Scorer: Conte 25

**21.04.99 v Manchester United FC (h) Lost 2-3**
Peruzzi, Birindelli (Amoruso 46), Ferrara, Juliano (Montero 46), Pessotto, Di Livio (Fonseca 80), Davids, Deschamps, Conte, Zidane, F Inzaghi. Scorers: F Inzaghi 6, 11

**2000-2001**
**GROUP STAGE 1**
**13.09.00 v Hamburger SV (a) Drawn 4-4**
Van der Sar, Ferrara, Tudor, O'Neill (Bachini 73), Pessotto, F Inzaghi, Del Piero (Kovacevic 59), Juliano (Birindelli 59), Tacchinardi, Zidane, Davids. Scorers: Tudor 6, F Inzaghi 36, 52, 88

**19.09.00 v Panathinaikos FC (h) Won 2-1**
Van der Sar, Ferrara, Paramatti, Tudor, Pessotto (Bachini 46), Conte (Birindelli 60), F Inzaghi, Del Piero (Trezeguet 62), Tacchinardi, Zidane, Davids. Scorers: Tacchinardi 35, Trezeguet 83

**26.09.00 v RC Deportivo La Coruna (h) Drawn 0-0**
Van der Sar, Ferrara, Tudor, Pessotto, F Inzaghi (Del Piero 65), Juliano, Birindelli (Paramatti 73), Trezeguet, Tacchinardi (Conte 60), Zidane, Davids. Sent off: Zidane 68

**18.10.00 v RC Deportivo La Coruna (a) Drawn 1-1**
Van der Sar, Ferrara, Tudor, Pessotto, Conte, F Inzaghi (Trezeguet 71), Del Piero, Juliano, Kovacevic (Bachini 62), Tacchinardi (Birindelli 89), Davids. Scorer: F Inzaghi 10

**24.10.00 v Hamburger SV (h) Lost 1-3**
Van der Sar, Ferrara (Zanchi 55), Paramatti, Tudor, Pessotto, Conte, F Inzaghi (Del Piero 55), Juliano, Trezeguet (Kovacevic 55), Zidane, Davids. Scorer: Kovacevic 56. Sent off: Zidane 29, Davids 33

**08.11.00 v Panathinaikos FC (a) Lost 1-3**
Van der Sar, Ferrara, O'Neill (Birindelli 60), Pessotto, Conte, F Inzaghi (Trezeguet 63), Del Piero, Juliano, Zanchi (Rampulla 57), Kovacevic, Tacchinardi. Scorer: F Inzaghi 24. Sent off: Van der Saar 56, Kovacevic 68

**2001-2002**
**GROUP STAGE 1**
**10.10.01* v FC Porto (a) Drawn 0-0**
Buffon, Birindelli (Paramatti 12), Montero, Thuram, Pessotto (C Zenoni 65), Zambrotta, Tacchinardi, Tudor, Davids, Del Piero, Salas (O'Neill 84)
*postponed from 12 September

**18.09.01 v Celtic FC (h) Won 3-2**
Buffon, C Zenoni, Montero, Thuram, Pessotto (Birindelli 63), Tacchinardi, Iuliano, Davids, Del Piero (Amoruso 83), Salas (O'Neill 69), Trezeguet. Scorers: Trezeguet 43, 55, Amoruso 90pen. Sent off: Davids 75

**25.09.01 v Rosenborg BK (a) Drawn 1-1**
Buffon, Thuram, Montero, Iuliano, Pessotto, C Zenoni (Maresca 78), Tacchinardi, O'Neill (Salas 59), Zambrotta, Del Piero, Trezeguet. Scorer: Del Piero 85

**17.10.01 v Rosenborg BK (h) Won 1-0**
Buffon - Maresca (Iuliano 62), Montero, Thuram, Pessotto - Zambrotta, Tudor, Davids, Nedved (Paramatti 84) - Del Piero (Salas 90), Trezeguet. Scorer: Trezeguet 25

**23.10.01 v FC Porto (h) Won 3-1**
Buffon, Tudor, Montero, Thuram, Paramatti, Zambrotta (C Zenoni 72), Tacchinardi, Davids (Birindelli 86), Nedved, Del Piero (Maresca 76), Trezeguet. Scorers: Del Piero 32, Montero 47, Trezeguet 73

**31.10.01 v Celtic FC (a) Lost 3-4**
Carini, Birindelli, Montero, Thuram, Paramatti, C Zenoni, Tacchinardi, Maresca (Frara 81), Nedved, Del Piero (Trezeguet 46), Amoruso. Scorers: Del Piero 19, Trezeguet 51, 77

**GROUP STAGE 2**

**29.11.01* v Bayer 04 Leverkusen (h) Won 4-0**
Buffon, Birindelli, Thuram, Iuliano, Pessotto, Zambrotta, Tacchinardi, Tudor, Nedved (Davids 84), Del Piero, Trezeguet (Amoruso 77). Scorers: Trezeguet 8, 60, Del Piero 37, Tudor 44
*postponed from 21 and 28 November (fog)

**04.12.01 v Arsenal FC (a) Lost 1-3**
Buffon, Birindelli, Thuram, Montero, Pessotto (Paramatti 78), Zambrotta, Tacchinardi, Tudor (Davids 21), Nedved (Amoruso 71), Del Piero, Trezeguet. Scorer: Taylor 49og

**19.02.02 v RC Deportivo (h) Drawn 0-0**
Buffon, Thuram, Ferrera, Iuliano, Pessotto (C Zenoni 79), Zambrotta, Tacchinardi (Maresca 61), Conte (Zalayeta 79), Davids, Del Piero, Trezeguet

**27.02.02 v RC Deportivo (a) Lost 0-2**
Buffon, Ferrera, Montero (Davids 46), Iuliano, Pessotto, Birindelli, Tacchinardi (Zalayeta 68), Maresca (Conte 46), Nedved, Del Piero, Trezeguet. Sent off: Davids 74

**12.03.02 v Bayer 04 Leverkusen (a) Lost 1-3**
Buffon, C Zenoni, Birindelli, Ferrera, Pessotto (Tudor 46) , Zambrotta, Tacchinardi, Conte (Maresca 46), Nedved, Amoruso (Zalayeta 61), Trezeguet

**20.03.02 v Arsenal FC (h) Won 1-0**
Carini, C Zenoni, Birindelli, Iuliano, Pramatti (Pessotto 24), Zambrotta (Amoroso 70), Conte, Maresca, Davids, Zalayeta, Guzman (Pericard 61). Scorer: Zelayeta 76

**2002-2003**

**GROUP STAGE 1**

**18.09.02 v Feyenoord (a) Drawn 1-1**
Buffon, Thuram, Ferrara, Montero, Birindelli, Tacchinardi, Davids (Fresi 65), Camoranesi (Baiocco 81), Nedved, Del Piero (Salas 76), Di Vaio. Scorer: Camoranesi 32

**24.09.02 v FC Dynamo Kyiv (h) Won 5-0**
Buffon, Thuram, Ferrara, Montero (Baiocco 76), Moretti, Tacchinardi (Tudor 68), Davids, Camoranesi, Nedved, Del Piero, Di Vaio (Trezeguet 72). Scorers: Di Vaio 14, 52, Del Piero 22, Davids 67, Nedved 79

**01.10.02 v Newcastle United FC (h) Won 2-0**
Buffon, Thuram, Ferrara, Montero, Moretti, Baiocco (Fresi 86), Tudor (Birindelli 84), Davids, Nedved, Del Piero, Di Vaio (Trezeguet 17). Scores: Del Piero 66, 81

**23.10.02 v Newcastle United FC (a) Lost 0-1**
Buffon, Thuram, Ferrara, Iuliano, Birindelli, Camoranesi (Zambrotta 69), Tacchinardi, Davids (Conte 45), Nedved, Del Piero, Di Vaio (Zalayeta 55)

**29.10.02 v Feyenoord (h) Won 2-0**
Buffon, Thuram (Iuliano 71), Ferrara, Tudor (Zambrotta 89), Birindelli, Camoranesi, Tacchinardi, Davids (Moretti 82), Nedved, Del Piero, Di Vaio. Scorer: Di Vaio 4, 69

**13.11.02 v Dynamo Kyiv (a) Won 2-1**
Chimenti, Birindelli, Fresi, Iuliano, Pessotto, Conte (Paro 27), Baiocco, Olivera (Davids 76), Zambrotta, Zalayeta, Salas (Cassani 90). Scorers: Salas 53, Zalayeta 61

**GROUP STAGE 2**

**26.11.02 v RC Deportivo (a) Drawn 2-2**
Buffon, Thuram, Montero, Iuliano, Birindelli, Camoranesi (Zambrotta 75), Tacchinardi, Davids, Nedved, Del Piero, Di Vaio (Zalayeta 75). Scorers: Birindelli 38, Nedved 57

**11.12.02 v FC Basel (h) Won 4-0**
Buffon, Thuram (Ferrera 59), Montero, Iuliano, Birindelli, Zambrotta, Tacchinardi, Davids, Nedved, Del Piero (Conte 72), Trezeguet (Zalayeta 75). Scorers: Trezeguet 3, Montero 34, Tacchinardi 43, Del Piero 51pen

**19.02.03 v Manchester United FC (a) Lost 1-2**
Chimenti, Zenoni, Ferrara, Montero, Pessotto, Camoranesi, Tacchinardi, Davids, Nedved, Trezeguet (Olivera 66), Zalayeta. Scorer: Nedved 90

**25.02.03 v Manchester United FC (h) Lost 0-3**
Buffon, Thuram, Montero, Ferrara, Zambrotta (Pessotto 67), Camoranesi, Conte (Tudor 46), Davids, Nedved, Trezeguet, Di Vaio (Salas 46)

**12.03.03 v RC Deportivo (h) Won 3-2**
Buffon, Thuram, Montero, Ferrara, Zambrotta, Camoranesi (Pessotto 46) Tacchinardi (Tudor 77), Davids, Nedved, Trezeguet, Di Vaio (Zalayeta 46). Scorers: Ferrara 12, Trezeguet 63, Tudor 90

**18.03.03 v FC Basel (a) Lost 1-2**
Buffon, Thuram (Del Piero 70), Montero, Iuliano, Birindelli, Zenoni, Tacchinardi, Tudor (Pessotto 46), Zambrotta, Nedved, Trezeguet (Salas 30). Scorer: Taccinardi 30

**QUARTER FINAL**
**09.04.03 v FC Barcelona (h) Drawn 1-1**
Buffon, Thuram, Montero, Ferrara, Zambrotta (Zalayeta 67), Camoranesi, Tacchinardi, Tudor (Birindelli 61), Davids, Nedved, Del Piero (Di Viao 82). Scorer: Montero 16

**22.04.03 v FC Barcelona (a) Won 2-1**
Buffon, Thuram, Montero, Ferrara, Zambrotta, Camoranesi (Birindelli 46), Tacchinardi, Davids, Nedved, Del Piero (Tudor 83), Di Viao (Zalayeta 46). Scorers: Nedved 53, Zalayeta 114. Sent off: Davids 79

**SEMI FINAL**
**06.05.03 v Real Madrid CF (a) Lost 1-2**
Buffon, Thuram, Ferrara, Iuliano (Pessotto 46), Zambrotta, Birindelli, Conte, Tudor (Camoranesi 80), Nedved (Dio Vaio 82), Del Piero, Trezeguet. Scorer: Trezeguet 45

**14.05.03 v Real Madrid CF (h) Won 3-1**
Buffon, Thuram, Ferrara, Montero, Birindelli (Pessotto 62), Zambrotta, Tacchinardi, Davids (Conte 85), Nedved, Del Piero, Trezeguet (Camoranesi 77). Scorers: Trezeguet 12, Del Piero 43, Nedved 70

**FINAL**
**28.05.03 v AC Milan (n) Drawn 0-0 (lost 2-3pens)**
Buffon, Thuram, Ferrara, Tudor (Birindelli 42), Montero, Zambrotta, Tacchinardi, Davids (Zalayeta 65), Camoranesi (Conte 46), Del Piero, Trezeguet. Penalties: Trezeguet (missed), Birindelli, Zalayeta & Montero (missed), Del Piero

| SEASONS | PLAYED | WON | DRAWN | LOST | FOR | AGAINST |
|---|---|---|---|---|---|---|
| 6 | 78 | 36 | 22 | 20 | 136 | 89 |

## FC KAISERSLAUTERN

**1998-1999**
**GROUP STAGE 1**
**16.09.98 v SL Benfica (h) Won 1-0**
Reinke, Roos (Reich 72), Ramzy, Schjonberg, Buck, Ratinho (Riedl 90), Sforza, Wagner, Koch, Hristov, Marschall. Scorer: Wagner 41

**30.09.98 v HJK Helsinki (a)** **Drawn 0-0**
Reinke, Samir, Ramzy, Ojigwe, Buck (Rische 66), Riedl (Koch 85), Sforza, Wagner, Reich (Rosler 70), Hristov, Marschall

**21.10.98 v PSV Eindhoven (a)** **Won 2-1**
Reinke, Koch, Ramzy, Samir, Roos, Sforza, Ballack (Riedl 60), Ojigwe, Reich, (Hrutka 79), Rosler (Rische 75), Hristov. Scorers: Riedl 67, Rische 81

**04.11.98 v PSV Eindhoven (h)** **Won 3-1**
Reinke, Koch (Reich 34), Ballack, Samir, Buck (Junior 67), Roos, Sforza, Riedl, Hristov, Marschall, Rosler (Rische 46). Scorers: Rische 68, Reich 77, Hristov 90

**26.11.98 v SL Benfica (a)** **Lost 1-2**
Reinke, Samir, Ramzy, Roos (Koch 46), Buck (Junior 46), Riedl, Ballack, Ojigwe (Rische 56), Reich, Hristov, Marschall. Scorer: Rische 90

**09.12.98 v HJK Helsinki (h)** **Won 5-2**
Reinke, Samir, Sforza (Riedl 85), Hrutka, Buck, Ramzy, Ballack (Rische 46), Koch (Rosler 37), Reich, Hristov, Marschall. Scorers: Rosler 43, 61, 80, Marschall 49, Rische 85

**QUARTER FINAL**
**03.03.99 v FC Bayern Munchen (a)** **Lost 0-2**
Reinke, Sforza, Ramzy, Hrutka (Koch 69), Buck (Ratinho 56), Riedl, Ballack, Wagner, Reich, Rische (Samir 73), Rosler. Sent off: Ramzy 71

**17.03.99 v FC Bayern Munchen (h)** **Lost 0-4**
Reinke, Sforza, Hrutka, Koch, Ratinho (Roos 46), Riedl (Junior 59), Ballack, Wagner, Reich, Rische, Rosler (Ojigwe 76). Sent off: Hrutka 8

| SEASONS | PLAYED | WON | DRAWN | LOST | FOR | AGAINST |
|---|---|---|---|---|---|---|
| 1 | 8 | 4 | 1 | 3 | 12 | 12 |

## FC KOSICE

**1997-1998**
**GROUP STAGE 1**
**17.09.97 v Manchester United (h)** **Lost 0-3**
Molnar, Semenik, Telek, Kral, Kozak, Sovic, Spilar, Zvara, Janocko, Ljubarskij (Rusnak 46), Kozlej (Faktor 76)

**01.10.97 v Feyenoord (a) Lost 0-2**
Molnar, Telek, Kozak, Spilar, Dzurik, Sovic (Ljubarskij 86), Zvara, Semenik (Rusnak 72), Kral (Faktor 67), Janocko, Kozlej

**22.10.97 v Juventus FC (h) Lost 0-1**
Molnar, Telek, Kozak, Spilar, Dzurik, Sovic (Ljubarskij 26), Zvara, Janocko, Toth (Bochnovic 87), Kozlej, Semenik (Rusnak 79)

**05.11.97 v Juventus FC (a) Lost 2-3**
Molnar, Semenik, Telek, Kozak, Toth, Kral (Faktor 70), Sovic , Zvara, Ljubarskij (Rusnak 76), Janocko (Bochnovic 82), Kozlej. Scorers: Ljubarskij 66, Ferrara og 71

**27.11.97 v Manchester United FC (a) Lost 0-3**
Molnar, Semenik, Kozak, Spilar, Toth, Sovic, Dzurik, Zvara (Faktor 80), Janocko (Rusnak 31), Ljubarskij, Kozlej (Bochnovic 84)

**10.12.97 v Feyenoord (h) Lost 0-1**
Molnar, Semenik, Kozak, Spilar, Dzurik, Sovic, Zvara, Janocko (Bochnovic 84), Toth, Ljubarskij (Lapsansky 84), Kozlej

| SEASONS | PLAYED | WON | DRAWN | LOST | FOR | AGAINST |
|---|---|---|---|---|---|---|
| 1 | 6 | 0 | 0 | 6 | 2 | 13 |

## SS LAZIO

**1999-2000**
**GROUP STAGE 1**
**14.09.99 v Bayer 04 Leverkusen (a) Drawn 1-1**
Marchegiani, Negro, Mihajlovic, Nesta, Pancaro, Lombardo, Stankovic, Veron (Simeone 50), Almeyda, Boksic (Salas 80), Mancini (Nedved 76). Scorer: Mihaljovic 18

**22.09.99 v Dynamo Kyiv (h) Won 2-1**
Ballotta, Negro, Favalli, Mihajlovic, Nesta, Nedved, Stankovic (Salas 52), Veron (Lombardo 81), Almeyda, Boksic, Mancini (Simeone 75). Scorers: Negro 70, Salas 72

**29.09.99 v NK Maribor (h) Won 4-0**
Marchegiani, Negro, Sensini, Sergio Conceicao, Mancini, Mihajlovic (Almeyda 72), Nesta, Pancaro, Lombardo (Veron 23), Stankovic (Salas 46), S Inzaghi. Scorers: S Inzaghi 60, Conceicao 62, Salas 71, 76

**19.10.99 v NK Maribor (a) Won 4-0**
Ballotta, Favalli, Sensini, Sergio Conceicao (Marcolin 75), Mihajlovic, Nesta (Fernando Couto 19), Simeone, Pancaro, Nedved (Gottardi 70), Stankovic, S Inzaghi. Scorers: Mihajlovic 36, S Inzaghi 50, 74, Stankovic 63

**27.10.99 v Bayer 04 Leverkusen (h) Drawn 1-1**
Marchegiani, Favalli, Sergio Conceicao (Stankovic 76), Fernando Couto, Mihajlovic, Pancaro, Nedved, Veron (Simeone 89), Fernando Couto, Almeyda, Boksic (S Inzaghi 59), Salas. Scorer: Nedved 1

**02.11.99 v Dynamo Kyiv (a) Won 1-0**
Ballotta, Negro, Marcolin, Sensini, Fernando Couto, Mancini, Simeone, Pancaro, Gottardi, Stankovic (Pinzi 64), S Inzaghi. Scorer: Mamedov og 18

**GROUP STAGE 2**
**24.11.99 v Olympique de Marseille (a) Won 2-0**
Marchegiani, Favalli, Sensini, Sergio Conceicao, Mihajlovic, Nesta, Pancaro, Nedved (Almeyda 81), Stankovic, Salas (Boksic 79), Mancini (Veron 74). Scorers: Stankovic 64, Sergio Conceicao 77

**07.12.99 v Chelsea FC (h) Drawn 0-0**
Marchegiani, Favalli, Fernando Couto, Mancini (Sergio Conceicao), Nesta, Simeone, Lombardo (Boksic 69), Gottardi, Nedved, S Inzaghi (Salas 46), Veron

**29.02.00 v Feyenoord (h) Lost 1-2**
Marchegiani, Sensini, Fernando Couto, Mihajlovic (Negro 40), Simeone, Lombardo, Gottardi, S Inzaghi (Stankovic 60), Veron (Nedved 69), Boksic, Mancini. Scorer: Veron 37

**08.03.00 v Feyenoord (a) Drawn 0-0**
Marchegiani, Negro, Sensini, Mihajlovic, Nesta, Pancaro, Nedved, Veron, Sergio Conceicao, Salas, Mancini (S Inzaghi 66),

**14.03.00 v Olympique de Marseille (h) Won 5-1**
Marchegiani, Negro, Sergio Conceicao, Mihajlovic (Fernando Couto 50), Nesta, Simeone, Pancaro (Gottardi 74), Nedved, Stankovic (Sensini 68), S Inzaghi, Boksic Scorers: S Inzaghi 17, 37, 38, 71, Boksic 82

**22.03.00 v Chelsea FC (a) Won 2-1**
Marchegiani, Negro, Mihajlovic, Simeone, Pancaro, Nedved, Stankovic (Boksic 46), Veron, Fernando Couto, Almeyda, S Inzaghi (Salas 68, Gottardi 87). Scorers: S Inzaghi 54, Mihajlovic 66. Sent off: Fernando Couto 83

**QUARTER FINAL**

**05.04.00 v Valencia CF (a) Lost 2-5**

Ballotta, Negro, Mihajlovic, Simeone (Salas 76), Pancaro, Gottardi, Nedved, Stankovic (Sergio Conceicao 62), S Inzaghi (Boksic 68), Veron, Almeyda. Scorers: S Inzaghi 28, Salas 87

**18.04.00 v Valencia CF (h) Won 1-0**

Marchegiani, Negro, Sergio Conceicao, Mihajlovic, Nesta, Pancaro (Mancini 76), Nedved (S Inzaghi 46), Veron, Almeyda (Simeone 84), Boksic, Salas. Scorer: Veron 52

**2000-2001**

**GROUP STAGE 1**

**12.09.00 v FC Shakhtar Donetsk (a) Won 3-0**

Peruzzi, Mihajlovic (Couto 53), Netsa, Simeone (Sensini 83), Pancaro, Nedved, Favalli, Stankovic (Lombardo 81), S Inzaghi, Veron, C Lopez. Scorers: Lopez 27, Nedved 68, Inzaghi 78

**20.09.00 v AC Sparta Praha (h) Won 3-0**

Marchegiani, Fernando Couto, Nesta, Simeone, Pancaro, Nedved (Sensini 80), Favalli (Colonnese 80), Stankovic, S Inzaghi (Lombardo 73), Veron, Salas. Scorers: S Inzaghi 35, 70, Simeone 58

**27.09.00 v Arsenal FC (a) Lost 0-2**

Marchegiani, Negro, Claudio Lopez, Mihajlovic, Nesta, Simeone, Pancaro, Nedved, Stankovic (Lombardo 46, Ravanelli 74), S Inzaghi (Salas 57), Veron

**17.10.00 v Arsenal FC (h) Drawn 1-1**

Peruzzi, Negro, Salas, Mihajlovic, Nesta, Simeone, Pancaro, Nedved, Stankovic (C Lopez 46), S Inzaghi (Crespo 69), Veron. Scorer: Nedved 24

**25.10.00 v FC Shakhtar Donetsk (h) Won 5-1**

Peruzzi, Baronio (Stankovic 46), Nesta, Pancaro, Nedved, Favalli, S Inzaghi (Crespo 46), Veron, Couto, Lombardo (Sensini 71), C Lopez. Scorers: C Lopez 48, 68, 90, Favalli 54, Veron 57

**07.11.00 v AC Sparta Praha (a) Won 1-0**

Marchegiani, Pesaresi, Gottardi, Stankovic, S Inzaghi (Ruggiu 85), Fernando Couto, Lombardo, Ravanelli, Colonnese, Baronio, Salas (Berrettoni 46, Luciani 90). Scorer: Ravanelli 43

**GROUP STAGE 2**

**22.11.00 v RSC Anderlecht (a) Lost 0-1**

Peruzzi, Pancaro, Nesta, Mihajlovic, Favalli, Stankovic, Lombardo (Baronio 62), Simeone, Nedved, Crespo (Ravanelli 62), Salas (S Inzaghi 78)

**05.12.00 v Leeds United AFC (h) Lost 0-1**
Peruzzi, Pancaro, Nesta, Fernando Couto, Favalli, Lombardo (Gottardi 82), Veron (Ravanelli 71), Simeone, Nedved, Crespo, Salas

**13.02.01 v Real Madrid CF (a) Lost 2-3**
Peruzzi, Negro, Nesta, Fernando Couto, Pancaro, Castroman (Gottardi 60), Veron, Simeone (Mihajlovic 90), Nedved, Crespo, Salas. Scorers: Crespo 4, Gottardi 84

**21.02.01 v Real Madrid CF (h) Drawn 2-2**
Peruzzi, Negro, Fernando Couto, Pancaro, Favalli, Castroman, Simeone, Mihajlovic (Baronio 81), Nedved, Crespo, Salas (S Inzaghi 74). Scorers: Nedved 4, Crespo 54

**06.03.01 v RSC Anderlecht (h) Won 2-1**
Marchegiani, Negro, Mihajlovic, Colonnese, Pancaro, Baronio, Stankovic, Pesaresi, Ravanelli, S Inzaghi, C Lopez (Luciani 78). Scorers: C Lopez 40, Baronio 77

**14.03.01 v Leeds United AFC (a) Drawn 3-3**
Marchegiani, Pesaresi, Fernando Couto, Mihajlovic, Colonnese, Castroman (Ruggiu 89), Baronio, Stankovic, Nedved, Ravanelli, C Lopez (Salas 73). Scorers: Ravanelli 21, Mihajlovic 29pen, 90

**2001-2002**
**GROUP STAGE 1**
**11.09.01 v Galatasaray SK (a) Lost 0-1**
Peruzzi, Fernando Couto, Nesta, Stam, Pancaro (S Inzaghi 81), Mendieta (Stankovic 52), Fiore, Simeone, Favalli (Cesar 72), C Lopez, Crespo

**19.09.01 v FC Nantes Atlantique (h) Lost 1-3**
Peruzzi, Fernando Couto, Nesta, Stam (Pancaro 73), Mendieta (C Lopez 65), Stankovic, Fiore, Simeone, Favalli, Crespo (Kovacevic 77), S Inzaghi. Scorer: F Couto 7

**26.09.01 v PSV Eindhoven (a) Lost 0-1**
Peruzzi, Fernando Couto, Colonnese, D Baggio, Mendieta (Poborsky 71), Fiore, Simeone (Stankovic 38), Giannichedda, Pancaro, C Lopez, Kovacevic (S Inzaghi 74)

**16.10.01 v PSV Eindhoven (h) Won 2-1**
Peruzzi, Fernando Couto, Stam, Favalli, Poborsky (Negro 74), Mendieta, Fiore (D Baggio 82), Giannichedda, Pancaro, C Lopez, S Inzaghi (Crespo 61). Scorers: Fiore 39, C Lopez 55pen

**24.10.01 v Galatasaray SK (h) Won 1-0**
Peruzzi, Stam (Pancaro 46), Nesta, Favalli, Negro, Mendieta, Fiore (Stankovic 62), Giannichedda, Cesar, C Lopez (S Inzaghi 71), Crespo. Scorer: Stankovic 76

**30.10.01 v FC Nantes Atlantique (a) Lost 0-1**
Peruzzi, Stam, Nesta, Favalli, Negro, Mendieta (Kovacevic 68), Fiore (Stankovic 83), Giannichedda, Cesar, C Lopez (S Inzaghi 46), Crespo

| SEASONS | PLAYED | WON | DRAWN | LOST | FOR | AGAINST |
|---|---|---|---|---|---|---|
| 3 | 32 | 15 | 7 | 10 | 52 | 34 |

## LEEDS UNITED AFC

**2000-2001**
**GROUP STAGE 1**
**13.09.00 v FC Barcelona (a) Lost 0-4**
Martyn, Kelly, Harte, Dacourt, Radebe (Hay 90), Bridges, Bowyer, McPhail (Hackworth 73), Smith, Mills, Duberry

**19.09.00 v Milan AC (h) Won 1-0**
Martyn, Kelly, Harte, Dacourt, Bridges, Bowyer, Smith, Mills, Bakke, Matteo, Duberry. Scorer: Bowyer 89

**26.09.00 v Besiktas JK (h) Won 6-0**
Martyn, Kelly, Harte, Dacourt (McPhail 75), Radebe, Viduka, Bowyer, Smith (Huckerby 80), Mills, Bakke, Matteo. Scorers: Bowyer 7, 90, Viduka 12, Matteo 22, Bakke 65, Huckerby 90

**18.10.00 v Besiktas JK (a) Drawn 0-0**
Robinson, Kelly, Harte, Woodgate, Bridges (Huckerby 28, McPhail 86), Viduka, Bowyer, Mills, Bakke, Matteo, Burns

**24.10.00 v FC Barcelona (h) Drawn 1-1**
Robinson, Kelly, Harte, Dacourt (Burns 75), Woodgate, Viduka, Bowyer, Smith, Mills, Bakke, Matteo. Scorer: Bowyer 5

**08.11.00 v Milan AC (a) Drawn 1-1**
Robinson, Kelly, Harte, Dacourt, Radebe, Viduka, Bowyer, Smith, Mills, Bakke, Matteo. Scorer: Matteo 45

**GROUP STAGE 2**
**22.11.00 v Real Madrid CF (h) Lost 0-2**
Robinson, Kelly, Harte, Radebe, Woodgate, Viduka, Bowyer, Smith, Mills, Matteo, Burns (Wilcox 60)

# CHAMPIONS LEAGUE HISTORY

**05.12.00 v SS Lazio (a) Won 1-0**
Robinson, Kelly, Dacourt, Radebe, Woodgate, Viduka, Bowyer, Wilcox (Kewell 76), Smith, Bakke, Matteo. Scorer: Smith 80

**13.02.01 v RSC Anderlecht (h) Won 2-1**
Martyn, Harte, Dacourt (Bakke 73), Radebe, Viduka, Bowyer, Smith, Mills, Matteo (Kewell 54), Batty, Ferdinand. Scorers: Harte 74, Bowyer 87

**21.02.01 v RSC Anderlecht (a) Won 4-1**
Martyn, Harte, Dacourt, Radebe, Viduka (Kewell 83), Smith, Mills, Bakke, Matteo, Batty, Ferdinand. Scorers: Smith 13, 38, Viduka 34, Harte 81 pen

**06.03.01 v Real Madrid CF (a) Lost 2-3**
Martyn, Harte, Dacourt, Radebe (Kelly 65), Viduka, Kewell, Smith, Bakke (Wilcox 86), Matteo, Batty, Ferdinand. Scorers: Smith 6, Viduka 54

**14.03.01 v SS Lazio (h) Drawn 3-3**
Robinson, Kelly, Harte, Viduka (Hackworth 64), Kewell, Bowyer, Wilcox, Mills, Matteo, Burns, Maybury (Batty 90). Scorers: Bowyer 28, Wilcox 43, Viduka 62

**QUARTER FINAL**

**04.04.01 v RC Deportivo la Cortuna (h) Won 3-0**
Martyn, Harte, Dacourt, Viduka, Kewell (Wilcox 84), Bowyer, Smith, Mills, Matteo, Batty, Ferdinand. Scorers: Harte 26, Smith 51, Ferdinand 66

**17.04.01 v RC Deportivo la Coruna (a) Lost 0-2**
Martyn, Harte, Dacourt, Viduka, Kewell (Bakke 78), Bowyer, Smith, Mills, Matteo, Batty, Ferdinand

**SEMI FINAL**

**02.05.01 v Valencia CF (h) Drawn 0-0**
Martyn, Harte, Dacourt, Viduka, Kewell, Bowyer, Smith, Mills, Matteo, Batty, Ferdinand

**08.05.01 v Valencia CF (a) Lost 0-3**
Martyn, Harte, Dacourt, Viduka, Kewell, Smith, Mills, Bakke, Matteo, Batty, Ferdinand. Sent off: Smith 90

| SEASONS | PLAYED | WON | DRAWN | LOST | FOR | AGAINST |
|---|---|---|---|---|---|---|
| 1 | 16 | 6 | 5 | 5 | 24 | 21 |

## LEGIA WARSZAWA

**1995-1996**
**GROUP STAGE 1**
**13.09.95 v Rosenborg BK (h) Won 3-1**
Szczesny, Jozwiak, Zielinski, Ratajczak, Mandziejewicz, Bednarz (Fedoruk 84), Lewandowski, Pisz, Wieszczycki (Michalski 81), Staniek, Kubica (Kucharski 46). Scorers: Pisz 65, Staniek 69, Jamtfall og 70

**27.09.95 v FC Spartak Moscow (a) Lost 1-2**
Szczesny, Mandziejewicz, Jozwiak, Zielinski, Bednarz, Lewandowski (Ratajczak 34), Pisz, Michalski (Fedoruk 71), Wieszczycki, Staniek (Kubica 83), Kucharski. Scorer: Jozwiak 82

**18.10.95 v Blackburn Rovers FC (h) Won 1-0**
Szczesny, Mandziejewicz, Jozwiak, Zielinski, Bednarz, Lewandowski, Pisz, Michalski, Podbrozny, Staniek, Kucharski. Scorer: Pobdrozny 26

**01.11.95 v Blackburn Rovers FC (a) Drawn 0-0**
Szczesny, Mandziejewicz, Jozwiak (Mosor 66), Bednarz, Jalocha, Lewandowski, Pisz, Staniek, Michalski, Podbrozny (Kucharski 46), Wieszczycki

**22.11.95 v Rosenborg BK (a) Lost 0-4**
Szczesny, Mandziejewicz, Jozwiak, Zielinski, Jalocha, Lewandowski, Pisz (Kucharski 17), Michalski, Wieszczycki (Bednarz 62), Podbrozny, Staniek

**06.12.95 v FC Spartak Moscow (h) Lost 0-1**
Szczesny, Mandziejewicz, Jozwiak, Zielinski, Bednarz, Lewandowski, Pisz, Michalski, Staniek (Wieszczycki 82), Podbrozny, Kucharski

**QUARTER FINAL**
**06.03.96 v Panathinaikos FC (h) Drawn 0-0**
Szczesny, Mandziejewicz, Zielinski, Jozwiak, Bednarz, Lewandowski (Wieszczycki 77), Pisz, Michalski, Staniek, Podbrozny, Kucharski (Sokolowski 65)

**20.03.96 v Panathinaikos FC (a) Lost 0-3**
Szczesny, Jalocha, Mandziejewicz, Zielinski, Lewandowski, Wieszczycki, Pisz, Michalski, Sokolowksi (Kacprzak 82), Podbrozny, Staniek (Kucharski 75)

| SEASONS | PLAYED | WON | DRAWN | LOST | FOR | AGAINST |
|---|---|---|---|---|---|---|
| 1 | 8 | 2 | 2 | 4 | 5 | 11 |

## RC LENS

**1998-1999**
**GROUP STAGE 1**
**16.09.98 v Arsenal FC (h) Drawn 1-1**
Warmuz, Sikora, Meride (Rool 76), Dehu, Etchi Oben (Sankhare 82), Debeve, Dalmat, Nyarko, Smicer, Nouma (Moreira 70), Vairelles. Scorer: Vairelles 90

**30.09.98 v FC Dynamo Kyiv (a) Drawn 1-1**
Warmuz, Meride, Magnier, Dehu, Etchi Oben, Debeve (Moreira 74), Nyarko, Rool, Dalmat, Vairelles (Nouma 67), Smicer (Eloi 82). Scorer: Vairelles 62

**21.10.98 v Panathinaikos FC (h) Won 1-0**
Warmuz, Sikora, Dehu, Meride, Debeve, Dalmat (Eloi 66), Nyarko, Rool, Smicer (Moreira 72), Vairelles, Nouma. Scorer: Eloi 80

**04.11.98 v Panathinaikos FC (a) Lost 0-1**
Warmuz, Sikora, Dehu, Magnier, Meride, Debeve (Smicer 59), Dalmat, Nyarko, Rool, Nouma (Eloi 70), Vairelles

**26.11.98 v Arsenal FC (a) Won 1-0**
Warmuz, Sikora, Dehu, Magnier, Lachor, Debeve, Smicer (Moreira 80), Nyarko, Rool, Nouma (Eloi 60), Vairelles. Scorer: Debeve 72. Sent off: Vairelles 90

**09.12.98 v FC Dynamo Kyiv (h) Lost 1-3**
Warmuz, Meride (Brunel 82), Dehu, Magnier, Lachor, Debeve, Smicer, Dalmat (Moreira 88), Nyarko, Nouma, Eloi (Foe 64). Scorer: Smicer 78. Sent off: Dehu 6

**2002-2003**
**GROUP STAGE 1**
**18.09.02 v AC Milan (a) Lost 1-2**
Warmuz, Coly, Song, J Bak, Coulibaly, Sibierski, Blanchard (Bakari 84), PB Diop, Diagne-Faye (Keita 64), Thomert (Utaka 64), Moreira. Scorer: Moreira 74

**24.09.02 v FC Bayern Munchen (h) Drawn 1-1**
Warmuz, Coly, Song, J Bak, Rool, Sibierski, Blanchard (Bakari 68), PB Diop, Keita, Utaka, Moreira. Scorer: Utaka 76

**01.10.02 v RC Deportivo La Coruna (a) Lost 1-3**
Warmuz, Coly, Song, J Bak (Coulibaly 65), Rool, Sibierski (Bakari 84), Blanchard, Coridon, Pedron (Diagne-Faye 76), Utaka, Moreira. Scorer: Moreira 10

**23.10.02 v RC Deportivo La Coruna (h) Won 3-1**
Warmuz, Coulibaly, Song, J Bak, Rool, Sibierski (Bakari 73), Thomert (Coridon 73), PB Diop, Keita, Utaka, Moreira. Scorers: Coulibaly 61, Moreira 79, Thomert 84

**29.10.02 v AC Milan (h) Won 2-1**
Warmuz, Coulibaly, Song, J Bak, Rool, Sibierski (Diagne-Faye 87), Coridon, PB Diop (Coly 57), Keita, Utaka, Moreira (Thomert 90). Scorers: Moreira 41, Utaka 49

**13.11.02 v FC Bayern Munchen (a) Drawn 3-3**
Warmuz, Coulibaly, Song, J Bak, Rool (Keita 69), Sibierski, Blanchard, Coridon (Diagne-Faye 29), Bakari (Thomert 76), Utaka, Moreira. Scorers: Fink 20og, Bakari 54, Blanchard 90

| SEASONS | PLAYED | WON | DRAWN | LOST | FOR | AGAINST |
|---|---|---|---|---|---|---|
| 2 | 12 | 4 | 4 | 4 | 16 | 17 |

## K LIERSE SK

**1997-1998**
**GROUP STAGE 1**
**17.09.97 v Bayer 04 Leverkusen (a) Lost 0-1**
Vande Walle, Eftevaag, Van Meir, Seernels, Hoefkens (Van de Weyer 68), Zdebel, Leen, Van Kerckhoven, Haagdoren, Hasenhuttul, Huistra (Scavone 80)

**01.10.97 v Sporting Clube de Portugal (h) Drawn 1-1**
Vande Walle, Van Meir, Brocken, Eftevaag, Scavone, Haagdoren, Bovri, Zdebel, Leen, Huistra (Hoefkens 90), Hasenhuttul. Scorer: Huistra 88

**22.10.97 v AS Monaco (a) Lost 1-5**
Vande Walle, Brocken, Van Meir, Eftevaag, Scavone (Van de Weyer 73), Leen, Zdebel, Van Kerckhoven, Haagdoren (Seernels 73), Huistra, Hasenhuttul (Uwuigbe 80). Scorer: Van Meir 64

**05.11.97 v AS Monaco (h) Lost 0-1**
Vande Walle, Brocken (Van de Weyer 79), Van Meir (Hoefkens 70), Eftevaag, Van Kerckhoven, Seernels, Leen, Zdebel, Haagdoren (Cavens 83), Huistra, Hasenhuttul

**26.11.97 v Bayer 04 Leverkusen (h) Lost 0-2**
Vande Walle, Seernels, Brocken (Uwuigbe 77), Hoefkens, Eftevaag (Cavens 70), Scavone, Zdebel, Haagdoren, Leen, Van de Weyer, Hasenhuttul (De Kayser 70)

**10.12.97 v Sporting Clube de Portugal (a) Lost 1-2**
Deman, Van Meir, Brocken, Hoefkens, Scavone, Seernels, Zdebel, Leen (Bovri 72), Huistra (Cavens 77), Haagdoren, Van de Weyer (Uwuigbe 84). Scorer: Haagdoren 28

| SEASONS | PLAYED | WON | DRAWN | LOST | FOR | AGAINST |
|---|---|---|---|---|---|---|
| 1 | 6 | 0 | 1 | 5 | 3 | 12 |

## LILLE OSC

**2001-2002**
**GROUP STAGE 1**
**10.10.01 v Deportivo La Coruna (h) Drawn 1-1**
Wimbee, Pichot, Cygan, Fahmi, Ecker, N'Diaye, D'Amico, Sterjovski (Olufade 74), Landrin (Bassir 61) , Benoit Cheyrou (Murati 78), Bakari. Scorer: Olufade 87.
* Postponed to 10 October after 11 September atrocities

**18.09.01 v Manchester United FC (a) Lost 0-1**
Wimbee, Pichot, Cygan, Fahmi, Ecker, N'Diaye, D'Amico, Benoit Cheyrou (Boutoille 75), Tafforeau (Schmitz 86), Sterjovski (Olufade 90), Bakari

**25.09.01 v Olympiakos Piraeus FC (h) Won 3-1**
Wimbee, Pichot, Cygan, Fahmi, Ecker, N'Diaye, D'Amico, Bruno Cheyrou (Tafforeau 76), Boutoille (Delpierre 66), Sterjovski, Bakari (Olufade 88). Scorers: Bakari 33, Bruno Cheyrou 44, Tafforeau 79

**17.10.01 v Olympiakos Piraeus FC (a) Lost 1-2**
Wimbee, Landrin, Cygan, Fahmi, Ecker, Murati (Beck 84), D'Amico, Benoit Cheyrou, Delpierre, Bakari (Bassir 5), Olufade (Pichot 60). Scorer: Bassir 38

**23.10.01 v RC Deportivo La Coruna (a) Drawn 1-1**
Wimbee, Delpierre, Fahmi, Ecker, Pichot, Sterjovski (Collot 88), Landrin, D'Amico, N'Diaye (Benoit Cheyrou 81), Bruno Cheyrou, Bassir (Beck 90). Scorer: Bruno Cheyrou 20pen

**31.10.01 v Manchester United FC (h) Drawn 1-1**
Wimbee, Pichot, Fahmi, Ecker, Cygan, Sterjovski, D'Amico, N'Diaye (Landrin 86), Bruno Cheyrou, Boutoille (Beck 59), Bassir (Murati 78). Scorer: Bruno Cheyrou 65

| SEASONS | PLAYED | WON | DRAWN | LOST | FOR | AGAINST |
|---|---|---|---|---|---|---|
| 1 | 6 | 1 | 3 | 2 | 7 | 7 |

## LIVERPOOL FC

**2001-2002**
**GROUP STAGE 1**
**11.09.01 v Boavista FC (h) Drawn 1-1**
Dudek, Vignal, Hyppia, Henchoz, Carragher, Gerrard, McAllister, Hamann, Murphy (Riise 71), Owen, Heskey. Scorer: Owen 29

**19.09.01 v BV Borussia Dortmund (a) Drawn 0-0**
Dudek, Vignal, Hyppia, Henchoz, Riise (McAllister 75), Murphy, Gerrard, Hamann, Carragher, Owen, Heskey

**26.09.01 v FC Dynamo Kyiv (h) Won 1-0**
Dudek, Vignal, Hyppia, Henchoz, Carragher, Gerrard, Barmby (Murphy 62), Hamann, Riise (McAllister 79), Litmanen (Fowler 64), Heskey. Scorer: Litmanen 23

**16.10.01 v FC Dynamo Kyiv (a) Won 2-1**
Dudek, Carragher, Hyppia, Henchoz, Riise, Smicer (Redknapp 79), Gerrard, McAllister, Murphy, Barmby (Berger 62), Heskey. Scorers: Murphy 43, Gerrard 67

**24.10.01 v Boavista FC (a) Drawn 1-1**
Dudek, Carragher, Hyppia (Wright 6), Henchoz, Riise, Smicer, McAllister (Berger 76), Hamann, Murphy, Fowler, Heskey. Scorer: Murphy 17

**30.10.01 v BV Borussia Dortmund (h) Won 2-0**
Dudek, Wright, Henchoz, Carragher, Riise, Smicer (Berger 65), Gerrard (Redknapp 85), Hamann, Murphy, Owen (Fowler 76), Heskey. Scorers: Smicer 15, Wright 82

**GROUP STAGE 2**
**20.11.01 v FC Barcelona (h) Lost 1-3**
Dudek, Carragher, Hyppia, Henchoz, Riise, Smicer (Litmanen 80), Gerrard, McAllister (Berger 69), Murphy, Owen, Heskey (Fowler 66). Scorer: Owen 27

**05.12.01 v AS Roma (a) Drawn 0-0**
Dudek, Carragher, Hyppia, Henchoz, Riise, Smicer (McAllister 63), Gerrard (Biscan 84), Hamann, Murphy (Berger 61), Owen, Heskey

**20.02.02 v Galatasaray SK (h) Drawn 0-0**
Kirkland, Abel Xavier, Hyppia, Henchoz, Carragher (Smicer 67), Murphy, Gerrard (McAllister 73), Hamann, Riise, Owen, Heskey

**26.02.02 v Galatasaray SK (a)** **Drawn 1-1**
Kirkland, Abel Xavier, Hyppia, Henchoz, Carragher, Smicer (Litmanen 74), Murphy, Hamann, Riise, Owen, Heskey. Scorer: Heskey 79

**13.03.02 v FC Barcelona (a)** **Drawn 0-0**
Dudek, Abel Xavier, Hyppia, Henchoz, Carragher, Murphy, Gerrard (Barmby 80), Hamann, Riise, Litmanen (Smicer 70), Heskey (Baros 74)

**19.03.01 v AS Roma (h)** **Won 2-0**
Dudek, Abel Xavier, Hyppia, Henchoz, Carragher, Smicer (McAllister 90), Murphy, Gerrard, Riise, Litmanen (Biscan 88), Heskey. Scorers: Litmanen 7pen, Heskey 64

**QUARTER FINAL**
**02.04.02 v Bayer 04 Leverkusen** **Won 1-0**
Dudek, Carragher, Hyppia, Henchoz, Riise, Murphy, Gerrard, Hamann, Smicer (Berger 75), Owen (Litmanen 70), Heskey. Scorer: Hyppia 44

**10.04.02 v Bayer 04 Leverkusen** **Lost 2-4**
Dudek, Abel Xavier (Berger 75), Hyppia, Henchoz, Carragher, Murphy, Gerrard, Hamann (Smicer 61), Riise, Owen, Heskey (Litmanen 41). Scorers: Abel Xavier 42, Litmanen 79

**2002-2003**
**GROUP STAGE 1**
**17.09.02 v Valencia CF (a)** **Lost 0-2**
Dudek, Carragher, Hyypia, Diao (Cheyrou 46), Traore, Murphy (Baros 76), Hamann, Gerrard, Riise, Heskey, Diouf (Owen 46). Sent off: Hamann 77

**25.09.02 v FC Basel (h)** **Drawn 1-1**
Dudek, Carragher, Henchoz, Hyypia, Riise, Gerrard, Murphy, Cheyrou, Heskey (Diouf 71), Baros, Owen (Berger 79). Scorer: Baros 34

**02.10.02 v FC Spartak Moskva (h)** **Won 5-0**
Dudek, Carragher, Henchoz (Traore 67), Hyypia, Riise, Gerrard (Diao 76), Murphy, Hamann, Cheyrou (Diouf 82), Heskey, Owen. Scorers: Heskey 7, 89, Cheyrou 15, Hyypia 28, Diao 81

**22.10.02 v FC Spartak Moskva (a)** **Won 3-1**
Dudek, Carragher, Traore, Hyypia, Riise, Diao, Murphy, Hamann, Heskey (Vignal 56, Biscan 76), Owen, Baros (Diouf 70). Scorer: Owen 29, 70, 90

**30.10.02 v Valencia CF (h)** **Lost 0-2**
Dudek, Carragher (Cheyrou 82), Traore, Hyypia, Riise, Gerrard, Diao, Murphy (Smicer 61), Hamann, Heskey, Owen (Baros 61)

**12.11.02 v FC Basel (a)** **Drawn 3-3**
Dudek, Carragher (Diouf 79), Traore, Hyypia, Riise, Gerrard (Diao 46), Murphy, Hamann, Smicer, Heskey (Baros 61), Owen. Scorers: Murphy 60, Smicer 63, Owen 85

| SEASONS | PLAYED | WON | DRAWN | LOST | FOR | AGAINST |
|---|---|---|---|---|---|---|
| 2 | 20 | 7 | 9 | 4 | 26 | 20 |

## FC LOKOMOTIV MOSCOW

**2001-2002**
**GROUP STAGE 1**
**11.09.01 v RSC Anderlecht (h)** **Drawn 1-1**
Nigmatullin, Obradovic, Drozdov, Sennikov, Lekcetho, Tchougainov, Izmailov, Maminov, Ignachevich, Buznikin (Vucicevic 66), Pimenov (Janashia 75). Scorer: Maminov 18

**19.09.01 v Real Madrid CF (a)** **Lost 0-4**
Nigmatullin, Obradovic, Drozdov, Lekcetho, Tchougainov, Loskov, Izmailov, Maminov, Obiorah (Buznikin 60), Tcherevtchenko, Pimenov (Vucicevic 75)

**26.09.01 v AS Roma (a)** **Lost 1-2**
Nigmatullin, Obradovic, Drozdov, Lekcetho, Tchougainov, Loskov, Izmailov, Maminov, Ignachevich, Tcherevtchenko, Pimenov (Buznikin 75)

**16.10.01 v AS Roma (h)** **Lost 0-1**
Nigmatullin, Obiorah, Obradovic, Lekcetho, Tchougainov, Izmailov, Maminov, Ignachevich, Loskov Tcherevtchenko, Pimenov

**24.10.01 v RSC Anderlecht (a)** **Won 5-1**
Nigmatullin, Sennikov, Lekcetho (Nizhegorodov 84), Tchougainov, Loskov, Izmailov, Maminov, Ignachevich, Obiorah (Buznikin 55), Tcherevtchenko, Pimenov (Drozdov 75). Scorers: Izmailov 13, Sennikov 28, Pimenov 58, Buznikin 63, 69

**30.10.01 v Real Madrid CF (h)** **Won 2-0**
Nigmatullin, Sennikov, Lekcetho, Tchougainov (Obradovic 24), Loskov, Izmailov, Maminov, Ignachevich, Buznikin (Obiorah 75), Tcherevtchenko (Drozdov 78), Pimenov. Scorers: Buznikin 30, Tcherevtchenko 50

**2002-2003**
**GROUP STAGE 1**
**18.09.02 v Galatasaray SK (h)** **Lost 0-2**
Ovchinnikov, Nizhegorodov, Ignashevich, Pashinin (Sennikov 60), Lekgetho, Mamimov, Drozdov, Loskov, Evseev, Buznikin (Pimenov 46), J Cesar (Adamu 74)

**24.09.02 v Club Brugge KV (a) Drawn 0-0**
Ovchinnikov, Nizhegorodov, Ignashevich, Sennikov, Lekgetho, Mamimov (Obradovic 46), Loskov, Evseev, Buznikin (Sirkayev 46), Pimenov, J Cesar (Obiorah 74)

**01.10.02 v FC Barcelona (h) Lost 1-3**
Ovchinnikov, Nizhegorodov, Ignashevich, Sennikov, Lekgetho, Mamimov, Drozdov, Obradovic, Evseev, Pimenov, Obiorah (Buznikin 66). Scorer: Obiorah 56

**23.10.02 v FC Barcelona (a) Lost 0-1**
Ovchinnikov, Ignashevich, Sennikov, Pashinin, Mamimov, Loskov, Obradovic, Evseev, Pimenov, Obiorah, J Cesar (Buznikin 84)

**29.10.02 v Galatasaray SK (a) Won 2-1**
Ovchinnikov, Nezhegorodov, Ignashevich, Sennikov, Pashinin, Mamimov, Loskov, Lekgetho, Evseev, Pimenov, Obiorah (J Cesar 78). Scorers: Loskov 70, Evseev 75

**13.11.02 v Club Brugge KV (h) Won 2-0**
Ovchinnikov, Nezhegorodov, Ignashevich, Sennikov, Pashinin, Mamimov, Loskov, Lekgetho, Evseev, Buznikin (Obiorah 66), J Cesar (Adamu 90). Scorers: J Cesar 44, Loskov 90

**26.11.02 v BV Borussia Dortmund (h) Lost 1-2**
Ovchinnikov, Nezhegorodov, Ignashevich, Sennikov, Pashinin, Mamimov (Obradovic 46), Loskov, Lekgetho, Evseev, Obiorah (Buznikin 65), Pimenov (Adamu 74). Scorer: Ignashevich 31

**11.12.02 v Real Madrid CF (a) Drawn 2-2**
Ovchinnikov, Nezhegorodov, Ignashevich, Pashinin, Mamimov, Loskov, Mnguni, Lekgetho, Evseev, Pimenov (Drozdov 81), J Cesar (Obiorah 46). Scorers: Obiorah 47, Mnguni 74

**19.02.03 v AC Milan (a) Lost 0-1**
Ovchinnikov, Nezhegorodov, Ignashevich (Parks 83), Pashinin, Sennikov, Mamimov, Loskov, Obradovic, Lekgetho, Buznikin (Izmailov 46), Pimenov

**25.02.03 v AC Milan (h) Lost 0-1**
Ovchinnikov, Nezhegorodov, Ignashevich, Sennikov, Evseev, Mamimov, Loskov, Izmailov, Sirkayev (Pimenov 58), Mnguni, Julio Cesar (Parks 82)

**12.03.03 v BV Borussia Dortmund (h) Lost 0-3**
Ovchinnikov, Ignashevich, Pashinin, Sennikov, Mamimov, Evseev, Mnguni, Obradovic (Julio Cesar 46), Lekgetho, Izmailov, Pimenov

**18.03.03 v Real Madrid CF (h) Lost 0-1**
Ovchinnikov, Nezhegorodov, Ignashevich, Pashinin, Sennikov, Mamimov (Sirkayev 81), Evseev, Mnguni (Julio Cesar 72), Loskov, Izmailov, Pimenov

| SEASONS | PLAYED | WON | DRAWN | LOST | FOR | AGAINST |
|---|---|---|---|---|---|---|
| 2 | 12 | 4 | 3 | 11 | 17 | 26 |

## LYON (OLYMPIQUE LYONNAIS)

**2000-2001**
**GROUP STAGE 1**
**12.09.00 v SC Heerenveen (h) Won 3-1**
Coupet, Deflandre, Edmilson, Laville (Muller 60), Marlet (Govou 90), Laigle, Anderson (Malbranque 76), Dhorasoo, Foe, Linares, Brechet. Scorers: Anderson 2, Houttuin og 10, Marlet 58

**20.09.00 v Olympiakos Piraeus FC (a) Lost 1-2**
Coupet, Deflandre, Edmilson, Laville, Violeau (Laigle 65), Marlet, Anderson, Dhorasoo (Muller 65), Foe, Linares (Malbranque 65), Brechet. Scorer: Foe 88

**27.09.00 v Valencia CF (a) Lost 0-1**
Coupet, Edmilson, Laville, Marlet, Anderson, Foe, Malbranque, Chanelet, Muller, Linares (Govou 82), Brechet

**17.10.00 v Valencia CF (h) Lost 1-2**
Coupet, Deflandre, Edmilson, Laville, Marlet, Laigle (Violeau 67), Anderson, Delmotte (Vairelles 46), Foe, Malbranque (Linares 67), Brechet. Scorer: Marlet 90. Sent off: Foe 62

**25.10.00 v SC Heerenveen (a) Won 2-0**
Coupet, Deflandre, Edmilson, Laville, Violeau, Marlet, Anderson (Malbranque 33), Vairelles (Muller 83), Delmotte (Dhorasoo 60), Linares, Brechet. Scorers: Malbranque 68, Marlet 78

**07.11.00 v Olympiakos Piraeus (h) Won 1-0**
Coupet, Deflandre, Edmilson, Laville (Blanc 71), Violeau, Marlet, Laigle, Anderson (Govou 85), Vairelles (Linares 59), Foe, Brechet. Scorer: Laigle 2

**GROUP STAGE 2**
**22.11.00 v FC Bayern Munchen (a) Lost 0-1**
Coupet, Deflandre, Edmilson, Muller, Brechet, Violeau (Malbranque 74), Foe, Linares (Vairelles 74), Laigle, Anderson, Marlet (Govou 81)

**05.12.00 v FC Spartak Moscow (h) Won 3-0**
Coupet, Deflandre, Edmilson, Muller, Brechet, Violeau, Laigle, Linares, Dhorasoo (Malbranque 82), Anderson (Bak 71), Marlet (Vairelles 89). Scorers: Marlet 2, Anderson 31, 42

**13.02.01 v Arsenal FC (h) Lost 0-1**
Coupet, Deflandre, Edmilson, Muller, Brechet, Violeau (Malbranque 75), Foe, Laigle (Delmotte 83) Dhorasoo (Govou 75), Anderson, Marlet

**21.02.01 v Arsenal FC (a) Drawn 1-1**
Coupet, Deflandre, Edmilson, Muller, Brechet, Violeau, Foe (Linares 67), Laigle (Dhorasoo 67), Govou (Loko 79), Anderson, Marlet. Scorer: Edmilson 90

**06.03.01 v FC Bayern Munchen (h) Won 3-0**
Coupet, Deflandre, Cacapa, Brechet, Delmotte, Violeau, Linares, Laigle, Dhorasoo (Malbranque 87), Govou (Loko 83), Anderson (Chanelet 76). Scorers: Govou 13, 20 Laigle 71

**14.03.01 v FC Spartak Moscow (a) Drawn 1-1**
Coupet, Cacapa, Edmilson, Muller, Delmotte (Govou 57), Violeau (Brechet 85), Laigle, Dhorasoo, Chanelet, Anderson, Marlet (Loko 83). Scorer: Anderson 68pen

**2001-2002**
**GROUP STAGE 1**
**10.10.01* v FC Barcelona (a) Lost 0-2**
Coupet, Deflandre, Muller, Cacapa, Edmilson, Brechet, Linares (Delmotte 83), Foe, Laigle, Anderson (Lyindula 48, Nee 84), Govou
*played 10 October after 11 Sept atrocities

**18.09.01 v Bayer 04 Leverkusen (h) Lost 0-1**
Coupet, Deflandre, Muller, Edmilson, Brechet, Carriere (Juninho P 67), Foe, Violeau, Laigle (Delmotte 79), Nee (Lyindula 61), Govou. Sent off: Juninho P 84

**25.09.01 v Fenerbahce SK (a) Won 1-0**
Coupet, Deflandre, Muller, Edmilson (Cacapa 63), Brechet, Violeau, Carriere (Laigle 84), Foe, Delmotte, Lyindula (Linares 90), Govou. Scorer: Delmotte 89

**17.10.01 v Fenerbahce SK (h) Won 3-1**
Coupet, Violeau, Muller, Edmilson, Chanelet, Delmotte, Juninho P (Brechet 67), Carriere, Foe, Lyindula (Nee 79), Govou (Linares 86). Scorers: Govou 45, Carriere 53, Delmotte 68

**23.10.01 v FC Barcelona (a) Lost 2-3**
Coupet, Chanelet (Delmotte 53), Muller, Edmilson (Cacapa 26), Brechet (Laigle 78), Juninho P, Carriere, Foe, Violeau, Lyindula, Govou. Scorers: Lyindula 66, Carriere 88

**31.10.01 v Bayer 04 Leverkusen (a) Won 4-2**
Coupet, Deflandre, Muller, Laville, Delmotte, Chanelet, Linares, Carriere (Violeau 77), Juninho P (Govou 68), Laigle, Nee. Scorers: Carriere 32, 38, Nee 64, Govou 81

**2002-2003**
**GROUP STAGE 1**
**17.09.02 v AFC Ajax (a) Lost 1-2**
Coupet, Chanelet (Diarra 79), Cacapa, Edmilson, Brechet, Dhorasoo, Carriere, Violeau (Laville 46), Juninho, Anderson, Govou (Vairelles 41). Scorer: Anderson 84

**25.09.02 v Rosenborg BK (h) Won 5-0**
Coupet, Deflandre, Muller, Cacapa, Brechet, Dhorasoo (Delmotte 78), Carriere, Violeau, Diarra, Anderson (Juninho 67), Vairelles (Lyindula 72)
Scorers: Carriere 6, Vairelles 26, 45, Anderson 34, Lyindula 75

**02.10.02 v FC Internazionale (a) Won 2-1**
Coupet, Muller, Cacapa, Edmilson, Brechet, Dhorasoo, Carriere (Juninho 88), Violeau, Diarra, Anderson (Laville 77), Govou (Vairelles 90). Scorers: Govou 21, Anderson 60

**22.10.02 v FC Internazionale (h) Drawn 3-3**
Coupet, Muller, Cacapa, Edmilson, Brechet, Dhorasoo, Carriere, Violeau (Vairelles 69), Juninho (Laville 58), Diarra, Anderson. Scorers: Anderson 21,74, Carriere 44

**30.10.02 v AFC Ajax (h) Lost 0-2**
Coupet, Muller, Cacapa, Edmilson, Brechet, Dhorasoo, Carriere (Lyindula 80), Violeau (Vairelles 59), Juninho, Anderson, Govou

**12.11.02 v Rosenborg BK (h) Drawn 1-1**
Coupet, Muller, Cacapa, Edmilson, Brechet, Dhorasoo (Delmotte 72), Carriere (Lyindula 72), Violeau (Juninho 66), Diarra, Anderson, Govou. Scorer: Govou 84

| SEASONS | PLAYED | WON | DRAWN | LOST | FOR | AGAINST |
|---|---|---|---|---|---|---|
| 3 | 24 | 10 | 4 | 10 | 38 | 28 |

## MACCABI HAIFA

**2002-2003**
**GROUP STAGE 1**
**10.09.02 v Manchester United FC (a) Lost 2-5**
Awate, Harazi (Cohen 74), Benado, Ejiafor, Keise, Almoshnino (Zano 56), Pralija, Badir, Zandberg (Israilevich 65), Katan, Rosso. Scorers: Katan 8, Cohen 86

**24.09.02 v Olympaikos Piraeus FC (h) Won 3-0**
Awate, Harazi (Zano 52), Benado, Ejiafor, Keise, Zutauttas, Pralija (Israilevich 87), Badir, Katan (Zandberg 79), Ayegbeni, Rosso. Scorer: Ayegbeni 27pen, 60, 86

**01.10.02 v Bayer 04 Leverkusen (h) Lost 0-2**
Awate, Zano, Benado, Ejiafor, Keise, Zutauttas, Pralija (Israilevich 70), Badir (Zandberg 60), Katan (Cohen 60), Ayegbeni, Rosso

**23.10.02 v Bayer 04 Leverkusen (a) Lost 1-2**
Awate, Harazi, Zano (Sivilia 80), Benado, Keise, Zutauttas, Pralija (Israilevich 74), Badir, Zandberg (Katan 74), Ayegbeni, Rosso. Scorer: Pralija 53

**29.10.02 v Manchester United FC (h) Won 3-0**
Awate, Harazi, Zano, Benado, Keise, Zutauttas (Zandberg 81), Pralija, Badir, Katan, Ayegbeni (Almoshnino 84), Rosso. Scorers: Katan 40, Zutauttas 56, Ayegbeni 76pen

**13.11.02 v Olympiakos Piraeus FC (a) Drawn 3-3**
Awate, Harazi, Zano, Benado, Keise, Pralija (Almoshnino 79), Badir, Eijofor, Katan (Zandeberg 68), Ayegbeni, Rosso. Scorers: Badir 9, Ayegbeni 10, Katan 41

| SEASONS | PLAYED | WON | DRAWN | LOST | FOR | AGAINST |
|---|---|---|---|---|---|---|
| 1 | 6 | 2 | 1 | 3 | 12 | 12 |

## RCD MALLORCA

**2001-2002**
**GROUP STAGE 1**
**11.09.01 v Arsenal FC (h) Won 1-0**
Leo Franco, Olaizola, Nino, Nadal, M Soler, Campano, Engonga (Vicente 67), Marcos, Ibagaza (Novo 46), Luque (Paunovic 76), Eto'o. Scorer: Engonga 12pen

**19.09.01 v Panathinaikos FC (a) Lost 0-2**
Leo Franco, Fatih, Nino, Nadal, M Soler, Campano (Novo 70), Engonga, Marcos (Riera 86), Paunovic, Luque (Carlos 60), Eto'o

**26.09.01 v FC Schalke 04 (a) Won 1-0**
Roa, Olaizola, Nadal, M Soler, Novo, Engonga, Marcos, Vicente (Fatih 46), Diaz (F Soler 86), Luque (Paunovic 72), Eto'o. Scorer: Eto'o 66

**16.10.01 v FC Schalke 04 (h)** **Lost 0-4**
Roa, Olaizola, Nino, Nadal (Fatih 26), M Soler, Campano (Novo 76), Diaz (Carlos 56), Marcos, Paunovic Luque, Eto'o. Sent off: Eto'o 26

**24.10.01 v Arsenal FC (a)** **Lost 1-3**
Leo Franco, Fatih (Biagini 64), Olaizola, Nadal, M Soler, Campano, Marcos (Robles 68), Novo, Diaz, Paunovic, Luque (Carlos 79). Scorer: Novo 74

**30.10.01 v Panathinaikos FC (h)** **Won 1-0**
Miki, Olaizola, Nino, Nadal, M Soler, Campano, Marcos, Novo (F Soler 63), Paunovic (Robles 70), Biagini (Luque 78), Eto'o. Scorer: Biagini 57

| SEASONS | PLAYED | WON | DRAWN | LOST | FOR | AGAINST |
|---|---|---|---|---|---|---|
| 1 | 6 | 3 | 0 | 3 | 4 | 9 |

## MANCHESTER UNITED FC

**1994-1995**
**GROUP STAGE 1**
**14.09.94 v IFK Goteborg (h)** **Won 4-2**
Schmeichel, May, Irwin, Bruce, Sharpe, Pallister, Kanchelskis, Ince, Butt, Hughes, Giggs. Scorers: Giggs 33, 65, Kanchelskis 48, Sharpe 70

**28.09.94 v Galatasaray SK (a)** **Drawn 0-0**
Schmeichel, May, Sharpe, Bruce, Butt, Pallister, Kanchelskis, Ince, Keane, Hughes, Giggs (Parker 64)

**19.10.94 v FC Barcelona (h)** **Drawn 2-2**
Schmeichel, Parker, Irwin, May (Bruce 69), Butt (Scholes 67), Pallister, Kanchelskis, Ince, Keane, Hughes, Sharpe. Scorers: Hughes 19, Sharpe 79

**02.11.94 v FC Barcelona (a)** **Lost 0-4**
Walsh, Parker, Irwin, Bruce, Butt, Pallister, Kanchelskis, Ince, Keane, Hughes, Giggs (Scholes 79)

**23.11.94 v IFK Goteborg (a)** **Lost 1-3**
Walsh, May (G Neville 69), Irwin, Bruce, Pallister, Kanchelskis, Ince, Cantona, McClair, Hughes, Davies (Butt 76). Scorer: Hughes 64. Sent off: Ince 83

**07.12.94 v Galatasaray SK (h)** **Won 4-0**
Walsh, G Neville, Irwin, Bruce, Keane, Pallister, Cantona, Butt, McClair, Beckham, Davies. Scorers: Davies 2, Beckham 37, Keane 48, Bulent og 87

# CHAMPIONS LEAGUE HISTORY

**1996-1997**
**GROUP STAGE 1**
**11.09.96 v Juventus FC (a) Lost 0-1**
Schmeichel, G Neville, Johnsen, Pallister, Irwin, Beckham, Butt, Giggs (McClair 46), Poborsky (Solskjaer 78), Cantona, Cruyff (Cole)

**25.09.96 v SK Rapid Wien (h) Won 2-0**
Schmeichel, G Neville, Johnsen (May 19), Pallister, Irwin, Poborsky (Butt 79), Beckham, Keane, Giggs, Cantona, Solskjaer (Cole 74). Scorers: Solskjaer 20, Beckham 27

**16.10.96 v Fenerbahce SK (a) Won 2-0**
Schmeichel, Pallister, G Neville, May, Johnsen, Irwin, Beckham, Butt, Cruyff (Poborsky 73), Cantona, Solskjaer. Scorers: Beckham 55, Cantona 60

**30.10.96 v Fenerbahce SK (h) Lost 0-1**
Schmeichel, G Neville (P Neville 82), May, Johnsen, Irwin, Beckham, Keane, Butt, Poborsky (Solskjaer 68), Cantona, Cruyff (Scholes 68)

**20.11.96 v Juventus FC (h) Lost 0-1**
Schmeichel, G Neville, May, Johnsen, P Neville (McClair 12), Beckham, Butt, Keane, Giggs, Cantona, Solskjaer (Cruyff 83)

**04.12.96 v SK Rapid Wien (a) Won 2-0**
Schmeichel, G Neville (Casper 89), May, Pallister, Irwin, Beckham, Butt (Poborsky 81), Keane (McClair 76), Giggs, Cantona, Solskjaer. Scorers: Giggs 24, Cantona 72

**QUARTER FINAL**
**05.03.97 v FC Porto (h) Won 4-0**
Schmeichel, G Neville, May, Pallister, Irwin, Beckham, Johnsen, Giggs, Cantona, Cole, Solskjaer. Scorers: May 22, Cantona 34, Giggs 61, Cole 80

**19.03.97 v FC Porto (a) Drawn 0-0**
Schmeichel, G Neville, May, Pallister, Irwin (Poborsky 80), Beckham (P Neville 80), Butt, Johnsen, Cantona, Solskjaer (Scholes 69), Keane

**SEMI FINAL**
**09.04.97 v BV Borussia Dortmund (a) Lost 0-1**
Van der Gouw, G Neville, Johnsen, Pallister, Irwin, Beckham, Butt, Keane, Giggs (Scholes 82), Cantona, Solskjaer (Cole 74)

**23.04.97 v BV Borussia Dortmund (h) Lost 0-1**
Schmeichel, G Neville, Pallister, May (Scholes), P Neville, Beckham, Johnsen, Butt, Cantona, Solskjaer (Giggs 57), Cole

# CHAMPIONS LEAGUE HISTORY

**1997-1998**
**GROUP STAGE 1**
**17.09.97 v 1 FC Kosice (a) Won 3-0**
Schmeichel, G Neville, Berg, Pallister, Irwin, Beckham (McClair 74), Poborsky, Butt, Keane, Cole, Scholes. Scorers: Irwin 30, Berg 61, Cole 88

**01.10.97 v Juventus FC (h) Won 3-2**
Schmeichel, G Neville, Berg, Pallister, Irwin, Beckham, Johnsen, Butt (Scholes 38), Sheringham, Giggs, Solskjaer (P Neville 49). Scorers: Sheringham 38, Scholes 69, Giggs 90

**22.10.97 v Feyenoord (h) Won 2-1**
Schmeichel, Irwin, G Neville, Pallister, P Neville, Beckham, Butt, Giggs, Scholes, Cole (Solskjaer 82), Sheringham. Scorers: Scholes 32, irwin 72 pen

**05.11.97 v Feyenoord (a) Won 3-1**
Schmeichel, G Neville, Berg, Pallister, Irwin (P Neville 84), Beckham, Butt, Giggs, Scholes (Solskjaer 78), Sheringham, Cole (Poborsky 78). Scorer: Cole 31, 44, 75

**27.11.97 v 1 FC Kosice (h) Won 3-0**
Schmeichel, G Neville, Pallister, Johnsen, P Neville (Berg 75), Beckham, Butt (Solskjaer 55), Giggs (Poborsky 75), Scholes, Sheringham, Cole. Scorers: Cole 40, Faktor og 85, Sheringham 90

**10.12.97 v Juventus FC (a) Lost 0-1**
Schmeichel, G Neville, Berg, Pallister, P Neville, Beckham, Johnsen, Poborsky (McClair 80), Giggs, Sheringham, Solskjaer (Cole 74)

**QUARTER FINAL**
**04.03.98 v AS Monaco (a) Drawn 0-0**
Schmeichel, G Neville, Johnsen, Berg, Irwin (McClair 66), P Neville, Scholes, Butt, Beckham, Solskjaer, Sheringham, Cole

**18.03.98 v AS Monaco (h) Drawn 1-1**
Van der Gouw, P Neville, G Neville (Berg 33), Johnsen, Irwin, Scholes (Clegg 46), Butt, Beckham, Sheringham, Solskjaer, Cole. Scorer: Solskjaer 53

**1998-1999**
**GROUP STAGE 1**
**16.09.98 v FC Barcelona (h) Drawn 3-3**
Schmeichel, G Neville, Stam, Berg, Irwin (P Neville 79), Beckham, Keane, Scholes, Giggs (Blomqvist 84), Solskjaer (Butt 55), Yorke. Scorers: Giggs 17, Scholes 24, Beckham 64. Sent off: Butt 70

# CHAMPIONS LEAGUE HISTORY

**30.09.98 v FC Bayern Munchen (a) Drawn 2-2**
Schmeichel, G Neville, Stam, P Neville, Irwin, Beckham, Keane, Scholes, Blomqvist (Jordi Cruyff 69), Sheringham, Yorke. Scorers: Yorke 30, Scholes 49

**21.10.98 v Brondby IF (a) Won 6-2**
Schmeichel, Brown, Stam, G Neville, P Neville, Scholes, Keane, Giggs (Jordi Cruyff 60), Blomqvist, Yorke (Wilson 65), Cole (Solskjaer 60). Scorers: Giggs 2, 21, Cole 28, Keane 55, Yorke 60, Solskjaer 62

**04.11.98 v Brondby IF (h) Won 5-0**
Schmeichel, G Neville, P Neville (Brown 32), Stam, Irwin, Beckham, Keane, Scholes, Blomqvist (Jordi Cruyff 46), Yorke, Cole (Solskjaer 56). Scorers: Beckham 7, Cole 13, P Neville 16, Yorke 28, Scholes 62

**25.11.98 v FC Barcelona (a) Drawn 3-3**
Schmeichel, Brown, G Neville, Stam, Irwin, Beckham (Butt 82), Keane, Scholes, Blomqvist, Yorke, Cole. Scorers: Yorke 25, 68, Cole 53

**09.12.98 v FC Bayern Munchen (h) Drawn 1-1**
Schmeichel, Brown, G Neville, Stam, Irwin (Johnsen 46), Beckham, Keane, Scholes, Giggs, Yorke (Butt 64), Cole. Scorer: Keane 43

**QUARTER FINAL**
**03.03.99 v FC Internazionale (h) Won 2-0**
Schmeichel, G Neville, Stam, Johnsen (Berg 46), Irwin, Beckham, Keane, Scholes (Butt 69), Giggs, Yorke, Cole. Scorer: Yorke 7, 48

**17.03.99 v FC Internazionale (a) Drawn 1-1**
Schmeichel, G Neville, Stam, Berg, Irwin, Beckham, Johnsen (Scholes 77), Keane, Giggs (P Neville 82), Yorke, Cole. Scorer: Scholes 88

**SEMI FINAL**
**07.04.99 v Juventus FC (h) Drawn 1-1**
Schmeichel, G Neville, Berg (Johnsen 46), Stam, Irwin, Beckham, Keane, Scholes, Giggs, Yorke (Sheringham 80), Cole. Scorer: Giggs 90

**21.04.99 v Juventus FC (a) Won 3-2**
Schmeichel, G Neville, Johnsen, Stam, Irwin, Beckham, Keane, Butt, Blomqvist (Scholes 68), Yorke, Cole. Scorers: Keane 24, Yorke 34, Cole 84

**FINAL**
**26.05.99 v FC Bayern Munchen (n) Won 2-1**
Schmeichel, G Neville, Stam, Johnsen, Irwin, Beckham, Butt, Blomqvist (Sheringham 67), Giggs, Yorke, Cole (Solskjaer 81). Scorers: Sheringham 90, Solskjaer 90

# CHAMPIONS LEAGUE HISTORY

**1999-2000**
**GROUP STAGE 1**
**14.09.99 v NK Croatia/Dinamo Zagreb (h) Drawn 0-0**
Van der Gouw, Stam, Beckham, Cole, Giggs, P Neville, Scholes, Yorke, Berg, Clegg (Fortune 76), Wilson (Sheringham 61)

**22.09.99 v SK Sturm Graz (a) Won 3-0**
Van der Gouw, Irwin, Stam, Beckham, Cole (Solskjaer 76), P Neville, Cruyff (Sheringham 68), Keane (Wilson 62), Scholes, Yorke, Berg. Scorers: Keane 16, Yorke 31, Cole 33

**29.09.99 v Olympique de Marseille (h) Won 2-1**
Van der Gouw, Irwin, Stam, Beckham, Butt, Cole (Clegg 86), P Neville, Scholes, Yorke, Solskjaer (Fortune 72), Berg (Sheringham 77). Scorers: Cole 79, Scholes 83

**19.10.99 v Olympique de Marseille (a) Lost 0-1**
Bosnich, Irwin, Stam, Beckham, Cole, Giggs, P Neville, Keane, Scholes, Yorke, Berg (Solskjaer 83)

**27.10.99 v NK Croatia/Dinamo Zagreb (a) Won 2-1**
Bosnich, Irwin, Stam, Beckham, Cole (Cruyff 79), Giggs, P Neville, Keane, Scholes (Greening 68), Yorke (Solskjaer 59), Berg. Scorers: Beckham 32, Keane 49

**02.11.99 v SK Sturm Graz (h) Won 2-1**
Bosnich, G Neville, Irwin (Higginbotham 76), May, Cole, Giggs, Keane, Solskjaer, Berg, Wilson (P Neville 54), Greening (Cruyff 65). Scorers: Solskjaer 56, Keane 69

**GROUP STAGE 2**
**23.11.99 v AC Fiorentina (a) Lost 0-2**
Bosnich, G Neville, Irwin, Stam, Beckham, Cole (Sheringham 63), Giggs, Keane, Scholes, Yorke (Solskjaer 63), Berg (P Neville 63)

**08.12.99 v Valencia CF (h) Won 3-0**
Van der Gouw, G Neville, Irwin, Stam, Beckham, Cole (Yorke 72), Giggs, P Neville, Keane, Scholes (Butt 72), Solskjaer. Scorers: Keane 38, Solskjaer 47, Scholes 70

**01.03.00 v FC Girondins de Bordeaux (h) Won 2-0**
Van der Gouw, G Neville, Irwin, Stam, Beckham, Butt, Cole (P Neville 81), Sheringham, Giggs (Solskjaer 88), Keane (Fortune 88), Silvestre. Scorers: Giggs 42, Sheringham 84

**07.03.00 v Girondins de Bordeaux (a) Won 2-1**
Van der Gouw, G Neville, Irwin (Solskjaer 83), Stam, Beckham, Butt, Cole (Berg 86), Sheringham (Yorke 77), Giggs, Keane, Silvestre. Scorers: Keane 33, Solskjaer 84

**15.03.00 v AC Fiorentina (h) Won 3-1**
Bosnich, G Neville, Irwin, Stam, Beckham, Cole, Giggs, Keane, Scholes, Yorke, Berg
Scorers: Cole 20, Keane 33, Yorke 70

**21.03.00 v Valencia CF (a) Drawn 0-0**
Bosnich, G Neville, Irwin, Stam, Butt, Sheringham, Keane, Scholes, Solskjaer (Cruyff 67), Berg, Fortune

**QUARTER FINAL**

**04.04.00 v Real Madrid CF (a) Drawn 0-0**
Bosnich, G Neville, Irwin (Silvestre 87), Stam, Beckham, Cole, Giggs, Keane, Scholes (Butt 81), Yorke (Sheringham 76), Berg

**19.04.00 v Real Madrid CF (h) Lost 2-3**
Van der Gouw, G Neville, Irwin (Silvestre 46), Stam, Beckham, Cole (Solskjaer 62), Giggs, Keane, Scholes, Yorke, Berg (Sheringham 62). Scorers: Beckham 64, Scholes 88 pen

**2000-2001**

**GROUP STAGE 1**

**13.09.00 v RSC Anderlecht (h) Won 5-1**
Barthez, G Neville, Irwin (P Neville 69), Johnsen, Beckham, Cole (Yorke 74), Sheringham, Giggs (Solskjaer 59), Keane, Scholes, Silvestre. Scorers: Cole 15, 50, 72, Irwin 32 pen, Sheringham 42

**19.09.00 v FC Dynamo Kyiv (a) Drawn 0-0**
Van der Gouw, G Neville, Irwin, Johnsen, Beckham, Butt, Cole (Solskjaer 78), Giggs, Keane, Yorke (Sheringham 67), Silvestre

**26.09.00 v PSV Eindhoven (a) Lost 1-3**
Van der Gouw, G Neville, Butt, P Neville, Keane, Scholes (Beckham 70), Yorke, Solskjaer, Brown, Silvestre (Wallwork 70), Greening (Giggs 70). Scorer: Scholes 3 pen

**18.10.00 v PSV Eindhoven (h) Won 3-1**
Barthez, G Neville, Irwin (Brown 80), Johnsen, Beckham (Butt 88), Cole, Sheringham (Yorke 74), Giggs, Keane, Scholes, Silvestre. Scorers: Sheringham 8, Scholes 82, Yorke 87

**24.10.00 v RSC Anderlecht (a) Lost 1-2**
Barthez, G Neville, Irwin (Solskjaer 78), Johnsen, Beckham, Butt, Cole, Giggs, Scholes, Yorke, Silvestre (Brown 63). Scorer: Irwin 36 pen

**08.11.00 v Dynamo Kyiv (h) Won 1-0**
Barthez, G Neville, Irwin, Beckham, Butt, Cole, Sheringham (Yorke 74), Giggs (Fortune 34, Silvestre 88), P Neville, Keane, Brown. Scorer: Sheringham 18

**GROUP STAGE 2**

**21.11.00 v Panathinaikos FC (h) Won 3-1**

Barthez, G Neville, Beckham, Butt, Sheringham, P Neville, Keane, Scholes, Yorke, Brown, Silvestre. Scorers: Sheringham 48, Scholes 81, 90

**06.12.00 v SK Sturm Graz (a) Won 2-0**

Barthez, G Neville, Irwin (P Neville 89), Beckham, Butt (Giggs 80), Sheringham, Keane, Scholes, Yorke (Solskjaer 89), Brown, Silvestre. Scorers: Scholes 18, Giggs 89

**14.02.01 v Valencia CF (a) Drawn 0-0**

Barthez, G Neville, Stam, Beckham (Butt 75), Cole (Solskjaer 85), Sheringham, Giggs, Keane, Scholes, Brown, Silvestre

**20.02.01 v Valencia CF (h) Drawn 1-1**

Barthez, G Neville, Stam, Beckham, Cole, Sheringham (Solskjaer 63), Giggs (Butt 18), Keane, Scholes, Brown, Silvestre. Scorer: Cole 12

**07.03.01 v Panathinaikos FC (a) Drawn 1-1**

Barthez, G Neville, Stam, Beckham, Cole (Solskjaer 78), P Neville (Sheringham 78), Keane, Scholes, Yorke, Brown, Silvestre (Chadwick 64). Scorer: Scholes 90

**13.03.01 v SK Sturm Graz (h) Won 3-0**

Barthez, G Neville, Irwin, Stam, Butt, Sheringham, Keane, Scholes (Greening 74), Solskjaer, Silvestre, Chadwick. Scorers: Butt 5, Sheringham 20, Keane 86

**QUARTER FINAL**

**03.04.01 v FC Bayern Munchen (h) Lost 0-1**

Barthez, G Neville, Stam, Beckham (Yorke 86), Cole, Giggs, Keane, Scholes, Solskjaer, Brown, Silvestre

**18.04.01 v FC Bayern Munchen (a) Lost 1-2**

Barthez, G Neville, Stam, Butt (Solskjaer 78), Cole, Giggs, Keane, Scholes, Yorke (Sheringham 66), Brown (Chadwick 85), Silvestre. Scorer: Giggs 49

**2001-2002**

**GROUP STAGE 1**

**10.10.01* v Olympiakos Piraeus (a) Won 2-0**

Barthez, G Neville, Johnsen, Blanc, Irwin (Silvestre 90), Beckham, Scholes, Keane, Veron (Cole 80), Giggs, Van Nistelrooy (Solskjaer 85). Scores: Beckham 66, Cole 82
*played 10 October after 11 Sept atrocities

**18.09.01 v Lille OSC (h) Won 1-0**
Barthez, G Neville (Silvestre 12), Brown, Blanc, Irwin, Beckham, Scholes, Keane, Veron (Cole 80), Giggs (Solskjaer 76), Van Nistelrooy. Scorer: Beckham 90

**25.09.01 v RC Deportivo La Coruna (a) Lost 1-2**
Barthez, G Neville, Johnsen, Blanc, Irwin, Beckham (Cole 90), Scholes, Keane, Veron, Giggs, Van Nistelrooy (Solskjaer 90). Scorer: Scholes 40

**17.10.01 v RC Deportivo La Coruna (h) Lost 2-3**
Barthez, G Neville, Johnsen (Brown 7), Blanc, Irwin (Solskjaer 85), Beckham, Scholes (Cole 63), Keane, Veron, Giggs, Van Nistelrooy. Scorers: Van Nistelrooy 7, 40

**23.10.01 v Olympiakos Piraeus (h) Won 3-0**
Barthez, G Neville, Brown, Blanc, Irwin, Beckham, Scholes, Butt (Solskjaer 73), Veron, Giggs, Van Nistelrooy. Scorers: Solskjaer 79, Giggs 88, Van Nistelrooy 90

**31.10.01 v Lille OSC (a) Drawn 1-1**
Carroll, Irwin, May (O'Shea 69) P Neville, Silvestre, Beckham, Butt, Scholes, Fortune, Cole (Yorke 76), Solskjaer. Scorer: Solskjaer 6

**GROUP STAGE 2**
**20.11.01 v FC Bayern Munchen (a) Drawn 1-1**
Barthez, G Neville, Brown, Blanc, Irwin (Silvestre 85), Beckham, Scholes, Keane, Veron, Fortune, Van Nistelrooy (Yorke 85). Scorer: Van Nistelrooy 74

**05.12.01 v Boavista FC (h) Won 3-0**
Barthez, P Neville, G Neville (O'Shea 77),, Blanc, Silvestre, Butt, Scholes (Fortune 85), Keane, Veron, Yorke, Van Nistelrooy (Solskjaer 88). Scorers: Van Nistelrooy 31, 62, Blanc 55

**20.02.02 v FC Nantes Atlantique (a) Drawn 1-1**
Barthez, P Neville (Forlan 78), G Neville, Blanc, Silvestre, Beckham, Scholes, Keane, Veron (Solskjaer 64), Giggs, Van Nistelrooy. Scorer: Van Nistelrooy 90pen

**26.02.02 v Nantes Atlantique (h) Won 5-1**
Barthez, Irwin, G Neville, Blanc (Johnsen 69), Silvestre, Beckham, Keane (Butt 75), Veron,Solskjaer, Giggs, Van Nistelrooy (Forlan 75). Scorers: Beckham 18, Solskjaer 31, 78, Silvestre 38, Van Nistelrooy 64pen

**13.03.02 v FC Bayern Munchen (h) Drawn 0-0**
Barthez, G Neville, Johnsen, Blanc, Silvestre, Beckham, Keane, Veron, Solskjaer (Forlan 78), Giggs, Van Nistelrooy

**19.03.02 v Boavista FC (a) Won 3-0**
Barthez, G Neville, Johnsen (P Neville 73), Blanc (O'Shea 73), Silvestre, Beckham, Butt, Scholes (Stewart 59), Solskjaer, Forlan, Giggs. Scorers: Blanc 14, Solskjaer 29, Beckham 52pen

**QUARTER FINAL**
**02.04.02 v RC Deportivo la Coruna (a) Won 2-0**
Barthez, G Neville, Johnsen, Blanc, Silvestre, Beckham (P Neville 90), Keane (Fortune 45), Butt, Scholes, Giggs, Van Nistelrooy (Solskjaer 76). Scorers: Beckham 15, Van Nistelrooy 41

**10.04.02 v RC Deportivo la Coruna (h) Won 3-2**
Barthez, G Neville, Johnsen (Brown 37), Blanc, Silvestre, Beckham (Solskjaer 21), Fortune, Butt, Veron (P Neville 74), Giggs, Van Nistelrooy. Scorers: Solskjaer 23, 56, Giggs 59

**SEMI FINAL**
**24.04.02 v Bayer 04 Leverkusen (h) Drawn 2-2**
Barthez, G Neville (P Neville 18, Irwin 89), Brown, Blanc, Silvestre, Veron, Butt, Scholes (Keane 62), Giggs, Van Nistelrooy, Solskjaer. Scorers: Zivkovic 29og, Van Nistelrooy 67pen

**30.04.02 v Bayer 04 Leverkusen (a) Drawn 1-1**
Barthez, Brown (Forlan 81), Johnsen (Irwin 60), Blanc, Silvestre, Veron, Keane, Butt (Solskjaer 61), Scholes, Giggs, Van Nistelrooy. Scorer: Keane 28

**2002-2003**
**GROUP STAGE 1**
**18.09.02 v Maccabi Haifa (h) Won 5-2**
Barthez (Ricardo 67), O'Shea, Ferdinand, Blanc, Silvestre, Beckham, P Neville, Veron, Giggs (Forlan 56), Solskjaer, Van Nistelrooy (Pugh 75). Scorers: Giggs 10, Solskjaer 35, Veron 46, Van Nistelrooy 54, Forlan 89pen

**24.09.02 v Bayer 04 Leverkusen (a) Won 2-1**
Barthez, O'Shea (G Neville 46), Ferdinand, Blanc, Silvestre, Beckham, P Neville, Butt, Veron (Solskjaer 88), Giggs, Van Nistelrooy (Forlan 46). Scorer: Van Nistelrooy 31, 44

**01.10.02 v Olympiakos Piraeus FC (h) Won 4-0**
Barthez, G Neville, Ferdinand, Blanc (O'Shea 69), Silvestre, Beckham, Scholes (Forlan 77), Butt, Veron, Solskjaer, Giggs (Fortune 69). Scorers: Giggs 19, 66, Veron 26, Solskjaer 77

**23.10.02 v Olympiakos Piraeus FC (a) Won 3-2**
Barthez, G Neville, O'Shea, Blanc, Silvestre, Beckham (Chadwick 63), P Neville, Scholes, Veron (Richardson 87), Giggs (Fortune 63), Forlan. Scorers: Blanc 21, Veron 59, Scholes 84

**29.10.02 v Maccabi Haifa (a) Lost 0-3**
Ricardo, G Neville, Ferdinand, O'Shea, Silvestre, P Neville, Scholes, Richardson (Nardiello 61), Fortune, Solskjaer, Forlan (Timm 79)

**13.11.02 v Bayer 04 Leverkusen (h) Won 2-0**
Ricardo, O'Shea, Blanc (G Neville 77), Ferdinand, Silvestre, Beckham (Solskjaer 78), Veron, Scholes, Fortune, Van Nistelrooy, Giggs (Chadwick 81). Scorers: Veron 42, Van Nistelrooy 69

**26.11.02 v FC Basel (a) Won 3-1**
Barthez, P Neville, Brown (May 90), O'Shea, Silvestre, Fortune, Scholes, Veron, Giggs, Solskjaer (Chadwick 90), Van Nistelrooy (Forlan 73). Scorers: Van Nistelrooy 62, 63, Solskjaer 68

**11.12.02 v RC Deportivo La Coruna (h) Won 2-0**
Barthez, G Neville, Brown, Silvestre, O'Shea (Beckham 81), P Neville (Forlan 81), Veron, Scholes, Giggs, Solskjaer, Van Nistelrooy (Richardson 89). Scorer: Van Nistelrooy 7, 55

**19.02.03 v Juventus FC (h) Won 2-1**
Barthez, G Neville, Ferdinand, Brown, Silvestre (O'Shea 52), Beckham, Keane, Butt, Scholes (Solskjaer 80), Giggs (Forlan 90), Van Nistelrooy. Scorers: Brown 4, van Nistelrooy 85

**25.02.03 v Juventus FC (a) Won 3-0**
Barthez, G Neville, Ferdinand, Keane,O'Shea (Pugh 60), Beckham, P Neville, Butt, Veron, Forlan (Giggs 8, Van Nistelrooy 49), Solskjaer. Scorers: Giggs 15, 41, Van Nistelrooy 63

**12.03.03 v FC Basel (h) Drawn 1-1**
Carroll, G Neville, Ferdinand, Blanc (Scholes 74), O'Shea, Fletcher (Beckham 74), P Neville, Butt, Richardson (Giggs 46), Solskjaer, Forlan. Scorer: G Neville 53

**18.03.03 v RC Deportivo La Coruna (a) Lost 0-2**
Ricardo, Roche (Stewart 46), Blanc, O'Shea, Lynch, Butt, P Neville, Pugh, Fletcher, Giggs (Richardson 72), Forlan (Webber 72)

**08.04.03 v Real Madrid CF (a) Lost 1-3**
Barthez, G Neville (Solskjaer 86), Ferdinand, Brown, Silvestre (O'Shea 58), Beckham, Keane, Butt, Scholes, Giggs, Van Nistelrooy. Scorer: Van Nistelrooy 52

**23.04.03 v Real Madrid CF (h) Won 4-3**
Barthez, Brown, Ferdinand, Silvestre (P Neville 79), O'Shea, Veron (Beckham 63), Keane (Fortune 82), Butt, Solskjaer, Giggs, Van Nistelrooy. Scorers: Van Nistelrooy 43, Helguera 52og, Beckham 71, 85

| SEASONS | PLAYED | WON | DRAWN | LOST | FOR | AGAINST |
|---|---|---|---|---|---|---|
| 8 | 93 | 48 | 25 | 20 | 171 | 95 |

## NK MARIBOR

**1999-2000**
**GROUP STAGE 1**
**14.09.99 v FC Dynamo Kyiv (a) Won 1-0**
Simeunovic, Seslar, Zidan, Karic, Simundza (Filipovic 82), Cipi, Balajic (Vugdalic 64), Djuranovic, Galic, Bozgo (Pregelj 90), Sarkezi. Scorer: Simundza 73

**22.09.99 v Bayer 04 Leverkusen (h) Lost 0-2**
Simeunovic, Vugdalic, Seslar, Zidan, Simundza, Filekovic (Pregelj 52), Cipi, Balajic (Dragusha 85), Djuranovic, Galic, Bozgo

**29.09.99 v SS Lazio (a) Lost 0-4**
Simeunovic, Vugdalic, Seslar, Zidan (Pregelj 81), Karic, Simundza (Sarkezi 46), Cipi, Balajic, Djuranovic, Galic, Bozgo (Filipovic 68). Sent off: Cipi 20

**19.10.99 v SS Lazio (h) Lost 0-4**
Simeunovic, Vugdalic, Seslar (Dargusha 84), Zidan, Karic, Simundza (Pregelj 78), Balajic, Djuranovic, Galic, Bozgo (Filipovic 61), Sarkezi

**27.10.99 v FC Dynamo Kyiv (h) Lost 1-2**
Gresak, Vugdalic, Seslar, Zidan, Karic, Filipovic (Pregelj 69), Simundza, Cipi, Balajic (Bozgo 61), Djuranovic, Sarkezi (Filekovic 87). Scorer: Balajic 50

**02.11.99 v Bayer 04 Leverkusen (a) Drawn 0-0**
Gresak, Vugdalic, Seslar, Zidan, Karic, Filipovic (Filekovic 90), Simundza (Bozgo 56), Balajic (Dragusha 90), Djuranovic, Galic, Sarkezi

| SEASONS | PLAYED | WON | DRAWN | LOST | FOR | AGAINST |
|---|---|---|---|---|---|---|
| 1 | 6 | 1 | 1 | 4 | 2 | 12 |

## MARSEILLE (OLYMPIQUE DE MARSEILLE)

**1992-1993**
**GROUP STAGE 1**
**25.11.92 v Rangers FC (a)** **Drawn 2-2**
Barthez, Angloma, Di Meco, Boli, Sauzee, Desailly, Casoni, Boksic (Durand 84), Voller (Eydelie 90), Ayew Pele, Deschamps. Scorers: Boksic 31, Voller 56

**09.12.92 v Club Brugge KV (h)** **Won 3-0**
Barthez, Thomas, Di Meco, Angloma, Sauzee, Desailly, Casoni, Boksic (Ferreri 86), Eydelie (Durand 82), Ayew Pele, Deschamps. Scorers: Sauzee 5 pen, Boksic 10, 27

**03.03.93 v CSKA Moscow (a)** **Drawn 1-1**
Barthez, Eydelie, Di Meco, Angloma, Sauzee, Desailly, Casoni, Boksic, Dobrovolski (Durand 57), Ayew Pele, Deschamps. Scorer: Pele 27

**17.03.93 v CSKA Moscow (h)** **Won 6-0**
Barthez, Angloma, Di Meco, Boli, Sauzee (Eydelie 67), Desailly, Durand, Boksic, Voller (Ferreri 65), Ayew Pele, Deschamps. Scorers: Sauzee 5 pen, 35, 49, Pele 43, Ferreri 71, Desailly 79

**07.04.93 v Rangers FC (h)** **Drawn 1-1**
Barthez, Angloma, Di Meco, Boli, Sauzee, Desailly, Eydelie, Boksic, Voller, Ayew Pele, Deschamps. Scorer: Sauzee 15

**21.04.93 v Club Brugge KV (a)** **Won 1-0**
Barthez, Angloma, Thomas, Boli, Eydelie, Desailly, Ferreri (Sauzee 46), Boksic, Voller (Durand 89), Ayew Pele, Deschamps. Scorer: Boksic 3

**FINAL**
**26.05.93 v Milan AC (n)** **Won 1-0**
Barthez, Angloma (Durand 62), Di Meco, Boli, Sauzee, Desailly, Eydelie, Boksic, Voller (Thomas 79), Ayew Pele, Deschamps. Scorer: Boli 44

**1992-2000**
**GROUP STAGE 1**
**14.09.99 v SK Sturm Graz (h)** **Won 2-0**
Porato, Blondeau, Perez, Berizzo, Pires, Brando, Maurice (Diawara 83), Ravanelli (Keita 88), Dalmat (Belmadi 76), Gallas, Luccin. Scorers: Pires 9, Ravanelli 33

**22.09.99 v NK Croatia/Dinamo Zagreb (a)** **Won 2-1**
Porato, Blondeau (Brando 53), Perez, Issa, Berizzo, Pires, Dalmat, Keita (Ravanelli 67), Bakayoko (Diawara 86), Gallas, Luccin. Scorers: Bakayoko 5, Perez 77

**29.09.99 v Manchester United FC (a) Lost 1-2**
Porato, Blondeau, Perez, Issa (Belmadi 82), Brando, Ravanelli (Pires 62), Dalmat, Bakayoko, Gallas, Fischer, Luccin (De La Pena 77). Scorer: Bakayoko 41

**19.10.99 v Manchester United FC (h) Won 1-0**
Porato, Blondeau, Perez, Issa, Berizzo, Pires, Brando (De La Pena 64), Ravanelli (Maurice 74), Dalmat (Reina 88), Gallas, Luccin. Scorer: Gallas 69

**27.10.99 v SK Sturm Graz (a) Lost 2-3**
Porato, Blondeau, Perez, Issa (De La Pena 46, Dugarry 51), Berizzo, Pires, Maurice (Reina 70), Ravanelli, Dalmat, Gallas, Luccin. Scorer: Dugarry 53, 78. Sent off: Blondeau 68

**02.11.99 v NK Croatia/Dinamo Zagreb (h) Drawn 2-2**
Porato, Perez, Berizzo, Brando, Belmadi, Montenegro (Dalmat 59), Diawara, Dugarry (Pires 66), Bakayoko (Ravanelli 78), Luccin, Reina. Scorers: Bakayoko 53, Diawara 89

**GROUP STAGE 2**
**24.11.99 v SS Lazio (h) Lost 0-2**
Porato, Perez (Maurice 67), Berizzo, Pires, Brando, Dalmat, Diawara (Ravanelli 58), Dugarry, Gallas, Fischer, Luccin

**07.12.99 v Feyenoord (a) Lost 0-3**
Porato, Perez, Berizzo (Issa 46), Pires (Martin 68), Brando, Maurice (Bakayoko 81), Dalmat, Dugarry, Gallas, Fischer, Luccin. Sent off: Fischer 62, Perez 79

**29.02.00 v Chelsea FC (h) Won 1-0**
Trevisan, Blondeau, Pires, Brando, Pouget (De La Pena 72), Dalmat, Leroy, Cyprien, Bakayoko (Moses 90), Luccin, Abardonado. Scorer: Pires 16

**08.03.00 v Chelsea FC (a) Lost 0-1**
Trevisan, Perez (Fischer 38), Pires, Brando, Pouget, Dalmat, Leroy, Cyprien (De La Pena 66), Bakayoko, Luccin, Abardonado

**14.03.00 v SS Lazio (a) Lost 1-5**
Porato, Martin (Bakayoko 46), Pires, Brando, De La Pena, Pouget (Moses 61), Dalmat, Leroy, Fischer (Martini 46), Luccin, Abardonado. Scorer: Leroy 50

**22.03.00 v Feyenoord (h) Drawn 0-0**
Porato, Brando, De La Pena, Leroy, Keita (Gavanon 90), Martini, Bakayoko (Moses 62), Fischer, Luccin, Abardonado, Reina. Sent off: Martini 75

| SEASONS | PLAYED | WON | DRAWN | LOST | FOR | AGAINST |
|---|---|---|---|---|---|---|
| 2 | 19 | 8 | 5 | 6 | 27 | 23 |

## AC MILAN (MILAN AC)

**1992-1993**
**GROUP STAGE 1**
**25.11.92 v IFK Goteborg (h) Won 4-0**
Antonioli, Tassotti, Massaro, Albertini, Costacurta (Nava 66), Baresi, Lentini, Rijkaard, Van Basten, Papin, Eranio. Scorers: Van Basten 34, 52, 61, 62 pen

**09.12.92 v PSV Eindhoven (a) Won 2-1**
Rossi, Tassotti, Maldini, Albertini, Costacurta, Baresi, Lentini, Rijkaard, Van Basten, Gullit (Eranio 60), Simone (Massaro 89). Scorers: Rijkaard 20, Simone 63

**03.03.93 v FC Porto (a) Won 1-0**
Rossi (Cudicini 87), Tassotti, Maldini, Albertini, Costacurta, Baresi, Lentini, Boban, Papin, Gullit, Simone (Evani 87). Scorer: Papin 71

**17.03.93 v FC Porto (h) Won 1-0**
Rossi, Gambaro, Maldini, Albertini, Costacurta, Baresi, Lentini (Massaro 65), Eranio, Papin, Evani, Simone (Savicevic 77). Scorer: Eranio 31

**07.04.93 v IFK Goteborg (a) Won 1-0**
Rossi, Tassotti, Nava, Evani, Costacurta, Maldini, Lentini, Rijkaard, Boban, Savicevic, Massaro (Gambaro 87). Scorer: Massaro 71

**21.04.93 v PSV Eindhoven (h) Won 2-0**
Cudicini, Nava, Gambaro, De Napoli, Costacurta, Maldini, Donadoni, Boban, Simone (Massaro 34), Savicevic, Evani. Scorer: Simone 5, 19

**FINAL**
**26.05.93 v Olympique de Marseille (n) Lost 0-1**
Rossi, Tassotti, Maldini, Albertini, Costacurta, Baresi, Lentini, Rijkaard, Van Basten (Eranio 86), Donadoni (Papin 58), Massaro

**1993-1994**
**GROUP STAGE 1**
**24.11.93 v RSC Anderlecht (a) Drew 0-0**
Rossi, Panucci, Maldini, Albertini, Costacurta, Baresi, Orlando, Donadoni, Papin, Brian Laudrup, Simone (Massaro 75)

**01.12.93 v FC Porto (h) Won 3-0**
Rossi, Panucci, Maldini, Albertini, Costacurta, Baresi, Massaro, Donadoni, Papin (Tassotti 65), Savicevic, Raducioiu (Carbone 82). Scorers: Raducioiu 17, Panucci 38, Massaro 63

**02.03.94 v SV Werder Bremen (h) Won 2-1**
Rossi, Tassotti, Maldini, Donadoni, Costacurta, Baresi, Eranio (Simone 46), Desailly, Boban, Savicevic (Albertini 88), Massaro. Scorers: Maldini 48, Savicevic 67

**16.03.94 v SV Werder Bremen (a) Drawn 1-1**
Rossi, Tassotti, Maldini, Donadoni, Costacurta, Filippo Galli, Eranio (Simone 56), Desailly, Boban, Savicevic (Albertini 87), Massaro. Scorer: Savicevic 74

**30.03.94 v RSC Anderlecht (h) Drawn 0-0**
Rossi, Tassotti, Maldini, Albertini, Costacurta, Baresi, Donadoni, Desailly, Raducioiu (Carbone 69), Brian Laudrup (Simone 46), Massaro

**13.04.94 v FC Porto (a) Drawn 0-0**
Rossi, Tassotti, Maldini, Albertini, Costacurta, Baresi, Carbone, Desailly, Boban, Savicevic (Panucci 84), Massaro

**SEMI FINAL**
**27.04.94 v AS Monaco (h) Won 3-0**
Rossi, Tassotti, Panucci, Albertini, Costacurta, Baresi, Donadoni, Desailly, Boban, Savicevic (Simone 87), Massaro (Lentini 84). Scorers: Desailly 14, Albertini 48, Massaro 66

**FINAL**
**18.05.94 v FC Barcelona (n) Won 4-0**
Rossi, Tassotti, Panucci, Albertini, Filippo Galli, Maldini (Nava 83), Donadoni, Desailly, Boban, Savicevic, Massaro. Scorers: Massaro 22, 45, Savicevic 47, Desailly 58

**1994-1995**
**GROUP STAGE 1**
**14.09.94 v AFC Ajax (a) Lost 0-2**
Rossi, Nava, Galli, Baresi, Maldini, Sordo (Lentini 74), Gullit, Boban, Donadoni, Savicevic, M Orlando (Stroppa 64)

**28.09.94 v SV Austria Salzburg (h) Won 3-0**
Rossi, Tassotti, Maldini, Baresi (Galli 22), Panucci, Gullit, Desailly, Albertini, Boban, Simone (Massaro 75), Stroppa. Scorers: Stroppa 39, Simone 60, 63

**19.10.94 v AEK Athens (a) Drawn 0-0**
Rossi, Tassotti, Costacurta, Baresi, Maldini (Panucci 11), Desailly, Albertini, Boban, Donadoni, Massaro (Stroppa 89), Gullit

**02.11.94 v AEK Athens (h) Won 2-1**
Rossi, Tassotti (Lentini 46), Costacurta, Baresi, Maldini, Panucci, Albertini, Desailly, Donadoni (Stroppa 74), Massaro, Simone. Goals: Panucci 67, 73

**23.11.94 v AFC Ajax (h) Lost 0-2**
Rossi, Panucci, Costacurta, Baresi, Maldini, Donadoni (Stroppa 75), Albertini, Desailly, Boban (Lentini 56), Massaro, Simone

**07.12.94 v SV Austria Salzburg (a) Won 1-0**
Rossi, Panucci, Galli, Baresi, Maldini, Desailly, Albertini, Savicevic (Sordo 75), Donadoni, Simone (Tassotti 60), Massaro. Scorer: Massaro 71

**QUARTER FINAL**
**01.03.95 v SL Benfica (h) Won 2-0**
Rossi, Panucci, Galli, Baresi, Maldini, Desailly, Albertini, Boban, Savicevic, Massaro (Stroppa 46), Simone. Scorer: Simone 63, 75

**15.03.95 v SL Benfica (a) Drawn 0-0**
Rossi, Panucci, Desailly, Baresi (Costacurta 85), Maldini, Eranio, Donadoni, Boban, Savicevic, Massaro, Simone (Stroppa 88)

**SEMI FINAL**
**05.04.95 v Paris Saint-Germain (a) Won 1-0**
Rossi, Panucci, Costacurta, Baresi, Maldini, Eranio, Albertini, Desailly, Boban, Simone (Massaro 84), Savicevic. Scorer: Boban 90

**19.04.95 v Paris Saint-Germain (h) Won 2-0**
Rossi, Tassotti (Galli 15), Maldini, Baresi, Panucci, Eranio, Albertini, Desailly, Boban, Savicevic, Simone (Donadoni 79). Scorer: Savicevic 21, 68

**FINAL**
**24.05.95 v AFC Ajax (n) Lost 0-1**
Rossi, Panucci, Costacurta, Baresi, Maldini, Donadoni, Desailly, Albertini, Boban (Lentini 84), Massaro (Eranio 88), Simone

**1996-1997**
**GROUP STAGE 1**
**11.09.96 v FC Porto (h) Lost 2-3**
Rossi, Reiziger (Tassotti 40), Galli, Maldini, Panucci, Boban (Eranio 71), Albertini, Desailly, Simone, Weah (Davids 72), Baggio. Scorers: Simone 15, Weah 69

**25.09.96 v Rosenborg BK (a) Won 4-1**
Rossi, Panucci, Costacurta, Desailly, Maldini, Savicevic (Eranio 42), Albertini, Ambrosini, Davids, Simone (Baggio 73), Weah. Scorers: Simone 6, 23, 26, Weah 56

**16.10.96 v IFK Goteborg (a) Lost 1-2**
Rossi, Panucci, Costacurta, Desailly, Maldini, Locatelli, Albertini, Ambrosini, Boban, Simone, Weah. Scorer: Weah 53

**30.10.96 v IFK Goteborg (h) Won 4-2**
Rossi, Panucci, Costacurta, Desailly, Maldini, Locatelli, Albertini, Boban, Davids (Coco 84) Simone (Baggio 64), Weah. Scorers: Boban 4, Albertini 14 pen, Locatelli 44, Baggio 90

**20.11.96 v FC Porto (a) Drawn 1-1**
Rossi, Panucci, Costacurta, Baresi, Maldini, Eranio (Dugarry 89), Boban, Desailly (Ambrosini 82), Davids, Weah, Baggio (Simone 79). Scorer: Davids 56

**04.12.96 v Rosenborg BK (h) Lost 1-2**
Rossi, Reiziger (Locatelli 77), Costacurta, Baresi, Maldini, Savicevic, Ambrosini (Panucci 46), Albertini, Boban, Baggio (Simone 46), Dugarry. Scorer: Dugarry 45

**1999-2000**
**GROUP STAGE 1**
**15.09.99 v Chelsea FC (a) Drawn 0-0**
Abbiati, Helveg, Maldini, Albertini, Costacurta, Shevchenko, Gattuso, Ayala, Leonardo (Giunti 83), Bierhoff, Guly

**21.09.99 v Galatasaray SK (h) Won 2-1**
Abbiati, Helveg, Maldini, Albertini, Costacurta (N'Gotty 83), Shevchenko (Ganz 88), Gattuso, Ayala, Leonardo (Giunti 69), Bierhoff, Serginho. Scorers: Leonardo 44, Shevchenko 45

**28.09.99 v Hertha BSC Berlin (h) Drawn 1-1**
Abbiati, Helveg (Guly 57), Maldini, Albertini (Giunti 75), Costacurta, Shevchenko, Gattuso, Ayala, Leonardo, Bierhoff, Serginho. Scorer: Bierhoff 74

**20.10.99 v Hertha BSC Berlin (a) Lost 0-1**
Abbiati, Maldini, Albertini, Costacurta (Ayala 46), Shevchenko, Leonardo, Bierhoff, Ambrosini (Giunti 64), Guly, Sala, Serginho (Orlandini 75)

**26.10.99 v Chelsea FC (h) Drawn 1-1**
Abbiati, Maldini, Costacurta, Shevchenko, Gattuso, Ayala, Leonardo (Boban 57), Bierhoff, Ambrosini, Guly, Serginho (Orlandini 86). Scorer: Bierhoff 74

**03.11.99 v Galatasaray SK (a) Lost 2-3**
Abbiati, Helveg, Maldini, Albertini, Shevchenko, Gattuso, Weah (Boban 83), Ayala, Giunti (Bierhoff 88), Guly (Serginho 57), N'Gotty. Scorers: Weah 20, Giunti 51

**2000-2001**
**GROUP STAGE 1**
**13.09.00 v Besiktas JK (h) Won 4-1**
Dida, Helveg, Maldini, Albertini, Costacurta, Shevchenko, Chamot, Bierhoff, Giunti (Brncic 85), Saudati (Guglielminpietro 62), Coco (Serginho 76). Scorers: Coco 36, Bierhoff 44, Shevchenko 45 pen, 77

**19.09.00 v Leeds United AFC (a) Lost 0-1**
Dida, Helveg, Maldini, Albertini, Costacurta, Shevchenko, Chamot, Bierhoff, Giunti (Saudati 90), Guglielminpietro (De Ascentis 59), Coco

**26.09.00 v FC Barcelona (a) Won 2-0**
Dida, Maldini, Albertini, Costacurta, Shevchenko, Gattuso (Guglielminpietro 90), Chamot, Bierhoff (Comandini 76), Giunti, Ambrosini (Helveg 85), Coco. Scorers: Coco 45, Bierhoff 71

**18.10.00 v FC Barcelona (h) Drawn 3-3**
Abbiati, Maldini, Albertini, Costacurta, Shevchenko, Gattuso, Jose Mari (Boban 69), Bierhoff, Ambrosini, Roque Junior, Coco. Scorers: Albertini 26, 39, Jose Mari 45

**24.10.00 v Besiktas JK (a) Won 2-0**
Dida, Maldini, Albertini, Costacurta, Shevchenko, Gattuso (Helveg 84), Jose Mari (Serginho 88), Bierhoff (Boban 72), Ambrosini, Roque Junior, Coco. Scorers: Shevchenko 38, Jose Mari 43

**08.11.00 v Leeds United AFC (h) Drawn 1-1**
Dida, Helveg, Maldini, Albertini, Shevchenko, Gattuso, Leonardo (Boban 54), Chamot, Bierhoff, Roque Junior, Serginho. Scorer: Serginho 68

**GROUP STAGE 2**
**21.11.00 v Galatasaray SK (h) Drawn 2-2**
Abbiati, Roque Junior, Chamot (Sala 51), Maldini, Gattuso, Giunti, Albertini, Serginho, Jose Mari, Bierhoff, Shevchenko. Scorers: Jose Mari 47, Shevchenko 73pen

**06.12.01 v RC DeportivoLa Coruna (a) Won 1-0**
Abbiati, Roque Junior, Costacurta, Maldini, Helveg (Gugly 90), Gattuso, Ambrosini, Coco, Leonardo, Boban (Giunti 67), Jose Mari (Serginho 81), Shevchenko. Scorer: Helveg 45

**14.02.01 v Paris Saint-Germain (h) Drawn 1-1**
Abbiati, Sala, Roque Junior, Maldini, Helveg, Giunti, Albertini, Serginho, Leonardo (Comandini 77), Bierhoff (Ba 46), Shevchenko. Scorer; Leonardo 27. Sent off: Roque Junior 42

**20.02.01 v Paris Saint-Germain (a) Drawn 1-1**
Abbiati, Sala, Maldini, Helveg, Ba (Chamot 71), Gattuso, Albertini, Serginho (Jose Mari 78), Coco, Leonardo (Boban 82), Shevchenko. Scorer: Jose Mari 90

**07.03.01 v Galatasaray SK (a) Lost 0-2**
Dida, Sala, Chamot, Maldini, Ba (Jose Mari 79), Giunti, Garcia, Coco, Boban (Serginho 70), Leonardo (Bierhoff 54), Shevchenko

**13.03.01 v RC Deportivo La Coruna (h) Drawn 1-1**
Rossi, Costacurta (Ba 60), Roque Junior, Maldini, Helveg, Gattuso, Albertini, Boban (Bierhoff 60), Coco (Serginho 70), Jose Mari, Shevchenko. Scorer: Shevchenko 86pen

**2002-2003**
**GROUP STAGE 1**
**18.09.02 v RC Lens (h) Won 2-1**
Dida, Simic, Maldini, Nesta, Kaladze, Gattuso, Pirlo, Rui Costa, Seedorf, F Inzaghi (Laursen 85), Rivaldo (Ambrosini 77). Scorer: F Inzaghi 57, 61

**24.09.02 v RC Deportivo La Coruna (a) Won 4-0**
Dida, Simic, Maldini, Nesta, Kaladze, Gattuso, Pirlo (Ambrosini 64), Rui Costa (Dalla Bona 84), Seedorf, F Inzaghi (Tomasson 80), Rivaldo. Scorers: Seedorf 17, F Inzaghi 33, 55, 62

**01.10.02 v FC Bayern Munchen (a) Won 2-1**
Dida, Simic, Maldini, Nesta, Kaladze, Gattuso, Pirlo (Serginho 77), Rui Costa (Laursen 87), Seedorf, F Inzaghi, Rivaldo (Ambrosini 66). Scorer: F Inzaghi 52, 84

**23.10.02 v FC Bayern Munchen (h) Won 2-1**
Dida, Simic, Maldini, Nesta, Kaladze, Ambrosini (Gattuso 46), Pirlo, Rui Costa (Laursen 85) Seedorf, Serginho (Dalla Bona 79), F Inzaghi. Scorers: Serginho 11, F Inzaghi 64

**29.10.02 v RC Lens (a) Lost 1-2**
Abbiati, Helveg, Costacurta, Laursen, Maldini, (Kaladze 65) Dalla Bona, Pirlo, Ambrosini, Serginho (Seedorf 65), Tomasson, Shevchenko (Boriello 46). Scorer: Shevchenko 31

**13.11.02 v RC Deportivo La Coruna (h) Lost 1-2**
Abbiati, Helveg, Maldini, Simic, Kaladze (Aubameyang 85), Dalla Bona, Pirlo, Rui Costa (F Inzaghi 75), Serginho, Tomasson, Shevchenko. Scorer: Tomasson 34

**GROUP STAGE 2**
**26.11.02 v Real Madrid CF (h) Won 1-0**
Dida, Simic (Chamot 89), Maldini, Costacurta, Kaladze, Gattuso, Ambrosini, Rui Costa (Serginho 76), Seedorf, Shevchenko (Tomasson 82), Rivaldo. Scorer: Shevchenko 40

**11.12.02 v BV Borussia Dortmund (a) Won 1-0**
Dida, Simic, Maldini, Nesta, Kaladze, Ambrosini, Pirlo, Rui Costa (Serginho 78), Seedorf, F Inzaghi (Rivaldo 86), Shevchenko (Laursen 90). Scorer: F Inzaghi 49

**19.02.03 v FC Lokomotiv Moskva (h) Won 1-0**
Dida, Brocchi (Simic 79), Costacurta, Nesta, Maldini, Gattuso, Pirlo, Rui Costa (Serginho 63), Rivaldo, F Inzaghi, Tomasson (Seedorf). Scorer: Tomasson 62

**25.02.03 v FC Lokomotiv Moskva (a) Won 1-0**
Dida, Costacurta, Maldini, Nesta, Kaladze, Gattuso, Redondo (Brocchi 76), Seedorf, Serginho (Rui Costa 87), F Inzaghi (Tomasson 84), Rivaldo. Scorer: Rivaldo 34pen

**12.03.03 v Real Madrid CF (a) Lost 1-3**
Abbiati, Simic (Nesta 62), Costacurta, Laursen, Maldini, Brocchi, Redondo (Pirlo 79), Seedorf, Dalla Bona (Rui Costa 46), Rivaldo, Shevchenko. Scorer: Rivaldo 81

**18.03.03 v BV Borussia Dortmund (h) Lost 0-1**
Abbiati, Simic, Nesta, Laursen, Maldini (Costacurta 46), Gattuso, Redondo, Rui Costa (F Inzaghi 62), Brocchi (Pirlo 82), Rivaldo, Tomasson

**QUARTER FINAL**
**08.04.03 v AFC Ajax (a) Drawn 0-0**
Dida, Simic, Nesta, Maldini, Costacurta, Rui Costa, Gattuso, Ambrosini, Seedorf, Shevchenko (Rivaldo 79), F Inzaghi (Tomasson 73)

**23.04.03 v AFC Ajax (h) Won 3-2**
Dida, Simic (Tomasson 83), Nesta, Maldini, Costacurta, Brocchi, Rui Costa (Redondo 85), Ambrosini, Kaladze (Rivaldo 80), Shevchenko, F Inzaghi. Scorers: F Inzaghi 30, Shevchenko 65, Tomasson 90

**SEMI FINAL**
**07.05.03 v Internazionale FC (h) Drawn 0-0**
Dida, Costacurta, Maldini, Nesta, Kaladze, Gattuso (Redondo 78), Rui Costa, Brocchi (Serginho 73), Seedorf, F Inzaghi, Shevchenko (Rivaldo 81)

**13.05.03 v Internazionale FC (a) Drawn 1-1**
Abbiati, Costacurta, Maldini, Nesta, Kaladze, Gattuso, Rui Costa (Ambrosini 64), Pirlo (Brocchi 89), Seedorf, F Inzaghi (Serginho 80), Shevchenko. Scorer: Shevchenko 45

**FINAL**

**28.05.03 v Juventus FC (n)** **Drawn 0-0 (won 3-2pens)**
Dida, Costacurta (Roque Junior 66), Maldini, Nesta, Kaladze, Gattuso, Rui Costa (Ambrosini 87), Pirlo (Serginho 71), Seedorf, F Inzaghi, Shevchenko. Penalties: Serginho, Seedorf & Kaladze (missed), Nesta, Shevchenko

| SEASONS | PLAYED | WON | DRAWN | LOST | FOR | AGAINST |
|---|---|---|---|---|---|---|
| 7 | 67 | 32 | 20 | 15 | 93 | 56 |

## MOLDE FK

**1999-2000**

**GROUP STAGE 1**

**15.09.99 v FC Porto (h)** **Lost 0-1**
Bakke, Fostervold, Berg Hestad, Tessem, Fjortoft (Sundgot 88), Lund, Olsen, Mork (Lindbaek 46), Dos Santos, Hoseth, Strande

**21.09.99 v Real Madrid CF (a)** **Lost 1-4**
Bakke, Lydersen (Singsaas 85), Fostervold, Berg Hestad, Tessem, Fjortoft, Lund, Olsen, Lindbaek (Sundgot 89), Hoseth (Mork 66), Strande. Scorer: Lindbaek 80

**28.09.99 v Olympiakos Piraeus FC (a)** **Lost 1-3**
Bakke, Lydersen, Fostervold, Berg Hestad, Tessem, Fjortoft, Lund, Olsen, Mork (Lindbaek 54), Strande (Dos Santos 72), Sundgot (Hoseth 74). Scorer: Lund 58

**20.10.99 v Olympiakos Piraeus FC (h)** **Won 3-2**
Bakke, Singaas, Lydersen, Fostervold, Berg Hestad, Tessem, Fjortoft, Lund, Olsen, Dos Santos, Hoseth (Mork 89). Scorers: Lund 54, 59, Berg Hestad 72

**26.10.99 v FC Porto (a)** **Lost 1-3**
Bakke, Singaas, Lydersen, Berg Hestad, Tessem (Lindbaek 61), Fjortoft, Lund, Olsen (Sundgot 84), Dos Santos, Hoseth (Mork 86), Strande. Scorer: Berg Hestad 82

**03.11.99 v Real Madrid CF (h)** **Lost 0-1**
Bakke, Singaas, Lydersen, Fostervold (Dos Santos 46), Berg Hestad, Tessem (Mork 87), Fjortoft, Lund, Olsen, Hoseth (Lindbaek 61), Strande

| SEASONS | PLAYED | WON | DRAWN | LOST | FOR | AGAINST |
|---|---|---|---|---|---|---|
| 1 | 6 | 1 | 0 | 5 | 6 | 14 |

## AS MONACO

**1993-1994**
**GROUP STAGE 1**
**24.11.93 v FC Spartak Moscow (h) Won 4-1**
Ettori, Valery, Sonor, Petit, Dumas, Puel, Klinsmann, Djorkaeff (Passi 75), Thuram, Scifo, Ikpeba (Gnako 79). Scorers: Klinsmann 17, Ikpeba 40, Djorkaeff 61 pen, Thuram 89

**08.12.93 v FC Barcelona (a) Lost 0-2**
Ettori, Valery, Sonor, Petit, Dumas, Puel, Klinsmann, Djorkaeff (Simba 71), Thuram (Gnako 46), Scifo, Ikpeba

**02.03.94 v Galatasaray SK (h) Won 3-0**
Ettori, Blondeau, Petit (Valery 46), Thuram, Grimandi, Puel, Klinsmann, Djorkaeff, Viaud, Scifo, Ikpeba. Scorers: Scifo 36, Djorkaeff 40, Klinsmann 55

**16.03.94 v Galatasaray SK (a) Won 2-0**
Ettori, Valery, Blondeau, Thuram, Dumas, Puel, Klinsmann, Djorkaeff, Viaud, Scifo (Grimandi 79), Ikpeba (Gnako 72). Scorers: Scifo 54, Gnako 88

**30.03.94 v FC Spartak Moscow (a) Drawn 0-0**
Ettori, Blondeau, Petit, Thuram, Dumas, Puel, Klinsmann, Djorkaeff (Wreh 69), Viaud, Scifo (Perez 84), Grimandi

**13.04.94 v FC Barcelona (h) Lost 0-1**
Ettori, Blondeau, Petit, Thuram, Dumas, Puel (Perez 77), Klinsmann, Djorkaeff, Gnako (Ikpeba 46), Scifo, Viaud

**SEMI FINAL**
**27.04.94 v Milan AC (a) Lost 0-3**
Ettori, Blondeau (Wreh 53), Petit, Grimandi, Dumas, Puel (Simba 78), Klinsmann, Djorkaeff, Gnako, Scifo, Viaud

**1997-1998**
**GROUP STAGE 1**
**17.09.97 v Sporting Clube de Portugal (a) Lost 0-3**
Barthez, Dumas, Diao, Leonard, Pignol (Konjic 46), Legwinski, Benarbia, Da Costa (Ikpeba 46), Collins, Spehar, Trezeguet

**01.10.97 v Bayer 04 Leverkusen (h) Won 4-0**
Barthez, Djetou, Dumas, Konjic (Irles 46), Legwinski (Christanval 54), Collins, N'Doram (Benarbia 63), Pignol, Ikpeba, Trezeguet, Henry. Scorers: Henry 30, 84, Ikpeba 74, 90

**22.10.97 v K Lierse SK (h) Won 5-1**
Barthez, Sagnol, Dumas (Irles 46), Konjic, Pignol, Legwinski, Benarbia, Djetou, Collins (N'Doram 78), Ikpeba (Trezeguet 78), Henry. Scorers: Henry 34, Collins 51, Ikpeba 66, Trezeguet 88, 90

**05.11.97 v K Lierse SK (a) Won 1-0**
Barthez, Sagnol, Irles, Konjic, Leonard (Diao 80), Benarbia (Carnot 73), Collins, Djetou, Legwinski, Henry (Trezeguet 66), Ikpeba. Scorer: Ikpeba 74

**26.11.97 v Sporting Clube de Portugal (h) Won 3-2**
Barthez, Sagnol, Irles, Dumas, Pignol, Legwinski, Djetou (Henry 19), Benarbia (Carnot 74), Collins, Trezeguet, Ikpeba. Scorers: Trezeguet 66, Henry 75, 90

**10.12.97 v Bayer 04 Leverkusen (a) Drawn 2-2**
Barthez, Pignol, Irles, Sagnol, Dumas, Legwinski, Djetou (Diao 9), Benarbia (Carnot 64), Collins (Henry 59), Trezeguet, Ikpeba. Scorers: Pignol 63, Henry 81

**QUARTER FINAL**
**04.03.98 v Manchester United FC (h) Drawn 0-0**
Barthez, Konjic, Dumas, Leonard, Sagnol, Djetou, Legwinski, Benarbia (Carnot 75), Collins, Ikpeba (Spehar 61), Henry

**18.03.98 v Manchester United FC (a) Drawn 1-1**
Barthez, Sagnol, Dumas, Leonard, Konjic (Da Costa 75), Djetou, Diawara, Benarbia (Carnot 66), Collins, Ikpeba (Henry 61), Trezeguet. Scorer: Trezeguet 6

**SEMI FINAL**
**01.04.98 v Juventus FC (a) Lost 1-4**
Barthez, Martin (Henry 67), Sagnol, Christanval, Pignol (Da Costa 40), Konjic, Diawara (Carnot 74), Benarbia, Djetou, Ikpeba, Trezeguet. Scorer: Da Costa 46

**14.04.98 v Juventus FC (h) Won 3-2**
Barthez, Diawara, Christanval, Leonard (Sagnol 64), Martin, Djetou, Benarbia, Collins, Ikpeba (Spehar 69), Trezeguet, Henry. Scorers: Leonard 38, Henry 50, Spehar 82

**2000-2001**
**GROUP STAGE 1**
**12.09.00 v Galatasaray SK (a) Lost 2-3**
Porato, Marquez, Christanval, Djetou, Giuly, Simone, Dabo, Leonard (Riise 11), Nonda (Prso 78), Bonnal (Farnerud 90), Irles. Scorers: Nonda 50, Simone 62 pen. Sent off: Dabo 72

**20.09.00 v Rangers FC (h) Lost 0-1**
Porato, Riise (Prso 46), Marquez, Djetou, Giuly, Simone, Nonda (Courville 84), Bonnal (Gravelaine 69), Irles, Abidal, Rodriguez

**27.09.00 v SK Sturm Graz (h)** **Won 5-0**
Porato, Marquez, Christanval, Djetou (Famerud 74), Giuly (Bonnal 46), Gravelaine, Simone (Prso 56), Jurietti, Nonda, Di Tommaso, Irles. Scorers: Simone 13, 38, 41, Famerud 77, Nonda 84

**17.10.00 v SK Sturm Graz (a)** **Lost 0-2**
Porato, Conteras, Christanval, Djetou, Giuly, Gallardo, Simone, Dabo (Bonnal 46), Jurietti, Prso (Eloi 83), Irles

**25.10.00 v Galatasaray SK (h)** **Won 4-2**
Porato, Conteras, Marquez (Irles 42), Christanval, Djetou, Giuly (Dabo 63), Gallardo, Simone, Jurietti, Nonda (Leonard 66), Bonnal. Scorers: Conteras 6, Bonnal 19, Simone 22, Nonda 26. Sent off: Jurietti 60, Djetou 64

**07.11.00 v Rangers FC (a)** **Drawn 2-2**
Porato, Conteras, Christanval, Da Costa, Giuly (Eloi 69), Gallardo (Gravelaine 26), Simone, Dabo, Nonda (Prso 57), Bonnal, Irles. Scorers: Da Costa 39, Simone 78

| SEASONS | PLAYED | WON | DRAWN | LOST | FOR | AGAINST |
|---|---|---|---|---|---|---|
| 3 | 23 | 10 | 5 | 8 | 42 | 32 |

## FC NANTES ATLANTIQUE

**1995-1996**
**GROUP STAGE 1**
**13.09.95 v FC Porto (h)** **Drawn 0-0**
Marraud, Le Dizet, Guyot, Decroix, Pignol, Makelele, Cauet, Carotti, N'Doram, Kosecki, Renou (Garcion 63)

**27.09.95 v Panathinaikos FC (a)** **Lost 1-3**
Marraud, Le Dizet, Pignol, Decroix (Chanelet 69), Guyot, Carotti, Makelele (Renou 76), Cauet, N'Doram, Ouedec (Peyrelade 69), Kosecki. Scorer: N'Doram 88

**18.10.95 v Aalborg BK (h)** **Won 3-1**
Casagrande, Chanelet, Pignol, Decroix, Guyot, Cauet, Makelele, Pedros, N'Doram, Ouedec (Carotti 78), Kosecki (Savinaud 89). Scorers: Ouedec 51, Pedros 55, Kosecki 74

**01.11.95 v Aalborg BK (a)** **Won 2-0**
Casagrande, Carotti, Cauet (Pignol 75), Decroix, Guyot, Ferri, Makelele (Chanelet 58), Pedros, N'Doram, Ouedec (Peyrelade 86), Kosecki. Scorers: Guyot 10, Ouedec 68

**22.11.95 v FC Porto (a) Drawn 2-2**
Casagrande, Chanelet, Le Dizet, Decroix, Guyot, Ferri, Pedros (Ouedec 70), Cauet, Makelele, Carotti, Kosecki (Renous 76, Savinaud 90). Scorer: Pedros 3, 33

**06.12.95 v Panathinaikos FC (h) Drawn 0-0**
Casagrande, Chanelet, Le Dizet, Decroix, Guyot, Ferri, Makelele, Pedros, N'Doram, Ouedec, Kosecki (Renou 85)

**QUARTER FINAL**
**06.03.96 v FC Spartak Moscow (h) Won 2-0**
Casagrande, Le Dizet (Chanelet 70), Decroix, Guyot, Pignol, Makelele, Pedros, N'Doram (Ferri 64), Cauet, Ouedec (Gourvennec 82), Kosecki. Scorers: N'Doram 28, Ouedec 67. Sent off: Pedros 77

**20.03.96 v FC Spartak Moscow (a) Drawn 2-2**
Casagrande, Le Dizet, Decroix, Carotti, Capron, Pignol, Makelele, Cauet, Gourvennec (Ferri 63), Ouedec, Kosecki (Chanelet 83). Scorer: Ouedec 63, 86

**SEMI FINAL**
**03.04.96 v Juventus FC (a) Lost 0-2**
Casagrande, Le Dizet, Capron, Decroix, Pignol, Ferri, Carotti, Cauet, Gourvennec (Chanelet 46), Ouedec (Peyrelade 86), Kosecki (Guyot 69). Sent off: Carotti 45

**17.04.96 v Juventus FC (h) Won 3-2**
Casagrande, Chanelet, Capron, Decroix, Pignol (Peyrelade 89), Ferri, N'Doram, Cauet, Makelele, Ouedec (Gourvennec 40), Kosecki (Renou 61). Scorers: Decroix 44, N'Doram 69, Renou 82

**2001-2002**
**GROUP STAGE 1**
**11.09.01 v PSV Eindhoven (h) Won 4-1**
Landreau, Laspalles, Gillet, Fabbri, Olembe, Savinaud (Berson 79), Quint, Ziani, Armand, Andre (Vahirua 71), Dalmat (Djemba-Djemba 86). Scorers: Andre 5, Quint 10pen, Dalmat 44, Vahirua 75

**19.09.01 v SS Lazio (a) Won 3-1**
Landreau, Deroff, Gillet, Fabbri, Armand, Ahamada (Quint 63), Delhommeau, Berson, Djemba-Djemba, Ziani, Andre (Dalmat 71). Scorrs: Fabbri 3, Armand 63, Ziani 86

**26.09.01 v Galatasaray SK (h) Lost 0-1**
Landreau, Deroff, Delhommeau, Fabbri, Armand, Dalmat, Olembe (Aristouy 88), Berson, Quint, Devinaud (Djemba-Djemba 73), Ahamada (Pujol 88)

**16.10.01 v Galatasaray SK (a) Drawn 0-0**
Landreau, Delhommeau, Deroff, Fabbri, Armand, Ahamada (Da Rocha 65), Berson, Djemba-Djemba, Quint, Ziani, Andre (Vahirua 70)

**24.10.01 v PSV Eindhoven (a) Drawn 0-0**
Landreau, Laspalles, Gillet, Fabbri, Armand, Da Rocha, Quint (Olembe 83), Berson (Savinaud 46), Djemba-Djemba, Ziani, Andre (Deroff 83)

**30.10.01 v SS Lazio (h) Won 1-0**
Landreau, Laspalles, Gillet, Fabbri, Armand, Ahamada (Da Rocha 66), Delhommeau, Djemba-Djemba, Olembe, Ziani, Andre (Deroff 87). Scorer: Andre 72

**GROUP STAGE 2**
**20.11.01 v Boavista FC (a) Lost 0-1**
Landreau, Laspalles, Gillet, Fabbri, Armand, Ahamada (Dalmat 67), Delhommeau, Berson, Da Rocha, Olembe (Ziani 78) Andre (Vahirua 67)

**05.12.01 v FC Bayern Munchen (h) Lost 0-1**
Landreau, Laspalles, Gillet, Fabbri, Armand, Quint, Devineau (Olembe 59), Da Rocha, Ahamada (Moldovan 63), Berson, Ziani (Andre 77)

**20.02.02 v Manchester United FC (h) Drawn 1-1**
Landreau, Cetto, Yepes, Fabbri, Armand, Ziani, Savinaud, Berson, Quint (Ateba 79), Moldovan (Andre 76), Vahirua (Da Rocha 62). Scorer: Moldovan 7. Sent-off: Yepes 90

**26.02.02 v Manchester United FC (a) Lost 1-5**
Landreau, Deroff, Cetto, Fabbri, Armand, Ateba (Vahirua 63), Djemba (Savinaud 57), Da Rocha, Ziani (Quint 77), Berson, Andre. Scorer: Da Rocha 17

**12.03.02 v Boavista FC (h) Drawn 1-1**
Landreau, Cetto, Yepes, Gillet, Ateba, Djemba, Savinaud (Laspalles 52), Da Rocha, Quint (Devineaud 61), Moldovan (Vahirua 46), Andre. Scorer: Moldovan 43

**19.03.02 v FC Bayern Munchen (a) Lost 1-2**
Grondin, Deroff, Cetto, Gillet, Ateba (Laspalles 64), Rubil, Paillieres, Toulalan, Armand, Devineau (Berson 78), Ahamada (N'Zigou 64). Scorer: Ahamada 54

| SEASONS | PLAYED | WON | DRAWN | LOST | FOR | AGAINST |
|---|---|---|---|---|---|---|
| 2 | 22 | 7 | 8 | 7 | 27 | 26 |

## NEWCASTLE UNITED FC

**1997-1998**
**GROUP STAGE 1**
**17.09.97 v FC Barcelona (h) Won 3-2**
Given, Barton, Watson, Albert, Beresford, Gillespie, Lee, Batty, Barnes (Ketsbaia 81), Tomasson (Peacock 78), Asprilla. Scorer: Asprilla 22 pen, 31, 49

**01.10.97 v FC Dynamo Kyiv (a) Drawn 2-2**
Given, Watson, Peacock, Barton, Albert, Batty, Barnes, Lee (Ketsbaia 46), Beresford, Gillespie, Asprilla (Tomasson 28). Scorer: Beresford 78, 85

**22.10.97 v PSV Eindhoven (a) Lost 0-1**
Given, Barton (Albert 81), Peacock, Howey, Watson, Gillespie, Batty, Lee Beresford (Ketsbaia 67), Tomasson, Asprilla

**05.11.97 v PSV Eindhoven (h) Lost 0-2**
Given, Watson, Albert, Pistone, Beresford, Gillespie, Hamilton, Barton, Barnes, Ketsbaia, Tomasson

**27.11.97 v FC Barcelona (a) Lost 0-1**
Given, Watson, Peacock (Pearce 31), Albert (Hughes 46), Pistone, Hamilton, Batty, Beresford, Ketsbaia, Tomasson, Barnes

**10.12.97 v FC Dynamo Kyiv (h) Won 2-0**
Hislop, Watson, Pearce, Albert, Peacock, Pistone (Hughes 46), Gillespie, Batty, Lee, Barnes, Asprilla (Ketsbaia 57). Scorers: Barnes 10, Pearce 21

**2002-2003**
**GROUP STAGE 1**
**18.09.02 v FC Dynamo Kyiv (a) Lost 0-2**
Given, Griffin, Dabizas, O'Brien, Bernard, Dyer, Hughes (Solano 69), Speed, Viana (Robert 69), Shearer (Ameobi 79), Bellamy

**24.09.02 v Feyenoord (h) Lost 0-1**
Given, Griffin, Dabizas, O'Brien, Hughes, Solano, Dyer, Speed, Robert, Shearer, Bellamy (Lua Lua 77)

**01.10.02 v Juventus FC (a) Lost 0-2**
Given, Griffin (Ameobi 79), Dabizas, O'Brien, Hughes, Dyer, Solano (Viana 70), Speed, Jenas (Lua Lua 80), Robert, Shearer

## CHAMPIONS LEAGUE HISTORY

**23.10.02 v Juventus FC (h) Won 1-0**
Harper, Griffin, Bramble, O'Brien, Hughes, Solano, Speed, Jenas, Robert (Viana 85), Shearer, Lua Lua (Ameobi 86). Scorer: Griffin 62

**29.10.02 v FC Dynamo Kyiv (h) Won 2-1**
Harper, Griffin, Bramble (Dabizas 27), O'Brien (Bernard 46), Hughes, Solano (Dyer 82), Speed, Jenas, Robert, Shearer, Ameobi. Scorers: Speed 58, Shearer 69pen

**13.11.02 v Feyenoord (a) Won 3-2**
Given, Griffin, Dabizas O'Brien, Hughes, Dyer, Speed, Jenas, Viana (Bernard 82), Shearer, Bellamy. Scorers: Bellamy 45, 89, Viana 49

**27.11.02 v Internazionale FC (h) Lost 1-4**
Given, Griffin, Dabizas O'Brien, Hughes (Caldwell 86), Dyer, Speed, Solano, Viana (Robert 46), Shearer, Bellamy. Scorer: Solano 72. Sent off: Bellamy 6

**11.12.02 v FC Barcelona (a) Lost 1-3**
Given, Griffin, O'Brien, Hughes, Bernard, Solano, Dyer, Speed, Bernard, Ameobi, Lua Lua (Chopra 84). Scorer: Ameobi 24

**18.02.03 v Bayer 04 Leverkusen (a) Won 3-1**
Given, Hughes, O'Brien, Bramble, Bernard, Jenas, Speed, Dyer, Robert, Ameobi (Cort 84), Lua Lua (Chopra 84). Scorers: Ameobi 5, 16, Lua Lua 32

**26.02.03 v Bayer 04 Leverkusen (h) Won 3-1**
Given, Griffin, Caldwell, Bramble, Bernard, Kerr (Viana 82), Speed, Dyer, Robert (Solano 70), Ameobi, Shearer (Lua Lua 81). Scorer: Shearer 5, 11,36pen

**11.03.03 v Internazionale FC (a) Drawn 2-2**
Given, Griffin, O'Brien (Hughes 59), Bramble, Bernard, Solano, Jenas, Speed, Robert (Viana 83), Bellamy, Shearer (Lua Lua 83). Scorer: Shearer 42, 49

**19.03.03 v FC Barcelona (h) Lost 0-2**
Given, Griffin, O'Brien, Bramble, Bernard, Solano (Ameobi 67), Jenas, Dyer, Robert (Viana 67), Bellamy, Shearer

| SEASONS | PLAYED | WON | DRAWN | LOST | FOR | AGAINST |
|---|---|---|---|---|---|---|
| 2 | 18 | 7 | 2 | 8 | 23 | 29 |

## OLYMPIAKOS PIRAEUS FC

**1997-1998**
**GROUP STAGE 1**
**17.09.97 v FC Porto (h) Won 1-0**
Tochoroglou, Varesanovic, Anatolakis, Karataidis, Djordjevic, Giannakopoulos, Passalis, Niniadis, Georgatos (Gogic 81), Alexandris (Dabizas 60), Ivic (Sabanadzovic 90). Scorer: Giannakopoulos 6

**01.10.97 v Rosenborg BK (a) Lost 1-5**
Tochoroglou, Varesanovic, Karataidis, Anatolakis, Georgatos (Ofori-Quaye 69), Giannakopoulos (Niniadis 55), Passalis, Poursanidis, Djordjevic, Ivic (Gogic 74), Alexandris. Scorer: Ofori-Quaye 69

**22.10.97 v Real Madrid CF (a) Lost 1-5**
Tochoroglou, Bandovic, Anatolakis, Poursanidis (Georgatos 84), Karataidis, Mavrogenidis (Gogic 72), Passalis, Dabizas, Djordjevic, Karapialis (Niniadis 72), Ofori-Quaye. Scorer: Dabizas 19

**05.11.97 v Real Madrid CF (h) Drawn 0-0**
Tochoroglou, Bandovic, Karataidis, Anatolakis, Amanatidis (Dabizas 78), Giannakopoulos (Mavrogenidis 74), Poursanidis, Passalis, Georgatos, Ivic (Alexandris 90), Ofori-Quaye

**27.11.97 v FC Porto (a) Lost 1-2**
Tochoroglou, Amanatidis (Karapialis 78), Karataidis, Anatolakis, Georgatos, Mavrogenidis, Dabizas, Passalis, Djordjevic, Alexandris (Ofori-Quaye 55), Ivic (Giannakopoulos 88). Scorer: Georgatos 25

**10.12.97 v Rosenborg BK (h) Drawn 2-2**
Tochoroglou, Dabizas, Karataidis, Anatolakis (Alexandris 73), Bandovic, Passalis, Poursanidis (Mitropoulos 87), Georgatos (Giannakopoulos 73), Mavrogenidis, Djordjevic, Ivic. Scorers: Mavrogenidis 48, Djordjevic 88

**1998-1999**
**GROUP STAGE 1**
**16.09.98 v FC Porto (a) Drawn 2-2**
Eleftheropoulos, Karataidis, Mavrogenidis, Amanatidis (Karapialis 83), Georgatos, Luciano De Souza (Gogic 87), Poursanidis, Anatolakis, Djordjevic, Ivic (Giannakopoulos 79), Ofori-Quaye. Scorers: Giannakopoulos 86, Gogic 90

**30.09.98 v NK Croatia/Dinamo Zagreb (h) Won 2-0**
Eleftheropoulos, Amanatidis (Antzas 75), Karataidis, Anatolakis, Mavrogenidis, Poursanidis, Karapialis (Niniadis 72), Giannakopoulos, Djordjevic, Gogic, Alexandris (Luciano De Souza 90). Scorers: Alexandris 21, Gogic 80

**21.10.98 v AFC Ajax (h) Won 1-0**
Eleftheropoulos, Amanatidis, Anatolakis, Karataidis, Poursanidis, Karapialis (Niniadis 86), Georgatos, Giannakopoulos, Djordjevic, Gogic (Ofori-Quaye 74), Alexandris (Passalis 69). Scorer: Alexandris 39

**04.11.98 v AFC Ajax (a) Lost 0-2**
Eleftheropoulos, Mavrogenidis, Karataidis, Anatolakis, Georgatos, Karapialis, Passalis, Djordjevic (Niniadis 69), Giannakopoulos, Gogic (Ivic 80), Alexandris (Ofori-Quaye 55)

**25.11.98 v FC Porto (h) Won 2-1**
Eleftheropoulos, Mavrogenidis, Karataidis, Giannakopoulos (Passalis 54), Karapialis (Antzas 70), Poursanidis, Georgatos (Luciano De Souza 83), Djordjevic, Gogic, Alexandris. Scorers: Gogic 18, Pedrag Djordjevic 55. Sent off: Passalis 84

**09.12.98 v NK Craotai/Dinamo Zagreb (a) Drawn 1-1**
Eleftheropoulos, Amanatidis, Anatolakis, Karataidis, Georgatos, Mavrogenidis, Poursanidis, Niniadis, Djordjevic (Luciano De Souza 62), Giannakopoulos (Alexandris 80), Gogic (Ofori-Quaye 85). Scorer: Giannakopoulos 64

**QUARTER FINAL**
**03.03.99 v Juventus FC (a) Lost 1-2**
Eleftheropoulos, Amanatidis, Anatolakis, Karataidis, Georgatos (Niniadis 90), Mavrogenidis, Poursanidis, Karapialis (Alexandris 74), Giannakopoulos (Ivic 74), Djordjevic, Gogic. Scorer: Niniadis 90 pen

**17.03.99 v Juventus FC (h) Drawn 1-1**
Eleftheropoulos, Amanatidis (Luciano De Souza 90), Anatolakis, Karataidis, Georgatos (Alexandris 90), Mavrogenidis, Poursanidis, Karapialis (Amponsah 78), Giannakopoulos, Djordjevic, Gogic. Scorer: Gogic 12

**1999-2000**
**GROUP STAGE 1**
**15.09.99 v Real Madrid CF (h) Drawn 3-3**
Eleftheropoulos, Karataidis, Amanatidis, Poursanidis, Giannakopoulos (Gogic 60), Giovanni, Djordjevic, Mavrogenidis (Amponsah 46), Ofori-Quaye, Zahovic (Niniadis 86), Anatolakis. Scorers: Giovanni 11, 64, Zahovic 67

**21.09.99 v FC Porto (a) Lost 0-2**
Eleftheropoulos, Karataidis, Niniadis, Amanatidis, Poursanidis, Giovanni, Djordjevic (Alexandris 90), Amponsah (Gogic 59), Ofori-Quaye, Zahovic (Luciano 75), Anatolakis

**28.09.99 v Molde FK (h) Won 3-1**
Eleftheropoulos, Karataidis, Amanatidis, Poursanidis, Giovanni, Djordjevic, Passalis, Karapialis (Gogic 62), Ofori-Quaye (Luciano 67, Antzas 79), Zahovic, Anatolakis. Scorers: Giovanni 16, 70, Luciano 77

**20.10.99 v Molde FK (a) Lost 2-3**
Eleftheropoulos, Karataidis (Antzas 58), Amanatidis, Poursanidis, Giovanni, Djordjevic, Mavrogenidis, Passalis (Giannakopoulos 77), Karapialis (Ofori-Quaye 46), Zahovic, Anatolakis. Scorers: Mavrogenidis 36, Zahovic 40

**26.10.99 v Real Madrid CF (a) Lost 0-3**
Eleftheropoulos, Karataidis, Amanatidis, Poursanidis, Gogic, Djordjevic, Amponsah (Giannakopoulos 62), Mavrogenidis (Niniadis 76), Passalis, Zahovic, Anatolakis

**03.11.99 v FC Porto (h) Won 1-0**
Eleftheropoulos, Karataidis, Amanatidis (Karapialis 46), Giannakopoulos, Giovanni, Djordjevic, Mavrogenidis, Passalis, Ofori-Quaye (Gogic 46), Zahovic, Antzas (Amponsah 79). Scorer: Giannakopoulos 56

**2000-2001**
**GROUP STAGE 1**
**12.09.00 v Valencia CF (a) Lost 1-2**
Eleftheropoulos, Patsatzoglou, Amanatidis, Poursanidis (Giannakopoulos 85), Luciano (Choutos 90), Giovanni, Djordjevic, Ze Elias, Mavrogenidis (Ofori-Quaye 73), Zetterberg, Kontis. Scorer: Djordjevic 74

**20.09.00 v Olympique Lyonnais (h) Won 2-1**
Eleftheropoulos, Patsatzoglou, Amanatidis, Luciano (Giannakopoulos 74), Giovanni, Djordjevic, Ze Elias (Poursanidis 72), Zetterberg, Georgatos, Ofori-Quaye (Mavrogenidis 82), Antzas. Scorers: Ofori-Quaye 19, Giovanni 34

**27.09.00 v SC Heerenveen (h) Won 2-0**
Eleftheropoulos, Patsatzoglou, Amanatidis, Luciano (Giannakopoulos 83), Giovanni, Djordjevic, Ze Elias, Zetterberg (Poursanidis 86), Georgatos, Ofori-Quaye (Niniadis 89), Antzas. Scorer: Giovanni 52, 69

**17.10.00 v SC Heerenveen (a) Lost 0-1**
Eleftheropoulos, Patsatzoglou, Amanatidis, Luciano (Anatolakis 75), Giovanni, Djordjevic, Ze Elias, Zetterberg, Georgatos (Choutos), Kontis, Ofori-Quaye

**25.10.00 v Valencia CF (h) Won 1-0**
Eleftheropoulos, Patsatzoglou, Amanatidis, Luciano (Giannakopoulos 59), Choutos (Anatolakis 74), Giovanni, Djordjevic, Ze Elias, Zetterberg, Georgatos (Alexandris 59), Kontis. Scorer: Djordjevic 65 pen

**07.11.00 v Olympique Lyonnais (a) Lost 0-1**
Eleftheropoulos, Patsatzoglou (Giannakopoulos 75), Amanatidis, Poursanidis (Mavrogenidis 54), Giovanni (Ofori-Quaye 51), Djordjevic, Ze Elias, Alvez, Zetterberg, Kontis, Antzas

**2001-2002**
**GROUP STAGE 1**
**10.10.01* v Manchester United FC (h) Lost 0-2**
Eleftheropoulos, Kostoulas (Ofori-quaye 70), Bermudez, Anatolakis, Venetidis, Patsatzoglou, Giannakopoulos, Karembeu, Zetterberg (Niniadis 66), Djordjevic (Alexandris 80), Giovanni
*postponed to 10 October after September 11 atrocities

**18.09.01 v Deportivo La Coruna (a) Drawn 2-2**
Eleftheropoulos, Mavrogenidis (Patsatzoglou 76), Bermudez, Anatolakis, Venetidis, Giannakopoulos, Ze Elias, Karembeu, Djordjevic, Zetterberg (Ofori-quaye 60), Giovanni (Atmanatidis 84). Scorers: Giannakopoulos 80, Oforiquaye 83

**25.09.01 v Lille OSC (a) Lost 1-3**
Eleftheropoulos, Mavrogenidis (Niniadis 64), Bermudez, Anatolakis, Venetidis, Giannakopoulos, Karembeu, Patsatzoglou, Ofori-quaye, Giovanni, Roberts (Alexandris 77). Scorer: Giannakopoulos 90

**17.10.01 v Lille OSC (h) Won 2-1**
Eleftheropoulos, Mavrogenidis, Bermudez (Amanatidis 46), Anatolakis (Niniadis 63), Venetidis, Patsatzoglou, Karembeu, Zetterberg (Giovanni 46), Djordjevic, Alexandris, Ofori-quaye. Scorers: Alexandris 53, Niniadis 64. Sent off: Giovanni 88

**23.10.01 v Manchester United FC (a) Lost 0-3**
Eleftheropoulos, Patsatzoglu, Anatolakis, Amanatidis, Kontis, Mavrogenidis (Poursanidis 46), Karembeu, Giannakopoulos (Roberts 83), Djordjevic, Alexandris (Alves 63), Ofori-quaye

**31.10.01 v RC Deportivo La Coruna (h) Drawn 1-1**
Georgiou, Patsatzoglu, Anatolakis, Amanatidis (Kostoulas 21), Kontis, Mavrogenidis (Niniadis 46), Karembeu, Giannakopoulos, Djordjevic, Alexandris, Ofori-quaye (Pousanidis 66). Scorer: Alexandris 51

**2002-2003**
**GROUP STAGE 1**
**18.09.02 v Bayer 04 Leverkusen (h) Won 6-2**
Eleftheropoulos, Patsatzoglou, Antzas, Anatolakis, Venetidis, Karembeu, Ze Elias, Zetterberg, Giannakopoulos (Oforiquaye 83), Giovanni (Alexandris 83), P Djordjevic (Edu 90). Scorers: Kleine 47og, Giannakopoulos 38, P Djordjevic 44, 64pen, 73, Zetterberg 83

**24.09.02 v Maccabi Haifa (a) Lost 0-3**
Eleftheropoulos, Patsatzoglou, Antzas, Anatolakis (Alexandris 55), Venetidis, Karembeu, Ze Elias, Zetterberg (Niniadis 79), Giannakopoulos (Oforiquaye 80), Giovanni, P Djordjevic

**01.01.02 v Manchester United FC (a) Lost 0-4**
Eleftheropoulos, Amanatidis (Patsatzoglu 73), Antzas, Anatolakis, Venetidis, Karembeu, Ze Elias, Zetterberg, Giannakopoulos (Edu 46), Oforiquaye (Alexandris 59), P Djordjevic. Sent off: Ze Elias 45

**23.10.02 v Manchester United FC (h) Lost 2-3**
Eleftheropoulos, Patsatzoglu, Antzas, Anatolakis, Venetidis, Karembeu, Zetterberg (Oforiquaye 71), Giannakopoulos (Mavrogenidis 87), Edu, Giovanni (Choutos 46), P Djordjevic. Scorers: Choutos 70, P Djordjevic 74

**29.10.02 v Bayer 04 Leverkusen (a) Lost 0-2**
Eleftheropoulos, Patsatzoglu, Antzas (Oforiquaye 63), Anatolakis (Zetterberg 46), Venetidis, Karembeu, Mavrogenidis, Giannakopoulos, Edu, Choutos (Giovanni 24), P Djordjevic

**13.11.02 v Maccabi Haifa (h) Drawn 3-3**
Eleftheropoulos, Patsatzoglu, Antzas, Venetidis, Karembeu, Zetterberg (Niniadis 46), Giannakopoulos, Edu, Giovanni (Oforiquaye 71), P Djordjevic, Alexandris
Scorers: Alexandris 37, Niniadis 57, Antzas 79

| SEASONS | PLAYED | WON | DRAWN | LOST | FOR | AGAINST |
|---|---|---|---|---|---|---|
| 6 | 38 | 11 | 9 | 18 | 48 | 69 |

## PANATHINAIKOS FC

**1995-1996**
**GROUP STAGE 1**
**13.09.95 v FC Dynamo Kyiv (a) Lost 0-1**
Nikpolidis, Apostolakis, Kapouranis, Ouzinidis, Savva Georgiadis, Markos, Borelli (Christodoulou 68), Maragos (Lagonikakis 79), Donis, Alexoudis, Warzycha
*FC Dynamo banned from competition and replaced by Aalborg BK*

**27.09.95 v FC Nantes-Atlantique (h) Won 3-1**
Wandzik, Ouzinidis, Charalambous Georgiadis, Kalitzakis, Savva Georgiadis, Markos, Borelli (Nioplias 80), Maragos (Kolitsidakis 87), Alexoudis (Kapouranis 68), Warzycha, Donis. Scorers: Charalambous Georgiadis 17, Warzycha 30, 46

**18.10.95 v FC Porto (a) Won 1-0**
Wandzik, Apostolakis, Savva Georgiadis, Ouzinidis, Charalambous Georgiadis (Lagonikakis 90), Kalitzakis, Borelli (Kapouranis 77), Donis (Kolitsidakis 82), Markos, Warzycha, Alexoudis. Scorer: Markos 40. Sent off: Alexoudis 35

**25.10.95 v Aalborg BK (a) Lost 1-2**
Wandzik, Apostolakis, Ouzinidis, Charalambous Georgiadis, Kalitzakis, Borelli (Maragos 77), Kapouranis, Savva Georgiadis, Markos, Warzycha, Donis. Scorer: Warzycha 42. Sent off: Kalitzakis 55

**01.11.95 v FC Porto (h) Drawn 0-0**
Wandzik, Apostolakis, Ouzinidis, Charalambous Georgiadis, Savva Georgiadis, Markos, Borelli, Alexoudis (Kapouranis 53), Maragos, Warzycha, Donis (Lagonikakis 90)

**22.11.95 v Aalborg BK (h) Won 2-0**
Wandzik, Apostolakis, Ouzinidis, Charalambous Georgiadis, Kolitsidakis, Markos, Borelli (Kapouranis 67), Maragos, Warzycha (Lagonikakis 89), Donis

**06.12.95 v FC Nantes-Atlantique (a) Drawn 0-0**
Wandzik, Apostolakis, Ouzinidis, Christodoulou, Kalitzakis, Markos, Borelli (Goumas 89), Savva Georgiadis, Kapouranis, Lagonikakis, Maragos

**QUARTER FINAL**

**06.03.96 v Legia Warszawa (a) Drawn 0-0**
Wandzik, Apostolakis, Charalambous Georgiadis, Savva Georgiadis, Kalitzakis, Kolitsidakis, Borelli, Markos, Maragos (Kapouranis 79), Warzycha, Alexoudis

**20.03.96 v Legia Warszawa (h) Won 3-0**
Wandzik, Apostolakis, Ouzinidis, Savva Georgiadis, Kalitzakis, Kolitsidakis, Borelli (Goumas 90), Maragos (Nioplias 80), Kapouranis, Warzycha (Lagonikakis 90), Donis. Scorers: Warzycha 34, 58, Borelli 72

**SEMI FINAL**

**03.04.96 v AFC Ajax (a) Won 1-0**
Wandzik, Apostolakis, Ouzinidis, Savva Georgiadis, Kalitzakis, Kolitsidakis, Borelli (Markos 84), Kapouranis, Maragos (Charalambous Georgiadis 63), Warzycha (Nioplias 90), Donis. Scorer: Warzycha 87

**17.04.96 v AFC Ajax (h) Lost 0-3**
Wandzik, Apostolakis, Markos (Lagonikakis 84), Charalambous Georgiadis, Kalitzakis, Kolitsidakis, Borelli, Kapouranis, Maragos (Nioplias 74), Warzycha, Donis

**1998-1999**
**GROUP STAGE 1**
**16.09.98 v FC Dynamo Kyiv (h) Won 2-1**
Wandzik, Kostantinidis, Kiassos, Apostolakis, Goumas, Milojevic, Vokolos (Kola 69), Mykland, Asanovic, Warzycha (Strandli 87), Liberopoulos (Alexpoulos 90). Scorers: Mykland 57, Liberopoulos 69

**30.09.98 v Arsenal FC (a) Lost 1-2**
Wandzik, Kostantinidis, Goumas, Milojevic, Kiassos (Kola 70), Lagonikakis, Asanovic, Apostolakis, Mykland, Liberopoulos (Mauro 82), Strandli (Sypniewski 82). Scorer: Mauro 88

**21.10.98 v RC Lens (a) Lost 0-1**
Wandzik, Kiassos (Basinas 46), Goumas, Lagonikakis (Mykland 83), Apostolakis, Vokolos, Kostantinidis, Asanovic, Kola, Mauro (Alexoudis 59), Liberopoulos

**04.11.98 v RC Lens (h) Won 1-0**
Wandzik, Lagonikakis, Goumas, Vokolos, Basinas, Kostantinidis, Milojevic, Apostolakis, Asanovic (Kiassos 81), Warzycha (Mauro 87), Liberopoulos. Scorer: Vokolos 53. Sent off: Milojevic 90

**26.11.98 v FC Dynamo Kyiv (a) Lost 1-2**
Wandzik, Kiassos (Mauro 85), Alexopoulos, Vokolos, Basinas, Lagonikakis, Apostolakis (Kola 78), Asanovic, Kostantinidis, Warzycha, Liberopoulos. Scorer: Lagonikakis 36

**09.12.98 v Arsenal FC (h) Lost 1-3**
Wandzik, Apostolakis, Milojevic, Lagonikakis, Kostantinidis (Strandli 69), Goumas, Basinas (Vokolos 78), Kola (Sypniewski 56), Asanovic, Warzycha, Liberopoulos. Scorer: Sypniewski 74

**2000-2001**
**GROUP STAGE 1**
**13.09.00 v RC Deportivo La Coruna (h) Drawn 1-1**
Nikopolidis, Henriksen, Percy Olivares, Paulo Sousa (Pflipsen 56), Warzycha (Koutsoures 69), Vokolos, Kola (Sypniewski 77), Basinas, Liberopoulos, Karagounis, Fissas. Scorer: Warzycha 29

**19.09.00 v Juventus FC (a) Lost 1-2**
Nikopolidis, Henriksen, Percy Olivares, Goumas, Warzycha (Nasiopoulos 77), Vokolos, Kola, Basinas, Liberopoulos, Karagounis (Pflipsen 82), Fissas (Sypniewski 87). Scorer: Goumas 45

**26.09.00 v Hamburger SV (a) Won 1-0**
Chalkias, Henriksen, Percy Olivares, Galetto (Kola 73), Goumas, Vokolos, Nasiopoulos (Saric 58), Basinas (Koutsoures 86), Liberopoulos, Karagounis, Fissas. Scorer: Nasiopoulos 36

**18.10.00 v Hamburger SV (h) Drawn 0-0**
Chalkias, Henriksen, Percy Olivares (Pflipsen 61), Galetto (Warzycha 71), Vlaovic (Nasiopoulos 81), Goumas, Vokolos, Basinas, Liberopoulos, Karagounis, Fissas

**24.10.00 v RC Deportivo La Coruna (a) Lost 0-1**
Chalkias (Nikopolidis 65), Henriksen, Galetto (Paulo Sousa 46), Goumas, Warzycha, Vokolos, Saric, Basinas, Liberopoulos, Karagounis (Kola 61), Fissas

**08.11.00 v Juventus FC (h) Won 3-1**
Nikopolidis, Henriksen, Paulo Sousa (Galetto 46), Goumas, Warzycha (Vlaovic 75), Vokolos, Saric, Basinas, Liberopoulos, Karagounis (Sypniewski 81), Fissas. Scorers: Paulo Sousa 7, Basinas 58 pen, Warzycha 65

**GROUP STAGE 2**

**21.11.00 v Manchester United FC (a) Lost 1-3**
Nikopolidis, Sypniewski (Olivares 79), Vokolos, Henriksen, Fissas, Basinas, Goumas, Karagounis (Vlaovic 67), Galetto, Liberopoulos, Warzycha (Kiasos 75). Scorer: Karagounis 65

**06.12.00 v Valencia CF (h) Drawn 0-0**
Nikopolidis, Vokolos, Henriksen, Koutsouris (Sypniewski 74), Fissas (Olivares 64), Basinas, Goumas, Saric, Karagounis, Warzycha (Vlaovic 75), Liberopoulos

**14.02.01 v SK Sturm Graz (a) Lost 0-2**
Nikopolidis, Vokolos, Henriksen, Koutsouris, Olivares (Boateng 53), Basinas, Goumas (Nasiopoulos 77), Saric, Karagounis (Paulo Sousa 66) , Warzycha (Vlaovic 75), Liberopoulos

**20.02.01 v SK Sturm Graz (h) Lost 1-2**
Nikopolidis, Olivares, Vokolos (Boateng 54), Henriksen, Fyssas (Saric 46), Basinas, Goumas, Nasiopoulos, Karagounis, Warzycha (Vlaovic 70), Liberopoulos. Scorer: Goumas 73

**07.03.01 v Manchester United FC (h) Drawn 1-1**
Nikopolidis, Olivares, Henriksen, Fyssas, Basinas (Plipsen 85), Goumas, Boateng, Seitaridis, Karagounis, Vlaovic (Galetto 59), Liberopoulos (Warzycha 66). Scorer: Seitaridis 25

**13.03.01 v Valencia CF (a) Lost 1-2**
Chalikias, Olivares, Vokolos, Fyssas, Basinas (Plipsen 85), Goumas, Nasiopoulos (Koutsouris 46), Seitaridis, Karagounis, Vlaovic (Warzycha 57), Liberopoulos (Sigurdsson 72). Scorer: Basinas 28pen

**2001-2002**
**GROUP STAGE 1**
**11.09.01 v FC Schalke 04 (a) Won 2-0**
Nikopolidis, Seitaridis, Henriksen, Kirgiakos, Fissas, Michaelsen, Paulo Sousa, Karagounis, Basinas, Konstantinou (Saric 89), Kolkka (Vlaovic 68). Scorers: Vlaovic 75, Bassinas 80

**19.09.01 v RCD Mallorca (h) Won 2-0**
Nikopolidis, Seitaridis, Henriksen, Kirgiakos, Fissas, Michaelsen, Paulo Sousa, Karagounis (Kolkka 80), Basinas, Konstantinou (Olisadebe 80), Vlaovic (Vokolos 84). Scorers: Vlaovic 25, Konstantinou 28

**26.09.01 v Arsenal FC (h) Won 1-0**
Nikopolidis, Kirgiakos, Vokolos, Henriksen, Fissas, Michaelsen, Paulo Sousa, Karagounis (Saric 85), Basinas, Olisadebe (Kolkka 70), Vlaovic (Konstantinou 65). Scorer: Karagounis 23

**16.10.01 v Arsenal FC (a) Lost 1-2**
Nikopolidis, Kirgiakos, Vokolos, Henriksen, Fissas, Michaelsen, Paulo Sousa (Seitaridis 78), Karagounis (Kolkka 78), Basinas, Olisadebe, Konstantinou (Vlaovic 78). Scorer: Olisadebe 50

**24.10.01 v FC Schalke 04 (h) Won 2-0**
Nikopolidis, Seitaridis (Saric 69), Vokolos, Henriksen, Fissas, Michaelsen, Paulo Sousa, Karagounis, Basinas (Goumas 64), Olisadebe, Konstantinou (Vlaovic 73). Scorers: Olisadebe 60, Konstantinou 60

**30.10.01 v RCD Mallorca (a) Lost 0-1**
Nikopolidis, Goumas, Vokolos, Kirgiakos, Fissas, Saric, Karagounis (Warzycha 82), Boateng, Kolkka (Galetto 73), Liberopoulos, Vlaovic (Konstantinou 82)

**GROUP STAGE 2**
**21.11.01 v FC Porto (h) Drawn 0-0**
Nikopolidis, Seitaridis, Kirgiakos, Henriksen, Fissas, Michaelsen (Liberopoulos 70), Paulo Sousa (Kolkka 80), Karagounis, Basinas, Olisadebe (Vlaovic 80), Konstantinou

**04.12.01 v Real Madrid CF (a) Lost 0-3**
Nikopolidis, Seitaridis, Kirgiakos, Henriksen, Goumas, Fissas, Michaelsen (Karagounis 46), Paulo Sousa (Boateng 46), Basinas, Olisadebe, Konstantinou (Vlaovic 70)

**19.02.02 v AC Sparta Praha (a) Won 2-0**
Nikopolidis, Kirgiakos, Henriksen, Goumas, Saric, Karagounis, Galetto (Jarni 66), Basinas, Pitsos, Liberopoulos, Konstantinou (Vokolos 86). Scorers: Karagounis 39, Konstantinou 71

**27.02.02 v AC Sparta Praha Won 2-1**
Nikopolidis, Kirgiakos, Henriksen, Goumas, Saric, Karagounis, Michaelsen (Galetto 62), Basinas, Pitsos (Jarni 77), Liberopoulos, Konstantinou (Kolkka 82). Scorer: Konstantinou 15, 47

**12.03.02 v FC Porto Lost 1-2**
Nikopolidis, Kirgiakos, Henriksen, Goumas, Saric, Karagounis, Vokolos (Vlaovic 71), Basinas, Jarni (Kolkka 35), Liberopoulos, Konstantinou (Olisadebe 31). Scorer: Kolkka 65

**20.03.02 v Real Madrid CF Drawn 2-2**
Nikopolidis, Seitaridis, Galetto, Henriksen, Fissas, Michaelsen, Karagounis, Goumas, Liberopoulos (Vokolos 77), Konstantinou (Olisadebe 71), Vlaovic (Warzycha 86) Scorers: Liberopoulos 9, Goumas 64

**QUARTER FINAL**
**03.04.02 v FC Barcelona (h) Won 1-0**
Nikopolidis, Kirgiakos, Henriksen, Fissas, Saric, Basinas, Goumas, Kolkka, Liberopoulos (Boateng 60), Konstantinou (Vokolos 90), Vlaovic (Olisadebe 74). Scorer: Basinas 79pen

**09.04.02 v FC Barcelona (a) Lost 1-3**
Nikopolidis, Kirgiakos, Henriksen, Fissas, Saric, Basinas, Karagounis (Michaelsen 44), Goumas, Kolkka (Vlaovic 46), Liberopoulos (Olisadebe ), Konstantinou. Scorer: Konstantinou 8

| SEASONS | PLAYED | WON | DRAWN | LOST | FOR | AGAINST |
|---|---|---|---|---|---|---|
| 4 | 42 | 16 | 9 | 17 | 44 | 44 |

## PARIS SAINT-GERMAIN FC

**1994-1995**
**GROUP STAGE 1**
**14.09.94 v FC Bayern Munchen (h) Won 2-0**
Lama, Cobos, Dieng, Ricardo Gomes, Roche, Le Guen, Bravo, Guerin (Llacer 82), Weah, Valdo (Kombuoare 84), Ginola. Scorers: Weah 39, Bravo 80

**28.09.94 v FC Spartak Moscow (a) Won 2-1**
Lama, Cobos (Llacer 80), Dieng, Kombuoare, Roche, Le Guen, Bravo, Guerin, Weah, Valdo, Ginola (Nouma 85). Scorers: Le Guen 52, Valdo 59

**19.10.94 v FC Dynamo Kyiv (a) Won 2-1**
Lama, Cobos, Dieng, Kombuoare, Roche, Le Guen, Bravo, Guerin, Weah (Colleter 88), Valdo, Ginola (Rai 54). Scorers: Guerin 25, Weah 75

**02.11.94 v FC Dynamo Kyiv (h) Won 1-0**
Lama, Cobos (Llacer 79), Colleter, Kombuoare, Roche, Le Guen, Bravo, Guerin, Weah, Rai (Nouma 79), Dieng. Scorer: Weah 69

**23.11.94 v FC Bayern Munchen (a) Won 1-0**
Lama, Cobos, Colleter, Dieng, Roche, Llacer, Bravo (Le Guen 58), Guerin, Nouma, Sechet, Ginola (Weah 64). Scorer: Weah 80

**07.12.94 v FC Spartak Moscow (h) Won 4-1**
Lama, Llacer, Colleter, Kombouare, Roche, Le Guen (Guerin 52), Bravo, Dieng, Weah (Allou 65), Rai, Ginola. Scorers: Weah 27, 50, Ginola 41, Rai 58

**QUARTER FINAL**
**01.03.95 v FC Barcelona (a) Drawn 1-1**
Lama, Cobos, Colleter, Kombouare, Roche, Le Guen, Bravo, Guerin, Weah, Valdo, Ginola (Rai 61). Scorer: Weah 57

**15.03.95 v FC Barcelona (h) Won 2-1**
Lama, Cobos, Colleter, Kombouare, Le Guen, Bravo, Guerin, Rai, Weah, Valdo, Ginola Scorers: Rai 73, Guerin 83

**SEMI FINAL**
**05.04.95 v Milan AC (h) Lost 0-1**
Lama, Llacer, Cobos, Ricardo Gomes, Roche, Le Guen, Bravo, Rai, Guerin, Weah, Ginola (Borrelli 83)

**19.04.95 v Milan AC (a) Lost 0-2**
Lama, Cobos (Sechet 76), Colleter, Ricardo Gomes, Roche, Le Guen, Bravo, Guerin, Weah, Valdo (Nouma 68), Ginola

**1997-1998**
**GROUP STAGE 1**
**17.09.97 v IFK Goteborg (h) Won 3-0**
Revault, Fournier (Guerin 79), Roche, Le Guen, Domi, Leroy (Algerino 73), Ngotty, Rai (Cisse 86), Gava, Maurice, Simone. Scorers: Ngotty 27, Lucic og 51, Rai 82 pen

**01.10.97 v Besiktas JK (a) Lost 1-3**
Revault, Fournier, Roche, Le Guen (Guerin 65), Domi, Edmilson (Algerino 46), Ngotty, Rai, Gava (Leroy 62), Maurice, Simone. Scorer: Simone 66

**22.10.97 v FC Bayern Munchen (a) Lost 1-5**
Revault, Fournier (Algerino 60), Le Guen, Ngotty (Rabesandratana 53), Roche, Domi (Llacer 46), Leroy, Rai, Gava, Maurice, Simone. Scorer: Simone 48

**05.11.97 v FC Bayern Munchen (h) Won 3-1**
Revault, Algerino, Le Guen, Rabesandratana, Llacer (Leroy 68), Fournier, Cisse, Guerin, Gava, Rai, Maurice (Ducroq 82). Scorers: Gava 18, Maurice 73, Leroy 75

**26.11.97 v IFK Goteborg (a) Won 1-0**
Revault, Fournier (Edmilson 79), Roche (Algerino 61), Le Guen, Domi, Leroy, Ngotty, Rabesandratana, Gava, Rai, Maurice (Llacer 90). Scorer: Rabesandratana 88. Sent off: Algerino 74

**10.12.97 v Besiktas JK (h) Won 2-1**
Revault, Le Guen, Kelban, Ducroq, Llacer, Edmilson (Cisse 70), Leroy, Rai, Gava, Simone, Maurice. Scorers: Gava 23, Simone 58

**2000-2001**
**GROUP STAGE 1**
**13.09.00 v Rosenborg BK (a) Lost 1-3**
Letizi, Talal, Luccin, Christian (Leroy 82), Anelka, Robert (Okocha 67), Dalmat, Dehu, Algerino, Edouard Cisse, Distin. Scorer: Christian 7

**19.09.00 v Helsingborgs IF (h) Won 4-1**
Letizi, Talal, Luccin, Christian (Leroy 89), Benarbia (Edouard Cisse 75), Anelka, Robert, Dalmat (Yanovski 82), Rabesandratana, Algerino, Mendy. Scorers: Anelka 25, Robert 63, Christian 81, Talal 90

**26.09.00 v FC Bayern Munchen (h) Won 1-0**
Letizi, Luccin, Christian (Leroy 79), Benarbia (Ducrocq 69), Anelka, Robert, Dalmat, Dehu, Rabesandratana, Algerino, Mendy. Scorer: Leroy 90

**18.10.00 v FC Bayern Munchen (a) Lost 0-2**
Letizi, Luccin (Edouard Cisse 84), Christian, Anelka, Robert, Dalmat, Dehu, Rabesandratana, Algerino, Distin, Mendy (Okocha 71)

**24.10.00 v Rosenborg BK (h) Won 7-2**
Letizi, Luccin (Ducrocq 60), Christian (Leroy 73), Anelka, Robert, Dalmat, Dehu, Rabesandratana, Algerino, Distin, Mendy. Scorers: Dehu 16, Christian 25, Anelka 35, 90, Luccin 45, Leroy 76, Robert 87 pen

**08.11.00 v Helsingborgs IF (a) Drawn 1-1**
Letizi, Anelka (Talal 85), Okocha, Robert (Yanovski 75), Dehu, Rabesandratana, Leroy, Edouard Cisse, Distin, Ducrocq, Aliou Cisse. Scorer: Anelka 34

**GROUP STAGE 2**
**21.11.00 v RC Deportivo La Coruna (h) Lost 1-3**
Letizi, Algerino, Distin, Dehu (Okpara 74), Mendy (Paisley 90), Luccin, Ducrocq (E Cisse 74), Okocha, Robert, Christian L Leroy. Scorer: Algerino 37

**06.12.00 v Galatasaray SK (a) Lost 0-1**
Letizi, E Cisse, Rabesandratana, Distin (Algerino 85), El-Kharkouri, Luccin, Ducrocq, Dalmat (Anelka 71), Yanovski, Robert, L Leroy (Christian)

**14.02.01 v Milan AC (a) Drawn 1-1**
Letizi, Mendy, A Cisse, Distin, Dehu, Domi, Ducrocq, Arteta (Okocha 69), Benarbia (Robert 57), E Cisse (L Leroy 90), Anelka. Scorer: Anelka 30

**20.02.01 v Milan AC (h) Drawn 1-1**
Letizi, A Cisse (Ducrocq 62), Distin, Dehu, Domi, Arteta, Benarbia (Luccin 70), Robert, E Cisse, L Leroy (Rabesandratana 87), Anelka. Scorer: Robert 75

**07.03.01 v RC Deportivo La Coruna (a) Lost 3-4**
Letizi, Mendy, A Cisse, Distin, Dehu, Algerino, Ducrocq, Arteta (Luccin 56), Okocha (Yanovsky 74), Benarbia (Rabesandratana 62), L Leroy. Scorers: Okocha 29, L Leroy 43, 55

**13.03.01 v Galatasaray SK (h) Won 2-0**
Letizi, Rabesandratana, Distin, Dehu, Ducrocq, Luccin, Algerino, Arteta (Benarbia 36), E Cisse, L Leroy (Benachour 88), Christian (Madar 68). Scorer: Christian 3, 27. Sent off: Ducrocq 89

| SEASONS | PLAYED | WON | DRAWN | LOST | FOR | AGAINST |
|---|---|---|---|---|---|---|
| 3 | 28 | 15 | 4 | 9 | 48 | 37 |

## PARMA AC

**1997-1998**
**GROUP STAGE 1**
**17.09.97 v AC Sparta Praha (a) Drawn 0-0**
Buffon, Ze Maria, Cannavaro, Thuram, Benarrivo, Crippa, Sensini, D Baggio, Strada, Chiesa, Crespo (Maniero 80)

**01.10.97 v Galatasaray SK (h) Won 2-0**
Buffon, Ze Maria (Mussi 77), Cannavaro, Thuram, Milanese, Crippa, Sensini, D Baggio, Strada (Fiore 67), Chiesa (Maniero 87), Crespo. Scorers: Sensini 24, Crespo 39

**22.10.97 v BV Borussia Dortmund (h) Won 1-0**
Buffon, Ze Maria (Mussi 77), Cannavaro, Thuram, Benarrivo, Crippa, Sensini, D Baggio, Strada (Stanic 78), Chiesa (Fiore 89), Crespo. Scorer: Crespo 62

**05.11.97 v BV Borussia Dortmund (a) Lost 0-2**
Buffon, Mussi, Thuram, Cannavaro, Benarrivo, Stanic (Maniero 70), Sensini, D Baggio, Strada (Crippa 32), Chiesa (Fiore 79), Crespo

**27.11.97 v AC Sparta Praha (h) Drawn 2-2**
Buffon, Ze Maria, Thuram, Cannavaro, Milanese, Stanic (Orlandini 85), Giunti, D Baggio, Fiore, Chiesa, Crespo (Maniero 85). Scorer: Chiesa 22, 90 pen

**10.12.97 v Galatasaray SK (a) Drawn 1-1**
Buffon, Ze Maria (Mussi 72), Thuram, Apolloni, Milanese (Adailton 72), Stanic Fiore, D Baggio, Crippa, Chiesa, Maniero (Crespo 84). Scorer: Chiesa 47

| SEASONS | PLAYED | WON | DRAWN | LOST | FOR | AGAINST |
|---|---|---|---|---|---|---|
| 1 | 6 | 2 | 3 | 1 | 6 | 5 |

## FC PORTO

**1992-1993**
**GROUP STAGE 1**
**25.11.92 v PSV Eindhoven (h) Drawn 2-2**
Vitor Baia, Joao Pinto, Andre, Aloisio, Jose Carlos, Rui Felipe, Jaime Magalhaes, Kostadinov, Domingos, Semedo (Toze 62), Jorge Couto. Scorers: Jaime Magalhaes 34, Jose Carlos 80

**09.12.92 v IFK Goteborg (a) Lost 0-1**
Vitor Baia, Joao Pinto, Bandeirinha, Aloisio, Fernando Couto, Antonio Carlos (Toze 65), Jorge Couto, Kostadinov, Domingos, Semedo, Andre

**03.03.93 v Milan AC (h) Lost 0-1**
Vitor Baia, Joao Pinto, Rui Jorge, Aloisio, Fernando Couto, Timofte, Jorge Costa, Kostadinov (Toni Nelson 77), Jorge Couto (Domingos 68), Semedo, Paulinho Santos

**17.03.93 v Milan AC (a)** **Lost 0-1**
Vitor Baia, Joao Pinto, Rui Jorge, Aloisio, Fernando Couto, Timofte (Domingos 64), Paulinho Santos, Kostadinov, Jorge Couto, Semedo, Andre (Bino 78)

**07.04.93 v PSV Eindhoven (a)** **Won 1-0**
Vitor Baia, Bandeirinha, Vik (Rui Jorge 66), Ze Carlos, Fernando Couto, Paulinho Santos, Jorge Couto, Jorge Costa, Paulo Cesar, Bino, Toze (Domingos 38). Scorer: Ze Carlos 77 pen

**21.04.93 v IFK Goteborg (h)** **Won 2-0**
Vitor Baia, Bandeirinha, Rui Jorge (Jorge Costa 46), Jose Carlos, Fernando Couto, Timofte, Jaime Magalhaes, Kostadinov (Bino 81), Domingos, Semedo, Andre. Scorers: Jose Carlos 42, Timofte 56

**1993-1994**
**GROUP STAGE 1**
**24.11.93 v SV Werder Bremen (h)** **Won 3-2**
Vitor Baia, Joao Pinto, Rui Jorge, Aloisio, Jorge Costa, Jose Carlos, Secretario, Kostadinov (Jaime Magalhaes 75), Domingos Oliveira, Semedo, Paulinho Santos (Rui Felipe 85). Scorers: Domingos Oliveira 6, Rui Jorge 32, Jose Carlos 81

**01.12.93 v Milan AC (a)** **Lost 0-3**
Vitor Baia, Joao Pinto, Paulo Pereira (Rui Felipe 46), Aloisio, Fernando Couto, Jose Carlos, Secretario, Rui Jorge, Domingos Oliveira, Semedo, Paulinho Santos (Vinha 46)

**02.03.94 v RSC Anderlecht (a)** **Lost 0-1**
Vitor Baia, Bandeirinha, Rui Jorge, Aloisio, Fernando Couto, Jorge Costa, Secretario, Kostadinov, Andre (Folha 86), Semedo (Rui Felipe 79), Drulovic

**16.03.94 v RSC Anderlecht (h)** **Won 2-0**
Vitor Baia, Joao Pinto, Rui Jorge, Aloisio, Jorge Costa, Secretario, Andre, Semedo, Timofte (Folha 74), Domingos Oliveira (Fernando Couto 87), Drulovic. Scorers: Drulovic 10, Secretario 89

**30.03.94 v SV Werder Bremen (a)** **Won 5-0**
Vitor Baia, Joao Pinto, Rui Jorge, Jorge Costa, Fernando Couto, Andre, Secretario, Kostadinov (Domingos Oliveira 72), Timofte, Paulinho Santos (Rui Felipe 8), Drulovic. Scorers: Wiedener og 11, Kostadinov 35, Secretario 60, Domingos Oliveira 63, Timofte 88 pen

**13.04.94 v Milan AC (h)** **Drawn 0-0**
Vitor Baia, Joao Pinto, Rui Jorge, Aloisio, Fernando Couto, Andre, Jorge Couto (Jaime Magalhaes 76), Rui Felipe, Domingos Oliveira, Timofte (Folha 68), Drulovic

**SEMI FINAL**

**27.04.94 v FC Barcelona (a) Lost 0-3**

Vitor Baia, Joao Pinto, Jorge Costa, Aloisio, Fernando Couto, Andre (Paulinho Santos 80), Secretario, Kostadinov, Folha (Semedo 66), Rui Felipe, Drulovic

**1995-1996**

**GROUP STAGE 1**

**13.09.95 v FC Nantes-Atlantique (a) Drawn 0-0**

Vitor Baia, Joao Pinto, Aloisio, Jose Carlos, Paulinho Santos, Emerson (Bino 90), Secretario, Rui Barros, Latapy, Domingos (Folha 78), Mielcarsky

**27.09.95 v Aalborg BK (h) Won 2-0**

Vitor Baia, Joao Pointo (Bino 73), Paulinho Santos, Jorge Costa, Jose Carlos, Laptapy, Emerson, Secretario, Domingos, Drulovic (Folha 79), Mielcarski (Rui Barros 36). Scorers: Rui Barros 41, 62

**18.10.95 v Panathinaikos FC (h) Lost 0-1**

Vitor Baia, Joao Pinto (Folha 55), Paulinho Santos, Aloisio, Jose Carlos, Emerson, Latapy, Secretario (Bino 84), Rui Barros (Jorge Couto 76), Drulovic, Domingos

**01.11.95 v Panathinaikos FC (a) Drawn 0-0**

Vitor Baia, Secretario, Rui Jorge, Aloisio, Jorge Costa, Emerson, Paulinho Santos, Edmilson, Rui Barros (Bino 78), Drulovic (Folha 85), Domingos

**22.11.95 v FC Nantes-Atlantique (h) Drawn 2-2**

Vitor Baia, Secretario, Paulinho Santos, Jose Carlos, Jorge Costa, Emerson (Folha 81), Licpsei, Edmilson, Rui Barros (Jorge Couto 59), Domingos, Drulovic (Bino 81). Scorers: Drulovic 10, Jose Carlos 56

**06.12.95 v Aalborg BK (a) Drawn 2-2**

Vitor Baia, Joao Pinto (Rui Barros 52), Rui Jorge (Folha 68), Aloisio, Jose Carlos (Joao Manuel Pinto 74), Emerson, Secretario, Edmilson, Paulinho Santos, Drulovic, Domingos. Scorer: Emerson 63, 75

**1996-1997**

**GROUP STAGE 1**

**11.09.96 v Milan AC (a) Won 3-2**

Wozniak, Sergio Conceicao, Lula, Jorge Costa, Aloisio (Drulovic 74), Fernando Mendes, Edmilson, Paulinho Santos, Barroso (Jardel 63), Zahovic, Artur (Rui Barros 87). Scorers: Artur 54, Jardel 76, 82

**25.09.96 v IFK Goteborg (h) Won 2-1**

Wozniak, Jorge Costa, Lula, Aloisio, Sergio Conceicao, Paulinho Santos, Rui Jorge, Fernando Mendes, Edmilson (Folha 67), Jardel (Drulovic 83), Artur. Scorer: Artur 27, 51

**16.10.96 v Rosenborg BK (a) Won 1-0**
Hilario, Paulinho Santos, Aloisio, Barroso, Jorge Costa, Fernando Mendes, Sergio Conceicao (Rui Barros 78), Edmilson, Drulovic (Jardel 69), Artur, Zahovic. Scorer: Jardel 90

**30.10.96 v Rosenborg BK (h) Won 3-0**
Hilario, Joao Pinto, Jorge Costa, Aloisio, Fernando Mendes, Edmilson (Barroso 73), Paulinho Santos, Zahovic, Rui Barros (Sergio Conceicao 59), Artur (Jardel 61), Drulovic. Scorers: Zahovic 32, Drulovic 41, Artur 60

**20.11.96 v Milan AC (h) Drawn 1-1**
Hilario, Sergio Conceicao, Jorge Costa, Aloisio, Fernando Mendes, Bino (Folha 66), Barroso, Zahovic, Edmilson, Artur (Joao Manuel Pinto 84), Drulovic (Jardel 54). Scorer: Edmilson 71

**04.12.96 v IFK Goteborg (a) Won 2-0**
Hilario, Sergio Conceicao, Aloisio, Zahovic, Joao Manuel Pinto, Fernando Mendes (Artur 46), Drulovic (Folha 90), Barroso, Paulinho Santos, Edmilson, Jardel (Rui Barros 80). Scorers: Jardel 64, Edmilson 90

**QUARTER FINAL**

**05.03.97 v Manchester United FC (a) Lost 0-4**
Hilario, Sergio Conceicao, Jorge Costa, Barroso, Aloisio, Paulinho Santos, Joao Costa (Jardel 25), Zahovic, Drulovic, Edmilson, Artur (Rui Barros 46)

**19.03.97 v Manchester United (h) Drawn 0-0**
Wozniak, Joao Pinto (Zahovic 37), Joao Manuel Pinto, Rui Jorge, Jorge Costa, Paulinho Santos, Fernando Mendes (Mielcarski 50), Barroso (Wetl 48), Drulovic, Edmilson, Jardel

**1997-1998**

**GROUP STAGE 1**

**17.09.97 v Olympiakos Piraeus FC (a) Lost 0-1**
Rui Correia, Sergio Conceicao, Joao Manuel Pinto (Barroso 33), Aloisio, Fernando Mendes, Zahovic, Paulinho Santos, Rui Barros (Capucho 52), Drulovic, Jardel, Folha (Artur 60)

**01.10.97 v Real Madrid CF (h) Lost 0-2**
Rui Correia, Paulinho Santos, Neves (Drulovic 40), Joao Manuel Pinto, Aloisio, Kenedy, Sergio Conceicao, Barroso (Folha 59), Rui Barros (Artur 46), Zahovic, Jardel

**22.10.97 v Rosenborg BK (a) Lost 0-2**
Rui Correia, Paulinho Santos, Lula, Aloisio, Fernando Mendes, Costa (Drulovic 40), Barroso, Chippo, Rui Barros (Zahovic 46), Jardel (Capucho 46), Artur. Sent off: Chippo 66

**05.11.97 v Rosenborg BK (h) Drawn 1-1**
Rui Correia, Paulinho Santos, Joao Manuel Pinto, Aloisio, Rui Jorge, Sergio Conceicao (Capucho 24, Artur 80), Rui Barros, Costa (Barroso 33), Zahovic, Drulovic, Jardel. Scorer: Jardel 8

**27.11.97 v Olympiakos Piraeus FC (h) Won 2-1**
Rui Correia, Buturovic, Lula, Joao Manuel Pinto, Kenedy (Costa 47), Sergio Conceicao (Rui Barros 20), Paulinho Santos, Rui Jorge, Capucho (Costa 46), Drulovic, Jardel. Scorer: Jardel 29, 52

**10.12.97 v Real Madrid CF (a) Lost 0-4**
Rui Correia, Barroso, Neves, Aloisio, Joao Manuel Pinto (Gaspar 34), Fernando Mendes (Mielcarksi 62), Paulinho Santos, Rui Barros, Zahovic, Folha (Capucho 34), Drulovic

**1998-1999**
**GROUP STAGE 1**
**16.09.98 v Olympiakos Piraeus FC (h) Drawn 2-2**
Kralj, Secretario, Jorge Costa, Aloisio, Fernando Mendes, Doriva, Paulinho Santos, Capucho, Zahovic (Chippo 70), Drulovic (Artur 59), Jardel (Panduru 90). Scorers: Zahovic 65, Jardel 82

**30.09.98 v AFC Ajax (a) Lost 1-2**
Rui Correia, Secretario, Jorge Costa, Aloisio, Fernando Mendes (Chippo 46), Doriva, Zahovic, Paulinho Santos, Capucho, (Artur 68), Drulovic (Rui Barros 83), Jardel. Scorer: Zahovic 68

**21.10.98 v NK Croatia/Dinamo Zagreb (h) Won 3-0**
Kralj, Secretario, Jorge Costa, Aloisio, Fernando Mendes, Capucho (Rui Barros 80), Doriva, Zahovic (Chippo 90), Paulinho Santos, Drulovic (Artur 63), Jardel. Scorers: Doriva 33, Zahovic 43, 75

**04.11.98 v NK Croatia/Dinamo Zagreb (a) Lost 1-3**
Kralj, Secretario, Joao Manuel Pinto, Aloisio (Mielcarski 75), Fernando Mendes (Chippo 75), Doriva, Paulinho Santos, Rui Barros (Jardel 28), Zahovic, Capucho, Drulovic. Scorer: Jardel 39

**25.11.98 v Olympiakos Piaeus FC (a) Lost 1-2**
Rui Correia, Secretario, Jorge Costa, Aloisio, Fernando Mendes (Joao Manuel Pinto), Chainho (Rui Barros 53), Doriva, Capucho (Miki 63), Zahovic, Drulovic, Jardel. Scorer: Zahovic 76

**09.12.98 v AFC Ajax (h) Won 3-0**
Rui Correia, Joao Manuel Pinto, Jorge Costa, Aloisio, Paulinho Santos, Panduru (Chippo 51), Doriva, Zahovic (Rui Barros 83), Chainho, Drulovic (Mielcarski 88), Jardel. Scorers: Zahovic 54, 73, Drulovic 79

**1999-2000**
**GROUP STAGE 1**
**15.09.99 v Molde FK (a) Won 1-0**
Vitor Baia, Jorge Costa, Argel, Peixe, Secretario, Drulovic, Jardel, Chainho, Capucho (Alessandro 54), Deco, Esquerdinha. Scorer: Deco 89

**21.09.99 v Olympiakos Piraeus FC (h) Won 2-0**
Vitor Baia, Jorge Costa, Argel, Peixe, Secretario, Drulovic, Jardel, Chainho (Rui Barros 76), Capucho (Alessandro 62), Deco (Aloisio 90), Esquerdinha. Scorers: Esquerdinha 6, Jardel 47

**28.09.99 v Real Madrid CF (a) Lost 1-3**
Vitor Baia, Jorge Costa, Argel, Peixe, Secretario, Drulovic (Miki 88), Jardel, Chainho (Rubens Junior 58), Capucho (Alessandro 51), Deco, Esquerdinha. Scorer: Jardel 24

**20.10.99 v Real Madrid CF (h) Won 2-1**
Vitor Baia, Jorge Costa, Rubens Junior (Drulovic 36), Argel (Aloisio 74), Peixe, Secretario, Drulovic, Jardel, Chainho, Capucho (Paulinho Santos 72), Deco, Esquerdinha. Scorer: Jardel 13, 35

**26.10.99 v Molde FK (h) Won 3-1**
Vitor Baia, Jorge Costa, Aloisio, Peixe, Secretario, Drulovic, Jardel (Domingos 76), Chainho (Ricardo Sousa 69), Capucho, Deco (Alessandro 29), Esquerdinha. Scorers: Deco 1, 28, Jardel 58

**03.11.99 v Olympiakos Piraeus FC (a) Lost 0-1**
Hilario, Rubens Junior, Aloisio, Secretario, Ricardo Sousa (Miki 64), Drulovic, Rodolfo (Chaino 64), Alessandro, Paulinho Santos, Romeu (Duda 72), Ricardo Silva

**GROUP STAGE 2**
**23.11.99 v AC Sparta Praha (a) Won 2-0**
Vitor Baia, Jorge Costa, Rubens Junior (Drulovic 73), Aloisio, Secretario, Jardel (Argel 87), Chaino (Domingos 90), Paulinho Santos, Capucho, Deco, Esquerdinha. Scorers: Drulovic 77, Jardel 84

**08.12.99 v Hertha BSC Berlin (h) Won 1-0**
Vitor Baia (Hilario 75), Jorge Costa, Rubens Junior (Drulovic 56), Aloisio, Secretario, Jardel (Ricardo Silva 90), Chaino, Paulinho Santos, Capucho, Deco, Esquerdinha. Scorer: Drulovic 79. Sent off: Paulinho Santos 90

**01.03.00 v FC Barcelona (a) Lost 2-4**
Hilario, Jorge Costa, Aloisio, Peixe (Alessandro 74), Secretario, Rui Barros (Domingos 39), Drulovic, Jardel, Chaino, Capucho (Clayton 74), Esquerdinha. Scorer: Jardel 5, 79

**07.03.00 v FC Barcelona (h) Lost 0-2**
Hilario, Rubens Junior (Domingos 45), Aloisio, Peixe (Chaino 46), Secretario, Drulovic, Jardel, Paulinho Santos (Clayton 64), Capucho, Esquerdinha, Ricardo Silva

**15.03.00 v AC Sparta Praha (h) Drawn 2-2**
Vitor Baia, Jorge Costa, Secretario, Domingos (Paulinho Santos 89), Drulovic, Jardel, Chaino (Peixe 53), Capucho (Rui Barros 82), Deco, Esquerdinha, Ricardo Silva. Scorers: Jorge Costa 16, Capucho 64

**21.03.00 v Hertha BSC Berlin (a) Won 1-0**
Vitor Baia, Jorge Costa, Aloisio, Secretario, Drulovic (Clayton 67), Jardel, Chaino, Paulinho Santos, Capucho (Alessandro 76), Deco (Peixe 90), Esquerdinha. Scorer: Clayton 70

**QUARTER FINAL**

**04.04.00 v FC Bayern Munchen (h) Drawn 1-1**
Hilario, Jorge Costa, Aloisio, Drulovic, Jardel, Chaino (Domingos 84), Paulinho Santos, Capucho (Clayton 73), Deco, Esquerdinha, Nelson. Scorer: Jardel 47

**19.04.00 v FC Bayern Munchen (a) Lost 1-2**
Hilario, Jorge Costa, Aloisio, Drulovic, Jardel, Chaino (Rui Barros 44, Domingos 77), Paulinho Santos, Capucho, Deco (Clayton 60), Esquerdinha, Nelson. Scorer: Jardel 90

**2001-2002**

**GROUP STAGE 1**

**10.10.01* v Juventus FC (h) Drawn 0-0**
Ovchinnikov, Ibarra, J Andrade, Ricardo Cavalho, Mario Silva, Paredes, Clayton (Soderstrom 71), Capucho (Alenitchev 77), Deco, Costinha - Pena (Helder 67)
*played 10 October after 11 Sept atrocities

**18.09.01 v Rosenborg BK (a) Won 2-1**
Ovchinnikov, Ibarra, J Costa, Ricardo Cavalho, Mario Silva, Costinha, J Andrade, Capucho (Alenitchev 90), Deco, R Junior (Paredes 37), Pena (Helder 84). Scorers: Pena 10, Deco 60

**25.09.01 v Celtic FC (a) Lost 0-1**
Ovchinnikov, Ibarra (Helder 76), J Costa, Ricardo Cavalho, Mario Silva (Alenitchev 46), Costinha (R Junior 46), J Andrade, Capucho, Deco, Paredes, Pena

**17.10.01 v Celtic FC (h) Won 3-0**
Ovchinnikov, Ibarra, Ricardo Cavalho, Mario Silva, Costinha (Sodertstrom 71), J Andrade, Capucho (J Costa 86), Clayton (R Junior 75), Deco, Paredes, Pena. Scorers: Clayton 1, 61, Mario Silva 45

**23.10.01 v Juventus (a) Lost 1-3**
Ovchinnikov, Ibarra (R Junior 75), Ricardo Cavalho, Mario Silva, Costinha, J Andrade, Capucho, Clayton (Helder 61), Deco (Rafael 67), Soderstrom, Pena. Scorer: Clayton 13

**31.10.01 v Rosenborg BK (h) Won 1-0**
P Santos, Ibarra, Ricardo Cavalho, Mario Silva, Costinha (R Junior 78), J Andrade, Capucho (Esnaider 68), Clayton (Soderstrom 69), Deco, Paredes, Pena. Scorer: Pena 37

**GROUP STAGE 2**

**21.11.01 v Panathinaikos FC (a) Drawn 0-0**
P Santos, Ibarra, Ricardo Cavalho, Mario Silva, Costinha (R Junior 90), J Andrade, Capucho, Clayton (Soderstrom 78), Deco, Paredes, Pena (Ricardo Silva 88)

**04.12.01 v AC Sparta Praha (h) Lost 0-1**
P Santos, Ibarra (Candido Costa 76), Ricardo Cavalho, Mario Silva, Soderstrom, J Andrade, Capucho, Clayton (Helder 73), Deco, Paredes, Pena (Paulo Costa 46)

**19.02.02 v Real Madrid CF (a) Lost 0-1**
Vitor Baia, Secretario, Jorge Andrade, Ricardo Silva, Mauro Silva (Candido Costa 84), Costinha (Alenitchev 85), Deco, Paredes, Capucho, Helder Postiga (Pena 66), Soderstrom

**27.02.02 v Real Madrid CF Lost 1-2**
Vitor Baia, Secretario, Jorge Andrade, Ricardo Silva (Alenitchev 68), Mauro Silva, Candido Costa, (Clayton 56), Deco, Paredes, Pavlin, Capucho, Helder Postiga (Pena 67). Scorer: Capucho 29

**12.03.02 v Panathinaikos FC (h) Won 2-1**
P Santos, Secretario, J Andrade, R Silva, Paredes, Costinha, Soderstrom, Capucho, Clayton (Candido Costa 68), Pena (Pavlin 84), Deco (Helder Postiga 90). Scorers: Deco 12, Pena 54. Sent off: Secretario 79

**20.03.02 v AC Sparta Praha (a) Lost 0-2**
P Santos, Ibarra, J Andrade, R Silva, M Silva, Paredes, Costinha (Rafael 64), Capucho, Clayton, Deco (Soderstrom 73), Helder Postiga (Pena 46)

| SEASONS | PLAYED | WON | DRAWN | LOST | FOR | AGAINST |
|---|---|---|---|---|---|---|
| 8 | 65 | 25 | 14 | 26 | 76 | 76 |

## PSV EINDHOVEN

**1992-1993**
**GROUP STAGE 1**
**25.11.92 v FC Porto (a) Drawn 2-2**
Van Breukelen, Linskens, Van Tiggelen, Erwin Koeman (Beerens 78), Heintze (Faber 33), Popescu, Ellerman, Vanenburg, Romario, Kieft, Numan. Scorer: Romario 44, 60. Sent off: Van Tiggelen

**09.12.92 v Milan AC (h) Lost 1-2**
Van Breukelen, Beerens, Faber, Linskens, Heintze, Popescu, Ellerman (Hoekstra 38), Vanenburg, Romario, Kieft, Numan. Scorer: Romario 66

**03.03.93 v IFK Goteborg (h) Lost 1-3**
Van Breukelen, Van Aerle, Van Tiggelen, Faber, Heintze, Popescu, Numan, Linskens (Vanenburg 46), Romario, Kieft, Hoekstra. Scorer: Numan 7

**17.03.93 v IFK Goteborg (a) Lost 0-3**
Van Breukelen, Van Aerle, Van Tiggelen, Erwin Koeman, Heintze, Faber, Linskens, Vanenburg, Romario, Numan (Bwalya 13), Hoekstra

**07.04.93 v FC Porto (h) Lost 0-1**
Van Breukelen, Beerens, Faber, Erwin Koeman, Heintze, Klomp, Linskens, Vanenburg, Romario, Kieft (Ellerman 63), Hoekstra (Bwalya 83)

**21.04.93 v Milan AC (a) Lost 0-2**
De Rom, Van Aerle (Beerens 37), Van Tiggelen, Erwin Koeman, Van der Gaag, Popescu, Linskens (Klomp 77), Vanenburg, Romario, Ellerman, Hoekstra

**1997-1998**
**GROUP STAGE 1**
**17.09.97 v FC Dynamo Kyiv (h) Lost 1-3**
Waterreus, Van der Weerden (Iwan 73), Stam, Valckx, Numan, Jonk, Petrovic, Degryse (Nilis 53), Cocu, De Bilde (Moller 77), Zenden. Scorer: Jonk 40

**01.10.97 v FC Barcelona (a) Drawn 2-2**
Waterreus, Van der Weerden, Stam, Faber, Numan, Jonk (Moller 82), Petrovic, Cocu, De Bilde, Iwan (Vampeta 40), Zenden (Nilis 68). Scorers: Cocu 70, Moller 86. Sent off: Van der Weerden 35

**22.10.97 v Newcastle United FC (h) Won 1-0**
Waterreus, Vampeta, Stam, Faber, Numan, Petrovic (Moller 81), Jonk, Cocu, Iwan (Stinga 63), De Bilde, Nilis (Bruggink 81). Scorer: Jonk 38

**05.11.97 v Newcastle United FC (a) Won 2-0**
Waterreus, Vampeta, Stam, Faber, Numan, Petrovic, Jonk, Cocu, Iwan, De Bilde, Nilis
Scorers: Nilis 33, De Bilde 90

**27.11.97 v FC Dynamo Kyiv (a) Drawn 1-1**
Waterreus, Vampeta, Stam, Faber, Numan, Stinga, Jonk, Cocu, Iwan (Valckx 38), De Bilde (Degryse 82), Nilis. Scorer: De Bilde 65

**10.12.97 v FC Barcelona (h) Drawn 2-2**
Waterreus, Faber, Valckx, Cocu, Numan, Iwan (Moller 46), Stinga, Jonk (Van Ede 90), Zenden, De Bilde, Bruggink. Scorers: Abelardo og 54, De Bilde 56. Sent off: Waterreus 90

**1998-1999**
**GROUP STAGE 1**
**16.09.98 v HJK Helsinki (h) Won 2-1**
Waterreus, Lucius, Abel Xavier, Marcos dos Santos, Oye, Iwan (Rommedahl 60), Ooijer, Nikiforov (Bruggink 54), Kolkka, Khokhlov, De Bilde (Claudio 90). Scorers: Ooijer 57, Bruggink 90

**30.09.98 v SL Benfica (a) Lost 1-2**
Waterreus, Lucius, Marcos dos Santos, Faber, Iwan (Rommedahl 61), Khokhlov, Van der Doelen (Bruggink 80), Abel Xavier, Kolkka, Van Nistelrooy, De Bilde (Nilis 61). Scorer: Rommedahl 70

**21.10.98 v 1 FC Kaiseralautern (h) Lost 1-2**
Waterreus, Lucius, Skerla, Nikiforov (Bruggink 73), Van der Weerden, Rommedahl, Khokhlov, Van der Doelen (Iwan 80), Kolkka (De Bilde 73), Nilis, Van Nistelrooy. Scorer: Kholkhov 78

**04.11.98 v 1 FC Kaiserslautern (a) Lost 1-3**
Lodewijks, Abel Xavier, Skerla, Nikiforov, Oyen, Van der Weerden (Marcos dos Santos 63), Iwan, Kholkhov, Van der Doelen (Rommedahl 74), Nilis (Need 29), Van Nistelrooy. Scorer: Van Nistelrooy 18

**26.11.98 v HJK Helsinki (a) Won 3-1**
Waterreus, Van der Weerden, Nikiforov, Abel Xavier, Oyen, Iwan, Kholkhov, Van der Doelen, Kolkka (Lucius 75), Nilis (Bruggink 85), Van Nistelrooy. Scorers: Van Nistelrooy 30, 67, 82 pen

**09.12.98 v SL Benfica (h) Drawn 2-2**
Waterreus, Abel Xavier, Skerla, Lucius, Van der Weerden, Iwan (Rommedahl 73), Kholkhov, Van der Doelen (Bruggink 82), Kolkka (Gakhokidze 73), Nilis, Van Nistelrooy. Scorers: Kholkhov 41, Van Nistelrooy 89

**1999-2000**
**GROUP STAGE 1**
**15.09.99 v FC Bayern Munchen (a) Lost 1-2**
Waterreus, Dirkx (Bruggink 77), Faber, Heintze, Van Bommel, Khokhlov, Van Nistelrooy, Nilis, Vogel, Nikiforov (Bouma 82), Iwan. Scorer: Khokhlov 59. Sent off: Van Bommel 90

**21.09.99 v Valencia CF (h) Drawn 1-1**
Waterreus, Dirkx, Faber (Wielaert 56), Heintze, Khokhlov, Van Nistelrooy, Bruggink, Vogel, Rommedahl (Kolkka 74), Nikiforov, Stinga (Bouma 73). Scorer: Van Nistelrooy 72

**28.09.99 v Rangers FC (h) Lost 0-1**
Waterreus, Dirkx, Heintze, Khokhlov, Van Nistelrooy, Nilis, Van der Doelen (Bruggink 80), Rommedahl (Kolkka 63), Nikiforov, Stinga (Bouma 68), Wielaert

**20.10.99 v Rangers FC (a) Lost 1-4**
Kralj, Faber, Heintze, Van Bommel, Khokhlov, Van Nistelrooy, Nilis (Bruggink 86), Vogel, Nikiforov, Stinga (Rommedahl 74), Wielaert (Kolkka 32). Scorer: Van Nistelrooy 45 pen

**26.10.99 v FC Bayern Munchen (h) Won 2-1**
Waterreus, Dirkx, Faber, Heintze, Van Bommel, Van Nistelrooy, Nilis (Bruggink 72), Kolkka (Iwan 88), Vogel, Addo, Stinga. Scorers: Van Nistelrooy 40, Nilis 57

**03.11.99 v Valencia CF (a) Lost 0-1**
Waterreus, Faber (Dirkx 59), Heintze, Van Bommel, Khokhlov, Van Nistelrooy, Nilis (Rommedahl 71), Kolkka, Addo, Nikiforov, Stinga

**2000-2001**
**GROUP STAGE 1**
**13.09.00 v FC Dynamo Kyiv (h) Won 2-1**
Waterreus, Heintze, Van Bommel, Kezman, Bruggink (De Jong 85), Van der Weerden, Vogel, Nikiforov, Bouma, Hofland (Ooijer 82), Claudio (Lucius 37). Scorers: Lucius 39, Bruggink 53

**19.09.00 v RSC Anderlecht (a) Lost 0-1**
Waterreus, Ooijer, Heintze, Van Bommel, Kezman, Bruggink (De Jong 72), Van der Weerden, Vogel, Rommedahl (Lucius 63), Nikiforov, Bouma (Kolkka 78)

**26.09.00 v Manchester United FC (h) Won 3-1**
Waterreus, Heintze, Van Bommel, Kezman (Kolkka 84), Bruggink, Van der Weerden, Vogel, Van der Doelen (Lucius 77), Nikiforov, Bouma (Rommedahl 80), Hofland. Scorers: Bouma 17, Van Bommel 38, Kezman 64

**18.10.00 v Manchester United FC (a) Lost 1-3**
Waterreus, Heintze, Van Bommel, Ramzi (Kolkka 65), Kezman, Bruggink (Lucius 29), Van der Weerden, Vogel, Van der Doelen (De Jong 73), Nikiforov, Hofland. Scorer: Van Bommel 76

**24.10.00 v FC Dynamo Kyiv (a) Won 1-0**
Waterreus, Ooijer, Heintze, Van Bommel, Ramzi, Kezman (Kolkka 90), Van der Weerden, Vogel, De Jong (Iwan 85), Lucius (Rommedahl 73), Nikiforov. Scorer: Ooijer 45

**08.11.00 v RSC Anderlecht (h) Lost 2-3**
Waterreus, Ooijer, Heintze, Van Bommel, Ramzi (Claudio 84), Kolkka, Vogel, De Jong (Bruggink 38), Rommedahl (Kezman 42), Nikiforov, Hofland. Scorer: Ramzi 45, 47. Sent off: Hofland 89

**2001-2002**
**GROUP STAGE 1**
**11.09.01 v FC Nantes-Atlantique (a) Lost 1-4**
Waterreus, Wielart, Nikiforov (Colin 58), Hofland, Hientze, Ramzi (Rommedahl 53), Vogel, Bouma (Gakhokidze 76), De Jong, Bruggink, Kezman. Scorer: De Jong 90

**19.09.01 v Galatasaray SK (h) Won 3-1**
Waterreus, Colin, Faber, E Addo, Bouma, Rommedahl (Lucius 79), Vogel, Van Bommel, Ramzi (De Jong 85), Bruggink (Vennegor of Hesselink 75), Kezman. Scorers: Bruggink 38, Faber 53, Kezman 90

**26.09.01 v SS Lazio Won 1-0**
Kralj, Faber, Nikiforov, Hofland, Bouma, Rommedahl (Gakhokidze 73), Vogel (Lucius 62), Van Bommel, Ramzi, Bruggink (Vennegor of Hesselink 89), Kezman. Scorer: Hofland 40

**16.10.01 v SS Lazio (a) Lost 1-2**
Lodewijks, Ooijer, Nikiforov (Vennegor of Hesselink 66), Hofland, Faber, Heintze (Bruggink 84), Rommedahl, Vogel, De Jong (Lucius 46), Bouma, Kezman. Scorer: Kezman 56

**24.10.01 v FC Nantes-Atlantique (a) Drawn 0-0**
Lodewijks, Ooijer, Faber, Hofland, Heintze, Rommedahl (Bruggink 62), Lucius, Vogel (De Jong 80), Bouma (Gakhokidze 84), Vennegor of Hesselink, Kezman

**30.10.01 v Galatasaray SK (a) Lost 0-2**
Lodewijks, Ooijer, Faber, Hofland, Heintze, Rommedahl, Lucius (Vennegor of Hesselink 60), Vogel, Bouma (Gakhokidze 71), De Jong (Bogelund 82), Kezman

**2002-2003**
**GROUP STAGE 1**
**17.09.02 v AJ Auxerre (a) Drawn 0-0**
Ten Rouwelaar, Bogelund, Ooijer, Hofland, Heintze, Rommedahl, Van der Schaaf (Lucius 40) Vogel, Bouma, Bruggink (Leandro 86), Kezman

**25.09.02 v Arsenal FC (h) Lost 0-4**
Waterreus, Bogelund, Ooijer, Hofland (Vennegoor of H 46), Heintze (Lucius 61), Rommedahl, Van Bommel, Vogel (Leandro 27), Bouma, Bruggink, Kezman

**02.10.02 v BV Borussia Dortmund (h) Lost 1-3**
Waterreus, Bogelund, Ooijer, Faber, Bouma, Rommedahl, Van Bommel, Vogel, Van der Schaaf, Leandro (Robben 55), Kezman (Vennegoor of H 75). Scorer: van der Schaaf 74

**22.10.02 v BV Borussia Dortmund (a) Drawn 1-1**
Waterreus, Bogelund, Ooijer, Faber, Heintze (Robben 46), Rommedahl, Van Bommel, Vogel, Bouma, Bruggink (Ramzi 80), Kezman (Vennegoor of H 85). Scorer: Bruggink 47

**30.10.02 v AJ Auxerre (h) Won 3-0**
Waterreus, Bogelund, Faber, Hofland, Bouma, Rommedahl, Van Bommel (van der Schaaf 65), Vogel (Lucius 78), Robben (Ramzi 70), Bruggink, Kezman. Scorers: Bruggink 34, Rommedahl 48, Robben 64

**12.11.02 v Arsenal FC (a) Drawn 0-0**
Waterreus, Bogelund, Ooijer (Vennegoor of H 80), Hofland, Bouma, Rommedahl, Van Bommel, Vogel (Lucius 42), Robben, Bruggink (Van der Schaaf 71), Kezman

| SEASONS | PLAYED | WON | DRAWN | LOST | FOR | AGAINST |
|---|---|---|---|---|---|---|
| 7 | 42 | 11 | 10 | 21 | 48 | 68 |

## RANGERS FC

**1992-1993**
**GROUP STAGE 1**
**25.11.92 v Olympique de Marseille (h) Drawn 2-2**
Goram, Murray, David Robertson, Gough (Pressley 46), McPherson, Brown, Steven (McSwegan 77), McCall, Durrant, Hateley, Mikhailichenko. Scorers: McSwegan 78, Hateley 83

**09.12.92 v CSKA Moscow (a) Won 1-0**
Goram, McCall, David Robertson, Durrant, McPherson, Brown, Steven, Ferguson, McCoist, Hateley, Mikhailichenko. Scorer: Ferguson 8

**03.03.03 v Club Brugge KV (a) Drawn 1-1**
Goram, Nisbet (Pressley 64), David Robertson, Murray, McPherson, Brown, Mikhailichenko, McCall, McCoist, Hateley, Huistra. Scorer: Huistra 73

**17.03.93 v Club Brugge KV (h) Won 2-1**
Goram, Nisbet, Murray, Gough, McPherson, Brown, Steven, McCall, McCoist, Hateley, Durrant (Hagen 87). Scorers: Durrant 41, Nisbet 72

**07.04.93 v Olympique de Marseille (a) Drawn 1-1**
Goram, McCall, Alex Robertson (Murray 53), Gough, McPherson, Brown, Steven, Ferguson, McCoist, Durrant, Huistra (McSwegan 85). Scorer: Durrant 52

**21.04.93 v CSKA Moscow (h) Drawn 0-0**
Goram, McCall, Alex Robertson, Gough, McPherson, Brown, Steven (McSwegan 82), Ferguson, McCoist, Durrant, Huistra

**1995-1996**
**GROUP STAGE 1**
**13.09.95 v Steaua Bucaresti (a) Lost 0-1**
Goram, Wright, Cleland, Gough, McLaren, Petric, Miller (Durie 72), Gascoigne, Durrant (Murray 82), McCoist, B Laudrup. Sent off: McLaren 77

**27.09.95 v BV Borussia Dortmund (h) Drawn 2-2**
Goram, Wright, Cleland, Gough, Petric, McCall, Miller, Gascoigne, McCoist, Durie (Durrant 75), B Laudrup (Ferguson 46). Scorers: Gough 64, Ferguson 73

**18.10.95 v Juventus FC (a) Lost 1-4**
Goram, Wright (Brown 46), Robertson, Gough, Moore, Petric, Durie, McCall (Murray 69), Cleland, McCoist, Salenko. Scorer: Ferrara og 79. Sent off: Cleland 55

**01.11.95 v Juventus FC (h) Lost 0-4**
Goram (Thomson 46), Wright (Durrant 25), Bollan, Brown, Petric, Gough, Ferguson, Gascoigne, Miller (McCoist 70), Salenko, McCall

**22.11.95 v Steaua Bucaresti (h) Drawn 1-1**
Goram, Brown (Bollan 75), Robertson, McLaren, Petric, Durrant (Miller 46), Gough, Gascoigne, McCall (Murray 87), McCoist, B Laudrup. Scorer: Gascoigne 33

**06.12.95 v BV Borussia Dortmund (a) Drawn 2-2**
Goram, McLaren, Gough, Bollan, Robertson, Cleland (Durrant 78), Miller (McCoist 82), Gascoigne, McCall, B Laudrup, Durie. Scorers: B Laudrup 11, Durie 84. Sent off: Gascoigne 75

**1996-1997**
**GROUP STAGE 1**
**11.09.96 v Grasshopper-Club (a) Lost 0-3**
Goram, Cleland (McInnes 60), Petric, Gough, Bjorklund, McCall, Gascoigne, Albertz, Durie (Miller 80), McCoist (Van Vossen 69), B Laudrup

**25.09.96 v AJ Auxerre (h) Lost 1-2**
Goram, Moore (Andersen 78), Gough, Bjorklund, Cleland, McInnes, Durie (Ferguson 65), Albertz, Gascoigne, B Laudrup, Van Vossen. Scorer: Gascoigne 71

**16.10.96 v AFC Ajax (a) Lost 1-4**
Goram, Moore, Gough, Bjorklund, Cleland, Ferguson (Durrant 84), McInnes (Van Vossen 81), McCall, Gascoigne, B Laudrup (Miller 81), Albertz. Scorer: Durrant 88

**30.10.96 v AFC Ajax (h) Lost 0-1**
Goram, Petric, Wilson (Andersen 85), Bjorklund, Shields, McInnes (McCoist 81), Albertz, Durrant, Robertson, B Laudrup, Miller (Van Vossen 59)

**20.11.96 v Grasshopper-Club (h) Won 2-1**
Goram, Petric, Gough, Wilson, Cleland, Miller, Moore, Albertz, Robertson, Van Vossen (Andersen 81), McCoist. Scorer: McCoist 67 pen, 73

**04.12.96 v AJ Auxerre (a) Lost 1-2**
Goram, Shields, Petric (McCoist 63), Gough, Moore, Robertson, Ferguson, Steven, McInnes, Van Vossen (Wilson 46), Andersen. Scorer: Gough 36

**1999-2000**
**GROUP STAGE 1**
**15.09.99 v Valencia CF (a) Lost 0-2**
Charbonnier, Porrini (Kanchelskis 72), Moore, Amoruso, Ferguson, Van Bronckhorst (Johansson 85), Mols, Reyna, Vidmar, Amato, McCann (Albertz 46)

**21.09.99 v FC Bayern Munchen (h) Drawn 1-1**
Charbonnier, Porrini, Moore, Amoruso, Numan, Ferguson, Van Bronckhorst, Mols (Hendry 84), Albertz, Reyna, Johansson (McCann 90). Scorer: Albertz 22

**28.09.99 v PSV Eindhoven (a) Won 1-0**
Charbonnier, Porrini, Moore, Amoruso, Numan, Ferguson, Van Bronckhorst, Mols, Wallace, Reyna (Albertz 24), McCann. Scorer: Albertz 85

**20.10.99 v PSV Eindhoven (h) Won 4-1**
Klos, Porrini, Moore, Amoruso, Ferguson, Van Bronckhorst, Mols (Johansson 81), Wallace (Kanchelskis 88), Vidmar, McCann (Albertz 71), McInnes. Scorers: Amoruso 19, Mols 39, 80, McCann 56

**26.10.99 v Valencia CF (h) Lost 1-2**
Klos, Porrini, Moore, Amoruso, Ferguson, Van Bronckhorst, Mols, Wallace (Johansson 75), Vidmar (Albertz 61), McCann, McInnes (Kanchelskis 38). Scorer: Moore 60

**03.11.99 v FC Bayern Munchen (a) Lost 0-1**
Klos, Porrini, Moore, Amoruso, Numan (McCann 72), Ferguson, Van Bronckhorst, Mols (Johansson 30), Wallace (Amato 80), Albertz, Reyna

**2000-2001**
**GROUP STAGE 1**
**12.09.00 v SK Sturm Graz (h) Won 5-0**
Klos, Amoruso, Numan, Ferguson, Van Bronckhorst, Mols (Dodds 59), Albertz, Reyna, R De Boer (McCann 72), Konterman, Johnston (Kanchelskis 77). Scorers: Mols 9, De Boer 19, Albertz 29, Van Bronckhorst 72, Dodds 85

**20.09.00 v AS Monaco (a) Won 1-0**
Klos, Amoruso, Numan, Ferguson, Van Bronckhorst, Mols (McCann 58), Reyna (Vidmar 87), R De Boer, Konterman, Tugay, Johnston. Scorer: Van Bronckhorst 8

**27.09.00 v Galatasaray SK (a) Lost 2-3**
Klos, Amoruso, Numan, Ferguson, Van Bronckhorst, Mols (Dodds 67), Reyna, R De Boer, Konterman, Tugay, Johnston (Kanchelskis 59). Scorers: Kanchelskis 72, Van Bronckhorst 90

**17.10.00 v Galatasaray SK (h) Drawn 0-0**
Klos, Ferguson, Kanchelskis, Albertz, Reyna, R De Boer, Konterman, Tugay, Porrini, Vidmar (Wilson 72), Lovenkrands (McCann 56)

**25.10.00 v SK Sturm Graz (a) Lost 0-2**
Christiansen, Amoruso, Numan, Ferguson, Kanchelskis, Van Bronckhorst (McCann 55), Wallace (Dodds 73), R De Boer, Konterman, Tugay, Porrini (Negri 78). Sent off: Numan 85

**07.11.00 v AS Monaco (h) Drawn 2-2**
Christiansen, Ricken, Amoruso, Numan, Ferguson, Mols (Tugay 56), Albertz (McCann 86), R De Boer (Wallace 78), Wilson, Miller, Vidmar. Scorers: Miller 3, Mols 52

| SEASONS | PLAYED | WON | DRAWN | LOST | FOR | AGAINST |
|---|---|---|---|---|---|---|
| 5 | 30 | 7 | 10 | 13 | 35 | 46 |

## SK RAPID WIEN

**1996-1997**
**GROUP STAGE 1**
**11.09.96 v Fenerbahce SK (h) Drawn 1-1**
Konsel, Schottel, Ivanov, Lesiak, Prosenik, Heraf, Zingler, Guggi (Jovanovic 57), Wagner (Stumpf 57), Kuhbauer, Penksa (Stoger 57). Scorer: Stumpf 71

**25.09.96 v Manchester United FC (a) Lost 0-2**
Konsel, Prosenik, Lesiak, Ivanov, Schottel, Ratajczyk, Heraf, Kuhbauer, Zingler (Jovanovic 72), Stoger (Barisic 64), Wagner (Stumpf 64)

**16.10.96 v Juventus FC (h) Drawn 1-1**
Konsel, Schottel, Ivanov, Zingler, Prosenik, Kuhbauer, Heraf, Stoger, Lesiak, Stumpf, Wagner (Mandreko 69). Scorer: Lesiak 20

**30.10.96 v Juventus FC (a) Lost 0-5**
Konsel, Ivanov, Schottel, Heraf, Zingler, Prosenik, Kuhbauer, Stoger (Pivarnik 65), Penksa (Jovanovic 46), Stumpf (Ratajczyk 46), Mandreko

**20.11.96 v Fenerbahce SK (a) Lost 0-1**
Konsel, Schottel, Ivanov, Lesiak, Prosenik (Guggi 82), Kuhbauer, Heraf, Stoger, Ratajczyk (Jovanovic 84), Wagner, Penksa (Stumpf 82)

**04.12.96 v Manchester United FC (h) Lost 0-2**
Konsel, Schottel, Ivanov, Zingler, Prosenik, Kuhbauer, Heraf, Stoger (Mandreko 66), Ratajczyk, Wagner, Stumpf (Penksa 72)

| SEASONS | PLAYED | WON | DRAWN | LOST | FOR | AGAINST |
|---|---|---|---|---|---|---|
| 1 | 6 | 0 | 2 | 4 | 2 | 12 |

## REAL MADRID CF

**1995-1996**
**GROUP STAGE 1**
**13.09.95 v AFC Ajax (a) Lost 0-1**
Buyo, Chendo, Hierro, Sanchis, Lasa, Redondo, Luis Enrique, Sandro (Rincon 54), Amavisca (Michel 69), Raul, Zamorano

**27.09.95 v Grasshopper-Club (h) Won 2-0**
Buyo, Quique Flores, Hierro, Sanchis, Lasa, Milla, Rincon (Michel 46), Michael Laudrup (Luis Enrique 74), Amavisca (Soler 59), Raul, Zamorano. Scorers: Zamorano 69, 89

**18.10.95 v Ferencvarosi TC (h) Won 6-1**
Buyo, Quique Flores, Hierro (Nando 63), Sanchis, Soler, Milla, Michel, Michael Laudrup (Esnaider 58), Amavisca (Luis Enrique 58), Raul, Zamorano. Scorers: Raul 24, 25, 84, Zamorano 34, 47, Hierro 54

**01.11.95 v Ferencvarosi TC (a) Drawn 1-1**
Buyo, Quique Flores, Alkorta, Sanchis, Soler, Redondo, Michel (Luis Enrique 61), Michael Laudrup, Raul, Esnaider, Amavisca. Scorer: Raul 73

**22.11.95 v AFC Ajax (h) Lost 0-2**
Buyo, Chendo (Michel 73), Alkorta, Sanchis, Quique Flores, Redondo, Luis Enrique, Michael Laudrup (Milla 73), Raul, Amavisca, Zamorano

**06.12.95 v Grasshopper-Club (a) Won 2-0**
Buyo, Quique Flores, Hierro (Alkorta 62), Sanchis, Lasa, Luis Enrique, Milla, Michael Laudrup (Rincon 69), Raul, Esnaider, Amavisca (Michel 62). Scorers: Raul 55, Michel 67

**QUARTER FINAL**
**06.03.96 v Juventus FC (h) Won 1-0**
Buyo, Chendo, Alkorta, Hierro, Garcia Calvo, Redondo, Soler (Quique Flores 27), Michael Laudrup (Michel 66), Luis Enrique, Raul, Zamorano. Scorer: Raul 20

**20.03.96 v Juventus FC (a) Lost 0-2**
Canizares, Chendo, Lasa, Alkorta, Garcia Calvo, Quique Flores (Rincon 57), Milla, Michel (Esnaider 65), Luis Enrique, Raul, Michael Laudrup

**1997-1998**
**GROUP STAGE 1**
**17.09.97 v Rosenborg BK (h) Won 4-1**
Canizares, Panucci, Hierro, Sanchis, Roberto Carlos, Seedorf, Karanka, Ze Roberto (Victor 74), Raul, Mijatovic (Redondo 58), Suker (Morientes 58). Scorers: Panucci 7, Ze Roberto 39, Raul 43, Morientes 83

**01.10.97 v FC Porto (a) Won 2-0**
Canizares, Panucci, Hierro, Sanchis, Roberto Carlos, Seedorf (Victor 84), Redondo, Raul, Amavisca, Mijatovic (Morientes 81), Suker (Jaime 61). Scorers: Hierro 14, Raul 78

**22.10.97 v Olympiakos Piraeus FC(h) Won 5-1**
Canizares, Jaime, Hierro, Karanka, Roberto Carlos, Seedorf (Victor 80), Redondo, Ze Roberto (Amavisca 70), Morientes (Sanchis 77), Raul, Suker. Scorers: Suker 33 pen, 67 pen, Morientes 44, Victor 86, Roberto Carlos 90

**05.11.97 v Olympiakos Piraeus FC (a) Drawn 0-0**
Canizares, Karanka, Hierro, Sanchis, Panucci, Seedorf (Jaime 63), Redondo, Ze Roberto, Raul, Suker (Victor 63), Mijatovic

**27.11.97 v Rosenborg BK (a) Lost 0-2**
Canizares, Chendo, Hierro, Sanchis, Karanka, Seedorf (Victor 80), Redondo, Ze Roberto (Jaime 46), Raul, Mijatovic, Morientes (Dani 80)

**10.12.97 v FC Porto (h) Won 4-0**
Canizares, Jaime, Hierro, Sanchis (Karanka 78), Roberto Carlos, Seedorf, Redondo, Amavisca, Raul (Guti 62), Suker, Morientes (Victor 70). Scorers: Hierro 6, Suker 30, 73 pen, Roberto Carlos 50

**QUARTER FINAL**

**04.03.98 v Bayer 04 Leverkusen (a) Drawn 1-1**
Illgner, Panucci, Hierro, Sanchis, Roberto Carlos, Redondo, Karembeu, Seedorf, Savio (Amavisca 88), Raul (Morientes 71), Mijatovic. Scorer: Karembeu 74

**18.03.98 v Bayer 04 Leverkusen (h) Won 3-0**
Illgner, Panucci, Hierro, Sanchis, Roberto Carlos (Amavisca 88), Redondo, Karembeu, Seedorf, Savio (Morientes 36), Raul, Mijatovic (Jaime 81). Scorers: Karembeu 49, Morientes 56, Hierro 90 pen

**SEMI FINAL**

**01.04.98 v BV Borussia Dortmund (h) Won 2-0**
Illgner, Panucci, Sanz, Sanchis, Roberto Carlos, Redondo, Karembeu, Seedorf, Raul, Mijatovic (Suker 52), Morientes (Jaime 88). Scorers: Morientes 24, Karembeu 67

**14.04.98 v BB Borussia Dortmund (a) Drawn 0-0**
Illgner, Panucci, Hierro, Sanz, Roberto Carlos, Redondo, Karembeu, Seedorf (Guti 88), Amavisca, Mijatovic (Victor 90), Raul (Jaime 75)

**FINAL**

**23.05.98 v Juventus FC (n) Won 1-0**
Illgner, Paucci, Sanchis, Hierro, Roberto Carlos, Redondo, Karembeu, Seedorf, Raul (Amavisca 90), Mijatovic (Suker 89), Morientes (Jaime 82). Scorer: Mijatovic 67

**1998-1999**

**GROUP STAGE 1**

**16.09.98 v FC Internazionale (h) Won 2-0**
Illgner, Panucci, Hierro, Sanchis, Roberto Carlos, Raul, Redondo, Seedorf, Savio (Karembeu 90), Mijatovic, Morientes (Jarni 86). Scorers: Hierro 80 pen, Seedorf 90

**30.09.98 v FC Spartak Moscow (a) Lost 1-2**
Illgner, Panucci, Hierro, Sanchis, Roberto Carlos, Karembeu (Morientes 81), Raul, Redondo, Seedorf, Savio, Mijatovic. Scorer: Raul 63

**21.10.98 v SK Sturm Graz (h) Won 6-1**
Illgner, Panucci, Hierro, Sanchis, Roberto Carlos, Karembeu (Jaime 46), Seedorf, Jarni, Savio, Raul (Guti 81), Mijatovic (Suker 76). Scorers: Savio 13, 90, Raul 22, Jarni 61, 79, Popovic og 67

**05.11.98 v SK Sturm Graz (a) Won 5-1**
Illgner, Panucci (Karembeu 76), Hierro, Sanchis, Roberto Carlos, Seedorf (Guti 71), Redondo, Jarni, Savio (Suker 62), Raul, Mijatovic. Scorers: Panucci 8, 61, Mijatovic 35, Seedorf 57, Suker 74

**25.11.98 v FC Internazionale (a) Lost 1-3**
Illgner, Jaime, Ivan Campo, Sanchis (Suker 89), Fernando Sanz, Roberto Carlos (Jarni 81), Seedorf , Redondo, Savio, Raul, Mijatovic. Scorer: Seedorf 59

**09.12.98 v FC Spartak Moscow (h) Won 2-1**
Illgner, Ivan Campo, Hierro, Fernando Sanz, Panucci (Jaime 60), Seedorf, Redondo, Roberto Carlos, Savio, Raul, Mijatovic. Scorers: Raul 34, Savio 66

**QUARTER FINAL**

**03.03.99 v FC Dynamo Kyiv (h) Drawn 1-1**
Illgner, Panucci, Sanchis (Ivan Campo 58), Hierro, Roberto Carlos, Seedorf (Savio 58), Redondo, Guti, Raul, Mijatovic, Morientes (Suker 76). Scorer: Mijatovic 67

**17.03.99 v FC Dynamo Kyiv (a) Lost 0-2**
Illgner, Panucci, Ivan Campo, Sanchis (Guti 70), Hierro, Roberto Carlos, Seedorf (Suker 65), Redondo, Jarni (Karembeu 80), Raul, Morientes

**1999-2000**

**GROUP STAGE 1**

**15.09.99 v Olympiakos Piraeus FC (a) Drawn 3-3**
Casillas, Michel Salgado, Roberto Carlos, Hierro (Helguera 60), Redondo (Guti 73), Raul, McManaman, Morientes (Anelka 54), Savio, Geremi, Julio Cesar. Scorers: Savio 24, Roberto Carlos 32, Raul 80

**21.09.99 v Molde FK (h) Won 4-1**
Casillas, Michel Salgado, Roberto Carlos, Redondo, McManaman (Balic 64), Morientes, Savio (Eto'o 74), Ivan Campo, Helguera, Anelka (Guti 56), Julio Cesar. Scorers: Morientes 27, Savio 60, 70 pen, Guti 81

**28.09.99 v FC Porto (h) Won 3-1**
Bizzarri, Michel Salgado, Roberto Carlos, Hierro, Redondo, Raul, McManaman (Seedorf 58), Morientes, Savio (Eto'o 90), Helguera (Sanchis 84), Julio Cesar. Scorers: Morientes 23, Helguera 37, Hierro 68 pen

**20.10.99 v FC Porto (a) Lost 1-2**
Illgner, Michel Salgado, Roberto Carlos, Hierro, Redondo, Raul, Morientes, Savio, Ivan Campo, Anelka (Seedorf 47), Geremi (Guti 66). Scorer: Peixe og 68

**26.10.99 v Olympiakos Piraeus FC (h) Won 3-0**
Bizzarri, Roberto Carlos, Hierro (Ivan Campo 41), Redondo, Raul, Morientes, Seedorf, Guti (McManaman 71), Helguera, Geremi (Michel Salgado 62), Julio Cesar. Scorers: Raul 21, Morientes 64, Roberto Carlos 83

**03.11.99 v Molde FK (a) Won 1-0**
Bizzarri, Michel Salgado, Roberto Carlos, Sanchis, Seedorf, Ivan Campo, Helguera, Karanka, Karembeu, Julio Cesar, Aranda (Etoo 55). Scorer: Karembeu 43

**GROUP STAGE 2**

**24.11.99 v FC Dynamo Kyiv (a) Won 2-1**
Bizzarri, Michel Salgado (Ivan Campo 27), Roberto Carlos, Raul, Morientes, Seedorf (Karanka 90), Savio (Sanchis 69), Guti, Helguera, Karembeu, Julio Cesar. Scorers: Morientes 17, Raul 48

**07.12.99 v Rosenborg BK (h) Won 3-1**
Casillas, Roberto Carlos, Hierro, Redondo, Raul, Morientes (Julio Cesar 89), Savio, Guti (Seedorf 65, Anelka 90), Helguera, Karanka, Karembeu. Scorers: Raul 18, Savio 85, Roberto Carlos 90

**29.02.00 v FC Bayern Munchen (h) Lost 2-4**
Casillas, Michael Salgado, Roberto Carlos, Hierro, Redondo, Raul, Morientes (Ogjenovic 79), Guti (McManaman 62), Karanka, Anelka, Geremi. Scorers: Morientes 25, Raul 48

**08.03.00 v FC Bayern Munchen (a) Lost 1-4**
Casillas, Michael Salgado, Roberto Carlos, Hierro, Redondo, Raul, Morientes (Ivan Campo 84), Guti, Helguera, Karanka (Anelka 69), Geremi (McManaman 63). Scorer: Helguera 69

**14.03.00 v FC Dynamo Kyiv (h) Drawn 2-2**
Casillas, Michael Salgado, Roberto Carlos, Hierro, Redondo, Raul, McManaman (Meca Garcia 61), Morientes, Guti, Karanka, Geremi (Helguera 72). Scorers: Raul 14 pen, Roberto Carlos 72

**22.03.00 v Rosenborg BK (a) Won 1-0**
Casillas, Michael Salgado, Roberto Carlos, Hierro (Karanka 46), Redondo, Raul, McManaman, Ivan Campo, Guti, Helguera, Aganzo Mendez (Balic 57, Karembeu 85). Scorer: Raul 3. Sent off: Guti 54

**QUARTER FINAL**
**04.04.00 v Manchester United FC (h) Drawn 0-0**
Casillas, Michael Salgado, Roberto Carlos, Redondo, Raul, McManaman, Morientes (Ogjenovic 86), Savio (Balic 76), Ivan Campo, Helguera, Karanka

**19.04.00 v Manchester United FC (a) Won 3-2**
Casillas, Michael Salgado, Roberto Carlos, Redondo, Raul, McManaman (Julio Cesar 89), Morientes (Anelka 72), Savio (Geremi 65), Ivan Campo, Helguera, Karanka. Scorers: Keane og 21, Raul 50, 52

**SEMI FINAL**
**03.05.00 v FC Bayern Munchen (h) Won 2-0**
Casillas, Michael Salgado, Roberto Carlos, Redondo, Raul, McManaman, Morientes (Savio 61), Ivan Campo, Helguera, Karanka, Anelka (Balic 80). Scorers: Anelka 4, Jeremies og 33

**09.05.00 v FC Bayern Munchen (a) Lost 1-2**
Casillas, Roberto Carlos, Redondo, Raul, McManaman (Balic 90), Savio (Karembeu 81), Ivan Campo, Helguera, Anelka (Sanchis 89), Geremi, Julio Cesar. Scorer: Anelka 31

**FINAL**
**24.05.00 v Valencia CF (n) Won 3-0**
Casillas, Michel Salgado (Hierro 85), Roberto Carlos, Redondo, Raul, McManaman, Morientes (Savio 72), Ivan Campo, Helguera, Karanka, Anelka (Sanchis 80). Scorers: Morientes 39, McManaman 67, Raul 75

**2000-2001**
**GROUP STAGE 1**
**12.09.00 v Sporting Clube de Portugal (a) Drawn 2-2**
Casillas, Michel Salgado, Roberto Carlos, Helguera, Raul, Figo, Savio, Ivan Campo, Flavio Conceicao (Guti 60), Munitis (Julio Cesar 90), Makelele (Celades 60). Scorers: Roberto Carlos 50, Rui Jorge og 76

**20.09.00 v FC Spartak Moscow (h) Won 1-0**
Casillas, Michel Salgado, Roberto Carlos, Helguera, Figo, Savio (McManaman 65), Guti, Munitis (Tote 89), Karanka, Celades (Hierro 81), Makelele. Scorer: Helguera 51

**27.09.00 v Bayer 04 Leverkusen (a) Won 3-2**
Casillas, Michel Salgado, Roberto Carlos, Hierro, Helguera, Figo, Guti, Flavio Conceicao (Ivan Campo 90), Munitis (Sanchis 87), Karanka, Solari (Raul 51). Scorers: Roberto Carlos 32, 75, Guti 69

**17.10.00 v Bayer 04 Leverkusen (h) Won 5-3**
Cesar, Roberto Carlos, Hierro (Celades 46), Helguera, Raul, Figo (Munitis 89), Savio (Solari 71), Ivan Campo, Guti, Geremi, Makelele. Scorers: Guti 4, 64, Helguera 24, Raul 75, Figo 87 pen

**25.10.00 v Sporting Clube de Portugal (h) Won 4-0**
Cesar, Roberto Carlos (Solari 69), Helguera, Figo (McManaman 52), Savio, Ivan Campo, Guti, Geremi, Munitis (Morientes 61), Celades, Makelele. Scorers: Guti 12, Savio 42, Morientes 62, 70

**07.11.00 v FC Spartak Moscow (a) Lost 0-1**
Cesar, Michel Salgado, Sanchis (Pavon 86), McManaman, Morientes, Geremi, Munitis (Tote 74), Karanka, Solari, Rivera, Makelele

**GROUP STAGE 2**

**22.11.01 v Leeds United AFC (a) Won 2-0**
Casillas, Geremi, Hierro, Ivan Campo, Roberto Carlos, Figo (Savio 84), Helguera, Guti (Munitis 89), Makelele, McManaman, Raul. Scorers: Hierro 66, Raul 68

**05.12.01 v RSC Anderlecht (h) Won 4-1**
Casillas, Geremi, Hierro (Flavio Conceicao 65), Karanka, Roberto Carlos, Figo, Helguera, Makelele (Celades 78), McManaman, Raul (Savio 58), Morientes. Scorers: Morientes 12, Figo 23pen, Helguera 44, R Carlos 73

**13.02.01 v SS Lazio (h) Won 3-2**
Casillas, Michel Salgado, Hierro, Karanka, Roberto Carlos, Figo, Helguera (Solari 90), Makelele, McManaman (Guti 76), Raul, Morientes (Munitis 66). Scorers: Morientes 32, Helguera 82, Figo 89pen

**21.02.01 v SS Lazio (a) Drawn 2-2**
Cesar, Michel Salgado, Hierro, Helguera (Celades 64), Roberto Carlos, Figo (Karanka 90), Solari, Makelele, Geremi, Guti (Munitis 69), Raul. Scorers: Solari 32, Raul 73

**06.03.01 v Leeds United AFC (h) Won 3-2**
Cesar, Geremei, Hierro, Karanka, Solari, Figo (Rivera 90), Celades, Makelele (Savio 87), McManaman, Morientes (Munitis 79), Raul. Scorers: Raul 7, 60 Figo 41

**14.03.01 v RSC Anderlecht (a) Lost 0-2**
Casillas, Michel Salgado, Geremei, Helguera, Roberto Carlos (Solari 70), Rivera, Sanchis, Celades, Savio, McManaman, Morientes (Tote 62), Munitis

**QUARTER FINAL**
**03.04.01 v Galatasaray SK (a) Lost 2-3**
Casillas, Michel Salgado, Hierro, Karanka, Roberto Carlos, Figo, Helguera, Makelele (Celades 62), McManaman (Solari 89), Raul, Morientes (Guti 66). Scorers: Helguera 33, Makelele 41

**18.04.01 v Galatasaray SK (h) Won 3-0**
Casillas, Michel Salgado, Hierro, Karanka, Roberto Carlos (Solari 90), Figo (Savio 86), Helguera, Makelele, McManaman, Raul, Guti (Flavio Conceicao 75). Scorrs: Raul 15, 37, Helguera 28

**SEMI FINAL**
**01.05.01 v FC Bayern Munchen (h) Lost 0-1**
Casillas, Michel Salgado (Munitis 77), Hierro, Karanka, Roberto Carlos, Figo, Helguera, Makelele, McManaman, Raul, Guti (Savio 55)

**09.05.01 v FC Bayern Munchen (a) Lost 1-2**
Casillas, Michel Salgado, Hierro, Karanka (Morientes 66), Roberto Carlos, Figo, Helguera, Makelele, McManaman (Savio 61), Raul, Guti. Scorer: Figo 18

**2001-2002**
**GROUP STAGE 1**
**11.09.01 v AS Roma (a) Won 2-1**
Casillas, Michel Salgado, Hierro, Karanka, Roberto Carlos, Figo, F Conceicao, Makelele, McManaman, Raul, Guti (I Campo 87). Scorers: Figo 50, Guti 63

**19.09.01 v FC Lokomotiv Moscow (h) Won 4-0**
Casillas, Michel Salgado, Hierro, Karanka, Roberto Carlos (Solari 83), Figo (McManaman 88), F Conceicao (Celades 76), Makelele, Munitis, Raul, Savio. Munitis 39, Figo 64pen, R Carlos 81, Savio 87

**26.09.01 v RSC Anderlecht (h) Won 4-1**
Casillas, Michel Salgado (Geremei 69), Hierro, Karanka, Roberto Carlos, Figo, Celades, Makelele (Baljic 81), Solari, Raul, Munitis (Morientes 72). Scorers: Celades 49, Raul 51, 68, Solari 79

**16.10.01 v RSC Anderlecht (a) Won 2-0**
Cesar, Michel Salgado, Hierro (Ruben 60), Pavon, Roberto Carlos, Figo, Celades, Makelele, McManaman (Savio 70), Raul, Guti (Morientes 72). Scorers: Raul 19, McManaman 35

**24.10.01 v AS Roma (h) Drawn 1-1**
Cesar, Michel Salgado, Hierro (Helguera 46), Pavon, Roberto Carlos (Solari 46), Figo, Celades, Makelele, Zidane, Raul, Morientes (Munitis 77). Scorer: Figo 75pen

**30.10.01 v FC Lokomotiv Moscow (a) Lost 0-2**
Cesar, Sanchez, Oscar, Helguera, Pavon, Raul Bravo, Solari, Celades, Makelele (Ruben 72), McManaman (Valdo 61), Munitis, Morientes (Aranda 61)

**GROUP STAGE 2**

**21.11.01 v AC Sparta Praha (a) Won 3-2**
Casillas, Michel Salgado, Hierro, Pavon, Roberto Carlos, Figo (Guti 89), Makelele, Zidane, Helguera, Raul, Morientes (McManaman 85). Scorers: Zidane 20, Morientes 36, 74

**04.12.01 v Panathinaikos FC (h) Won 3-0**
Casillas, Michel Salgado, Hierro (Karanka 52), Pavon, Roberto Carlos (Solari 77), Figo, Celades, Zidane, Helguera, Raul, Morientes (Munitis 85). Scorers: Helguera 41, Raul 66, 72

**19.02.02 v FC Porto (h) Won 1-0**
Casillas, Michel Salgado, Hierro, Karanka, Roberto Carlos, Figo (McManaman 17), Makelele, Zidane, Helguera (Solari 77), Morientes, Guti (Munitis 41). Scorer: Solari 83

**27.02.02 v FC Porto (a) Won 2-1**
Cesar, Pavon, Hierro, Karanka (Celades 46), Raul Bravo (Michel Salgado 75), Minambres, McManaman (Munitis 63), Flavio Conceicao, Helguera, Guti, Solari. Scorers:Solari 7, Helguera 20

**12.03.02 v AC Sparta Praha (h) Won 3-0**
Casillas, Geremei, Helguera (Morientes 76), Pavon, Raul Bravo, McManaman (Savio 53), Celades, Flavio Conceicao, Solari (Minambres 63), Munitis, Guti. Scorers: Solari 60, Guti 64, Savio 71

**20.03.02 v Panathinaikos FC (a) Drawn 2-2**
Casillas, Geremei, Campo, Ruben, Raul Bravo, McManaman (Solari 80), Celades, Falvio Conceicao, Minambres, Morientes (Portillo 60), Savio (Valdo 74). Scorers: Morientes 11, Portillo 80

**QUARTER FINAL**

**02.04.02 v FC Bayern Munchen (a) Lost 1-2**
Cesar, Michel Salgado, Hierro, Pavon, Roberto Carlos, Solari (McManaman 76), Helguera, Makelele, Geremi (Flavio Conceicao 83), Zidane, Raul. Scorer: Geremi 11

**10.04.02 v FC Bayern Munchen (h) Won 2-0**
Cesar, Michel Salgado, Hierro, Helguera, Roberto Carlos, Solari, Makelele, Figo (Geremi 90), Zidane, Raul, Morientes (Guti 81). Scorers: Helguera 69, Guti 85

**SEMI FINAL**
**23.04.02 v FC Barcelona (a) Won 2-0**
Cesar, Michel Salgado, Hierro, Pavon, Helguera, Roberto Carlos, Solari (F Conceicao 89), Makelele, Zidane, Raul, Guti (McManaman 80). Scorers: Zidane 55, McManaman 90

**01.05.02 v FC Barcelona (h) Drawn 1-1**
Cesar, Michel Salgado, Hierro, Helguera, Roberto Carlos, Figo (McManaman 68), Zidane (Flavio Conceicao 46), Makelele, Solari, Raul, Guti (Pavon 87). Scorer: Raul 44

**FINAL**
**15.05.02 v Bayer 04 Leverkusen (n) Won 2-1**
Cesar (Casillas 68), Michel Salgado, Hierro, Helguera, Roberto Carlos, Figo (McManaman 61), Zidane, Makelele (Flavio Conceicao 46), Solari, Raul, Morientes. Scorers: Raul 9, Zidane 45

**2002-2003**
**GROUP STAGE 1**
**17.09.02 v AS Roma (a) Won 3-0**
Casillas, Michel Salgado, Hierro, Helguera, R Carlos, Figo, Makelele (McManaman 78), Cambiasso, Zidane (Solari 70), Raul, Guti. Scorers: Guti 41, 74, Raul 56

**25.09.02 v KRC Genk (h) Won 6-0**
Casillas, Michel Salgado, Hierro, Helguera, R Carlos (R Bravo 70), Figo, Celades, Cambiasso (Morientes 67), Solari, Raul (Portillo 76), Guti. Scorers: Zokora 33og, M Salgado 45, Figo 55pen, Guti 64, Celades 74, Raul 76

**02.10.02 v AEK Athens (a) Drawn 3-3**
Casillas, Michel Salgado, Pavon, Helguera, R Carlos, Figo, Makelele, Cambiasso, Zidane (Portillo 84), Raul (Morientes 81), Guti McManaman 87). Scorers: Zidane 15, 39, Guti 60

**22.10.02 v AEK Athens (h) Drawn 2-2**
Casillas, Michel Salgado, Hierro, Helguera, R Carlos (R Bravo 75), McManaman (Minambres 82), Celades, Cambiasso, Zidane (Solari 71), Ronaldo, Guti. Scorers: McManaman 24, 43

**30.10.02 v AS Roma (h) Lost 0-1**
Casillas, Michel Salgado, Hierro, Helguera, R Carlos, Figo, Makelele, Cambiasso (Guti 86), Zidane (Solari 78), Raul, Ronaldo (Morientes 78)

**12.11.02 v KRC Genk (a) Drawn 1-1**
Casillas, Minambres, Hierro (Helguera 30), Pavon, R Carlos, Figo (McManaman 67), Celades, F Conceicao, Tote, Morientes (Solari 77), Guti. Scorer: Tote 21

**26.11.02 v AC Milan (a) Lost 0-1**
Casillas, Michel Salgado, Pavon, Helguera, R Carlos, Figo, Celades, Cambiasso (Solari 76), Zidane, Raul, Morientes (Portillo 61)

**11.12.02 v FC Lokomotiv Moskva (h) Drawn 2-2**
Casillas, Michel Salgado, Hierro, Pavon, R Carlos, Figo, Makelele (F Conceicao 32), Cambiasso (Morientes 77), Zidane, Raul, Ronaldo (Guti 46). Scorers: Raul 21, 76

**19.02.03 v BV Borussia Dortmund (h) Won 2-1**
Casillas, Michel Salgado, Helguera, Pavon, R Carlos, Figo, Makelele, F Conceicao, Zidane (Solari 81), Raul, Ronaldo (Guti 74). Scorers: Raul 43, Ronaldo 56

**25.02.03 v BV Borussia Dortmund (a) Drawn 1-1**
Casillas, Michel Salgado, Helguera, Pavon (Portillo 90), R Carlos, Figo (Minambres 72), Makelele, F Conceicao (Guti 68), Zidane, Raul, Ronaldo. Scorer: Portillo 90

**12.03.03 v AC Milan (h) Won 3-1**
Casillas, Michel Salgado, Helguera, Pavon, R Carlos, Figo, Makelele, F Conceicao, Zidane (Solari 88), Raul (Portillo 90), Ronaldo (Guti 67). Scorers: Raul 12, 57, Guti 86

**18.03.03 v FC Lokomotiv Moskva (a) Won 1-0**
Casillas, Michel Salgado, Helguera, Pavon, Solari, Figo, Makelele, F Conceicao, Zidane (Cambiasso 90), Raul, Ronaldo (Guti 81). Scorer: Ronaldo 35

**08.04.03 v Manchester United FC (h) Won 3-1**
Casillas, Michel Salgado, Hierro, Helguera, Roberto Carlos, F Conceicao, Makelele, Figo, Raul, Zidane, Ronaldo (Guti 84). Scorers: Figo 12, Raul 28, 49

**23.04.03 v Manchester United FC (a) Lost 3-4**
Casillas, Michel Salgado, Hierro, Helguera, Roberto Carlos, McManaman (Portillo 69), Makelele, Figo (Pavon 88), Guti, Zidane, Ronaldo (Solari 67). Scorer: Ronaldo 12, 50, 59

**06.05.03 v Juventus FC (h) Won 2-1**
Casillas, Michel Salgado, Hierro, Helguera, Roberto Carlos, Makelele, Figo, Guti, Zidane, Ronaldo (Portillo 50), Morientes (Solari 79)
Scorers: Ronaldo 23, Roberto Carlos 73

**14.05.03 v Juventus FC (a) Lost 1-3**
Casillas, Michel Salgado, Hierro, Helguera, Roberto Carlos, F Conceicao (Ronaldo 52), Figo, Guti, Zidane, Cambiasso (McManaman 76), Raul. Scorer: Zidane 89

| SEASONS | PLAYED | WON | DRAWN | LOST | FOR | AGAINST |
|---|---|---|---|---|---|---|
| 7 | 93 | 53 | 18 | 22 | 170 | 105 |

## AS ROMA

**2001-2002**
**GROUP STAGE 1**
**11.09.01 v Real Madrid CF (h) Lost 1-2**
Pelizzoli, Zebina, Zago, Samuel, Cafu (Balbo 82), Assuncao, Emerson, Candela, Totti, Batistuta, Montella (Lima 46). Scorer: Totti 73pen

**19.09.01 v RSC Anderlecht (a) Drawn 0-0**
Antonioli, Zebina, Zago, Samuel, Cafu, Tommasi, Lima, Emerson, Candela, Totti, Batistuta (Montella 82)

**26.09.01 v FC Lokomotiv Moscow (h) Won 2-1**
Antonioli, Zebina, Zago, Samuel, Cafu (Guigou 63), Tommasi (Assuncao 62), Lima, Candela, Totti, Delvecchio, Montella (Batistuta 46). Scorers: Tchougainov 69og, Totti 79

**16.10.01 v FC Lokomotiv Moscow (a) Won 1-0**
Antonioli, Zebina, Zago, Samuel, Cafu (Fuser 89), Tommasi (Assuncao 83), Emerson, Lima, Guigou, Totti, Batistuta. Scorer: Cafu 78

**24.10.01 v Real Madrid CF (a) Drawn 1-1**
Antonioli, Zebina, Zago (Aldair 46), Samuel, Cafu, Tommasi (Assuncao 65), Emerson, Lima, Candela, Totti, Batistuta (Delvecchio 88). Scorer: Totti 35

**30.10.01 v RSC Anderlecht (h) Drawn 1-1**
Pelizzoli, Siviglia, Aldair, Samuel, Cafu, Tomic (De Rossi 71), Assuncao, Emerson, Guigou, Cassano (Balbo 76), Delvecchio. Scorer: Delvecchio 52

**GROUP STAGE 2**
**20.11.01 v Galatasaray SK (a) Drawn 1-1**
Antonioli, Zebina (Fuser 81), Aldair, Samuel, Cafu, Tommasi (Cassano 46), Emerson, Lima (Assuncao 75), Candela, Totti, Batistuta. Scorer: Emerson 90

**05.12.01 v Liverpool FC (h) Drawn 0-0**
Antonioli, Zebina, Aldair, Samuel, Guigou (Assuncao 46), Tommasi (Fuser 78), Emerson, Lima, Candela, Totti, Batistuta

**20.02.02 v FC Barcelona (a) Drawn 1-1**
Antonioli, Zebina, Samuel, Panucci, Cafu, Tommasi, Emerson, Lima (Guigou 74), Candela, Totti (Delvecchio 81), Batistuta. Scorer: Panucci 57

**26.02.02 v FC Barcelona (h) Won 3-0**
Antonioli, Zebina, Samuel, Panucci, Cafu, Emerson, Lima, Candela, Totti (Cassano 87), Delvecchio (Montella 46), Batistuta (Tommasi 72). Scorers: Emerson 61, Montella 74, Tommasi 90

**13.03.02 v Galatasaray SK (h) Drawn 1-1**
Antonioli, Zebina (Aldair 46), Samuel, Panucci, Cafu, Emerson, Lima, Candela, Totti, Delvecchio (Assuncao 82), Montella (Batistuta 55). Scorer: Cafu 52

**19.03.02 v Liverpool FC (a) Lost 0-2**
Antonioli, Aldair, Samuel, Panucci, Cafu, Emerson, Lima (Montella 46), Tommasi, Candela, Totti, Assuncao (Cassano 69), Batistuta (Delvecchio 46)

**2002-2003**
**GROUP STAGE 1**
**17.09.02 v Real Madrid CF (h) Lost 0-3**
Antonioli, Cufre (Guardiola 46), Dellas, Samuel, Panucci, Cafu, Tommasi, Emerson, Candela, Montella, Cassano (Delvecchio 64)

**25.09.02 v AEK Athens (a) Drawn 0-0**
Antonioli, Cufre, Samuel, Panucci, Cafu, Tommasi, Lima, Emerson, Candela, Montella, Batistuta (Cassano 90)

**02.10.02 v KRC Genk (a) Won 1-0**
Antonioli, Zebina, Samuel, Panucci, Cafu (Cassano 46), Tommasi (Tomic 53), Lima, Emerson, Candela, Totti, Batistuta (Montella 68). Scorer: Cassano 81

**22.10.02 v KRC Genk (h) Drawn 0-0**
Antonioli, Zebina, Samuel, Panucci, Cafu (Bombardini 84), Tommasi (Guigou 60), Lima, Emerson, Candela, Cassano (Montella 46), Batistuta

**30.10.02 v Real Madrid CF (a) Won 1-0**
Antonioli, Aldair (Zebina 90), Samuel, Panucci, Cafu, Tommasi, Totti, Emerson, Candela, Delvecchio (Lima 88), Montella (Batistuta 72). Scorer: Totti 27

**12.11.02 v AEK Athens (h) Drawn 1-1**
Antonioli, Zebina, Samuel, Panucci, Cafu (Bombardini 90), Tommasi, Lima (Guigou 81), Emerson, Cassano (Cufre 65), Delvecchio, Montella. Scorer: Delvecchio 40

**27.11.02 v Arsenal FC (h) Lost 1-3**
Antonioli, Zebina, Samuel, Panucci, Cafu, Lima (Batistuta 73), Emerson, Candela, Cassano (Montella 65), Delvecchio (Guigou 57) Totti. Scorer: Cassano 4

**10.12.02 v AFC Ajax (a) Lost 1-2**
Antonioli, Zebina, Samuel, Dellas (Montella 61), Panucci, Cafu, Lima, Emerson, Cassano (Batistuta 72), Candela, Totti. Scorer: Batistuta 89

**18.02.03 v Valencia CF (h) Lost 0-1**
Pelizzoli, Zebina, Aldair, Dellas (Cufre 54), Panucci, Cafu, Lima, Tommasi, Guigou, Delvecchio (Bombardini 54), Montella (Cassano 46)

**26.02.03 v Valencia (a) Won 3-0**
Antonioli, Samuel, Aldair, Zebina (Cufre 63), Cafu, Emerson, Tommasi, Lima, Candela, Totti (Fuser 88), Cassano (Guigou 90). Scorers: Totti 24, 30, Emerson 36

**11.03.02 v Arsenal (a) Drawn 1-1**
Pelizzoli, Panucci, Samuel, Aldair, Cafu, Emerson, Tommasi, Lima, Candela, Totti, Cassano (Montella 62). Scorer: Cassano 45. Sent off: Totti 23

**19.03.02 v AFC Ajax (h) Drawn 1-1**
Pelizzoli, Panucci, Aldair, Cufre, Cafu (Fuser 80), Emerson, Tommasi (Guigou 80), Lima (Montella 60), Candela, Delvecchio, Cassano. Scorer: Cassano 24

| SEASONS | PLAYED | WON | DRAWN | LOST | FOR | AGAINST |
|---|---|---|---|---|---|---|
| 2 | 24 | 6 | 12 | 6 | 22 | 22 |

## ROSENBORG BK

**1995-1996**
**GROUP STAGE 1**
**13.09.95 v Legia Warszawa (a) Lost 1-3**
Jamtfall, Kvarme, Hoftun, Bragstad, Stensaas, Strand, Soltvedt (Heggem 79), Skammelsrud, Loken, Iversen (Staurvik 90), Jakobsen. Scorer: Jakobsen 64

**27.09.95 v Blackburn Rovers FC (h) Won 2-1**
Rise, Kvarme, Hoftun, Bragstad, Stensaas, Strand (Starvik 82), Soltvedt, Skammelsrud, Loken (Iversen 71), Brattbakk (Heggem 90), Jakobsen. Scorers: Loken 30, Stensaas 86

**18.10.95 v FC Spartak Moscow (h) Lost 2-4**
Jamtfall, Kvarme (Heggem 46), Hoftun, Bragstad, Stensaas, Strand (Starvik 78), Soltvedt (Iversen 66), Skammelsrud, Loken, Brattbakk, Jakobsen. Scorers: Loken 2, Brattbakk 44

**01.11.95 v FC Spartak Moscow (a) Lost 1-4**
Rise, Loken, Hoftun, Bragstad, Stensaas, Strand (Heggem 61), Skammelsrud, Brattbakk, Starvik, Iversen, Jakobsen. Scorer: Loken 90

**22.11.95 v Legia Warszawa (h) Won 4-0**
Rise, Kvarme, Hoftun, Starvik, Stensaas, Strand (Heggem 88), Soltvedt, Iversen, Skammelsrud, Brattbakk, Jakobsen. Scorers: Strand 17, Brattbakk 45, Jakobsen 63, Heggem 88

**06.12.95 v Blackburn Rovers FC (a) Lost 1-4**
Rise, Kvarme, Hoftun, Bragstad (Heggem 46), Stensaas, Strand (Starvik 46), Soltvedt, Iversen, Skammelsrud, Brattbakk, Jakobsen. Scorer: Iversen 30

**1996-1997**
**GROUP STAGE 1**
**11.09.96 v IFK Goteborg (a) Won 3-2**
Jamtfall, Loken, Hoftun, Bragstad (Starvik 73), Stensaas, Strand (Heggem 84), Skammelsrud, Soltvedt, Jakobsen, Brattbakk, Iversen. Scorers: Jakobsen 32, Iversen 52, Brattbakk 64

**25.09.96 v Milan AC (h) Lost 1-4**
Jamtfall, Loken, Hoftun, Bragstad, Stensaas, Strand (Heggem 81), Skammelsrud, Soltvedt, Jakobsen (Kvarme 76), Brattbakk (Starvik 34), Iversen. Scorer: Soltvedt 16

**16.10.96 v FC Porto (h) Lost 0-1**
Jamtfall, Heggem, Kvarme, Hoftun, Stensaas (Starvik 85), Strand, Skammelsrud, Soltvedt, Jakobsen, Brattbakk, Iversen. Sent off: Jakobsen 76

**30.10.96 v FC Porto (a) Lost 0-3**
Jamtfall, Kvarme, Bragstad (Sorli 45), Hoftun, Stensaas, Strand (Fjortoft 79), Skammelsrud, Soltvedt, Heggem, Brattbakk, Iversen

**20.11.96 v IFK Goteborg (h) Won 1-0**
Jamtfall, Kvarme, Hjelde, Hoftun, Stensaas, Strand (Fjortoft 87), Skammelsrud, Soltvedt, Heggem, Brattbakk, Iversen. Scorer: Skammelsrud 66

**04.12.96 v Milan AC (a) Won 2-1**
Jamtfall, Kvarme, Hjelde, Hoftun, Stensaas, Strand (Jakobsen 90), Skammelsrud, Soltvedt, Heggem, Brattbakk, Iversen. Scorers: Brattbakk 29, Heggem 70

**QUARTER FINAL**
**05.03.97 v Juventus FC (h) Drawn 1-1**
Jamtfall, Bergdolmo, Hoftun, Stensaas, Strand, Skammelsrud, Heggem, Hjelde, Soltvedt, Rushfeldt (Brattbakk 67), Jakobsen (Bragstad 87). Scorer: Soltvedt 51

**19.03.97 v Juventus FC (a) Lost 0-2**
Jamtfall, Bergdolmo, Hoftun, Stensaas, Strand (Brattbakk 60), Skammelsrud, Heggem, Hjelde, Soltvedt, Rushfeldt, Jakobsen (Fjortoft 66). Sent off: Stensaas 89

**1997-1998**
**GROUP STAGE 1**
**17.09.97 v Real Madrid CF (a) Lost 1-4**
Jamtfall, Heggem, Bragstad, Hoftun, Bergdolmo, Strand, Skammelsrud, Berg, Brattbakk, Rushfeldt (Boateng 58), Jakobsen (Mayer 74). Scorer: Jakobsen 22

**01.10.97 v Olympiakos Piraeus FC (h) Won 5-1**
Jamtfall, Heggem, Steen, Hoftun, Bergdolmo, Strand, Skammelsrud, Berg, Brattbakk, Rushfeldt, Jakobsen. Scorers: Brattbakk 13, 79, Strand 33, 43, Rushfeldt 56

**22.10.97 v FC Porto (h) Won 2-0**
Jamtfall, Heggem, Bragstad, Hoftun, Bergdolmo, Strand (Winsnes 58), Skammelsrud, Berg, Brattbakk, Rushfeldt, Jakobsen (Dahlum 79). Scorers: Rushfeldt 10, Brattbakk 37

**05.11.97 v FC Porto (a) Drawn 1-1**
Jamtfall, Heggem, Bragstad, Hoftun, Bergdolmo, Strand (Winsnes 90), Skammelsrud, Berg, Brattbakk, Rushfeldt, Dahlum (Hernes 65). Scorer: Strand 88

**27.11.97 v Real Madrid CF (h) Won 2-0**
Jamtfall, Heggem, Bragstad, Hoftun, Bergdolmo, Strand, Skammelsrud, Berg, Brattbakk, Rushfeldt, Jakobsen. Scorers: Strand 42, Brattbakk 53

**10.12.97 v Olympiakos Piraeus FC (a) Drawn 2-2**
Jamtfall, Heggem, Bragstad, Hoftun, Bergdolmo, Strand, Skammelsrud, Berg, Brattbakk, Rushfeldt, Jakobsen. Scorer: Rushfeldt 49, 69

**1998-1999**
**GROUP STAGE 1**
**16.09.98 v Athletic Club Bilbao (a) Drawn 1-1**
Jamtfall, Basma, Bragstad, Hoftun, Bergdolmo, Strand, Skammelsrud, Berg, Hernes (Jan Derek Sorensen 80), Rushfeldt, Jakobsen (Dahlum 90). Scorer: Strand 65

**30.09.98 v Juventus FC (h) Drew 1-1**
Jamtfall, Basma, Bragstad, Hoftun, Bergdolmo, Strand (Winsnes 84), Skammelsrud, Berg, Jan Derek Sorensen (Hernes 55), Rushfeldt (Dahlum 62), Jakobsen. Scorer: Skammelsrud 69 pen

**21.10.98 v Galatasaray SK (h) Won 3-0**
Arason, Basma, Bragstad, Hoftun, Bergdolmo, Strand, Skammelsrud, Winsnes (Mayer 76), Jan Derek Sorensen (Dahlum 76), Rushfeldt, Jakobsen (Hernes 55). Scorer: Rushfeldt 69, 86, 90

**04.11.98 v Galatasaray SK (a) Lost 0-3**
Arason, Basma, Johnsen, Hoftun, Bergdolmo, Strand, Skammelsrud, Berg, Dahlum (Hernes 65), Rushfeldt, Jakobsen (Jan Derek Sorensen 61)

**25.11.98 v Athletic Club Bilbao (h) Won 2-1**
Jamtfall, Bergdolmo, Bragstad, Hoftun, Pedersen, Strand (Winsnes 79), Skammelsrud, Berg, (Mayer 90), Jan Derek Sorensen (Dahlum 84), Rushfeldt, Jakobsen. Scorer: Jan Derek Sorensen 2, 50

**09.12.98 v Juventus FC (a) Lost 0-2**
Jamtfall, Bergdolmo, Bragstad, Hoftun, Pedersen (Hernes 66), Strand, Johnsen (Winsnes 57), Berg, Jan Derek Sorensen (Dahlum 46), Rushfeldt, Jakobsen

**1999-2000**
**GROUP STAGE 1**
**14.09.99 v Boavista FC (a) Won 3-0**
Jamtfall, Bergdolmo, Hoftun, Bragstad, Strand (Winsnes 89), Berg, Sorensen (Dahlum 82), Carew, Skammelsrud, Jakobsen, Bent Johnsen. Scorers: Sorensen 10, Berg 43, Strand 73

**22.09.99 v Feyenoord (h) Drawn 2-2**
Jamtfall, Bergdolmo, Hoftun, Bragstad, Strand, Berg, Sorensen, Carew, Skammelsrud, Jakobsen (Dahlum 59), Bent Johnsen (Winsnes 65). Scorer: Carew 21, 24

**29.09.99 v BV Borussia Dortmund (h) Drawn 2-2**
Jamtfall, Bergdolmo, Hoftun, Bragstad, Basma (Winsnes 25), Strand, Berg, Sorensen, Carew, Skammelsrud, Jakobsen (Dahlum 64). Scorers: Sorensen 35, Carew 68

**19.10.99 v BV Borussia Dortmund (a) Won 3-0**
Jamtfall, Bergdolmo, Hoftun, Bragstad, Strand, Berg, Sorensen, Carew, Skammelsrud, Jakobsen, Winsnes. Scorers: Sorensen 17, 58, Winsnes 70

**27.10.99 v Boavista FC (h) Won 2-0**
Jamtfall, Bergdolmo, Hoftun, Bragstad, Strand, Berg (Bent Johnsen 89), Sorensen, Carew, Skammelsrud, Jakobsen (Dahlum 58), Winsnes. Scorers: Berg 61, Dahlum 66

**02.11.99 v Feyenoord (a)** **Lost 0-1**
Jamtfall, Bergdolmo, Hoftun, Bragstad, Strand, Berg, Sorensen, Carew, Skammelsrud, Jakobsen (Dahlum 62), Winsnes

**GROUP STAGE 2**
**24.11.99 v FC Bayern Munchen (h)** **Drawn 1-1**
Jamtfall, Bergdolmo, Hoftun, Bragstad, Basma, Strand, Berg, Sorensen, Carew, Skammelsrud, Winsnes (Dahlum 71). Scorer: Skammelsrud 47

**07.12.99 v Real Madrid CF (a)** **Lost 1-3**
Jamtfall, Bergdolmo, Hoftun, Basma, Strand (Aaroy 90), Berg, Sorensen, Carew, Skammelsrud, Jakobsen (Winsnes 52), Bent Johnsen. Scorer: Carew 48

**29.02.00 v FC Dynamo Kyiv (a)** **Lost 1-2**
Arason, Bergdolmo, Hoftun, Bragstad, Basma, Strand (Storflor 46, Bent Johnsen 90), Berg, Carew, Skammelsrud, Jakobsen, Winsnes. Scorer: Jakobsen 48

**08.03.00 v FC Dynamo Kyiv (h)** **Lost 1-2**
Arason, Hoftun, Bragstad, Basma, Strand (Storvik 78), Berg, Sorensen, Carew, Skammelsrud, Jakobsen (Knutsen 78), Bent Johnsen. Scorer: Berg 38

**14.03.00 v FC Bayern Munchen (a)** **Lost 1-2**
Arason, Bergdolmo, Bragstad, Basma, Strand (Winsnes 82), Berg, Sorensen, Carew, Skammelsrud, Bent Johnsen, Knutsen (Jakobsen 73). Scorer: Carew 64. Sent off: Bragstad 90

**22.03.00 v Real Madrid CF (h)** **Lost 0-1**
Arason, Bergdolmo, Hoftun, Basma, Strand, Berg, Sorensen, Carew, Skammelsrud, Jakobsen (Knutsen 70), Bent Johnsen

**2000-2001**
**GROUP STAGE 1**
**13.09.00 v Paris Saint-Germain (h)** **Won 3-1**
Arason, Hoftun, Basma, Strand (Knutsen 78), Berg, Sorensen, Frode Johnsen, Skammelsrud, Winsnes, Bent Johnsen, Stensaas. Scorers: Berg 18, F Johnsen 62, Skammelsrud 90

**19.09.00 v FC Bayern Munchen (a)** **Lost 1-3**
Jamtfall, Hoftun, Basma, Strand (Knutsen 81), Berg, Sorensen, Frode Johnsen, Skammelsrud, Winsnes, Bent Johnsen, Stensaas. Scorer: Sorensen 38

**26.09.00 v Helsingborgs IF (h)** **Won 6-1**
Jamtfall, Hoftun, Basma (Belsvik 82), Strand (Knutsen 75), Berg, Sorensen, Frode Johnsen, Skammelsrud, Winsnes (Storvik 87), Bent Johnsen, Stensaas. Scorers: Frode Johnsen 21, 29, 79, Strand 51, 52, S Johansen og 65

**18.10.00 v Helsingborgs IF (a)** **Lost 0-2**
Arason, Hoftun, Basma, Strand, Berg, Sorensen, Frode Johnsen (Belsvik 60), Skammelsrud, Winsnes (Storvik 88), Bent Johnsen, Stensaas. Sent off: Hoftun 72

**24.10.00 v Paris Saint-Germain (a)** **Lost 2-7**
Jamtfall, Basma, Strand (Trondsen 71), Berg, Sorensen, Frode Johnsen, Skammelsrud, George, Winsnes (Belsvik 55), Bent Johnsen, Stensaas (Boateng 85). Scorer: George 36, 38

**08.11.00 v FC Bayern Munchen (h)** **Drawn 1-1**
Arason, Hoftun, Basma (Belsvik 86), Sorensen, Frode Johnsen, Skammelsrud, Knutsen, George (Strand 82), Winsnes, Bent Johnsen, Stensaas. Scorer: Frode Johnsen 27

**2001-2002**
**GROUP STAGE 1**
**10.10.01 v Celtic FC (a)** **Lost 0-1**
Arason, Bl Johnsen, Basma, Hoftun, Saarinen, Berg, Skammelsrud, Strand (Wisnes 82), Olsen (F Johnsen 86), Brattbakk (George 74), Rushfeldt
*Postponed to 10 October after 11 September atrocities

**18.09.01 v FC Porto (h)** **Lost 1-2**
Arason, Bl Johnsen (El Fakiri 29), Basma, Hoftun, Saarinen, Berg, Skammelsrud, Strand, Brattbakk (Enerly 84) Rushfeldt, F Johnsen. Scorer: Rushfeldt 90

**25.09.01 v Juventus FC (h)** **Drawn 1-1**
Arason, Berg, Basma, Hoftun, Saarinen (Stensaas 72), Enerly (Bl Johnsen 79), Skammelsrud, Strand (Olsen 46), Brattbakk, Rushfeldt, F Johnsen. Scorer: Skammelsruud 90pen

**17.10.01 v Juventus FC (a)** **Lost 0-1**
Arason, Berg, Basma, Hoftun, Saarinen, Bl Johnsen, El Fakiri (Enerly 46), Skammelsrud, Strand, Brattbakk (George 59), Rushfeldt (F Johnsen 75)

**23.10.01 v Celtic FC (h)** **Won 2-0**
Arason, Olsen, Basma, Hoftun, Saarinen, Strand, Skammelsrud, Berg (Winsnes 74), Brattbakk, George (Bl Johnsen 83), Rushfeldt. Scorer: Brattbakk 19, 36

**31.10.01 v FC Porto (a)** **Lost 0-1**
Arason, Olsen, Basma, Hoftun (Enerly 46), Bl Johnsen, Strand, Skammelsrud, Berg (Winsnes 88), Stensaas, Brattbakk, (George 65) F Johnsen

**2002-2003**
**GROUP STAGE 1**
**17.09.02 v Internazionale FC (h) Drawn 2-2**
Arason, Strand (Stensaas 75), Hoftun, Basma, Saarinen, Olsen, Skammelsrud, Berg, Karadas, Brattbakk, F Johnsen. Scorer: Karadas 52, 65

**25.09.02 v Olympique Lyonnais (a) Lost 0-5**
Arason, Olsen (Sibaya 65), Hoftun, Basma, Saarinen (Blixt 83), Stensaas (Ludvigsen 72), Skammelsrud, Berg, Karadas, Brattbakk, F Johnsen

**02.10.02 v AFC Ajax (h) Drawn 0-0**
Arason, Olsen, Hoftun, Basma, Saarinen, Strand, Skammelsrud, Berg, Karadas, Brattbakk (George 40), F Johnsen (Enerly 35)

**22.10.02 v AFC Ajax (a) Drawn 1-1**
Arason, Strand, Hoftun, Basma, Saarinen, Enerly, Skammelsrud, Berg, Karadas, Brattbakk (Ludvigsen 74), F Johnsen. Scorer: Enerly 84pen

**30.10.02 v Internazionale FC (a) Lost 0-3**
Arason, Strand, Hoftun, Basma, Saarinen, Enerly (Ludvigsen 80), Skammelsrud, Berg, Karadas, Brattbakk (Olsen 57), F Johnsen

**12.11.02 v Olympique Lyonnais (h) Drawn 1-1**
Arason, Strand, Hoftun, Basma, Saarinen, Enerly (Ludvigsen 79), Skammelsrud, Berg, Karadas, Brattbakk, F Johnsen. Scorer: Brattbakk 69

| SEASONS | PLAYED | WON | DRAWN | LOST | FOR | AGAINST |
|---|---|---|---|---|---|---|
| 8 | 56 | 16 | 14 | 26 | 77 | 12 |

## SALZBURG (SV AUSTRIA SALZBURG)

**1994-1995**
**GROUP STAGE 1**
**14.09.94 v AEK Athens (h) Drawn 0-0**
Konrad, Lainer, Winklhofer, Mladenovic, Pfeifenberger, Aigner, Jurcevic, Artner (Freisegger 67), Hasunhuttl (Stadler 46), Feiersinger, Hutter

**28.09.94 v Milan AC (a) Lost 0-3**
Konrad (Illsanker 60), Lainer, Winklhofer, Fyrstaller, Mladenovic, Aigner (Hutter 60), Jurcevic, Artner, Pfeifenberger, Freisegger, Kocijan (Hiden 60)

**19.10;94 v AFC Ajax (h) Drawn 0-0**
Konrad, Lainer, Kocijan (Hasunhuttl 78), Furstaller, Mladenovic (Hutter 75), Winklhofer, Jurcevic, Artner, Pfeifenberger, Feiersinger, Hiden

**02.11.94 v AFC Ajax (a) Drawn 1-1**
Konrad, Lainer, Kocijan, Furstaller, Mladenovic (Hutter 75), Winklhofer, Jurcevic, Artner (Hasenhuttl 83), Pfeifenberger, Feiersinger, Hiden. Scorer: Mladenovic 62

**23.11.94 v AEK Athens (a) Won 3-1**
Konrad, Lainer, Kocijan (Hutter 86), Furstaller, Mladenovic, Winklhofer, Hasenhuttl (Stadler 82), Artner, Pfeifenberger, Feiersinger, Hiden. Scorers: Pfeifenberger 7, 9, Hasenhuttl 76

**07.12.94 v Milan AC (h) Lost 0-1**
Konrad, Lainer, Kocijan, Furstaller, Mladenovic, Winklhofer (Hasenhuttl 60), Jurcevic, Artner, Pfeifenberger, Feiersinger, Hiden (Hutter 75)

| SEASONS | PLAYED | WON | DRAWN | LOST | FOR | AGAINST |
|---|---|---|---|---|---|---|
| 1 | 6 | 1 | 3 | 2 | 4 | 6 |

## FC SHAKHTAR DONETSK

**2000-2001**
**GROUP STAGE 1**
**12.09.00 v SS Lazio (h) Lost 0-3**
Virt, Gleveckas, Tymoschuk, Popov, Bakharev, Zubov, Atelkin, Vorobyev, Chmarko, Shevchuk, Abramov (Bielik 77)

**20.09.00 v Arsenal FC (a) Lost 2-3**
Virt, Starostyak, Gleveckas, Tymoschuk, Popov, Bakharev (Bielik 70), Zubov, Atelkin (Kovalov 77), Vorobyev, Shevchuk, Abramov (Kryventsov 58). Scorers: Bakharev 26, Vorobyev 29. Sent off: Popov 45

**27.09.00 v AC Sparta Praha (a) Lost 2-3**
Virt, Starostyak, Gleveckas, Tymoschuk, Bakharev, Kovalov (Abramov 78), Zubov, Atelkin (Bielik 79), Vorobyev, Shevchuk, Aliuta. Scorers: Zubov 56, Hornak og 84

**17.10.00 v AC Sparta Praha (h) Won 2-1**
Virt, Starostyak (Bielik 67), Gleveckas, Tymoschuk, Popov, Bakharev, Zubov, Atelkin, Vorobyev (Kovalov 90), Abramov (Kryventsov 58), Okoronkwo. Scorers: Gleveckas 35, Zubov 87 pen

**25.10.00 v SS Lazio (a)** **Lost 1-5**
Virt, Gleveckas, Tymoschuk, Popov (Chmarko 75), Bakharev, Kovalov (Starostyak 84), Zubov, Atelkin, Vorobyev, Aliuta (Bielik 71), Okoronkwo. Scorer: Vorobyev 41

**07.11.00 v Arsenal FC (h)** **Won 3-0**
Virt, Starostyak, Gleveckas, Tymoschuk, Popov, Bakharev, Zubov, Atelkin (Bielik 52), Vorobyev (Savu 86), Abramov (Aliuta 77), Okoronkwo. Scorers: Atelkin 34, Vorobyev 57, Bielik 66

| SEASONS | PLAYED | WON | DRAWN | LOST | FOR | AGAINST |
|---|---|---|---|---|---|---|
| 1 | 6 | 2 | 0 | 4 | 10 | 15 |

## SCHALKE 04

**2001-2002**
**GROUP STAGE 1**
**11.09.01 v Panathinaikos FC (h)** **Lost 0-2**
Reck, Hajto, Waldoch, Van Kerckhoven, Nemec, Oude Kamphuis, Van Hoogdalem (Djordjevic 78), Moller (Wilmots 59), Bohme (Asamoah 68), Agali, Mpenza

**19.09.01 v Arsenal FC (a)** **Lost 2-3**
Reck, Hajto, Waldoch, Van Kerckhoven, Vermant (Asamoah 54), Oude Kamphuis, Van Hoogdalem, Moller (Djordjevic 72), Bohme (Mulder 82), Agali, Mpenza. Scorers: Van Hoogdalem 43, Mpenza 59

**26.09.01 v RCD Mallorca (h)** **Lost 0-1**
Reck, Hajto, Waldoch (Asamoah 70), Van Kerckhoven, Nemec (Mulder 82), Oude Kamphuis, Van Hoogdalem, Moller, Bohme (Buskens 67), Agali, Mpenza

**16.10.01 v RCD Mallorca (a)** **Won 4-0**
Reck, Hajto, Waldoch, Van Kerckhoven, Asamoah, Vermant, Thon (Nemec 80), Van Hoogdalem (Kmetsch 78), Matellan, Wilmots (Buskens 74), Sand. Scorers: Van Hoogdalem 15, Hajto 22pen, Asamoah 77, Sand 84

**24.10.01 v Panathinaikos FC (a)** **Lost 0-2**
Reck, Hajto, Waldoch, Van Kerckhoven, Asamoah, Vermant (Thon 79), Moller, Kmetsch, Matellan (Bohme 50), Wilmots (Mulder 67), Sand

**30.10.01 v Arsenal FC (h)** **Won 3-1**
Reck, Hajto, Waldoch, Matellan, Nemec (Thon 67), Van Hoogdalem (Kmetsch 63), Vermant (Djordjevic 74), Moller, Bohme, Sand, Mulder. Scorers: Mulder 2, Vermant 60, Moller 64

| SEASONS | PLAYED | WON | DRAWN | LOST | FOR | AGAINST |
|---|---|---|---|---|---|---|
| 1 | 6 | 2 | 0 | 4 | 9 | 9 |

## AC SPARTA PRAHA

**1997-1998**
**GROUP STAGE 1**
**17.09.97 v AC Parma (h) Drawn 0-0**
Postulka, Novotny, Svoboda, Repka, Mistr (Lalik 71), Martin Hasek, Baranek, Nemecek, Cizek (Gabriel 46), Siegl (Obajdin 86), Lokvenc

**01.10.97 v BV Borussia Dortmund (a) Lost 1-4**
Postulka, Repka, Svoboda, Novotny, Hornak (Obajdin 30), Nemecek, Martin Hasek (Gabriel 54), Ivan Hasek, Cizek, Siegl, Lokvenc (Nemeth 71). Scorer: Siegl 76

**22.10.97 v Galatasaray SK (h) Won 3-0**
Postulka, Repka, Svoboda, Novotny, Hornak, Nemecek, Martin Hasek, Gabriel (Cifranic 85), Baranek (Obajdin 77), Siegl, Lokvenc. Scorers: Siegl 34, Gabriel 66, Obajdin 87

**05.11.97 v Galatasaray SK (a) Lost 0-2**
Postulka, Repka, Svoboda, Novotny, Votava (Gabriel 66), Hornak, Cizek, Baranek (Obajdin 23), Hasek, Siegl (Nemecek 66), Lokvenc

**27.11.97 v AC Parma (a) Drawn 2-2**
Postulka, Hornak, Svoboda, Repka, Gabriel (Nemecek 70), Votava, Baranek (Obajdin 62), Novotny, Mistr (Lokvenc 50), Siegl, Cizek. Scorers: Novotny 87, Obajdin 89

**10.12.97 v BV Borussia Dortmund (h) Lost 0-3**
Postulka, Votava, Svoboda, Novotny (Baranek 51), Hasek, Obajdin (Mistr 67), Nemecek, Cizek, Gabriel, Lokvenc, Siegl (Pospisil 75)

**1999-2000**
**GROUP STAGE 1**
**15.09.99 v Girondins de Bordeaux (h) Drawn 0-0**
Postulka, Gabriel, Labant, Hasek, Svoboda (Pavel Novotny 90), Jiri Novotny, Lokvenc, Siegl (Sionko 58), Baranek, Rosicky (Prohaszka 84), Fukal

**21.09.99 v FC Spartak Moscow (a) Drawn 1-1**
Postulka, Gabriel, Labant, Hasek, Hornak, Jiri Novotny, Lokvenc, Sionko, Baranek (Prohaszka 86), Rosicky (Obajdin 76), Fukal. Scorer: Lokvenc 17

**28.09.99 v Willem II (h) Won 4-0**
Postulka, Gabriel, Labant, Hasek, Hornak, Jiri Novotny, Sionko (Siegl 84), Prohaszka (Jarosik 36), Baranek (Obajdin 82), Rosicky, Fukal. Scorers: Jiri Novotny 26, Prohaszka 29 pen, Rosicky 40, Jarosik 58

**20.10.99 v Willem II (a) Won 4-3**
Postulka, Gabriel, Labant, Hasek, Svoboda, Jiri Novotny, Lokvenc (Jarosik 80), Sionko, Baranek (Obajdin 86), Rosicky (Siegl 61), Fukal. Scorers: Jiri Novotny 17, Labant 54 pen, 90 pen, Baranek 62

**26.10.99 v Girondins de Bordeaux (a) Drawn 0-0**
Postulka, Gabriel, Labant, Hasek, Hornak, Jiri Novotny, Lokvenc (Siegl 81), Sionko, Baranek (Svoboda 89), Rosicky (Jarosik 90), Fukal

**03.11.99 v FC Spartak Moscow (h) Won 5-2**
Postulka, Gabriel, Labant, Hasek, Hornak, Jiri Novotny, Lokvenc, Obajdin (Jarosik 80), Sionko (Siegl 85), Rosicky (Svoboda 69), Fukal. Scorers: Lokvenc 1, 66, Rosicky 11, Fukal 49, Labant 63 pen

**GROUP STAGE 2**

**23.11.99 v FC Porto (h) Lost 0-2**
Postulka, Gabriel, Hasek, Hornak, Jiri Novotny, Lokvenc, Obajdin (Jarosik 80), Sionko (Siegl 81), Baranek, Rosicky (Svoboda 88), Fukal

**08.12.99 v FC Barcelona (a) Lost 0-5**
Postulka, Gabriel, Hasek, Hornak, Jiri Novotny, Lokvenc, Svoboda (Bolf 17), Sionko (Jarosik 70), Baranek, Rosicky, Fukal. Sent off: Hasek 38

**01.03.00 v Hertha BSC Berlin (a) Drawn 1-1**
Blazek, Gabriel, Jiri Novotny, Lokvenc (Siegl 68), Obajdin (Hapal 75), Bolf, Sionko, Jarosik, Baranek, Rosicky, Fukal. Scorer: Siegl 84

**07.03.00 v Hertha BSC Berlin (h) Won 1-0**
Blazek, Gabriel, Jiri Novotny, Lokvenc, Bolf, Sionko (Svoboda 74), Jarosik, Baranek, Rosicky, Fukal, Hapal (Siegl 65). Scorer: Fukal 90

**15.03.00 v FC Porto (a) Drawn 2-2**
Blazek, Gabriel, Svoboda (Siegl 85), Jiri Novotny, Lokvenc, Bolf (Hornak 81), Sionko (Obajdin 54), Jarosik, Baranek, Rosicky, Fukal. Scorers: Lokvenc 74, Fukal 90

**21.03.00 v FC Barcelona (h) Lost 1-2**
Blazek, Gabriel, Svoboda (Hapal 59), Jiri Novotny, Lokvenc, Obajdin (Flachbart 71), Bolf, Sionko, Jarosik, Rosicky, Fukal. Scorer: Svoboda 18

**2000-2001**
**GROUP STAGE 1**
**12.09.00 v Arsenal FC (h) Lost 0-1**
Postulka, Grygera, Svoboda, Jiri Novotny, Kincl (Siegl 61), Obajdin, Bolf, Pavel Novotny, Papousek (Prohaszka 79), Rosicky, Mynar (Flachbart 86)

**20.09.00 v SS Lazio (a) Lost 0-3**
Postulka, Grygera, Hornak, Svoboda (Kolousek 78), Jiri Novotny, Kincl (Siegl 82), Obajdin, Bolf, Jarosik, Rosicky, Mynar (Labant 46)

**27.09.00 v FC Shakhtar Donetsk (h) Won 3-2**
Postulka, Grygera, Labant, Hornak, Svoboda (Kolousek 87), Jiri Novotny, Obajdin (Prohaszka 76), Bolf, Sionko (Papousek 90), Jarosik, Rosicky. Scorers: Rosicky 54, Hornak 73, Jarosik 82

**17.10.00 v Shakhtar Donetsk (a) Lost 1-2**
Postulka, Grygera, Labant, Hasek (Pavel Novotny 90), Hornak, Jiri Novotny, Obajdin (Kolousek 80), Bolf (Kincl 90), Sionko, Jarosik, Rosicky. Scorer: Jarosik 16. Sent off: Grygera 87

**25.10.00 v Arsenal FC (a) Lost 2-4**
Postulka, Labant, Hasek, Hornak, Jiri Novotny, Kincl, Bolf, Sionko (Papousek 85), Jarosik, Jun (Mynar 46), Rosicky. Scorers: Labant 40 pen, Rosicky 90

**07.11.00 v SS Lazio (h) Lost 0-1**
Blazek, Grygera, Labant, Hasek (Mynar 86), Svoboda (Prohaszka 61), Jiri Novotny, Siegl (Kincl 81), Bolf, Jarosik, Papousek, Rosicky

**2001-2002**
**GROUP STAGE 1**
**10.10.01 v FC Spartak Moscow (h) Won 2-0**
Cech, Grygera, Hubschmann, Novotny, Labant, Sionko, Jarosik, Hasek, Michalik (Zelenka 60), Kincl (Papousek 90), Hartig (Holub 80). Scores: Kincl 57, Sionko 88
* Postponed to 10 October after 11 September atrocities

**18.09.01 v FC Bayern Munchen (a) Drawn 0-0**
Cech, Grygera, Hubschmann, Novotny, Labant, Sionko, Jarosik, Hasek, Michalik (Flachbart 90), Kincl, Hartig (Babnic 57, Zelenka 90)

**25.09.01 v Feyenoord (h) Won 4-0**
Cech, Grygera, Hubschmann, Novotny, Labant, Sionko, Jarosik, Hasek, Michalik (Zelenka 80), Kincl, Hartig (Holub). Scorers: Hartig 24, Labant 37pen, Kincl 71, Michalik 74

**17.10.01 v Feyenoord (a) Won 2-0**
Cech, Grygera, Hubschmann, Novotny, Labant, Sionko, Jarosik, Hasek, Michalik (Zelenka 88), Kincl, Hartig. Scorers: Jarosik 43, Novotny 78

**23.10.01 v FC Spartak Moscow (a) Drawn 2-2**
Cech, Grygera, Hubschmann, Novotny, Labant, Sionko (Sloncik 83), Jarosik, Hasek, Michalik (Babnic 73), Kincl, Holub (Zelenka 57). Scorers: Holub 29, Babnic 90

**31.10.01 v FC Bayern Munchen (h) Lost 0-1**
Cech, Grygera, Hubschmann, Novotny, Labant, Sionko, Jarosik, Hasek (Sloncik 70), Michalik (Holub 80), Babnic (Zelenka 53), Kincl

**GROUP STAGE 2**

**21.11.01 v Real Madrid CF (h) Lost 2-3**
Cech, Flachbart, Hubschmann, Novotny, Labant, Sionko, Jarosik, Hasek (Sloncik 71), Michalik (Zelenka 52), Hartig (Papousek 78), Kincl. Scorers: Michalik 30, Sionko 72

**04.12.01 v FC Porto (a) Won 1-0**
Cech, Flachbart, Hubschmann, Novotny, Labant, Sionko (Papousek 83), Jarosik, Hasek (Zelenka 90), Michalik, Hartig (Holub 90), Kincl. Scorer: Sionko 75

**19.02.02 v Panathinaikos FC (h) Lost 0-2**
Cech, Mynar (Zelenka 53), Hubschmann, Novotny, Flachbart, Sionko, Jarosik, Zavadil, Michalik, Hartig (Cizek 46), Kincl. Sent off: Hubschmann 86

**27.02.02 v Panathinaikos FC (a) Lost 1-2**
Cech, Mynar, Cizek, Novotny, Flachbart, Sionko, Jarosik, Zavadil (Klein 38), Michalik, Zelenka, Kincl. Scorer: Klein 90

**12.03.02 v Real Madrid CF (a) Lost 0-3**
Cech, Cizek, Hubschmann, Novotny, Flachbart, Sionko, Jarosik, Abanda (Babnic 66), Michalik, Klein, Kincl

**20.03.02 v FC Porto (h) Won 2-0**
Cech, Flachbart, Novotny, Grygera, Mares, Sionko (Klein 90), Jarosik, Hubschmann, Cizek, Hartig (Babnic 79), Kincl (Zavadil 46). Scorers: Sionko 63, Jarosik 71

| SEASONS | PLAYED | WON | DRAWN | LOST | FOR | AGAINST |
|---|---|---|---|---|---|---|
| 4 | 36 | 11 | 9 | 16 | 47 | 55 |

## SPARTAK MOSCOW

**1993-1994**
**GROUP STAGE 1**
**24.11.93 v AS Monaco (a) Lost 1-4**
Pomazoun, Khlestov, Ivanov, Tsymbalar, Pisarev, Nikiforov, Onopko, Karpin, Mamedov, Lediakhov (Piatnitsky 46), Beschastnykh (Rodionov 61). Scorer: Pisarev 48

**08.12.93 v Galatasaray SK (h) Drawn 0-0**
Pomazoun, Khlestov (Ivanov 31), Mamedov, Tsymbalar, Pisarev, Nikiforov, Onopko, Karpin, Piatnitsky, Lediakhov, Beschastnykh

**02.03.94 v FC Barcelona (h) Drawn 2-2**
Stauche, Khlestov, Ivanov, Tsymbalar, Pisarev (Rodionov 46), Nikiforov, Ternavski, Karpin, Piatnitsky, Lediakhov, Beschastnykh. Scorers: Rodionov 76, Karpin 87

**16.03.94 v FC Barcelona (a) Lost 1-5**
Stauche, Khlestov, Ivanov, Tsymbalar, Ternavski, Nikiforov, Onopko, Karpin, Piatnitsky, Lediakhov (Rodionov 46), Beschastnykh (Pisarev 72). Scorer: Karpin 3

**30.03.94 v AS Monaco (h) Drawn 0-0**
Stauche, Mamedov, Ternavski (Khlestov 75), Tsymbalar, Rodionov, Nikiforov, Onopko, Karpin, Piatnitsky, Lediakhov, Beschastnykh

**13.04.94 v Galatasaray SK (a) Won 2-1**
Stauche, Mamedov, Ternavski, Tsymbalar (Lediakhov 75), Pisarev, Nikiforov, Onopko, Karpin, Piatnitsky, Massalitine (Alenitchev 78), Beschastnykh. Scorers: Onopko 54, Karpin 84

**1994-1995**
**GROUP STAGE 1**
**14.09.94 v FC Dynamo Kyiv (a) Lost 2-3**
Tyapushkin, Mamedov, Ternavski, Tsymbalar, Rakhimov, Tchoudin, Naduda, Alenitchev (Moukhamadiev 59), Piatnitsky, Pisarev, Tikhonov (Rodionov 43). Scorers: Pisarev 12, Tikhonov 38

**28.09.94 v Paris Saint-Germain (h) Lost 1-2**
Tyapushkin, Mamedov, Tikhonov, Tsymbalar, Rakhimov, Nikiforov, Onopko, Khlestov, Piatnitsky, Pisarev, Moukhamadiev (Alenitchev 67). Scorer: Rakhimov 39. Sent off: Mamedov 58

**19.10.94 v FC Bayern Munchen (h) Drawn 1-1**
Tyapushkin, Ananko, Ketchinov, Tsymbalar, Rakhimov, Nikiforov (Ternavski 85), Onopko, Tikhonov, Piatnitsky, Pisarev, Moukhamadiev (Konovalov 75). Scorer: Matthaus og 77

**02.11.94 v FC Bayern Munchen (a) Drawn 2-2**
Tyapushkin, Ananko, Khlestov, Alenitchev, Rakhimov, Nikiforov, Onopko, Tikhonov, Piatnitsky, Pisarev (Naduda 85), Ketchinov. Scorers: Tikhonov 4, Alenitchev 32

**23.11.94 v FC Dynamo Kyiv (h) Won 1-0**
Tyapushkin, Khlestov, Lipko, Alenitchev, Rakhimov, Nikiforov, Onopko, Tikhonov, Piatnitsky (Naduda 88), Pisarev (Konovalov 62), Moukhamadiev. Scorer: Moukhamadiev 51

**07.12.94 v Paris Saint-Germain (a) Lost 1-4**
Tyapushkin, Khlestov, Lipko, Alenitchev, Ketchinov (Konovalov 74), Nikiforov, Onopko, Tikhonov, Piatnitsky, Pisarev, Moukhamadiev (Rodionov 46). Scorer: Rodionov 64

**1995-1996**
**GROUP STAGE 1**
**13.09.95 v Blackburn Rovers FC (a) Won 1-0**
Tcherchesov, Khlestov, Nikiforov, Mamedov, Onopko, Tsymbalar, Kulkov, Shmarov (Ketchinov 89), Piatnitsky, Yuran, Tikhonov. Scorer: Yuran 41

**27.09.95 v Legia Warszawa (h) Won 2-1**
Tcherchesov, Khlestov, Nikiforov, Mamedov, Onopko, Tsymbalar, Kulkov, Shmarov, Piatnitsky, Yuran, Tikhonov. Scorers: Nikiforov 13 pen, Yuran 52

**18.10.95 v Rosenborg BK (a) Won 4-2**
Tcherchesov, Mamedov, Nikiforov, Khlestov, Tsymbalar, Onopko, Kulkov, Shmarov (Ketchinov 56), Piatnitsky (Alenitchev 46), Yuran, Tikhonov. Scorers: Alenitchev 58, Nikiforov 67, Ketchinov 76, 83

**01.11.95 v Rosenborg BK (h) Won 4-1**
Tcherchesov, Khlestov, Nikiforov, Ananko, Onopko, Tsymbalar (Ketchinov 46), Kulkov, Shmarov, Alenitchev (Titov 85), Yuran, Tikhonov. Scorers: Shmarov 2, Yuran 9, Tsymbalar 19, Tikhonov 80

**22.11.95 v Blackburn Rovers FC (h) Won 3-0**
Tcherchesov, Khlestov, Nikiforov, Mamedov, Onopko, Tsymbalar, Kulkov, Shmarov (Ketchinov 66), Alenitchev, Yuran (Piatnitsky 72), Tikhonov (Moukhamadiev 87). Scorers: Alenitchev 23, Nikoforov 47, Mamedov 55

**06.12.95 v Legia Warsaw (a) Won 1-0**
Tcherchesov, Khlestov, Nikiforov, Tsymbalar, Mamedov, Onopko (Ananko 82), Kulkov, Shmarov, Alenitchev, Ketchinov, Tikhonov. Scorer: Mamedov 41

**QUARTER FINAL**

**06.03.96 v FC Nantes-Atlantique (a) Lost 0-2**
Nigmatullin, Lipko, Nikiforov, Mamedov (Tchudin 34), Evseiev, Ananko, Tsymbalar (Shmarov 46), Piatnitsky, Alenitchev (Bezrodny 71), Ketchinov, Tikhonov

**20.03.96 v FC Nantes-Atlantique (h) Drawn 2-2**
Nigmatullin, Ananko, Nikiforov, Evseiev, Lipko, Tsymbalar, Nagorniak (Bezrodny 74), Alenitchev, Shmarov (Piatnitsky 59), Ketchinov, Tikhonov. Scorer: Nikiforov 32, 38

**1998-1999**

**GROUP STAGE 1**

**16.09.98 v SK Sturm Graz (a) Won 2-0**
Filimonov, Parfionov, Ananko, Khlestov, Baranov, Bushmanov, Titov, Tsymbalar, Shirko (Kanischev 46), Pisarev (Samarone 77), Tikhonov. Scorers: Titov 60, Tsymbalar 63

**30.09.98 v Real Madrid CF (h) Won 2-1**
Filimonov, Parfionov, Ananko, Bushmanov, Khlestov, Baranov, Titov, Tsymbalar, Tikhonov, Pisarev (Kanischev 67), Robson (Buznikin 90). Scorers: Tsymbalar 72, Titov 78

**21.10.98 v FC Internazionale (a) Lost 1-2**
Filimonov, Parfionov, Ananko, Bushmanov, Khlestov, Baranov (Meleshin 81), Tsymbalar, Romaschenko, Tikhonov, Pisarev (Kanischev 66), Robson. Scorer: Tsymbalar 65

**04.11.98 v FC Internazionale (h) Drawn 1-1**
Filimonov, Parfionov, Ananko, Bushmanov, Romaschenko, Baranov (Meleshin 63), Titov, Tsymbalar, Tikhonov, Robson, Buznikin (Pisarev 46). Scorer: Tikhonov 68

**25.11.98 v SK Sturm Graz (h) Drawn 0-0**
Filimonov, Gorlukovitch, Ananko, Bushmanov, Khlestov, Baranov, Tsymbalar, Titov, Tikhonov, Shirko (Buznikin 70), Robson (Kanischev 57)

**09.12.98 v Real Madrid CF (a) Lost 1-2**
Filimonov, Parfionov, Ananko, Bushmanov, Khlestov, Baranov, Tsymbalar, Titov, Tikhonov, Shirko, Robson (Kanischev 75). Scorer: Khlestov 89

**1999-2000**

**GROUP STAGE 1**

**15.09.99 v Willem II (a) Won 3-1**
Filimonov, Kovtun, Khlestov, Bushmanov, Baranov, Titov (Evseev 71), Ketchinov (Tsymbalar 46), Tikhonov, Parfionov, Bezrodny, Robson. Scorers: Tikhonov 27 pen, 37, 53 pen

**21.09.99 v AC Sparta Praha (h) Drawn 1-1**
Filimonov, Kovtun, Khlestov, Tsymbalar (Shirko 56), Bushmanov, Baranov (Ketchinov 63), Bulatov (Bezrodny 70), Titov, Tikhonov, Parfionov, Robson. Scorer: Bezrodny 73. Sent off: Kovtun 68, Robson 82

**28.09.99 v Girondins de Bordeaux (a) Lost 1-2**
Filimonov, Khlestov, Bushmanov, Baranov (Ketchinov 55), Bulatov (Tsymbalar 46), Titov, Tikhonov, Eseev, Parfionov, Shirko, Bezrodny. Scorer: Bezrodny 64

**20.10.99 v Girondins de Bordeaux (h) Lost 1-2**
Filimonov, Kovtun, Khlestov, Bushmanov, Baranov (Ketchinov 55), Bulatov, Titov, Tikhonov, Parfionov, Shirko, Bezrodny. Scorer: Tikhonov 55 pen

**26.10.99 v Willem II (h) Drawn 1-1**
Filimonov, Kovtun, Khlestov, Bushmanov, Baranov (Eseev 46), Bulatov (Ketchinov 58), Titov, Tikhonov, Parfionov, Shirko, Bezrodny. Scorer: Bezrodny 25. Sent off: Kovtun 90

**03.11.99 v AC Sparta Praha (a) Lost 2-5**
Filimonov, Khlestov, Bushmanov, Ananko, Bulatov, Titov, Tikhonov, Parfionov, Shirko (Meleschin 73), Bezrodny, Robson (Baranov 53). Scorers: Bulatov 34, Bezrodny 45. Sent off: Tikhonov 62

**2000-2001**
**GROUP STAGE 1**
**12.09.00 v Bayer 04 Leverkusen (h) Won 2-0**
Filimonov, Kovtun, Ananko, Bulatov, Titov, Stolcers (Baranov 46), Tikhonov, Parfenov, Shirko (Marcao 74), Bezrodny, Robson (Kalynychenko 75). Scorers: Titov 51, Bezrodny 89

**20.09.00 v Real Madrid CF (a) Lost 0-1**
Filimonov, Kovtun, Tchuisse (Shirko 58), Ananko, Bulatov, Titov, Stolcers (Bezrody 65), Tikhonov, Kalynychenko, Parfenov, Robson (Marcao 75)

**27.09.00 v Sporting Clube de Portugal (h) Won 3-1**
Filimonov, Kovtun, Tchuisse, Ananko, Bulatov, Titov, Stolcers (Baranov 46), Parfenov, Shirko (Marcao 46), Bezrodny, Robson. Scorers: Robson 44, Marcao 68, 82

**17.10.00 v Sporting Clube de Portugal (a) Won 3-0**
Filimonov, Kovtun, Tchuisse, Ananko, Baranov, Bulatov, Titov, Marcao (Kalynychenko 62), Parfenov, Bezrodny, Robson (Pisarev 85). Scorers: Dimas og 16, Titov 52, 68

**25.10.00 v Bayer 04 Leverkusen (a) Lost 0-1**
Filimonov, Kovtun, Tchuisse, Ananko, Baranov, Bulatov, Titov, Marcao (Kalynychenko 58), Parfenov, Bezrodny, Robson

**07.11.00 v Real Madrid CF (h) Won 1-0**
Filimonov, Kovtun, Tchuisse, Ananko, Baranov, Bulatov, Titov, Kalynychenko, Marcao (Shirko 64), Bezrodny, Robson. Scorer: Geremi og 47

**2001-2002**
**GROUP STAGE 1**
**10.10.01 v AC Sparta Praha (a) Lost 0-2**
Levytsky, Ananko, Kovtun, Mitreski, Parfenov, Baranov, Titov, Bulatov, Bezrodny (Tsykhmeistruk 58), Beschastnykh, Robson (Lovchev 61)

**18.09.01 v Feyenoord (h) Drawn 2-2**
Kabanov, Tchouisse (Ananko 32), Kovtun, Mitreski, Parfenov, Baranov, Titov, Bulatov, Tsykhmeistruk, Beschastnykh, Robson. Scorers: Robson 62, Beschastnykh 69

**26.09.01 v FC Bayern Munchen (h) Lost 1-3**
Kabanov, Ananko, Kovtun, Mitreski, Parfenov (Tchouisse 46), Baranov, Titov, Bulatov, Bezrodny (Tsykhmeistruk 46), Beschastnykh, Robson. Scorer: Baranov 64

**17.10.01 v FC Bayern Munchen (a) Lost 5-1**
Levytsky, Ananko, Kovtun, Mitreski, Parfenov, Baranov, Titov, Bulatov, Tsykhmeistruk, Beschastnykh, Robson. Scorer: Beschastnykh 58

**23.10.01 v AC Sparta Praha (h) Drawn 2-2**
Levytsky, Ananko, Kovtun, Kebe, Parfenov, Baranov, Titov, Bulatov, Tsykhmeistruk (Mitreski 46), Beschastnykh, Robson. Scorers: Robson 4, Beschastnykh 34

**31.01.01 v Feyenoord (a) Lost 1-2**
Levytsky, Mjavanadze, Kovtun, Mitreski, Parfenov, Baranov, Titov, Bulatov, Tsykhmeistruk, Beschastnykh, Robson (Danishevsky 76). Scorer: Beschastnykh 14

**2002-2003**
**GROUP STAGE 1**
**17.09.02 v FC Basel (a) Lost 0-2**
Cherchasov, Tchuisse, Moises, Kovtun, Kebe, Baranov (Da Silva 56), Kudryashov, Khlestov, Kalynychenko (Mitreski 72), Beschastnykh, Danishevskiy

**25.09.02 v Valencia CF (h) Lost 0-3**
Cherchasov, Tchuisse, Moises, Kovtun (Baranov 46) Mitreski, Kudryashov, Khlestov, Kalynychenko, Kebe, Beschastnykh, Danishevskiy (Okon Flo 54)

**02.10.02 v Liverpool FC (a) Lost 0-5**
Cherchasov, Kebe, Moises, Mitreski, Kovtun (Abramidze 63), Khlestov (Bezrodny 26), Kudryashov (Da Silva 50), Pavlenko, Kalynychenko, Beschastnykh, Danishevskiy

**22.10.02 v Liverpool FC (a)** **Lost 1-3**
Levitsky, Mitreski (Kudryashov 82), Kovtun (Kebe 36), Abramidze, Khlestov, Sonin (Torbinskiy 60), Pavlenko, Kalynychenko, Beschastnykh, Danishevskiy, Bezrodny
Scorer: Danishevskiy 23

**05.11.02 v FC Basel (h)** **Lost 0-2**
*Postponed from 30.10.02 due to Moscow theatre siege.*
Levitsky, Khlestov, Moises, Abramidze, Kovtun, Pavlenko, Beschastnykh, Bezrodny (Kudryashov 46), Kebe (Mitreski 77), Kalynychenko (Torbinskiy 71), Danishevskiy

**12.11.02 v Valencia CF (a)** **Lost 0-3**
Levitsky, Mitreski (Ogunsanya 77), Moises, Abramidze, Kovtun, Pavlenko, Beschastnykh, Bezrodny (Da Silva 46), Kudryashov (Sonin 62), Kalynychenko, Danishevskiy

| SEASONS | PLAYED | WON | DRAWN | LOST | FOR | AGAINST |
|---|---|---|---|---|---|---|
| 8 | 56 | 16 | 13 | 27 | 69 | 18 |

## SPORTING LISBON

**1997-1998**
**GROUP STAGE 1**
**17.09.97 v AS Monaco (h)** **Won 3-0**
De Wilde, Saber, Marco Aurelio, Beto, Vinicius, Pedro Martins, Oceano, Lang (Ramirez 84), Pedro Barbosa (Afonso Martins 74), Leandro Machado, Hadji (Quim Berto 89).
Scorers: Oceano 4, Hadji 8, Leandro Machado 65

**01.10.97 v K Lierse SK (a)** **Drawn 1-1**
De Wilde, Quim Berto, Beto, Marco Aurelio, Vinicius, Lang, Oceano, Pedro Martins, Pedro Barbosa (Simao Sabrosa 64), Leandro Machado, Hadji. Scorer: Leandro Machado 86

**22.10.97 v Bayer 04 Leverkusen (h)** **Lost 0-2**
De Wilde, Saber, Marco Aurelio, Beto (Ramirez 76), Vinicius, Lang, Vidigal, Pedro Martins (Nene 54), Simao Sabrosa, Leandro Machado, Hadji (Gimenez 36)

**05.11.97 v Bayer 04 Leverkusen (a)** **Lost 1-4**
De Wilde, Quim Berto, Marco Aurelio, Vidigal, Nene, Vinicius (Saber 40), Oceano, Pedro Martins (Luis Miguel 89), Hadji, Pedro Barbosa, Leandro Machado (Gimenez 75).
Scorer: Hadji 44. Sent off: Vidigal 22, Pedro Barbosa 82

**26.11.97 v AS Monaco (a) Lost 2-3**
De Wilde (Tiago 23), Saber, Nene, Marco Aurelio, Quim Berto (Vinicius 73), Oceano (Afonso Martins 79), Lang, Pedro Martins, Leandro Machado, Hadji, Luis Miguel. Scorers: Luis Miguel 31, Oceano 38 pen

**10.12.97 v K Lierse SK (h) Won 2-1**
De Wilde, Quim Berto, Beto, Marco Aurelio, Vinicius, Lang, Vidigal, Pedro Martins (Carlos Miguel 46), Afonso Martins (Gimenez 46), Leandro Machado (Iordanov 87), Ramirez. Scorers: Ramirez 46, Gimenez 67

**2000-2001**
**GROUP STAGE 1**
**12.09.00 v Real Madrid CF (h) Drawn 2-2**
Schmeichel, Sa Pinto (Edmilson 80), Acosta, Horvath, Hugo (Bruno Caires 73), Bino, Beto, Rui Jorge, Joao Pinto (Tonito 85), Prates, Andre Cruz. Scorers: Sa Pinto 39, Andre Cruz 42

**19.09.00 v Bayer 04 Leverkusen (a) Lost 2-3**
Schmeichel, Sa Pinto, Acosta (Mpenza 74), Horvath (Babb 61), Hugo, Bino, Beto, Rui Jorge (Tonito 75), Joao Pinto, Prates, Andre Cruz. Scorers: Andre Cruz 12, Sa Pinto 79. Sent off: Joao Pinto 41

**27.09.00 v FC Spartak Moscow (a) Lost 1-3**
Schmeichel, Dimas, Sa Pinto, Horvath, Hugo (Acosta 70), Bino, Beto, Rui Jorge (Tonito 70), Prates, Mpenza (Rodrigo 82), Andre Cruz. Scorer: Sa Pinto 24

**17.10.00 v FC Spartak Moscow (h) Lost 0-3**
Schmeichel, Dimas, Sa Pinto, Acosta, Horvath (Pedro Barbosa 57), Bino, Beto, Rui Jorge (Rodrigo 38), Joao Pinto (Mpenza 57), Prates, Andre Cruz

**25.10.00 v Real Madrid CF (a) Lost 0-4**
Nelson, Dimas, Delfim (Bino 46), Sa Pinto, Hugo (Pedro Barbosa 71), Mahon (Acosta 46), Beto, Joao Pinto, Prates, Mpenza, Andre Cruz

**07.11.00 v Bayer 04 Leverkusen (h) Drawn 0-0**
Nelson, Dimas, Babb, Delfim, Pedro Barbosa, Acosta, Hugo (Edmilson 46), Bino, Joao Pinto (Rodrigo 81), Prates, Andre Cruz

| SEASONS | PLAYED | WON | DRAWN | LOST | FOR | AGAINST |
|---|---|---|---|---|---|---|
| 2 | 12 | 2 | 3 | 7 | 14 | 26 |

## STEAUA BUCARESTI

### 1994-1995

**GROUP STAGE 1**

**14.09.94 v RSC Anderlecht (a) Drawn 0-0**
Stingaciu, Panait, Pirvu, Dobos, Csik, Prodan, Lacatus, Militaru (Rosu 89), Ilie (Iftode 83), Panduru, Stan. Sent off: Lacatus 87

**28.09.94 v NK Hajduk Split (h) Lost 0-1**
Stingaciu, Panait, Pirvu, Dobos, Gilca, Prodan, Rosu, Militaru (Stan 76), Ilie (Popa 76), Panduru, Csik

**19.10.94 v SL Benfica (a) Lost 1-2**
Stingaciu, Panait, Pirvu, Dobos, Gilca, Prodan, Filipescu, Militaru, Rosu (Bucur 65), Panduru (Iftode 80), Stan. Scorer: Militaru 89. Sent off: Dobos 57

**02.11.94 v SL Benfica (h) Drawn 1-1**
Stingaciu, Panait, Filipescu, Bucur, Gilca, Prodan, Csik, Iftode (Ion 70), Rosu (Popa 80), Panduru, Stan. Scorer: Panduru 27

**23.11.94 v RSC Anderlecht (h) Drawn 1-1**
Stingaciu, Panait, Pirvu, Dobos, Gilca, Prodan, Lacatus, Csik, Ilie (Popa 75), Panduru (Rosu 79), Stan. Scorer: Dobos 55

**07.12.94 v NK Hajduk Split (a) Won 4-1**
Stingaciu (Gherasim 89), Csik, Pirvu, Dobos, Gilca, Prodan, Lacatus (Ion 88), Militaru, Ilie (Filipescu 74), Rosu, Stan. Scorers: Ilie 11, 32, Lacatus 23, Gilca 89

### 1995-1996

**GROUP STAGE 1**

**13.09.95 v Rangers FC (h) Won 1-0**
Stelea, Csik, Pirvu, Dobos, Gilca, Prodan, Raducan, Militaru, Bucur (Filipescu 46), Vladoiu (Sabin Ilie 79), Adrian Ilie (Rosu 61). Scorer: Prodan 85. Sent off: Militaru 77

**27.09.95 v Juventus FC (a) Lost 0-3**
Stelea, Csik, Pirvu, Dobos, Gilca, Prodan, Raducan, Adrian Ilie (Panait 79), Filipescu (Nagy 83), Lacatus (Rosu 54), Vladoiu

**18.10.95 v BV Borussia Dortmund (a) Lost 0-1**
Stelea, Dobos, Panait (Rosu 86), Gilca, Prodan, Pirvu, Adrian Ilie (Raducan 64), Filipescu (Nagy 70), Csik, Lacatus, Vladoiu

**01.11.95 v BV Borussia Dortmund (h) Drawn 0-0**
Stelea, Csik, Pirvu, Dobos, Panait, Prodan, Bucur, Adrian Ilie (Nagy 79), Filipescu (Raducan 66), Lacatus (Rosu 59), Vladoiu

**22.11.95 v Rangers FC (a) Drawn 1-1**
Stelea, Csik, Pirvu, Dobos, Prodan, Bucur, Filipescu, Militaru (Rosu 89), Adrian Ilie (Nagy 75), Lacatus (Raducan 88), Vladoiu. Scorer: Adrian Ilie 55

**06.12.95 v Juventus FC (h) Drawn 0-0**
Stelea, Panait, Dobos, Nagy, Prodan, Csik, Pirvu (Rosu 46), Militaru (Sabin Ilie 83), Galca, Vladoiu, Filipescu (Raducan 63). Sent off: Vladoiu 60

**1996-1997**
**GROUP STAGE 1**
**11.09.96 v Clube Atletico de Madrid (a) Lost 0-4**
Gherasim, Csik, Baciu, Prodan, Nagy, Militaru, Bucur, Rosiu, Calin (Zamfirescu 75), Serban (Nemtanu 90), Sabin Ilie (Ciocoiu 53). Sent off: Baciu 28

**25.09.96 v BV Borussia Dortmund (h) Lost 0-3**
Gherasim (Stelea 46), Csik, Prodan, Nagy, Militaru, Serba, Filipescu, Bucur (Zamfirescu 46), Sabin Ilie (Rosu 62), Lacatus, Calin

**16.10.96 v Widzew Lodz (h) Won 1-0**
Stelea, Zamfirescu, Baciu, Csik, Filipescu, Militaru, Serban, Nagy, Lacatus, Calin (Rosu 46), Sabin Ilie (Ciocoiu 46). Scorer: Bogusz og 82

**30.10.96 v Widzew Lodz (a) Lost 0-2**
Stelea, Zamfirescu, Prodan, Csik, Nagy, Calin (Stan Ilie 57), Serban (Rosu 65), Adrian Ilie, Militaru, Miu, Lacatus (Ciocoiu 75)

**20.11.96 v Clube Atletico de Madrid (h) Drawn 1-1**
Stelea, Miu, Prodan, Baciu, Nagy, Serban, Calin (Ciocoiu 27), Bucur (Nemtanu 71), Militaru (Rosu 72), Stan Ilie, Lacatus. Scorer: Ilie 46

**04.12.96 v BV Borussia Dortmund (a) Lost 3-5**
Stelea, Miu, Csik, Bucur, Baciu, Serban (Nemtanu 65), Militaru, Rosu (Ciocoiu 46), Nagy, Calin, Sabin Ilie. Scorers: Sabin Ilie 17 pen, Baciu 52, Calin 79

| SEASONS | PLAYED | WON | DRAWN | LOST | FOR | AGAINST |
|---|---|---|---|---|---|---|
| 3 | 18 | 3 | 7 | 8 | 14 | 26 |

## SK STURM GRAZ

### 1998-1999
### GROUP STAGE 1

**16.09.98 v FC Spartak Moscow (h) Lost 0-2**
Sidorczuk, Neukirchner, Milanic, Popovic, Posch, Schopp, Mahlich, Schupp, Vastic, Haas, Reinmayr (Angibeaud 61)

**30.09.98 v FC Internazionale (a) Lost 0-1**
Sidorczuk, Milanic (Angibeaud 79), Foda, Neukirchner, Schopp (Popovic 58), Mahlich, Schupp, Posch, Reinmayr (Minavand 90), Vastic, Haas

**21.10.98 v Real Madrid CF (a) Lost 1-6**
Sidorczuk, Popovic, Foda, Neukirchner (Kocijan 68), Schopp, Mahlich, Schupp (Martens 89), Posch, Reinmayr, Vastic, Haas. Scorer: Vastic 8

**05.11.98 v Real Madrid CF (h) Lost 1-5**
Sidorczuk, Milanic, Popovic (Babalade 71), Foda, Neukirchner, Schupp, Posch, Minavand, Reinmayr (Kocijan 71), Vastic, Haas (Martens 75). Scorer: Haas 3

**25.11.98 v FC Spartak Moscow (a) Drawn 0-0**
Sidorczuk, Milanic, Schupp, Popovic, Schopp, Kocijan (Martens 88), Mahlich, Prilasnig, Posch, Vastic, Haas (Babalade 90)

**09.12.98 v FC Internazionale (h) Lost 0-2**
Sidorczuk, Milanic (Martens 46), Foda, Popovic, Schopp, Neukirchner (Prilasnig 77), Schupp, Posch, Reinmayr, Haas, Kocijan (Wallner 84)

### 1999-2000
### GROUP STAGE 1

**14.09.99 v Olympique de Marseille (a) Lost 0-2**
Schicklgruber, Neukirchner (Kutsupias 82), Foda, Mahlich, Schupp, Reinmayr (Korsos 46), Vastic, Prilasnig, Martens (Pantelic 46), Feldhofer, Kocijan

**22.09.99 v Manchester United FC (h) Lost 0-3**
Sidorczuk, Neukirchner, Foda, Mahlich (Reinmayr 75), Strafner, Schupp, Vastic, Prilasnig (Katsupias 71), Martens, Feldhofer (Korsos 72), Kocijan

**29.09.99 v NK Croatia/Dinamo Zagreb (a) Lost 0-3**
Schicklgruber, Neukirchner, Milanic (Feldhofer 66), Foda, Mahlich (Pantelic 73), Strafner, Vastic, Prilasnig, Martens, Schopp (Korsos 50), Kocijan

**19.10.99 v NK Croatia/Dinamo Zagreb (h) Won 1-0**
Schicklgruber, Neukirchner, Mahlich, Schupp, Vastic, Korsos, Prilasnig, Martens (Strafner 89), Feldhofer, Schopp, Kocijan (Reinmayr 80). Scorer: Kocijan 40

**27.10.99 v Olympique de Marseille (h) Won 3-2**
Schicklgruber, Neukirchner, Mahlich, Schupp, Vastic, Prilasnig, Martens, Feldhofer (Strafner 39), Schopp (Reinmayr 81), Minavand (Bardel 76), Kocijan. Scorers: Mahlich 18, Kocijan 61, 84

**02.11.99 v Manchester United FC (a) Lost 1-2**
Schicklgruber, Neukirchner, Mahlich, Strafner, Vastic, Prilasnig, Martens (Reinmayr 71), Angibeaud (Bardel 71), Schopp, Minavand, Kocijan (Bochtler 74). Scorer: Vastic 88 pen

**2000-2001**
**GROUP STAGE 1**
**12.09.00 v Rangers FC (a) Lost 0-5**
Schicklgruber, Foda, Strafner, Schupp, Reinmayr (Mahlich 80), Korsos, Prilasnig, Mamedov, Schopp, Yuran (Szabics 80), Fleurquin

**20.09.00 v Galatasaray SK (h) Won 3-0**
Schicklgruber, Neukirchner, Schupp, Reinmayr (Strafner 71), Prilasnig, Schopp, Minavand, Kocijan (Mamedov 46), Popovic, Yuran (Korsos 83), Fleurquin. Scorers: Yuran 32, Schopp 64, Schupp 81

**27.09.00 v AS Monaco (a) Lost 0-5**
Schicklgruber, Foda (Feldhofer 46), Reinmayr, Korsos, Prilasnig, Mamedov (Strafner 46), Schopp, Minavand, Popovic (Szabics 69), Yuran, Fleurquin

**17.10.00 v AS Monaco (h) Won 2-0**
Sidorczuk (Schicklgruber 82), Neukirchner, Schupp, Reinmayr (Strafner 70), Vastic, Korsos, Mamedov, Schopp, Kocijan, Popovic (Prilasnig 59), Fleurquin. Scorer: Schopp 39, 88

**25.10.00 v Rangers FC (h) Won 2-0**
Schicklgruber, Neukirchner, Schupp, Reinmayr (Minavand 46), Korsos, Prilasnig, Mamedov (Feldhofer 83), Kocijan, Popovic, Yuran (Strafner 65), Fleurquin. Scorers: Yuran 20, Prilasnig 90

**07.11.00 v Galatasaray SK (a) Drawn 2-2**
Sidorczuk, Neukirchner, Schupp (Korsos 61), Reinmayr (Yuran 46), Vastic, Prilasnig, Mamedov, Schopp, Minavand (Strafner 87), Kocijan, Fleurquin. Scorers: Yuran 64, Hakan Unsal og 80

**GROUP STAGE 2**

**21.11.00 v Valencia CF (a) Lost 0-2**

Sidorczuk, Mamedov, Neukirchner, Prilasnig, Schopp (Feldhoffer 78), Schupp, Reinmayr (Szabics 84), Korsos, Minavand, Vastic, Kocjian

**06.12.00 v Manchester United FC (h) Lost 0-2**

Sidorczuk, Mamedov (Mahlich 85), Neukirchner (Strafner 82), Popovic, Prilasnig, Schopp, Korsos (Reinmayr 70) Fleurquin, Minavand, Vastic, Kocjian

**14.02.01 v Panthinaikos FC (h) Won 2-0**

Sidorczuk, Korsos, Neukirchner, Prilasnig, Schopp (Ibertsberger 79), Schupp, Fleurquin, Minavand, Vastic, Kocjian (Szabics 89), Yuran (Haas 56). Scorers: Haas 60, Kocijan 85

**20.02.01 v Panathinaikos FC (a) Won 2-1**

Sidorczuk, Korsos, Neukirchner, Prilasnig, Schopp (Ibertsberger 79), Schupp, Fleurquin, Minavand, Vastic, Kocjian (Hlinka 90), Haas (Szabics 70). Scorers: Schopp 25, Haas 42

**07.03.01 v Valencia CF (h) Lost 0-5**

Sidorczuk, Korsos, Strafner, Prilasnig, Ibertsberger, Schupp, Fleurquin (Feldhoffer 62), Minavand (Martens 75), Vastic, Kocjian (Scabics 62), Haas. Sent off: Prilasnig 35

**13.03.01 v Manchester United FC (a) Lost 0-3**

Sidorczuk, Korsos, Neukirchner, Ibertsberger, Schopp, Schupp (Martens 65), Fleurquin, Mahlich (Hlinka 46), Minavand (Szabics 46), Vastic, Haas

| SEASONS | PLAYED | WON | DRAWN | LOST | FOR | AGAINST |
|---|---|---|---|---|---|---|
| 3 | 24 | 7 | 2 | 15 | 20 | 53 |

## VALENCIA CF

**1999-2000**

**GROUP STAGE 1**

**15.09.99 v Rangers FC (h) Won 2-0**

Canizares, Pellegrino, Bjorklund, Mendieta, Claudio Lopez (Ilie 71), Gerard, Carboni, Sanchez (Angulo 80), Kily Gonzalez, Angloma, Albelda. Scorers: Kily Gonzalez 57, 74

**21.09.99 v PSV Eindhoven (a) Drawn 1-1**

Canizares (Palop 64), Pellegrino, Bjorklund, Mendieta, Claudio Lopez (Oscar 90), Gerard, Carboni, Sanchez (Angulo 74), Kily Gonzalez, Angloma, Albelda. Scorer: Claudio Lopez 4

**28.09.99 v FC Bayern Munchen (a) Drawn 1-1**
Palop, Pellegrino, Bjorklund, Mendieta (Angulo 87), Claudio Lopez, Gerard, Carboni, Sanchez (Ilie 62), Kily Gonzalez (Farinos 84), Angloma, Albelda. Scorer: Gerard 80

**20.10.99 v FC Bayern Munchen (h) Drawn 1-1**
Palop, Pellegrino, Bjorklund (Djukic 20), Mendieta (Farinos 69), Claudio Lopez, Angulo, Ilie, Gerard, Carboni, Kily Gonzalez (Oscar 85), Albelda. Scorer: Ilie 11

**26.10.99 v Rangers FC (a) Won 2-1**
Palop, Pellegrino, Djukic, Mendieta (Soria 80), Claudio Lopez, Angulo, Ilie (Sanchez 61), Gerard, Carboni, Kily Gonzalez (Farinos 67), Albelda. Scorers: Mendieta 35, Claudio Lopez 45

**03.11.99 v PSV Eindhoven (h) Won 1-0**
Palop, Pellegrino, Djukic, Mendieta, Claudio Lopez, Farinos, Angulo, Gerard, Carboni, Sanchez (Oscar 77), Kily Gonzalez. Scorer: Caludio Lopez 70

**GROUP STAGE 2**
**23.11.99 v Girondins de Bordeaux (h) Won 3-0**
Palop, Pellegrino, Djukic, Mendieta, Claudio Lopez (Sanchez 90), Farinos (Angulo 80), Ilie (Albelda 75), Gerard, Carboni, Kily Gonzalez, Angloma. Scorers: Farinos 60, Ilie 68, Kily Gonzalez 90

**08.12.99 v Manchester United FC (a) Lost 0-3**
Palop, Pellegrino, Bjorklund, Djukic, Mendieta, Claudio Lopez (Vlaovic 85), Farinos, Oscar (Sanchez 69), Carboni, Angloma, Milla

**01.03.00 v AC Fiorentina (a) Lost 0-1**
Canizares, Pellegrino, Djukic, Claudio Lopez, Farinos, Ilie (Sanchez 80), Gerard, Carboni, Kily Gonzalez, Angloma, Milla (Angulo 26)

**07.03.00 v AC Fiorentina (h) Won 2-0**
Canizares, Pellegrino, Djukic, Mendieta, Claudio Lopez, Farinos, Ilie (Oscar 77), Gerard, Carboni, Kily Gonzalez (Angulo 90), Angloma. Scorers: Ilie 35, Mendieta 90 pen

**15.03.00 v Girondins de Bordeaux (a) Won 4-1**
Canizares, Pellegrino, Djukic, Mendieta (Bjorklund 56), Farinos, Ilie (Angulo 73), Gerard, Carboni, Sanchez, Kily Gonzalez (Oscar 86), Angloma. Scorers: Djukic 41, Mendieta 48 pen, Kily Gonzalez 72, Sanchez 90

**21.03.00 v Manchester United (h) Drawn 0-0**
Canizares, Pellegrino, Djukic, Claudio Lopez, Farinos, Angulo, Gerard, Carboni, Sanchez (Ilie 70), Kily Gonzalez, Angloma

**QUARTER FINAL**

**05.04.00 v SS Lazio (h) Won 5-2**

Canizares, Pellegrino, Djukic, Claudio Lopez, Farinos, Angulo, Gerard, Carboni, Sanchez (Oscar 81), Kily Gonzalez, Angloma. Scorers: Angulo 2, Gerard 4, 40, 80, Claudio Lopez 90

**18.04.00 v SS Lazio (a) Lost 0-1**

Canizares, Pellegrino, Bjorklund, Djukic, Mendieta (Albelda 61), Claudio Lopez, Farinos, Angulo (Oscar 82), Gerard, Kily Gonzalez, Angloma

**SEMI FINAL**

**02.05.00 v FC Barcelona (h) Won 4-1**

Canizares, Pellegrino, Djukic, Mendieta, Claudio Lopez (Ilie 90), Farinos, Angulo (Albelda 78), Gerard (Sanchez 83), Carboni, Kily Gonzalez, Angloma. Scorers: Angulo 10, 43, Mendieta 45 pen, Claudio Lopez 90

**10.05.00 v FC Barcelona (a) Lost 1-2**

Canizares, Pellegrino, Djukic, Mendieta, Claudio Lopez, Farinos (Sanchez 90), Angulo, Gerard, Carboni, Kily Gonzalez (Albelda 74), Angloma (Gerardo 86). Scorer: Mendieta 69

**FINAL**

**24.05.00 v Real Madrid CF (n) Lost 0-3**

Canizares, Pellegrino, Djukic, Mendieta, Claudio Lopez, Farinos, Angulo, Gerard, Kily Gonzalez, Angloma, Gerardo (Ilie 69)

**2000-2001**

**GROUP STAGE 1**

**12.09.00 v Olympiakos Piraeus FC (h) Won 2-1**

Canizares, Pellegrino, Deschamps, Djukic, Mendieta, Zahovic (Sanchez 66), Diego Alonso (Carew 86), Carboni, Kily Gonzalez, Baraja, Angloma. Scorers: Baraja 36, Diego Alonso 45

**20.09.00 v SC Heerenveen (a) Won 1-0**

Canizares, Pellegrino, Deschamps (Milla 10), Djukic, Mendieta, Diego Alonso (Carew 80), Carboni, Sanchez, Kily Gonzalez (Vicente 46), Baraja, Angloma. Scorer: Kily Gonzalez 38

**27.09.00 v Olympique Lyonnais (h) Won 1-0**

Canizares, Pellegrino, Djukic, Mendieta, Diego Alonso (Carew 62), Carboni, Sanchez, Kily Gonzalez (Vicente 80), Baraja, Angloma, Milla (Zahovic 71). Scorer: Zahovic 78

**17.10.00 v Olympique Lyonnais (a) Won 2-1**

Canizares, Pellegrino, Djukic, Mendieta (Angulo 61), Carew (Diego Alonso 81), Zahovic (Albelda 71), Carboni, Sanchez, Kily Gonzalez, Baraja, Angloma. Scorers: Sanchez 45, Baraja 86

**25.10.00 v Olympiakos Piraeus FC (a) Lost 0-1**
Canizares, Pellegrino, Deschamps, Djukic, Diego Alonso (Carew 66), Angulo, Vicente, Carboni, Parri (Angloma 80), Albelda (Milla 49), Gerardo

**07.11.00 v SC Heerenveen (h) Drawn 1-1**
Palop, Pellegrino, Bjorklund, Djukic, Zahovic, Diego Alonso, Angulo, Vicente, Baraja, Parri (Sanchez 46), Albelda (Carew 78). Scorer: Diego Alonso 10

**GROUP STAGE 2**
**21.11.01 v SK Sturm Graz (h) Won 2-0**
Canizares, Angloma, Djukic, Pellegrino, Bjorklund (Amarilla 59), Mendieta, Albelda, Baraja (Milla 90), Kili Gonzalez (Vicente 82), Sanchez, Carew. Scorers: Carew 45, Sanchez 47

**06.12.01 v Panathinaikos FC (a) Drawn 0-0**
Canizares, Angloma, Djukic, Pellegrino, Carboni, Mendieta, Albelda, Baraja (Milla 90), Kili Gonzalez (Vicente 74), Angulo (Ilie 75), Carew (D Alonso 86)

**14.02.01 v Manchester United FC (h) Drawn 0-0**
Canizares, Angloma, Ayala, Pellegrino, Carboni - Angulo, Mendieta, Baraja, Kili Gonzalez, Aimar, Carew (D Alonso 76)

**20.02.01 v Manchester United (a) Drawn 1-1**
Canizares, Angloma, Ayala, Pellegrino, Carboni, Angulo (Sanchez 65), Mendieta, Baraja, Kili Gonzalez (Vicente 76), Aimar (Albelda 89), Carew. Scorers: Brown 88og

**07.03.01 v SK Sturm Graz (a) Won 5-0**
Canizares, Angloma, Ayala, Pellegrino, Djukic, Angulo, Mendieta (Albelda 82), Deschamps, Kili Gonzalez (Vicente 76), Aimar, Sanchez, Carew (D Alonso 79)
Scorers: Ayala 5, Carew 50, Kili Gonzalez 52, D Alonso 84, 90

**13.03.01 v Panathinaikos FC (h) Won 2-1**
Canizares, Angloma, Ayala, Djukic, Albelda (Aimar 66), Deschamps (Bjorklund 28), Baraja, Zahovic, Vicente, Sanchez, D Alonso (Carew 70). Sanchez 39, Angloma 75

**QUARTER FINAL**
**04.04.01 v Arsenal FC (a) Lost 1-2**
Canizares, Angloma, Ayala, Pellegrino, Carboni, Mendieta (Vicente 89), Baraja, Aimar (Angulo 68), K Gonzalez, Sanchez, Carew. Scorer: Ayala 41

**17.04.01 v Arsenal FC (h) Won 1-0**
Canizares, Angloma, Ayala (Djukic 50), Pellegrino, Carboni, Angulo (Aimar 67), Mendieta, Baraja, Vicente, Sanchez (Zahovic 72), Carew. Scorer: Carew 75

**SEMI FINAL**

**02.05.01 v Leeds United AFC (a) Drawn 0-0**
Canizares, Angloma, Ayala, Pellegrino, Carboni, Albelda, Mendieta, Baraja, Kili Gonzalez (Vicente 90), Sanchez (Zahovic 67), Carew

**08.05.01 v Leeds United AFC (h) Won 3-0**
Canizares, Angloma, Ayala, Pellegrino, Fabio Aurelio, Albelda, Mendieta (Angulo 73), Aimar (Deschamps 70), Kili Gonzalez (Vicente 65), Sanchez, Carew. Scorers: Sanchez 16, 47 Mendieta 52

**FINAL**

**23.05.01 v FC Bayern Munchen (n) Drawn 1-1 Lost 5-4pens**
Canizares, Angloma, Ayala (Djukic 90), Pellegrino, Carboni, Baraja, Mendieta, Kili Gonzalez, Aimar (Albelda 46), Sanchez (Zahovic 66), Carew. Scorer: Mendieta 3pen. Penalty scorers: Mendieta, K Gonzalez, Carew, Baraja Missed: Zahovic, Carboni, Pellegrino

**2002-2003**

**GROUP STAGE 1**

**17.09.02 v Liverpool FC (h) Won 2-0**
Canizares, Curro Torres, Ayala, Pellegrino, Carboni, Albelda (De los Santos 84), Baraja, Rufete (Angulo 75), Vicente, Aimar (Mista 71), Carew. Scorers: Aimar 20, Baraja 38

**25.09.02 v Spartak Moscow (a) Won 3-0**
Canizares, Curro Torres, Ayala, Pellegrino, Carboni, Albelda, Baraja, Angulo (Sanchez 74), Vicente (Rufete 75), Aimar, Carew (Mista 58). Scorers: Angulo 6, Mista 71, Sanchez 83

**02.10.02 v FC Basel (h) Won 6-2**
Canizares, Curro Torres, Ayala, Pellegrino, Fabio Aurelio, Albelda, Baraja (Mista 46), Angulo, Vicente (Garrido 60), Aimar (Sanchez 71), Carew. Scorers: Carew 10, 13, Fabio Aurelio 17, Baraja 28, Aimar 58, Mista 60

**22.10.02 v FC Basel (a) Drawn 2-2**
Canizares, Curro Torres, Ayala, Pellegrino, Fabio Aurelio, De los Santos, Baraja (Marchena 76), Rufete (Angulo 71), K Gonzalez, Mista, Sanchez (Carew 80). Scorers: Baraja 38, Curro Torres 72

**30.10.02 v Liverpool FC (a) Won 1-0**
Canizares, Curro Torres, Marchena, Pellegrino, Carboni, Rufete, Albelda, Baraja, K Gonzalez (Vicente 88), Carew (Mista 79), Aimar (Angulo 68). Scorer: Rufete 34

**12.11.02 v Spartak Moscow (h) Won 3-0**
Palop, Garrido, Djukic, Marchena, Fabio Aurelio, Angulo, Mista, De los Santos (David 87), K Gonzalez, Salva (Albiol 71), Sanchez (Navarro 88). Scorers: Sanchez 38, 46, Fabio Aurelio 78

**GROUP STAGE 2**

**27.11.02 v AFC Ajax (h) Drawn 1-1**

Canizares, Curro Torres, Ayala, Pellegrino, Carboni (Fabio Aurelio 74), Angulo (De los Santos 84), Baraja, Albelda, Vicente, Mista (Sanchez 67), Carew. Scorer, Angulo 90

**10.12.02 v Arsenal FC (a) Drawn 0-0**

Palop, Curro Torres, Ayala, Pellegrino, Carboni, Angulo, Baraja (Fabio Aurelio 87), Albelda, Vicente (Rufete 68), Aimar (Marchena 90), Carew. Sent off: Angulo 72

**18.02.03 v AS Roma (a) Won 1-0**

Canizares, Reveillere, Djukic, Pellegrino, Carboni, Rufete (Mista 73), Albelda, Baraja, Vicente (K Gonzalez 63), Carew, Aimar (Marchena 89). Scorer: Carew 78

**26.02.03 v AS Roma (h) Lost 0-3**

Canizares, Reveillere, Ayala, Pellegrino (Carboni 77), Fabio Aurelio, Rufete (Aimar 64), Albelda, Baraja, Vicente (K Gonzalez 53), Carew, J Sanchez

**11.03.03 v AFC Ajax (a) Drawn 1-1**

Canizares, Reveillere, Ayala (Marchena 88), Pellegrino, Carboni, Rufete, Albelda, Baraja, K Gonzalez, Carew (Mista 64), Aimar (J Sanchez 84). Scorer: K Gonzalez 28pen

**19.03.03 v Arsenal FC (h) Won 2-1**

Canizares (Palop 71), Reveillere, Ayala, Pellegrino, Carboni, Rufete, Albelda, Vicente, Carew, Aimar, J Sanchez (Angulo 68). Scorer: Carew 34, 56

**QUARTER FINAL**

**09.04.03 v Internazionale FC (a) Lost 0-1**

Canizares, Reveilliere, Ayala, Marchena, Carboni, Rufete (Mista 80), Albelda, Baraja, Vicente (Fabio Aurelio 85), Aimar, Carew (Angulo 66). Sent off: Albelda 57

**22.04.03 v Internazionale FC (h) Won 2-1**

Canizares, Reveilliere, Ayala, Marchena, Carboni (Fabio Aurelio 80), Angulo, Baraja, Vicente, Aimar (Mista 84), Carew (Rufete 73), Sanchez. Scorers: Aimar 7, Baraja 51

| SEASONS | PLAYED | WON | DRAWN | LOST | FOR | AGAINST |
|---|---|---|---|---|---|---|
| 3 | 48 | 25 | 14 | 9 | 74 | 39 |

## SV WERDER BREMEN

**1993-1994**
**GROUP STAGE 1**
**24.11.93 v FC Porto (a) Lost 2-3**
Reck, Basler, Bode (Neubarth 65), Bratseth, Beiersdorfer (Wolter 46), Legat, Eilts, Votava, Hobsch, Herzog, Rufer. Scorers: Hobsch 84, Rufer 85

**012.12.93 v RSC Anderlecht (h) Won 5-3**
Reck, Basler (Wiedener 84), Bode, Bratseth, Beiersdorfer, Borowka, Eilts, Votava, Hobsch, Herzog (Wolter 54), Rufer. Scorers: Rufer 66, 89, Bratseth 72, Hobsch 81, Bode 84

**02.03.94 v Milan AC (a) Lost 1-2**
Reck, Wolter, Legat, Neubarth, Beiersdoffer, Basler, Eilts, Votava, Bode (Hobsch 76), Herzog, Rufer. Scorer: Basler 54

**16.03.94 v Milan AC (h) Drawn 1-1**
Reck, Wiedener, Legat, Bratseth, Beiersdorfer, Basler, Bode (Unger 88), Votava, Hobsch, Neubarth, Rufer. Scorer: Rufer 52 pen

**30.03.94 v FC Porto (h) Lost 0-5**
Reck, Wolter, Legat, Bratseth, Wiedener, Harttgen (Neubarth 46), Basler, Votava, Bode, Herzog, Rufer (Bockenfeld 77)

**13.04.94 v RSC Anderlecht (a) Won 2-1**
Reck, Schaaf, Legat, Bratseth, Beiersdorfer, Borowka, Basler, Votava, Bode, Neubarth, Rufer. Scorer: Bode 33, 65

| SEASONS | PLAYED | WON | DRAWN | LOST | FOR | AGAINST |
|---|---|---|---|---|---|---|
| 1 | 6 | 2 | 1 | 3 | 11 | 15 |

## WIDZEW LODZ

**1996-1997**
**GROUP STAGE 1**
**11.09.96 v BV Borussia Dortmund (a) Lost 1-2**
Szczesny, Wojtala, Lapinski, Michalczuk, Szymkowiak (Bajor 73), Michalski, Czerwiec, Siadaczka (Szarpak 80), Majak, Dembinski, Citko. Scorer: Citko 84

**25.09.96 v Clube Atletico de Madrid (h) Lost 1-4**
Szczesny, Wojtala, Bajor, Michalczuk, Szymkowiak (Zajac 76), Michalski, Szarpak (Wyciszkiewicz 12, Miaszkiewicz 62), Majak, Bogusz, Dembinski, Citko. Scorer: Citko 45

**16.10.96 v Steaua Bucaresti (a) Lost 0-1**
Szczesny, Wojtala, Bajor, Lapinski, Bogusz, Szymkowiak, Michalski, Majak, Citko, Miaszkiewicz (Zajac 84), Dembinski

**30.10.96 v Steaua Bucaresti (h) Won 2-0**
Szczesny, Wojtala, Lapinski, Bogusz, Czerwiec, Szymkowiak, Michalski, Majak, Michalczuk, Dembinski (Wyciszkiewicz 87), Citko. Scorers: Majak 40, Czerwiec 48

**20.11.96 v BV Borussia Dortmund (h) Drawn 2-2**
Szczesny, Wojtala, Lapinski, Bogusz, Czerwiec, Szymkowiak (Wyciszkiewicz 56), Michalski, Majak, Michalczuk, Dembinski, Citko. Scorer: Dembinski 15, 20

**04.12.96 v Clube Atletico de Madrid (a) Lost 0-1**
Szczesny, Wojtala, Lapinski, Bogusz, Szymkowiak (Miaszkiewicz 88), Michalski, Czerwiec, Majak, Michalczuk (Wyciszkiewicz 78), Dembinski, Citko

| SEASONS | PLAYED | WON | DRAWN | LOST | FOR | AGAINST |
|---|---|---|---|---|---|---|
| 1 | 6 | 1 | 1 | 4 | 6 | 10 |

## WILLEM II (TILBURG)

**1999-2000**
**GROUP STAGE 1**
**15.09.99 v FC Spartak Moscow (h) Lost 1-3**
Mampaey, Prommayon, Hill, Victoria, Valk (Sanou 62), Ceesay, Arts, Bombarda, Galasek, Shoukov (Schenning 90), Jaliens. Scorer: Arts 56

**21.09.99 v Girondins de Bordeaux (a) Lost 2-3**
Mampaey, Hill, Victoria, Valk, Ceesay, Arts, Bombarda (Schenning 74), Galasek, Abdellaoui (Sanou 58), Shoukov, Jaliens. Scorers: Abdellaoui 40, Sanou 70

**28.09.99 v AC Sparta Praha (a) Lost 0-4**
Mampaey, Prommayon, Hill, Gentile (Bombarda 46), Victoria, Ceesay, Arts, Galasek, Abdellaoui (Sanou 81), Shoukov, Jaliens

**20.10.99 v AC Sparta Praha (h) Lost 3-4**
Mampaey (Van Fessem 65), Prommayon, Hill, Victoria, Ceesay, Bombarda (Valk 59), Galasek, Shoukov (Sanou 77), Landzaat, Schenning, Jaliens. Scorers: Bombarda 1, Shoukov 6, Schenning 50. Sent off: Galasek 53

**26.10.99 v FC Spartak Moscow (a) Drawn 1-1**
Van Fessem, Prommayon, Hill, Gentile, Victoria, Ceesay, Shoukov (Hermes 76), Landzaat (Valk 84), Schenning, Sanou (Schulp 86), Van Nieuwstadt. Scorer: Sanou 69

**03.11.99 v Girondins de Bordeaux (h) Drawn 0-0**
Van Fessem, Prommayon, Gentile, Victoria (Valk 87), Ceesay, Galasek, Shoukov, Landzaat (Ramzi 76), Schenning (Hill 90), Sanou, Jaliens

| SEASONS | PLAYED | WON | DRAWN | LOST | FOR | AGAINST |
|---|---|---|---|---|---|---|
| 1 | 6 | 0 | 2 | 4 | 7 | 15 |

# NOTES

# NOTES